lonely planet

Y0-CKP-073

Ireland

Donegal p373

Derry & Antrim p526

BELFAST p460

Fermanagh & Tyrone p557

Down & Armagh p503

Mayo & Sligo p336

Meath, Louth, Monaghan & Cavan p431

The Midlands p400

Galway p303

DUBLIN p48

Wicklow & Kildare p115

Clare p278

Limerick & Tipperary p257

Wexford, Waterford, Carlow & Kilkenny p140

Kerry p218

Cork p183

Isabel Albiston, Brian Barry, Fionn Davenport, Noelle Kelly, Catherine le Nevez, Neil Wilson

CONTENTS

Plan Your Trip

Ireland: The Journey Begins Here 4
Ireland Map 8
Our Picks 10
Regions & Cities 22
Itineraries 24
When to Go 36
Get Prepared 38
The Food Scene 40
The Outdoors 42

The Guide

Dublin 48
Find Your Way 50
Plan Your Days 52
Grafton Street & St Stephen's Green 54
Merrion Square & Georgian Dublin 66
Temple Bar 75
Kilmainham & the Liberties 81
North of the Liffey 90
Docklands 100
Beyond the city centre 107

Wicklow & Kildare 115
Find Your Way 116
Plan Your Time 117
Wicklow Mountains 118
Kildare & the Curragh 134

Wexford, Waterford Carlow & Kilkenny 140
Find Your Way 142
Plan Your Time 144
Wexford Town 146
Waterford city 155

Carlow town 166
Kilkenny city 171

Cork 183
Find Your Way 184
Plan Your Time 186
Cork city 188
Clonakilty 201
Bantry 209

Kerry 218
Find Your Way 220
Plan Your Time 222
Killarney National Park 224
Dingle 242
Tralee 250

Limerick & Tipperary 257
Find Your Way 258
Plan Your Time 259
Limerick city 260
Cashel 266
The Galtees & Glen of Aherlow 274

Clare 278
Find Your Way 280
Plan Your Time 281
The Burren 282
Cliffs of Moher 289
Loop Head Peninsula 295

Galway 303
Find Your Way 304
Plan Your Time 306
Galway city 308
Connemara National Park 318
Aran Islands 324
Clifden 329

White Island (p565)

Mayo & Sligo 336
Find Your Way 338
Plan Your Time 340
Westport 342
Achill Island 349
Esnnicrone 358
Mullaghmore 366

Donegal 373
Find Your Way 374
Plan Your Time 375
Glenveagh National Park 376
Malin Head 385
Slieve League Cliffs 392

The Midlands 400
Find Your Way 402
Plan Your Time 403
Clonmacnoise 404
Strokestown 415
Belvedere House & Gardens 425

Meath, Louth, Monaghan & Cavan 431
Find Your Way 432
Plan Your Time 434
Brú na Bóinne 436
Trim Castle 450
County Cavan 454

Belfast 460
Find Your Way 462
Plan Your Days 464
City centre 466
Cathedral Quarter 474
Titanic Quarter & East Belfast 481

Titanic Experience (p483)

Skellig Michael (p236)

| Queen's Quarter & South Belfast | 488 |
| West & North Belfast | 495 |

Down & Armagh ...503
- Find Your Way ...504
- Plan Your Time ...506
- Newcastle ...508
- Armagh city ...520

Derry & Antrim ...526
- Find Your Way ...528
- Plan Your Time ...530
- Derry city ...532
- Ballycastle ...543

Fermanagh & Tyrone ...557
- Find Your Way ...558
- Plan Your Time ...559
- Enniskillen ...560

Toolkit

- Arriving ...574
- Getting Around ...575
- Money ...576
- Accommodation ...577
- Family Travel ...578
- Health & Safety ...579
- Food, Drink & Nightlife ...580
- Responsible Travel ...582
- LGBTIQ+ Travellers ...584
- Accessible Travel ...585
- How to Drive the Wild Atlantic Way ...586
- Nuts & Bolts ...587
- Language ...588

Storybook

A History of Ireland in 15 Places ...592

Meet the Irish ...596

Gaelic Games: More than Sport ...598

WB Yeats ...601

Ireland's Red Deer ...603

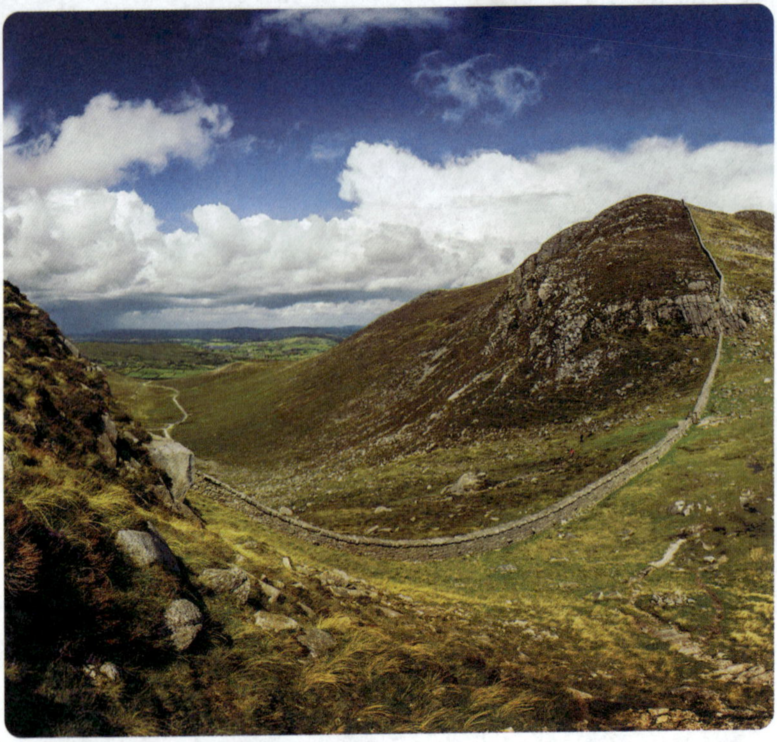

MIKE-HUBERT.COM/SHUTTERSTOCK ©

Mourne Mountains (p511)

IRELAND

THE JOURNEY BEGINS HERE

Though I grew up in Ireland, I spent most of my adult life elsewhere until I returned to Belfast a few years ago. Living here again, I see that the country has moved forward; its people are more accepting of differences and no longer so entrapped by conflicts of religious and national identity. A generation of people born after the Good Friday Agreement of 1998, who grew up in a time of peace and relative economic prosperity, have come of age.

Isabel Albiston

@isabel_albiston

Isabel is a travel writer and journalist who lives in Belfast.

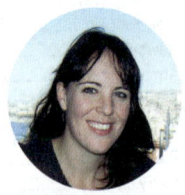

My favourite experience is cycling through the **Mournes** (p511), passing valleys, reservoirs and fields of sheep contained by dry brick walls, with sweeping views of the sea.

WHO GOES WHERE

Our writers and experts choose the places that, for them, define Ireland.

PLAN YOUR TRIP

The sense of renewal in Ireland's southeast is palpable. Even the smallest places have new and reinvigorated sights and an emerging generation of artists and artisans producing innovative creations. **Waterford** (p155) tops the lot for its incredible pace of change. Its revitalised Viking Triangle has unique new museums from watchmaking to wakes, vivid street art murals are proliferating, and a vast redevelopment on the northern riverbank is opening up a whole new side to the city.

Catherine Le Nevez

lonelyplanet.com/authors/catherine-le-nevez

A Lonely Planet author since 2004, Catherine has a Doctorate in Creative Arts (Writing) and insatiable wanderlust.

There's nothing quite like the visual treats that await in **Connemara** (p318). Stone walls and long narrow winding roads hem in green grass, lost sheep, stone bridges, dramatic coastline, towering mountains and postcard-perfect villages. You'd be forgiven for thinking your surroundings are a scene from a film – and actually these landscapes have been featured in quite a few. With Irish still the main language in parts, the culture and heritage of this region give visitors a true experience of Ireland.

Noelle Kelly

@noellemarieyoga

A recovering travel addict, Noelle has visited 50 countries and previously co-ran a travel blog. She's now a yoga teacher, and sharing her yoga practice has replaced her vagabonding ways.

The thing with Ireland's most beautiful spaces is that a lot of people already know they're there. But that's not the case with the **Fore Valley** (p428) in County Westmeath, which ticks all the boxes – a beautiful valley dotted with the remains of an ancient monastic site – but gets barely any visitors and is all the better for it.

Fionn Davenport

A travel writer since the olden times (before the internet), Fionn has written countless guides for Lonely Planet and others. Over the last couple of decades, he's focused on the regions and countries closest to his Dublin home, which he periodically leaves but always returns to.

The **Sheep's Head Peninsula** (p215) in West Cork is one of Ireland's most enchanting landscapes, a narrow spine of knife-edge hills leading to a dramatically perched lighthouse at the end of a satisfying hike. The views from here and the spectacular Goat's Path road range from the rugged hills of the Beara Peninsula to the sea cliffs of Mizen Head, and they sum up all that is best about this wild stretch of Ireland's coast.

Neil Wilson

@neil3965

Neil is a freelance travel writer who has covered Ireland for Lonely Planet for more than 20 years.

Mayo (pictured) **and Sligo** (p336) are home to some of the most idyllic, picturesque and jaw-droppingly beautiful scenes of Ireland you're likely to encounter. Magnificent mountains, spectacular beaches, unspoilt countryside and lively pubs all await in the west of Ireland. Get off the beaten track, follow your nose and you never know what gems you might uncover!

Brian Barry

@Brian_DeBarra

Cork-native Brian is a travel writer, photographer and tour guide who has explored more than fifty countries. An adventure sports enthusiast, lover of the outdoors and independent travel advocate, Brian prefers the road less travelled.

Connemara (p318)

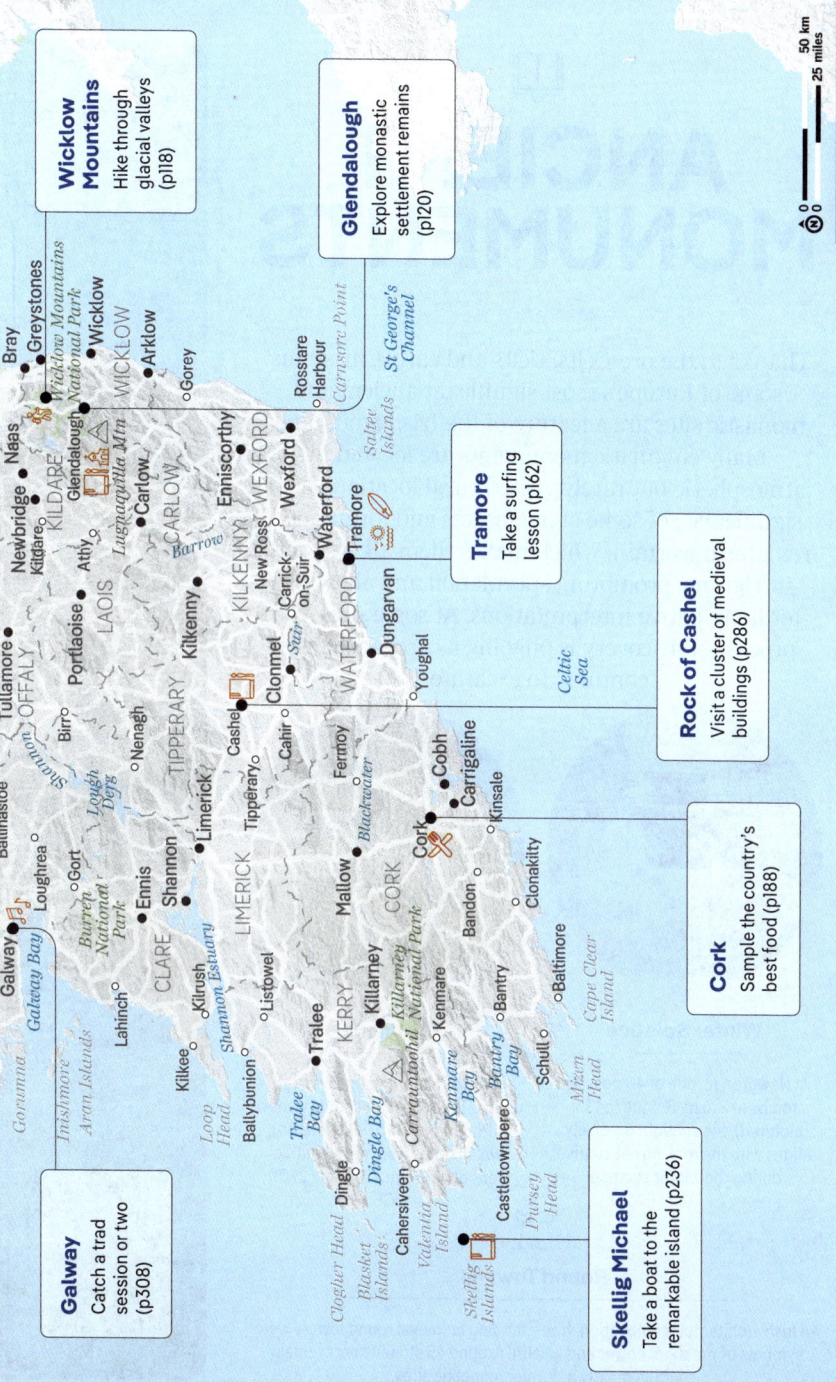

ANCIENT MONUMENTS

Thanks to the pre-Celts, Celts and early Christians, some of Europe's most significant ancient and monastic sites are a feature of the Irish landscape. Many enigmatic monuments are located in atmospheric but rarely visited rural locations. The significance of some stone figures and formations remains uncertain, which makes them all the more intriguing, prompting speculation and allowing for imaginative interpretations. At some sites, the process of discovery is ongoing as archaeologists continue to excavate.

Winter Solstice

At Newgrange, one of 40 passage tombs at Brú na Bóinne (p436; pictured), the sunlight precisely aligns with the roof-box at sunrise during the winter solstice.

Dolmens

Ireland has 172 dolmen portal tombs. The oldest (and most visited) is Poulnabrone (p288; pictured), which dates from the Neolithic period, between 4200 and 2900 BCE.

Round Towers

An Irish architectural innovation, free-standing medieval round towers were symbols of prestige, power and wealth. Around 65 stone towers remain intact, mostly at former monastic sites.

Skellig Michael (p236)

PLAN YOUR TRIP — OUR PICKS

❹ ❺
❶
❷
❸

BEST ANCIENT MONUMENT EXPERIENCES

Visit the remains of the ❶ **Glendalough** monastic settlement, located in a magical setting on the edge of a glacial lake in a forested valley. (p120)

Discover the impressive cluster of medieval buildings, including a round tower and Romanesque frescoes, at the ❷ **Rock of Cashel**, a hilltop fortress. (p268)

Take a boat trip out to the remains of a 1400-year-old monastery on the rocky island of ❸ **Skellig Michael**. (p236)

Avoid the crowds and visit the moody and evocative Stone Age passage graves strewn about the ❹ **Loughcrew Hills**. (p445)

Marvel at Newgrange's immense, round, white stone walls topped by a grass dome, part of the vast Neolithic necropolis ❺ **Brú na Bóinne**. (p436)

11

INTO THE WILD

Ireland's moody mountains, rolling hills, blanket bogs, inland loughs and rivers are home to a range of wildlife. Six of Ireland's wildest and most untouched areas are national parks, where the ecosystem is protected and wildlife thrives. A variety of marine life visits Irish waters and can be spotted on boat trips or from the shore. Ireland is an important breeding area for seabirds and a destination or stop-off point for many migrating birds.

Marine Life

Ireland's coasts are visited by basking sharks and whale species, including minke, humpback and killer whales. At least 145 bottlenose dolphins live in the Shannon Estuary.

Red Deer

The red deer at Killarney National Park (p224; pictured) are thought to be the only herd of indigenous deer in Ireland. Elsewhere, red deer were introduced from Scotland.

Golden Eagles

There are estimated to be around 20 to 25 golden eagles in Donegal following efforts over the past 20 years to reintroduce the species.

Rathlin Island (p546)

BEST WILDLIFE EXPERIENCES

Spot seals, Irish hares, puffins, fulmars, guillemots and kittiwakes on ❶ **Rathlin Island** in County Antrim. (p546)

Visit ❷ **Wild Nephin National Park**, home to a range of wildlife, including otters, mountain hares, native red deer and rare birdlife. (p355)

Take a boat trip to see the bird sanctuary of ❸ **Little Skellig** in County Kerry, home to the second-largest colony of breeding gannets in the world. (p236)

Look out for red deer, badgers, foxes and otters as well as a variety of birdlife in ❹ **Glenveagh National Park** in County Donegal. (p376)

Hear the squawks of puffins, garnets, Manx shearwaters, razorbills and guillemots, just some of the 220 species recorded at the ❺ **Saltee Islands** in County Wexford. (p154)

Matt Molloy's (p343)

PINTS & TRAD SESSIONS

Finding yourself swept up in a foot-tapping trad music session in a pub is an invigorating, quintessential experience of visiting Ireland. The trad scene is most active on the west coast, but you can catch sessions all over the country. As the Guinness flows, you'll be joining in by the end of the night.

Oral Tradition

In the past, trad music was never written down but passed on from one player to another, with musicians adding their own personal flair.

Trad Recordings

In the 1960s, the ensemble group Ceoltóirí Chualann was the first to reach a wider audience. From it came the Chieftains, perhaps Ireland's most important traditional group.

BEST TRAD EXPERIENCES

Head out on a trad music pub crawl in ❶ **Galway city**, where several pubs with daily trad sessions are located within stumbling distance of one another. (p310)

Catch an impromptu trad session at a family-owned pub in ❷ **Doolin**, where local musicians gather in corner snugs to play. (p294)

Join locals and musicians crammed in for trad sessions at ❸ **Matt Molloy's**, the Westport pub of a member of the band the Chieftains. (p343)

Tap your feet to trad music in the world-famous pubs of Dublin's ❹ **Temple Bar**. (p77)

Discover why the family-run pub ❺ **De Barra's** in Clonakilty has gained the reputation of being one of Ireland's best folk music venues. (p202)

BEACH LIFE

Ireland's coastline combines rugged cliffs with soft white sands. All around the country, you'll find sheltered beaches suitable for bathing and patrolled by lifeguards in summer. Though the water might be cold, Ireland is a top surfing destination, offering excellent surf schools, gentle beginner breaks and more challenging swells for expert surfers.

Wheelchair-Accessible Beaches

Beach wheelchairs are available to use free of charge at certain beaches. The best-equipped county is Wexford, where beach wheelchairs can be reserved at eight different beaches.

Sand Dunes

Ireland's north and west coasts are home to the country's most extensive sand dune systems, in which Neolithic and Bronze Age artefacts have been discovered.

Big-Wave Surfers

When, in 2020, unusual weather events created huge waves off Mullaghmore in County Sligo, Irish surfer Conor Maguire surfed monster swells estimated to have been around 18m high.

BEST BEACH EXPERIENCES

Descend steep steps from the cliffs to reach the soft sands of ❶ **Malin Beg**, an off-the-beaten-track beach in western County Donegal. (p294)

Stroll the dunes, take a dip in clear waters and catch the sunset at ❷ **Fanore Beach** in County Clare. (p284; pictured near left)

Sink into the fine white sand flanked by grassy hills at County Mayo's ❸ **Keem Bay**, one of the most beautiful beaches in Ireland. (p351)

Spot butterflies and rabbits among the wildflower-strewn dunes and listen for the hum of the sands at ❹ **White Park Bay** in County Antrim. (p548)

Join in the seaside fun, take a surf lesson or relax on the sands of ❺ **Tramore**, County Waterford's summer playground. (p162)

CASTLES & COUNTRY HOUSES

Ireland's castles and country houses tell the story of its past, from the fortified homes of Gaelic earls and Anglo-Norman knights to those built post-plantation. These days, many of the country's finest properties are open to the public to explore on tours and to enjoy the grounds, which often include outstanding gardens and extensive walking trails. You'll usually find a coffee shop and sometimes biking trails and other activities, making for a great day out.

Northern Estates

In Northern Ireland, the National Trust manages a number of the area's grand country houses, which are mostly open for guided tours and have extensive grounds.

The Garden of Ireland

In part because of its climate, County Wicklow has some of the country's best gardens, including those at Killruddery House and the world-renowned grounds of Powerscourt Estate (p125; pictured).

Stay in a Castle

Some of Ireland's historic castles are now luxurious hotels, complete with turrets, where you can live out your fairy-tale fantasies during an overnight stay.

Glenveagh Castle (p377)

BEST CASTLE & COUNTRY HOUSE EXPERIENCES

Take a tour to learn the dark history of ❶ **Glenveagh Castle** and then explore the gardens and expansive parkland. (p377)

Discover *Game of Thrones* filming locations on the grounds of ❷ **Castle Ward**, a grand country house built in two architectural styles, and then take a kayak out onto Strangford Lough. (p517)

Explore the magnificent country estate of ❸ **Powerscourt**, where the main draw is the impressive gardens with views of Great Sugarloaf mountain. (p126)

Get swept up in the fantasy of ❹ **Kilkenny Castle**, where the themed rooms can be visited on guided tours. (p172)

Clamber over the ruins of ❺ **Dunluce Castle** and gawp at its spectacular setting on the Causeway Coast. (p551)

HAPPY HIKING

Ireland's wild beauty is constantly in motion and impossible to capture, from the ripples in the water of inland loughs in the breeze and the still or stormy seas to the ever-shifting light and the rolling mist. One of the best ways to experience it is on foot, hiking along a range of coastal trails, parkland walks, and inland river and canal paths. From dramatic clifftop walks to gentle woodland hikes, Ireland has a trail for everyone.

Ireland's Highest Mountain

In County Kerry, Carrauntoohil (1040m; p232) in the Macgillycuddy's Reeks mountain range is the country's highest peak. Several routes go to the top.

Changeable Weather

Trails that seem straightforward in sunny conditions can become treacherous in mist and rain. When hillwalking, bring a map, a compass and warm clothes.

Accessible Trails

Ireland has a number of wheelchair-accessible trails, including the Green Road Walk in the Wicklow Mountains, several forest park trails and canal towpaths.

Cuilcagh Mountain (p455)

BEST HIKING EXPERIENCES

Hike the trails that traverse the spine of the ❶ **Wicklow Mountains** and marvel at the wild topography and glacial valleys. (p119)

Explore the remarkable hexagonal rocks of the ❷ **Giant's Causeway** and visit a host of nearby attractions on a coastal hike. (p548)

Pull on your walking boots to explore the rugged wilderness atop the soaring sea cliffs of ❸ **Slieve League**. (p393)

Take the so-called 'stairway to heaven', a boardwalk trail over the blanket bogs of ❹ **Cuilcagh Mountain**, with views over the Fermanagh lakes. (p455)

Tackle the Diamond Hill trail for panoramic views of the moody mountains and Galway coastline and then stroll the nature trails at ❺ **Connemara National Park**. (p319)

URBAN DELIGHTS

Ireland's metropolitan centres are home to some of the country's most cutting-edge architecture and cultural centres, with contemporary art and music scenes that reflect Ireland's increasingly diverse population. Many of the most significant events in Irish history are commemorated in excellent museums in Dublin, the city where they mostly occurred. From ever-evolving street art to innovative restaurants, Irish cities are a place to experience what makes Ireland the country it is today.

City Bikes

Cycling can be a fun way to explore Ireland's cities, most of which now have bike-share schemes and an improving network of urban cycle paths.

Dublin's Museums

The capital is where you'll find Ireland's most important archaeological artefacts and artworks, many of them housed in the three Dublin branches of the National Museum.

Street Art

Ireland's street art scene is thriving. Look out for vibrant pieces in Belfast, Dublin, Galway and Cork, including work by Irish artist Conor Harrington.

Titanic Experience (p483)

BEST URBAN EXPERIENCES

Learn all about the *Titanic* in a multimedia ❶ **museum** in the former Belfast shipyards where the ship was built. (p483)

Stroll the grounds and cobbled squares of Dublin's ❷ **Trinity College** and take a look at the *Book of Kells*. (p55; p58)

Visit the Museum of Free Derry and view the nearby murals of the People's Gallery that pay tribute to the turbulent history of ❸ **Derry's Bogside neighbourhood**. (p536)

Admire ❹ **Limerick city**'s fine Georgian architecture, view the artefacts from ancient Greece and Rome in the Hunt Museum, and visit the Limerick City Gallery of Art. (p260)

Discover the dark history of ❺ **Cork City Gaol**, a Victorian-era prison that is now a fascinating museum. (p190)

REGIONS & CITIES

Find the places that tick all your boxes.

Donegal

IRELAND'S UNMISSABLE FORGOTTEN COUNTY

Quietly dramatic, Ireland's most northerly county is home to the country's highest cliffs, broad sandy beaches and an active surf scene, as well as misty, heather-covered mountains, isolated castles, red deer and golden eagles. Its Irish-speaking areas have a rich culture of trad music.

p373

Fermanagh & Tyrone

ANCIENT LANDSCAPE OF LAKELANDS AND HILLS

In County Fermanagh, Lough Erne's islands are home to an array of wildlife, mysterious stone figures and the remains of a monastery. The starry dark skies of neighbouring County Tyrone can be observed through telescopes at Davagh Forest, which is connected by a boardwalk trail to the Beaghmore Stone Circles.

p557

Donegal
p373

Mayo & Sligo

IDYLLIC ISLANDS, BREATHTAKING BEACHES AND OUTDOOR ADVENTURES

Remote mountain passes, spirited towns, crumbling castles and islands rich in folklore await in counties Mayo and Sligo. Here you can watch big-wave surfers at Mullaghmore and then visit the tombs of Carrowmore Megalithic Cemetery and the 5000-year-old stone enclosures preserved beneath the bogs at Céide Fields.

p336

The Midlands

THE IRISH HEARTLAND

Many visitors to Ireland skip the Midlands, but they miss out on experiencing a taste of authentic rural life in unhurried villages surrounded by verdant fields and stops at grand country houses. There are sacred monastic sites to visit and waterways to cruise at a delightfully relaxed pace.

p400

Mayo & Sligo
p336

The Midlands
p400

Derry & Antrim

HOME TO THE CAUSEWAY COAST

The remarkably beautiful stretch of coast between Belfast and Derry has numerous attractions, including the undulating Glens of Antrim, the seabird colonies of Rathlin Island, the dramatic hexagonal rocks of the Giant's Causeway, the world's oldest licensed whiskey distillery and the walled city of Derry itself, to name just a few.

p526

Belfast

CHARACTERFUL PORT CITY

Belfast has lived through dark times, but these days, the focus is on fun: coming together for a meal in one of the city's restaurants, catching a gig or attending an arts event. The city's history, including its links to *Titanic*, is explored in a number of worthwhile museums.

p460

Down & Armagh

COASTLINE, MOUNTAINS AND LEGENDS

County Down's coastline and Armagh city's religious sights are reachable on day trips from Belfast, but don't rush through. The Mournes, Strangford Lough and the Ring of Gullion are designated areas of natural beauty, and historical sites date from as far back as the Stone Age.

p503

Derry & Antrim
p526

Fermanagh & Tyrone
p557

BELFAST
✪ p460

Down & Armagh
p503

Meath, Louth, Monaghan & Cavan

THE STORY OF IRELAND

Ireland's earliest inhabitants lived in Meath and Louth, in an area that is now a commuter belt for Dublin. The tombs at Brú na Bóinne and Loughcrew are their legacy. Nearby, the Hill of Tara was the seat of Ireland's high kings. Monaghan and Cavan offer walking trails through unspoilt landscapes.

p431

Meath, Louth, Monaghan & Cavan
p431

Galway

FESTIVALS, RUGGED LANDSCAPES AND WINDSWEPT ISLANDS

Ireland's largest Gaeltacht (Irish-speaking area) is found in County Galway, home of the country's finest oysters and wild and moody Connemara National Park. Galway city is a cultural hot spot with a packed schedule of festivals and a vibrant trad music scene.

p303

Clare

CAVES, CLIFFS, COAST AND CRAIC

County Clare is home to Ireland's famous Cliffs of Moher, as well as the wildflower-strewn lunar landscapes of the Burren. But it is not only Clare's natural beauty that brings the crowds. Come evening, the county's pub floors shudder under the weight of feet tapping to the beat of trad sessions.

p278

Limerick & Tipperary

HEARTLANDS, HISTORY AND CULTURE

At the mouth of the River Shannon, Limerick, Ireland's third city, is rich in history. Nearby are the thatched cottages of Adare, the medieval buildings of Rock of Cashel and dairies producing Cashel Blue cheese. The surrounding hills of Tipperary are home to castles, ancient abbeys and walking trails.

p257

Kerry

THE JEWEL IN IRELAND'S SCENIC CROWN

Kerry is home to Ireland's highest mountains, wildlife-rich Killarney National Park and a number of charming peninsulas to explore. Remote islands, including the remarkable Skellig Michael, sit amid the crashing waves. Given its natural beauty, it's no wonder Kerry is a popular destination, but it's always possible to escape the crowds.

p218

Cork

FINE FOOD, FINE SCENERY, FINE FOLK

Ireland's largest county is where you'll find the country's second city and its best food, from the artisan producers and suppliers to the markets and the restaurants. The county's wild west has outstanding scenery, where narrow roads traverse enchanting headlands, passing picture-perfect fishing villages.

p183

Dublin
⭐ DUBLIN p48

IRELAND'S CAPITAL OF COOL

Ireland's capital city has no shortage of museums and galleries to visit, but beyond the major sights, there are vintage shops and neighbourhood brunch cafes to discover, not to mention elegant Georgian architecture, distilleries and breweries, and Dublin's legendary nightlife. The city's rich literary heritage is celebrated at a number of sites.

p48

Wicklow & Kildare p115

Limerick & Tipperary p257

Wexford, Waterford, Carlow & Kilkenny p140

Wicklow & Kildare

MOUNTAINS, MEADOWS AND RACEHORSES

South of Dublin, the Wicklow Mountains form a bracken-covered spine replete with waterfalls, deep glacial valleys and important early Christian sites, including Glendalough. On the fringes are spectacularly located aristocratic houses with landscaped gardens to visit. The paddocks of neighbouring County Kildare are home to Ireland's finest racehorses.

p115

Wexford, Waterford, Carlow & Kilkenny

SWEEPING COASTLINE, WOODED VALLEYS AND VIBRANT STREETLIFE

Known as the 'sunny southeast' because of these counties' warm and dry weather, this sheltered corner of Ireland offers outdoor activities ranging from gentle riverside walks to kitesurfing. History abounds in the counties' mystical standing stones, castles, abbey ruins and medieval buildings, while the county towns are burgeoning creative centres.

p140

ITINERARIES

Wild West Coast

Allow: 6 days   **Distance:** 809km

Ireland's wild Atlantic coast offers windswept adventures and craggy islands. This route will have you gazing over the precipice of towering sea cliffs, surfing waves or relaxing on pristine beaches, feasting on oysters washed down with creamy pints of Guinness, and catching trad sessions performed by some of the country's best musicians.

Sheep's Head, Cork (p215)

① BANTRY ⏱ 1 DAY

Start your wild west adventure in **Bantry** (p209), where you can visit 18th-century Bantry House and its spectacular gardens and dine on Bantry Bay mussels. If you're up for a challenge, you can drive, cycle or climb the single-track road up to Priest's Leap for sweeping bay views. Next, take an afternoon drive to the scenic peninsulas of Mizen Head, Sheep's Head or Beara.

② DINGLE ⏱ 1 DAY

Make a stop in the colourful harbour town of **Dingle** (p242), one of Ireland's largest Gaeltacht (Irish-speaking) spots. Pop into craft shops, take a seal-spotting boat trip or head out with a kayak or stand-up paddleboard before retiring with a pint in one of Dingle's pubs.

Detour: Book well ahead for a boat trip to the remarkable early Christian monastic island of Skellig Michael (p236). 🚗 3 hours

③ CLIFFS OF MOHER ⏱ 1 DAY

To beat the crowds, arrive early at the **Cliffs of Moher** (p289) for walks along a narrow path high above the Atlantic Ocean. Next, view the sheer cliff face from the water on a boat trip. In the evening, head to nearby Doolin to hear trad music and eat seafood.

Detour: Walk through the wildflowers, wildlife and karst limestone landscapes of the Burren (p282). 🚗 3½ hours

④
GALWAY CITY ⏱1 DAY

Start your day at one of **Galway city's** (p308) highly rated coffee shops for a flat white or espresso to fuel you as you explore the city on foot. Later, head out for oysters and other freshly caught seafood. In the evening, experience Galway's trad music scene on a pub crawl.
Detour: Take in the savage beauty of the landscape on a road trip through **Connemara National Park** (p318). 1½ hours

⑤
WESTPORT ⏱1 DAY

The picturesque planned town of **Westport** (p342) in County Sligo is packed with pubs and near some beautiful beaches. Take a surf lesson and then visit the town's boutiques. Alternatively, start your day with a hike up the nearby holy mountain of Croagh Patrick before catching a trad session in Matt Malloy's.
Detour: Take a ferry to Clare Island (p346) for peaceful hillwalks. 50 minutes

⑥
SLIEVE LEAGUE ⏱1 DAY

Head west to the soaring cliffs of **Slieve League** (p392), which are Ireland's highest. Put on your walking boots to tackle the trails, from which you can spot sure-footed sheep grazing near the sheer drop. Hear stories about the area and gaze up at the cliffs from below on a boat trip.
Detour: Catch the sunset on the crescent of silver sand at Malin Beg (p294; pictured). 25 minutes

Glenveagh Castle, Donegal (p377)

ITINERARIES

Northern Highlights

Allow: 4 days   **Distance:** 324km

The North is packed with outstanding scenery, from the lakelands of Fermanagh to the wilds of Donegal to the hexagonal rocks of the Giant's Causeway. Along the way, discover fascinating historical sites, including the intriguing islands of Lough Erne and the walled city of Derry.

❶ ENNISKILLEN ⏱ 1 DAY

Start in **Enniskillen** (p560), the island town that's the gateway to water-based adventures on Lough Erne. After checking out the town's castle museums, take a boat trip to explore the monastic ruins and round tower of Devenish Island, or paddle out by kayak to see the mysterious stone figures of White Island. Sample the local produce, which includes meat from livestock that graze on the islands.

❷ GLENVEAGH NATIONAL PARK ⏱ DAY

Cross the border into Donegal and drive into the Derryveagh Mountains that surround **Glenveagh National Park** (p376). Hike trails around Lough Veagh and take a tour of Glenveagh Castle. Stroll the landscaped gardens, see the red deer and discover the waterfalls. Bring your binoculars to spot birds. You might even see one of the area's golden eagles.

❸ INISHOWEN PENINSULA ⏱ ½ DAY

Ireland's most northerly point is **Malin Head** (p385), at the tip of the Inishowen Peninsula and reachable by car or by bike via the Inishowen 100 scenic route. At Malin Head, you can walk along clifftop trails, spot basking sharks and dolphins, and stop for a pint at family-run Farren's Bar. Come on a clear night for a chance to see the northern lights.

④ DERRY ⏱ 1 DAY

Spend a day in **Derry** (p532), on the banks of the River Foyle. Get your bearings by strolling the city walls and then explore the Bogside murals and the Museum of Free Derry. Next, cross the Peace Bridge to Ebrington Sq, where you can sample the beer at Walled City Brewery. In the evening, catch some live music in one of the city's bars.

⑤ GIANT'S CAUSEWAY ⏱ ½ DAY

One of the best ways to take in the scenery of the North Antrim coast is to hike a section of the Causeway Coast Way. Allow time to explore the dramatic hexagonal rocks of the area's star attraction, the **Giant's Causeway** (p546).

Detour: A 5km walking and cycling trail connects the Giant's Causeway to Old Bushmills Distillery (p549), open for tours and whiskey tastings.

⑥ BALLYCASTLE ⏱ ½ DAY

The seaside town of **Ballycastle** (pp543) has a sandy beach, pier-side fish and chips, and pubs with trad music to enjoy. Nearby is the Carrick-a-Rede Rope Bridge, which links the mainland to a small island; cross it if you dare.

Detour: From Ballycastle, a short ferry trip transports you to wildlife-rich Rathlin Island (p546), where nesting puffins and their chicks can be spotted on nearby sea stacks in summer.

ITINERARIES

East Coast Cities & Sights

Allow: 6 days   **Distance:** 332km

If you love to combine days hiking and biking in the hills with urban culture and nightlife, this itinerary is for you. Ireland's two largest cities sit just two hours apart by road or rail, each packed with museums, restaurants and pubs. To the south of both are scenic mountain ranges.

Temple Bar, Dublin (p77)

❶ BELFAST ⏱ 1 DAY

Begin in **Belfast** (p460), where you can learn about the *Titanic* at a number of attractions in Titanic Quarter. Next, head to the city centre for a spot of shopping and take a look at the street art in the Entries and Cathedral Quarter. Make a reservation to eat at one of the city's top restaurants in the evening. End the day with a pint in the Crown.

❷ NEWCASTLE ⏱ 1 DAY

Take the scenic route via the Ards Peninsula and the Strangford Lough ferry to reach **Newcastle** (p508). Walking trails through the Mournes start from town, including routes up Slieve Donard, the North's highest peak. You can also hire an e-bike and hit the hills on two wheels.
➤ *Detour: Catch some folk or trad music in one of several pubs in the village of Rostrevor (p515).*

❸ BRÚ NA BÓINNE ⏱ 1 DAY

Arrive early to secure a spot on a passage tomb tour and spend the day exploring the remarkable collection of prehistoric burial sites and museum at **Brú na Bóinne** (p436), including Newgrange – which dates from around 3200 BCE – and Knowth, with an impressive collection of passage-grave art.
➤ *Detour: Explore the lesser visited Stone Age passage graves at Loughcrew (p445).*

4 DUBLIN ⏱ 2 DAYS

Two days in **Dublin** (p48) gives you enough time to see the major sights. Stroll through Trinity College and take a look at the artefacts in the Chester Beatty. Visit the Archaeology and Natural History museums or the National Gallery and then hit the pubs of Temple Bar. On day two, learn how the black stuff is brewed at the Guinness Storehouse and then visit more museums and parks.

5 POWERSCOURT ⏱ ½ DAY

The main attraction at the **Powerscourt Estate** (p125) is the magnificent gardens; the grand house is closed to the public. Take time to explore the Japanese Gardens and Pepperpot Tower and stop at the cafe and gift shops before driving out to view the 121m-high Powerscourt Waterfall, Ireland's highest. From here, nature trails lead through giant redwoods and ancient oak trees. Nearby are two par-72 golf courses.

6 GLENDALOUGH ⏱ ½ DAY

You have plenty to do and see at the ancient monastic site of **Glendalough** (p120). With half a day to spend, wander around the ruins, including the 10th-century round tower and St Kevin's Kitchen, a classic early Irish church. Afterwards, walk to the Upper Lake and back. If you have more time, you can hike the 19km Miners' Way trail through the Wicklow Mountains.

ITINERARIES

Sunny Southeast

Allow: 4 days   **Distance:** 242km

Ireland's southeastern corner enjoys a (relatively) sunny and dry climate and serves up the country's best food. Work up an appetite with surfing lessons, bike rides and visits to Viking-themed museums and then take a culinary tour of the country's foodie hotspots, grazing at artisan markets and dining at acclaimed restaurants.

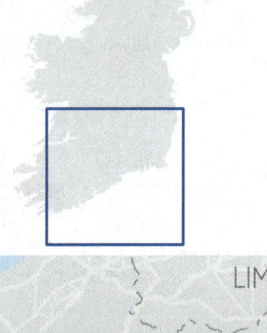

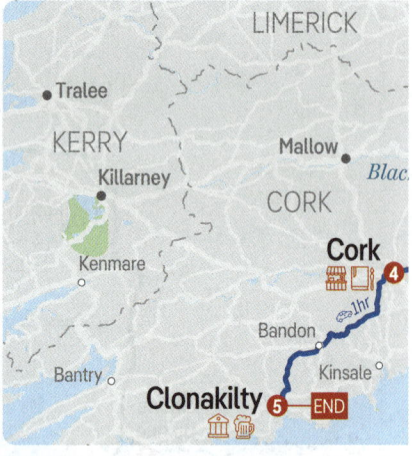

❶ WEXFORD ⏱ 1 DAY

Begin your day with a walk around the historic buildings of **Wexford** (p146) and then head to nearby Johnstown Castle. Next, visit the Irish National Heritage Park, which encompasses the site of the first Anglo-Norman settlement in Ireland as well as reconstructed sites from other historical periods. If you like opera, catch a performance during the Wexford Festival Opera season in autumn.

❷ WATERFORD ⏱ 1 DAY

Ireland's oldest city is the place to discover Viking history. Start at **Waterford**'s (p155) Viking Triangle, headed by a replica longboat, and take a look at the giant outdoor Viking Triangle chessboard. Next, head to the King of the Vikings immersive VR experience that recreates life in what was then known as Vadrarjfordr.

🚲 *Detour: Rent a bike in Waterford and cycle the traffic-free 48km Waterford Greenway (p161) to Dungarvan.*

❸ DUNGARVAN ⏱ ½ DAY

Stop to see the boats and colourful pubs of **Dungarvan** (p163) quay front and sample seafood, farmhouse cheeses and other artisan produce at the farmers market. Also worth a visit is the Anglo-Norman castle that guards the harbour. Hopheads can book a tour of Dungarvan Brewing Company.

🚲 *Detour: Take in spectacular scenery along the Copper Coast on your way to the surf town of Tramore (p162).*

④ CORK CITY ⏱ 1 DAY

Arrive in **Cork** (p188) ready to eat. Begin grazing at the English Market and then sample the artisan produce of the Marina Market. Next, stroll the university campus and discover the grim history of Cork City Gaol. If you still have energy to spare, view the city from the water on an urban kayaking tour. End the day with a slap-up meal in one of the city's excellent restaurants.

⑤ CLONAKILTY ⏱ ½ DAY

In the market town of **Clonakilty** (p201), you can sample the famous Clonakilty black pudding and taste triple-distilled whiskey at Clonakilty Distillery. Learn about local independence hero Michael Collins at a museum in what was once his home and at the Michael Collins Centre on the outskirts of town. Finally, catch a folk music session at the pub De Barra's.

PIOTR MACHOWCZYK/SHUTTERSTOCK ©

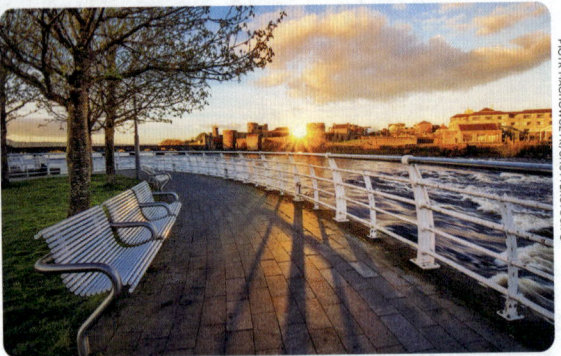

Limerick City (p260)

ITINERARIES

Inland Ireland

Allow: 4 days **Distance:** 304km

Heading inland offers an alternative insight into Irish life, from horse racing to hurling to dairy farming, with stops at thriving towns with vibrant arts scenes and lively pubs. Travel along quiet rural roads leading to impressive medieval castles and monastic sites on this route through the Irish heartlands.

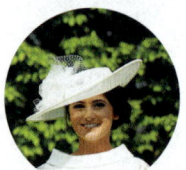

1

KILDARE ½ DAY

The biggest attraction in **Kildare** (p134) is the Irish National Stud, 1.5km south of town, where you can wander the paddocks and see the thoroughbreds. If you are in town for race day, don your finest hat and take the shuttle bus from Kildare to the Curragh Racecourse to bet on the horses. At other times, you can see the racecourse on a behind-the-scenes tour.

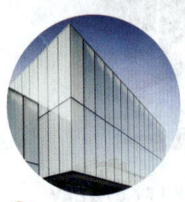

2

CARLOW ½ DAY

The landmark sights of **Carlow** (p166) are located in the compact town centre, overlooking the River Barrow. Start at Carlow Castle and then take a look at the cathedral and visit the museum to see intriguing archaeological finds. Next, dip into Carlow's thriving arts scene at the Centre for Contemporary Arts. If time allows, visit some of the gardens located near the town, including the accessible Delta Sensory Gardens.

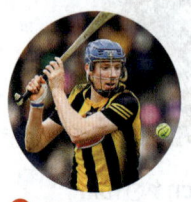

3

KILKENNY 1 DAY

With a day to spend in **Kilkenny** (p171), begin by exploring the medieval mile that connects the cathedral and castle. Stop to browse Irish crafts and designs in the castle stables and then walk along the riverbanks or take a boat trip. While in town, try to catch a hurling game. In the evening, head to the city's legendary pubs for live music.

BRENDAN MORAN/SPORTSFILE VIA GETTY IMAGES ©, VIEW PICTURES/UNIVERSAL IMAGES GROUP VIA GETTY IMAGES ©, PIARAS Ó MÍDHEACH

PLAN YOUR TRIP ITINERARIES

❹ CASHEL ⏱ 1 DAY

Head straight to **Cashel**'s (p266) most important sight, the impressive cluster of medieval buildings on a high limestone bluff known as the Rock of Cashel. Afterwards, go to the ruins of Hore Abbey, from where you can snap photos of the Rock of Cashel. Then, spend some time exploring the museums of pretty Cashel town and sample some Cashel Blue cheese.

❺ LIMERICK ⏱ ½ DAY

Stop in the city of **Limerick** (p260) to see the Georgian architecture and visit the art gallery and Hunt Museum, which houses artefacts from ancient Greece and Rome. On Saturday mornings, the Milk Market is crammed with stalls selling artisan produce and local cheeses. You can also take an *Angela's Ashes* walking tour, which includes places mentioned in the book by Frank McCourt.

❻ CLONMACNOISE ⏱ ½ DAY

Overlooking a bend in the River Shannon, the monastic ruins of **Clonmacnoise** (p404) are located in a bucolic setting. Ireland's most significant monastic site attracts scholars from around the world. Allow a couple of hours to explore the ruins, which include early Christian tombstones, two round towers, three high crosses and nine churches. You can also reach the ruins by boat from Athlone Castle.

35

WHEN TO GO

Ireland is a year-round destination, with festivals and seasonal highlights to enjoy whatever the month.

There's no getting around it: Ireland is green because it rains a lot, all year round. Rather than planning to avoid wet weather, it's best to factor the probability of rain into your plans. With a raincoat in your backpack, Ireland really is a country where every season offers something special.

In spring, the hills are covered with wildflowers and sweet-smelling yellow gorse. Summer is the best time for the beach and enjoying the long days outdoors. In autumn, the sea is still warm enough for bathing, the forest leaves turn red and gold, and the sunsets can be stunning. In winter, you can take a crisp walk in the frosty hills and then while away the long dark night enjoying a trad session by the fire in a cosy pub. There are festivals across the country throughout the year, so it's worth timing your visit to coincide with an event that takes your fancy.

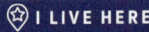

I LIVE HERE

MAY AT THE CLIFFS OF MOHER

Michelle Moroney is a yoga teacher and owner of the Cliffs of Moher Retreat in County Clare. @_michellemoroney

In late spring, we often get good weather. It always seems to be sunny for my son's birthday in May. The beaches are quiet too; I like to take sunset walks in Lahinch. In Ennistymon woods, the forest floor is covered with a blanket of bluebells, yellow celandine, and white wild garlic flowers. There is hope and magic in the air in May.

WET WEST

Over the last few years, weather stations in Kerry and Mayo have topped annual lists of Ireland's wettest places. Valentia Island in Kerry gets almost twice as much rain each year as Dublin.

St Patrick's Day, Dublin

Weather through the year (Dublin)

JANUARY	**FEBRUARY**	**MARCH**	**APRIL**	**MAY**	**JUNE**
Avg. daytime max: 8°C	Avg. daytime max: 8°C	Avg. daytime max: 9°C	Avg. daytime max: 11°C	Avg. daytime max: 13°C	Avg. daytime max: 16°C
Days of rainfall: 8	Days of rainfall: 7	Days of rainfall: 8	Days of rainfall: 8	Days of rainfall: 8	Days of rainfall: 8

NORTH ATLANTIC DRIFT

Ireland's temperate climate is a result of the North Atlantic Drift. This warm ocean current extends from the Gulf Stream, which brings warm water from the Gulf of Mexico. The Gulf Stream is predicted to weaken in the coming years, which will cause temperatures in Ireland to drop.

Big Festivals, Events & Parades

Ireland's most famous festivity is **St Patrick's Day**. It's celebrated all over the country, but the biggest party is in Dublin (p48), where the five days of events and the parade are attended by hundreds of thousands of spectators. **March**

The **Galway International Arts Festival** (p306) is the country's most important cultural festival, with music, dance performances and comedy events. **July**

Northern Ireland's biggest festival is the **Belfast International Arts Festival**, which attracts performers from all over the world. Everything from visual arts to dance is on offer. **October**

Derry Halloween (p539) brings in visitors from around the globe, who dress up as witches and ghouls to join the massive street party. The celebrations feature fireworks, aerial performances, pyrotechnics and a parade. **October**

Local Festivals & Sporting Events

Hundreds of thousands of people head to the north Atlantic coast to cheer on the motorcyclists competing in the **North West 200 Motorcycle Race** (p539). Spectators watch the action from five grandstands, located between Portstewart and Portrush. **May**

Fiddlers, accordionists, drummers, flute and whistle players, and singers gather in Ennis, County Clare, for **Fleadh Nua** (p301), a trad music festival. Events include ticketed concerts, free singing sessions and walking tours in the town's streets. **May**

Kilkenny fills with local and international comedians who come to tell jokes at the **Cat Laughs Comedy Festival** (p174). Come for performances of improv, sketch and stand-up comedy. **June**

Swimmers take to the waters around Ireland for a chilly **Christmas Day dip**. Locations include Forty Foot in the Dublin suburb of Sandycove (p113). **December**

I LIVE HERE

SUMMER ON LOUGH ERNE

Barry Flanagan is a tour guide and owner of Erne Water Taxi in County Fermanagh.
@ernewatertaxi

It's a different world out on the lough, and no two days are the same. The ever-changing wind affects how the boat moves and the way that the light is reflected on the water. In summer, the islands are a luscious green. I love to catch a glimpse of a kingfisher near the banks of the River Erne and listen for the call of curlews on Devenish Island.

Devenish Island monastic site (p564)

SUNNY SOUTHEAST

The driest, sunniest part of the country is the southeastern corner, which includes counties Carlow, Kilkenny, Tipperary, Waterford and Wexford. It gets an Avg. of seven hours of sunshine a day in early summer.

JULY	AUGUST	SEPTEMBER	OCTOBER	NOVEMBER	DECEMBER
Avg. daytime max: **18°C**	Avg. daytime max: **17°C**	Avg. daytime max: **16°C**	Avg. daytime max: **14°C**	Avg. daytime max: **11°C**	Avg. daytime max: **8°C**
Days of rainfall: **9**	Days of rainfall: **9**	Days of rainfall: **8**	Days of rainfall: **9**	Days of rainfall: **9**	Days of rainfall: **9**

Giant's Causeway (p548)

GET PREPARED FOR IRELAND

Useful things to load in your bag, your ears and your brain.

Clothes

Raincoat: In summer, bring a lightweight jacket that you can carry in your day bag in case of showers. In winter, you'll need a warm coat that's also waterproof. Umbrellas are useful only when there's no wind.

Layers: Sunny spring and summer days can look like t-shirt weather, but if the sky clouds over, it can suddenly feel cool. It's always a good idea to carry an extra layer, especially for the evening.

Boots: If you plan on hiking, bring waterproof trail shoes or boots. You'll be glad of them on muddy trails.

Denim: Jeans are fine pretty much everywhere. In smarter restaurants and bars, you can wear a more dressed-up top or shirt with jeans.

Shoes: Some Dublin clubs require that you wear shoes and not trainers (sneakers).

Manners

Most Irish people are friendly and inclined to stop for a chat. It's polite to greet the people you pass by, especially in rural areas.

Avoid discussing religion and politics in Northern Ireland, unless you are sure the topic won't cause offence. Some people there identify as Irish, some as British and others as Northern Irish, so try not to make assumptions.

📖 READ

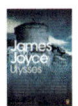

Ulysses (James Joyce; 1922) Joyce's experimental modernist masterpiece takes place over the course of a single day in Dublin.

Milkman (Anna Burns; 2018) A darkly funny perspective on life in West Belfast during the Troubles.

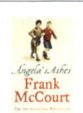

Angela's Ashes (Frank McCourt; 1996) A bleak story of a poverty-stricken childhood in Limerick.

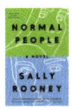

Normal People (Sally Rooney; 2018) This best-selling novel depicts a relationship between two teenagers from different socioeconomic backgrounds.

Words

'What's the craic?' (crack) can be used to ask what's happening in general, to ask for gossip or to ask what's going on with a particular situation: 'What's the craic with your man at the bar?'

Great craic is used to describe a situation, place or person that is fun, jolly or good company: 'She's great craic.'

Eejit (ee-jit) means an idiot or a fool. Often used affectionately: 'Don't be an eejit, now.'

Bold Naughty, usually used with children. 'Don't be bold.'

Banjaxed means broken beyond repair ('The remote control is banjaxed') or very drunk ('He got banjaxed last night').

Wrecked, plastered, battered and **hammered** are more words to describe being very drunk.

Bang on means just right, accurate or correct. 'You're bang on.'

Fair play Well done, good for you.

Gas means funny. Can be used to describe a person or a situation.

Grand is great, fine or good. 'You're grand' means it's fine; don't worry.

So Often used at the end of a sentence, particularly in the west of Ireland; eg 'It'll be grand, so.'

So it is Sometimes used in Northern Ireland at the end of sentences. 'That's the last train, so it is.'

No bother Not a problem. Usually said when being thanked for something or after agreeing to do someone a favour.

Take a dander means to go for a walk or explore. 'Do you want to take a dander to the shops?'

Wee means small.

Yoke is any nearby object.

📺 WATCH

Derry Girls (Michael Lennox; 2018–22; pictured) This comedy TV series follows the high jinks of four schoolgirls in 1990s Derry.

Good Vibrations (Lisa Barros D'Sa and Glenn Leyburn; 2013) The story of record-label owner Teri Hooley and Belfast's punk rock scene.

Michael Collins (Neil Jordan; 1996) Liam Neeson stars in this Oscar-winning biopic about the Irish fight for independence.

The Secret of Kells (Tomm Moore and Nora Twomey; 2009) The first in a trilogy of animated films depicting themes from Irish folklore.

The Banshees Of Inisherin (Martin McDonagh; 2022) Colin Farrell and Brendan Gleeson play longtime best mates whose friendship is thrown into crisis.

🎧 LISTEN

The Blindboy Podcast (2017–present) Hosted by Blindboy of comedy hip-hop duo the Rubberbandits, this podcast features interviews, fiction and comedy.

Whiskey in the Jar (Dubliners; 1967) A traditional Irish folk song that's essential listening on a road trip around Kerry and Cork.

Sunday Bloody Sunday (U2; 1983) This song depicts the horror of the Bloody Sunday killings in Derry during the Troubles.

Teenage Kicks (The Undertones; 1978) A catchy punk anthem that captures feelings of teenage infatuation; best played at full volume.

Oysters

THE FOOD SCENE

Irish cuisine hasn't always been a source of national pride, but the food produced across the country is gaining acclaim.

Ireland's culinary scene has come a long way over recent years. These days, produce from the country's fertile farmlands and surrounding seas is whipped up into flavoursome dishes in kitchens across the country. Though farming has long been a way of life for rural communities, a renewed value has been placed on quality local produce. Farms and suppliers are name-checked on menus, and there has been a move towards embracing organic farming methods and seasonal produce.

Irish Cuisine

Traditional Irish cuisine involves simply prepared staples: potatoes and root vegetables served with lamb, beef or pork. Nowadays, the same ingredients are treated with creativity to produce innovative dishes in the country's best restaurants. Some of Ireland's best food is prepared by international chefs from countries as diverse as Finland and Japan.

For many, eating fresh local seafood within view of the ocean is one of the highlights of a trip to Ireland. Kilmore Quay in Wexford is known across the country for its crab, mussels, scallops and prawns. For oysters, head to Galway.

Finding vegetarian and vegan food is no problem in most places in Ireland, but the quality varies.

Time for Tea

Many Irish people drink a lot of tea, and you'll certainly be offered a cup if you visit a local's home. It is usually taken with milk and accompanied by biscuits. (Dunking them in the tea is optional.) Coffee is increasingly popular, and in most areas of the country, it's possible to find coffee shops that use high-quality, locally roasted beans.

For a midmorning or late afternoon snack, head to a cafe for a freshly baked scone or tray bake (sweet cakes or biscuits that are baked in the oven on a flat tray and then cut into small rectangular slices).

Whiskey & Stout

As recently as the 1990s, Ireland had only three working distilleries: Jameson's, Bushmills and Cooley's. But an explosion in artisan distilling has seen the number grow to more than 40, producing a range of aged whiskeys, which the Irish call *uisce beatha* (water of life).

Known as the black stuff, Guinness is one of Ireland's best-known products, but it's not the country's only stout. Murphy's and Beamish are both brewed in Cork city, and breweries across the country produce their own stouts. Some of the most highly rated are Porterhouse's Oyster Stout and Dungarvan Brewing Company's Black Rock Irish Stout.

Specialities

Abernethy butter a slow-churned butter produced in County Down.

Boxty A savoury potato pancake patty.

Champ and **Colcannon** Mashed-potato dishes made with spring onion and cabbage, respectively.

Chowder Creamy seafood soup, usually accompanied by soda bread.

Clonakilty black pudding This County Cork blood sausage has its own dedicated museum.

Irish stew Comforting dish made with meat, potatoes and root vegetables.

Oysters Irish waters produce exceptional, subtly flavoured oysters.

Soda bread Made with buttermilk and bicarbonate of soda. Guinness is sometimes added, giving the loaf a rich, malty taste.

Waterford blaa A doughy white bread roll.

Wexford strawberries Widely considered the country's best.

Seaweed

Carrageen moss A reddish seaweed that can be found in dishes as diverse as salads and ice cream.

Dulse A purple seaweed that is dried and eaten as a snack or as a seasoning; also known as dillisk.

Kelp A nutritious seaweed that can be cooked and eaten.

Irish Cheeses

Ardrahan Farmhouse pasteurised cow's milk cheese with an earthy taste.

Corleggy Handmade raw goat's milk cheese.

Gubbeen Cow's milk cheese; includes a crumbly, oak-smoked variety.

Durrus A creamy, fruity farmhouse cheese made using traditional techniques.

Cashel Blue Creamy blue cheese from Tipperary.

Cooleeney Soft cheese made with the raw and pasteurised milk of a Friesian dairy herd.

FOOD FESTIVALS

Baltimore Seafood & Wooden Boat Festival (p208) In late May, vendors ply punters with west Cork's best smoked fish, cheese and organic vegetables.

Cork on a Fork (p192) Cooking demonstrations, food trails and cooking classes are all part of a packed schedule of events in August.

Galway International Oyster & Seafood Festival (p307) This huge annual festival features oyster-eating championships and piles of fresh seafood.

All Ireland Chowder Festival (p186) Restaurants and pubs from all over the country compete for the title of Best Chowder in Ireland in Kinsale.

Taste of Wicklow Food Festival (p133) Celebrity chefs offer demonstrations, and the festival field is packed with artisan food stalls in Wicklow town.

West Waterford Festival of Food (p164) In Dungarvan, this festival includes foraging trails and themed food markets.

THE YEAR IN FOOD

SPRING
Market stalls overflow and restaurant chefs get creative with seasonal asparagus, spinach, broccoli, scallions (spring onions) and rhubarb. Woodland areas carry the scent of abundant wild garlic.

SUMMER
The early crop of potatoes is ready for harvesting. It's the best time of year for crustaceans, including langoustines, lobster and crab. In late summer, Ireland's hedgerows offer juicy blackberries for picking.

AUTUMN
In September, Ireland's apples are harvested to be sold in markets or brewed into cider. Seasonal vegetables include parsnips, squash, turnip and pumpkins. September and October are the best months for foraging mushrooms.

WINTER
It's the best time of year for wild game, including venison, rabbit and pheasant. The native oyster season runs from September to April. Look out for winter cabbage, sprouting broccoli and carrots.

Carrick-a-Rede rope bridge (p547)

THE OUTDOORS

One of the best ways to experience Ireland's wild beauty is to embrace the outdoors, be it on foot, by bike, or on horseback.

Gentle hills, rocky ridges, wild boglands, soaring sea cliffs, remote islands and unpredictable weather are all part of experiencing the great Irish outdoors. There are several scenic mountain ranges to hike, including the Wicklow Mountains in the east, the Mournes in the north and the mountains of Kerry in the southwest, while Ireland's coastal waters, rivers and lakes can be explored by canoe, kayak or SUP. Ireland's wild Atlantic waves are popular with surfers, who don thick wetsuits and brave the waters year-round.

Walking & Hiking

Ireland's coastline, hills and inland waterways are traversed by a network of walking trails, with options ranging from gentle strolls to multiday hikes. The country's forest parks have graded waymarked trails that are excellent for short walks. These trails often include options that are wheelchair- and pushchair-accessible and ideal for families, including interpretative trails and themed trails with carvings of woodland characters to spot along the way. Many hill and mountain walks are also waymarked, but you'll need to bring a compass and a map. In areas of blanket bog, boardwalks have been constructed to protect the delicate natural habitat, adding an element of fun and making for drier feet too. Two useful websites for finding local hiking routes are Walk NI (walkni.com) and Sport Ireland (sportireland.ie/outdoors).

Long-distance walking trails include the Ulster Way, a 1024km circular route through Northern Ireland. It has a 50km section

---

Popular Sports

GOLF
Tee off at the spectacularly situated links courses of **Royal Portrush** (p542), with views over the north Atlantic.

ROCK CLIMBING
In County Clare, tackle the **Blind Man's Cliff** at Ailladie (p384), an 800m-long limestone sea cliff.

CANOEING & KAYAKING
Explore **Strangford Lough** by kayak or canoe, entering the water at Castle Ward in County Down (p518).

FAMILY ADVENTURES

Clamber over rocks and jump into the sea on a **coasteering session** (p548) in County Antrim.

Kids will love **Beyond the Trees**, a 1.4km-long treetop walkway at Avondale Forest Park in County Wicklow (p129).

Pull on a wetsuit, grab a surfboard and **ride the waves** at **Tramore** (p162) in County Waterford.

Meander around the islands and inlets of County Fermanagh's **Upper Lough Erne** by kayak (p569).

Cycle the 48km **Waterford Greenway**, suitable for all abilities, including families with kids (p161).

Surf the waves at **Rossnowlagh Beach** near Bundoran in County Donegal (p399).

Pet piglets, lambs, ducklings and chicks at **Muckross Traditional Farms** (p226) in Co Kerry, where 1930s farming practices are recreated.

---

known as the Causeway Coast Way on the north Antrim coast and the 27km Mourne Way trail across the Mourne Mountains in County Down. In the Republic, the 650km Coast to Coast Walk is made up of five linked sections, beginning in Dublin with the Wicklow Way and ending with the Kerry Way.

Ireland's mountains and hills can be climbed on day hikes. Carrauntoohil in County Kerry and the Twelve Bens in Connemara are the most challenging. In County Down, Slieve Donard is a straightforward climb. Other peaks include Errigal Mountain in County Donegal and Mt Brandon in County Kerry.

Cycling

Ireland has a huge network of minor roads traversing the wildest corners of the island that are perfect for exploring by bike, with the help of a good map. Waymarked routes include the Kingfisher Trail, which extends 370km along the back roads of Counties Fermanagh, Leitrim, Cavan and Monaghan. Looped cycle routes run from Clifden Cycle Hub in Connemara, County Galway, and through Killarney National Park in County Kerry. Sustrans (sustrans.org.uk) has maps of signed cycling routes in the North, including traffic-free rides.

A number of forest parks have purpose-built, graded mountain-biking trails, and several have bike rental and uplift services. Some of the best include Davagh Forest (p570) in County Tyrone and Kilbroney Park (p515) in County Down.

Surfing

Despite its cold waters, Ireland is an increasingly popular destination for surfing and is considered by many to have some of the world's best waves. Surf schools offer lessons and equipment hire at the major surf spots in Counties Donegal, Sligo, Clare, Antrim, Derry and Waterford. Expert surfers test their skills with the towering waves at Mullaghmore in County Sligo.

Surfing, Tramore (p162)

SUP
Paddle out to see the **Samson** wreck in the waters around Ardmore (p165), County Waterford.

FISHING
County Fermanagh's lakes, including **Lough Erne** (p567), are popular for both coarse and game fishing.

HORSE RIDING
Take in the wild scenery of **Connemara National Park** in County Galway on horseback (p320).

DIVING
Discover wrecks in the waters near **Rathlin Island** in County Antrim on a dive with Aquaholics (p546).

ACTION AREAS

Where to find Ireland's best outdoor activities.

National Parks

1. Killarney National Park (p224)
2. Burren National Park (p282)
3. Wicklow Mountains National Park (p118)
4. Connemara National Park (p318)
5. Wild Nephin National Park (p355)
6. Glenveagh National Park (p376)

Walking/Hiking

1. Causeway Coast, County Antrim (p550)
2. Mourne Mountains, County Down (p517)
3. Wicklow Mountains, County Wicklow (p119)
4. Errigal Mountain, County Donegal (p381)
5. The Burren, County Clare (p286)
6. Croagh Patrick, County Mayo (p348)
7. Slieve League, County Donegal (p393)

PLAN YOUR TRIP THE OUTDOORS

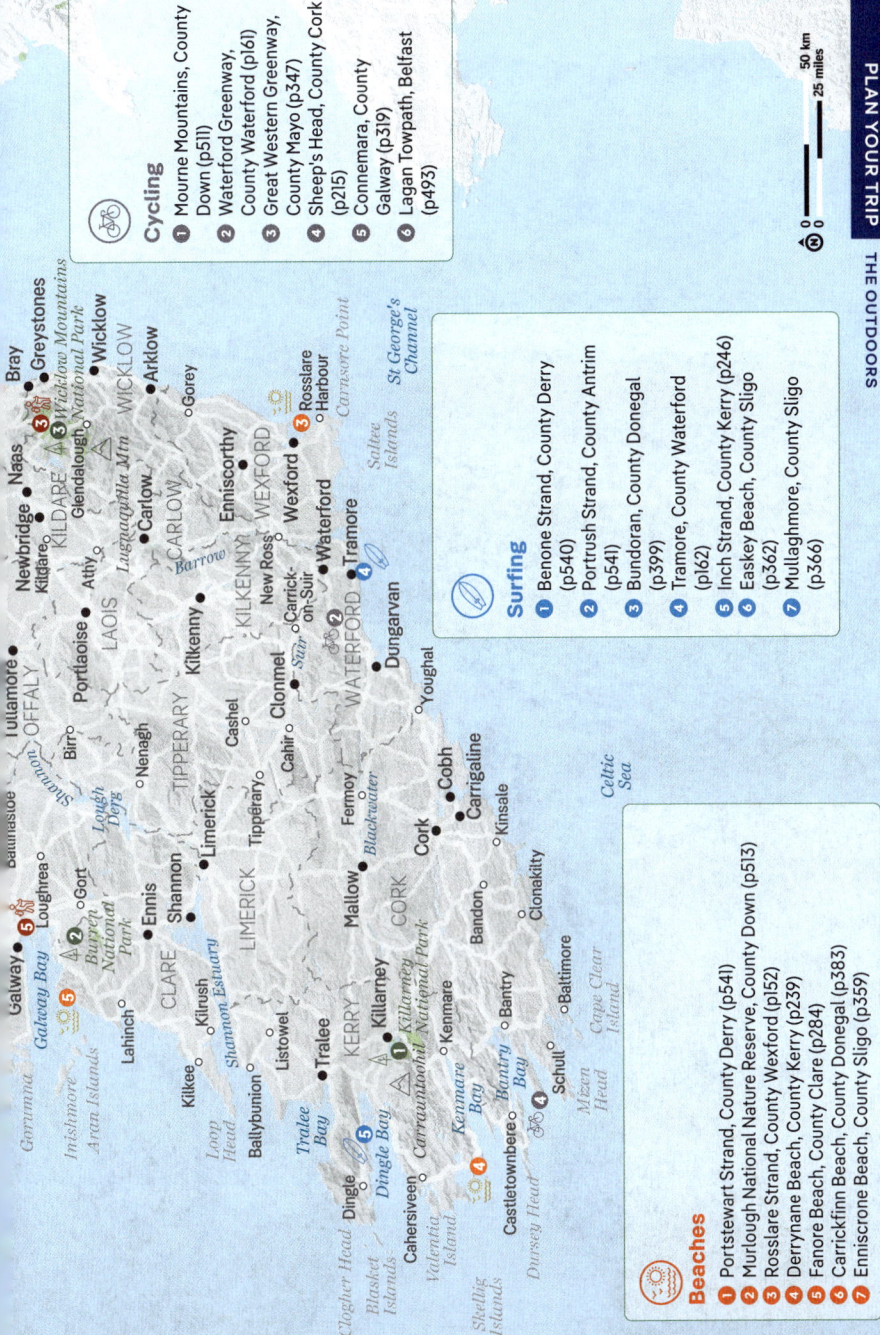

Cycling
1. Mourne Mountains, County Down (p511)
2. Waterford Greenway, County Waterford (p161)
3. Great Western Greenway, County Mayo (p347)
4. Sheep's Head, County Cork (p215)
5. Connemara, County Galway (p319)
6. Lagan Towpath, Belfast (p493)

Surfing
1. Benone Strand, County Derry (p540)
2. Portrush Strand, County Antrim (p541)
3. Bundoran, County Donegal (p399)
4. Tramore, County Waterford (p162)
5. Inch Strand, County Kerry (p246)
6. Easkey Beach, County Sligo (p362)
7. Mullaghmore, County Sligo (p366)

Beaches
1. Portstewart Strand, County Derry (p541)
2. Murlough National Nature Reserve, County Down (p513)
3. Rosslare Strand, County Wexford (p152)
4. Derrynane Beach, County Kerry (p239)
5. Fanore Beach, County Clare (p284)
6. Carrickfinn Beach, County Donegal (p383)
7. Enniscrone Beach, County Sligo (p359)

THE GUIDE

IRELAND

THE GUIDE

Donegal
p373

Derry & Antrim
p526

BELFAST
p460

Fermanagh
& Tyrone
p557

Down &
Armagh
p503

Mayo & Sligo
p336

Meath, Louth,
Monaghan
& Cavan
p431

Galway
p303

The
Midlands
p400

DUBLIN
p48

Wicklow
& Kildare
p115

Clare
p278

Limerick &
Tipperary
p257

Wexford,
Waterford, Carlow
& Kilkenny
p140

Kerry
p218

Cork
p183

Chapters in this section are organised by hubs and their surrounding areas. We see the hub as your base in the destination, where you'll find unique experiences, local insights, insider tips and expert recommendations. It's also your gateway to the surrounding area, where you'll see what and how much you can do from there.

Cuilcagh Mountain (p455)
DAVI COSTA/SHUTTERSTOCK ©

DUBLIN
IRELAND'S CAPITAL OF COOL

A small city with a huge reputation, Dublin has a mix of heritage and hedonism that won't disappoint.

Dublin's been making noise since around 500 BCE, when a bunch of intrepid Celts camped at a ford over the River Liffey, giving us the tough-to-pronounce Irish name of Baile Átha Cliath (*bawl-ya aw-ha kleeya*, meaning Town of the Hurdle Ford). Fast forward a couple of thousand years, past a bunch of invaders from the Vikings to the Normans, and contemporary Dublin is still making noise. But this time, it's generally in the spirit of revelry rather than rebellion.

And it's still a popular spot – Dublin is by far the most populated county in Ireland, with roughly one-quarter of the country's population living and working within its borders. Unsurprisingly, it's where you'll find the biggest concentration and range of hotels and restaurants and the largest choice of attractions and things to do, plus virtually all of the services that Ireland has available.

While a lot of the action is crammed into the (fairly small) city centre, Dublin is also a city of villages, each with its own architectural styles, quirks and residents who staunchly declare their neighbourhood to be the best. Some of the city's must-see spots are in these neighbourhoods of Dublin, from a cool brunch cafe in the Docklands to a vintage shop in the Liberties.

It's not all perfect, of course, and Dubliners will admit theirs isn't always the prettiest city. But they will remind you that pretty things are as easy to like as they are to forget, and then point out the showstopper Georgian bits to prove that Dublin has a fine line in sophisticated elegance. True love is demonstrated with brutal unsentimentality, but they'll go soft at the knees when talking about the character and personality of the 'greatest city in the world, if you ignore all the others'. But heaven help the outsider who dares criticise the place!

Garrulous, amiable and witty, Dubliners are great hosts, a charismatic bunch with compelling souls and sociability, giving you all the more reason to make yourself an honorary Dubliner, if only for a few days, and see for yourself what all the fuss is about.

THE MAIN AREAS

GRAFTON STREET & ST STEPHEN'S GREEN
Heart of the city.
p54

MERRION SQUARE & GEORGIAN DUBLIN
Elegant architecture and top museums. **p66**

TEMPLE BAR
Nightlife central.
075

KILMAINHAM & THE LIBERTIES
Distilleries and breweries.
p81

Above: Grand Canal Square, the Docklands (p100); left: Jameson Distillery (p95)

NORTH OF THE LIFFEY	**DOCKLANDS**	**BEYOND THE CITY CENTRE**
Grandeur of old Dublin.	Dublin's tech hub.	Beaches, parks and stadiums.
p90	**p100**	**p107**

Find Your Way

Dublin is small and flat enough to get around on foot; most of the city's primary sights are within walking distance of one another. The city's rent-and-ride Dublinbikes scheme is the ideal way to cover ground quickly. Otherwise, there's the bus and the two-line light rail system called the Luas.

Beyond the City Centre
p107

Kilmainham & the Liberties
p81

BUS
Dublin Bus covers most areas in the city, with 12 night bus routes (called Nitelink) at the weekend. The easiest way to pay for public transport in Dublin is with a prepaid Leap card. Leap Visitor Cards can be purchased for one, three or seven days.

TRAM
The Luas tram system has two lines, red and green, which run through the city centre. For visitors, the handiest routes are down into Ranelagh, or from the Docklands out to Smithfield. You can buy a ticket at each station or use a Leap card.

THE GUIDE
DUBLIN

North of the Liffey
p90

- Chapter One
- 14 Henrietta Street
- General Post Office
- Famine
- Temple Bar Food Market
- Temple Bar
- Project Arts Centre

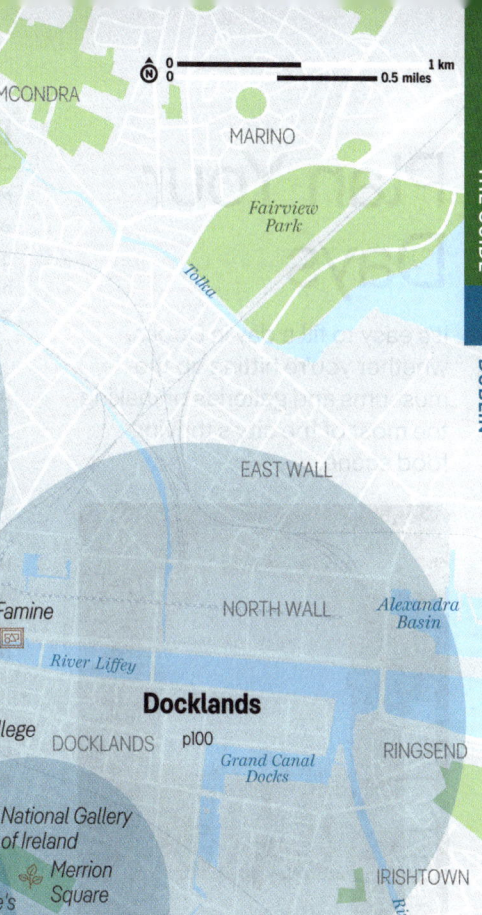

Temple Bar
p75

- Chester Beatty
- Trinity College Dublin
- Little Museum of Dublin
- National Gallery of Ireland
- O'Donoghue's
- Merrion Square
- St Stephen's Green

Docklands
p100

Merrion Square & Georgian Dublin
p66

Grafton Street & St Stephen's Green
p54

WALK
Dublin's city centre is flat and eminently walkable. It's less than 2km from one end of the city centre to the other. An increasing number of roads are pedestrianised, particularly in the summer, which makes the whole experience even more pleasant.

FROM THE AIRPORT
The best way to get into town is by bus. Journeys take around 30 minutes. Aircoach and Dublin Express have regular services to the city centre and the suburbs, or you can hop on the cheaper but slower Dublin Bus.

51

Plan Your Days

It's easy to fill a day in Dublin, whether you're hitting up the museums and galleries or making the most of the city's thriving food scene.

Trinity College (p55)

Day 1

Morning
● Start with a stroll through the grounds of **Trinity College** (p55) before ambling up Grafton St to **St Stephen's Green** (p60). To see some beautiful books and artefacts up close, drop into the **Chester Beatty** (p55).

Afternoon
● Pick your heavyweight institution, or visit all three: the **National Museum of Ireland – Archaeology** (p70), the **National Gallery** (p68) and the **Museum of Natural History** (p69) are all in the same neighbourhood.

Evening
● It wouldn't be a night in Dublin without a pint and a bit of trad music. Hit up one of the pubs in **Temple Bar** (p75) to get acquainted.

You'll Also Want to...

Soak up the spirit of the city with a visit to distilleries and design boutiques and then take a jaunt along the coast.

VISIT THE DISTILLERIES
Dublin's whiskey scene has seen a resurgence, with cool distilleries like **Teeling** and **Roe & Co** (p86) opening their doors.

HIT THE BEACH
A short trip on the DART train gets you to coastal **Dalkey** (p111) or the fishing village of **Howth** (p111).

CATCH A MATCH
There's no game on Earth like hurling. It's fast-paced, thrilling and ferocious. See it yourself at **Croke Park Stadium** (p110).

Day 2

Morning
- Begin with a little penance at either (or both) of Dublin's medieval cathedrals, **St Patrick's** (p84) and **Christ Church** (p78), before pursuing pleasure at Dublin's most popular tourist attraction, the **Guinness Storehouse** (p83).

Afternoon
- Go further west to **Kilmainham** (p81), visiting first the fine collection at the **Irish Museum of Modern Art** (p85) before going out the back entrance and stepping into **Kilmainham Gaol** (p89). If the weather is good, take a stroll around the **War Memorial Gardens** (p86).

Evening
- Check out the restaurant and bar scene in **Stoneybatter** (p97), whether you fancy a traditional pub or a hipster bistro.

Day 3

Morning
- Head **North of the Liffey** (p90), starting with a walk up O'Connell St to see the **General Post Office** (p91). Afterwards, check out the collection at the **Hugh Lane Gallery** (p94), including Francis Bacon's reconstructed studio, before discovering the city's Georgian past at **14 Henrietta Street** (p91).

Afternoon
- Explore the excellent collection of the **National Museum of Ireland – Decorative Arts & History** (p95) and then head to **Phoenix Park** (p109).

Evening
- Watch a play at one of Dublin's theatres, be it a traditional show at the **Gate Theatre** (p99) or something a little more experimental at the **Abbey Theatre** (p98).

UNDERSTAND DUBLIN
Dubliners tell the story of their city at the **Little Museum of Dublin** (p55), whose collection is made from local contributions.

GO GREEN
Phoenix Park (p109) is home to the president, the US ambassador, the zoo and a herd of wild deer.

SHOP UNTIL YOU DROP
Hit up the design shops and indie boutiques of the wonderfully elegant **Powerscourt Townhouse** (p63).

VISIT A GEORGIAN TOWNHOUSE
One of the city's best museum experiences is **14 Henrietta Street** (p91), where 250 years of history are laid bare.

GRAFTON STREET & ST STEPHEN'S GREEN

HEART OF THE CITY

If you were to limit your sightseeing to only one neighbourhood, Grafton St and St Stephen's Green would be it (not that we'd recommend anything of the sort, of course). Busy, pedestrianised Grafton St is both the city's most famous street and its unofficial centre. At its northern end is the neighbourhood's main attraction, Trinity College, whose pleasures and treasures can be explored in a couple of hours.

At the other end of the street is the centrepiece of Georgian Dublin, St Stephen's Green, beautifully landscaped and dotted with statuary that provides a veritable who's who of Irish history.

West of Grafton St is a warren of narrow lanes and streets – think funky boutiques, great restaurants and a huge choice of bars and cafes. Further west again are Dublin Castle and Chester Beatty, both of which can be explored in half a day.

TOP TIP

The area around Grafton St is by far the most popular neighbourhood in the city, but Dublin's compact size means you don't have to stay here to have it all at your doorstep. If you do, be aware that most of the lodgings are among the priciest in town.

St Stephen's Green (p60)

Little Museum of Dublin
Artefacts Sourced By Citizens

The award-winning Little Museum of Dublin tells the city's story via quirky memorabilia, photographs and artefacts donated by the general public. The collection includes a lectern used by JFK on his 1963 visit to Ireland and a whole room on the 2nd floor devoted to the history of U2. To visit, you must take a guided tour that goes on the hour every hour. The museum also runs a daily walking tour of St Stephen's Green, as well as a themed weekly tour telling the story of Ireland's influential women.

Little Museum of Ireland

Blue Quran, Chester Beatty Library

Chester Beatty
A Trove Of Beautiful Objects

On the grounds of Dublin Castle, the world-famous Chester Beatty has a breathtaking assembly of more than 20,000 manuscripts, including the world's second-oldest biblical fragment and a collection of Qurans from the 9th to the 19th centuries that is considered among the best examples of illuminated Islamic texts in the world. Other treasures include ancient Egyptian texts on papyrus, intricately designed little medicine boxes and perhaps the finest selection of Chinese jade books on the planet. Keep an eye on the calendar of events – it regularly runs qigong workshops on the rooftop garden, as well as sound baths and meditation sessions.

Trinity College Dublin
The Capital's Most Prestigious University

Step through the front arch of Trinity College Dublin, and you'll feel like you're being transported back in time. Ireland's most prestigious university is a 16th-century bucolic retreat in the heart of the city. Ambling about its cobbled squares, it's easy to imagine it in those far-off days when all good gentlemen (for they were only men until 1904) came equipped with a passion for philosophy and a love of empire. Thankfully, the student body is a lot more diverse these days.

A great way to see the grounds is on a walking tour, departing from the entrance on College Green. On sunny days, head to the campus bar on the cricket grounds to lounge around with a cold beer.

GRAFTON STREET & ST STEPHEN'S GREEN

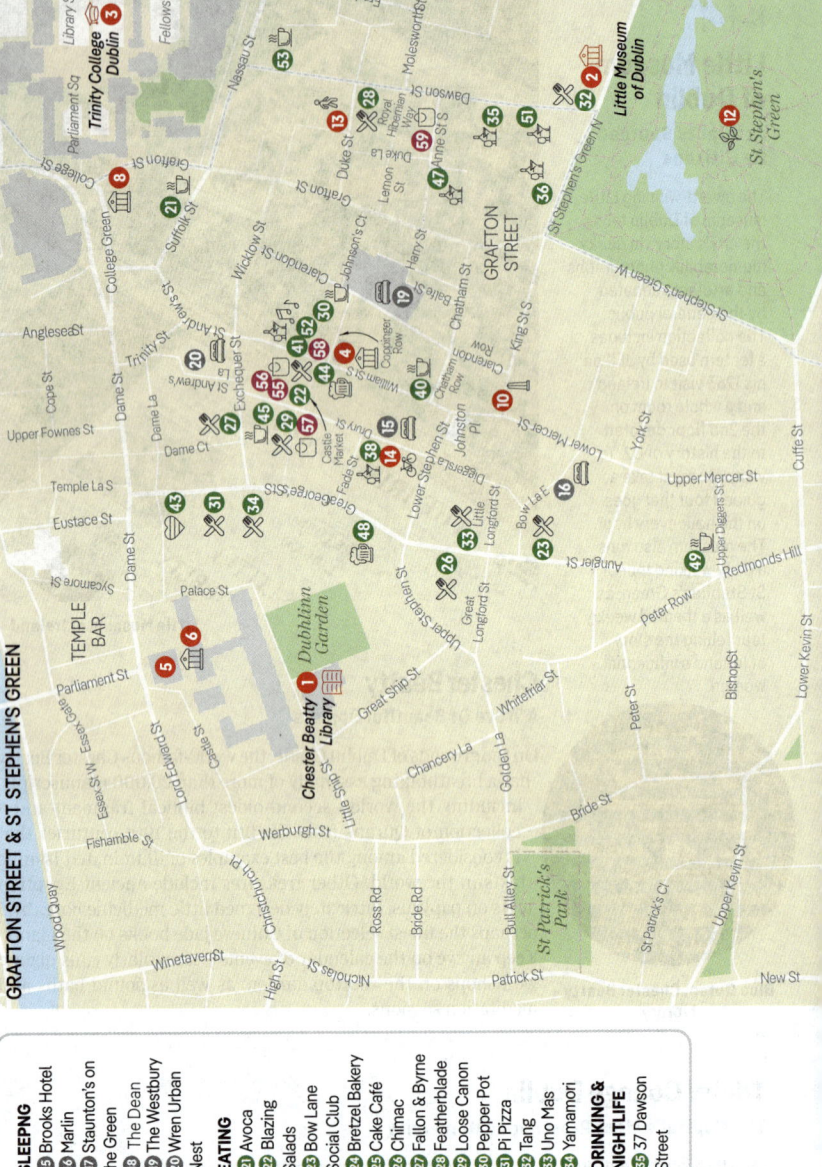

HIGHLIGHTS
1. Chester Beatty Library
2. Little Museum of Dublin
3. Trinity College Dublin

SIGHTS
4. City Assembly House
5. City Hall
6. Dublin Castle
7. Irish Jewish Museum
8. Irish Whiskey Museum
9. Iveagh Gardens
10. Luke Kelly Statue
11. Museum of Literature Ireland
12. St Stephen's Green

ACTIVITIES, COURSES & TOURS
13. Dublin Literary Pub Crawl
14. Lazy Bike Tour

SLEEPNG
15. Brooks Hotel
16. Marlin
17. Staunton's on the Green
18. The Dean
19. The Westbury
20. Wren Urban Nest

EATING
21. Avoca
22. Blazing Salads
23. Bow Lane Social Club
24. Bretzel Bakery
25. Cake Café
26. Chimac
27. Fallon & Byrne
28. Featherblade
29. Loose Canon
30. Pepper Pot
31. Pi Pizza
32. Tang
33. Uno Mas
34. Yamamori

DRINKING & NIGHTLIFE
35. 37 Dawson Street

DUBLIN GRAFTON STREET & ST STEPHEN'S GREEN

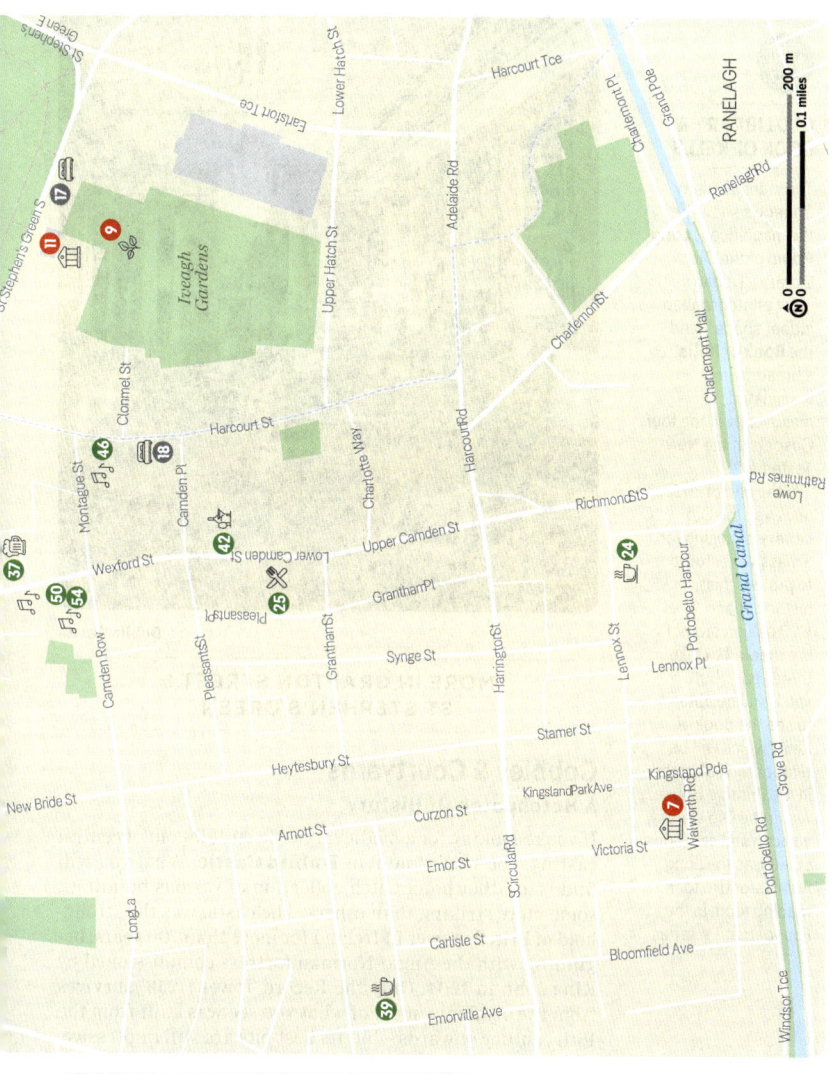

RANELAGH

36 9 Below
37 Against the Grain
38 Un Amy Austin o
39 Bibi's
40 Clement & Pekoe
41 Farrier & Draper
42 Frank's
43 George
44 Grogan's Castle Lounge
45 Kaph
46 Krystle
47 Un La Cave o
48 Long Hall
49 Network
50 Opium
51 Peruke & Periwig
52 Pygmalion
53 Sprout
54 Whelan's

SHOPPING
55 Industry
56 Irish Design Shop
57 Om Diva
58 Powerscourt Townhouse
59 Sheridans Cheesemongers

57

OLD LIBRARY & BOOK OF KELLS

The stars of Trinity College's show are the magnificent **Long Room** of the Old Library – Dublin's most photographed indoor space – and the **Book of Kells**, a breathtaking, illuminated manuscript of the four Gospels of the New Testament.

At the end of 2023, however, the Old Library is closing for a massive restoration to protect this historic space. The €90 million project is expected to take three years, but you'll still be able to see the Book of Kells, which will be temporarily rehomed in the Printing House. As for the Old Library, you can still see it on screen, as the Long Room stood in for a reading room in the *Foundation* TV series.

Dublin Castle

MORE IN GRAFTON STREET & ST STEPHEN'S GREEN

Cobbles & Courtyards
A Hotchpotch Of History

If you're looking for a medieval castle straight out of central casting, you won't find it at **Dublin Castle**. What you will find is a rather hotchpotch collection of various buildings, some more striking than others. The castle was the stronghold of British power in Ireland for more than 700 years, beginning with the Anglo-Norman fortress commissioned by King John in 1204. Only the Record Tower (1258) survives from the original – most of what you see was built from the 18th century onwards – but its best bits are still impressive.

The castle was officially handed over to Michael Collins, representing the Irish Free State, in 1922, when the British viceroy is reported to have rebuked him for being seven minutes late. Collins replied, 'We've been waiting 700 years. You can have the seven minutes.'

WHERE TO EAT IN GRAFTON STREET & ST STEPHEN'S GREEN

Featherblade
With an emphasis on more unusual cuts of beef, this steakhouse offers amazing value for money. €€

Pi Pizza
A buzzing restaurant with a simple menu of excellent Neapolitan pizza and organic wines. €€

Chimac
This hipster spot serves Korean fried chicken with a side of frozen rosé. €

Nowadays, the castle can be visited only on a guided tour, during which you'll get to see the **State Rooms**, many of which are decorated in dubious taste. There are beautiful chandeliers (ooh!), plush Irish carpets (aah!), splendid rococo ceilings and the throne of King George V. You also get to see the room in which the wounded James Connolly was tied to a chair while convalescing after the 1916 Easter Rising, brought back to health to be executed by firing squad.

If you're not taking a tour, a stroll through the cobbled courtyard is a pleasant way to see the buildings. At Christmas, this whole area is taken over by a traditional **market**.

Literary Legends
The Epicentre Of Irish Writing

The motherland of Ireland's literary heritage, the **Museum of Literature Ireland** (MoLI) is an interactive space dedicated to writers old and new. The museum is in two stunning Georgian townhouses collectively known as Newman House, which in 1865 saw the establishment of the Catholic University of Ireland, the alma mater of James Joyce, Pádraig Pearse and Eamon de Valera.

Inside, the entire timeline of Irish literature is explored, from the Middle Ages to the present day. Highlights include Joyce's *Ulysses* notebooks as well as the first print of the novel, but Ireland's newest writers are also celebrated in a rotating series of exhibitions. You might see an artsy installation created by the author Claire-Louise Bennett or a multimedia experience curated by Patrick McCabe.

On the first Friday of every month, the museum is open late and feels like a literary happening. There are live readings, discussions and music throughout the evening. Best of all, admission on those nights is free. The Commons Cafe is open late for the occasion, but it's a lovely spot for a bite whenever you visit, with outdoor seating for pleasant days.

At the back of the museum, the **Courtyard** and **Readers Gardens** are well worth a visit, be it for a moment of calm or a continuation of the literary experience. There's an ash tree where Joyce had his graduation photo taken, as well as sculptures of reading figures spread throughout.

Dublin's HQ
You Can't Fight City Hall

The beautiful Georgian structure of **City Hall** was originally built by Thomas Cooley as the Royal Exchange between 1769 and 1779, and botched in the mid-19th century

---

BEST SPOTS FOR A QUICK LUNCH

Sprout
Made using ingredients grown on the restaurant's own farm, the salads are massive, colourful and downright delicious. €

Pepper Pot
In the Powerscourt Townhouse (p63), this cute cafe is best known for its roasted pear, bacon and cheddar sandwich. €

Tang
Hop in for quick Middle Eastern food on the go, such as Lebanese flatbreads and spicy rice bowls. €

Blazing Salads
If you want to be virtuous, this is the place to be – this Californian-style salad bar is the epitome of wellness. €

WHERE TO EAT IN GRAFTON STREET & ST STEPHEN'S GREEN

Loose Canon
Grab a cheeseboard or a buttery toasted sandwich at this wine and cheese shop. €

Uno Mas
A chichi tapas joint with dishes like octopus with kale and ham croquettes. €€

Yamamori
A Dublin classic, serving sushi, noodles and a well-priced lunch bento box. €€

when it became the offices of the local government (hence its name). Thankfully, a renovation in 2000 restored it to its gleaming Georgian best.

The rotunda and its ambulatory form a breathtaking interior, bathed in natural light from enormous windows to the east. A vast marble statue of former mayor and Catholic emancipator Daniel O'Connell stands here as a reminder of the building's links with Irish nationalism. (The funerals of 19th-century nationalist politician Charles Stewart Parnell and Irish revolutionary Michael Collins were held here.)

There was a sordid precursor to City Hall on this spot: the Lucas Coffee House and the adjoining Eagle Tavern, in which Richard Parsons, Earl of Rosse, founded the notorious Hellfire Club in 1735. Although the city abounded with gentlemen's clubs, this particular one gained a reputation for messing about in the arenas of sex and Satan, two topics guaranteed to fire the lurid imaginings of the city's gossipmongers.

Sadly, the in-house museum that told the story of City Hall closed during the COVID-19 pandemic and is yet to return. However, you can still go inside and see the glorious rotunda when there's not a wedding on. There are also occasional free history talks.

The Secret Garden
Smell The Roses

St Stephen's Green might get all the glory, but the **Iveagh Gardens** are every bit as lovely (and half as crowded). Ninian Niven designed them in 1863 as the private grounds of Iveagh House, and they include a rustic grotto, a cascade, a fountain, a maze and a rosarium, with a plethora of rose varieties that smell heavenly in the spring. Regular big-ticket gigs take place here in the summer, along with the **Comedy Festival** and **Taste of Dublin**. Enter the gardens from Clonmel St (off Harcourt St) or from Upper Hatch St, which brings you straight into the rose garden.

Whiskey a Go-Go
Sink A Dram

If there's one thing Dublin's not short of, it's whiskey distilleries. The industry underwent something of a resurgence, and now numerous distilleries are on the go, most of which are spread around the Liberties (p86). But if you want to taste a few different spirits and not just one brand, head to the **Irish Whiskey Museum** near Trinity College.

THE TWO LUKES

In 2018, Dublin's legendary folk singer Luke Kelly (1940–84) was immortalised in sculpture not once, but twice – on the same day. The first figure to be erected was a traditional bronze sculpture on South King St by John Coll, capturing Kelly mid-song while playing the banjo.

The second figure is a 2m marble head with eyes closed and 3000 strands of copper hair. It's on Sheriff St, where Kelly was born. Like all bold pieces of art, it has generated much comment, with some declaring that the artist did a great job capturing Kelly mid-orgasm.

WHERE TO STAY IN GRAFTON STREET & ST STEPHEN'S GREEN

Brooks Hotel
A boutique, family-run hotel with huge beds and a cosy residents lounge. €€

The Westbury
This Dublin stalwart may be pricey, but it's worth it for the sheer quality. Some suites have terraces. €€€

Marlin
The rooms are small but functional in this 2019-opened hotel, and the prices are great. €€

Irish Whiskey Museum

You'll learn all about the history of Irish whiskey on a guided tour before tasting a few different varieties at the end. Serious fans will want to book the premium tour for more exclusive sips or the blending experience, where you can create your own whiskey. However, you don't have to do a tour to have a taste. Head straight to the bar and order a whiskey flight from the knowledgeable barkeeps.

Walk with the Writers
An Upmarket Pub Crawl

How do you justify an evening of drinking? By calling it the **Dublin Literary Pub Crawl**, of course. On this two-hour performance tour, two actors lead you on a jaunt between pubs associated with famous Dublin writers, such as Samuel Beckett, Oscar Wilde and Brendan Behan. (Just don't try to match Behan's drinking prowess.)

BEST SPOTS FOR PICNIC SHOPPING

Fallon & Byrne
Dublin's prime foodie emporium, where you can buy sandwiches, salads, fancy baked goods, coffee and cold-pressed juices.

Sheridans Cheesemongers
This fancy cheese shop has everything you could desire, from Wicklow brie to the stinkiest blue. It also sells olives and charcuterie.

Avoca
Pick up premade salads, sandwiches made to order and rotisserie chicken in the basement of this classic homeware shop.

Bretzel Bakery
Serving everything from house-made bagels to slices of cake, this old-school bakery has been going since 1870.

WHERE TO STAY IN GRAFTON STREET & ST STEPHEN'S GREEN

The Dean
Funky rooms, Smeg fridges and a hopping rooftop bar – light sleepers beware. €€

Staunton's on the Green
This handsome Georgian house has charming bedrooms and a beautiful garden. €€

Wren Urban Nest
With eco-credentials and calming decor, this is a great base for exploring the neighbourhood. €€

We Are Scientists performing at Whelan's

BEST FESTIVALS IN DUBLIN

Dublin International Film Festival
Two weeks of screenings, premieres and celebrities around the city.

St Patrick's Festival
As well as the parade, the Festival Quarter is the hub of live music, DJs and comedy, usually held at Collins Barracks (p95).

Pride
Pride is a big deal in Dublin, and the LGBTIQ+ festival is only growing. Expect gigs, parties and one hell of a parade.

Forbidden Fruit
The city's foremost music festival, with huge acts playing on the grounds of Royal Hospital Kilmainham (p85).

Along the way, the actors recite the words of these poets and writers and tell the stories of the pubs and the city itself. The tour leaves from the Duke on Duke St, where you can grab a bite beforehand to line the stomach. If you don't drink, join the Monday morning tour, which has all of the lit without getting you lit.

Musical Magnet
The Musician's Favourite Venue

Whelan's isn't just a pub – it's many an Irish musician's spiritual home. From the outside, it looks like a run-of-the-mill bar on Wexford St, but the venue inside has played host to an incredible array of visiting artists over the years, from Jeff Buckley to David Gray.

They don't just come to perform. You'll often see a famous face milling around the back of the crowd, checking out their competition. The main stage is in a midsized room attached to the bar, and when the show is done, you can often find the

WHERE TO DRINK IN GRAFTON STREET & ST STEPHEN'S GREEN

Grogan's Castle Lounge
A city institution, Grogan's has long been a favourite haunt of Dublin's writers and artists.

Long Hall
One of the oldest pubs in Dublin, with a decor that's barely changed since the 1860s.

Against the Grain
A craft beer bar run by Galway Bay Brewery, with a dizzying selection of beers on tap.

acts filling up in the bar along with their fans. In the smaller room upstairs, you might see an up-and-coming band or an act trying out new material.

Live Like a Viscount
Shop In Style

On sunny days, you'll always see a crowd of Dubliners sitting on the wide stone steps of the **Powerscourt Townhouse**. Whether they're waiting to meet a friend or just soaking up the sun with a coffee, it's seemingly the hangout spot of choice. This makes sense, considering this 18th-century Georgian townhouse was built solely for the purpose of entertaining. Richard Wingfield, 3rd Viscount Powerscourt, bought the building just to host guests during Parliament season.

Nowadays, it's a swish shopping centre, with each of the floors filled with upmarket boutiques trading in antique and modern jewellery, wedding dresses and high-end homewares. But the original architecture still shines through, from the elaborate chandeliers to the glossy mahogany handrails on the stairs. The main attraction is the atrium, now home to the **Little Pyg** pizzeria and wine bar, where groups of friends share food and cocktails under the skylights.

If you're looking to pick up a unique piece of jewellery, head to **Chupi** or **MoMuse** for delicate gold necklaces and bracelets. The antique shops huddle together in one row, with prices ranging from the reasonable to the wacky. It's always worth browsing in **The Garden** if only to soak up the scent of the freshly cut flowers.

There's plenty of great shopping to be found nearby too. Head to Drury St to pick up vintage clothing in Om Diva, designy bits in **Industry** or homegrown pieces in the **Irish Design Shop**.

Historic Neighbourhood
Dublin's Jewish Past

Housed in an old synagogue, the **Irish Jewish Museum** tells the story of the country's Jewish community over the last 150 years through a wealth of materials. But unless you were looking for it, you might walk straight past its door. The original synagogue consisted of two adjoining terraced houses on a quiet street in Portobello, so the entrance seamlessly blends in.

Irish Jewish Museum

BEST LATE-NIGHT BARS

George
One of Dublin's best (and original) gay bars, with drag nights and karaoke. Open until 3am Wednesday to Saturday and 1.30am the rest of the week.

Opium
State-of-the-art nightclub with the feel of an upmarket Chinese-themed Vegas lounge. Closes at 2.30am Fridays and Saturdays.

Pygmalion
It's party central at the 'Pyg', with live DJs and pounding music. Open to 3am every day but Sunday.

Krystle
Chart hits and club classics abound at this old-school nightclub. The doors don't even open until 11pm.

WHERE TO GET COFFEE IN GRAFTON STREET & ST STEPHEN'S GREEN

Clement & Pekoe
A cool version of an Edwardian tearoom, with carefully made drip coffees and cold brews.

Kaph
A magnet for caffeine fiends, with homemade cakes and coffee as strong as rocket fuel.

Network
A tiny cafe with swoon-worthy latte art and all kinds of coffee paraphernalia.

At one stage, the synagogue was the epicentre of the Jewish community in Dublin before an increasing number of people migrated out to the suburbs, and the synagogue closed its doors in the 1970s. The museum opened around 15 years later. Among the old photos and artefacts are memorabilia from WWII, including a Star of David arm patch and the marriage certificate of Ester Steinberg, the only known Irish victim of the Holocaust.

Check the opening hours in advance, as they change seasonally, but it's often open on Sundays.

Citizens Assemble!
Georgian Townhouse

The Society of Artists built the **City Assembly House** between 1766 and 1771 as the first purpose-built public exhibition room in the British Isles. During the 19th century, it served as an unofficial city hall – Daniel O'Connell, former mayor and leader of the 19th-century Catholic Emancipation movement, delivered one of his most famous speeches here in 1843 – but it is now the headquarters of the Irish Georgian Society, which is restoring it to its original purpose. The organisation hosts occasional exhibitions and architectural talks, as well as walking tours of the city, which are open to nonmembers.

Dublin on Two Wheels
On Yer Bike

Want to tick off a load of sights in one go? Join a **Lazy Bike Tour**, where guides take you between all the big attractions without you having to worry about plotting a route or navigating Dublin's one-way streets. The tours cover a big chunk of the city, from Dublin Castle and the surrounding neighbourhoods to Christchurch and the Liberties, but a great option is the Taste of Dublin tour, which combines the city's highlights as well as not-so-obvious sights. The best bit? You can choose to cycle an e-bike to make your spin that little bit easier.

The outfit is based in the bike storage area on the ground floor of the car park on Drury St, and you can also rent a bike here if you want to explore on your own.

ANY RESERVATIONS?

Dublin has a thriving food scene, but that means it's often tricky to nab a dinner reservation, particularly in the popular spots around the Grafton St area. Tables are even harder to find at the weekend when it feels like the whole city is out for dinner.

If you haven't secured your reservations weeks in advance, don't panic. It's always worth ringing or stopping by to see if there have been any last-minute cancellations. You can also follow @lastminutetabledublin on Instagram to keep track of 11th-hour availability or check out EarlyTable (earlytable.ie), which gets you up to 50% off your bill if you book an early sitting. Hooray for the early birds!

WHERE TO DRINK WINE IN GRAFTON STREET & ST STEPHEN'S GREEN

Amy Austin
Uber cool wine bar inside a car park (trust us, it works). It's dog friendly too.

Frank's
With a communal table and loads of natural wines, it's the hip oenophile's favoured spot.

La Cave
An old-school basement bar that will transport you to Paris.

37 Dawson Street

Foodie Rambles
Eat Your Way Through Dublin

Feeling peckish? Join a foodie tour of the city with **Fab Food Trails**. The 2½- to three-hour tasting walks take in some of the city centre's choicest independent producers, with plenty of nibbles along the way. You'll visit up to eight bakeries, cheesemongers and delis, learning about the food culture of each neighbourhood you explore – you might tuck into an artisan toasted cheese sandwich or a little tub of gelato. The guides keep well up to speed with Dublin's ever-changing food trends, and the tours all start in the city centre. The company also runs Food & Fashion tours, as well as *Balade Gourmande à Dublin* for French speakers.

BEST COCKTAIL BARS

Peruke & Periwig
This teeny little Tardis of a bar has an eccentric apothecary vibe, with hipster mixologists and a lengthy menu.

9 Below
On the edge of St Stephen's Green, this basement bar is the epitome of luxury, with table service and high-end liquors.

37 Dawson Street
Antiques, eye-catching art and elegant bric-a-brac adorn this bar that's a favourite with the trendy crowd.

Farrier & Draper
This opulent bar in the 18th-century Powerscourt Townhouse (p63) combines a luxe aesthetic with well-made cocktails.

WHERE TO GET BRUNCH IN GRAFTON STREET & ST STEPHEN'S GREEN

Bow Lane Social Club
Did somebody say drag brunch? Weekends here are boozy, raucous and oh-so-fun. €€

Cake Café
House-made baked beans, avocado toast and towering slices of cake – need we say more? €

Bibi's
This neighbourhood favourite is perfect for a languid Saturday morning with pancakes or poached eggs. €€

MERRION SQUARE & GEORGIAN DUBLIN

ELEGANT ARCHITECTURE AND TOP MUSEUMS

Georgian Dublin's apotheosis occurred in the exquisite architecture and elegant spaces of Merrion and Fitzwilliam Sqs. Here you'll find the perfect mix of imposing public buildings, museums, and private offices and residences. It is around these parts that much of moneyed Dublin works and plays, amid the neoclassical beauties thrown up during Dublin's 18th-century prime. These include the home of the Irish parliament at Leinster House and, immediately surrounding it, the National Gallery, the main branch of the National Museum of Ireland and the Museum of Natural History.

But it's not just a neighbourhood for the upper crust. At weekends, artists sell their wares in Merrion Sq, and food trucks pop up during the week, where you can pick up a pizza or gourmet taco. You'll find some of the city's top fine-dining restaurants on the streets surrounding the parks too.

TOP TIP

As much of this neighbourhood is the domain of office workers, it's pleasantly calm at the weekend. If you want to have a nosy around the park or nab a bench under a cherry tree for a quiet half hour, a Sunday morning is the best time to visit.

Leinster House (p73)

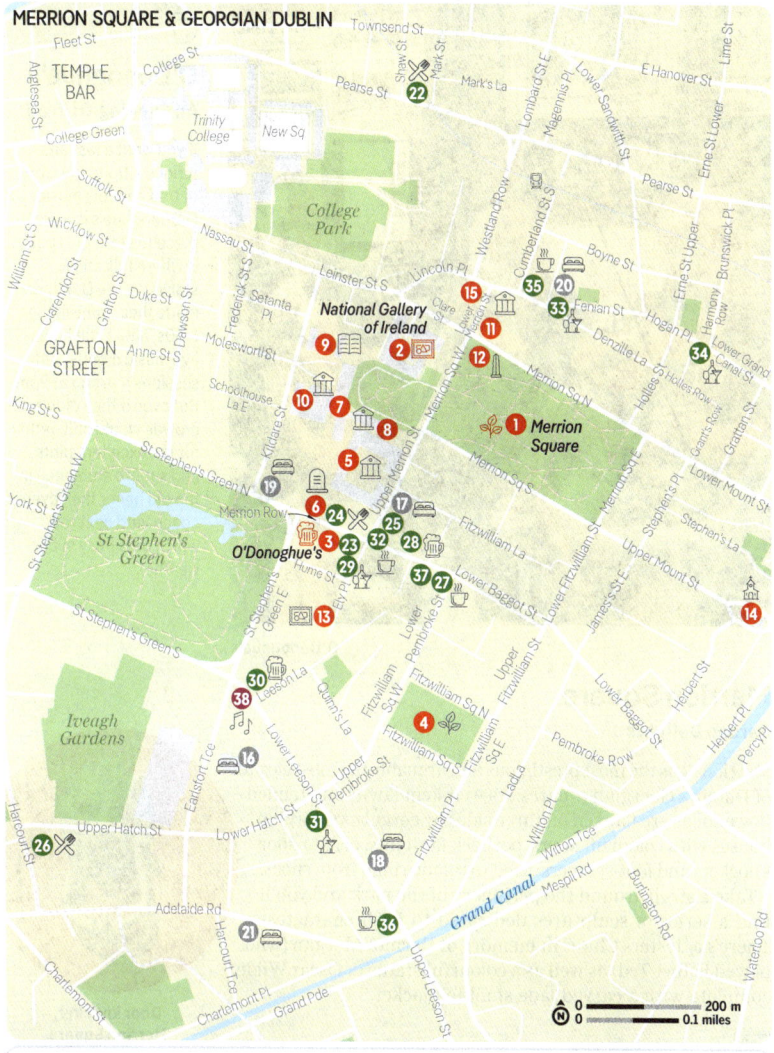

MERRION SQUARE & GEORGIAN DUBLIN

HIGHLIGHTS
1. Merrion Square
2. National Gallery of Ireland
3. O'Donoghue's

SIGHTS
4. Fitzwilliam Square
5. Government Buildings
6. Huguenot Cemetery
7. Leinster House
8. Museum of Natural History
9. National Library of Ireland
10. National Museum of Ireland – Archaeology
11. Oscar Wilde House
12. Oscar Wilde Statue
13. Royal Hibernian Academy of Arts
14. St Stephen's Church
15. Sweny's Pharmacy

SLEEPING
16. Conrad
17. Merrion
18. Number 31
19. Shelbourne
20. The Alex
21. Wilder Townhouse

EATING
22. Bread 41
23. Etto
24. Hugo's
25. Restaurant Patrick Guilbaud
26. Tir

DRINKING & NIGHTLIFE
27. Bear Market
28. Doheny & Nesbitt's
29. Ely Wine Bar
30. Hartigan's
31. House
32. Lolly & Cooks
33. Note
34. Square Ball
35. Steam Café
36. The Kiosk
37. Toners

ENTERTAINMENT
38. Sugar Club

67

O'Donoghue's

O'Donoghue's
An Evening Of Trad

If you want a fast and furious intro to the world of trad and folk music, O'Donoghue's is a great place to start. This pub is where folk music stalwarts The Dubliners made their name in the 1960s, and it still hosts live music nightly, with sessions starting at 9pm. But even if they didn't, the crowds would still gather for the excellent pints and superb ambience in the old bar or the covered coach yard next to it, which gets busy in fine weather.

Merrion Square
Garden Delights

Merrion Sq is the most prestigious and arguably the most elegant of Dublin's Georgian squares. Its well-kept lawns and tended flower beds are flanked on three sides by gorgeous Georgian houses with colourful doors, peacock fanlights, ornate door knockers and foot-scrapers, used to remove mud from shoes.

Take a stroll around the periphery of the park and you'll find a series of sculptures dedicated to Irish characters. There's a 'Jesters Chair' in memory of Dermot Morgan (who played Father Ted) as well as a colourful statue of Oscar Wilde, complete with a carved jade smoking jacket.

Door knocker, Merrion Square

National Gallery of Ireland
World-Class Collection

A magnificent Caravaggio and a breathtaking collection of works by Jack B Yeats are the main reasons to visit the National Gallery of Ireland, but not the only ones. Its excellent collection is strong in Irish art, and there are also high-quality collections of every major European school of painting.

You'll find works by Rembrandt and his circle; paintings by El Greco, Goya and Picasso; and a well-represented display of Italian pieces from the early Renaissance to the 18th century.

Insider tip: to protect FW Burton's gorgeous watercolour, *Hellelil and Hildebrand, the Meeting on the Turret Stairs* from the light, it is displayed only twice a week, for an hour at a time, on Thursdays (11.30am) and Sundays (2pm).

Museum of Natural History

MORE IN MERRION SQUARE & GEORGIAN DUBLIN

The Dead Zoo
The Weird And The Wonderful

Affectionately known as the 'Dead Zoo', the dusty, weird and utterly compelling **Museum of Natural History** is a fine example of the scientific wonderment of the Victorian age. Its enormous collection of stuffed beasts and carefully annotated specimens has barely changed since Scottish explorer Dr David Livingstone opened it in 1857 – before disappearing into the African jungle for a meeting with explorer Henry Stanley.

The **Irish Room** on the ground floor is filled with taxidermy mammals, sea creatures, birds and butterflies all found in Ireland at some point, including the massive skeletons of three 10,000-year-old Irish elk that greet you as you enter.

Take the stairs up to the 1st floor and you'll find the **Mammals of the World**, with a combination of skeletons, models and taxidermy creatures, including zebras, giraffes and one very angry hippopotamus. Evolutionists will love the lineup of orang-utan, chimpanzee, gorilla and human skeletons – it's a great spot for a photo too.

BEST COFFEE SHOPS

Lolly & Cooks
This branch on Merrion St is great for a morning pick-me-up. The coffee and pastry combo is a bargain.

The Kiosk
This cute red brick kiosk is the place to pick up a coffee from The Perch roasters before a stroll around Leeson St.

Bear Market
Grab a coffee and a giant croissant at this cool cafe on Pembroke St.

Steam Café
Just inside the lobby of The Alex (p70), this is the place to go for Cloud Picker coffee and an energy ball.

WHERE TO STAY IN MERRION SQUARE & GEORGIAN DUBLIN

Number 31
The former home of modernist architect Sam Stephenson, with elegant rooms and a cool sunken lounge. €€

Wilder Townhouse
Set in a striking red-brick building, the Wilder has a delightfully quirky vibe. €€

Shelbourne
Dublin's most famous hotel was founded in 1824 and is the height of old-school luxury. €€€

MORE OF THE NATIONAL MUSEUM

The museum's sister institutions are made up of the stuffed beasts of the **Museum of Natural History** (p69), the decorative arts section at **Collins Barracks** (p95) and a **Country Life** (p345) museum in County Mayo, on Ireland's west coast.

Wilde's Homeplace
Behind The Curtain

Hanging in the middle of the space, spanning all of the floors and stealing the spotlight, is the skeleton of a 20m-long fin whale found beached in County Sligo.

Blue plaques adorn several townhouses in this neighbourhood, but the most prestigious address is 1 Merrion Sq, the **Oscar Wilde House**. This home is where Oscar and his siblings were raised by his parents William and Jane, who were exceptional people in their own right. His father was a noted ear and eye surgeon, and his mother was a revolutionary poet and writer; both also have their own plaques by the door.

The American College Dublin now resides here, and tours take you through the various rooms of the house, from the grand library up to the picturesque balcony, complete with a bust of Wilde. Along the way, you'll learn all about the scandals and insecurities that plagued Wilde over the years, as well as get an insight into his childhood.

Stand in the living room of the house and you can see the flamboyant statue of Wilde down in the park below, usually surrounded by people snapping photos or reading the quotes inscribed around the edges of the plinths nearby.

Go Back in Time
Historical Treasures

Established in 1877 as the primary repository of the nation's cultural and archaeological treasures, the **National Museum of Ireland – Archaeology** is the country's most important museum. In the original 1890 building, you'll find stunning Celtic metalwork and Ireland's most famous crafted artefacts: the 12th-century Ardagh Chalice and the Tara Brooch, dating from the 8th century.

Also part of the Treasury is the exhibition **Ór-Ireland's Gold**, featuring stunning jewellery and decorative objects created by Celtic artisans in the Bronze and Iron Ages. Among them are the Broighter Hoard, which includes a 1st century BCE large gold collar, unsurpassed anywhere in Europe, and an extraordinarily delicate gold boat. There's also the wonderful Loughnashade bronze war trumpet from the 1st century BCE.

The other showstopper is the collection of Iron Age 'bog bodies' in the **Kingship and Sacrifice** exhibit. These four figures were dug out of the midland bogs in varying states of

BEST MUSEUM TOURS

National Museum of Ireland – Archaeology
There are regular highlight tours of the museum, alongside a series of special events that cater particularly well to families – think ogham stone crafting and drop-in sessions about Viking Ireland where kids can dress up.

National Gallery
As well as the usual gallery tours, the National Gallery also runs themed tours, drawing classes and sensory family-friendly workshops. There are often special curator-led tours based around particular exhibitions.

WHERE TO STAY IN MERRION SQUARE & GEORGIAN DUBLIN

Merrion
A resplendent five-star hotel in a terrace of beautifully restored Georgian townhouses. €€€

Conrad
The style here is contemporary chic: marble bathrooms, wonderful beds and a clutter-free aesthetic. €€€

The Alex
A beautifully sleek hotel where gorgeous design meets comfort. The lobby has a cool co-working space. €€

The Cavan, or 'Queen's' Brooch, National Museum of Ireland

preservation. The bodies' various eerily preserved details – a distinctive tangle of hair, sinewy legs and fingers with fingernails intact – are memorable, but it's the accompanying detail that will make you pause: scholars now believe that all of these bodies were victims of the most horrendous ritualistic torture and sacrifice – the cost of being notable figures in the Celtic world.

Upstairs are **Medieval Ireland 1150–1550**, **Viking Ireland** – which features exhibits from the excavations at Wood Quay, the area between Christ Church Cathedral and the river – and **Ancient Egypt**, displaying items acquired from excavations conducted between 1890 and 1930.

Ireland's Library
The Ultimate Archive

Home to 12 million documents, photographs and books, the **National Library of Ireland** is the country's library of record. The main branch on Kildare St was built between 1884 and 1890 by Sir Thomas Newenham Deane to echo the design of the facade of the National Museum of Ireland – Archaeology.

MERRION SQUARE MARKETS

If you fancy picking up a photograph or painting directly from the artist, visit the **Sunday Art Market** in Merrion Sq, where the work is hung on the railings around the park. It's been going since 1985, and there's no commission charged, as you're buying directly from the artists.

On Thursdays, office workers flock to the **Merrion Square Food Market**, where loads of food trucks park up and people spread out on the lawn or under a tree for their lunch. You might get Peruvian ceviche, Korean bulgogi or traditional fish and chips. It's on from 11.30am to 2pm – expect longer lines at 1pm.

WHERE TO EAT IN MERRION SQUARE & GEORGIAN DUBLIN

Note
A cool wine bar where you can enjoy a languid dinner or just a few snacks. €€

Etto
Award-winning restaurant and wine bar that does contemporary versions of classic Italian cuisine. €€€

Ely Wine Bar
Choose between the dinner menu or 'bites and flights', with small plates and sampler glasses of wine. €€

RELIGIOUS EXPERIENCE

Built in 1825 in Greek Revival style and commonly known as the 'pepper canister' on account of its appearance, **St Stephen's Church** is one of the most attractive and distinctive in Dublin, and looks particularly fetching at twilight when its exterior lights have just come on.

But that's not the main reason to visit. There are often gigs in this intimate space, particularly during TradFest, which takes place every January in unusual venues like this alongside pubs in Temple Bar. At other times, there are concerts by artists like James Vincent McMorrow and Joan As Police Woman, as well as regular performances by the Chamber Choir Ireland.

National Library of Ireland (p72)

The similarities are clear to see, particularly in the elaborate dome of the reading room.

This space is the main visitor highlight, and it was here that Stephen Dedalus expounded his views on Shakespeare in James Joyce's *Ulysses*. For everyone else, it's an important repository of early manuscripts, first editions and maps. If you want to trace your family history, the Genealogy Advisory Service is on the 2nd floor.

The permanent exhibition on WB Yeats is vast, with manuscripts of his famous poems *The Lake Isle of Innisfree* and *Easter, 1916* alongside photographs, his old school reports and even his Nobel Prize medal.

There are occasional tours of the building, some led by the director of the NLI, as well as events and readings.

People & Politics

Home Of The Government

Walk up Upper Merrion St and you'll usually see a few *gardaí* (Irish police) hovering outside the entrance to the **Government Buildings**, which house the Department of the Taoiseach (Prime Minister). This gleaming Edwardian pile opened as the Royal College of Science in 1911 before being

---

WHERE TO EAT IN MERRION SQUARE & GEORGIAN DUBLIN

Bread 41
An artisan bakery with fresh loaves and pastries at the entrance and lunch tables at the back. €

Hugo's
A homey bistro with fresh Irish ingredients and a well-priced pretheatre menu. €€

Tír
A cool deli on Baggot St, open for breakfast baps and artisan sandwiches at lunchtime. €

transformed into government offices in 1989. Free 40-minute tours include the Taoiseach's office, the Cabinet Room and the ceremonial staircase with a stunning stained-glass window designed by Evie Hone (1894–1955) for the 1939 New York Trade Fair. Tours don't run every day (or even particularly regularly), but when they do, there are usually three different times available. Pick up tickets from 9.30am on the day of the tour at the Clare St entrance of the National Gallery.

To the rear of the Government Buildings, you'll find **Leinster House**, where the Oireachtas (Parliament) sits. This Palladian mansion was built as a city residence for James Fitzgerald, the Duke of Leinster and Earl of Kildare, by Richard Cassels between 1745 and 1748, and is a remarkable building. Unfortunately, public tours of this building are currently postponed – the only tours available are those sponsored by a TD or Senator.

Secret Graveyard
Hidden In Plain Sight

The tiny **Huguenot Cemetery** was established in 1693 by French Protestant refugees. The cemetery is closed, but you can see graves through the railings. Of the 239 surnames, one is Becquett, a relation of the writer Samuel Beckett. In the spring, the graveyard is covered in a blanket of bluebells, which makes for a rather enchanting sight.

Michelin Dining
Under The Cloche

This neighbourhood has plenty of chichi restaurants, which makes sense when you consider the proliferation of visiting dignitaries and business diners with hefty expense accounts. But the long-running favourite in Dublin is **Restaurant Patrick Guilbaud**. This fine-dining experience, set underneath the Merrion Hotel, opened in 1981, was awarded a Michelin star in 1988 and a second star in 1996 – it's retained both stars ever since.

While Dubliners are quick to fawn over the latest food trend or fad (check out the lines for an Instagrammable doughnut or burger, if you don't believe us) Guilbaud's has retained a level of elegance and innovation, with a menu of largely Irish dishes prepared in the classical French style. Sadly, the set lunch menu is no longer the bargain it once was, but it's still a good way of experiencing haute cuisine at a cheaper price.

FAMOUS RESIDENTS

Over the years, plenty of renowned characters have lived in this corner of Dublin, which is why it's worth keeping an eye out for blue plaques bolted to the doorways around the neighbourhood. Famous residents of Merrion Sq include the Wilde family (p70), Daniel O'Connell and WB Yeats, who lived at No 82.

Just around the corner is Fitzwilliam Sq, the smallest of Dublin's Georgian squares and the only one where the inner garden remains the private domain of the square's residents. Artist Jack B Yeats lived at No 18, and the founder of the National Gallery, William Dargan, lived at No 2.

WHERE TO DRINK IN MERRION SQUARE & GEORGIAN DUBLIN

Toners
The closest thing to a country pub in the city, with an award-winning snug.

Doheny & Nesbitt's
A standout, even in a city of wonderful pubs, with antique snugs and excellent whiskeys.

House
An elegant bar spread across two Georgian townhouses, with a nightclub vibe at weekends.

Joycean Pilgrimage
A Literary Favourite

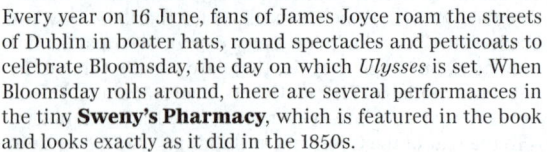

Every year on 16 June, fans of James Joyce roam the streets of Dublin in boater hats, round spectacles and petticoats to celebrate Bloomsday, the day on which *Ulysses* is set. When Bloomsday rolls around, there are several performances in the tiny **Sweny's Pharmacy**, which is featured in the book and looks exactly as it did in the 1850s.

If you're not around for the big day, fear not – the shop is open throughout the year, with readings held on Thursday evenings. You can copy Leopold Bloom and buy a bar of lemon soap or check out the prized artefacts in the Victorian cabinets – there are lotions, potions, old photographs and books.

Contemporary Art
Fine Art And Fine Dining

The **RHA Gallery** (or Royal Hibernian Academy of Arts, to give its proper name), has an exalted reputation as one of the most prestigious exhibition spaces for modern and contemporary art in Ireland.

The biggest event of the year is the **RHA National Exhibition**, which usually runs from May to the end of July and shows the work of those artists deemed worthy enough by the selection committee made up of members of the academy.

But what makes this gallery really special is the cafe and wine bar, **Margadh**. During the week, there's a casual lunch menu of soup, salads and sandwiches, made with well-sourced ingredients like crab, crayfish or fresh burrata. But in the evenings, the space turns into a fancy wine bar with a curated list of bottles from around the world, along with an excellent selection of wines by the glass. You can order food a la carte, but doing so would be a shame, as the tasting menu is one of the best in the city (and almost certainly the best priced, at €49 for a seven-course meal). Expect to see dishes like kingfish with kumquat and chilli, or a baked Flaggy Shore oyster with nduja sausage and lime. The bite of Cantabrian anchovy toast and preserved lemon aioli has a legion of foodie fans, so it will likely stick around on the menu for some time.

OPEN DAYS

If you're the kind of person who likes to peek behind closed doors, time your trip to Dublin to coincide with two events. The first is **Culture Night**, an all-island event usually on the third Friday in September. In Dublin, it means a series of free events in cool locations, some of which are otherwise closed to the public.

Open House Dublin is a free festival of architecture in October, with guided tours of buildings you can't usually access, as well as interesting private homes.

WHERE TO DRINK IN MERRION SQUARE & GEORGIAN DUBLIN

Square Ball
A busy sports bar for craft beer, board games and quiz nights.

Sugar Club
A top music venue for gigs, live DJ sets and 'story slam' nights.

Hartigan's
A spartan, no-frills bar for serious drinkers during the day and UCD students at night.

TEMPLE BAR

NIGHTLIFE CENTRAL

Dublin's best-known district is the cobbled playpen of Temple Bar, where mayhem and merriment are standard fare, especially at night when the pubs are full and the party spills out onto the streets. It's loud, raucous and a hell of a lot of fun.

If you visit during the day, the district's bohemian bent is on full display. You can browse for vintage clothes, get your nipples pierced, nibble on sushi, pick up the latest musical releases or watch an indie movie. If that's not enough, the neighbourhood is home to some excellent art galleries, as well as one of Dublin's best independent bookstores – and that's all before the pints start flowing come evening.

If you wanted to, you could visit all of Temple Bar's top sights in less than half a day, but that's not really the point. This neighbourhood is more about ambience than attractions.

TOP TIP

Keep an eye on your receipts if you're drinking in the evening. In some bars, the price of a pint sneaks up at 11pm or midnight (or both) when the bar owners assume people stop paying attention. Our advice? Take your business elsewhere if you see it happen.

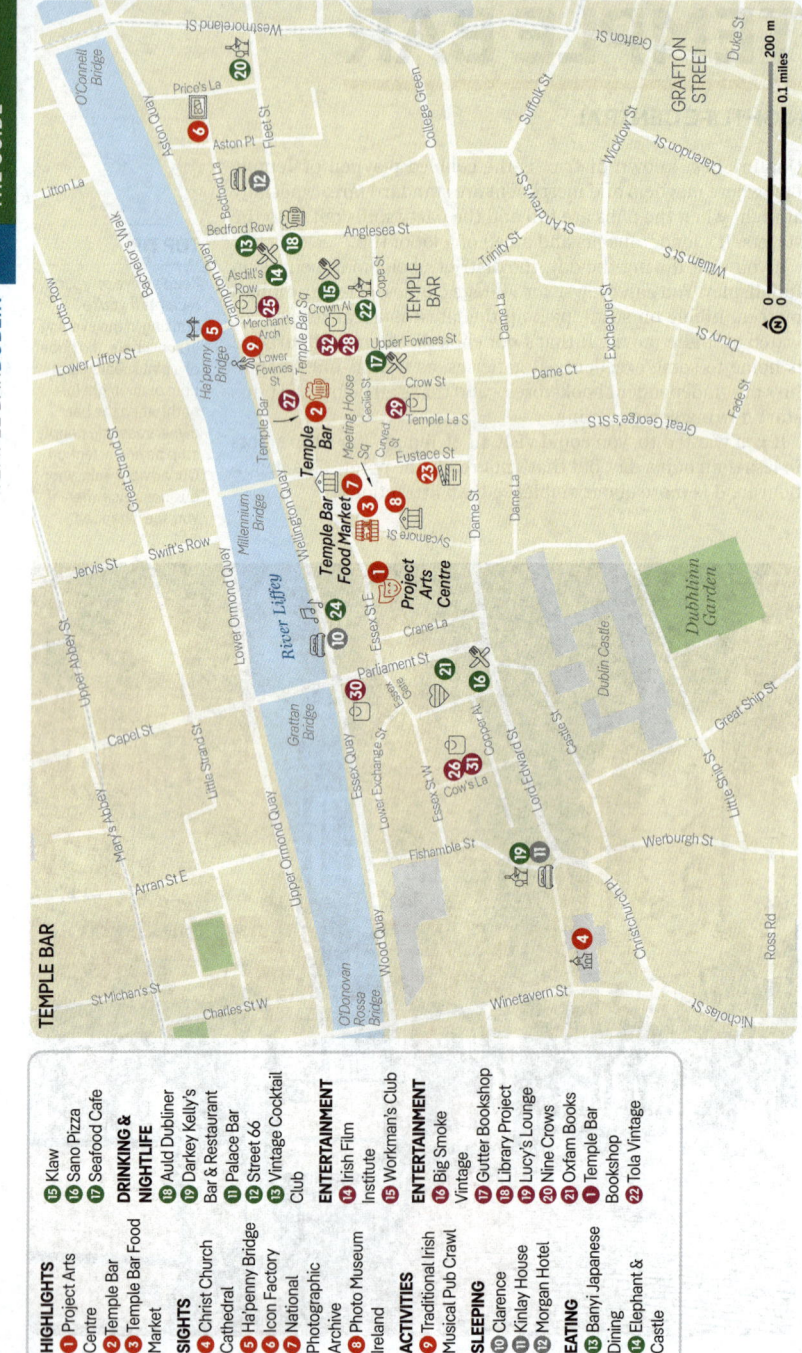

TEMPLE BAR

HIGHLIGHTS
1. Project Arts Centre
2. Temple Bar
3. Temple Bar Food Market

SIGHTS
4. Christ Church Cathedral
5. Ha'penny Bridge
6. Icon Factory
7. National Photographic Archive
8. Photo Museum Ireland

ACTIVITIES
9. Traditional Irish Musical Pub Crawl

SLEEPING
10. Clarence
11. Kinlay House
12. Morgan Hotel

EATING
13. Banyi Japanese Dining
14. Elephant & Castle
15. Klaw
16. Sano Pizza
17. Seafood Cafe

DRINKING & NIGHTLIFE
18. Auld Dubliner
19. Darkey Kelly's Bar & Restaurant
20. Palace Bar
21. Street 66
22. Vintage Cocktail Club

ENTERTAINMENT
23. Irish Film Institute
24. Workman's Club

ENTERTAINMENT
25. Big Smoke Vintage
26. Gutter Bookshop
27. Library Project
28. Lucy's Lounge
29. Nine Crows
30. Oxfam Books
31. Temple Bar Bookshop
32. Tola Vintage

Temple Bar Food Market
Weekend Eats

The Temple Bar Food Market is one of the longest-running in town. Held in Meeting House Sq every Saturday, this market sees various stall holders setting up shop to sell everything from Gruyère-stuffed crêpes to apple pies. You'll usually find the longest line in front of the van with sizzling artisan sausages on the grill. But it's not the only resident of the square – in the summer months, there are often screenings of outdoor movies, as well as circus performances and family fun days.

Temple Bar Food Market

Leonie McDonagh, Project Arts Centre

Project Arts Centre
Theatrical Hub

The Project Arts Centre is the city's most interesting venue for challenging new work, be it drama, dance, live art or film. You never know what to expect, which makes it all that more fun. We've seen some awful rubbish here, but we've also watched some of the best shows in town. It's worth a visit if only to see the hint of the Maser mural outside. This artwork was created in support of the Repeal the 8th movement for abortion reform but was partially painted over to avoid the centre losing its charitable (and therefore politically neutral) status.

Temple Bar
Popular Pints

With the most photographed pub facade in Dublin, and perhaps the world, the Temple Bar is smack bang in the middle of the tourist precinct and is usually chock-a-block with visitors. But despite its enduring popularity (and long lines on busier days), it still presses all the right buttons. There's live music every day, starting at 10.30am and going right through until the wee hours, with traditional musicians playing on the tiny stage in the middle of the bar.

There's a beer garden with a retractable roof, and you can get a bite to eat during the day and early in the evening – just don't expect to get grub once the hardy drinking kicks off after 8pm.

Christ Church

BEST BOOKSHOPS IN TEMPLE BAR

Gutter Bookshop
Named after the famous Oscar Wilde quote, this indie bookshop has all the latest releases and loads of Irish authors.

Library Project
With a focus on photography, this is the place to pick up thick coffee table books or art magazines.

Oxfam Books
If you fancy picking up a cheap read, this secondhand bookshop is the place to go.

Temple Bar Bookshop
On Cow's Lane, this cosy antiquarian bookshop specialises in rare books and first editions.

MORE IN TEMPLE BAR

Cathedral Quarter
An Iconic Structure

Its hilltop location and eye-catching flying buttresses make **Christ Church** the most photogenic of Dublin's cathedrals. It was founded in 1030 and rebuilt from 1172, mostly under the impetus of Richard de Clare, Earl of Pembroke (better known as Strongbow), the Anglo-Norman noble who invaded Ireland in 1170 and whose monument has pride of place inside.

Once the original wooden church was replaced by the building you see today, the cathedral vied for supremacy with nearby St Patrick's Cathedral (p84), but like its sister church, it fell on hard times in the 18th and 19th centuries – the nave had been used as a market, and the crypt housed taverns – and was virtually derelict by the time restoration took place.

The monument to Strongbow is in the southern aisle. The armoured figure on the tomb is unlikely to be Strongbow (it's more probably the Earl of Drogheda), but his internal organs may have been buried here. A popular legend relates that the half figure beside the tomb is Strongbow's son, who was cut in two by his father when his bravery in battle was suspect.

WHERE TO DRINK IN TEMPLE BAR

Palace Bar
With its mirrors and wooden niches, the Palace is one of Dublin's great 19th-century pubs.

Darkey Kelly's Bar & Restaurant
Once the home of Ireland's first female serial killer, Darkey now boasts a killer whiskey selection instead.

Workman's Club
This cool music venue is the place to be for a post-gig beer or a late-night bop.

An entrance by the south transept descends to the unusually large arched crypt, which dates from the original Viking church. Curiosities in the crypt include a glass display case housing a mummified cat chasing a mummified rat (known as Tom and Jerry), which were trapped inside an organ pipe in the 1860s. Now, that's something you don't see every day...

Photography Exhibitions
Worth A Thousand Words

Formerly the Gallery of Photography, **Photo Museum Ireland** is a small but mighty space celebrating the best in – you guessed it – photography. The exhibitions change fairly regularly and might feature homegrown talent or international artists, with the work displayed in small spaces on the upper floors.

It also runs photography classes and workshops led by renowned photographers, and the bookshop downstairs is well stocked with all manner of photographic tomes and manuals, as well as a hefty supply of arty postcards. At the other end of Meeting House Sq, the **National Photographic Archive**, a branch of the National Library of Ireland (p71), has a rotation of works from its extensive collection on display, which changes a few times a year.

Arthouse Cinema
Catch A Film

The cinephile's movie theatre of choice, the **Irish Film Institute** is the place to watch both artsy new releases and old movies from the archive. It opened in 1992 in what was an 18th-century Quaker meeting house and has been a city favourite ever since, frequently hosting premieres and film festival screenings.

The cafe-bar is a great spot for a pre-movie bite, and it does a well-priced combo deal with a ticket and a meal. During the day, it shows free movies as part of the Archive at Lunchtime series, where you can see short films from the IFI Irish Film Archive.

Lost in Music
Pints And Trad

Want to get a taste of the traditional music scene but not sure where to start? Head off on a **Traditional Irish Musical Pub Crawl**. Kicking off at Ha'penny Bridge Inn, the 2½-hour tour is led by two professional musicians who play a

---

BEST VINTAGE SHOPS IN TEMPLE BAR

Lucy's Lounge
This colourful, jampacked shop has been trading for decades and is well and truly part of the furniture.

Big Smoke Vintage
Opened in 2023, this boutique in Merchant's Arch has old band t-shirts and battered motorcycle jackets.

Nine Crows
A favourite among Dublin's cool kids, with pieces organised by theme.

Tola Vintage
Stock up on loads of secondhand gear and pay by the weight, not by the label.

WHERE TO DRINK IN TEMPLE BAR

Vintage Cocktail Club
A not-so-secret speakeasy with dark, cosy rooms and a rooftop terrace. Booking essential.

Auld Dubliner
Sure, it's a tourist favourite, but it's still a reliable place for a singsong and a laugh.

Street 66
A fantastic LGBTIQ+ venue with live music, great cocktails and a wide range of gins behind the bar.

Ha'penny Bridge

BEST PLACES TO EAT IN TEMPLE BAR

Elephant & Castle
Feeling delicate? A giant plate of spicy chicken wings will cure what ails you. €€

Sano Pizza
Excellent Neapolitan pizza at an even better price, and you don't need to book in advance. €

Banyi Japanese Dining
This compact restaurant has arguably the best Japanese cuisine in Dublin. €€

Klaw
Crab-shack-style spot specialising in oysters and shellfish. €

Seafood Cafe
Same owners as Klaw, but with a broader seafood menu. €€

few tunes while they talk about the history, culture and heritage around trad.

Be warned, though – this isn't a tour for those who want a bit of rowdiness. In the spirit of a proper session, it's described as a 'listening tour', designed for you to take in the music without a load of chatter in the background.

Icon Walk
Punk Gallery

The artists' collective **Icon Factory** hosts tiny exhibitions of up-and-coming new talent. You'll also find colourful souvenirs celebrating the best in Irish music and literature, and the proceeds from every sale go to the artists themselves. Take a stroll around the **Icon Walk** outside and get better acquainted with Irish playwrights, rock stars, sporting heroes and actors.

A Picturesque Bridge
Penny For Your Thoughts

Dublin's most famous bridge is the **Ha'penny Bridge**, built in 1816. One of the world's oldest cast-iron bridges, it was built to replace the seven ferries that plied a busy route between the two banks of the river. Officially known as the Liffey Bridge, it gets its name from the ha'penny (halfpenny) toll that was charged until 1919. For a time, the toll was 1.5 pence, and so it was called the Penny Ha'penny Bridge.

WHERE TO STAY IN TEMPLE BAR

Clarence
Refurbished in 2022, this slick hotel has a great cocktail bar. €€

Morgan Hotel
A hotel right in the middle of the action; some rooms have balconies. €€

Kinlay House
This huge hostel has basic rooms in a former boarding house. €

KILMAINHAM & THE LIBERTIES

DISTILLERIES AND BREWERIES

Stretching westward along the Liffey, the Liberties and Kilmainham are some of the oldest neighbourhoods in Dublin. Coming from the heart of the city centre, you'll first stumble into the Liberties, on the edge of which is St Patrick's Cathedral and, behind the cathedral, the wonderful Marsh's Library. This traditionally working-class enclave is one of the many neighbourhoods that's been transformed by gentrification, with cool cafes and restaurants, a growing list of hotels, and a collection of distilleries – modern echoes of its 18th-century past when the Liberties was a hub of whiskey-making.

The most famous landmark is between the two neighbourhoods: the Guinness Storehouse. As you move further west into the riverside burg of Kilmainham, you'll come across the country's greatest modern art museum and Kilmainham Gaol, which has played a key role in the tormented history of the country's slow struggle to gain its freedom.

TOP TIP

While Kilmainham is within walking distance from the city centre (with the furthest attraction roughly an hour's stroll away), you can make life easier by catching the bus. The hop-on, hop-off services stop at all the major attractions in the neighbourhood, and some include discounted entry.

Irish Museum of Modern Art (p85)

KILMAINHAM & THE LIBERTIES

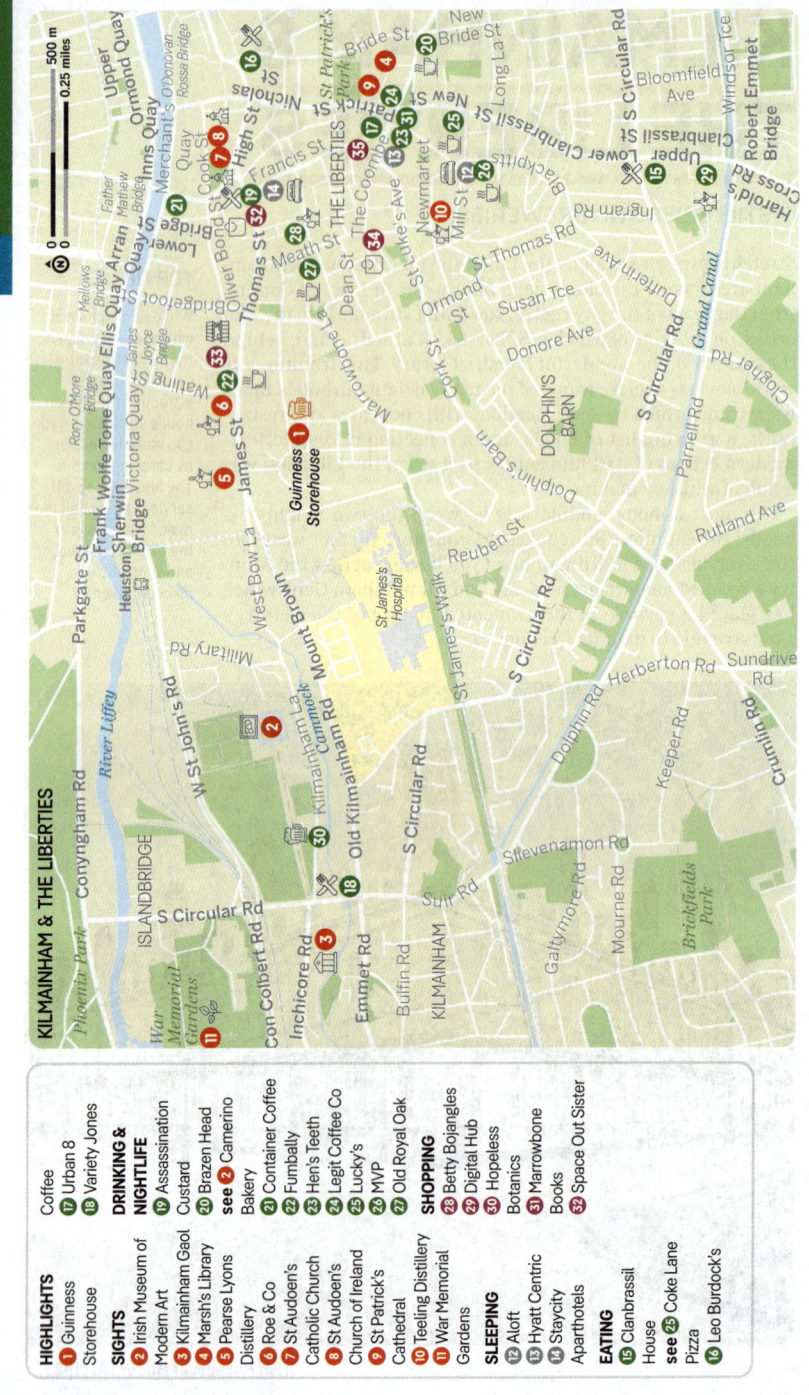

HIGHLIGHTS
1. Guinness Storehouse

SIGHTS
2. Irish Museum of Modern Art
3. Kilmainham Gaol
4. Marsh's Library
5. Pearse Lyons Distillery
6. Roe & Co
7. St Audoen's Catholic Church
8. St Audoen's Church of Ireland
9. St Patrick's Cathedral
10. Teeling Distillery
11. War Memorial Gardens

SLEEPING
12. Aloft
13. Hyatt Centric
14. Staycity Aparthotels

EATING
15. Clanbrassil House
see 25 Coke Lane Pizza
16. Leo Burdock's
17. Urban 8
18. Variety Jones

DRINKING & NIGHTLIFE
19. Assassination Custard
20. Brazen Head
see 2 Camerino Bakery
21. Container Coffee
22. Fumbally
23. Hen's Teeth
24. Legit Coffee Co
25. Lucky's
26. MVP
27. Old Royal Oak

SHOPPING
28. Betty Bojangles
29. Digital Hub
30. Hopeless Botanics
31. Marrowbone Books
32. Space Out Sister

Guinness Storehouse
My Goodness, My Guinness

The most popular attraction in Dublin is the Guinness Storehouse, a multimedia homage to the 'black stuff' that's part of their 26-hectare brewery. Across its seven floors, you'll discover everything about Guinness before getting to taste the brew in the top-floor Gravity Bar, fresh out of a €20 million refurb that has doubled its size – there are now two rounded bars at the top, designed to look like the head of two pints.

Before you get up there, you first walk through the extravaganza that is the Guinness floor show, spread across 1.6 hectares and involving an array of audiovisual and interactive displays that cover pretty much all aspects of the brewery's history and the brewing process. It's slick and sophisticated, but you can't ignore the man behind the curtain: the extensive exhibit on the company's incredibly successful history of advertising is a reminder that, for all the talk of mysticism and magic, it's all really about marketing and manipulation.

The point is made deliciously moot when you finally get a pint in your hand and let the cream pass your lips. It's the best pint of Guinness in the world, claim the cognoscenti, and die-hards can opt for the Connoisseur Experience for exclusive tastings. Other add-ons include the STOUTie, the stout equivalent of latte art, where a pretty good likeness of yourself is drawn in the creamy head of the pint.

HOW TO POUR THE PERFECT PINT

There's a five-step process to pouring a pint of Guinness. First off, the tulip pint glass must be dry and clean. The glass is then held beneath the tap at a 45-degree angle. A smooth pour should fill the glass to about three-quarters full before it sits on the counter to settle for a couple of minutes, during which time the head is formed. Then it's time to top it off, creating a domed effect across the top of the glass.

St Patrick's Cathedral

CATHEDRAL PARK

The park adjacent to St Patrick's Cathedral was once a slum, but it's now a lovely garden in which to sit and catch some sunshine. There's a small wooden playground for kids, loads of colourful flowerbeds and people lounging on the grass. On Sundays, there's a small market, with stalls selling secondhand books, antique maps and bric-a-brac. It's not particularly large, but it's a pleasant way to spend an hour or so. A small cafe sells coffee too.

MORE IN KILMAINHAM & THE LIBERTIES

Patron Saint
Ireland's Largest Church

St Patrick's Cathedral stands on the spot where St Patrick himself reputedly baptised the local Celtic chieftains in the 5th century. Fiction or not, it's a sacred bit of turf upon which this cathedral was built between 1191 and 1270.

Like Christ Church Cathedral (p78), the building has suffered a rather dramatic history of storm and fire damage and has been altered several times, most questionably in 1864 when the flying buttresses were added, thanks to the neogothic craze that swept the nation. Oliver Cromwell, during his 1649 visit to Ireland, converted St Patrick's to a stable for his army's horses, an indignity to which he also subjected numerous other Irish churches. Jonathan Swift, author of *Gulliver's Travels*, was the dean of the cathedral from 1713 to 1745, but after his tenure, the cathedral was neglected until its restoration in the 1860s. Also like Christ Church, St Patrick's is a Church of Ireland cathedral, which means that overwhelmingly Catholic Dublin has two Anglican cathedrals!

WHERE TO STAY IN KILMAINHAM & THE LIBERTIES

Aloft
This sleek hotel is right by the Teeling Distillery (p86) and has a great rooftop bar. €€

Hyatt Centric
Clean, modern rooms over the road from St Patrick's Cathedral. €€

Staycity Aparthotels
A range of one and two-bedroom apartments; ideal if you're travelling in a group. €€

The interior is breathtaking, with vaulted ceilings, stained glass windows and carved pillars. Entering the cathedral from the southwestern porch, you come almost immediately, on your right, to the tombs of Swift and his long-time companion Esther Johnson, aka Stella.

As well as the regular entrance and daily guided tours, you can visit during the Choral Evensong. At Christmas, the carol services are a beautiful way to get into the festive spirit. There are often other musical performances too.

Old-World Library
Step Back In Time

Trinity's Long Room (p58) might hog the limelight, but **Marsh's Library** is a worthy contender for the title of Dublin's most impressive library. This magnificently preserved scholars library, virtually unchanged in three centuries, is one of Dublin's most beautiful open secrets and an absolute highlight of any visit. Atop its ancient stairs are beautiful dark-oak bookcases, each topped with elaborately carved and gilded gables. The shelves are filled with ancient books, some of which are taken out and displayed in glass cabinets during periodic exhibitions, so you can see what lies within.

Founded in 1701 by Archbishop Narcissus Marsh (1638–1713) and opened in 1707, the library was designed by Sir William Robinson, the man also responsible for the Royal Hospital Kilmainham (p85). It's the oldest public library in the country and contains 25,000 books from the 16th century to the early 18th century, as well as maps, manuscripts (including one in Latin dating from 1400) and a collection of incunabula (books printed before 1500).

When you walk from the first hall into the second, strike up a conversation with the resident librarians. They can tell you their personal theories (or experiences) of the resident ghost and show you the spines of the books bearing bullet holes from the 1916 Easter Rising.

Modern Art
A Stellar Collection

The **Irish Museum of Modern Art** might be a bit of a trek from town, but it's definitely worth the effort. The gallery is home to Ireland's most important collection of modern and contemporary Irish and international art, and it's housed in the elegant, airy expanse of the Royal Hospital

---

BEST SHOPS IN KILMAINHAM & THE LIBERTIES

Hopeless Botanics
You may not be in the market for a giant houseplant, but the pots and candles in this botanic shop are beautiful.

Betty Bojangles
This vintage store is jampacked with clothes, from smoking jackets to sequinned dresses.

Space Out Sister
A beautiful boutique on Francis St selling vintage and handmade lingerie.

Marrowbone Books
This homely little shop is packed with secondhand books, and it sometimes puts on gigs.

Marsh's Library

BEST BRUNCH SPOTS IN KILMAINHAM & THE LIBERTIES

Two Pups Coffee
A beloved neighbourhood joint serving French toast, Turkish eggs and excellent coffee. €

Fumbally
A bright, airy warehouse cafe that serves healthy dishes and homemade kombucha. €

Urban 8
A brewery-owned restaurant in Kilmainham, with hefty burgers and spicy wings. €

Kilmainham, designed by Sir William Robinson and built between 1684 and 1687 as a retirement home for soldiers.

Inside the gallery, you'll find a mix of contemporary pieces from Irish artists and works from heavy hitters like Pablo Picasso and Joan Miró in the permanent collection. Temporary exhibitions change regularly and feature homegrown talent or work loaned by international galleries. New pieces are added to the collection every year.

In the summer months (between June and September), a huge array of outdoor activities and exhibitions are staged as part of **IMMA Outdoors**, from curator talks and guided walks to sound baths and open studios. There's also live music in the courtyard.

Garden Stroll
Kilmainham's Finest

Hardly anyone ever ventures this far west, but they're missing a lovely bit of landscaping in the shape of the **War Memorial Gardens** – by our reckoning as pleasant a patch of greenery as any you'll find in the heart of the Georgian centre. Designed by Sir Edwin Lutyens, the memorial commemorates the 49,400 Irish soldiers who died during WWI. Their names are inscribed in the two huge granite bookrooms that stand at one end.

Distillery District
Whiskey Is Back

Back in the 18th and 19th centuries, the Liberties was at the epicentre of the world's distilling and brewing industries. But when the industry fell into a decline, the Dublin operations suffered, with the city's last distillery closing in the 1970s.

Since 2015, however, whiskey production in the Liberties whiskey has flourished, with boutique distilleries opening their doors in derelict buildings and former powerhouses.

First on the scene was **Teeling Distillery**, which began production in 2015 and offers guided tours that end with a tasting. Book a Select Single Tasting if you want to sample the top-shelf whiskeys. You can also do the Bottle Your Own experience, where you fill your own bottle right from the still.

The boutique **Pearse Lyons Distillery** opened in the former St James' Church in 2017, with a cool glass spire on the old building. They distil small-batch, craft Irish whiskey, and tours include a history of distilling in the Liberties, as well as the obligatory tastings.

GIGS & EVENTS

For most Dubliners, a trip to Kilmainham means one thing: an epic gig. Royal Hospital Kilmainham is the home of IMMA, but on select evenings, it becomes a hub of live music, with everyone from Leonard Cohen to Primal Scream taking to the stage. It's a special setting – the sun sets behind the main stage, and the gentle slope makes it a natural amphitheatre (of sorts).

As well as the one-off gigs, this is also where **Forbidden Fruit** (p62) takes place every June.

WHERE TO DRINK IN KILMAINHAM & THE LIBERTIES

Brazen Head
Reputedly Dublin's oldest pub, the Brazen Head has been serving thirsty patrons since 1198.

Fallon's
A fabulously old-fashioned bar with a wood-burning stove and a great snug.

Old Royal Oak
Kilmainham locals are fiercely protective of this gorgeous traditional pub, which opened in 1845.

Teeling Whiskey Distillery

Roe & Co took up residence in 2019 in the old Guinness Power Station, a cool brick building opposite the main brewery entrance. The emphasis here is on cocktails. After a traditional tasting, you learn about flavour profiles in a mixology workshop before heading to the bar to sample the bartender's wares.

Places of Worship

Two Churches, Same Saint

On High St, two churches stand side by side, each bearing the same name, a tribute to St Audoen, the 7th-century bishop of Rouen (aka Ouen) and patron saint of the Normans. They built the older of the two, **St Audoen's Church of Ireland**, between 1181 and 1212, and today it is the only medieval church in Dublin still in use.

Through the Norman church's heavily moulded Romanesque Norman door, you can touch the 9th-century 'lucky stone' that was believed to bring good luck to business and check out the 9th-century slab in the porch that suggests it

FLEA MARKETS

Compared to most European cities (and even some Irish ones), Dublin's market scene is sadly lacking. The popular Dublin Flea Market was given the boot when development began in its former home, Newmarket, and for a few years, there was nothing in its place.

But now, a market is up and running at the **Digital Hub** on Thomas St. **We Love Markets** opens on the last Sunday of the month and has a similar setup. There's a mix of antique sellers, vintage clothes rails and Dubliners selling their own secondhand bits. There's a strong party vibe, too – the resident vinyl van blasts the tunes, and street food trucks sling out baked potatoes and lobster rolls.

WHERE TO DRINK IN KILMAINHAM & THE LIBERTIES

Lucky's
A favourite of art students from the nearby National College of Art and Design; craft beer and wine on tap.

Fourth Corner
A dark bar with loud music and food during the day.

MVP
A small and friendly bar just off the beaten path, with frequent quiz nights.

87

DUBLIN'S BEST NEIGHBOURHOOD

Nicola Brady is a writer who has made her home in Dublin's oldest neighbourhood. Here she shares her Liberties favourites.

'Anything you could want from a day in Dublin can be found in the Liberties. You've got the big attractions like the Guinness Storehouse and the neighbouring distilleries, as well as historical sights like St Patrick's Cathedral and the old city walls. The food scene here is the best in the city, with everything from Michelin-starred dining to casual brunch cafes, but it also feels like it's got a sense of the proper, old-school Dublin to it, from the women selling flowers off Thomas St to the fellas propping up the bar in an old pub. It feels like a neighbourhood with a soul.'

St Audoen's Church of Ireland

was built on an even older church. You can wander around on your own or chat with the staff at the visitor centre, who can take you on an informal tour of the present church, which has funerary monuments that were beheaded by Cromwell's purists. Its tower and door date from the 12th century, and the aisle is from the 15th century, but the church today is mainly the product of a 19th-century restoration.

Enter the church from the south off High St through St Audoen's Arch, which was built in 1240 and is the only surviving reminder of the city gates. The adjoining park is pretty but attracts unsavoury characters, particularly at night, so it's best avoided.

Attached is the bigger, 19th-century **St Audoen's Catholic Church**, which since 2006 has been home to the Polish chaplaincy in Ireland.

WHERE TO EAT IN KILMAINHAM & THE LIBERTIES

Clanbrassil House
Family-style sharing dishes are cooked over coals in this cool bistro. €€

Coke Lane Pizza
Excellent sourdough pizzas served fresh from the hatch on the terrace of Lucky's bar. €

Variety Jones
This edgy restaurant was awarded a Michelin star in 2020. World class. €€€

A Most Historic Prison
The Stark Sight Of Kilmainham Gaol

If you have any desire to understand Irish history – especially the long-running resistance to British rule – then a visit to the former prison of **Kilmainham Gaol** is a must. This threatening grey building, built in 1796, has played a role in virtually every act of Ireland's painful path to independence, and even today, despite closing in 1924, it still has the power to chill.

The uprisings of 1798, 1803, 1848, 1867 and 1916 ended with the leaders' confinement here. Robert Emmet, Thomas Francis Meagher, Charles Stewart Parnell and the 1916 Easter Rising leaders were all visitors, but it was the executions in 1916 that most deeply etched the jail's name into the Irish consciousness. Of the 15 executions that took place between 3 May and 12 May after the revolt, 14 were conducted here. As a finale, prisoners from the Civil War were held here from 1922.

Browsing the museum gives you excellent context and access to some of the former prisoners' personal belongings and letters. The enthusiastic guides provide a thought-provoking tour of the eerie prison, the largest unoccupied building of its kind in Europe. The tour finishes in the gloomy yard where the 1916 executions took place.

Visits are by guided tour only, and the group sizes are kept small. If you want to visit, you'll need to book as far in advance as possible, as time slots sell out quickly, particularly during the summer and at the weekend.

Kilmainham Gaol

> **BEST COFFEE SHOPS IN KILMAINHAM & THE LIBERTIES**
>
> **Soren & Son**
> Just over the road from St Patrick's Cathedral (p84), this trendy cafe serves an excellent flat white.
>
> **Camerino Bakery**
> IMMA's cafe is a great choice for a coffee and a slice of cake.
>
> **Legit Coffee Co**
> This hip cafe on Meath St has a great brunch menu but is also a handy spot to pick up a coffee to go.
>
> **Container Coffee**
> Excellent coffee on the walk from the city centre to the Guinness Storehouse.

WHERE TO EAT IN KILMAINHAM & THE LIBERTIES

Hen's Teeth
Part gallery, part hipster hangout, this cafe serves clever dishes and hosts cool pop-ups. €

Leo Burdock's
If you're hankering for some fish and chips, you can't go wrong with Burdock's. €

Assassination Custard
Two tables and a small menu that changes daily. It's only open during the week, for lunch only. €

NORTH OF THE LIFFEY

GRANDEUR OF OLD DUBLIN

Grittier than its more genteel southside counterpart, the area immediately north of the River Liffey offers a fascinating mix of 18th-century grandeur, traditional city life and the multicultural melting pot that is contemporary Dublin. At the heart of it is O'Connell St, Ireland's widest boulevard and once the elegant centre of the Georgian city. That lustre has faded somewhat, but around it, you'll still find superb art galleries and whiskey museums, bustling markets and some of the best restaurants for world cuisine in town.

A number of neighbourhoods fall under the wider northside umbrella, such as Smithfield, the former warehouse district that's now the land of coffee shops and slick bars. Just beyond is the hipster neighbourhood of Stoneybatter, with friendly pubs, brunch cafes and an annual street fair. It's all within walking distance of the city centre, but you can whizz out there on the Luas tram.

TOP TIP

By day, O'Connell St is a bustle of activity, with shoppers, hawkers, walkers and others going about their business. At night, however, it can be a different story, as alcohol and drugs can give the street an air of menace and, sadly, the odd spot of trouble. Give it a wide berth after dark.

O'Connell St

Chapter One
Two-Star Lunch

Awarded its second Michelin star in 2019, Chapter One is unquestionably one of the best restaurants in the country, courtesy of the Scandi-influenced, Irish-based menus created by superstar chef Mickael Viljanen. But while the multicourse dinner menu will set you back a pretty penny, the lunch deal gives you a taste of the dining experience without breaking the bank. Each dish arrives with an artistic flourish, but it's not snooty – this is simply incredible food served in style. You'll need to book far in advance.

Chapter One

General Post Office
Emblem Of Independence

If you're looking for a quintessential Dublin landmark, this is it. The General Post Office is at the heart of Ireland's struggle for independence. It served as command HQ for the rebels during the 1916 Easter Rising, and you can still see the pockmarks of the struggle in the Doric columns outside.

As a result, the GPO has become the focal point for all kinds of protests, parades and remembrances, as well as home to an interactive visitor centre, GPO Witness History. This interactive museum explores all facets of the Rising, from its origins to the events of Easter Week and on to its aftermath.

General Post Office

14 Henrietta Street
Dublin's Georgian Past

Dublin has its fill of Georgian townhouses, but most are a symbol of grandeur and pomp. That's not the case at 14 Henrietta Street, which has been carefully restored to gently peel back layers of complex social history over 250 years. Part museum, part community archive, it covers the magnificent elegance of upper-class life in the 1740s to the destitution of the early 20th century, when the house was occupied by 100 tenants living in near squalor.

You can visit only on a guided tour, which is also offered in Irish Sign Language. The museum also runs guided walking tours of the local neighbourhood, as well as themed talks (and the occasional singalong) led by former residents or social historians.

NORTH OF THE LIFFEY

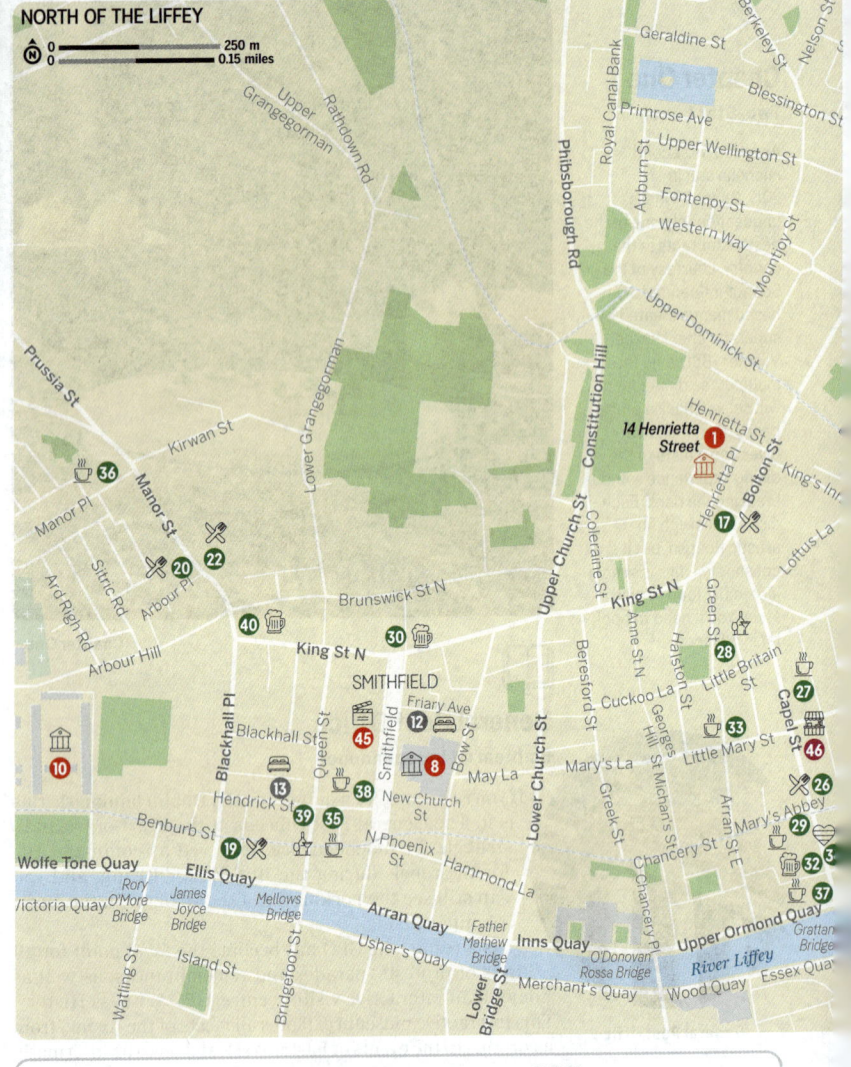

HIGHLIGHTS
1. 14 Henrietta Street
2. Chapter One
3. General Post Office

SIGHTS
4. Garden of Remembrance
5. Hugh Lane Gallery
6. James Joyce Centre
7. James Joyce Statue
8. Jameson Distillery
9. National Leprechaun Museum
10. National Museum of Ireland – Decorative Arts & History

SLEEPING
11. Address Connolly
12. Generator Hostel
13. Hendrick
14. Jacob's Inn
15. Morrison
16. Point A

EATING
17. Boco
18. El Grito
19. Fish Shop
20. Grano
21. Han Sung
22. L Mulligan Grocer
23. M&L
24. Moore Street Mall
25. Mr Fox
26. White Rabbit

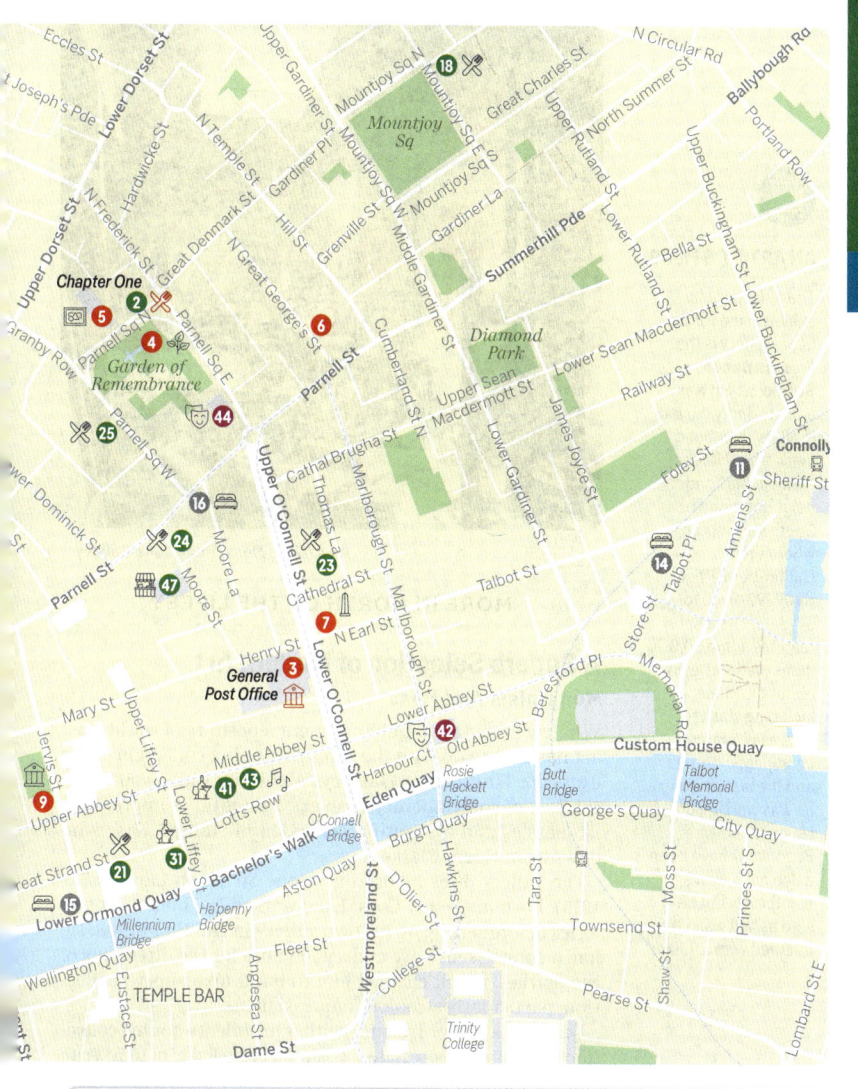

DRINKING & NIGHTLIFE
- 27 Aobaba
- 28 Bar 1661
- 29 Brother Hubbard
- 30 Cobblestone
- 31 Grand Social
- 32 Nealon's
- 33 Oxmantown
- 34 Pantibar
- 35 Proper Order
- 36 Slice
- 37 Soup Dragon
- 38 Third Space
- 39 Token
- 40 Walshs
- 41 Wigwam

ENTERTAINMENT
- 42 Abbey Theatre
- 43 Academy
- 44 Gate Theatre
- 45 Light House

SHOPPING
- 46 Ayla Turkish Foods Market
- 47 Moore Street Market

AN ARTIST'S MESS

The most popular exhibit in the Hugh Lane Gallery is the **Francis Bacon Studio**, which was painstakingly moved in all its shambolic mess from 7 Reece Mews in the London neighbourhood of South Kensington, where the Dublin-born artist (1909–92) lived for 31 years. The display features some 80,000 items madly strewn about the place, including slashed canvases, empty champagne bottles and the last painting he was working on. Neatniks, beware: Bacon may have been a dab hand with a paintbrush, but he sure as hell wasn't as talented with a duster.

An Artist's Mess, Hugh Lane Gallery

MORE IN NORTH OF THE LIFFEY

A Superb Selection of Modern Art
Modernism And Mess

Whatever reputation Dublin has as a repository of world-class art has a lot to do with the simply stunning collection at the exquisite **Hugh Lane Gallery**. Within its walls, you'll find the best of contemporary Irish art, a handful of impressionist classics and a beautiful collection of stained-glass windows from Harry Clarke.

The gallery owes its origins to one Sir Hugh Lane (1875–1915). Born in County Cork, Lane worked in London art galleries before setting up his own gallery in Dublin in 1908. He had a connoisseur's eye and a good nose for the directions of the market, which enabled him to build up a superb collection, particularly strong in impressionists.

Unfortunately for Ireland, neither his talents nor his collection were much appreciated. Irish rejection led him to rewrite his will and bequeath some of the finest works in his collection to the National Gallery in London. Later, he relented and added a rider to his will leaving the collection to Dublin, but he failed to have it witnessed, thus causing a long legal squabble over which gallery had rightful ownership.

WHERE TO STAY NORTH OF THE LIFFEY

Address Connolly
Snazzy rooms and a tiny rooftop lounge by Connolly Station. €€

Morrison
Dubbed a five-star in 2023, this Curio Collection by Hilton hotel is right on the River Liffey. €€

Generator Hostel
A funky, bright hostel with comfy dorms and a lively social scene. €

The collection of eight paintings (known as the Hugh Lane Bequest 1917) was split in two in a 1959 settlement that saw half of them moving back and forth every six years. However, in 2021, a new agreement was reached – now a collection of 10 paintings rotates in two groups of five, changing every five years.

At noon on Sundays, from September to June, the art gallery hosts concerts of contemporary classical music.

The Gritty City
A Moving Tour

If you want to see the realities of life in Dublin (or any major city), then a walking tour with **Secret Street Tours** is the way to go. Led by people affected by homelessness, these tours take you around Smithfield and the surrounding neighbourhood, starting off at Collins Barracks (p95). You'll see the local cultural and historical sights through the eyes of someone who knows what it's like to live on these streets. If there's one walking tour to take while in Dublin, this is it.

Raise a Glass
Smithfield Spirit

The distilleries of the Liberties (p86) might be coming for its throne, but the **Jameson Distillery** in Smithfield has been luring in visitors for decades, despite not producing a drop of whiskey in this location since 1971. But no matter – visit this museum and you get a slick tour through a recreation of the factory before sitting down for a tasting.

If you're really serious about whiskey, you can book the Secret Tasting, with four premium blends exclusive to the distillery, or taste it straight from the barrel on the Cask Draw. True aficionados can bottle their own from the barrel. If you wince at the thought of drinking whiskey straight, take the Cocktail Making Masterclass to learn how to make the perfect whiskey sour.

History, Home & Heritage
A Converted 18th-Century Barracks

Once the world's largest military barracks, this imposing greystone building is now home to the **National Museum of Ireland – Decorative Arts & History**. But the museum wears many hats, and you'll see a wide array of Irish treasures as

---

SEE ANOTHER NEIGHBOURHOOD

Secret Street Tours also runs a walking tour in the **Liberties** (p81), which kicks off on Palace St by **Dublin Castle** (p58) and wraps up near **St Stephen's Green** (p60).

BEST BARS NORTH OF THE LIFFEY

Bar 1661
Ireland's moonshine, poitín, is transformed into excellent cocktails at this world-class bar.

Pantibar
A raucous, fun gay bar owned by 'gender discombobulist' Rory O'Neill, aka Panti Bliss.

Wigwam
Loads of craft beers, loads of cocktails and a raucous bottomless brunch at the weekend.

Token
Gourmet junk food, great beers, and a room full of retro video games and pinball machines.

WHERE TO STAY NORTH OF THE LIFFEY

Hendrick
Cosy rooms and interior street art in a great location in Smithfield. €€

Point A
This 'budget boutique' hotel opened in 2023 and has slick rooms and a great bar. €€

Jacob's Inn
A modern hostel with pod-style bunks and private rooms, too. €

you walk from hall to hall, from classic pieces of Irish design to military memorabilia.

Start off at the **Soldiers & Chiefs** exhibition, which covers the history of Irish soldiery at home and abroad from 1550 to the 21st century. You'll get to see the muddied army coat of Michael Collins, a hero of the struggle for independence, who was killed in the Civil War in 1922. The barracks were renamed in his honour, and it's why most Dubliners still refer to the museum as the Collins Barracks.

The rest of the museum is dedicated to the arts, with a treasure trove of artefacts ranging from silver, ceramics and glassware to weaponry, furniture and folk-life displays. The fascinating **Way We Wore** exhibit displays Irish clothing and jewellery from the past 250 years, and **Reconstructed Rooms** features four different rooms decorated in styles from 1600 to the present day. Another highlight is the exhibit of the work of iconic Irish designer **Eileen Gray**, showcasing her avant-garde furniture and the renowned non-conformist chair.

In a hurry? Some of the best pieces are gathered in the **Curator's Choice** exhibition, a collection of 25 objects hand-picked by different curators and displayed alongside an account of why they were chosen.

Market Days
Old-School Dublin

Make your way up Moore St and your walk will be accompanied by the calls of the c traders, shouting out their daily deals. You might not want a sackful of apples, but you can't hear the shout of 'Ten for a euro!' without thinking it sounds like a deal. The market may not be as vibrant as it once was, but it's still going strong, and the permanent buildings on the street have brought an air of multiculturalism to this corner of the city. You'll find Brazilian restaurants, Asian markets and Indian spices.

For a real culinary adventure, head to the **Moore Street Mall** next to Lidl. It may not look like much, but this food court offers options from all over the world, such as Balkan cafes and Bolivian restaurants, along with noodle and curry vendors. The prices are fantastic.

Night at the Movies
Popcorn And Pilsner

If you like independent cinema, you'll love the **Light House**. This snazzy four-screener in a cool building just off

---

STREET ART IN SMITHFIELD

The laneway by Proper Order has two pieces by the street art collective Subset, one a striking black and white portrait.

At the other end of Smithfield Market by the Cobblestone (p98), there's a building a couple of doors down covered in a mural of two musicians, one with a fiddle and one with a flute.

On Stirrup Lane, another piece by Subset is called *Horseboy*, an incredible artwork with psychedelic colours and an optical illusion effect.

WHERE TO EAT NORTH OF THE LIFFEY

Fish Shop
Exceptional seafood in a tiny restaurant, from fresh mackerel to perfect fish and chips. €€

Brother Hubbard
A giant restaurant with midweek brunch and vegan-friendly dishes. €

Mr Fox
Fine dining in a gorgeous setting on Parnell Sq. €€€

Moore Street Mall

Smithfield Plaza shows a mix of art-house and mainstream releases, documentaries, and Irish films. The themed movie seasons are always worth checking out – you might catch the entire back catalogue of Wes Anderson films or an all-night marathon of the *Lord of the Rings* trilogy.

It also runs a Cinema Book Club, where a screening of a book adaptation is followed by a casual chat in the bar. Previous movies have included *Brokeback Mountain*, *The Shining* and *10 Things I Hate About You*.

All Things Joyce
Statues And Museums

From the bemused statue on North Earl St to the shrine-like museum on North Great George's St, there's no escaping James Joyce in this corner of town. You'll find the **James Joyce Centre** in a beautifully restored house, with exhibits of furniture from Joyce's Paris apartment, a life-size recreation of a typical Edwardian bedroom and the original door of 7 Eccles St, the home of Leopold and Molly Bloom in *Ulysses*. The centre also runs two walking tours, Introducing Joyce's Dublin and Footsteps of Leopold Bloom.

BEST CAFES NORTH OF THE LIFFEY

Proper Order
A small Smithfield cafe with excellent coffee and treats from No Messin' Bakery. €

Slice
This Stoneybatter joint is a local hotspot for brunch and hot chocolate. €

Oxmantown
Excellent sandwiches and decadent Vietnamese iced coffees. €

Third Space
A laidback cafe in Smithfield with a neighbourhood mindset and social vibe. €

WHERE TO EAT NORTH OF THE LIFFEY

Grano
An exceptional Italian restaurant in Stoneybatter, with homemade pasta and killer tiramisu. €€

L Mulligan Grocer
A gastropub in Stoneybatter with great beer and even better Scotch eggs. €€

M&L
The best Chinese restaurant in Dublin, with spicy Szechuan-style cuisine. €

GO CITY PASS

If you know you're going to be ticking off a few big attractions when you're in town, a **Go City** Dublin pass can save you some cash. Choose between an All-Inclusive Pass or an Explorer Pass, where you select how many sights you want to see.

The All-Inclusive Pass is probably the easiest bet. It can be purchased for one to five days and includes all the main attractions around Dublin, from the big (Guinness Storehouse, Christ Church and EPIC) to the small (Teeling Distillery, 14 Henrietta Street). And it's not just attractions – options include hop-on, hop-off bus tours, food walking tours and excursions to places like the Game of Thrones Studio Tour in Northern Ireland.

The Cobblestone

Dublin's Disney
One For The Kids

Ostensibly designed as a child-friendly museum of Irish folklore, the **National Leprechaun Museum** is really a romper room for kids sprinkled with bits of fairy tale. Which is no bad thing, even if the picture of the leprechaun painted here is more Lucky Charms and Walt Disney than sinister creature of pre-Christian mythology.

Memorial Garden
Peaceful And Quiet

Just over the road from the Hugh Lane Gallery (p94), the **Garden of Remembrance** is a rather austere little park, but it's a tranquil space to clear your head for a little while.

It was opened by President Eamon de Valera in 1966 for the 50th anniversary of the 1916 Easter Rising and is dedicated to all those who gave their lives. There's a pool in the centre and a bronze statue of the Children of Lir by Oisín Kelly. According to Irish legend, the children were turned into swans by their wicked stepmother.

NIGHTS OUT NORTH OF THE LIFFEY

Cobblestone
For top-notch trad, go to Smithfield's 'drinking pub with a music problem'.

Abbey Theatre
Head to Ireland's national theatre for homegrown talent and touring performances.

Walshs
A classic traditional pub in Stoneybatter with a cosy snug.

Capel St

A Glutton's Delight
A Haven Of World Cuisine

Ask Dublin foodies where their favourite neighbourhood is, and you'll hear the same place pop up time and time again: **Capel St**. This northside street was pedestrianised in 2022, making it the longest traffic-free road in the city. Take a walk up the road and you'll find loads of excellent restaurants along the way, with cuisines from all over the globe.

White Rabbit is at the back of an Asian supermarket and serves top-notch Korean food – think pork belly *cupbap*, platters of spicy fried chicken, and its signature corn dogs stuffed with sausage and mozzarella and served with mustard, ketchup and sugar. A few doors up the road is **Ayla Turkish Foods Market**, selling tempting slabs of sticky baklava, rows of cheesy *börek* (filo pastry with cheese) and *böreği* (pastries) stuffed with feta, the perfect snack that will set you back only a couple of euro.

From the outside, **Aobaba** looks like a run-of-the-mill bubble tea cafe. While it does serve plenty of those milk teas, it's also a great spot for Vietnamese dishes like summer rolls, banh mi and spicy pho. Some other cuisines have sneaked onto the street as well, like **Dash**, the smash burger bar where the patties are squashed down on the grill with onions and then slathered with truffle butter or chipotle sauce.

Wrap things up with a nightcap at the warm and cosy **Nealon's**, a traditional pub near the Liffey end of the street.

BUDGETS EATS NORTH OF THE LIFFEY

Soup Dragon
This cafe has been a budget favourite for years. The daily soup, bread and fruit deal is a bargain. €

Han Sung
A canteen at the back of a Korean supermarket, serving excellent bibimbap (a rice bowl with meat, vegetables and egg). €

El Grito
A cool taqueria on Mountjoy Sq, with tacos from €2.50. €

Boco
Buzzing pizza joint on Bolton St that's popular with students. €

NIGHTS OUT NORTH OF THE LIFFEY

Grand Social
This multipurpose venue is great fun and hosts club nights, comedy and live music.

Academy
A terrific midsize venue for live music and epic party nights.

Gate Theatre
An elegant theatre in a late 18th-century building, with big-name performances.

DOCKLANDS

DUBLIN'S TECH HUB

The gleaming modern buildings of the Docklands are the closest thing Dublin has to skyscrapers. The 79m-high Capital Dock is the tallest building in the Republic of Ireland – its 22 storeys tower over everything else around. Lines of shiny glass and steel towers line both sides of the River Liffey, from Talbot Bridge to Dublin Port, making the Docklands the only neighbourhood that incorporates both the north and south sides of the city.

The hub of the area is the 10,000-sq-m Grand Canal Sq, designed by American landscape architect Martha Schwartz. It's a handsome square, with benches along the canal and planters filled with greenery. You'll often find tech workers hanging out with a coffee – this neighbourhood has been known as the Silicon Docks ever since Google opened its European HQ at Grand Canal Dock, and others swiftly followed, including Facebook, X (the company formerly known as Twitter), LinkedIn and Indeed.

TOP TIP

If you want to explore the neighbourhood at a faster clip, sign up for Dublin Bikes (dublinbikes.ie or download the app). Bikes are parked at stations all over the Docklands, and the first 30 minutes are free. You can sign up for a one- or three-day ticket, and e-bikes are also available.

Google's European HQ, Docklands

DOCKLANDS

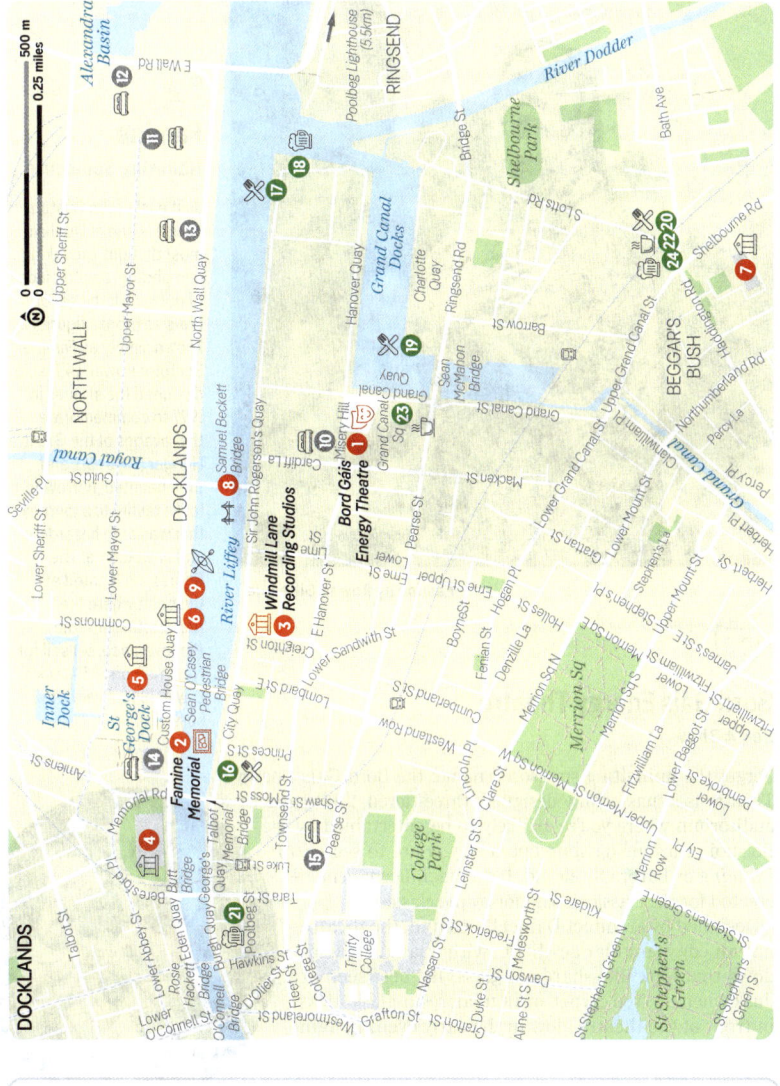

HIGHLIGHTS
1. Bord Gáis Energy Theatre
2. Famine Memorial
3. Windmill Lane Recording Studios

SIGHTS
4. Custom House
5. EPIC The Irish Emigration Museum
6. Jeanie Johnston
7. National Print Museum
8. Samuel Beckett Bridge

ACTIVITIES
9. City Kayaking

SLEEPING
10. Anantara The Marker
11. Beckett Locke
12. Gibson Hotel
13. Mayson
14. Spencer Hotel
15. Trinity City Hotel

EATING
16. As One
17. Bites by Kwanghi
18. Brewdog Outpost
19. Charlotte Quay
20. Old Spot
    see 13 Ryleigh's Rooftop Steakhouse

DRINKING & NIGHTLIFE
21. John Mulligan's
22. Juniors Deli & Cafe
23. Nutbutter
24. Slattery's

Famine by Rowan Gillespie

Famine
Haunting Sculpture

Just east of the Custom House is one of Dublin's most thought-provoking and photographed pieces of public art: the set of life-size bronze figures known simply as *Famine*. Sculptor Rowan Gillespie designed the statues in 1997 to commemorate the ravages of the Great Hunger (1845–51), and their haunted, harrowed looks testify to a journey that was both hazardous and unwelcome. The figures are located at the point where the first 'coffin ship,' the *Perseverance*, set sail for New York on St Patrick's Day in 1846. Everyone survived.

Bord Gáis Energy Theatre
See A Show

Forget the uninviting sponsored name: the Bord Gáis Energy Theatre is a masterfully designed, three-tiered, 2100-capacity auditorium where you're as likely to be entertained by the Bolshoi or a touring state opera as you are to see *Dirty Dancing* or Barbra Streisand. It's a magnificent venue – created for the classical, paid for by the classics.

Designed by architect Daniel Libeskind, the theatre has an edgy, angular aesthetic, with triangular windows that look like shards of glass. It's best seen at dusk when the 'red carpet' of angular, resin-glass sticks in front of the theatre glow in the early evening light.

Windmill Lane Recording Studios
Musical Legends

The Lion King, Bord Gáis Energy Theatre

What do the Rolling Stones, Metallica and Lady Gaga all have in common? They've all laid down tracks in the Windmill Lane Recording Studios. It opened its doors in 1978 and saw a rake of musicians walk through the doors in the years that followed, including U2, who recorded all of their first three albums (*Boy, October* and *War*) here. As a result, fans of the band graffitied the walls outside the recording space.

The studio opened its doors to the public in February 2020. (The timing was a little unfortunate.) Now you can walk around the recording rooms and hear the stories of the legends who recorded here and the songs they sang. It's hallowed ground for music fans.

Custom House

MORE IN THE DOCKLANDS

Neoclassical Building
James Gandon's Masterpiece

Though it's one of the most impressive buildings along the edge of the River Liffey, Dubliners and visitors to the city have never had much of a connection to **Custom House**. After all, this was traditionally the domain of government offices and rarely open to the public.

But that all changed with the arrival of the **Custom House Visitor Centre**, which opened in 2021. Now you can walk inside the central area of the building and learn about the history of this colossal neoclassical pile.

Inside, you'll get the full backstory, from its construction between 1781 and 1791 (you can even see the desk it was designed on, belonging to architect James Gandon) to the day it was set on fire in 1921. The 200-year story is told through audiovisual displays, models and touchscreens, with some of the displays plastered straight onto the curved walls.

If you want to get the best view of the building from the outside, cross over to the south side of the Liffey, where you

---

FESTIVE SEASON

At Christmas, the entire facade of Custom House is covered in a light installation, which is either fun and festive or a touch gaudy depending on your level of Scrooge-iness.

The area around the building really comes into its own on 31 December when it's transformed into the main stage for the **New Year's Festival Dublin**. Major acts put on an afternoon performance, and there's a fake countdown to midnight for the younger kids. The full-on extravaganza happens when the actual clock strikes 12. You need to book tickets in advance (nyfdublin.com), but it's as good a place as any to celebrate.

WHERE TO STAY IN THE DOCKLANDS

Anantara The Marker
This swish five-star rebranded in 2023 and is still the hotel of note in the area. €€€

Trinity City Hotel
There's a nice courtyard and refurbished rooms, some of which have balconies. €€

Gibson Hotel
Out by the 3 Arena, this modern hotel is ideal for gigs or people taking the ferry. €€

Jeanie Johnston

can see the whole building in all its glory. Below the frieze are heads representing the gods of Ireland's 13 principal rivers; the sole female head, above the main door, represents the River Liffey. The cattle heads honour Dublin's beef trade, and the statues behind the building represent Africa, America, Asia and Europe. Set into the dome are four clocks and, above that, a 5m-high statue of Hope.

Irish Emigration
An Epic Museum

Ireland has a long history of migration, and those stories are told in **EPIC The Irish Emigration Museum**. This high-tech, interactive museum explores the concept of emigration and its effect on Ireland, and the 70 million or so people around the world who claim Irish ancestry.

You start your visit with a 'passport' and proceed through 20 interactive – and occasionally moving – galleries examining why people left, where they went and how they maintained their relationship with their ancestral home. The setting is particularly striking – the exhibitions are in the basement of the building, kept between stone archways and tunnels.

WHERE TO EAT IN THE CHQ

Upshoots
Hearty burritos and rice bowls, with excellent breakfast options before 11am. €

Urban Brewing
Super cool brewery serving dishes like IPA-brined chicken and beer-battered halloumi. €€

Toss'd Noodles & Salads
The place to go for quick, filling food, such as Thai curry, yakisoba and noodle salads. €

The Bakehouse
Need a sugar fix? Pick up a pastel-hued cupcake or a chocolate brownie in this cafe. €

WHERE TO STAY IN THE DOCKLANDS

Spencer Hotel
A contemporary business hotel in the heart of the Irish Financial Services Centre (IFSC). €€

Mayson
A cool boutique hotel on the river, with a tiny pool and nifty rooftop bar. €€

Beckett Locke
Chic suites and apartments with full kitchens and working areas. €€

In 2022, EPIC launched a campaign called **This Is Not Us**, which saw a CGI character invented based on the stereotypical view of an Irish person: beer swilling, potato eating and free-fighting. Since then, the campaign to bust these clichés has only grown, with installations and special events around St Patrick's Day to tell the stories of the real Ireland rather than resorting to tired tropes.

If you want to discover your own family history, you can track your surname in the **Irish Family History Centre**, part of EPIC. Those who want to dig a little deeper can book a one-to-one consultation with one of the centre's genealogists, who can guide you along your journey and help with research. Appointments can be booked in 30-, 60- or 90-minute sessions.

EPIC is in the **CHQ building**, a massive glass structure on the northern side of the River Liffey, with several places to eat under its roof.

Famine Ships
Replica Sailing Boat

One of the city's most original tourist attractions is the **Jeanie Johnston**, an exact working replica of a 19th-century 'coffin ship', as the sailing boats that transported starving emigrants away from Ireland during the Famine were gruesomely known. However, the original Jeanie Johnston suffered no deaths in its 16 journeys between 1848 and 1855, which carried a total of 2500 passengers.

Step aboard for a guided tour, which starts on the upper deck so you can see the craftsmanship and the soaring sails. You then go below deck to hear about the harrowing plight of a typical journey, which took around 47 days. Up to 250 passengers would have been on board during a crossing, breathing in fresh air for only half an hour every day. You'll hear their stories as you see the cramped quarters up close.

Go Kayaking
Paddle The Liffey

Want to see the city from a different perspective? Then head out to explore the River Liffey with **City Kayaking**. You'll start at Custom House Quay and paddle your way towards the city centre, getting a unique angle on the riverside buildings on your way. The guided tours last around two hours and at least 90 minutes are spent on the water, where you'll paddle underneath the Ha'penny and O'Connell Bridges.

WATERSIDE DINING IN THE DOCKLANDS

As One
A sleek, sustainable restaurant on the Liffey that does an excellent brunch. €€

Nutbutter
Vegan-friendly cafe with massive salads, tacos and a great breakfast menu in Grand Canal Dock. €€

Ryleigh's Rooftop Steakhouse
Overlooking the River Liffey, this rooftop restaurant has one of the best views in town. €€

Charlotte Quay
A lively restaurant at Grand Canal for cocktails and beautiful plates of food. €€

WHERE TO EAT IN THE DOCKLANDS

Juniors Deli & Cafe
Designed to imitate a New York deli, Juniors has delicious food and a buzzing atmosphere. €€

Old Spot
A gorgeous gastropub that does an excellent Sunday roast. Bookings essential. €€

Bites by Kwanghi
A light-filled restaurant serving Asian street food with a contemporary twist. €€

For something special, book the **Music Under The Bridges** tour, where musicians park up on stage boats under the bridges to perform music and spoken-word pieces while you bob around on the water.

Lighthouse Keeper
A Seaside Stroll

One of the city's most rewarding walks is a stroll along the Great South Wall to the **Poolbeg Lighthouse**, the stumpy red tower visible in the middle of Dublin Bay. The lighthouse dates from 1768, but it was redesigned and rebuilt in 1820. To get there, take the bus from the city centre to Ringsend and then make your way past the power station to the start of the wall (it's about 1km).

It's not an especially long walk out to the lighthouse – about 800m or so – but it will give you a stunning view of the bay and the city behind you, best enjoyed just before sunset on a summer's evening.

Extra, Extra!
The History Of Print

You don't have to be into printing to enjoy the **National Print Museum**, a quirky little spot where personalised guided tours are offered in a delightfully casual and compelling way. Learn about the history of printing in Ireland and then wander through the various (still working) antique presses amid the smell of ink and metal.

The guides are excellent and can tailor the guided tours to suit your interests – for example, visitors interested in history can get a detailed account of the difficulties encountered by the rebels of 1916 when they tried to have the proclamation printed. While entry is free, tours are usually €5, though there's a free tour every Sunday. It also runs crafting workshops for adults and kids on topics like calligraphy or woodtype poster printing.

National Print Museum

SAMUEL BECKETT BRIDGE

Inspired by the shape of an Irish harp, the Samuel Beckett Bridge is the second Dublin bridge designed by the Spanish architect Santiago Calatrava (his other was the James Joyce Bridge). Compared to other bridges in Dublin, this one is a standout structure, with a contemporary shape that's often photographed by people walking past, particularly when it rotates 90 degrees to allow ships to sail up the Liffey.

WHERE TO DRINK IN THE DOCKLANDS

John Mulligan's
A brilliant old boozer dating from 1782, with an avid flock of regulars.

Slattery's
Popular with rugby fans who couldn't get tickets to the match at the nearby Aviva Stadium.

Brewdog Outpost
This funky red building has a microbrewery, beer school and loads of craft beer on tap.

BEYOND THE CITY CENTRE

BEACHES, PARKS AND STADIUMS

While Dublin's city centre is fairly small, there's a whole other world to explore just outside the confines of what Dubliners call 'town'. You don't have to journey far to see it – you can be on the coastline, with its hilltop walks and sandy beaches, within half an hour if you catch the train. Get on a bus and you could be hiking in the mountains within the hour, looking down on the city and the sea from a lookout and then sitting in a nearby pub for a platter of seafood and a pint.

If you don't have the time or the inclination to trek that far, you can get a taste of the countryside even closer to the city, with a walk through Phoenix Park or a trip to the Botanic Gardens. It's all on Dublin's doorstep.

TOP TIP

If you're heading out for a hike, make sure you're prepared for all weather. The skies can shift from glorious blue to dark and grey within a matter of minutes, so bring a rain jacket even if it's sunny.

GREAT WALKS IN DUBLIN

Dollymount Strand
Take a seaside stroll out to Bull Island on Dublin's north coast.

Ardgillan Demesne
Head to Skerries to walk the 5km loop through the gardens of this grand castle.

Malahide Castle
Trails lead through 101 hectares of parkland, as well as a fairy trail and butterfly house.

Sandymount Strand
This is the closest beach to the city centre, and a popular dog-walking spot.

Sandymount Strand

BEYOND THE CITY CENTRE DUBLIN

BEYOND THE CITY CENTRE

HIGHLIGHTS
1. Phoenix Park

SIGHTS
2. Baily Lighthouse
3. Croke Park Stadium
4. Dalkey
5. Dollymount Strand
6. Dún Laoghaire
7. Glasnevin Cemetery
8. Howth
9. James Joyce Tower & Museum
10. Killiney Hill Park
11. National Botanic Gardens
12. Sandycove
13. Sandymount Strand

ACTIVITIES
14. Dublin Bay Cruises
15. Dún Laoghaire Baths
16. Experience Gaelic Games
17. Forty Foot Pool
18. Howth Cliff Path Walk
19. Ireland's Eye Ferries
20. Pure Magic Watersports
21. Vico Bathing Place

SLEEPING
22. Croke Park Hotel
23. Devlin
24. Dylan
25. Haddington House
26. Intercontinental Dublin
27. Pembroke Townhouse

EATING
28. Aqua
29. Big Mike's
30. Butcher Grill
31. Howth Market
32. Kinara
33. Mamó
34. Manifesto
35. Octopussy's
36. People's Park Market
37. Shouk
38. Washerwoman

DRINKING & NIGHTLIFE
39. Abbey Tavern
40. Finnegan's
41. Hole in the Wall
42. John Kavanagh's

Phoenix Park
Bucolic Bliss

Measuring 709 glorious hectares, Phoenix Park is one of the biggest city parks in the world. Step through the pillared entrance on Conyngham Rd, and within minutes, the bustle of the city feels a million miles away. You'll see colourful flowerbeds, grannies pushing buggies and usually a gaggle of people hanging out under the giant Wellington Monument.

Meander off the main thoroughfare of Chesterfield Ave and things get quieter still, with pathways weaving through woodland and patches of wildflowers. There's a high chance you'll also meet the park's long-term residents, the herd of fallow deer. Introduced to the park by Lord Ormond in 1662 to create a royal hunting ground, the deer have stuck around ever since and are remarkably calm around the people taking their photographs – but whatever others are doing, remember to give the deer space and never feed them.

The other famous resident of Phoenix Park is the Irish president, who lives in the white Palladian lodge Áras an Uachtaráin. You can take a free tour of the residence by collecting tickets at the Phoenix Park Visitor Centre.

If you hear the distant roar of a lion or an elephant trumpet, don't panic – that's just the inhabitants of Dublin Zoo, one of the oldest in the world.

WHERE TO EAT IN PHOENIX PARK

The park has two cafes. The best known is the Victorian Tea Rooms, in a pretty building just off Chesterfield Ave. It serves the kind of classic fare that you crave halfway through a long walk: homemade cakes, giant cookies and bowls of soup.

If you're up as far as the Walled Garden and Ashtown Castle, **Phoenix Cafe** has a large outdoor courtyard and an excellent menu of colourful fresh salads and warm scones with house-made jam.

Deer, Phoenix Park

All-Ireland Championship Camogie Final

BOAT TRIPS IN DUBLIN

Dublin Bay Cruises
During the summer, you can hop on a boat into the city and head to Howth or Dún Laoghaire (or sail between the two).

Ireland's Eye Ferries
Take a tour around Howth and out to the island of Ireland's Eye, scanning the cliffs for local birdlife.

Dublin Under Sail
Set off from Dún Laoghaire to explore the bay on a giant traditional sailing vessel, the *Brian Ború*. You can even learn the ropes yourself.

MORE BEYOND THE CITY CENTRE

Stadium Tour
Home Of The Gaa

For fans of the GAA (Gaelic Athletic Association), **Croke Park Stadium** is sacred ground. But even if you're not a fan, a tour of the stadium is excellent, particularly the moment when you can run through the tunnel and out towards the pitch. Take it up a notch by booking a walk on the **Skyline** for a guided tour along the top of the building's roof. You can also do this at dusk for an even better view of the city at sunset.

There's also the **GAA Museum**, where you can learn about the history and the importance of Gaelic sports in Ireland. Test your skills in the Interactive Games Zone to see what you're like with a hurley.

Try it Yourself
Gaelic Athletic Association Action

Want to take your GAA skills up another level? Check out **Experience Gaelic Games**. Ostensibly created as a uniquely Irish version of a corporate bonding exercise, this centre allows you to experience the trio of Gaelic games: hurling, Gaelic football and handball. The staff have enormous passion for the sports, and their pride and delight at showing them to visitors is infectious. The centre is out in Glasnevin,

WHERE TO STAY BEYOND THE CITY CENTRE

Haddington House
A boutique hotel on the seafront in Dún Laoghaire, with a top-notch restaurant. €€

Devlin
Sister property to the Dean (p61) in Ranelagh, with small but stylish rooms and a rooftop bar. €€

Pembroke Townhouse
An elegant boutique hotel within walking distance of town. €€

and you can book into public sessions or private workshops for groups of six or more. As you might expect, it's a popular activity for hens and stags.

Fishing Village
Hills And Hikes In Howth

Tidily positioned at the foot of a bulbous peninsula, the pretty port village of **Howth** (the name rhymes with 'both') is a major fishing centre, a yachting harbour and one of the most sought-after addresses in town.

It's an easy hop out of the city – the DART drops you right by the harbour, where you can take a stroll among the fishing boats or pop into **Howth Market** for a coffee and a bun. But the real appeal comes a little further afield. Walk about 10 minutes along the coast and you'll be at the start of the **Howth Cliff Path Walk**, a 6km loop that takes you over the headland for gorgeous views over the grassy slopes to the sea. If you want to do a proper hike, there are longer routes that lead to the **Baily Lighthouse** and back over rough, mountainous terrain.

Back in the village, choose from plenty of excellent restaurants, many of which unsurprisingly focus on seafood. The bulk of these are on West Pier, as close to the fishing boats as you can get without stepping on board. Try **Octopussy's** for tasty seafood tapas or **Aqua** for top-quality fish dishes in an elegant dining room overlooking the harbour. Many Dubliners make the trek out just for a meal in **Mamó**, a modern bistro serving inventive, deconstructed dishes. The set lunch menu is great value.

On the Coast
See The Sea

A short DART ride brings you to the village of **Dalkey**, a well-to-do enclave favoured by resident celebrities like Bono and visitors like Matt Damon, who was based here during the first COVID-19 lockdown in 2020.

Start your exploration in the village, wandering between the chichi food stores and bookshops before heading out to the coast and the small park at **Sorrento Point**, where you'll get some great views.

If you want to head off on a longer walk (and you should), make your way along Vico Rd, stopping for a dip at the **Vico Bathing Place**, where you'll see swimmers almost every day of the year. Climb the 'Cat's Ladder' steps and you'll soon be in **Killiney Hill Park**, where you can stand on the top of the Pyramid of Dublin and feel like the king of the world.

A DAY BEYOND THE CITY CENTRE

Gaz Smith is a chef and owner of Michael's, Little Mike's and Big Mike's. Here he shares his idea of the perfect day spent outside the city.

'My idea of a perfect day in Dublin is spent out on the coast. The whole area from **Portmarnock** to **Howth** is just stunning. It's never overcrowded, and there's so much out there. Depending on the tides, you can walk for miles. There's a little estuary when the tide is out, and there's loads of wildlife. **St Anne's Park** is so big and diverse. There are BMX tracks, a rose garden, a playground and often a food market. I love to go for a few pints in **The Sheds** in Clontarf, which is a proper Irish boozer.'

WHERE TO STAY BEYOND THE CITY CENTRE

Dylan
A wonderfully quirky hotel with a buzzy bar and terrace that's a hit on sunny days. €€

Croke Park Hotel
Just over the road from the stadium, with a lovely big terrace for alfresco dining. €€

Intercontinental Dublin
This seriously plush hotel makes for a decadent getaway and has a great spa to boot. €€€

Family Castle
Historical Home
In the pretty village of **Malahide** is a castle well worth the short train ride. The former home of the Talbot family, **Malahide Castle** is packed with furniture and paintings. Highlights are a 16th-century oak room with decorative carvings, and the medieval Great Hall, which has family portraits, a minstrel's gallery and a painting of the Battle of the Boyne. Puck, the Talbot family ghost, is said to have last appeared in 1975.

While the castle is accessible only via a guided tour, a walk around the extensive gardens is self-guided.

Dublin's Graveyard
More Than A Million Souls
The tombstones at **Glasnevin Cemetery**, Ireland's largest and most historically important burial site, read like a who's who of Irish history. Most of the leading names of the past 150 years are buried here, including former mayor and Catholic emancipator Daniel O'Connell and 19th-century nationalist politician Charles Stewart Parnell. O'Connell established it in 1832 as a burial ground for people of all faiths, a high-minded response to Protestant cemeteries' refusal to bury Catholics.

The best way to visit the cemetery is to take one of the daily tours that will (ahem) bring to life the rich and important stories of those buried in what is jokingly referred to by Dubliners as 'Croak Park'.

While you're there, pay a visit to the **Glasnevin Cemetery Museum**, which tells the social and political story of Ireland through the lives of the people, known and unknown, buried here. If you want a great view of the city, buy a ticket to climb **O'Connell Tower**, the tallest round tower in Ireland, which marks O'Connell's tomb.

Botanical Delights
Garden Central
If you want to stop and smell the roses, there's no better place than the **National Botanic Gardens**. While there are acres of pretty flowers and plants outside, a highlight is the series of curvilinear glasshouses, dating from 1843 to 1869 and created by Richard Turner, who was also responsible for the glasshouse at Belfast Botanic Gardens and the Palm House in London's Kew Gardens. Within these Victorian masterpieces, you will find the latest in botanical technology, including a series of computer-controlled climates reproducing environments from different parts of the world.

BEST OUTDOOR ADVENTURES IN DUBLIN

Rock Climbing
Climb the jagged peaks of Dalkey Quarry and then abseil down with Adventure.ie.

Rafting
Whizz along the River Liffey on an adrenaline-filled whitewater rafting trip with Rafting.ie, starting in Palmerstown.

Mountain Biking
Hit the trails at Glencullen Adventure Park and then have a beer and burger afterwards.

Kite Surfing
Learn how to fly over the waves during a kitesurfing class with **Pure Magic Watersports**.

WHERE TO EAT BEYOND THE CITY CENTRE

Big Mike's
Blackrock outpost from Gaz Smith (p111) opened in 2022, with a slick terrace and incredible seafood. €€

Butcher Grill
Tiny Ranelagh steakhouse serving excellent beef; there are few spots in town where the meat sweats are so welcome. €€

Kinara
Impeccable Pakistani restaurant serving unusual curries, with outlets in Ranelagh and Clontarf. €€

National Botanic Gardens

If you're visiting from Glasnevin Cemetery, a little gate links the two places from the northeastern part of the cemetery.

Dive In
Embrace The Sea

These days, it feels like half of Dublin has a sea-swimming habit and the dry robe to match. One of the most popular spots for a dip is the **Forty Foot Pool** in **Sandycove**. This open-air seawater bathing pool was originally nudist and for men only. Nowadays, everyone is welcome, but generally, they're all wearing their swimsuits. Be warned, the waves can get fairly wild on windy days, and it's jampacked when the sun is shining.

The pool is featured at the close of the first chapter of *Ulysses* when Buck Mulligan heads off to the Forty Foot Pool for a morning swim. The **James Joyce Tower** is where the story begins – there's a tiny museum inside the Martello tower, which has photographs, letters, various editions of Joyce's work and two death masks of Joyce on display.

Walk 1km or so up the shore and you'll reach **Dún Laoghaire**. While there's not a huge amount to do here, a stroll along the East Pier up to the lighthouse is a lovely little amble, passing the sailboats docked in the marina. On Sundays, there's a market in **People's Park**, with a combination of farmers-market-style produce and food that's ready to eat. There's also a swimming spot nearby – in 2022, the **Dún Laoghaire Baths** reopened to the public after a multimillion-euro development. The actual baths themselves have yet to open (a source of contention), but you can jump into the sea from the baths' steps.

CLASSIC PUBS

John Kavanagh's
You can't go to Glasnevin without popping into the 'Gravediggers' for a pint.

Hole in the Wall
The longest pub in Ireland, with cosy snug and great bar food. It's on the edge of Phoenix Park.

Finnegan's
Bono's local in Dalkey, with a great atmosphere and outdoor seating.

Abbey Tavern
An old-style pub in Howth, with live music out the back.

WHERE TO EAT BEYOND THE CITY CENTRE

Manifesto
Classic pizzeria in Rathmines, with expertly charred pizzas and an inventive wine list. €€

Shouk
Top-notch Middle Eastern food at a great price; the platters are made for sharing. €

Washerwoman
Excellent gastropub fare in this charming restaurant in Glasnevin. €€

Above: Lough Bray Lower (p119); right: Kilmacurragh Botanic Gardens (p130)

WICKLOW & KILDARE

MOUNTAINS, MEADOWS AND RACEHORSES

Explore two contrasting counties on the edge of Dublin, with eagles soaring over granite crags and racehorses grazing in lush paddocks.

Wicklow and Kildare may be neighbours and have a boundary with Dublin in common, but that's where the similarities end. Immediately south of the capital is green and scenic County Wicklow, known as the 'Garden of Ireland'. Its most dramatic natural feature is the heather- and bracken-covered granite spine of the Wicklow Mountains, the east coast's most stunning landscape of deep glacial valleys, isolated mountain lakes, bridal-veil waterfalls and historical treasures dotted throughout, including Glendalough, one of Ireland's most important early Christian sites.

Spread around the fringes of the mountains are aristocratic estates such as Powerscourt, Killruddery and Russborough, with their 18th-century Palladian mansions and glorious landscaped gardens. The coastal town of Bray entices visitors with its lively seafront and stunning cliff walk while, further inland, Avondale Forest Park is home to a treetop walkway that opened in 2023.

To the west of Dublin is flat, fertile Kildare, known throughout Ireland as the 'Thoroughbred County'. Thousands of acres of grassland, meadow and paddock have raised generations of world-class racehorses. Some of the world's most lucrative stud farms are here, many with links to the horse-breeding centre of Kentucky in the USA. Kildare is also home to the Bog of Allen, the remains of the country's largest raised bog (a slightly dome-shaped peat bog), and now a focus for ecological and conservation projects.

THE MAIN AREAS

WICKLOW MOUNTAINS
Gorgeous scenery and ancient monastic settlement.
p118

KILDARE & THE CURRAGH
Heartland of Irish horse racing.
p134

THE GUIDE

WICKLOW & KILDARE

Kildare & the Curragh, p134
Ireland's most famous racecourse sits amid a lush hinterland of horse paddocks and stud farms.

Wicklow Mountains, p118
These scenic granite hills harbour a cradle of Irish Christianity as well as aristocratic estates and hiking trails galore.

Find Your Way

Bring your walking boots for Wicklow and Kildare. There are no cities, and even the region's largest town, Bray, is easily walkable. Buses and trains cover longer distances, though you'll need a car in more remote areas.

CAR
For motorists, the M4, M7 and M11 motorways provide fast and easy access to all parts of the region except the Wicklow Mountains and the Bog of Allen, where narrow, winding roads are the norm.

BUS & TRAIN
Both Wicklow and Kildare are easily accessed from Dublin. Frequent trains and buses run to Bray, Greystones, Wicklow town, Kildare town and Newbridge, while the specialist St Kevins Bus service runs daily from Dublin to Glendalough.

116

Happy Pear (p132)

Plan Your Time

The main sights in both Wicklow and Kildare lie within easy day-trip distance of Dublin and are well served by bus and train.

Pressed for Time

In the morning, head straight for **Glendalough** (p120), and after a wander around the impressive ruins of the ancient monastic site, take a walk to the Upper Lake and back. If you got here by bus, extend your walk to **The Spink** before catching the return bus to Dublin. If you're driving, you'll have time in the afternoon for a visit to the gorgeous gardens at **Powerscourt** (p125).

Three Days to Explore

If your trip doesn't coincide with a race day at the **Curragh** (p135), take a guided tour of the racecourse (Wednesday and Thursday only), which, combined with a visit to the **Irish National Stud** (p136), gives you a good insight into Irish horse racing. Spend a day exploring **Powerscourt** (p125) and **Glendalough** (p120), and another to visit Avondale's **Treetop Walk** (p129) and **Avoca Handweavers** (p130).

Seasonal Highlights

SPRING
The first classic race weekend of the horse-racing season kicks off at the Curragh with the **Irish 2000 Guineas festival** at the end of May.

SUMMER
Bray's famous **Air Display** takes place in late July with aerobatic manoeuvres, artisan food stalls, a fun fair, music and helicopter sightseeing flights.

AUTUMN
Autumn colours put on a show in woodlands all over Wicklow, notably at Mount Usher Gardens, Kilmacurragh Botanic Gardens and Powerscourt.

WINTER
Go Christmas shopping at Avoca Handweavers (and their Kilmacanogue shop), Powerscourt Gardens still look good, especially when the snowdrops bloom in February.

WICKLOW MOUNTAINS

○ DUBLIN
Wicklow Mountains

As you leave Dublin and cross into County Wicklow, the landscape changes dramatically. From Rathfarnham, the Military Rd begins a 40km southward journey along the spine of the Wicklow Mountains, crossing vast sweeps of heather-clad moors, bogs and hills dotted with small mountain lakes.

The road was built in the early 1800s to help the British military control rebels hiding in the mountains, and the deep glens still have a feeling of remoteness. No doubt it was this atmosphere of seclusion that drew a community of medieval monks to build the remarkable monastic settlement of Glendalough in the heart of the mountains, a place that now draws more visitors than anywhere else in the county.

But the mountains still have their secluded corners, and for those seeking adventure, there are ample opportunities for outdoor activities. The Wicklow Way, a long-distance walking trail, offers the chance to immerse yourself in the region's natural splendour.

TOP TIP

The Wicklow Mountains National Park Information Centre is near the Upper Lake car park in Glendalough. The centre provides info on wildlife and a free map titled *The Walking Trails of Glendalough*. Don't confuse it with the Glendalough Visitor Centre beside the lower car park, which deals only with the monastic site.

Lough Tay

HIGHLIGHTS
1. Glendalough
2. Powerscourt Estate

SIGHTS
3. Powerscourt Waterfall

ACTIVITIES
4. Great Sugarloaf Mountain
5. Lugnaquilla Mountain
see 2. Powerscourt Golf Club

SLEEPING
see 1. Glendalough International Hostel
6. Glenmalure Hostel
7. Heather House
see 2. Powerscourt Hotel

EATING
8. Byrne & Woods
9. Roundwood Stores

DRINKING & NIGHTLIFE
10. Bear Paw Deli
11. Glendalough Green
12. Glenmalure Lodge
13. Johnnie Fox's

SHOPPING
14. Annamoe Antiques
15. Avoca Kilmacanogue

INFORMATION
see 1. Glendalough Visitor Centre
16. Wicklow Mountains National Park Information Centre

Hike the Wicklow Mountains
Walking Trails Galore

The Wicklow Mountains rear up right on the edge of Dublin's suburban sprawl. From Rathfarnham, still within the city limits, the Military Rd (R115) provides easy access to the high moors, rounded granite hills and pretty mountain lakes that dominate the scenery. Look out for parking places that mark the starting points for many fine walks.

The wild topography is marvellously desolate and raw. Between the mountains are a number of deep glacial valleys – most notably Glenmacnass, Glenmalure and Glendalough – and corrie lakes such as Lough Bray Upper and Lower, and Lough Tay, gouged by ice at the head of the glaciers.

Continues on p124

PRACTICALITIES

Scan this QR code for prices and opening hours:

TOP SIGHT
Glendalough

Nestled in a narrow valley in the Wicklow Mountains, haunting Glendalough is one of the most significant early Christian sites in Ireland and one of the loveliest spots in the country. Despite its popularity, it remains a deeply spiritual place, and you will have little difficulty in understanding why those solitude-seeking monks came here more than 1000 years ago.

DON'T MISS

The Upper Lake

Round Tower

St Kevin's Kitchen

Reefert Church

St Kevin's Cell

Cathedral of St Peter and St Paul

Monastery Gatehouse

The Monastic Site

Glendalough was founded in the late 5th century by St Kevin, a bishop who established a monastery on the Upper Lake's southern shore and about whom there is much folklore. During the Middle Ages, when Ireland was known as 'the island of saints and scholars', Glendalough became a monastic city catering to thousands of students and teachers. The site is entered through the only surviving **monastery gatehouse** in Ireland.

Round Tower

The imposing 10th-century Round Tower is the focus of this early Christian settlement, standing 33m tall and 16m in circumference at the base. The upper storeys and conical roof were reconstructed in 1876.

Cathedral of St Peter & St Paul

The Cathedral of St Peter and St Paul, just southeast of the Round Tower, has a 10th-century nave. The chancel and sacristy date from the 12th century. At the centre of the graveyard, to the southwest of the cathedral, is the **Priest's House**. This odd building dates from 1170 but has been heavily reconstructed. It may have been the location of shrines to St Kevin. Later, during penal times, it became a burial site for local priests – hence the name.

St Kevin's Kitchen

Glendalough's trademark is St Kevin's Kitchen or Church, at the southern edge of the monastic site. This compact structure, with a miniature round-tower-like belfry, protruding sacristy and steep stone roof, is a medieval masterpiece. It was never a kitchen; it got its nickname because the belfry resembles a kitchen chimney. The oldest parts of the building date from the 11th century; the structure has been remodelled since, but it's still a classic early Irish church.

The Upper Lake

While the most fascinating ancient structures lie in the lower part of the valley east of the Lower Lake, the Upper Lake has the best scenery.

Reefert Church

The considerable remains of Reefert Church sit above the tiny River Poulanass, south of the Upper Lake car park. This small and plain 11th-century Romanesque church has some reassembled arches and walls. Traditionally, Reefert (meaning 'Royal Burial Place') was the burial site of the chiefs of the local O'Toole family.

Climb the steps at the back of the churchyard, follow the path to the west and at the top of a rise overlooking the Upper Lake, you'll find the scant remains of **St Kevin's Cell**, a small beehive hut.

Teampall na Skellig & St Kevin's Bed

The original site of St Kevin's settlement, **Teampall na Skellig**, is at the base of the cliffs towering over the southern side of the Upper Lake. The terraced shelf has the reconstructed ruins of a church and early graveyard. Rough wattle huts once stood on the raised ground nearby.

Just east of Teampall na Skellig is the 2m-deep artificial cave called **St Kevin's Bed**, said to be where Kevin lived. The earliest human habitation of the cave was long before St Kevin's era – there's evidence that people lived in the valley for thousands of years before any monks arrived.

There's no boat service to these sites, so you'll have to settle for gazing at them from the signposted viewpoint on the trail along the lake's north shore.

THE SPINK

One of the most popular waymarked hikes at Glendalough is the Spink, the steep ridge running along the southern flank of the Upper Lake. You can go part of the way and turn back, or complete a circuit of the Upper Lake by following the path down to the old mine workings and returning along the north shore (6km, allow three hours).

TOP TIPS

- The monastic site is free to enter, but you have to pay €4 for the car parks.
- The visitor centre car park is more convenient for the monastic site; the Upper Lake car park for picnics, the lake beach and walkers.
- At weekends and daily in July and August, the car parks can be full by 11am, so arrive early.
- Despite signs on the approach saying 'cash only', you can pay the Upper Lake car park fee by card.
- There is a large free car park by the Woollen Mills south of Laragh village, a 30-minute walk from the monastic site.

TOP SIGHT
Glendalough

A Walking Tour

A visit to Glendalough is a trip through ancient history and a refreshing hike in the hills. The ancient monastic settlement founded by St Kevin in the 5th century grew to be quite powerful by the 9th century, but it started falling into ruin from 1398 onwards. Still, you won't find more evocative clumps of stones anywhere.

Start at the **1 Main Gateway** to the monastic city, where you will find a cluster of important ruins, including the (nearly perfect) 10th-century **2 Round Tower**, the **3 cathedral** dedicated to Sts Peter and Paul, and **4 St Kevin's Kitchen**, which is really a church. Cross the stream past the famous **5 Deer Stone**, where Kevin was supposed to have milked a doe, and turn west along the path. It's a 1.5km walk to the **6 Upper Lake**. On the lake's southern shore is another cluster of sites, including the **7 Reefert Church**, a plain 11th-century Romanesque church where the powerful O'Toole family buried their kin, and **8 St Kevin's Cell**, the remains of a beehive hut where Kevin is said to have lived.

ST KEVIN

St Kevin came to the valley as a young monk in 498 CE, in search of a peaceful retreat. He was reportedly led by an angel to a Bronze Age tomb now known as St Kevin's Bed. For seven years he slept on stones, wore animal skins, survived on nettles and herbs and – according to legend – developed an affinity with the birds and animals. One legend has it that, when Kevin needed milk for two orphaned babies, a doe stood waiting at the Deer Stone to be milked.

Kevin soon attracted a group of disciples and the monastic settlement grew, until by the 9th century Glendalough rivalled Clonmacnoise as Ireland's premier monastic city. According to legend, Kevin lived to the age of 120. He was canonised in 1903.

❷ Round Tower
Glendalough's most famous landmark is the 33m-high Round Tower, which is exactly as it was when it was built a thousand years ago except for the roof; this was replaced in 1876 after a lightning strike.

❺ Deer Stone
The spot where St Kevin is said to have truly become one with the animals is really just a large mortar called a *bullaun*, used for grinding food and medicine.

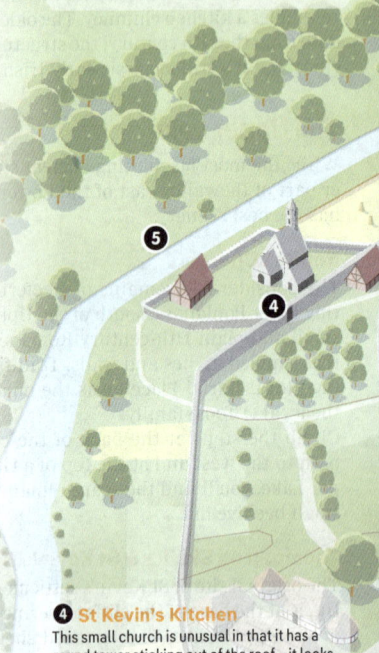

❹ St Kevin's Kitchen
This small church is unusual in that it has a round tower sticking out of the roof – it looks like a chimney, hence the church's nickname.

❼ Reefert Church
Its name derives from the Irish *righ fearta*, which means 'burial place of the kings'. Seven princes of the powerful O'Toole family are buried in this simple structure.

❻ Upper Lake
The site of St Kevin's original settlement is on the banks of the Upper Lake, one of the two lakes that give Glendalough its name – the 'Valley of the Two Lakes'.

❽ St Kevin's Cell
This beehive hut is reputedly where St Kevin would go for prayer and meditation; not to be confused with St Kevin's Bed, a cave where he used to sleep.

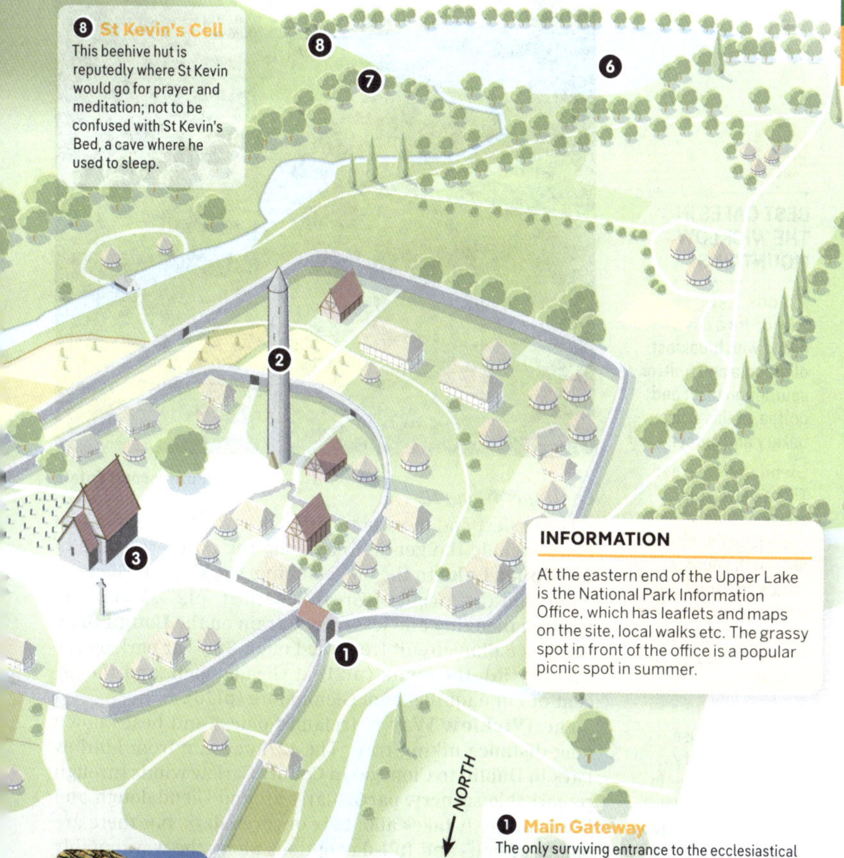

WICKLOW & KILDARE WICKLOW MOUNTAINS

THE GUIDE

INFORMATION
At the eastern end of the Upper Lake is the National Park Information Office, which has leaflets and maps on the site, local walks etc. The grassy spot in front of the office is a popular picnic spot in summer.

❶ Main Gateway
The only surviving entrance to the ecclesiastical settlement is a double arch; notice that the inner arch rises higher than the outer one in order to compensate for the upward slope of the causeway.

❸ Cathedral of St Peter & St Paul
The largest of Glendalough's seven churches, the cathedral was built gradually between the 10th and 13th centuries. The earliest part is the nave, where you can still see the *antae* (slightly projecting column at the end of the wall) used for supporting a wooden roof. slope of the causeway.

123

Powerscourt Estate

BEST CAFES IN THE WICKLOW MOUNTAINS

Roundwood Stores
Fuel up for a day's hiking with breakfast of granola and fruit, or sourdough toast and coffee, at this artisan bakery and grocer. €€

Glendalough Green
There's always a crowd of thirsty cyclists gathered around the outdoor tables on Laragh village green, guzzling great coffee and cake from this popular cafe. €

Bear Paw Deli
This no-nonsense cafe in Enniskerry village specialises in hearty US-style deli sandwiches. Big Kev's Reuben (pastrami, sauerkraut, cheese and Russian dressing) is a winner. €

Continues from p119

The easiest and most popular walks, which take about an hour, include the gentle hike along the northern shore of the **Upper Lake** to the old lead mine workings at Glendalough, and the ascent of Great Sugarloaf (p127). You'll find more challenging and less busy terrain on the **Lough Bray Loop**, a 6.6km circuit from the Lough Bray car park on the Military Rd, the Spink (p121) at Glendalough, and the ascent of Lugnaquilla from Glenmalure (p126).

The **Wicklow Way** is Ireland's oldest and best-known long-distance hiking trail. The 127km route from Marlow Park in Dublin to Clonegal in County Carlow winds through remarkable scenery, particularly around Glendalough and Glenmalure. It takes about six or seven days, but there are plenty of half- and full-day options along the way, notably the easy 11km from Roundwood to Glendalough.

WHERE TO EAT IN THE WICKLOW MOUNTAINS

Byrne & Woods
Elegant restaurant in an old cottage in Roundwood serving locally sourced dishes and well-chosen wines. €€

Johnnie Fox's
Northwest of Enniskerry, this traditional 19th-century pub has a standout seafood menu. €€

Glenmalure Lodge
Hearty all-day pub food includes steak and Guinness pie, lamb stew and a ploughman's lunch. €€

Explore an Aristocratic Estate

Gorgeous Gardens And Stunning Views

Just 500m south of the village of Enniskerry, the magnificent **Powerscourt Estate** lies within easy day-tripping distance of Dublin. At its heart is an elegant Georgian mansion, but the real draw is wandering around the gorgeous grounds and gardens and soaking up the stunning views towards Great Sugarloaf mountain.

The estate has existed more or less since 1300, when the LePoer (later anglicised to Power) family built themselves a castle here. The property came into the possession of Richard Wingfield, Marshall of Ireland, in 1603, and his descendants lived here for the next 350 years. In 1730, the Georgian wunderkind Richard Cassels was given the job of building a 68-room Palladian-style mansion around the core of the old castle.

The Wingfields left in the 1950s, after which the house underwent a massive restoration. On the eve of its opening to the public in 1974, a fire gutted the whole building. The estate was eventually bought by the Slazenger sporting-goods family, who have overseen a second restoration as well as the addition of all the amenities the estate now has to offer, including the two golf courses and the fabulous Powerscourt Hotel, part of Marriott's Autograph Collection.

The 20-hectare landscaped **gardens** are the star attraction, originally laid out in the 1740s but redesigned in the 19th century by Daniel Robinson, one of the foremost horticulturalists of his day. His masterpiece is a magnificent blend of sweeping terraces, elegant statuary, ornamental lakes, secret hollows, rambling walks and walled enclosures replete with more than 200 types of trees and shrubs, all designed to frame the ever-present backdrop of the Great Sugarloaf mountain.

Tickets come with a map laying out 40-minute and hour-long walks around the gardens. Don't miss the exquisite **Japanese Gardens** or the **Pepperpot Tower**, modelled on a 7.5cm-tall pepperpot owned by Lady Wingfield. The **animal cemetery** is the final resting place of the Wingfields' pets and even one of the family's favourite milking cows. Some of the epitaphs are surprisingly personal.

Powerscourt House itself is every bit as grand as the gardens. Though most of it is not open to the public, there's a fine cafe, a small exhibition, and several gift and homewares shops to browse.

WHY I LOVE THE WICKLOW MOUNTAINS

Neil Wilson, writer

For all my adult life, I have been an enthusiastic rock climber, hill walker and mountain biker, and here in the Wicklow Mountains, barely an hour's drive from central Dublin, I can indulge in all three. The massive granite blocks that litter the valley floor beyond Glendalough's Upper Lake provide some of the finest bouldering in Ireland, while the forest trails at Ballinastoe present challenging singletrack for the mountain biker. Though Lugnaquilla may not be the most exciting hill in Ireland, its ascent does make for a grand day out.

WHERE TO SHOP IN THE WICKLOW MOUNTAINS

Avoca Kilmacanogue
A hugely popular shop crammed with knitwear, textiles, ceramics, toys, homewares, gourmet foodstuffs and cookbooks.

Powerscourt House
Several shops sell Irish crafts, jewellery, giftware, clothing, furniture, books, and artisan food and drink.

Annamoe Antiques
A proper old-school antiques shop about halfway between Roundwood and Glendalough.

A 6km drive to a separate part of the estate takes you to the 121m-high **Powerscourt Waterfall**, the highest waterfall in Ireland, and at its most impressive after heavy rain. A nature trail has been laid out around the base of the waterfall – a popular picnic spot – taking you past giant redwoods, ancient oaks, beech, birch and rowan trees. There are plenty of birds in the vicinity, including the chaffinch, cuckoo, chiffchaff, raven and willow warbler. Walking from house to falls is not recommended as the route lies on narrow roads with no footpath.

Drive the Military Road
Scenic Mountain Route

The so-called Military Rd was first built in the early 1800s by the British army to help suppress Irish rebels in the wake of the 1798 Rising. This narrow, twisting road (now the R115) winds its way from the outskirts of Dublin through the most remote parts of the Wicklow Mountains, offering extraordinary views of the surrounding countryside.

If you're coming from Enniskerry, join the road at Glencree and follow it south through the Sally Gap and the Glenmacnass Valley to Laragh. On the way, you can divert east at the Sally Gap to a fantastic viewpoint overlooking **Lough Tay**. Further south, you pass the spectacular **Glenmacnass Waterfall** before dropping down into Laragh, with the magnificent monastic ruins of Glendalough (p120) nearby.

Tee Off at Powerscourt Golf Club
Championship Courses

Golfers have a choice of two stunning par-72 courses overlooked by the shapely peak of the Great Sugarloaf mountain. The **West Course**, with streams and ravines, was designed by David McLay Kidd (who also designed Bandon Dunes in Oregon, USA) and is a shade tougher than the **East Course**, designed by Peter McEvoy, which is arguably the more scenic, with hedges, ancient oaks and beech trees. You can rent clubs, hire a caddy or get lessons from a pro.

Glenmacnass Waterfall

GLENMALURE

Driving southwest over the mountains from Laragh to scenic Glenmalure, turn right at Drumgoff Bridge and continue 6km up a narrow dead-end road to a car park where trails head off in various directions.

A 500m walk beyond the car park leads to atmospheric **Glenmalure Hostel** – no phone, no electricity (lighting is by gas) and no running water, just a rustic two-storey cottage with 19 beds, a gas stove, water from the stream, and an open log fire.

You can walk up the hidden **Fraughan Rock Glen** west of the car park, and – for experienced hill walkers only – continue to the summit of **Lugnaquilla** (925m), the highest summit in the Wicklow Mountains. Allow six hours for the return trip.

WHERE TO STAY IN THE WICKLOW MOUNTAINS

Powerscourt Hotel
On the grounds of Powerscourt Estate, Wicklow's most luxurious hotel has massive rooms and a gourmet restaurant. €€€

Heather House
Understated country-house elegance radiates from the luxurious bedrooms at this superb-value B&B. €€

Glendalough International Hostel
Modern hostel conveniently situated near Glendalough monastic site; all dorms are en suite. €

Miners' Way

Walk the Miners' Way
Exploring Industrial Heritage

The granite rocks on the eastern edge of the Wicklow Mountains are laced with mineralised quartz veins that were once rich in galena and sphalerite. These ores of lead and zinc were mined extensively between 1726 and 1925, leaving the valleys of Glendasan, Glendalough and Glenmalure with a legacy of old mine workings, spoil heaps, rusting machinery and ruined buildings.

Opened in 2019, the **Miners' Way** is a 19km walking trail that links the main industrial heritage sites in the three glens. Pick up a map and guide at the **Glendalough Information Centre**.

GREAT SUGARLOAF MOUNTAIN

At 503m, it's nowhere near Wicklow's highest summit, but the Great Sugarloaf is one of the most distinctive hills in Ireland, its conical peak visible for many kilometres around. The mountain towers over the small village of Kilmacanogue, on the N11 about 35km south of Dublin, and can be climbed from a walkers' car park on the L1031 minor road (off the R755 road, 7.5km south of Enniskerry). It's a steep but straightforward hike – allow one hour round trip.

GETTING AROUND

Public transport in the Wicklow Mountains is thin on the ground, apart from St Kevins Bus (glendaloughbus.com), which runs from St Stephen's Green North in Dublin twice daily year-round (1½-hour journey, departing at 11am and 6pm) via Bray, Kilmacanogue, Roundwood and Laragh. Day-trip timings give you five hours at Glendalough, which is enough time to explore the monastic site, have lunch and enjoy a hike to the Upper Lake.

THE GUIDE

BEYOND THE WICKLOW MOUNTAINS WICKLOW & KILDARE

- Russborough House
- Bray Head Cliff Walk
- Killruddery House
- Wicklow Mountains
- Mount Usher Gardens
- Avondale Forest Park
- Kilmacurragh Botanic Gardens
- Avondale House

Beyond the Wicklow Mountains

Away from the mountains, Wicklow offers lush landscaped gardens, aristocratic mansions, artisan food shops, woodland walks and coastal scenery.

The coastal towns and rolling valleys of eastern Wicklow play second fiddle to the mountains in terms of dramatic scenery, but they are still popular weekend destinations for Dubliners – visit midweek to avoid the crowds. Highlights include the seaside town of Bray, the gardens at Killruddery House, the treetop walkway at Avondale Forest Park and the beautiful Vale of Avoca.

West of the Wicklow Mountains, the landscape is more rural than rugged, especially towards the borders of Kildare and Carlow. The wild moorland terrain gives way to rich pastures, woodland and lakes. The main attraction in this part of Wicklow is the magnificent Palladian pile at Russborough House, just outside Blessington.

TOP TIP

Wicklow has a load of food festivals, including Taste of Wicklow (p133), Wicklow Naturally's October Feast and Wicklow Christmas Market.

Beyond The Trees, Avondale Forest Park

DAVI COSTA/SHUTTERSTOCK ©

Bray

Tiptoe Through the Treetops
Forest Walkway And Lookout Tower

Avondale Forest Park, 2km south of Rathdrum on the road to Avoca, is the birthplace of Irish forestry. The country's first forestry school was established here in 1904, but the estate's pedigree goes back even further. Its original owner, Samuel Hayes, planted a forest that now has more than 100 species of trees, and wrote Ireland's first treatise on woodland management in 1794.

It's fitting that one of Ireland's most impressive new attractions, **Beyond The Trees**, is rooted here in Avondale. Opened in 2023, this 1.4km-long treetop walkway perched on slender timber pylons takes you high above the forest floor, where you can peer into a canopy of skyscraping redwoods, feathery eucalyptus and moss-draped boughs of mature oak, beech and larch.

AVONDALE HOUSE & CHARLES STEWART PARNELL

The fine Palladian **mansion** at the heart of Avondale estate was designed by James Wyatt in 1779 and was the birthplace and Irish headquarters of Charles Stewart Parnell (1846–91), the 'uncrowned king of Ireland' and one of the key figures in the Irish independence movement.

Guided tours of the house last around 90 minutes and include the elegant dining room, a stunning vermilion-hued library and a wealth of information on Irish history. Guides explain Parnell's part in the fight for Irish Home Rule and his sisters Fanny and Anna's founding of the Ladies Land League to raise money in the United States for poor tenant farmers in Ireland.

WHERE TO STAY BEYOND THE WICKLOW MOUNTAINS

Brook Lodge & Wells Spa
This luxurious country-house hotel 12km southwest of Rathdrum has two swimming pools and a sumptuous spa. €€€

Tinakilly Country House
Magnificent Victorian Italianate house 4km northwest of Wicklow town offers the most elegant B&B in the county. €€€

Strand Hotel
Period property once owned by Oscar Wilde. Reach 1st-floor rooms via a sweeping timber staircase. €€

AVOCA HANDWEAVERS

Although today it's a multimillion-euro business with branches all over Ireland, **Avoca Handweavers** began life in 1723 as a cooperative weaving mill in the picture-postcard village that gave it its name. You can wander around the whitewashed cottage-style mill buildings and take a tour of the weaving sheds. There are audio guides for hire (also available in German, French, Spanish and Italian), or you can just chat with the weavers as they work their traditional handlooms.

The colourful woollen and other fabrics produced here are made into throws, rugs, scarves, blankets, bags, cushion covers and more, which are sold in the neighbouring shop (and in Avoca branches and other shops around the country).

Mount Usher Gardens

The walkway, which includes educational displays and adventure-playground-style challenges for the kids, culminates in a viewing tower of engineered timber that spirals a giddy 38m above the ground, with breathtaking views over green fields and woods to the humpback forms of Lugnaquilla and the Wicklow Mountains 20km to the northwest.

It takes at least 10 minutes to walk up the tower, but you can get down in 10 seconds via a 90m-long spiral slide – don't forget to collect a mat on the way up. Both the walkway and the tower are wheelchair accessible. You'll need at least 90 minutes to explore the walkway, and the same again if you want to include a tour of Avondale House.

The Garden of Ireland
Green-Fingered Grandeur

County Wicklow is known as the 'Garden of Ireland' because its 'Goldilocks climate' – not too warm, not too cold, not too wet, not too dry, but 'just right' – means that it has an unusually high concentration of horticultural highlights.

Chief among these is **Kilmacurragh Botanic Gardens**, 7km east of Rathdrum, an outpost of the state-owned National

---

WHERE TO STAY BEYOND THE WICKLOW MOUNTAINS

Hidden Valley Holiday Park
The River Avonmore flows through this peaceful camping ground, with riverside pitches and safe swimming. €

Woodenbridge Hotel
Dating from 1608, this hotel 13km south of Rathdrum has hosted Sir Walter Scott among other notables. €€

Wicklow Head Lighthouse
This 1781 lighthouse has octagonal rooms with views of the Wicklow Mountains and the Irish Sea. €€€

Botanic Gardens. Surrounding the ruins of an 18th-century mansion, Kilmacurragh was originally laid out in 1712 and replanted in the 19th century to reflect the wilder, informal style of famous Irish gardener William Robinson (1838–1935). More recent projects include areas dedicated to Irish native woodlands, hedgerows and wildflower meadows, and a Chilean garden packed with South American species, but the biggest draw remains the colourful display of rhododendrons and azaleas (best in late May and June).

William Robinson's style is repeated in spades at the privately owned **Mount Usher Gardens**, 10km south of Greystones, where plantings are artfully laid out along the banks of the River Vartry. Pick up the *Tree Trail* map and guide, and head for the Palm Walk (lined with crocuses in early spring), the Azalea Walk (multicoloured blooms in late May and June) and the Maple Walk (ablaze with colour in autumn). There's the excellent **Avoca Garden Cafe** on the premises, as well as a shopping courtyard where you can buy freshly baked goods, ice cream, plants, furniture, clothing and art, including photography.

Killruddery House and Gardens, 2km south of Bray, has been home to the Brabazon family (the earls of Meath) since 1618, and has one of the oldest gardens in Ireland. The 320-hectare estate now encompasses a sustainable farm that promotes biodiversity in addition to the 17th-century gardens. As well as wandering amid ornamental beech hedges and walkways lined with yew trees and magnolia, you can explore the walled kitchen garden where chickens roam free beneath the apple trees, vegetables grow in neat ranks, and decorative flowers bloom in the glasshouse. You can sample the produce of the farm and garden at the **Grain Store** restaurant, and buy house-made chutney, jam, bread and cakes in the farm shop.

Hike the Bray Head Cliff Walk

Invigorating Coastal Trail

From the southern end of the seafront in Bray, a scenic **footpath** runs for 7km south along the steep, rocky coastline to Greystones. The track was first built in the 1840s as a supply road during the construction of the railway line, which runs below for most of the route. The path is mostly good, but it is a bit rough and narrow in places (not suitable for buggies or young children).

It's better to start from the Greystones end, as your walk climbs gradually towards the scenic (and literal) highpoint at Bray Head, where the coast is at its most rugged and the views are superlative. En route, look out for harbour porpoises,

BEST PUB FOOD BEYOND THE WICKLOW MOUNTAINS

Mickey Finn's
Many dishes at this cosy, low-ceilinged pub 14km southwest of Wicklow town incorporate beers brewed at the adjacent Wicklow Brewery. There's trad music on Wednesdays year-round. €€

Ballymore Inn
Gastropub using produce from local farms, its own polytunnels and gardens, plus seafood delivered daily from Duncannon. Located 5km west of Russborough House, just over the border in County Kildare. €€

Harbour Bar
Four former fisher's terraces in Bray make up this maze of rooms with vintage maritime bric-a-brac. The beer garden gets rammed on sunny days, and the fish and chips is outstanding. €€

WHERE TO EAT BEYOND THE WICKLOW MOUNTAINS

Strawberry Tree
Elegant organic restaurant at Brook Lodge, 12km southwest of Rathdrum. Dinner only; closed Monday and Tuesday. €€€

Dockyard No 8
This cafe in Bray is a fantastic spot for breakfast or lunch; sit outside in good weather. €€

Firehouse Bakery
Pastries are piled high on the counters at this artisan bakery-cafe-deli 3km southwest of Greystones. €

dolphins and basking sharks offshore, and seabirds, sparrowhawks and kestrels along the cliffs. You might even spot Ireland's only reptile, the viviparous lizard.

You can return to your starting point by rail in just 10 minutes. Trains run between Bray and Greystones two or three times per hour.

Tour a Palladian Palace
Country House And Gardens

Magnificent **Russborough House**, 5km southwest of Blessington, is one of Ireland's finest stately homes, a Palladian palace built for Joseph Leeson (1705–83), the first earl of Milltown and, later, Lord Russborough. The house was built between 1741 and 1751 to the design of Richard Cassels, who was at the height of his fame as an architect.

The house remained in the hands of Leeson's descendants until 1931, and in 1952, it was purchased by Sir Alfred Beit, whose uncle was a founder of the De Beers diamond-mining company. Sir Alfred and his wife Lady Clementine, a cousin of the notorious Mitford sisters, stocked the mansion with a remarkable art collection, including masterpieces by Velázquez, Vermeer, Goya, Rubens, Gainsborough and others. This famous art collection was soon to be the focus of a series of crimes.

In 1974, the IRA stole 19 of the paintings, all of which were later recovered. At the time, it was considered the biggest art theft in history, worth around £8 million. In 1986, Russborough was hit again – this time Dublin gangster Martin Cahill masterminded the heist. Although most of that haul was also recovered, some pieces were damaged beyond repair. In 1987, Beit donated 17 of the most valuable works to the National Gallery, but that didn't stop two more break-ins, in 2001 and 2002. One of the stolen paintings was a Gainsborough that had already been taken – and recovered – twice before.

Thankfully all of the paintings were recovered after both attempts, but where a succession of thieves couldn't succeed, the cost of upkeep did: in 2015, the trust that now owns Russborough had to sell some of its most valuable paintings to keep the house in good repair and open to the public.

On a guided tour of the house, which is decorated with strikingly ornate stucco plasterwork, you'll see all the remaining important paintings, which, given the history, is a monumental exercise in staying positive. There are superb views of the Wicklow Mountains from the front of the house, and 80 hectares of parklands encompass an 18th-century walled garden, a hedge maze, walking trails and the **National Birds**

WICKLOW BREWERY

Wicklow Brewery, 7km southeast of Rathdrum, offers engaging hour-long tours that guide you through the brewing process from milling local grains to mashing, fermenting, maturing and kegging. The beers are preservative-free and use the brewery's own well water. St Kevins Red Ale and the spicy GingerKnut IPA are standouts. The twice-daily tours include five tastings, often featuring experimental brews. On weekends, you can stop by the brewery's beer hall for a pint; live-music concerts regularly take place amid the kettles and tanks.

WHERE TO EAT BEYOND THE WICKLOW MOUNTAINS

Bates Restaurant
Housed in a 1785 coaching inn, this restaurant is hidden down an alley beside a pub. €€

Hollywood Cafe
A former post office, once home to the Irish emigrant who gave his village's name to Hollywood, USA. €

Happy Pear
Half of Greystones seems to meet at this popular cafe, deli and organic grocery. €

Russborough House

of Prey Centre where you can get up close and personal with eagles, owls and falcons.

Savour the Flavours of Wicklow
Markets, Festivals And Foraging

The lush farmland that lies east and west of the Wicklow Mountains is a source of quality produce for local restaurants and a source of pride for the locals, celebrated most weekends in **farmers markets** all over the county (see loveyourlocalmarket.ie/Wicklow.html) and annually during the **Taste of Wicklow Food Festival**, which takes place in Wicklow town on the last weekend in June. As well as celebrity chef workshops, live music, street food and kids events, the festival offers the opportunity to sample a wide range of artisan food.

If you can't make the festival, you can opt for a foraging walk with Geraldine Kavanagh of **Wicklow Wild Foods**. She will take you on a three-hour exploration of the woods at Avondale Forest Park near Rathdrum, introducing you to the wealth of edible plants that flourish here, from dandelion and nettles to gorse flowers, meadowsweet, pennywort, wood sorrel, fir tips and wild garlic, finishing up with a picnic of foraged foods. Walks run most weekends from March to October and should be booked in advance via the website (wicklowwildfoods.com).

BEST BEACH IN COUNTY WICKLOW

South of Wicklow town, a string of beaches with high dunes, safe bathing and powdery sand attracts droves of Dubliners in good weather. The cream of the crop is **Brittas Bay** 10km south of Wicklow town, the only Blue Flag beach in Wicklow, and one of the best in Ireland – 5km of clean white sand and sheltered water, with lifeguards in summer.

Two large car parks are open from May to September. Choose the north car park and walk north for the quietest part of the beach.

GETTING AROUND

Away from the coast, public transport is sparse, so it's better to have your own wheels. The M11/N11 runs south from Dublin through the heart of eastern Wicklow, providing easy car and bus access from the capital. A railway line links Dublin to Bray, Greystones, Wicklow town, Rathdrum and Arklow, continuing to Enniscorthy, Wexford and Rosslare.

To the west of the Wicklow Mountains, the N81 runs from Dublin to Blessington and on to Tullow in County Carlow, with two minor roads linking east across the mountains via the passes of Sally Gap and Wicklow Gap.

KILDARE & THE CURRAGH

Some of Ireland's best grazing land has made County Kildare (Cill Dara) prime agricultural real estate, especially for the horse-racing set. The county is dotted with stud farms where champion racehorses are reared and trained. In recent decades, it has had to contend with Dublin's ever-expanding commuter belt, which has swallowed up many of its towns and villages. The county isn't exactly packed with must-see attractions, but it has enough diversions – the Irish National Stud and the Museum of Style Icons, for example – to justify a day trip from the capital or a stop on your way out west.

Stretching from Kildare town to Newbridge, the Curragh is one of the country's largest tracts of unfenced grassland and the centre of the Irish horse-racing industry. If you get up early or pass by in the late evening, you'll see thoroughbreds exercising on the gallops and wide-open training grounds surrounding the world-famous Curragh Racecourse.

TOP TIP

On all race days, free shuttle buses run to the Curragh from Kildare and Newbridge railway stations. On the five Irish Classics race weekends – the 1000 Guineas, 2000 Guineas, Derby, Oaks and St Leger – Expressway operates a bus from Dublin Busàras direct to the racecourse.

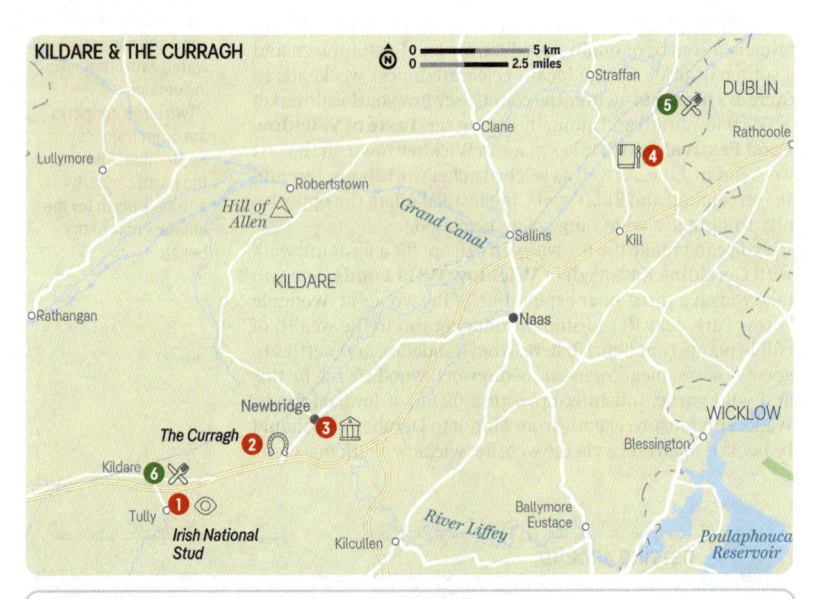

HIGHLIGHTS
1. Irish National Stud
2. The Curragh

SIGHTS
3. Museum of Style Icons
4. Oughterard Church & Round Tower

EATING
5. Cliff at Lyons
see 6. Firecastle Artisan Grocer & Café
6. Hartes of Kildare

DRINKING & NIGHTLIFE
see 3. Emporium

Irish National Stud (p136)

Enjoy a Day at the Races
Home Of Irish Horse Racing

The Curragh, 3km southwest of central Newbridge, is among the oldest, most famous and most prestigious racecourses in the world. It hosted its first recorded race in 1727 and was inaugurated as an official racing facility in 1868, but it had been a favoured place with the Irish nobility for hawking, hunting and horse racing since at least 1682, and chariot races took place here as long ago as the 3rd century CE. Its name comes from the Gaelic *cuirreach,* meaning 'the place of the running horse'.

Each year sees more than 20 race days, including the five Irish Classics from the Irish 2000 Guineas in May to the Irish St Leger in September. But race days are not just about the ponies. These are grand social occasions with people dressed to the nines cramming the terraces, restaurants and champagne bars, and sometimes with live music performances after the racing. Even if you're not the horsey type, it's worth experiencing the passion and atmosphere of the place.

The racecourse was redeveloped in 2019 and now sports a magnificent modern grandstand with a vast, floating, copper-coloured roof that reflects the horizontality of the surrounding grasslands. If you can't make a race day, guided

THE GUINNESS VAULT

The 10m-tall stump of an 8th-century round tower marks the ancient Christian site of **Oughterard Church and Round Tower**, 20km northeast of Newbridge. Its name in Irish means 'high place', and there are sweeping views across the green Kildare countryside. The cemetery here is best known for its most famous resident – a vault amid the ruins of the 14th-century church is the resting place of **Arthur Guinness** (1724–1803), the brewer who created the world-famous black beer.

You can take a train from Dublin to Hazelhatch station and walk to Oughterard via the **Arthur Guinness Heritage Trail** (7km each way), stopping for lunch at the **Cliff at Lyons** on the Grand Canal.

WHERE TO EAT IN KILDARE & NEWBRIDGE

Hartes of Kildare
Wood-panelled hotspot Hartes has plush green banquettes, gleaming timber furniture and a brilliant gastropub fare. €€

Firecastle Artisan Grocer & Café
Mouth-watering Kildare town deli serving inventive salads, vegan dishes and black pudding sausage rolls. €

Domo's Emporium
Excellent coffee and a tempting breakfast menu at this popular cafe in the Newbridge Silverware showroom. €€

behind-the-scenes tours of the racecourse take place on Wednesdays and Thursdays from April to October, during which you get to see the jockeys' changing rooms, the saddling areas and other places that are normally off-limits to the public.

It is worth noting that horse racing is a contentious issue, with animal welfare advocates highlighting the deaths of horses involved in the practice.

Admire the Art of Breeding Racehorses
Stallions, Fillies And Foals

The **Irish National Stud**, 1.5km south of Kildare town, is the big attraction in Kildare, and visitors have included the late Queen Elizabeth II. Owned and managed by the Irish government, the immaculately kept centre breeds high-quality stallions to mate with mares from all over the world. You can wander the paddocks and go eye-to-eye with famous stallions, or take a 45-minute guided tour (four daily; included in admission). Around 3pm in the spring, you'll see the foals being walked back to their stables.

The stud was founded in 1900 by Colonel Hall Walker (of Johnnie Walker whisky fame). He was remarkably successful with his horses, but his eccentric breeding technique relied heavily on astrology: the fate of a foal was decided by its horoscope, and the roofs of the stallion boxes opened on auspicious occasions to reveal the stars above and hopefully influence the horses' fortunes.

Guided tours take place every hour on the hour, with access to the intensive-care unit for newborn foals. If you visit between February and June, you might even see a foal being born. Alternatively, the foaling unit shows a 10-minute video with all the action. Given that most of those foals are now geldings, they probably have dim memories of their time in the Teasing Shed, the place where stallions are stimulated before 'covering' a mare. The fee for having a mare inseminated by the stud's top stallion can be as much as €120,000.

Other attractions on-site include lakeside walks, a 'fairy trail' for kids and the **Irish Horse Museum**, a celebration of championship horses and the history of horse racing. You can also visit Colonel Hall Walker's **Japanese Gardens** (part of the complex), considered to be the best of their kind in Europe. Created between 1906 and 1910, they trace the journey from birth to death through 20 landmarks, including the Tunnel of Ignorance, the Hill of Ambition and the Chair of Old Age.

MUSEUM OF STYLE ICONS

The otherwise unremarkable town of Newbridge, just off the M7, is home to one of Ireland's more unusual museums. Follow the signs upstairs from the Newbridge Silverware showroom on Athgarvan Rd to discover a hidden world of Hollywood glamour: the **Museum of Style Icons**.

Beneath a sparkle of glitter balls, you'll find a host of beautifully designed exhibits showcasing dresses, suits and stage costumes that were once worn by stars such as Audrey Hepburn, Marilyn Monroe, The Beatles, Elizabeth Taylor and Princess Diana, among many others. The accompanying photographs, letters and background information bring the exhibits to life. Look for the green suit worn by Tippi Hedren in Hitchcock's *The Birds*.

GETTING AROUND

County Kildare is within easy reach of Dublin via the M4 and M7 motorways, and there are fast and frequent train and bus services to Newbridge and Kildare town. However, you'll need a car to explore the attractions outside of the main towns.

You can walk from Kildare town train station to the Irish National Stud in 30 minutes, and from Newbridge station to Newbridge Silverware in 20 minutes, but you'll need to take a taxi or shuttle bus to the Curragh Racecourse.

Beyond Kildare & the Curragh

Rural County Kildare preserves contrasting legacies: of the Anglo-Irish aristocracy and large-scale industrial peat extraction.

County Kildare's lush green landscape and proximity to Dublin have always made it attractive to those with money wanting to be close to the capital. In the past, that meant estates and mansions belonging to the aristocracy, exemplified by the splendours of Castletown House; today it manifests as commuter belt communities, upmarket dormitory towns, luxury country hotels and golf resorts.

But the far west of the county is characterised by a very different landscape. The Bog of Allen, the largest area of raised bog in all of Ireland, spreads into the neighbouring counties of Offaly and Meath. Subject to large-scale peat extraction for 100 years, it provides a lesson in ecological destruction.

TOP TIP

County Kildare is within easy reach of Dublin via the M4 and M7 motorways, and frequent trains run to Maynooth, Newbridge and Kildare town.

Castletown House (p138)

Join the Gentry on a Georgian Estate
Elegant Country House

Magnificent **Castletown House** (open daily April to October), signposted from junction 6 on the M4 north of Celbridge, is Ireland's most imposing Palladian mansion, and a testament to the vast wealth enjoyed by the Anglo-Irish gentry during the 18th century. It was built between 1722 and 1732 for William Conolly (1662–1729), speaker of the Irish House of Commons and, at the time, Ireland's richest man. A highlight of the opulent interior is the **Long Gallery**, replete with family portraits and exquisite stucco work by the Francini brothers.

Entry is by guided tour only (hourly 10am to 4pm). Alternatively, you can explore the grounds for free. Stroll down to the river for grand views back to the house or ask at reception for directions to the **Wonderful Barn** (40 minutes walk each way), a picturesque conical tower with an exterior spiral staircase dating from 1743 (not open to the public).

Investigate an Irish Peat Bog
Nature Conservation In Action

Covering more than 950 sq km spread across six counties, the Bog of Allen is the largest raised peat bog in Ireland, but four centuries of exploitation have removed 90% of its 10,000-year-old peat reserves.

Run by the nonprofit Irish Peatland Conservation Council, the **Bog of Allen Nature Centre** (open Monday to Friday), at Lullymore in eastern County Kildare, celebrates the amazing biodiversity of Ireland's bogs and traces the history of peat extraction and the threat it poses to wildlife and the environment. The garden at the back has the largest carnivorous plant collection in Ireland, including sundews, butterworts and pitcher plants, and ponds filled with frogs and newts. A nearby boardwalk extends into **Lodge Bog**, one of the last surviving untouched fragments of the Bog of Allen.

EXPLORING THE GRAND CANAL

The Grand Canal runs for 132km from Dublin to the River Shannon, much of it through rural County Kildare. The towpath is ideal for leisurely walks and bike rides, and there are numerous access points. At **Sallins**, just north of Naas, you can rent bikes from Greenway Bike Hire, enjoy a canalside lunch at **Lock 13** gastropub or ride along the canal to the delightful **Cliff at Lyons**, a boutique country house hotel with a coffee shop, pub and Michelin-starred restaurant Aimsir.

The village of **Robertstown**, 15km northeast of Kildare town, is the hub of the Grand Canal, Kildare Way and Barrow towpath trails, the latter stretching all the way to St Mullins, 95km to the south in County Carlow.

GETTING AROUND

It's best to have a car for exploring beyond the Curragh and Kildare town. You'll certainly need one to reach the Bog of Allen.

Dublin Bus C4 runs every 30 minutes from Aston Quay in Dublin city centre to Celbridge Main St (a 45-minute journey), from where it's a 10-minute walk to Castletown House.

THE GUIDE

WICKLOW & KILDARE BEYOND KILDARE & THE CURRAGH

Wonderful Barn   139

WEXFORD, WATERFORD, CARLOW & KILKENNY

SWEEPING COASTLINE, WOODED VALLEYS AND VIBRANT STREETLIFE

Fringed by beaches and threaded by rivers, Ireland's southeast encompasses ancient castles, flower-filled gardens, charming villages and charismatic cities.

Protected from the wild Atlantic weather, these four counties – coastal Wexford and Waterford, and inland Carlow and Kilkenny – comprise Ireland's 'sunny southeast', as it's locally known. Blessed by what is typically the warmest and driest climate in the country, this is an outdoorsy paradise. Walking and cycling routes wind across the landscape, including trails in the region's flourishing gardens and gentle paths along the banks of its rivers. Getting out on the waterways with a kayak or SUP or aboard a cruise provides a different perspective as you see the scenery float past. Along the coast's secluded coves and broad beaches, activities range from surfing and kitesurfing to fishing trips from ports hauling in super-fresh seafood.

Rich seams of history run through this segment of Ireland's Ancient East. Mystical standing stones, imposing castles and religious relics including magnificent ruined abbeys are scattered across the region, along with churches and cathedrals. At the heart of each of these four counties, their eponymous county towns – Wexford town, Waterford city, Carlow town and Kilkenny city – also chronicle the past: the Vikings founded Wexford and Ireland's oldest city, Waterford. Carlow's ruined castle once guarded its river, and Kilkenny's medieval mile brings its Middle Ages heritage to life. Throughout the region, new stories continue to be written through tech innovations and creativity across food, music, design and art.

THE MAIN AREAS

WEXFORD TOWN
Atmospheric, cultural harbour town. **p146**

WATERFORD CITY
Age-old heritage; contemporary street art. **p155**

CARLOW TOWN
Artistic gateway to picturesque countryside. **p166**

KILKENNY CITY
Magnificent castle, cathedral and nightlife. **p171**

THE GUIDE

WEXFORD, WATERFORD, CARLOW & KILKENNY

Above: Duckett's Grove (p169); left: Puffin, Saltee Islands (p154)

Find Your Way

Covering just 7192 sq km, Ireland's southeasternmost corner is within two hours' drive of international airports north in Dublin and west in Cork. Ferries sail between Rosslare in County Wexford and Britain, France and Spain.

Kilkenny City, p171
Kilkenny's medieval castle, cathedral and tangle of pub-lined streets make the county's flagship city a magnet for visitors.

Waterford City, p155
Alongside its riverside quays, Ireland's oldest city is awash with Viking history, glassmaking heritage, gleaming museums and eye-popping street-art murals.

WEXFORD, WATERFORD, CARLOW & KILKENNY

Carlow Town, p166
The country's second-longest river, the beautiful River Barrow, flows through the history-rich, strategically important main town of Ireland's second-smallest county.

Wexford Town, p146
Wexford anchors its namesake county with its boat-filled waterfront and narrow streets lined with lively bars, restaurants, galleries and boutiques.

CAR
Driving is the ultimate way to reach out-of-the-way sights and make serendipitous discoveries. Main roads link larger destinations. On narrow, often single-lane backroads, go slow in anticipation of oncoming vehicles, including tractors.

BUS & TRAIN
Public transport is viable for many destinations. All four counties and their main cities/towns can be accessed by train, while buses typically run more frequently and serve a greater number of smaller regional locales.

Dungarvan (p163)

Plan Your Time

Soak up history and culture in Waterford and Kilkenny cities, set out into the rolling countryside on a driving, cycling or walking trail, and stroll wide sandy beaches along the coast.

Time-Limited Trip

Start in **Kilkenny** (p171) along the Marble City's famous medieval mile, linking its landmark cathedral and castle. Browse Irish crafts and design in the castle stables, stroll the riverbanks or board a cruise, cheer on a lightning-fast hurling game, and catch live music in the city's legendary pubs. Take a day trip via colourful **Thomastown** (p178) to the exquisite village of **Inistioge** (p179) and magical, wooded Woodstock Gardens.

Southeast in a Week

Traverse the **Blackwater Valley** (p165) to seaside **Ardmore** (p164) with its monastic ruins. Continue to foodie **Dungarvan** (p163) before taking in spectacular scenery along the **Copper Coast** (p162) to surf town **Tramore** (p162). Discover the Viking backstories of **Waterford city** (p155) and **Wexford town** (p146), and 1798 Rising history in **Enniscorthy** (p151). Finish by following the River Barrow to **Carlow town** (p166).

Seasonal Highlights

SPRING
Spring tends to arrive earlier here than elsewhere in Ireland. Flowers bring colour, and leaves green the trees, with most holidaymakers yet to descend.

SUMMER
Long days and warm temperatures make summer superb for enjoying the region's beaches and outdoor activities. Festivals are in full swing; book accommodation well ahead.

AUTUMN
Festivities continue across the region, and conditions can remain mild, especially early in the season. It's a glorious time for walking amid the autumnal colour.

WINTER
Cosy pubs provide refuge from the cold. Sights, accommodation and restaurants might reduce their opening hours or close altogether, especially outside the main towns.

Medieval Mile Museum, Kilkenny (p173) 145

WEXFORD TOWN

Set back from the fishing trawlers and shipping-container eateries along its quays, Wexford's engaging county town spills over with vibrantly hued buildings. Locally made art and crafts abound in Wexford's knot of narrow streets, which are crammed with independent shops, restaurants and bars, along with entertainment venues, including its renowned opera house.

Today home to some 20,000 inhabitants, Wexford (Irish: Loch Garman) has a tempestuous history. Vikings raided a monastery on this estuary of the River Slaney in 819 CE, naming the area Veisafjǫrðr ('inlet of the mudflats'). At the request of the deposed Irish King of Leinster, Diarmuid MacMurrough, sanctioned by England's King Henry II, the Anglo-Normans conquered in 1169. Oliver Cromwell's forces stormed and sacked the Irish Royalist city in 1649, wiping out three-quarters of Wexford's population. Rebels made a robust stand against British rule during the 1798 Rising. These epoch-defining events are explored at sights in and around the town and county.

DUBLIN
Wexford Town

TOP TIP

Look for Wexford's art and craft galleries throughout town. In a repurposed shopping arcade, the **Creative Hub** is home to more than 25 artists and craft makers. The **Wexford Arts Centre** hosts free contemporary art exhibitions and workshops. Grassroots arts and crafts feature at Friday and Saturday's Bullring Market.

National Opera House (p149)

WEXFORD TOWN

HIGHLIGHTS
1. Selskar Abbey

SIGHTS
2. Bullring
3. Cornmarket
4. Creative Hub
5. National Opera House
6. Westgate
7. Wexford Arts Centre

ACTIVITIES
see 2. WexWalks

SLEEPING
8. Blue Door
9. Talbot Hotel

EATING
10. Crust
11. Greenacres
12. Jasper's
13. La Côte
14. Nori

DRINKING & NIGHTLIFE
15. The Trough

Walking Through Wexford's Past
Historic Structures And Streetscapes

Vestiges of Wexford's history remain in its winding streets laid out by the Vikings. Notable sites in the town centre include the Cromwell-inflicted ruins of 1190-founded **Selskar Abbey**, where King Henry II did penance for murdering former ally Thomas Becket. The sister of Richard Fitz Gilbert de Clare (aka Strongbow), Basilia, is believed to have wed one of Henry II's lieutenants here. The structure itself occupies the site of a Viking temple dedicated to Odin. Nearby, the squat **Westgate** tower, constructed around 1300, is the only survivor of seven gates that accessed the walled town. The **Cornmarket**, dating from

BEST PLACES TO EAT IN WEXFORD TOWN

La Côte
Daily caught seafood such as scallops, lemon sole and mussels stars at this elegant harbourfront restaurant. €€€

Jasper's
Buzzing bar-restaurant in the Crown Quarter hotel and entertainment hub, with vivid decor and pub fare (vegan menu available). €€

The Trough
Scandinavian-style cafe serving all-day brunch and house-baked pastries such as wild-blackberry-filled doughnuts. €

Nori
Japanese cuisine using Wexford seafood. €€

Crust
Woodfired pizzas topped with artisan Irish meats and cheeses by a Naples-trained chef. €€

Greenacres
Epicurean bistro, deli and gallery space. €€

Johnstown Castle

1775, was once Wexford's central marketplace. During medieval times, bull baiting took place in the **Bullring**; in 1798, it was used for the manufacture and repair of pikes for the Rebellion. For an educational and highly entertaining stroll through the town's history, take a 75-minute tour with local Paul Walsh of **WexWalks**.

Roaming Johnstown's Hallowed Halls & Gardens

Aristocratic, Horticultural And Agricultural Legacies

See how the aristocracy lived at **Johnstown Castle**, 7km southwest of Wexford's centre. First established by the Esmonde family following the Anglo-Norman invasion and later expelled by Cromwell, this turreted Gothic Revival

WHERE TO STAY IN WEXFORD TOWN

Talbot Hotel
Harbourside landmark with stylish rooms, dining and leisure facilities (including a pool), and free parking. €€

Killiane Castle Country House
A 17th-century manor with eight rooms and four self-catering apartments adjoining a 15th-century castle, 5km south of town. €€

Blue Door
Central yet peacefully situated B&B in a restored Georgian townhouse run by a welcoming owner/chef. €

masterpiece was created between 1836 and 1872 by the Grogan family, who went on to marry into the powerful Fitzgerald dynasty. Highlights include the Apostles Hall, named for its elaborately carved sculptures; the dining room with a Grogan family portrait; the grand drawing room with its original French mirrors; the library; and its last resident Lady Fitzgerald's chamber; and the 86m-long servants' tunnel that concealed castle workers from view. After Lady Fitzgerald's death in 1942, it was donated to the state, becoming an agricultural college and research facility until its 2019 restoration, when the castle first opened to the public.

In the stable yard, the **Irish Agricultural Museum** depicts the changes to rural Irish life brought about by the industrial revolution, such as the shift from horse-drawn machinery to engine-powered equipment, through exhibits such as tractors, bicycles, and farming manuals and implements.

Surrounding the castle, the magnificent **Johnstown Castle Gardens** incorporate three lakes, a walled garden, hay meadows, woodland, follies, resident otters, waterfowl and iridescent peacocks, along with a visitor centre and cafe.

Diving Deep into Irish History
Open-Air Heritage Museum

For the full sweep of Irish history, head 5.5km west of Wexford's town centre to the **Irish National Heritage Park** at Ferrycarrig. Sprawled over 14 hectares of native woodland, marsh and banks of the River Slaney, it encompasses the site of the first Anglo-Norman settlement in Ireland. Ongoing archaeological excavations have unearthed stone foundations of the castle that replaced the original wooden fortifications, along with pottery and arrowheads.

Among the open-air museum's reconstructed sites are a Mesolithic camp, portal dolmen, monastic site, medieval ringfort and Viking harbour. Various activities and events range from panning for gold to blacksmithing and falconry demonstrations. Character-dressed guides lead themed tours ('prehistoric Ireland', 'early Christian Ireland' or 'age of invasion'), and there are also audio- and self-guided tours. To really get to grips with the past, you can stay off-grid within thatched, wattle-and-daub walls at the Viking settlement or ringfort overnight, complete with costumes and the opportunity to cook over an open fire.

OPERATIC WEXFORD

Wexford's **National Opera House** presents opera as well as comedy, concerts, dance, musicals, theatre, workshops and educational events throughout the year. Panoramic views of the town and harbour unfold from the top-floor cafe/restaurant, La Vista. The opera house comes into its own in autumn as the centrepiece for the world-famous **Wexford Festival Opera**, established in 1951 and held over 12 days from late October to early November each year, with a focus on revitalising forgotten masterpieces.

Alongside the main festival is the open-access **Wexford Fringe Festival**, ranging from art and photography to jazz and classical recitals and trad sessions, as well as the **Wexford Spiegeltent Festival**, named for its century-old wood, velvet and mirrored pavilion venue.

GETTING AROUND

Sloping gently towards the harbour, Wexford's compact town centre is easily walkable. Parallel to the quayside promenade, North Main St is the main shopping thoroughfare. Public car parks are plentiful, including by the waterfront. Buses serve the main outlying sights (Monday to Saturday only; no services on Sundays). Bike-share operator Bolt rents e-bikes with a 90km range; payment per minute is via the app. From Wexford's centrally located O'Hanrahan Station, trains run north to Dublin and south to Rosslare.

Beyond Wexford Town

History is etched across the landscapes of County Wexford, from ancient and ecclesiastical remains to strategic defensive and seafaring sites.

North of Wexford town, Enniscorthy, the county's second-largest town, is home to the National 1798 Rebellion Centre and the battlefield of Vinegar Hill. Birdlife flocks to the beaches along the east coast. To Wexford's south, Rosslare is synonymous with its ferry port, while its strand is a popular summer holiday spot. On the southern coast, Kilmore Quay, with its quaint thatched cottages, has a picturesque marina with a busy fishing fleet and access to the Saltee Islands bird sanctuary. Straddling the River Barrow as it makes its way to the sea, New Ross, with its replica Famine ship, is a gateway for a fascinating drive along the Hook Peninsula, capped by the world's oldest working lighthouse.

TOP TIP

Roadside stalls throughout the county sell sweet, juicy Wexford strawberries from around the May bank holiday weekend to late October.

Saltee Islands (p154)

Re-enactment at Vinegar Hill

Rebellion History in Enniscorthy
Castle, Interpretative Centre And Battlefield

On the River Slaney, **Enniscorthy** (Inis Córthaidh), County Wexford's second-largest town with a population of some 9500 inhabitants, sits 24km northwest of Wexford town. At its heart, 13th-century **Enniscorthy Castle** was occupied over the centuries by British armies, Irish rebels, prisoners and local merchant families. Today it houses an exhibition exploring the castle's Anglo-Norman origins and Enniscorthy's expansion in the 1600s as a prosperous market town. Self-guided tours include the dungeon and rooftop battlement looking over the town and across to Vinegar Hill.

Combined tickets are available for the castle and the **National 1798 Rebellion Centre**, which powerfully relates Wexford's ill-fated uprising against British rule in Ireland, emboldened by the French and American revolutions. An audiovisual presentation gives you the sense of being present at the Battle of Vinegar Hill, which saw the massacre of 1500 Irish men, women and children, whose pikes and knives were no match for the British muskets and cannons. Afterwards, contemplate the struggle while walking on windswept **Vinegar Hill**, 2.5km northeast of the National 1798 Rebellion Centre, with views across Enniscorthy.

WILDLIFE WATCHING ON WEXFORD'S EAST COAST

Wexford's sparsely populated east coast is a haven for wildlife, including 250-plus bird species. The **Wexford Wildfowl Reserve**, 7km northeast of Wexford town on the reclaimed land of the North Slob (derived from the Irish word slab, meaning mud or mire), is inhabited by mute swans, goldcrests and peregrine falcons year-round, and some 10,000 Greenland white-fronted geese each winter.

Just east at the forested **Raven Nature Reserve** are red squirrels, Irish hares, pine martens, and grey and harbour seals. To its north, rare little terns nest in the dunes of 11km-long white-sand **Curracloe Beach**. Further north in the seaside village of Courtown, volunteer-staffed **Courtown Seal Rescue** rehabilitates orphaned and injured seals, which you can meet on behind-the-scenes tours.

WHERE TO EAT IN ENNISCORTHY

The Wilds
Local, seasonal, organic cafe with fabulous soups, sandwiches and sweets inside an Irish design gallery space. **€**

Via Veneto
Paolo Fresilli cooks authentic pizzas, pasta, meat and shellfish dishes, using recipes from his home region of Lazio. **€€€**

Casa d'Galo
Chargrilled Portuguese dishes including piri-piri chicken served on colourful plates, with Douro and Beira Atlântico wines. **€€**

BEST DINING WITH ACCOMMODATION IN COUNTY WEXFORD

Dunbrody Country House
Celebrity chef Kevin Dundon's Georgian property incorporates restaurants, a cookery school and beautifully wallpapered guest rooms. €€€

Monart
High teas and fine dining at an ivy-draped 18th-century spa hotel with woodland and lake views. €€€

Marlfield House Hotel
Two modern Irish restaurants (the Duck and the Conservatory) in an antique-filled Regency house amid 14.5-hectare gardens. €€€

Ladyville House at Loftus Hall
Estate-grown produce at a 180-seat restaurant, plus 22 luxurious rooms at historic Loftus Hall, reopened in 2023. €€€

Rosslare Strand

Strolling Rosslare's Strand
More Than A Busy Port

Rosslare (Ros Láir) is best known for **Rosslare Europort**, 19km south of Wexford town, which has passenger ferries to Britain, France and Spain, as well as booming post-Brexit freight routes. A major expansion is in the pipeline, with the port also set to become Ireland's offshore renewable energy hub, but it will remain operating throughout.

Patrolled by lifeguards in summer, the 4.5km-long beach **Rosslare Strand** begins 8km northwest of the port. At its northern tip, the par-72, 18-hole links course at the **Rosslare Golf Club** follows the contours of the sand dunes. Rosslare Strand's village centre has holiday favourites like ice cream, cafes, pubs, bars and bike hire, as well as a 'sea spa' with a seawater pool and salt-infused steam room at Rosslare's iconic, fifth-generation-run **Kelly's Resort Hotel & Spa** (nonguests welcome).

South of Rosslare Harbour, beyond the lake-set early Augustinian priory ruins of **Our Lady's Island** (an annual pilgrimage site), a traditional moss-green-painted pub is the atmospheric setting for sublime seafood at the **Lobster Pot**.

WHERE TO EAT IN KILMORE QUAY

Quayside Deli & Fish Shop
Wave-muralled building with crab rolls, chowder, and fish and chips to eat in or take away. €

Mary Barry's
Memorabilia-filled, low-ceilinged pub with crackling open fireplaces serving seafood platters, grilled fish and whole lobsters. €€

Cocoa's Cafe
Scones, cakes, cookies and warm cinnamon buns, along with breakfast burritos, bagels and sourdough toasties. €

HEADING OUT ON THE HOOK PENINSULA

South of New Ross, between Bannow Bay to the east and Waterford Harbour to the west, County Wexford's Hook Peninsula is awash with history. This loop drive covers 60km, with plenty to see, so allow at least half a day.

Start in **1 Ballyhack**, whose Knights Hospitallers stone tower house, Ballyhack Castle, dates from the mid-15th century. Travel southeast through Arthurstown to **2 Duncannon**, home to the star-shaped Duncannon Fort, built in the 16th century to defend against the Spanish Armada and used as a WWI training facility. Duncannon's beach hosts a popular sand-sculpting festival each August. Continue south past Dollar Bay's caves, rock formations and pools and out onto **3 Hook Head**. Its black-and-white-striped lighthouse is the oldest continually operating in the world. Climb its 13th-century tower to spot dolphins, seals and migrating whales beyond the fossil-rich shore.

Drive through patchwork-field countryside to **4 Fethard-on-Sea**, with the crumbling remains of a 15th-century castle with a crenellated circular tower (and sea-cave kayaking and coasteering expeditions run by adventure company Irish Experience). Turn north to reach the ruins of Cistercian **5 Tintern Abbey**, built in the early 13th century for monks from its Welsh namesake. The abbey later became a private estate; a 350m walking path leads through woodland to the Colclough Walled Garden, laid out in 1838 and beautifully restored. Wind northwest past hedgerows and drystone walls to another ruined Cistercian abbey, 1170-founded **6 Dunbrody Abbey**.

Back in Ballyhack, sail the peninsula's coastline with By Hook or By Crooke Boat Tours, or cross by car ferry to Passage East, near the town of Crooke (hence Anglo-Norman military leader Strongbow's instruction en route to capturing Waterford to land 'by Hook or by Crooke') in County Waterford.

THE KENNEDYS OF WEXFORD

Near the Dunbrody Famine Ship in New Ross, a life-size bronze **statue of John F Kennedy** commemorates the US president's visit in summer 1963. JFK's great-grandfather, Patrick Kennedy, was born 7km south in Dunganstown at the **Kennedy Homestead**, which is still farmed by his descendants. Its museum covers both the Kennedys who stayed in Ireland and émigrés like Patrick who sailed to the United States in 1848.

Exhibits include the rosary beads JFK had with him at the time of his assassination. The 252-hectare memorial park **John F Kennedy Arboretum**, 6km southeast, has 4500 species of trees. Spanning the River Barrow, the **Rose Fitzgerald Kennedy Bridge** (Ireland's longest, at 887m) opened in 2020 and is named for JFK's mother.

Coastal Expeditions at Kilmore Quay
Wildlife Spotting On And Offshore

Some of Ireland's best seafood lands 23km southwest of Wexford town at photogenic fishing port **Kilmore Quay** (Cé na Cille Móire), where craned trawlers fill the harbour and thatched and slate-roofed cottages with whitewashed stone walls line its narrow lanes. From the village, the **Ballyteige Burrow Nature Reserve** extends 9km northwest. Behind the beach's dunes, the salt marsh and mudflats are a winter refuge for bird species, including brent geese.

Fishing is possible from the shore, or you can charter a boat at the harbour to head out to the reefs and wrecks. Boats also set sail from the harbour for one of Europe's most important bird sanctuaries, the **Saltee Islands** (90-hectare Great Saltee and 40-hectare Little Saltee), some 5km offshore of Kilmore Quay to the south. Inhabited as far back as 3500 BCE and used by marauding pirates, the islands were owned by Tintern Abbey (p153) until the monasteries' dissolution. They're now frequented by puffins, garnets, Manx shearwaters, razorbills and guillemots, among the 220 species recorded here. Nesting season, from spring to early summer, is the best time to visit. Landings are possible only on Great Saltee (weather depending); there are no toilets or shelter, so wear waterproofs, including footwear.

Understanding Irish Emigration in New Ross
Board A Replica Famine Ship

New Ross (Rhos Mhic Triúin), 36km west of Wexford town, is Ireland's only inland port, established by the Anglo-Normans on the River Barrow in the 12th century. As vessels outgrew it, shipping declined, but in the 19th century, it was a departure point for 'coffin ships' that left Famine-stricken Ireland for the promise of the New World. On the Quay, the moored replica **Dunbrody Famine Ship** provides an unflinching glimpse into emigrants' desperate voyages. During 45-minute tours, you'll see an introductory film before receiving a 'ticket' to board the ship, where costumed crew convey the grim conditions for passengers, who were allowed only an hour a day up on deck for the six weeks at sea. The dark, dank, cramped quarters and limited food and water meant countless passengers didn't survive the harrowing transatlantic journey.

Today, scenic trips with **Barrow Princess River Cruise** travel between New Ross' Quay and Waterford city (two hours one way); you can take bikes on board.

GETTING AROUND

Trains between Dublin and Rosslare Europort stop in Enniscorthy, Wexford town and Rosslare Strand. Buses serve the county's main towns, but you'll need your own wheels (car or bike) to access smaller destinations off the beaten track. Car ferries yo-yo between Ballyhack and Passage East, County Waterford, saving a large detour via New Ross. Journey time is just five minutes; pay on board.

WATERFORD CITY

Even in the context of more than 1100 years of history, Ireland's oldest city is undergoing a metamorphosis. The creative energy infusing this city of around 55,000 inhabitants is visible in scores of street-art canvases splashing colour across its architecture, major unveilings like Mount Congreve House and Gardens (Waterford's largest-ever investment in a visitor attraction), and a slew of new sights and museums in the city's ancient Viking Triangle. Work is underway on a massive redevelopment of Waterford's 8-hectare former industrial North Quays into a mixed-use zone with shopping and tourism and cultural facilities, as well as a new riverside walkway, train station and transport hub, and a 207m-long pedestrian, cycle and electric shuttle-bus bridge with an opening span for watercraft linking the river's banks.

Add to that local boutiques, artisan designers and producers, cafes, restaurants, bars, and a packed schedule of festivals. All make Waterford one of Ireland's most exciting places to be right now.

TOP TIP

For history buffs planning to visit several museums, the Freedom of Waterford Pass is a huge money saver. It includes an Epic Walking Tour, led by an expert guide, visiting Christ Church Cathedral, with access to Waterford's Medieval Museum, Irish Silver Museum, Bishop's Palace and the Irish Museum of Time.

House of Waterford Crystal (p158)

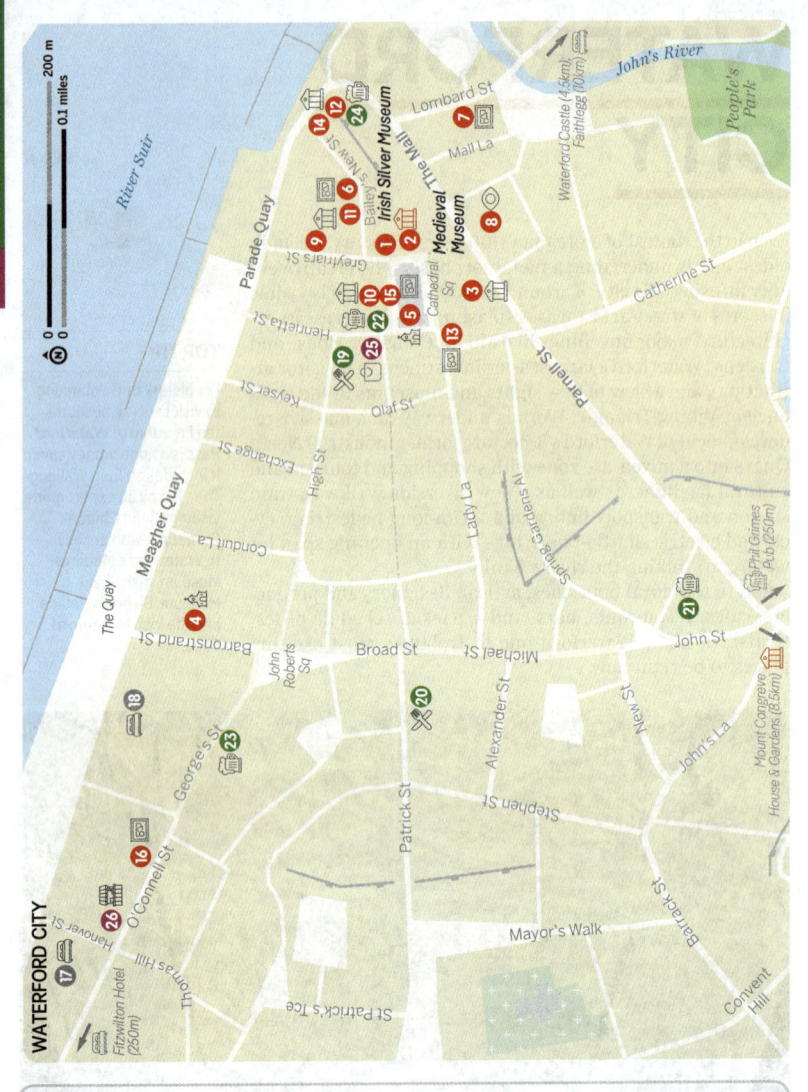

WATERFORD CITY

HIGHLIGHTS
1. Irish Silver Museum
2. Medieval Museum

SIGHTS
3. Bishop's Palace
4. Cathedral of the Most Holy Trinity
5. Christ Church Cathedral
6. Dragon Slayer Sword
7. GOMA
8. House of Waterford Crystal
9. Irish Museum of Time
10. Irish Wake Museum
11. King of the Vikings
12. Reginald's Tower
13. Strongbow & Aoife
14. Vadrarfjordr
15. Viking Triangle
16. Waterford Gallery of Art

SLEEPING
17. Dooley's Hotel
18. Granville Hotel

EATING
19. Everett's
20. Momo

DRINKING & NIGHTLIFE
21. Davy Mac's
22. Fat Angel
23. J & K Walsh Victorian Spirit Grocer
24. The Reg

SHOPPING
25. Irish Handmade Glass Company
26. Phoenix Yard Market

156

Vadrarfjordr replica

Exploring Waterford's Viking Triangle
Waterford Treasures: Museums And Architecture

Behind the riverside quays, northwest of the Mall, Waterford's Viking Triangle is the oldest part of the city. At its gateway, the 10m-long **Vadrarfjordr** replica Viking longboat was handcrafted in 2012 from Irish oak. It sits at the foot of **Reginald's Tower**, named for the Viking king who built a fort here in 914. Rebuilt by the Anglo-Normans in the 12th century, Ireland's earliest complete building formed part of the city's medieval walls. The tower's museum records the city's Viking history.

In the ruins of a 13th-century Franciscan friary, an immersive 30-minute VR experience **King of the Vikings** vividly recreates life in what was then known as Vadrarfjordr. By the entrance, the 23m-long **Dragon Slayer Sword** sculpture was carved from a single Douglas fir.

Waterford's giant outdoor **Viking Triangle chessboard** is modelled on a Viking-made set found in Scotland.

Silver in Ireland from Viking times to 18th-century Georgian dining is displayed at the **Irish Silver Museum**. The collection includes a coin minted in what's now Iraq, which arrived in 850 with Ireland's original Viking invaders. In Ireland's only building enclosing two medieval chambers (the 13th-century Chorister's Hall and 15th-century Mayor's Hall), the **Medieval Museum** exhibits include the Waterford Charter Roll (aka the Great Parchment Book of Waterford),

WATERFORD ART INDOORS & OUT

More than 60 colourful murals make Waterford's city centre a vibrant open-air gallery. For 10 days each August, the **Waterford Walls Street Art Festival** features workshops, guided walking and cycling tours, and live music, as Irish and international artists transform donated walls into urban works of art. Year-round, the **Waterford Walls Project** organises tours of the striking creations.

Indoor spaces to view art include the **Waterford Gallery of Art**, showcasing Irish painting and sculpture from the first half of the 20th century in a 19th-century former bank. **GOMA** (Gallery of Modern Art) mounts up to nine exhibitions each year by recent graduates and emerging and established artists, with a focus on innovation.

WHERE TO EAT IN WATERFORD CITY

Everett's
Award-winning modern Irish cuisine using premium mountain-to-sea produce in atmospheric surrounds including a vaulted cellar. €€€

Phoenix Yard Market
Street-food stalls spanning fish and chips from the Skipper's Kitchen to vegetarian dishes from the Crazy Vegetable. €

Momo
Artistically presented bistro dishes using quality local ingredients served at lunch and dinner. €€

WATERFORD FESTIVITIES

Waterford loves a party. Every weekend from June to August, **Summer in the City** hosts live music, film screenings, street performers and more.

On the August bank holiday weekend, **Spraoi** sees street theatre, circus acts, comedy, dance and music, plus a parade with hundreds of performers, floats and bands, and fireworks over the river.

Early September's **Harvest Festival** celebrates Waterford's restaurants and producers. Late September's **John Dwyer Weekend** is a trad-music fest with sessions, song and dance workshops, and scheduled and impromptu concerts. Visual and performing arts feature in late October's **Imagine Arts Festival**.

From mid-November to late December, **Winterval** is a wonderland of illuminations, quayside ice skating, secret music gigs, storytelling and Christmas activities.

---

documenting plagues through to Cromwell's invasion, with the earliest use of English in city records in Ireland.

Ireland's only neoclassical Georgian cathedral, the Church of Ireland **Christ Church Cathedral**, was built by John Roberts in 1779 on the site of an 11th-century Viking church where Irish princess Aoife, daughter of Leinster King Diarmuid MacMurrough, married Anglo-Norman leader Strongbow the day after he invaded Waterford on 24 August 1170. Ireland's oldest cathedral, the Catholic **Cathedral of the Most Holy Trinity**, on Barronstrand St in the city centre, was also designed by John Roberts and completed in 1793.

In a 15th-century almshouse (Ireland's oldest urban domestic building), the **Irish Wake Museum** delves into the rituals and superstitions around death. In partnership with Waterford Whisky, you can experience a traditional Irish wake and whiskey. Occupying a restored Gothic-style church on Greyfriars St, the **Irish Museum of Time** spans the evolution of Irish watchmakers from the late 17th to the 20th centuries. Timepieces include longcase (grandfather) clocks, table clocks and watches.

A **Strongbow & Aoife** sculpture stands on the grounds of the **Bishop's Palace**, a Georgian mansion. Dating from 1741, the palace charts Waterford's history from the 1700s to 1970. Irish independence, World Wars I and II, and Waterford sporting legends are covered on the top floor, while the ground floor is furnished as an elegant 18th-century townhouse with the 1789 Penrose Decanter, Waterford's oldest piece of crystal.

Learning About Waterford's Famous Crystal
Factory Visits – And Shopping Too

Waterford has been famous for its sparkling glassware since brothers George and William Penrose opened their factory on the riverside quays in 1783. Its 1952-created Lismore design is the world's best-selling crystal pattern. At today's gleaming modern **House of Waterford Crystal** premises opposite the Bishop's Palace, you can go behind the scenes on an hour-long factory tour that takes in the unchanged art of wooden mould-making; molten glass transformed in the blowing room; the marking department where temporary geometric grid guides are applied; the cutting department, where master cutters make unique deep cuts that refract light and give the glass its luminescence; the sculpting department; and the engraving area where copper wheels engrave designs on the

---

WHERE TO STAY IN WATERFORD CITY

Granville Hotel
Early 1700s quayside showpiece with antique-furnished rooms, spectacular stained glass and outstanding dining, including breakfasts. €€

Dooley's Hotel
Overlooking the river, with 112 individually styled rooms and regular live music in its bar. €€

Fitzwilton Hotel
Contemporary street-art-painted hotel with modern rooms (four wheelchair accessible), welcoming staff and limited free parking. €€

crystal. In the glittering shop, gifts range from a €60 tumbler to a €26,000 crystal Viking longboat.

Just 200m northwest in the city centre, you can also see glass being blown through the open doorway of the industrial workshop of the **Irish Handmade Glass Company**, attached to its contemporary design shop.

Visiting Magnificent Mount Congreve
Scented Strolls In Manor Gardens

Overlooking the River Suir 8km west of Waterford, with a direct entrance to the Waterford Greenway, **Mount Congreve House and Gardens** has been reinvigorated thanks to the biggest tourism-attraction investment in Waterford's history. At the 1760 Georgian manor, designed by renowned Waterford architect John Roberts, you'll see an audiovisual presentation, gallery and model of the building.

Mount Congreve's greatest draw is the 28-hectare garden set amid beautiful woodland. Its 16km of trails take in 3000 types of trees and shrubs, 1200-plus species of rhododendrons and 600 different camellias. The 750m **Fragrant Walk** is a kaleidoscope for the senses. The **Magnolia Walk** is Europe's largest planting. Walled vegetable and herb gardens provide produce for its Stables Cafe. Facilities also include a visitor centre and gift shop, along with gardener-led guided tours.

It's possible to stay on the property overnight in restored gatehouse **lodges**. Other historic places to stay in Waterford city's environs include turreted 19th-century **Waterford Castle**, 5km east of the city on its own island in the River Suir (reached round-the-clock by private car ferry), and 18th-century manor **Faithlegg**, 9km east of the city. Both have exceptional dining and golf courses.

CYCLING THE WATERFORD GREENWAY

Waterford city is linked to Dungarvan by one of Ireland's best vehicle-free bike rides, the **Waterford Greenway** (p161), with cycle rental available in both towns as well as along the route.

BEST PUBS IN WATERFORD CITY

The Reg
Incorporating the medieval city walls, with six bars, a rooftop terrace and nightly live music, plus summer gigs in the adjacent churchyard.

J&K Walsh Victorian Spirit Grocer
An 1889 jewel with timber cabinetry, original draught taps and Guinness served through the hatch in the snug.

Davy Mac's
Vintage-fitted pub and upstairs gin bar (110 varieties) at the Apple Market nightlife hub.

Fat Angel
Opposite the cathedral, with by-the-glass wines and craft beers.

Phil Grimes Pub
Legendary live-gig lineup and ivy-clad beer garden with a wood-burning stove.

GETTING AROUND

Waterford's city centre is relatively flat, making it easy to explore on foot. Buses serve outlying areas. The quayside has short- and long-stay car parking. Bike-share scheme TFI has stations around the city, with time-based payment via the app; the first half-hour is free. The Waterford Greenway cycling trail links riverside Waterford with seaside Dungarvan.

From Waterford's quays, boat cruises run to New Ross, County Wexford. Bikes can be taken on board. Passage East, 12km east of Waterford, has five-minute ferries for car, foot and bicycle passengers to Ballyhack, on County Wexford's Hook Peninsula. On the northern riverbank, Waterford's railway station, Plunkett Station, is on the line to Limerick Junction and to Dublin. While no commercial flights currently serve Waterford Airport, 9.5km south of the city, a proposed runway extension is expected to see international services resume.

Beyond Waterford City

County Waterford's coastal highlights include Tramore, Dungarvan and Ardmore. Venture inland to explore the Blackwater and Nire valleys.

TOP TIP

While spectacular in either direction, Waterford's coastal views are even more dramatic travelling west to east from Dungarvan towards Tramore.

On the doorstep of Waterford city is some of the southeast's most beautiful and varied scenery. Immediately to the city's southeast is the broad natural Waterford harbour at the mouth of the 'Three Sisters' (the Rivers Nore, Suir and Barrow), where pretty village Dunmore East faces County Wexford's Hook Peninsula.

South of Waterford city, Tramore combines old-fashioned seaside funfair attractions with ideal conditions for surfing. Restaurants and pubs cluster around the boat-filled harbour in Dungarvan. Beyond the Ring Peninsula are Ardmore's beautiful beaches and Ireland's earliest Christian ruins. To the north, the Blackwater Valley leads to lovely spots like Lismore with its monumental castle. Eastwards, the Nire Valley traverses mountainscapes and waterfalls.

Strand Inn

Waterford Greenway

Discovering Dunmore East's 19th-Century Charms

Cliffs, Coves And Aquatic Adventures

Perched above rose-hued sandstone cliffs 17km southwest of Waterford city, quaint **Dunmore East** (Dún Mór) was a 19th-century steamer port, and hallmarks of the era include its whitewashed thatched-roofed cottages, 1825-built **lighthouse** with a fluted Doric column and latticed cast-iron balcony, and once-segregated bathing spots **Mens Cove** and **Ladies Cove**, separated by the green expanse of Dunmore East's town park.

Beneath the cliffs, the largest of Dunmore's half-a-dozen cove beaches, **Lawlor's Strand**, and the adjacent **Councillor's Strand**, are close to the Lower Village's bars, cafes and restaurants. The outdoor terraces of the **Strand Inn** and **Spinnaker Bar and Restaurant** overflow on sunny days. Above the fishing harbour in Dunmore's Upper Village, nautical memorabilia-filled pub **Power's Bar** hosts legendary Tuesday-night trad sessions. All three bars are venues for the **Dunmore East Bluegrass Festival** in late August.

WATERFORD GREENWAY BY BIKE

Following a former railway line, the **Waterford Greenway** unfolds for 48km between Waterford city (an extension opened in 2023 reaches the quayfront) and Dungarvan's harbour. It's suitable for all abilities including families with kids, and can be cycled in either direction, though the descent is gentlest from east to west.

En route, you'll take in historic ruins, splendid gardens, farmland, three viaducts, 11 bridges and a 400m-long tunnel. Rent wheels in Waterford city, Dungarvan or midway at Kilmacthomas (you can pick up and drop off at all three locations). Allow around six hours on a standard bike (less on an electric model). A 24km section from Waterford city to New Ross is due for completion in 2025.

WHERE TO STAY IN TRAMORE

Majestic Hotel
Modern hotel with sea views from many of its 60 rooms (some opening to balconies). €€

Beach Haven House
Spotless property a short stroll from the beach with B&B and self-catering accommodation, and super-friendly hosts. €€

O'Shea's Hotel
Footsteps from the sand, with simple rooms above the pub and more modern rooms in an annex. €€

COUNTY WATERFORD'S COPPER COAST

Between Tramore and Dungarvan, the spectacular **Copper Coast** stretches from Kilfarrasy Beach in the east to Ballyvoyle Beach in the west. Some 460 million years ago, volcanoes, deserts and ice sheets shaped the rugged coastline of rocky headlands, cliffs and coves, and produced copper-rich quartz that was mined here in the 19th century.

Remains include the 1824 winding-engine house ruins at **Tankardstown**. In 2014, the Copper Coast was designated Ireland's first Unesco Geopark. At Bunmahon, the **Geological Garden** has rocks that form the area's foundations. Nearby, a restored 1828 church houses the **Copper Coast Geopark Visitor Centre**, with an exhibition on the coast's geological and mining history, and trail cards outlining walks in the area.

Swimming, snorkelling and sandcastle-building aside, there are plenty of opportunities to get active. Just north of the harbour, **Dunmore Adventure** has a host of water sports, from sailing and powerboating courses to kayaking and SUP, as well as Ireland's biggest inflatable aquapark. Gentle walks wind through the 17-hectare **Dunmore East Woods**. To take in the clifftop scenery, the bracing **Dunmore East Coastal Walk** runs from the harbour car park trailhead to Portally Cove (4km round trip; moderate fitness required; one to 1½ hours). An extension completed in 2020 continues on to Ballymacaw Cove (15km round trip from Dunmore East; strenuous; allow four to five hours in total).

Driving from Dunmore East to Tramore, the most scenic route is the signposted 16km drive via the narrow R684 and R685 backroads.

Riding the Waves at Tramore
Surf Schools And Seaside Attractions

Tramore, 13km south of Waterford city, is its summer playground. The town climbs up the hillside above its 5km-long sand-spit **strand** (Tramore's Irish name, Trá Mhór, means big beach), with funfair rides, amusement arcades and deep-fried, sugary snacks galore by the seafront promenade. Live music at Tramore's pubs in season adds to the carnival atmosphere.

The sheltered bay's slow-forming waves make Tramore a year-round hotspot for surfing, especially for beginner and intermediate surfers. With board and wetsuit rental as well as lessons, surf schools such as **Freedom Surf School**, **Oceanics** and **Tramore Surf Shop** get you up on the waves. **NCD Kiteboarding School** can get you above them.

At the strand's eastern end, its 30m-long, marram-grass-covered sand dunes have been evolving for more than 50,000 years and are some of the highest in Ireland. From here, you can walk to the **Back Strand** intertidal salt marsh lagoon, a haven for wading birds. Unpredictable currents make it unsafe for swimming. Brownstown Head bookends Tramore Bay to the east, with Great Newtown Head guarding the western end. Nearby, off Cliff Rd, are the rocky **Newtown Cove** and staircase accessed **Guillamene Cove** for sheltered swimming and picnics.

WHERE TO STAY IN DUNGARVAN

Kilcannon House
Enjoy poached kippers or whiskey-topped porridge for breakfast at this B&B 9km west of Dungarvan. €€

Park Hotel
Resort-style complex in landscaped grounds with 86 rooms, 15 self-catering lodges, a 20m swimming pool and gym. €€

Lawlors Hotel
Steps from Dungarvan's harbour, with views from some rooms, this family-run property dates from 1807. €€

Surfing, Tramore

Savouring the Flavours of Dungarvan
Food Festivities And Cooking Classes

With its boat-filled bay and colourful pubs along the quayfront, **Dungarvan** (Dún Garbhán), 47km southwest of Waterford city, has instant appeal. Guarding the harbour since 1209, Anglo-Norman **Dungarvan Castle** is distinguished by its rare polygonal shell keep and 18th-century military barracks behind its curtain wall, and it opens for free tours between June and September. Spanning the River Colligan as it flows into the bay is a single-arch stone bridge built in 1801, a legacy of the Duke of Devonshire, who rebuilt the town centre as it is today. The town's history is detailed in the late 18th-century former grain store housing the **Waterford County Museum** (until the 2014 merger of Waterford's county and city councils, Dungarvan was the county town).

At the western terminus of the **Waterford Greenway**, with bike rentals available in town, Dungarvan is within easy reach of beaches such as sandy **Clonea Strand**, 6km to the east, and more on the **Ring Peninsula** stretching around Dungarvan Bay to the south.

Dungarvan's fishing boats, shellfish beds and seaweed harvesting, along with the surrounding fertile farmland, shore up its reputation as a foodie hub. Marie Power of the **Sea Gardener** runs foraging walks, seaweed cookery workshops, beach picnics and talks. The lively **Dungarvan Farmers Market**, with stalls selling freshly baked artisan breads, farmhouse cheeses, cured

IRISH TRADITIONS ON THE RING PENINSULA

South of Dungarvan, rural backroads wind through green fields of the Gaeltacht (Irish-speaking area) of the **Ring Peninsula** (An Rinn; 'the headland'). Spirited trad-music sessions frequently take place at pubs including the **Marine Bar** and **Mooney's Tigh Tábhairne**.

From Mooney's, it's an invigorating 7km round-trip walk along the **Helvick Head Walking Trail** to **Helvick Harbour** (also accessible by car), with panoramic views of the ocean and bay.

By the harbour's fishing pier, wellness centre **Sólás na Mara** harnesses locally harvested seaweed's naturally occurring nutrients like iodine, calcium and magnesium to ease ailments from skin conditions to stress in traditional Irish seaweed baths. The private baths (single or double) are filled with freshly filtered, warmed seawater.

WHERE TO STAY IN ARDMORE

Cliff House Hotel
Cliff-perched property with luxurious sea-view rooms, swimming pool, spa, and Michelin-starred restaurant specialising in seafood. €€€

Round Tower Hotel
Family-run 1920s hotel beneath St Declan's monastery ruins, with an on-site bar and restaurant. €€

Newtown Farm
A 48-hectare dairy farm in the hills above Ardmore with B&B rooms overlooking the coast or fields. €€

EXPLORING CURRAGHMORE ESTATE

Once occupying a whopping 400 sq km, today **Curraghmore Estate** covers a 'mere' 10 sq km, accessed 1km west of the village of Portlaw (19km northwest of Waterford city). Granted by Henry II in 1177, Curraghmore ('great bog') remains the seat of Lord and Lady Waterford. Its original medieval tower was enhanced in the 18th century by Georgian architect James Wyatt, with Victorian refurbishments in the 19th century.

Tours give you an insight into its architectural and ancestral history, alongside its lavish furniture and art collections, and take in the 'shell house' folly constructed in 1754 from seashells. Afterwards, stroll the formal gardens and ancient oak woodland, and stop in at its wood-panelled courtyard tearooms.

St Declan's Monastery

meats, fruit and veggies, ready-to-eat dishes and more, fills the main square, Grattan Sq, on Thursday mornings. Throughout the week, you can pick up produce and delicacies at an array of deli-cafes around town and dine at excellent restaurants such as the **Tannery**, helmed by renowned Irish chef Paul Flynn, who also operates the **Tannery Cookery School**, with courses from 'seafood made easy' to masterclasses (plus boutique accommodation at the **Tannery Townhouse**).

At pubs around town, try brews named for local landmarks (such as Helvick Gold Blonde Ale, Greenway Waterford Pale Ale, Copper Coast Red Ale and Comeragh Challenger Gluten Free Ale, along with seasonals like Mahon Falls Rye Ale) from the **Dungarvan Brewing Company**, which runs summertime brewery tours. Dungarvan's epicurean celebrations peak during mid-April's **West Waterford Festival of Food**, with food trails and tours, cooking demonstrations, daily markets, dining events, talks, tastings, children's activities and street entertainment.

Taking a Pilgrimage at Seaside Ardmore
Monastic Ruins And Revered Beaches

In the county's southwestern corner, 71km from Waterford city, **Ardmore** is a pretty seaside village steeped in ecclesiastical history. Its 5km-long **cliff walk** loop trail starts from Ireland's oldest Christian settlement, **St Declan's Monastery**, where it's believed St Declan introduced Christianity in the 5th

---

WHERE TO EAT IN BLACKWATER VALLEY

Fuller's Bistro
Produce is sourced from within 20km of this Lismore restaurant with a conservatory and lavender-planted stone-walled garden. €€

Foley's on the Mall
Two-level Lismore townhouse dating from 1870 serving local specialities like Blackwater salmon and Comeragh Mountains lamb. €€

Vinilo
Bakery/cafe with fantastic sourdough (and gourmet sandwiches), croissants, and pastries like blackberry custard scrolls or fig-and-apple tartlets. €

century (predating St Patrick), with its 30m-high round tower, 8th-century oratory (St Declan's burial place) and remains of 12th-century Ardmore Cathedral. The cliff walk continues to Ardmore Head's 19th-century **lookout tower**. It returns to town along the coast past the **Samson wreck** (the crane barge blew ashore in 1987), and the ruins of **St Declan's Church** and sacred **St Declan's Well**, with its reputedly curative spring.

Ardmore Watersports runs kayaking and SUP tours to the wreck, as well as banana boat safaris, and rents bicycles to explore the area. Beyond the broad **strand** in the village, some 5km northeast, lies beautiful white-sand **Ballyquin Beach**, with tidal rock pools below ruins of a former stud; it is beloved by locals for swimming and surf fishing.

Traversing the Blackwater Valley
Grand Gardens Galore

In northwestern County Waterford, the River Blackwater flows through the enchanting landscape of the Blackwater Valley. At Ballyduff, the **Blackwater Distillery** crafts gin, vodka and whiskey, and the summertime **Booley Theatre** presents traditional Irish dance, music and storytelling. Lismore is dominated by its vast castle built in 1185. Within the defensive walls, the **Lismore Castle Gardens** unfold over 4 hectares, with a stately yew avenue and contemporary art gallery. You can 'see' inside the castle on a 30-minute VR experience at the town's **Lismore Heritage Centre**.

Downstream in Cappoquin, where the River Blackwater makes a 90-degree turn south, are late Georgian, John Roberts–designed **Cappoquin House and Gardens** ablaze with rhododendrons and azaleas in spring. Some 7km north of Cappoquin, at 1832-founded **Cistercian Mt Melleray Abbey**, Trappist monks run a heritage centre and tearooms.

Situated 9km downstream of Cappoquin, at the confluence with the River Finisk, the Brighton Pavilion–inspired, Indo-Gothic **Dromana Gate** heralds the entrance to **Dromana House and Gardens**, where more rhododendrons, azaleas and rare bulbs flourish. Looped walks lead through the woods to the river. In Villierstown, 3km south, **Blackwater Eco Tours** operates guided 90-minute River Blackwater boat tours and has kayak, SUP and motorboat rental. Each spring, performances, concerts and recitals take place at 12 different valley locations during the **Blackwater Valley Opera Festival**.

WALKING IN THE COMERAGH MOUNTAINS

The **Comeragh Mountains** (from 'coum', meaning 'hollow') climb from the coast near Dungarvan into the wilds of County Waterford to the County Tipperary border. From the car park, signposted 22km northeast of Dungarvan, an easy gravel walking path (2km one way) leads to the base of **Mahon Falls**, where waterfalls cascade over 80m-high sandstone cliffs.

On the western side of the Comeragh Mountains, several more challenging hikes depart from the **Nire Valley** car park (33km north of Dungarvan). A great taster is the Coumduala Loop Walk (8km round trip) along the slopes of Knockanaffrin to hidden lake Coumduala Lough.

To recharge, the charming guesthouse **Hanora's Cottage** has an evening-only gourmet restaurant and Jacuzzi-equipped rooms beside the River Nire.

GETTING AROUND

Buses serve most main towns, but your own wheels are best to reach destinations further afield, especially along the scenic backroads, and to allow for more flexibility in your schedule. The Waterford Greenway cycle route links Waterford city with Dungarvan.

CARLOW TOWN

The origins of Carlow's county town (Ceatharlach) stretch back into the mists of pre-written history. Winding through the town, the River Barrow was vital to Carlow's importance, evident in the remains of its castle and its military museum. While it might seem unlikely today, the town served as the capital of Ireland from 1361 to 1374 under King Edward III.

Carlow's Catholic cathedral is the country's second oldest, and its college is Ireland's second-oldest tertiary education institution, established to educate Catholic men in the late 18th century. Now a non-religious, coeducational college for liberal arts and social studies, with a lively 600-strong student population, it's also the site of the town's artistic hub, the Visual Centre for Contemporary Art. Its success has catapulted Carlow's visual and performing arts scenes to the fore and revitalised the town, which is today home to some 25,000 people in its busy centre and surrounds.

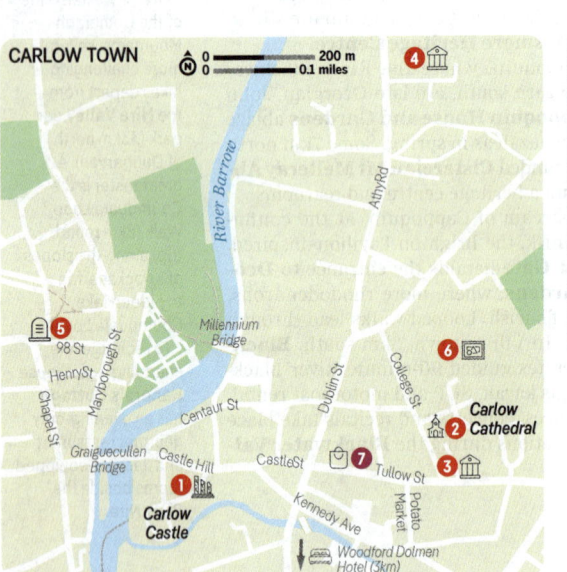

TOP TIP

Many of the most appealing places to stay are on Carlow's town fringes (such as the riverside Woodford Dolmen Hotel in 4-hectare grounds with an on-site restaurant and bar, 3km south of town) and in the surrounding countryside, including over the border in neighbouring counties like Laois and Kildare.

HIGHLIGHTS
1. Carlow Castle
2. Carlow Cathedral

SIGHTS
3. Carlow County Museum
4. County Carlow Military Museum
5. Croppies Grave
6. Visual Centre for Contemporary Art

SHOPPING
7. Made in Carlow

Checking Out Carlow's Landmarks
Castle, Cathedral And County Museum

Most of Carlow's landmark sights sit within its compact town centre. Above the River Barrow, the 13th-century **Carlow Castle** was once one of Ireland's most strategically important, but only the keep and two towers have survived, after a disastrous renovation attempt in 1814 to turn it into a psychiatric facility saw most of the structure destroyed.

The spire of **Carlow Cathedral** (Cathedral of the Assumption) rises 46m above the town's rooftops. Built in 1828 from blue-grey limestone and white granite, it's the second-oldest Catholic cathedral in Ireland. Just south in a former convent with stained-glass windows, a carved cathedral pulpit is among the exhibits at the **Carlow County Museum**. Some of its most intriguing displays are archaeological finds dating from 6700 BCE to the Middle Ages, including arrowheads, axes, granite hammers, pottery and an Iron Age glass bead, which were unearthed during the construction of the Carlow M9 bypass.

Discovering Carlow's Arts Scene
Galleries, Performances And Festivals

Carlow has an active arts scene. Adjacent to 1782-founded Carlow College, St Patrick's, the **Visual Centre for Contemporary Art** displays local and international works in five gallery spaces. It's also home to the **George Bernard Shaw Theatre**, presenting dance, film, music, plays and comedy. **Lennons**, its cafe by day and bistro by night, is the best place to eat in town. On Tullow St, Carlow's main shopping street, gallery and design shop **Made in Carlow** represents more than 100 Carlow artists, and the jewellery, prints, paintings, textiles, clothing, woodwork, ceramics, sculpture and photography make unique souvenirs. Cultural festivities include June's **Carlow Arts Festival** and August's **Carlow Fringe Festival**.

Cayisha Graham, Carlow Arts Festival

CARLOW'S MILITARY HISTORY

Given its strategic location on the Barrow and Slighe Cualann (one of the main roads to Tara), control of Carlow was crucial for prospective rulers of Leinster, and Carlow has seen plenty of military action over the centuries.

At the **County Carlow Military Museum**, you can see replica medieval suits of armour and swords, original 1798 Rebellion artefacts, including a Brown Bess musket, a display on WWII armoured vehicle production in Carlow and uniforms dating from the foundation of the Irish state to those currently in use.

On the Barrow's western bank, in Governey Park, **Croppies Grave** is a monument to the 600 Carlow men massacred by British troops during the 1798 Rebellion.

GETTING AROUND

Carlow's town centre is easily walkable, and car parks are plentiful. Buses serve outlying areas. From Carlow's railway station, trains run north to Kildare and Dublin, and south to Kilkenny and Waterford.

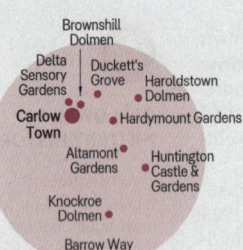

THE GUIDE | BEYOND CARLOW TOWN **WEXFORD, WATERFORD, CARLOW & KILKENNY**

Brownshill Dolmen
Delta Sensory Gardens
Duckett's Grove
Haroldstown Dolmen
Carlow Town
Hardymount Gardens
Altamont Gardens
Huntington Castle & Gardens
Knockroe Dolmen
Barrow Way

Beyond Carlow Town

Megalithic remains and majestic landscaped gardens lie in the fertile countryside fanning out into the county beyond Carlow town.

County Carlow covers just 897 sq km in its entirety (only County Louth is smaller), making it easy to get around it in a day. It's worth allowing longer though, especially to appreciate its famed gardens with vivid displays of colourful flowers to the east and south of Carlow town, with numerous walking opportunities. Outdoors enthusiasts will want to spend time exploring the River Barrow. Its towpath offers gentle walking and cycling between Carlow town and St Mullins (either the full distance or a shorter section). Paddling on the river in a kayak or canoe is a wonderful alternative to take in the scenery of this pretty part of the country.

TOP TIP

In late July and early August, the Carlow Garden Festival has open gardens, talks, workshops, tours and picnics all across the county.

Huntington Castle and Gardens (p170)

HUGH ROONEY/EYE UBIQUITOUS/UNIVERSAL IMAGES GROUP VIA GETTY IMAGES ©

Altamont Gardens

Following Carlow's Garden Trail
Walks Amid Woodland And Blooms

Carlow's renowned gardens stem from its aristocratic estates. Today, many are open to the public along the Carlow Garden Trail. Just 2km north of Carlow town, the not-for-profit **Delta Sensory Gardens** contain 20 interlocking, wheelchair-accessible gardens, including a 'five senses' garden, a musical fountain garden and a sculpture garden. Proceeds benefit the adjacent centre for adults with learning disabilities. At **Duckett's Grove**, 11km northeast of Carlow town, two interconnected walled gardens shelter historic varieties of roses and peonies, and a fruit orchard with heirloom Irish apple varieties such as Kerry Pippin and Irish Peach. A great kids' playground here has slides and an obstacle course.

One of Ireland's largest Spanish chestnut trees and a monumental beech tree guard the entrance to the 1-hectare **Hardymount Gardens**, 15km southeast of Carlow town. Espaliered apple trees, trailing wisteria, sunflowers, foxgloves and agapanthus shelter inside the granite-walled garden. **Altamont Gardens**, 24km southeast of Carlow town (5km east of

BEST PLACES TO STAY BEYOND CARLOW TOWN

Step House Hotel
Boutique gem on Borris' main street, with a brasserie and cellar restaurant. €€

Brandon View House
B&B 3km northeast of St Mullins with organically grown farm produce (including packed lunches) and views of the heather-clad mountains. €€

Kilgraney House
Georgian country house 7km north of Borris with guest suites, cottages and extensive gardens. €€

Lorum Old Rectory
At the foot of the Blackstairs Mountains, 6km north of Borris, this 1863 property has rooms and self-catering apartments. €€

WHERE TO EAT IN COUNTY CARLOW

Sha-Roe Bistro
Creations like Blackstairs Mountain lamb with roast root vegetables in an 18th-century Clonegal cottage. €€€

Mullicháin Café
Warming soups with house-baked bread, pizzas, open sandwiches and salads by the river in St Mullins. €

Clashganny House
An 1830s millhouse 5km south of Borris serving dishes like black truffle-stuffed wood pigeon with redcurrant jus. €€

Ballon) combine formal and informal gardens, and expansive lawns bordered by yews and hedges. An ice-age glen with mossy granite outcrops leads to riverside walks, with Sessile oaks dating from the 1750s towering above snowdrops and bluebells. Its herbaceous walled garden is home to a cafe.

At **Huntington Castle and Gardens**, 30km southeast of Carlow town in Clonegal (the southern terminus of the long-distance walking route the Wicklow Way), French lime trees line the avenue leading to the castle entrance and Italianate parterre gardens laid out in the 17th century. Gravel paths flanked by topiary and fountains pass fish ponds, rose gardens and manicured lawns. Beyond the 500-year-old yew walk lies woodland and farmland on the 65-hectare estate. Tours of the castle itself, parts of which date from 1625, take place in summer.

Navigating the River Barrow
Walking, Cycling And Paddling

Extending for 192km in all, Ireland's second-longest river, the River Barrow (thought to be named after Borvo, the ancient Celtic god of spring water and minerals), travels through County Carlow on its way to Waterford Harbour. The original towpath, the **Barrow Way**, runs 48km from Carlow town to St Mullins and can be walked or cycled. You'll pass small villages; tower house, mill and church ruins; and cascading weirs. Wildlife includes kingfishers, herons, dragonflies, damselflies, otters, hedgehogs and badgers.

To get out on the water, **Go With the Flow** and **Pure Adventure** run kayak and canoe tours, and have rentals to paddle yourself. Boats can be picked up and dropped off at various points on the river, such as **Clashganny** (Clais Ghainimh; 'sandy river trench'), a beautiful recreational area 5km south of Borris (9km north of St Mullins) with swimming, picnic facilities and looped forest trails.

At the Barrow Way's southern terminus, St Mullins, are the ruins of **St Mullins Monastery**, founded in the 7th century by St Moling, which became the burial place of the kings of Leinster. Remains include four church buildings, part of a round tower, and a 9th-century high cross. Nearby are the holy waters of **St Moling's Well**.

COUNTY CARLOW'S MEGALITHIC SITES

Dubbed 'dolmen county', County Carlow is home to numerous megalithic sites, including its most famous portal tomb **Brownshill Dolmen**, topped by Europe's largest capstone, weighing a hefty 103 tonnes. Believed to date back 4900 to 5500 years, it's visible from the R726 in a field 4km east of Carlow town.

Haroldstown Dolmen, 20km east of Carlow town, stands at a height of over 2m, with two overlapping capstones and a large doorstone. On the eastern slopes of Knockroe Mountain, 12km east of Borris, **Knockroe Dolmen** has a tilted capstone with a horseshoe-like engraving and a spiral motif on one of its portal walls. Carlow County Museum (p167) has details of other sites throughout the county.

GETTING AROUND

Buses serve main destinations in County Carlow, but to reach out-of-the-way sights (including the majority of its gardens), you'll need your own wheels. Many hotels and B&Bs in the county rent bikes.

KILKENNY CITY

With its turreted castle rising above the River Nore and the knot of narrow streets, Kilkenny is a medieval treasure. Known as the Marble City for its dark, fossil-speckled limestone, the city has played an outsize role throughout Ireland's history.

Kilkenny's Irish name, Cill Chainnigh, comes from the 6th-century monastery founded by St Canice. At the northern end of the medieval mile, which links the major sights, monumental St Canice's Cathedral dates from the 13th century. While Kilkenny's Anglo-Norman parliament instituted the 1366 Statutes of Kilkenny, intended to prevent the Anglo-Norman aristocracy's adoption of Irish culture and language, the 1641 Confederation of Kilkenny alliance of Irish and Anglo-Normans aimed to return Catholics' land and power, and Kilkenny was the capital of Ireland until Cromwell's invasion.

Today it's home to some 27,000 people, and legacies of Kilkenny's heritage resonate in its architecture, atmospheric pubs, sporting events (including Ireland's national game of hurling) and its many festivals.

TOP TIP

Given its proximity to Dublin, 130km north, Kilkenny's sights and vibrant drinking, dining and entertainment scenes make it a hugely popular destination year-round, especially on weekends and during festivals and events. Book central accommodation well ahead at peak times or consider visiting midweek or staying in its surrounds.

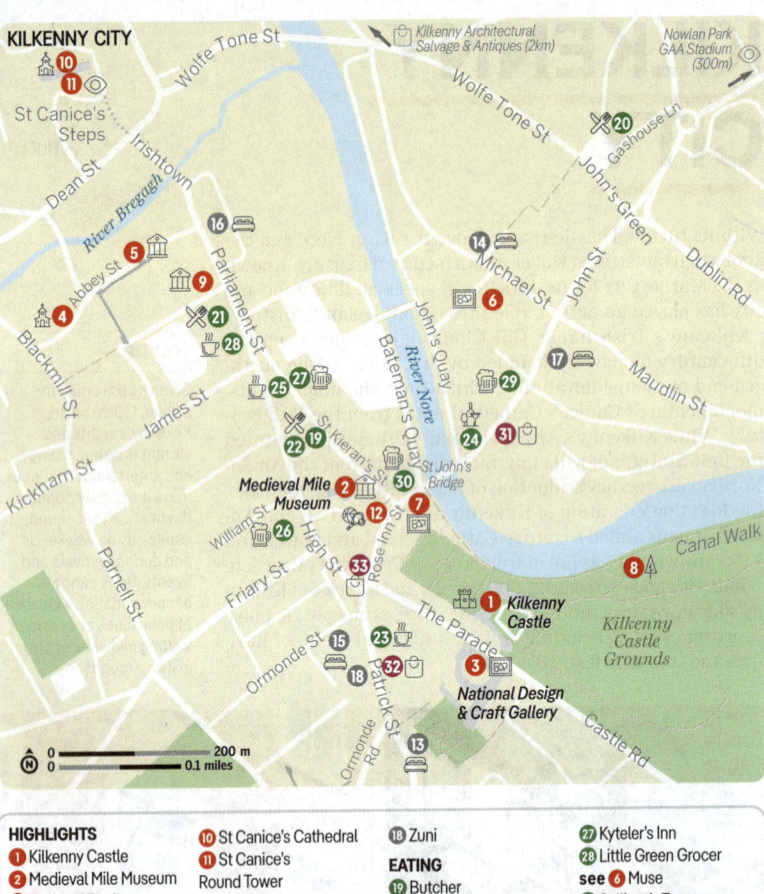

KILKENNY CITY

HIGHLIGHTS
1. Kilkenny Castle
2. Medieval Mile Museum
3. National Design & Craft Gallery

SIGHTS
4. Black Abbey
5. Black Freren Gate
6. Butler Gallery
7. Kilkenny Hurlers Statue
8. Nore Linear Park
9. Rothe House & Garden
10. St Canice's Cathedral
11. St Canice's Round Tower

ACTIVITIES
12. The Kilkenny Way

SLEEPING
13. Butler House
14. Celtic House
15. Hibernian Hotel
16. Kilkenny Tourist Hostel
17. Langton's Hotel
18. Zuni

EATING
19. Butcher
20. Campagne
21. Foodworks
22. Petronella

DRINKING & NIGHTLIFE
23. Cafe La Coco
24. Dylan Whisky Bar
25. Higgs Field
26. Hole in the Wall
27. Kyteler's Inn
28. Little Green Grocer
see 6. Muse
29. Sullivan's Taproom
30. Tynans Bridge House Bar

SHOPPING
31. Hurley Depot
see 3. Kilkenny Design Centre
32. Rudolf Heltzel
33. Yvonne Ross

Sightseeing Along Kilkenny's Medieval Mile
Castle, Cathedral And Intriguing Museums

Kilkenny's medieval mile connects its major sites in the city's historic heart. At the southern end, beside the River Nore in 21-hectare gardens, **Kilkenny Castle** fulfils every storybook fantasy of what a castle should look like. The castle occupies the site of a wooden defensive tower built by Strongbow. His son-in-law, William Marshal, replaced it in 1192 with a stone castle, and three of its four round towers still survive. Acquired in 1391 by the powerful

Kilkenny Castle

Butler family, who lived here for almost six centuries, it was sold to the city for a token £50 in 1967 and has been open to the public since 1976. In the chequered-floored entrance hall, the copper-green walls are hung with Butler family portraits, swords, daggers and (since extinct) Irish elk antlers. Also on the ground floor are the state dining room and beautifully wall-papered 'Chinese withdrawing room'. The 19th-century Jamaican mahogany grand staircase leads to the 1st-floor tapestry room, adorned with 15th- and 17th-century tapestries, as well as the anteroom, library and drawing room. The 2nd floor is home to the children's nursery, 'blue bedroom', 'Chinese bedroom' and the Moorish staircase to the east wing's superb picture gallery, displaying portraits, landscapes and religious paintings against deep-burgundy walls. Guided tours access otherwise off-limits areas, including the castle's west wing and medieval foundations.

St Mary's Church, northwest of the castle, was built by William Marshal in the early 13th century. It now houses the **Medieval Mile Museum**, whose interactive map and timeline put 800 years of city history into context. Artefacts include maces, sceptres, keys, coins, civic records and skeletons, along with tombs in the Rothe Chapel and graves in the former churchyard, where upwards of 40,000 Kilkenny citizens (more than the current population) lie buried.

BEST PLACES TO DINE IN KILKENNY

Butcher
County Kilkenny–farmed beef chargrilled in a post-industrial space with an in-house cocktail bar. €€

Campagne
Michelin-starred chef Garrett Byrne creates regional French cuisine from seasonal Irish produce. €€€

Higgs Field
Vegetarian cafe/restaurant transforming locally grown and foraged ingredients into dishes like lentil pâté with chickpea crackers and pickled ox-eye daisy capers. €

Petronella
Modern Irish cuisine in a romantic stone-walled, oak-beamed building in medieval passageway Butter Slip. €€

Foodworks
All-day brunch and evening bistro meals incorporate the owners' vegetables, herbs and reared pigs. €€

WHERE TO STAY IN KILKENNY

Hibernian Hotel
Central 18th-century Georgian bank housing 46 contemporary guest rooms, a brasserie restaurant and bar. €€

Celtic House
Superbly located B&B with full Irish breakfasts and four rooms decorated with its artist-owner's landscapes. €€

Kilkenny Tourist Hostel
Dorms, doubles and family rooms, a self-catering kitchen and turf-fire-warmed lounge at the medieval mile's northern end. €

KILKENNY FESTIVALS

Any weekend in Kilkenny feels like a festival but all the more so during its numerous dedicated events.

March's **Kilkenny Tradfest** has more than 100 trad-music gigs, and celebrations include a circus, hurling match and parade during **St Patrick's Festival Kilkenny**. Bluegrass, swing, folk, rockabilly and Cajun music play during May's **Kilkenny Roots Festival**.

The highlight of June's **Cat Laughs Comedy Festival** is the football match featuring Irish comedians versus the world. Events at historic venues during August's **Kilkenny Arts Festival** range from storytelling to digital art projections on the castle walls. October's **Savour Kilkenny** food fest has cookery demonstrations, markets, and a craft brewery and distillery marquee. From late November, **Yulefest** brings winter magic to the city.

St Canice's Cathedral

Further northwest, Ireland's only complete remaining burgage plot (a medieval rental property owned by the merchant class), **Rothe House and Garden**, dates from 1594. It's made up of three houses with three enclosed courtyards, with a restored 17th-century garden. Straw beehives, an Irish deer skull, an Ogham stone, clothing from the late 19th to early 20th centuries, local newspapers, maps and archives from families who lived at the property are among the diverse displays at its museum.

Continuing northwest brings you to **St Canice's Cathedral**, where elaborate tombs include the Butler dynasty. Built between 1202 and 1285, its tower collapsed in 1332 in circumstances linked to Dame Alice Kyteler's trial for witchcraft (which also saw her maid Petronella burned at the stake). Cromwell's forces caused further destruction during the 1650 siege, leaving it roofless until the cathedral's reconstruction. Rising 30m outside, the remarkably preserved **round tower** dates from the 9th century. Climb 121 steps up steep ladders for dizzying city views.

Heading southwest on Abbey St through the **Black Freren Gate** (the medieval city walls' only surviving arch), you'll reach the **Black Abbey** Dominican priory, built in 1225 by William Marshal. Measuring almost 45 sq m, Ireland's largest stained-glass window, which depicts the 15 mysteries of the rosary, was created in 1892. Among the abbey's other treasures are a

WHERE TO STAY IN KILKENNY

Butler House
With private gardens and an entrance to Castle Yard, this 1786 mansion has 17 period-furnished rooms. €€€

Langton's Hotel
Kilkenny empire with historic and modern rooms, gardens, two restaurants, four bars and a theatre. €€€

Zuni
In a converted 1902 theatre with 14 designer rooms above its exceptional modern Irish restaurant. €€

pre-Reformation statue of St Dominic carved from Irish oak and an alabaster sculpture of the holy trinity, which has a rare depiction of God holding Jesus on the crucifix and was hidden behind a wall until its 19th-century discovery.

Browsing Irish Crafts & Design
Galleries And Artisan Shops

Castle Yard, the former stables and coach houses of Kilkenny Castle, is now Ireland's showcase for contemporary craft and design, the **National Design & Craft Gallery**. Textiles, ceramics and jewellery are the focus of its exhibitions. It also hosts events and workshops. Irish-made homewares, clothing, stationery, art and other artisan wares are for sale at the adjacent **Kilkenny Design Centre**.

The **Butler Gallery**, in a former almshouse on the River Nore's eastern bank, mounts mainly modern and contemporary art exhibitions, and sculptures stud its walled garden. Its on-site shop sells arts and crafts made in Kilkenny and its surrounds, such as Jerpoint glass, Moth to a Flame candles, Caroline Dolan ceramics, and Tinnakeenly leather bags and wallets.

Jewellers worth seeking out in the city centre include **Yvonne Ross**, creating contemporary custom pieces, and **Rudolf Heltzel**, who uses traditional gold- and silversmithing techniques.

For vintage treasures like signs, furniture, art, industrial equipment and lighting, check out **Kilkenny Architectural Salvage & Antiques**.

Feeling Kilkenny's Hurling Pride
Catch A Game Or Tour

The oldest and fastest field sport in the world, Ireland's ancient game of hurling dates back almost 3000 years. In 2018, curling and the women's game of camogie were inscribed on Unesco's representative list for intangible cultural heritage. Founded in 1887, Kilkenny's hurling team, the Cats, are the most successful in Irish history, winning the Provincial Leinster Championships 75 times and the All-Ireland Championship 36 times to date. The Cats' home ground is **Nowlan Park GAA Stadium**, with a capacity of 30,000, and the season runs from April to July.

Even if you can't attend a match, you can take a two-hour 'ultimate hurling experience' with **The Kilkenny Way**. It includes a stadium tour, with the chance to try the game yourself, before watching classic games at Lanigan's Legends Bar, surrounded by sporting memorabilia.

BEST PLACES TO DRINK IN KILKENNY

Hole in the Wall
Hidden down a passage in the 1552 Archer Inner House, with intimate live music gigs.

Sullivan's Taproom
Reviving brewing in Kilkenny with its Black Marble Stout, Maltings Red Ale and Irish Gold.

Tynans Bridge House Bar
Charming former grocery-pub with original timber cabinetry opposite St John's Bridge.

Kyteler's Inn
Rambling inn first established by witchcraft-convicted Dame Alice in the 13th century.

Dylan Whisky Bar
Cosy snugs, old advertising-etched mirrors, open turf fire and tasting flights from its 280-strong whiskey collection.

WHERE TO GET COFFEE IN KILKENNY CITY

Little Green Grocer
Small, sustainable deli serving Cork-roasted Badger & Dodo coffee with organic dairy and plant-based milk in compostable cups.

Cafe La Coco
Coffee comes in edible vegan cups at this cute striped-awning cafe with a white-washed brick-walled interior.

Muse
Adjoining the Butler Gallery's walled garden, with Dublin microroaster Cloud Picker coffee and fabulous cafe dishes.

TOURING KILKENNY

While Kilkenny is easy to navigate, numerous guided tours offer insights into the city. Historian **Pat Tynan** leads informative walking tours, or try the Medieval Mile Museum's **Medieval Mile Trail**, humorous tours with **Shenanigan's** or a spooky evening with **Kilkenny Ghost Tours**. Both **Kilkenny Tasting Tours** and **Kilkenny Foodie Tours** run epicurean explorations that include tastings.

For a two-wheeled spin around town, **Kilkenny Cycling Tours** has various guided options, such as sunset tours, and rents bikes and 'hydrobikes' (pedal-powered canoes).

Boat Trips Kilkenny runs river cruises along the Nore that take you below the castle and let you see the city from a different angle. **Kilkenny Road Train Tours** tootles around town with commentary and singalongs on miniature 'trains' (on wheels).

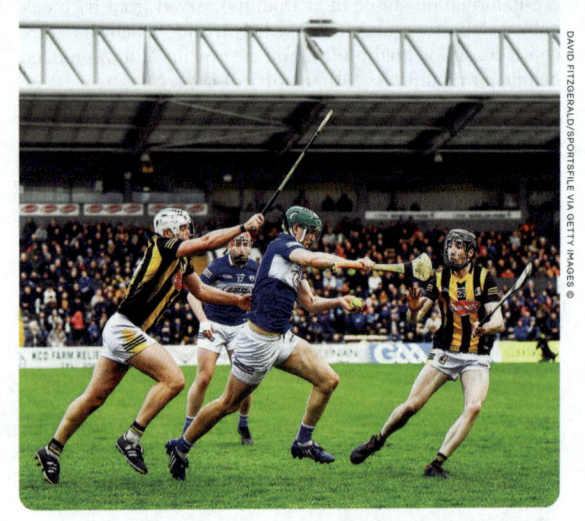

Nowlan Park GAA Stadium (p175)

Across the road from Lanigan's is the 4.2m-high, striped limestone **Kilkenny Hurlers statue**, featuring three players reaching for a sliotar (ball). At the **Hurley Depot**, you can buy equipment including Kilkenny-made hurleys (sticks) and black-and-amber Cats clothing.

Walking Along the Nore Linear Park
River Strolling And Summer Swimming

Tracing the banks of the River Nore, the **Nore Linear Park** is a series of signposted walking trails covering 6.5km. You can take on a short section or allow around two hours for the complete stretch, which starts on the eastern bank just south of the city centre on Maudlin St. From here, follow it downstream via a boardwalk to the city's ring road and then cross the pedestrian bridge to the western bank and head upstream past the castle and its gardens through the city centre and the Bishop Meadows parkland. Finish by cooling off at the weir swimming area, which is patrolled by lifeguards in summer.

GETTING AROUND

Kilkenny's ancient, gently sloping city centre is easily walkable. While there's little in the way of on-street parking, there are car parks in and around the centre, with the largest off Parliament St. Buses serve outlying suburbs. Bike-share scheme Bolt has e-bikes accessed via its app. Kilkenny Cycling Tours rents standard and electric bikes.

On the centre's eastern edge, Kilkenny's railway station, MacDonagh Station, has train services to south to Waterford, and north to Carlow and Dublin.

Beyond Kilkenny City

Leaving the lively city's limits, County Kilkenny's countryside is home to charming towns, villages, gardens, artisans and evocative monastic ruins.

The rural corners of County Kilkenny are some of the loveliest in Ireland. Thomastown's colourful streetscapes are the jumping-off point for the superbly preserved ruins of Jerpoint Abbey, fascinating medieval remains unexpectedly discovered at working farm Jerpoint Park, as well as a trove of artisan producers and craftspeople, the prestigious golf course at magnificent estate Mount Juliet, and rescued Romantic-era gardens. Grand Victorian gardens have been regenerated on the edge of Inistioge, a photogenic gem of a village above the River Nore. On the River Barrow, Graiguenamanagh's ancient abbey endures as a Catholic Parish church. Walking trails lead along the river and high up on Brandon Hill from where you can survey the surrounding landscapes.

TOP TIP

Check the reopening date for Dunmore Cave. Situated 11km north of Kilkenny, it's famed for its stalagmites, stalactites and fierce Viking history.

Graiguenamanagh (p180)

KELLS PRIORY'S ATMOSPHERIC RUINS

Sprawling across a hectare of pastoral landscapes 16km south of Kilkenny, **Kells Priory** was founded in 1193 by Geoffrey FitzRobert, brother-in-law of Strongbow. Extensive ruins of this fortified Augustinian monastery remain, including a nave, chancel, chapel, bread oven and mill – much of what you see today dates from the 15th century, before King Henry VIII's suppression of Catholic monasteries.

At dusk, the silhouetted ruins have an ethereal enchantment. Two kilometres south of the priory is the 29m-high **Kilree round tower**, dating from 1100, alongside the remains of a church. Outside, the Celtic high cross thought to date from the 9th century is believed to mark the non-Christian burial place of Irish high king Niall Caille.

Tearooms, Woodstock Gardens

Treasure Hunting in & around Thomastown
Abbey Ruins, Artisans, Gardens And Golfing

Thomastown (Baile Mhic Andáin; historically known as Grennan), 17km southeast of Kilkenny city, centres on a quadrant of streets lined by colourfully painted buildings and enticing cafes. Few fragments of its medieval town walls remain today; among them are the ruins of circa 1350 former toll house **Mullin's Castle** by the bridge spanning the River Nore, a popular spot for trout fishing.

More spectacular ruins are located 2km southwest of town at **Jerpoint Abbey**, one the most complete Cistercian abbey ruins in Ireland. The abbey dates from the 12th century, and the tower and cloister were constructed in the 15th century. Tours depart from the visitor centre, which has an exhibition on the abbey's history as well as details of children's 'treasure hunts' to find saints, knights, mythological beasts and exotic animals carved into the abbey's stonework. Nearby, **Jerpoint Park** occupies a once-thriving 12th-century medieval town known as Newtown, which vanished from records in the 1600s and was overgrown with oak trees until it became the working farm it remains today. Guided tours piece together its history, and you can catch sheepdog demonstrations.

For golfers, the treasure in this area is **Mount Juliet**, a Jack Nicklaus–designed course with 80 bunkers, five lakes and

WHERE TO STAY IN THOMASTOWN

Tower House
One of the three stylishly renovated rooms in this medieval tower house has an arrow-slit 'murder hole'. €€

Abbey House
Opposite Jerpoint Abbey in flower-filled gardens, with six rooms and a piano in the guest lounge. €€

Lawcus Farm
On the King's River with B&B rooms in an old stone farmhouse and a self-contained tree house. €€

a walled garden protecting the 16th green, 6km southwest of Thomastown. The surrounding estate has an equestrian centre as well as a luxurious 18th-century manor house and modern accommodation, and restaurants including the Michelin-starred Lady Helen.

Thomastown and its surrounds are home to numerous artisans and craftspeople whose work is displayed in Kilkenny City's galleries and shops. Studios open to visitors include **Jerpoint Glass** and woodturner **Eoghan Leadbetter**. Potter **Bernard Kavanagh** has a gallery in Thomastown, as does ceramicist **Brid Lyons**. Renowned potter and ceramicist **Nicholas Mosse** is based in nearby Bennettsbridge, 9km north of Thomastown. Mosse and his family have restored the 1790s Romantic-era garden **Kilfane Glen**, 7km northeast of Thomastown, where oak, chestnut, beech and larch trees tower above wild ferns, campanula, wood anemones, bluebells and foxgloves, and moss-covered paths and bridges wind through a narrow ravine alongside a stream that leads to a waterfall and thatched summerhouse.

Falling for Inistioge's Charms
Enchanting Village And Victorian Gardens

On the River Nore 26km southeast of Kilkenny, **Inistioge** (Inis Tíog), with its 18th-century, 10-arch stone bridge and central green ringed by quaint houses, churches, cafes and pubs, is one of Ireland's prettiest villages. Parallel to the river, the **Nore Valley Walk** links Inistioge with Thomastown on a beautiful 11km route through pastoral and wooded landscapes and passing the ruins of Dysart and Grennan castles.

Inistioge's greatest attraction lies just outside the village 1.5km to the south. **Woodstock Gardens'** 20 hectares of formal and informal gardens have been restored to the Victorian era of 1840 to 1890, when they were originally developed. Its long avenues are lined with noble fir and monkey puzzle trees. Foxgloves, lavender and cornflowers on the terraced flower garden are linked to the rose garden by the yew walk. Adjoining the walled kitchen garden, the cast-iron conservatory containing tearooms opens to a sunny outdoor terrace. In the arboretum is Ireland's tallest silver fir and a coast redwood, as well as Bentham cypress, beech and oak trees. Numerous walking paths include a waterfall trail past cascading streams. Allow at least a couple of hours to explore.

COUNTY KILKENNY TIPPLES

Kilkenny's lush landscapes and limestone soils are ripe for farms and producers. **Highbank Orchard**, 13km southwest of Kilkenny city, is an organic apple orchard making apple cider, rum, brandy and wine, along with apple juice, syrup and cider vinegar.

You can take tours of the orchard and production facilities, and buy direct from its farm shop.

Located 6km to the west, **Ballykeefe Distillery** produces whiskey, poitín, vodka and gin from grain grown on its farm and water from its 80m-deep aquifer. Tours of its facilities take in the millhouse, brewhouse, copper pot stills, barrel-aging room and bottling plant, finishing with tastings. For both Highbank and Ballykeefe, you'll need to book tours in advance.

WHERE TO STAY IN INISTIOGE

Ballyduff House
With open fires and a book-lined library, this 1760 property 5km west of Inistioge has five antique-furnished rooms. €€

Woodstock Arms
Third-generation-run pub on Inistioge's village green with seven guest rooms and a pool table in the bar. €€

Grove Farmhouse
Countryside views extend from this 200-year-old house's four rooms on a working farm 5km southwest of Inistioge. €€

Duiske Abbey

Walking in & around Graiguenamanagh
River, Hilltop And Town Strolls

Affable **Graiguenamanagh** (pronounced 'greg-nuh-mah-na' and referred to locally as Graig, ie 'greg') sits 28km southeast of Kilkenny. Its Irish name, Graig na Manach, means grange (valley or village) of the monks. **Duiske Abbey** was built in 1204 by William Marshal, making it one of the first and largest Cistercian abbeys in Ireland. Constructed mainly of imported yellow limestone, its remarkable carvings include a Norman knight with a sword and still leaf foliage. After 1536, when it was suppressed by Henry VIII, it fell into ruin, and in 1744, the tower collapsed into the nave, before a full restoration in the 1980s that retained its medieval floor tiles and processional door. Outside are two high crosses from the 8th and 9th centuries.

By the River Barrow that forms the border with County Carlow, converted 19th-century grain store **Waterside** rents bikes to traverse the 8km towpath to St Mullins, and has comfy guesthouse accommodation and the best restaurant in town. Outside, **Pure Adventure** has SUP, kayak and canoe hire. The river is the trailhead for the 19km loop hike to **Brandon Hill** (Cnoc Bhréanail), Ireland's eighth-highest peak at 515m. At the top, you're rewarded with a panorama of the Barrow Valley, Mt Leinster and the Blackstairs Mountains. Recharge afterwards with a pint at Graiguenamanagh's unchanged-in-generations grocery-pub **Mick Doyle's**.

BEST PLACES TO EAT BEYOND KILKENNY CITY

Kings Mill
A 13th-century stone mill overlooking a weir 13km west of Thomastown is the setting for authentic Italian cuisine. €€

Blackberry Cafe
Overlooking Inistioge's bridge, with open sandwiches on soda bread, pork and roast apple sausage rolls, and quiche with goat's cheese and pine nuts. €

Truffle Fairy
Handmade chocolates, muffins, slices and cookies at this aqua-painted Thomastown cafe/shop use sustainable cocoa beans. €

Tābú Tapas Thomastown
Local tapas twists include leek tortilla, black pudding croquettes, Irish stew empanadas and calamari frittura with wild garlic aioli. €€

GETTING AROUND

Thomastown is on the train line linking Kilkenny city with Waterford. Buses serve other main towns and villages, but you'll need your own wheels to reach sights further afield and to appreciate the area's lesser-explored corners. Some accommodation providers hire bikes or arrange wheels in Kilkenny city.

Jerpoint Abbey (p178)

Above: Mizen Head (p213); right: Ballymaloe tomatoes

CORK
FINE FOOD, FINE SCENERY, FINE FOLK

From Cork, the rebel city, and the foodie hotspots of Kinsale and Ballymaloe to the wild scenery of the far west peninsulas, Ireland's biggest county has it all.

Everything good about Ireland can be found in County Cork. Surrounding the country's second city – a thriving metropolis made glorious by location and its almost Rabelaisian devotion to the finer things of life – is a lush landscape dotted with villages that offer days of languor and idyll. The city's understated confidence is grounded in its plethora of food markets and ever-evolving cast of creative eateries, and in its selection of pubs, entertainment and cultural pursuits.

Ireland's largest county can fairly lay claim to being the foodie capital of Ireland. Lush pastures provide prime meat and dairy products, while superb seafood is landed around the coast. It seems as if you can't move here without bumping into a traditional cheesemaker, artisan baker or boutique coffee roaster. Kinsale is famous for its seafood, Clonakilty for its black pudding and Ballymaloe as the birthplace of Ireland's devotion to local produce.

Further west, you'll follow narrow roads around rugged, rock-girt coastlines and pass through a dozen or more old fishing villages where boats bob at their moorings and harbourside bars entice you in. The scenery is every bit as enchanting as the tourist brochures would have you believe, particularly along the Mizen Head, Sheep's Head and Beara peninsulas, where you can wander the wild hills and get in touch with Ireland's ancient past.

THE MAIN AREAS

CORK CITY
Ireland's second city.
p188

CLONAKILTY
Market towns and harbour villages. **p201**

BANTRY
Coast and mountain scenery.
p209

Find Your Way

Cork is Ireland's largest county, and it takes a fair bit of travelling to cover it all. Our chosen destinations capture its fascinating diversity, from city to coast to wild mountain scenery.

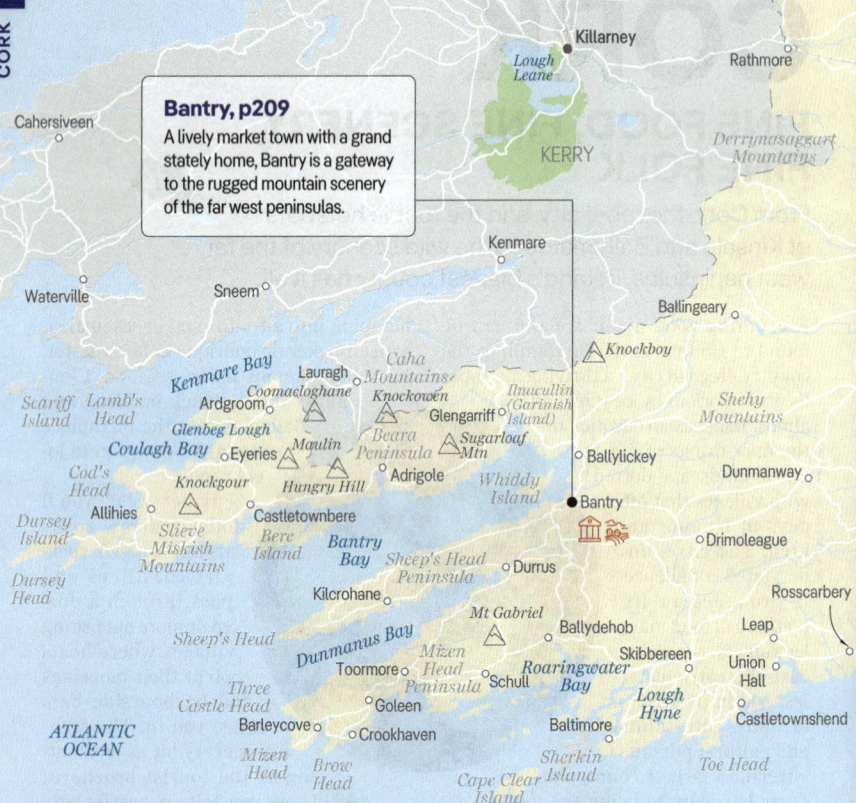

Bantry, p209

A lively market town with a grand stately home, Bantry is a gateway to the rugged mountain scenery of the far west peninsulas.

CAR

A car is pretty much essential for exploring County Cork away from the main towns, especially along the coast and around the Mizen Head, Sheep's Head and Beara peninsulas. Find car rental companies at Cork airport, south of the city.

BUS

Regular bus services run from Cork city to Youghal, Kinsale, Clonakilty, Skibbereen and Bantry, and from Skibbereen to Baltimore. Bus 270 links Skibbereen to Bantry, Glengarriff, Kenmare and Killarney five times a day year-round.

TRAIN

The only destinations that can be reached by train from Cork city are Midleton and Cobh. Trains depart every half-hour and are useful for making a day trip in either direction. Heading west from Cork city, you have to go by car or bus.

Cork City, p188
Set on an island amid a maze of river channels, Ireland's second-largest city is cosmopolitan and cultured, with a reputation for fine food and drink.

Clonakilty, p201
The birthplace of black pudding is a foodie town par excellence, with a fine farmers market, a choice of great eateries and its own distillery.

Plan Your Time

Cork city is well worth a visit, but make sure to check out Cobh and Kinsale and put aside at least a few days for touring the coast and the West Cork peninsulas.

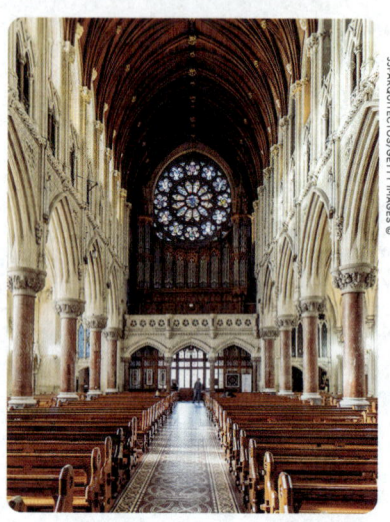

St Colman's Cathedral, Cobh (p197)

Pressed for Time

- If you only have a day to spend, it's a toss-up between **Cork city** (p188) and **Kinsale** (p195), though at a push you could visit both as they're only 30 minutes apart by car or bus.

- The best sight in Cork is the city itself – soak it up as you wander the streets, but don't miss the colourful food and drink stalls at the **English Market** (p190), followed by **Cork City Gaol** (p190) or an **urban kayak tour** (p191).

- If you stay in Cork, eat at **Market Lane** or **Paradiso** (p191), or opt for an early evening stroll around Kinsale followed by dinner at **Fishy Fishy** (p195).

Seasonal Highlights

Summer is peak season for whale watching around the Cork coastline and the best weather for sea-kayaking trips, while autumn has food festivals galore, notably in Skibbereen and Kinsale.

APRIL
Kinsale hosts the **All Ireland Chowder Festival**, including a competition for the best seafood chowder.

MAY
Enjoy seafood banquets, live music in the square and traditional sailboats racing round the harbour during the **Baltimore Wooden Boat Festival**.

JUNE
Cork Midsummer Festival is a week-long arts festival celebrating music, theatre, dance, literature and visual arts.

186

Three Days to Travel Around

● Visit **Blarney Castle** (p200) first thing and then explore **Cork city** (p188); visit **Cork City Gaol** (p190) and make sure not to miss the **English Market** (p190).

● Day two is for a boat trip from nearby **Cobh** (p197) to fascinating **Spike Island** (p198), followed by an hour's drive to **Kinsale** (p195) for a wander around **Charles Fort** (p196) and dinner at one of its many fine eateries.

● Finally, head west along the coastal road, stopping for lunch at **Clonakilty** (p201) or **Skibbereen** (p205); finish up with a visit to spectacular **Mizen Head** (p213).

More Than a Week

● After a few days of enjoying the sights and cuisine of Cork city, Kinsale and Mizen Head, take a deep dive into the wilds of West Cork.

● Go midnight kayaking on **Lough Hyne** (p206); devote two days to a leisurely cycle around the **Sheep's Head Peninsula** (p215) and walk to the lighthouse at the tip.

● Allow two days for the Beara Peninsula – take the cable car to **Dursey Island** (p214) and hike the **Copper Mine Trail** (p216).

● Take a tour of **Bantry House** (p210) and don't miss the boat trip to **Ilnacullin** (p216).

JULY
A week of music, parties and drag events during **Cork Pride** culminates in a colourful parade through the city centre.

AUGUST
Yacht races, children's dinghy racing, long-distance swims and a range of land-based entertainment enliven the **Schull** and **Kinsale regattas**.

SEPTEMBER
Hundreds of visitors flock to **Cape Clear Island International Storytelling Festival** for traditional storytelling, workshops and walks.

OCTOBER
Cork Jazz Festival has an all-star lineup of jazz, rock and pop in venues across town, plus a fringe offshoot in Kinsale.

CORK CITY

Ireland's second city is first in every important respect – at least according to the locals, who cheerfully refer to it as the 'real capital of Ireland'. It's a liberal, youthful and cosmopolitan place that was badly hit by economic recession but is busily reinventing itself with spruced-up streets, revitalised stretches of waterfront and seemingly an artisan coffee bar on every corner. There's a bit of a hipster scene, but the best of the city is still happily traditional: snug pubs with live-music sessions, restaurants dishing up top-quality local produce and a genuinely proud welcome from the locals.

The compact city centre is set on an island in the River Lee, surrounded by waterways and packed with grand Georgian avenues, cramped 17th-century alleys, modern masterpieces such as the opera house, and narrow streets crammed with pubs, shops, cafes and restaurants, fed by arguably the best foodie scene in the country.

TOP TIP

Avoid city centre parking problems by using Black Ash Park & Ride on the South City Link Rd, on the way to the airport. Parking costs €5 a day, with buses into the city centre at least every 15 minutes (10-minute journey time).

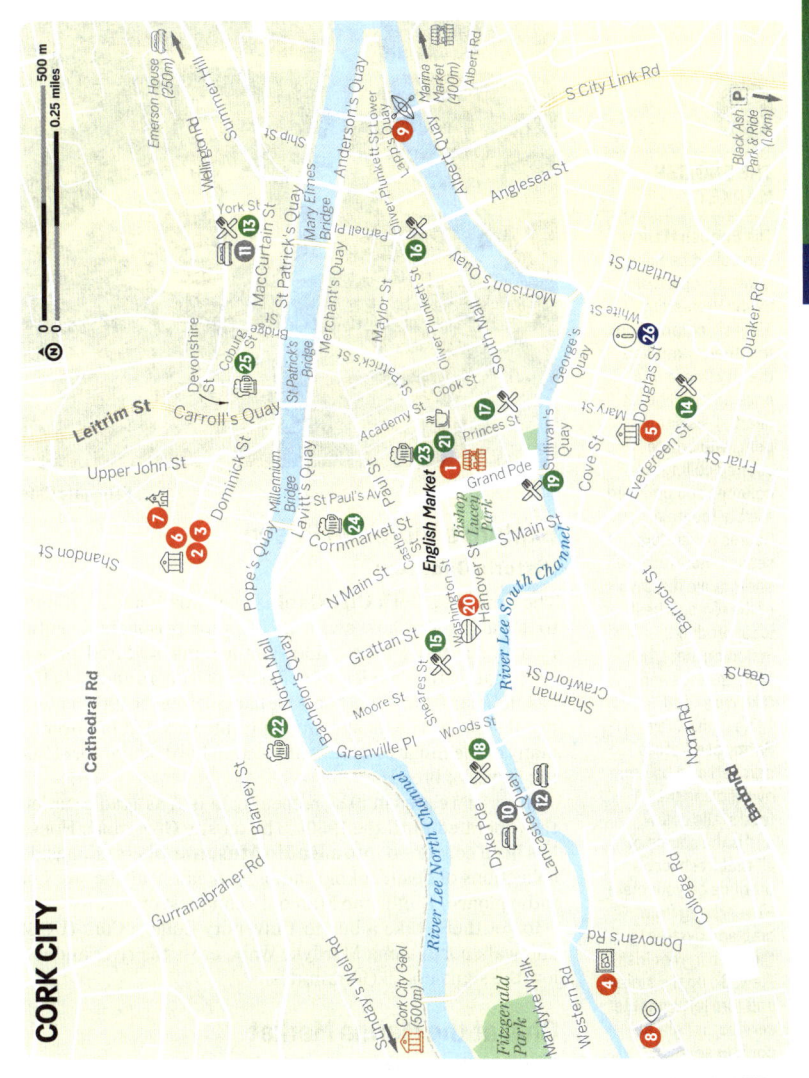

CORK CITY

HIGHLIGHTS
1. English Market

SIGHTS
2. Cork Butter Museum
3. Firkin Crane
4. Lewis Glucksman Gallery
5. Nano Nagle Place
6. Old Butter Market
7. St Anne's Church
8. University College Cork

ACTIVITIES
9. Atlantic Sea Kayaking

SLEEPING
10. Anam Cara B&B
11. Hotel Isaacs
12. River Lee Hotel

EATING
13. Glass Curtain
14. Good Day Deli
15. Ichigo Ichie
16. Market Lane
17. Nash 19
18. Paradiso
19. Quay Co-op

DRINKING & NIGHTLIFE
20. Chambers Bar
21. Farmgate Cafe
22. Franciscan Well Bar & Brewery
23. Mutton Lane Inn
24. Joh Rising Sons n
25. Sin É

INFORMATION
26. LInC

THE GUIDE

CORK CORK CITY

189

THE ENGLISH MARKET

The **English Market** – so called because it was set up in 1788 by the Protestant or 'English' corporation that then controlled the city (there was once an Irish Market nearby) – is a true gem, with ornate vaulted ceilings, columns and polished marble fountain. Scores of vendors set up colourful and photogenic displays of the region's best local produce, including meat, fish, fruit, cheeses and takeaway food.

The unmissable **Farmgate Cafe** is perched on a balcony overlooking the food stalls below, and is the source of all that fresh local produce on your plate – everything from crab and oysters to the lamb in your Irish stew. Go up the stairs and turn left for table service, or right for counter service.

Farmgate Cafe

Explore a Victorian Prison
Historic Gaol Tour

The imposing **Cork City Gaol** is well worth a visit, if only to get a sense of how awful life was for prisoners a century ago. An audio tour guides you around restored prison cells that feature models of suffering prisoners and sadistic-looking guards and bring home the harshness of the 19th-century penal system. The most common crime was that of poverty; many of the inmates were sentenced to hard labour for stealing loaves of bread.

The prison closed in 1923, reopening in 1927 as a radio station that operated until the 1950s. The on-site Governor's House has been converted into a **Radio Museum** where, alongside collections of beautiful old radios, you can hear the story of radio pioneer Guglielmo Marconi's conquest of the airwaves.

To get there, take a bus to University College Cork (UCC) and walk north along Mardyke Walk, cross the river and follow the signs uphill (10 minutes).

Chill at the Marina Market
Fun Foodie Hangout

Opened in 2020, the **Marina Market** has quickly become one of the city's favourite hangouts. Modelled on the (now-defunct) Paper Island in Copenhagen, the market is a hangar-like space lined with artisan food and drink stalls and has a

---

WHERE TO STAY IN CORK CITY

River Lee Hotel
Modern riverside hotel with a glass-walled atrium brings a touch of luxury to the city centre. €€€

Anam Cara B&B
Cute little Georgian-style cottage with a homely, country-house feel. €€

Hotel Isaacs
Hotel housed in a former Victorian furniture warehouse with a central location. €€

central seating area of tables and chairs and even some comfortable leather sofas. Try **Alchemy** for coffee, **Oak Fire** for pizza and **Nua Asador** for barbecue (all its meat comes from the English Market).

The venue is open daily from 8am to 8pm, but really comes to life at weekends when it hosts a crafts and farmers market. It's a 20-minute walk from the city centre along Centre Park Rd, or catch bus 212 from the train station.

Stroll a University Campus
Art And Architecture

Established in 1845 as one of three 'queen's colleges' (the others are in Galway and Belfast) set up to provide nondenominational alternatives to the Anglican Protestant Trinity College in Dublin, the campus of **University College Cork** spreads around an attractive collection of Victorian Gothic buildings, gardens and historical attractions, including a 19th-century astronomical observatory. Self-guided audio tours are available from the visitor centre.

The covered walkway on the north side of the main quad, known as the **Stone Corridor**, houses Ireland's biggest collection of Ogham stones, carved with runic inscriptions dating from the 4th to the 6th century CE.

In the northeast corner of the campus is the award-winning **Lewis Glucksman Gallery**, a startling construction of limestone, steel and timber built in 2004 by Dublin architects O'Donnell and Tuomey. Three floors of galleries display the best of national and international contemporary art and large-scale, mixed-media installations.

Go Urban Kayaking
Exploring Cork On The Water

Cork city centre is actually an island in the River Lee, with no fewer than 29 bridges linking to the 'mainland', so what better way to explore than on the water? From June to September (Thursday to Sunday only) **Atlantic Sea Kayaking** runs 2½-hour 'Under the Bridges' kayaking tours of the city, starting from the pontoon next to the boardwalk at Lapps Quay.

Afternoon tours start at 2pm, and the tide dictates how far upstream and how many bridges you can pass under. Guides provide entertaining and informative commentary as you go. If you're lucky, you might find a seal following you, and otters have been spotted too. Sunset tours begin at 7.30pm, and all are suitable for beginners.

LGBTIQ+ CORK

Cork has an out-and-proud gay scene that rivals Dublin's. Most nightlife venues are concentrated in the west end of the city centre, and many are mixed-crowd, all-welcome places.

Chambers Bar
Cork's biggest and liveliest gay bar, with DJs playing until 2am, themed entertainment nights and outrageous cocktails.

Cork Pride
Week-long July festival with events throughout the city.

Emerson House
Gay and lesbian B&B in an elegant Georgian house. Host Cyril is a mine of information.

Gay Cork
What's-on listings and directory (gaycork.com).

L.InC
Resource centre for lesbians and bisexual women.

WHERE TO EAT IN CORK CITY

Nash 19
Superb bistro and deli where locally sourced food is honoured at breakfast and lunch. €€

Market Lane
Bright corner bistro with a broad and hearty menu reflecting what's fresh at the English Market. €€

Paradiso
Contemporary vegetarian and vegan cuisine; contender for the best restaurant in town of any genre. €€

Discover a Green Oasis
Museum And Quiet Gardens

The part of the city south of the river, east of Gothic St Fin Barre's Cathedral and the 17th-century ramparts of Elizabeth Fort, is changing fast as restoration and gentrification take hold. Seek out the renovated red-brick complex of **Nano Nagle Place**, a former convent that houses an award-winning **museum** dedicated to Honora Nagle, a remarkable 18th-century woman who devoted herself to providing education for poor children in Cork. Beyond the museum is a wonderful oasis of peaceful terraced **gardens**, and home to an ideal lunch spot, the **Good Day Deli**.

Savour Cork's Food Scene
Artisan Food And Drink

Cork's food and drink scene is reason enough to visit the city. Dozens of restaurants and cafes make the most of County Cork's rightly famous local produce, ranging from beef and pork to seafood and dairy, while the renowned English Market (p190) - a cornucopia of fine food - is a national treasure.

Bonner Travel offers a three-hour **Cork Culinary Tour** (daily except Sundays, minimum four people) that explores the city's food markets and eating places and includes tasting sessions with food and drink producers, ending with a pint in a traditional pub, or coffee and cake at one of the city's artisan coffee shops.

The five-day **Cork on a Fork** food festival takes place in late August, with food trails, tours, tasting masterclasses, street events, talks, cooking demos, community events and farmers markets.

Explore the Shandon Cultural Quarter
Butter Museum And Bell Ringing

Shandon, perched on a hillside overlooking the city centre to the north, is a great spot for city views, but you'll also find galleries, antique shops and cafes along its lanes. Those tiny old row houses, where generations of workers raised huge families in basic conditions, are now sought-after urban pieds-à-terre.

Cross the bridge opposite the opera house, walk up Mulgrave St and turn left along narrow Dominick St until you reach a large, circular building. Built in 1855 and known as the **Firkin Crane** (a firkin is a wooden barrel, and a crane is a weighing device), this is where Cork's butter was weighed and packed for export (it now houses a dance centre).

BEST EVENTS IN CORK CITY

Cork World Book Fest
Huge literary festival in April that combines talks and readings by Irish and international writers with book stalls, music, street entertainment, workshops, film screenings and more.

Cork Harbour Festival
A week-long early June extravaganza of walks, talks, boat and bike tours, sailing, swimming, canoeing and stand-up paddleboarding, culminating in An Rás Mór (the Great Race), a mass rowing race from the harbour to the city centre.

Cork Midsummer Festival
A week-long arts festival in late June celebrating music, theatre, dance, literature and visual arts.

WHERE TO EAT IN CORK CITY

Ichigo Ichie
Michelin-starred Japanese restaurant immerses diners in *kappo* cuisine, where the chef prepares food as you watch. €€€

Glass Curtain
Understated, sophisticated dining experience devoted to the finest of Irish produce. €€

Quay Co-op
Famous for its inclusive atmosphere, this cafeteria offers a range of organic vegetarian dishes. €

St Anne's Church

Go around to the right and you'll find the neoclassical columns that adorn the facade of the **Old Butter Market**. Look out for the cow's head above the arched entrance. Cork had the largest butter market in the world during the 1860s, and the trade's history is told through the displays and dioramas of the **Cork Butter Museum** next door.

From here, head north along Exchange St to the tall clock tower at the junction with Church St. Shandon is dominated by the 1722 **St Anne's Church**, aka the 'Four-Faced Liar' – so called because each of the tower's four clocks used to tell a slightly different time. Wannabe campanologists can ring the **Shandon Bells** on the 1st floor of the Italianate clock tower and then continue up the 132 steps to the top for 360-degree views of the city.

BEST BARS IN CORK

Franciscan Well Bar & Brewery
Brews its own beer, best enjoyed in the enormous beer garden at the back. Holds regular beer festivals with other small independent Irish breweries.

Mutton Lane Inn
Tiny, inviting trad pub lit by candles and fairy lights, one of Cork's most intimate drinking holes.

Sin É
Everything a craic-filled pub should be: long on atmosphere and short on pretension, with live music almost every night.

Rising Sons
Huge red-brick building housing an award-winning microbrewery; try their lip-smacking trademark stout, MiDaza.

GETTING AROUND

Cork city centre is easy enough to get around on foot, with most sights lying within 20 minutes walking distance of Emmet Place, the pedestrianised main shopping square. If you need to get further afield, the city bus network is comprehensive.

Although Cork has a bike-sharing scheme (run by TFI Bikes), cycling is not good for navigating the city centre, as the network of bike lanes is fragmented and too often shared with buses or other motorised traffic.

On-street parking requires either the Park by Phone app or scratch-card parking discs available from many city centre shops. Be warned – traffic wardens are ferociously efficient. The central area has several signposted car parks, which charge by the hour. See also Black Ash Park & Ride (p188).

Beyond Cork City

Whether you're a nature lover, history buff or connoisseur of fine food, you'll find something to inspire you beyond Cork's city limits.

Cork city's hinterland is a treasure trove of foodie towns par excellence. The picturesque yachting harbour of Kinsale is famed for its seafood, while aficionados of a particularly fine Irish whiskey will recognise the name Midleton – the main reason to linger in this bustling market town is to visit the old Jameson whiskey distillery, along with a meal at one of the town's famously good restaurants. The surrounding region of East Cork is full of pretty villages and home to Ballymaloe House, the fountainhead of Irish gastronomy.

Cobh, on the other hand, is more famous for history than cuisine – this was *Titanic*'s last port of call before its disastrous maiden voyage.

TOP TIP

It's possible to stay in Cork city and make day trips to Cobh and Midleton by train and to Kinsale by bus.

Kinsale

Charles Fort (p196)

Hang Out in a Picturesque Harbour Town
Shopping And Seafood In Kinsale

The yachting harbour of **Kinsale** (Cionn tSáile), 25km south of Cork city, is one of many colourful gems strung along the coastline of County Cork. Narrow, winding streets lined with galleries, gift shops, lively bars and superb restaurants sit beside a handsome natural harbour guarded by a huge 17th-century fortress.

Take a boat trip with **Kinsale Harbour Cruises** or join **Dermot Ryan** for a one-hour walking tour of the town. Browse the boutiques along Main St: **Granny's Bottom Drawer** for Irish linen, woollens, leather goods and vintage-style homewares; **Giles Norman Gallery** for evocative black-and-white landscape photographs; and **Prim's Bookshop** for a treasure trove of interesting titles.

Kinsale has been labelled the seafood capital of southwest Ireland, and for such a small place, it certainly packs more than its fair share of international-standard restaurants. Most are within easy walking distance of the town centre, and you can eat well on any budget.

BEST PLACES TO EAT IN KINSALE

Fishy Fishy
One of the most famous seafood restaurants in the country; all the fish is caught locally. €€€

Black Pig Wine Bar
Mouth-watering menu of gourmet tapas and cheese and charcuterie platters sourced from local suppliers. €€

Bastion
Michelin-starred but a relaxed and informal entry into the world of haute cuisine. €€€

St Francis Provisions
Minuscule but mighty, with superb seafood and vegetarian dishes. €€

WHERE TO STAY IN EAST CORK

Knockeven House
Splendid Victorian guesthouse in Cobh with huge bedrooms done out with period furniture. €€

Ballymaloe House Hotel
Rooms decorated with period furnishings; breakfast includes bread from its own bakery and eggs from the farm. €€€

An Stór Townhouse
Midleton accommodation straddling the boundary between upmarket hostel and budget guesthouse. €€

I LIVE HERE: BEST THINGS TO DO IN KINSALE

Giles and **Catherine Norman** run the Giles Norman Gallery and Townhouse in Kinsale. Giles is one of Ireland's leading landscape photographers. (instagram.com/gilesnorman)

A perfect day in Kinsale starts with breakfast at **OHK Café**, followed by a relaxing stroll along **Scilly Walk**, which brings you to the spectacular **Charles Fort**. After you've experienced the fort's panoramic views, enjoy lunch by the sea at the **Bulman Bar** and then head back towards the town along the High Rd for more incredible views. Spend a couple of hours exploring Kinsale's many independent shops and galleries. End the day at **The Black Pig**, which has a delicious tapas-style menu and an incredible wine list.

Learn About the Lusitania
Maritime Museum And Viewpoint

The 200-year-old **Old Head Signal Tower** sits atop a prominent headland 13km south of Kinsale via the R604. It was built during the Napoleonic Wars as part of a network of 81 signal towers around the Irish coast, an early warning system in case of a French invasion.

The tower houses a museum dedicated to the **RMS Lusitania**, which was torpedoed by a German U-boat in 1915, with the loss of 1200 lives. You can walk to the nearby clifftops for impressive views south towards the Old Head, the nearest point of land to the disaster; a privately owned golf club prevents you from reaching the lighthouse at the tip of the headland.

Waterfront Walk to a 17th-Century Fortress
Seaside Views And Military History

You haven't 'done' Kinsale until you've done the **Scilly Walk**, a lovely coastal trail that leads to **Charles Fort**. One of Europe's best-preserved star-shaped artillery forts, this vast 17th-century fortification would be worth a visit for its spectacular views alone. But there's much more for you here: the 18th- and 19th-century ruins inside the walls make for some fascinating wandering.

Built in the 1670s to guard Kinsale Harbour, the fort was in use until 1921, when much of it was destroyed as the British withdrew. Displays explain the typically tough lives led by the soldiers who served here and the comparatively comfortable lives of the officers. Return along High Rd – this is Kinsale's '**Golden Mile**', lined with millionaires' holiday homes and superb views over the harbour (6km round trip).

Irish Whiskey at the Source
Distillery Tour And Tasting

The charming market town of Midleton, 20km east of Cork, is best known as the home of the **Old Jameson Whiskey Distillery**, where the art of creating world-famous Jameson Irish whiskey is brought vividly to life.

Coachloads of visitors pour into the 200-year-old distillery buildings (Jameson is today made in a nearby modern distillery), and 75-minute tours explain the process of converting barley into whiskey, leading past the old grain stores, malting floors and copper stills, including the world's largest pot

---

WHERE TO STAY IN KINSALE

Giles Norman Townhouse
Plush guest rooms with elegant bathrooms, espresso machines and a discount at the downstairs gallery. €€€

Old Presbytery
Luxury apartments set in a gorgeously refurbished 18th-century Georgian townhouse. €€€

Pier House
Pristine rooms, some opening to balconies with garden and harbour views. No breakfast. €€

Cobh

still, built in 1825. The tour ends with a tasting session, comparing Jameson with Scotch and bourbon.

The old distillery is undergoing a major restoration leading up to its 200th anniversary in 2025; until then, some parts of the site may be off limits.

Discover Cobh's Titanic Heritage
Historic Harbour Town

Cobh (pronounced 'cove') is a charming waterfront town 23km east of Cork city, dotted with brightly coloured houses and overlooked by a splendid cathedral. It's a far cry from the harrowing decades during and after the Great Famine – from 1848 to 1950, no fewer than 2.5 million emigrants passed through. Cobh (then called Queenstown) was also the final port of call for the RMS *Titanic*.

The original White Star Line offices on Cobh waterfront, where 123 passengers embarked on (and one lucky soul absconded from) *Titanic*, now house the **Titanic Experience**, which provides a powerful insight into the ill-fated liner's first and final voyage in 1912. You can find more exhibits on *Titanic* at the nearby **Cobh Heritage Centre**, an interactive museum that chronicles Irish emigration across the Atlantic in the wake of the Great Famine.

BEST PLACES TO EAT BEYOND CORK CITY

Seasalt
Cobh cafe run by a Ballymaloe-trained chef bringing fresh local produce to brunch dishes such as Gubbeen chorizo hash. €

Farmgate Restaurant
Sister establishment to Cork city's Farmgate Cafe, this Midleton branch offers the same superb blend of traditional and modern Irish cuisine. €€

Ballymaloe Cafe
Always-busy cafe next to Ballymaloe House Hotel serving freshly prepared seasonal and organic produce from its own farms and gardens (and elsewhere in County Cork). €€

WHERE TO GET A COFFEE IN KINSALE

Lemon Leaf
Popular local cafe with garden courtyard at the back serving an extensive breakfast menu.

Poet's Corner
Cheerful cafe and book exchange; great cakes, coffee and huge toasted sandwiches.

Diva Boutique Bakery
Takeaway coffee, pastries and artisan baked goods at Ballinspittle, 8km west of Kinsale.

THE GOURMET HEARTLAND OF BALLYMALOE

Drawing up at the Allen family's wisteria-clad **Ballymaloe House**, 12km southeast of Midleton, you know you've arrived somewhere special. **Myrtle Allen** (1924–2018) was a legend in her own lifetime, acclaimed internationally for her nearly single-handed creation of fine Irish cooking. The menu at Ballymaloe's celebrated **restaurant** changes daily to reflect the availability of produce from its own farms and other local sources, while the **Ballymaloe Cafe** serves freshly prepared seasonal lunches, including tasty quiche, salads, sandwiches and daily specials.

TV personality Darina Allen, daughter-in-law of the late Myrtle, runs the famous **Ballymaloe Cookery School**, 3km east of Ballymaloe House. Darina's own daughter-in-law, Rachel Allen, a high-profile TV chef and author, regularly teaches at the school.

Spike Island

Sail to an Island Fortress
Harbour Cruise And Open-Air Museum

Spike Island lies low and green in Cork Harbour, clearly visible from Cobh. It was once an important part of the port's defences, topped by a huge 18th-century artillery fort that commanded the harbour entrance. In the second half of the 19th century, during the Irish War of Independence and from 1984 to 2004, it served as a prison, gaining the nickname 'Ireland's Alcatraz'.

A trip to Spike Island begins with a 12-minute **boat trip** across the harbour, departing from Kennedy Pier in the middle of Cobh waterfront (book tickets online; ferry and guided tour included in admission price). On arrival, you get a guided walking tour of the **former prison buildings**, the old punishment block, the shell store (once used as a children's prison) and No 2 Bastion with its massive 6in gun. You're then free to explore on your own.

Highlights include the **Gun Park**, with a good display of mostly 20th-century artillery; the **Mitchell Hall**, with an exhibit on the SS *Aud,* a German ship loaded with arms for the 1916 Easter Rising that was sunk in the entrance to Cork Harbour; and the **Glacis Walk**, a 1.5km trail that leads around the walls of the fortress, with great views of Cobh town and the harbour entrance. You'll need around four hours to make the most of a visit.

If you're arriving by car, park either in the cathedral car park on Cathedral Pl or the Five Foot Way car park west of the town centre. There's a cafe and toilets on the island.

WHERE TO DRINK IN KINSALE

Bulman Bar
Enjoy chilled white wine at outdoor tables or beers in the wood-panelled interior.

Spaniard Bar
An old pub with a peat fire in winter; on sunny days, outdoor tables have views across the harbour.

Dalton's Bar
Cosy little pub with a roaring fire and live traditional music sessions on weekday evenings.

YOUGHAL TOWN WALKING TOUR

The ancient seaport of Youghal (pronounced 'yawl') has a rich history that may not be instantly apparent. The town was a hotbed of rebellion against the English in the 16th century when Sir Walter Raleigh was mayor here in 1588–89. Oliver Cromwell wintered here in 1649 as he tried to quell insurgency among the pesky Irish.

Starting from the **1 tourist office** head inland along Quay Lane to reach the curious **2 Clock Gate Tower** astride Main St. It was built in 1777 and served as a town gate, clock tower and jail. Several prisoners taken in the 1798 Rising were hanged from its windows. Continue north on Main St to the beautifully proportioned **3 Red House**, designed in 1706 by Dutch architect Leuventhen. Across the road is the 15th-century tower house **4 Tynte's Castle**, which originally had a defensive riverfront position.

A few doors further along are six **5 almshouses** built by the first Earl of Cork in 1610. Turn left on Church St, and at the end is 13th-century **6 St Mary's Collegiate Church**, which incorporates elements of an earlier Danish church dating from the 11th century. Hidden behind high walls to the north of the church, 15th- to 18th-century **7 Myrtle Grove** (not open to the public) is the former home of Sir Walter Raleigh and a rare Irish example of a late medieval Tudor-style house. The churchyard is bounded to the west by a fine stretch of the **8 old town wall**. Follow the parapet until you can go down a set of stairs to the outer side and then enter the next gate along to descend back to Main St through the 17th-century **9 College Gardens**, now restored and in use as a public park.

The Secrets of Smoking Salmon
Artisan Smokehouse

No trip to Cork is complete without a visit to an artisan food producer, and the effervescent Frank Hederman is more than happy to show you around **Belvelly Smoke House**, 19km east of Cork on the R624 towards Cobh. Belvelly is the oldest traditional smokehouse in Ireland – indeed, the only surviving one.

Seafood, cheese and butter are smoked here, but the speciality is fish, particularly mackerel and salmon. Belvelly uses only salmon that has been organically farmed in Ireland or harvested from a small, sustainable wild salmon fishery in County Cork. In a traditional process that takes 24 hours, the fish is filleted and cured before being hung to smoke over beech woodchips. The result is subtle and delectable.

Call ahead to arrange a tour of the smokehouse (Fridays only, minimum two people) or drop by any time to buy produce. Alternatively, stop by the Hederman stall at Cork's English Market (p190) or at the Cobh or Midleton farmers markets.

Kiss the Blarney Stone
Get The Gift Of The Gab

If you need proof of the power of a good yarn, then join the queue to get into **Blarney Castle**, 8km northwest of Cork, one of Ireland's most popular tourist attractions. Everyone's here, of course, to plant their lips on the **Blarney Stone**, which supposedly gives one the gift of the gab, a cliché that has entered every lexicon and tourist guidebook.

The Blarney Stone is perched at the top of a climb up claustrophobic spiral staircases. On the battlements, you bend backwards over a long, long drop (with a safety grill and attendant to prevent tragedy) to kiss the stone (post-COVID it gets sprayed with disinfectant between visitors); as your shirt rides up, coachloads of onlookers stare up your nose. Once you're upright again, don't forget to admire the stunning views before descending.

The famous stone aside, Blarney Castle itself is an impressive 16th-century tower set in gorgeous grounds. Escape the crowds on a walk around the **Fern Garden** and **Arboretum**, investigate toxic plants in the Harry Potterish **Poison Garden**, or explore the landscaped nooks and crannies of the **Rock Close**.

BEST FARMERS MARKETS

Cork is a hotbed of Ireland's 'eat local' food scene.

Midleton Farmers Market (9am to 1pm Saturdays) is one of Ireland's oldest and best, with bushels of local produce on offer. It's behind the big roundabout at the north end of Main St.

Cobh Farmers Market (10am to 2pm Friday) takes place on the waterfront, where a range of stalls offer a choice of fresh produce along with flowers and local crafts.

Kinsale Farmers Market (10am to 2pm Wednesdays) sets up on the square across from the tourist office; this is the place to buy artisan foods straight from the producer.

GETTING AROUND

Hourly buses run to Kinsale from Cork train and bus stations via Cork Airport. The bus stop in Kinsale is on Pier Rd near the tourist office. Both Midleton and Cobh are on the same railway line, with trains to and from Cork city every 30 minutes, making it possible to combine the two in a single day trip (eg Spike Island in the morning and Jameson distillery in the afternoon, or vice versa). Once there, you can easily get around Kinsale, Cobh or Midleton on foot.

CLONAKILTY

Cheerful, brightly painted Clonakilty is a bustling market town that serves as a hub for the scores of beguiling villages strung out along the West Cork coast. You'll find smart B&Bs, good restaurants and cosy pubs alive with music. Little waterways coursing through town add to the charm.

Clonakilty is famous for two things: it's the birthplace of Irish Free State commander-in-chief Michael Collins (1890–1922), embodied in a large statue on the corner of Emmet Sq and in two fascinating museums; and it's the home of the most famous black pudding in the country, mixed from a secret recipe in a factory on the edge of town.

Streets converge on Astna Sq, dominated by a 1798 Rising monument. Also in the square is the Kilty Stone, a piece of the original castle that gave Clonakilty – Cloich na Coillte in Irish, meaning 'castle of the woods' – its name.

TOP TIP

Clonakilty's compact farmers market combines local produce, such as black pudding, Baltimore bacon, Dunmanway free-range eggs and Inchydoney honey, with crafts like handmade candles and seaweed soaps, and hot-food stalls. It sets up in Emmet Sq from 9am to 3pm on Fridays.

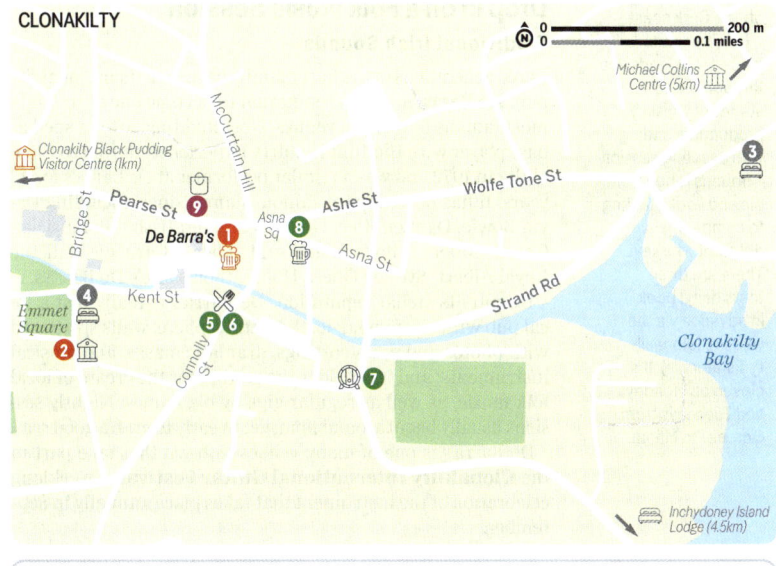

HIGHLIGHTS
1. De'Barra's

SIGHTS
2. Michael Collins House

SLEEPING
3. Bay View House
4. Emmet Hotel

EATING
5. Pike Deli
6. Scannells

DRINKING & NIGHTLIFE
7. Clonakilty Distillery
8. Craft & Co

NIGHTLIFE
9. Edward Twomey

CLONAKILTY DISTILLERY

A giant sculpture of a whale's tail marks the site of the state-of-the-art **Clonakilty Distillery**, established in 2016 by the local Scully family, who have farmed here for nine generations. It produces triple-distilled single pot still Irish whiskey made with grain grown on the owners' family farm nearby, as well as Minke brand gin and vodka. (Minke whales are common off the Cork coast.)

The 75-minute guided tour leads you through the various stages of whiskey production, ending with a tasting session – options range from gin and vodka tasting to comparing five different whiskeys. There are three tours daily; book in advance via the website (clonakiltydistillery.ie). It's closed on Mondays and Tuesdays from October to March.

Michael Collins Centre

Drop in on a Folk Music Session
Traditional Irish Sounds

Three generations of the Barry family have seen their Clonakilty pub, **De Barra's**, rise in reputation to become one of Ireland's most famous folk music venues. Noel Redding, after a spell as bass player with the Jimi Hendrix Experience, moved to Clonakilty in 1972 and was a regular performer at De Barra's for 20 years. It has hosted many famous names since, including David Bowie, Damien Rice, George Ezra and Irish folk musician Christy Moore, who famously said, 'There's Carnegie Hall, the Royal Albert, Sydney Opera House, then there's De Barra's...'.

Despite its stellar reputation, De Barra's is really just a local pub with a convivial, jostling atmosphere, walls splattered with photos and press cuttings, dramatic masks, and musical instruments, and it provides the setting for the cream of local folk music, as well as regular gigs by big names. Nightly sessions usually begin around 9pm; get in early to grab a good seat.

De Barra's is one of many venues in town that take part in the **Clonakilty International Guitar Festival**, a weeklong celebration of the instrument that takes place annually in September.

WHERE TO STAY IN CLONAKILTY

Bay View House
Spacious modern villa offers immaculate B&B accommodation, a genial welcome and great breakfasts. €€

Inchydoney Island Lodge
A seawater spa, plus luxurious rooms overlooking the ocean from private balconies; 5km south of Clonakilty. €€€

Emmet Hotel
Lovely Georgian hotel on the elegant main square mixes period charm with the perks of a modern hotel. €€

Immerse Yourself in Irish History
Museums And Storytelling

Born on a farm just outside Clonakilty, Michael Collins is one of County Cork's most famous sons. He played a central role in the War of Independence with Britain and in 1922 became commander-in-chief of the army of the newly founded Irish Free State. He lived for a time on Emmet Sq in Clonakilty town centre, where the **Michael Collins House** museum now sits. Videos, artefacts and interactive displays, along with passionate and knowledgeable staff, lead you through Collins' life and his importance in modern Irish history.

A visit to the **Michael Collins Centre**, signposted off the R600 to Timoleague 7km east of Clonakilty, is an excellent way to make sense of his life and the times in which he lived. A session with a storytelling guide reveals photos, letters and a reconstruction of the 1920s country lane where Collins was killed, complete with an armoured vehicle. Shows take place three times a day in July and August, less frequently in June and September, and must be booked in advance.

The Secret of Black Pudding
Local Food Speciality

Clonakilty's most treasured export is its black pudding, a sausage made from beef mince, blood, oatmeal and onion that features on most local restaurant menus. A self-guided audio tour of the **Clonakilty Black Pudding Visitor Centre**, on the western edge of town, leads you through the history of this famous speciality, based on an original recipe from the 1880s. After a glimpse into the factory where it is made, you get to taste a selection of the company's black pudding, white pudding, sausage and bacon.

If you are going no further than the town centre, the best place to buy Clonakilty black pudding is from butcher **Edward Twomey** on Pearse St.

BEST PLACES TO EAT IN CLONAKILTY

Scannells
Cosy gastropub with a flower-filled beer garden at the back; serves superb steak sandwiches and seafood chowder. €€

Pike Deli
This busy artisan bakery and deli turns out fresh breads, savoury tarts, pastries and pies to take away. Closed Sundays and Mondays. €

Craft & Co
Tables spill out onto the town square from this popular pub, the ideal spot to tuck into its delicious tacos and nachos. €

GETTING AROUND

The centre of Clonakilty has narrow streets and a one-way system. If you're arriving by car, park in Deasy's public car park on the N71 south of the town centre – it's just five minutes walk away from the distillery, Michael Collins House and the town centre.

You can easily reach all the in-town attractions on foot, but you'll need your own wheels to visit the Michael Collins Centre, Inchydoney and the Black Pudding Visitor Centre.

Beyond Clonakilty

Dive into west Cork: watch humpback whales breaching offshore and sunsets over Baltimore harbour, and kayak beneath the stars.

The West Cork coast begins the slow build-up of scenic beauty that culminates in County Kerry to the west, but what you find here is already enough to have you reaching for the camera. Picturesque villages, ancient stone circles and fine sandy beaches mark the meandering coastal route from Kinsale to Clonakilty and on to Skibbereen and Baltimore. Rather than follow the main N71 road, take the R600 and explore the maze of minor roads along the coast, perfect for aimless wandering.

West Cork is famed for its fine food, which is celebrated in farmers markets and food festivals throughout the region. Seafood is a speciality here – don't miss the opportunity to sample whatever is fresh from the quayside.

TOP TIP

In County Cork pubs, locally brewed Murphy's and Beamish stouts, not Guinness, are the preferred pints.

Fastnet Rock (p207)

Bridge House B&B

Learn About the Great Famine
Historic Town And Heritage Centre

The town of **Skibbereen** (Sciobairín), 30km west of Clonakilty, is a pleasant, workaday market town, with an attractive, upmarket centre on the banks of the River Ilen. During the Famine, however, Skibb was hit perhaps harder than any other town in Ireland, with huge numbers of the local population emigrating or dying of starvation or disease.

Skibbereen Heritage Centre houses a haunting exhibition about the Famine, with audio of actors reading heartbreaking contemporary accounts. A visit here puts Irish history into harrowing perspective. A kilometre west of town, beside the N71 road towards Schull, is **Abbeystrewry Famine Cemetery**, which contains the mass grave of 8000 to 10,000 local people who died during the Famine, marked by a memorial of polished black stone.

Lord Dufferin and GF Boyle, who journeyed from Oxford to Skibbereen in 1847 to see if reports of the Famine were true, reported: 'The accounts are not exaggerated – they cannot be exaggerated – nothing more frightful can be conceived'. Their eyewitness account makes horrific reading, and Dufferin was so appalled by what he saw that he contributed £1000 (about €100,000 in today's money) to the relief effort.

BEST PLACES TO EAT IN SKIBBEREEN & BALTIMORE

Dillon's Corner
You can be sure that the food served at Skibbereen's artisan bakery and restaurant uses locally sourced produce in its inventive pasta dishes, salads and sourdough sandwiches. Closed Mondays. €€

Antiquity Cafe
Skibbereen's first all-vegan eatery puts a lot of thought into its food, so you can expect more than just salad. The icing on the vegan cake? It's also a bookshop. €

Dede at the Customs House
Baltimore gets two Michelin stars for Turkish chef Ahmet Dede and a tasting menu that explodes with intriguing and exciting flavours. Book two months in advance; closed Monday to Wednesday. €€€

WHERE TO STAY BEYOND CLONAKILTY

Bridge House B&B
Mona Best's Skibbereen B&B is a work of art, filled with Victorian tableaux and period memorabilia. €€

Rolf's Country House
Upmarket B&B in a restored and extended farmhouse in restful gardens on the upper fringes of Baltimore. €€

Casey's of Baltimore
Most of the rooms in this super-comfortable hotel have sea views, as does its popular seafood restaurant. €€€

WHALE WATCHING

The waters off the coast of West Cork famously offer some of the best whale watching in the country. The most frequently spotted species include common dolphin, grey seal and harbour seal, but the big draws are **Minke whales** and **humpback whales**, which start to appear in April, with numbers peaking in May and June. Watching humpbacks breach is an unforgettable sight. **Fin whales**, the second largest species on the planet, can be seen later in summer.

Cork Whale Watch runs four-hour trips in a comfortable twin-hulled boat, departing daily, weather permitting, from Reen Pier, 4km south of Union Hall. Successful whale spotting is highly weather dependent, and trips can be cancelled if the wind is too strong or visibility too poor.

Lough Hyne

Enjoy Midnight Kayaking on Lough Hyne
Marine Nature Reserve

Lough Hyne, 8km southwest of Skibbereen, is one of Ireland's natural wonders and became the country's first marine nature reserve in 1981. Its glacier-gouged depths were originally filled with fresh water until rising sea levels breached one end around 4000 years ago. It is now linked to the sea by a narrow tidal channel known as the Rapids, where the tide pours in and out twice a day in a rush of white water.

Atlantic Sea Kayaking offers guided sea-kayak tours of the lough, including superbly atmospheric 2½-hour 'starlight paddles' after dark. On these trips, you are almost guaranteed to experience marine phosphorescence – bioluminescent plankton in the seawater emit sparkles of greenish light when disturbed by your kayak paddle, a truly magical experience. Tours last from around 9.30pm to midnight and are suitable for beginners.

There are also lovely walks along the loughside road and in the neighbouring **Knockomagh Wood Nature Reserve**. A waymarked nature trail leads up a steep hill through the forest, and you're rewarded with stunning views at the top.

WHERE TO EAT & DRINK BEYOND CLONAKILTY

Kalbo's Cafe
Skibbereen cafe using local produce in tasty breakfast and lunch dishes. Closed Sundays and Mondays. €

Glandore Inn
Picture-postcard views over the harbour from outdoor tables, and fresh seafood from Union Hall across the water. €€

Algiers Inn
Historic Baltimore pub with a pirate theme and a US-influenced gastropub menu. €€

Go Camping on a Hilltop Farm
Explore Off The Beaten Track

Top of the Rock Pod Pairc is a gorgeous campsite set on a remote farm near Drimoleague, 14km north of Skibbereen. Its hilltop location is a haven of peace, offering grand views of the Mullaghmesha hills. Goats, lambs, ducks and chickens wander freely, and the friendly owners offer free tours of the farm where kids can feed and pet the animals. As well as tent sites and a couple of campervan pitches, there are seven comfortable camping pods and a cute two-person caravan. A campfire is lit at 7pm most nights for socialising around.

The area to the north is laced with hiking trails, some of which you can begin right from the campsite. One of the more intriguing hikes is the **Glanaclohy Loop Walk**, leading from the impressive ruined tower of Castledonovan into the hills where you will find the **House of George the Sky**, the ruins of a farmhouse built way above the valley floor.

Take a Cruise to Cape Clear
Island Boat Trip

With its lonely inlets, pebble beaches, and gorse- and heather-clad cliffs, **Cape Clear Island** (Oileán Chléire) is an escapist's heaven – albeit one that is only 5km long and just over 1.5km wide at its broadest point. But that's just as well, as you'll want time to appreciate this small, rugged Gaeltacht (Irish-speaking) area, the southernmost inhabited island in the country.

Information boards near the harbour highlight a couple of marked **walking trails**, while unmarked roads wander all over the island – bring your bike on the boat to make exploring them easier. The **Cape Clear Heritage Centre**, signposted 1km east of the ferry landing, has exhibits on the island's history and culture, and fine views north across the water to Mizen Head. The remains of a 12th-century **church** and **holy well** are near the pier, while on the coast to the west, the ruins of 14th-century **Dunamore Castle**, the stronghold of the O'Driscoll clan, can be seen perched on a rock.

Cape Clear is one of the top **birdwatching** spots in Ireland, known for its seabirds including Manx shearwater, guillemot, gannet, fulmar and kittiwake. Tens of thousands of migrating birds can pass hourly, especially in the early morning and at dusk. The best time of year for twitching here is October.

A **passenger ferry** makes the 45-minute crossing from Baltimore to Cape Clear Island three or four times a day in summer and twice a day in winter.

FASTNET ROCK

Named 'Ireland's Teardrop' because it was the last sight of the 'ould country' for emigrants sailing to America, **Fastnet Rock** is the southernmost point of Ireland.

This isolated fang of rock, topped by a spectacular lighthouse built in 1904, stands 6.5km southwest of Cape Clear Island, and in good weather is visible from many places on the coastline, from Baltimore to Mizen Head. Its image – usually with huge waves crashing around it – graces a thousand postcards, coffee-table books and framed art photographs.

From May to August, **Cape Clear Ferries** operates boat trips to the rock (no landing), departing from Baltimore (May to October) and Schull (June to August) via Cape Clear Island. Tours are weather dependent and last from 11am to 5pm, with two or three hours ashore on Cape Clear.

WHERE TO EAT & DRINK BEYOND CLONAKILTY

Bushe's Bar
Outdoor tables on Baltimore's main square are the best spot in town for a sundowner; famous crab sandwiches. €€

The Dock Wall
Union Hall pub with an outdoor, harbour-view terrace at the back and a sure hand with the seafood chowder. €€

Connolly's of Leap
Famous music pub on the main road 7km east of Skibbereen; also has a tempting menu of homemade pizza. €€

DROMBEG STONE CIRCLE

On an exposed hillside, with fields falling away towards the coast, the **Drombeg Stone Circle** is superbly atmospheric. Its 17 stones, oriented towards the winter solstice sunset, once guarded the cremated bones of an adolescent. The 9m diameter circle probably dates from the 5th century CE and is a sophisticated Iron Age update of an earlier Bronze Age monument.

Just beyond the stones are the remains of a hut and an Iron Age cooking pit, known as a *fulachta fiadh*. Experiments have shown that its heated rocks could boil water and keep it hot for nearly three hours, long enough to cook meat. To get here, take the signposted turn on the R597, approximately 4km west of Rosscarbery.

Be a Salty Seadog in Baltimore
Boats, Pirates And Castles

Baltimore is a classic maritime village, its sheltered anchorage filled with pleasure yachts in summer. The harbour has long been a favourite of mariners and was the haunt of pirates in the 17th century. The most infamous date in its history is 20 June 1631, when the village was sacked by a fleet of Barbary pirates who carried off more than 100 prisoners to a life of slavery. The remaining villagers fled to Skibbereen, and Baltimore lay abandoned for many decades afterwards.

The village is dominated by the stone tower of the 13th-century castle of **Dun na Sead** (Fort of the Jewels). Inside, the great hall houses seasonal art displays and exhibits on the town's piratical history, but the main attraction is the view from the battlements.

The focus of life here is the **central terrace** overlooking the harbour, the ideal spot to sup a pint or slurp an ice cream while watching the boats go by. All around spreads a multitude of holiday cottages, catering to the summer swell of sailing folk, sea anglers, divers, and visitors to nearby Sherkin and Cape Clear Islands.

The best time to turn up is the last weekend in May when the **Baltimore Seafood & Wooden Boat Festival** provides a showcase for local seafood while traditional wooden sailboats race around the harbour.

If you fancy getting out on the water yourself, **Baltimore Sea Safari** runs trips in a fast rigid-hulled inflatable boat along the West Cork coast to see sea cliffs and wildlife, including whales and dolphins. **Aquaventures** also runs boat trips and rents out gear (including wetsuits) for confident, go-it-alone snorkellers (maps and advice supplied).

A white-painted landmark beacon called **Lot's Wife** stands on the headland 2km southwest of town, marking the entrance to Baltimore Harbour and making a good objective for a pleasant walk, especially at sunset.

Lot's Wife

GETTING AROUND

Cork city is as close as you'll get by train, but frequent bus services go along the N71 to Clonakilty and Skibbereen. However, you'll need your own transport for exploring the more interesting nooks and crannies further inland and along the minor coastal roads.

BANTRY

Framed by the Sheep's Head hills and the craggy Caha Mountains, magnificent and sprawling Bantry Bay is one of the country's most attractive seascapes. Sheltered by islands at the head of the bay, Bantry town is neat and respectable, with narrow streets of old-fashioned independent shops, lively traditional pubs, a choice of excellent seafood restaurants and a picturesque waterfront.

Pride of place goes to the splendid Georgian mansion of Bantry House, the former home of Richard White, who earned his place in history when, in 1798, he warned authorities of the imminent landing of Irish patriot Wolfe Tone and his French fleet, in support of the United Irishmen's rebellion. In the end, storms prevented the fleet from landing, and the course of Irish history was definitively altered. All Wolfe Tone got for his troubles was a square and a statue bearing his name.

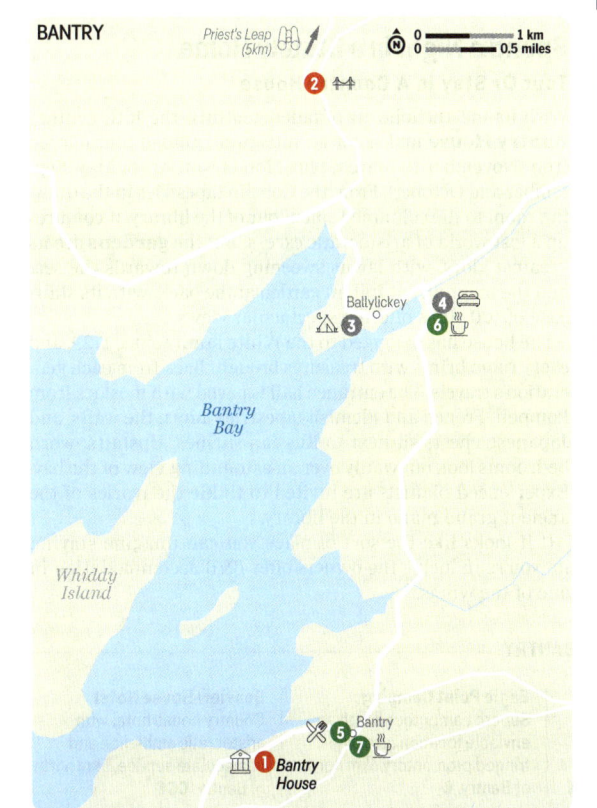

TOP TIP

Much of Bantry's income and employment derives from seafood. You'll see Bantry Bay mussels on menus in the town's many seafood restaurants and throughout County Cork. Bantry's weekly market sets up in Wolfe Tone Sq every Friday from 9.30am to 1pm.

HIGHLIGHTS
1. Bantry House

SIGHTS
2. Coomhola Bridge

SLEEPING
3. Eagle Point Camping
4. Seaview House Hotel

EATING
5. Fish Kitchen

DRINKING & NIGHTLIFE
6. Manning's Emporium
7. West Cafe-Wine Bar

BEST PLACES TO EAT IN BANTRY

West Cafe-Wine Bar
Good coffee, lush breakfasts and Sunday brunch; the bar opens late Thursday to Sunday with a tempting tapas menu. €€

Fish Kitchen
Friendly, unfussy little restaurant above a fishmonger's shop does freshly caught local seafood to perfection. Closed Sundays and Mondays. €€

Manning's Emporium
Grab a menu, choose a table and order at the counter at this gourmet deli and cafe; cheese and charcuterie platters are the best way to sample local artisan produce. Closed Tuesday. €€

Bantry House

Spend a Night in a Stately Home
Tour Or Stay In A Country House

With its melancholic air of faded gentility, the 18th-century **Bantry House** makes for an intriguing guided tour (closed from November to March, plus Mondays in April, May, September and October). From the Gobelin tapestries in the drawing room to the columned splendour of the library, it conjures up a lost world of aristocratic excess. But the **gardens** are its greatest glory, with lawns sweeping down towards the sea, and the magnificent Italian garden at the back, with its staircase of 100 steps offering spectacular views.

The house has belonged to the White family since 1729, and every room brims with treasures brought back from each generation's travels. The entrance hall is paved with mosaics from Pompeii, French and Flemish tapestries adorn the walls, and Japanese chests sit next to Russian shrines. Upstairs, worn bedrooms look out wanly over an astounding view of the bay. Experienced pianists are invited to tinkle the ivories of the ancient grand piano in the library.

If it looks like the sort of place you can imagine staying in, you're in luck – the owners offer B&B accommodation in one of the wings.

WHERE TO STAY IN BANTRY

Bantry House
The six guest bedrooms in this stately home are decorated with antiques and contemporary furnishings. €€€

Eagle Point Camping
Superb campground with an enviable location on a pine-fringed promontory 6km north of Bantry. €

Seaview House Hotel
Country house hotel with aristocratic ambience and immaculate service, 5km north of Bantry. €€€

Hike, Bike or Drive the Priest's Leap

Spectacular Mountain Road

If you're a faint-hearted driver, don't even think about heading up the vertiginous, single-track road to **Priest's Leap** (Léim an tSagairt), 15km north of Bantry. In fact, if your GPS points you this way, think again. If you're feeling intrepid, however, this wild ride – the original 400-year-old route between Bantry and Kenmare – rewards the brave with monumental views across the mountains to Bantry Bay.

From Bantry, take the N71 north for 8km and turn right after the bridge at the head of the bay. Keep the river on your right for 1.7km to **Coomhola Bridge**, but don't cross the bridge – turn left and then take the first right (signposted 'Priest's Leap'). A long straight gets increasingly steep before relenting a bit. There are big drops on the left and few passing places on the final climb to the small parking area at the top. You can complete a circular route by descending the far side to **Bonane**, on the main N71 road 11km south of Kenmare, and returning to Bantry (not suitable for motorhomes or caravans).

The road has long been a classic challenge for **cyclists**, climbing almost 400m in 4.5km, and it's exceptionally steep (15%) in parts. Any fit rider will make it to the top, but unless your thighs are Tour de France material, you'll be off and pushing the bike at three or four places. A mountain bike is recommended as you'll need that bottom gear, and the road surface is uneven in places with a grass strip in the middle. Make sure your brakes are in good order for the descent!

It's also possible to **hike** up the road. If you park at Coomhola Bridge, it's a straightforward, if steep, 6km walk to the top. Allow 1½ hours each way. The summit of the pass is marked by a memorial stone and a wind-buffeted crucifix.

Priest's Leap

LEGEND OF THE PRIEST'S LEAP

The story goes that around the start of the 17th century, Father James Archer was rallying Cork and Kerry's clans to resist the English. Enemy troops spotted him on the old road to Kerry and gave chase until he and his horse leapt from the top of the pass and escaped to Bantry. The spot where he is supposed to have landed is marked by a **memorial plaque** at the side of the main road just south of Lidl supermarket on the north edge of Bantry.

GETTING AROUND

Bantry is a small town, so you'll have no trouble getting around on foot. Although Bantry House has a large car park, you can walk to the house from the town centre in 15 minutes using the arched pedestrian entrance on the Quay between the cinema and the estate office.

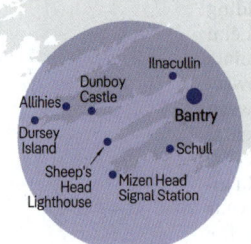

Beyond Bantry

Get your walking boots on – Cork's far west peninsulas and islands are laced with hiking trails.

Bantry is the jumping-off point for exploring County Cork's so-called 'far west peninsulas' – Mizen Head and Sheep's Head to the southwest and Beara to the northwest. Each has a distinct identity and atmosphere. The Mizen is mostly green and lush, with heathery hills backing the yachting harbour of Schull. The long, narrow finger of the Sheep's Head is more barren and rocky, with steep hills and narrow roads, but with a rugged charm all of its own. The Beara is the biggest of all. Its intricate coast and sharp-featured mountains are a geologist's paradise of exposed and contorted rock strata, making for dramatic scenery at almost every turn.

TOP TIP

Bring binoculars – there's every chance of spotting whales and dolphins from shore at places such as Mizen Head and Sheep's Head.

Ilnacullen (p216)

Mizen Head

Mix with the Yachting Crowd
Pretty harbour village

From Skibbereen, the N71 rolls west through Ballydehob, from where the R592 leads southwest to the pretty yachting harbour of **Schull** (pronounced 'skull'). Attracted by the deep-pocketed sailing crowd, local creatives have turned this former fishing village into a buzzing little hotspot, crammed with craft shops and art galleries.

Stroll the main street and drop into **Newman's West** for a glass of wine or **Hackett's Bar** for a pint of stout and a crab sandwich. Schull hosts the lively **Fastnet Film Festival** in late May, when 500 short films from more than 40 countries are entered into competition. In late August, the town is filled with sailors for five days of yacht and dinghy racing, jokingly named **Calves Week** (a smaller version of England's more famous Cowes Week), culminating in a weekend regatta that includes an outdoor market, children's sports, crab-fishing competitions and a fireworks display.

Brave the Bridge at Mizen Head
Spectacular Sea Cliffs

On a clear day, the road west from Schull enjoys great views out to Cape Clear Island and the Fastnet lighthouse. The landscape

THREE CASTLE HEAD HIKE

The remote cape immediately to the north of Mizen Head is the site of one of Ireland's most unusual medieval structures, a curtain wall with three towers that combines with a lake and sea cliffs to fortify an entire headland. Constructed in 1207, **Dunlough Castle** – its three towers give the headland its name – once commanded the sea route along the coast and was occupied by the O'Mahony family until 1627.

A pleasant 30-minute **walk** across sheep pastures leads to the castle from a car park at the end of the minor road beyond the Mizen Head turnoff. The path crosses private land and is closed from mid-January to April. No dogs allowed.

WHERE TO STAY BEYOND BANTRY

Dzogchen Beara
Buddhist meditation centre with self-catering cottages, hostel and cafe, 9km southwest of Castletownbere. **€**

Gallán Mór
Gorgeous boutique B&B halfway between Durrus and Ahakista. Minimum two-night stay; closed October to February. **€€**

Eccles Hotel
At the east end of Glengarriff, this historic hotel has counted George Bernard Shaw and WB Yeats as former guests. **€€€**

becomes wilder around Goleen, where narrowing roads run out to a dead end at the impressive cliffs of Mizen Head itself.

Completed in 1909 to help warn ships off the rocks, **Mizen Head signal station** is perched high above crashing waves and contorted sea cliffs on a small island connected to the mainland by a dizzying 45m-high footbridge. From the visitor centre, it's a 10-minute walk via 99 steps to reach the station, which houses exhibits on the station's history and on marine wildlife. Keep your eyes open for whales and dolphins.

Various ramps and steps lead to different viewpoints and photo opportunities. If you're pushed for time, the best cliff scenery is from **Dunlough Bay View** (across the bridge and up the steps to the right).

Cross the Sea to Dursey Island
Ride Ireland's Only Cable Car

At the end of the Beara peninsula, tiny **Dursey Island** is reached by cable car rather than ferry, a quaint 1960s contraption that sways precariously 30m above Dursey Sound. (It was thoroughly renovated in 2023.) In a perfect photo op, livestock take precedence over humans in the queue.

The island, just 6.6km long by 1.5km wide, is a **wildlife sanctuary**, and dolphins and whales can sometimes be seen in the surrounding waters. The **Beara Way** loops around the island for 14km; allow four hours for the complete loop. The **signal tower** is an obvious destination for a shorter walk (8km round trip).

Enjoy a Picnic Overlooking the Sea
Coastal Castle

The 15th-century **Dunboy Castle**, a former stronghold of the O'Sullivan Beare clan, was destroyed by English forces during the Siege of Dunboy in 1602. The ruins sit on a promontory overlooking the southern entrance to the sheltered harbour of Bere Haven, a fantastic spot for a summer picnic. Stock up at the farmers market or one of the delis in Castletownbere.

On the way to the castle, you pass the fenced-off shell of **Puxley Manor**, a grand Victorian mansion that was once home to a copper-mining magnate and provided the inspiration for Clonmere in Daphne du Maurier's 1943 novel *Hungry Hill*. The manor was burnt out by the IRA in 1921 and has lain abandoned since 2008, but it was purchased by an Irish businessman in 2022 with plans to turn it into a luxury hotel.

CASTLETOWNBERE

Bustling Castletownbere (Baile Chais Bhéara), the 'capital' of the Beara, is a fishing port first and a tourist town second. That gives it great appeal for those looking for the 'real' Ireland, although that's not to say it doesn't have some worthwhile sights, notably **Dunboy Castle** and the world-famous pub **MacCarthy's Bar**. If you're carrying an original copy of the late Pete McCarthy's bestseller *McCarthy's Bar*, you'll be thrilled to see the front-cover photo in real life.

There's a developing food scene on the Beara, and Castletownbere is at the centre of it. There's a **farmers market**, a couple of **artisan delis** and **coffee shops**, and a growing number of good restaurants.

WHERE TO EAT BEYOND BANTRY

Josie's Lakeview House
Captivating views over Glanmore Lake accompany scrumptious, home-cooked food, 4km south of Lauragh. €€

Copper Cafe
Healthy, hearty house-cooked lunches at this attractive cafe beside the Copper Mine Museum in Allihies. €

MacCarthy's Bar
Victorian-style wood-panelled Glengarriff bar with a menu of hearty pub grub; the house speciality is Bantry Bay mussels. €€

SHEEP'S HEAD CYCLING TOUR

This 70km route starts and finishes in Bantry, where you can hire bikes from O'Donovan's. Fit riders can complete the circuit in a day, but take two if you want to dawdle and take in a walk (overnight in Kilcrohane).

Head west from **1 Bantry** on the N71 and turn right on the minor road past the Westlodge Hotel. At a fork 10km further on, bear right (signposted Kilcrohane). **2 Goat's Path Farm and Pod Park** is a good overnight spot if you've made a late afternoon start. Past Gortnakilla Pier, keep left at a fork to begin the long climb up the Goat's Path road to the narrow spine of the peninsula 195m above sea level at **3 Seefin** (Sui Finn, or Finn's Seat, as in legendary giant Finn MacCool). The views here are spectacular.

Descend the hairpins on the far side to **4 Kilcrohane**, where you can get coffee and cake at the Old Creamery, and then continue southwest, following signs for the Sheep's Head Cafe to reach the end of the road at **5 Bernie's Cupán Tae**, a tiny tearoom famous for its scones and salmon sandwiches. From here, a superb waymarked walk leads for 2km to the **6 Sheep's Head lighthouse** at the tip of the peninsula amid jaw-dropping sea-cliff scenery; allow 1½ to two hours round trip.

Return to Kilcrohane and continue along the coast road to **7 Ahakista**, where you have a choice of watering holes: the Ahakista Bar, a charming, tin-roofed stone cottage known locally as the Tin Pub; the Heron Gallery Cafe for lunches, coffee and cake; or Arundel's for a waterfront beer garden. From here, it's a straightforward 19km back to Bantry via the pretty village of **8 Durrus**.

ILNACULLIN

The horticultural miracle of Ilnacullin, also known as Garinish Island, was created in the early 20th century when the island's owner commissioned architect Harold Peto to design a garden on the then-barren outcrop. Topsoil was shipped in, and subtropical species were planted: camellias, magnolias and rhododendrons now provide a seasonal blaze of colour.

The centrepiece of the island is a magical **Italianate garden**. Nearby, a cypress avenue leads to a faux-Grecian temple with a stunning view of Great Sugarloaf. There are more views from the island's highest point, a 19th-century **Martello tower**.

Harbour Queen and Blue Pool ferries take you to the island past colonies of basking seals and a nesting site for white-tailed eagles.

Dunboy is at the end of the narrow L8935, which leaves the main road 2.5km southwest of Castletownbere. There are parking spaces for two or three cars.

Walk the Copper Mine Trail
Industrial Heritage Hike

The isolated village of **Allihies** (Na hAilichí), 20km west of Castletownbere, whose colourfully painted houses grace many a postcard and guidebook cover, has a fascinating history of copper mining. Your first stop should be the community-run **Copper Mine Museum**, where you can get historical context and pick a map of the **Copper Mine Trail**, a waymarked hike among the remains of the old workings.

From the museum, the trail leads downhill and then goes left along a classic Irish *boreen* (small lane) that winds up to another minor road near the ruined engine house of **Kealoge Mine**. Follow the road for 1.5km and turn right on a gravel track past the scant remains of **Caminches Mine**. Follow the signposted trail to your ultimate objective: the **Mountain Mine**, the biggest and highest of the old copper mines.

The impressive **engine house** dates from 1862 and once contained the **Man Engine**, a primitive steam-powered elevator that transported miners to and from the bottom of the mine, as well as hoisting ore to the surface (the mine reached a depth of 421m below the surface, around 280m below sea level). The open pits and tunnels are safely fenced off, but you can explore the rest of the site and soak up the expansive views across the village to the beautiful white strand of **Ballydonegan Beach**, largely made of crushed quartz washed out from the old mine workings.

Ballydonegan Beach

You can return to the village by following the yellow marker posts of the Beara Way from the narrow road just below the Mountain Mine.

GETTING AROUND

Regular bus services ply the main N71 road from Cork city, Clonakilty and Skibbereen through Bantry and Glengarriff and on to Kenmare and Killarney. Local Link Cork runs a network of minibus routes connecting Bantry to Castletownbere, Allihies, Kilcrohane, Goleen and other villages on the peninsulas, but most services are limited to two or three times a week. To properly explore the Mizen Head, Sheep's Head and Beara peninsulas, it's far better to have your own wheels.

Engine house, Copper Mine Trail

KERRY
THE JEWEL IN IRELAND'S SCENIC CROWN

Home to Ireland's highest mountain range, the country's most beautiful national park and its most remote islands, Kerry is crammed with superlatives.

County Kerry contains some of Ireland's most iconic scenery: surf-pounded sea cliffs, soft golden strands, emerald-green farmland crisscrossed by tumbledown stone walls, mist-shrouded bogs and mountain peaks that tear the clouds. Off the coast, the jagged, improbable outpost of Skellig Michael is one of Ireland's two Unesco World Heritage sites.

With one of the country's finest national parks as its backyard, the lively tourism hub of Killarney spills over with colourful shops, restaurants and pubs loud with spirited trad music. The town is the jumping-off point for Kerry's famed circular driving route, the Ring of Kerry, which skirts the mountainous, island-fringed Iveragh Peninsula, with photo-worthy views unfolding at every twist and turn.

The more compact Dingle Peninsula is like a condensed version of its southern neighbour, with the Slea Head Drive linking ancient prehistoric ring forts, beehive huts, Christian sites, sandy beaches and glimpses of a hard, unforgiving land. The lively town of Dingle is known for its seafood restaurants. For those seeking a taste of Gaelic culture, the nearby Gaeltacht (Irish-speaking) region of West Kerry provides a unique opportunity to experience the Irish language and customs firsthand.

Kerry's exquisite beauty makes it one of Ireland's most popular tourist destinations, but if you need to escape from the crowds, there's always a mountain pass, an isolated cove or an untrodden trail to discover.

ATTILA JANDI/SHUTTERSTOCK ©

THE MAIN AREAS

KILLARNEY NATIONAL PARK
Lakes and mountains. **p224**

DINGLE
Charming harbour town. **p242**

TRALEE
Historic market town. **p250**

Above: Great Blasket Island (p246); left: Kilmalkedar Church (p249)

Find Your Way

County Kerry covers a large area, much of it mountainous and remote with narrow winding roads. Regular public transport is confined to the main towns and villages, so a car is essential to make the most of your time.

Tralee, p250

The enchanting capital of North Kerry offers a delightful blend of historical charm, elegant Georgian streets and friendly locals.

Dingle, p242

Charming harbour town packed with colourful streets, lively pubs, and warm-hearted locals, where the spirit of the Gaeltacht dances on every corner.

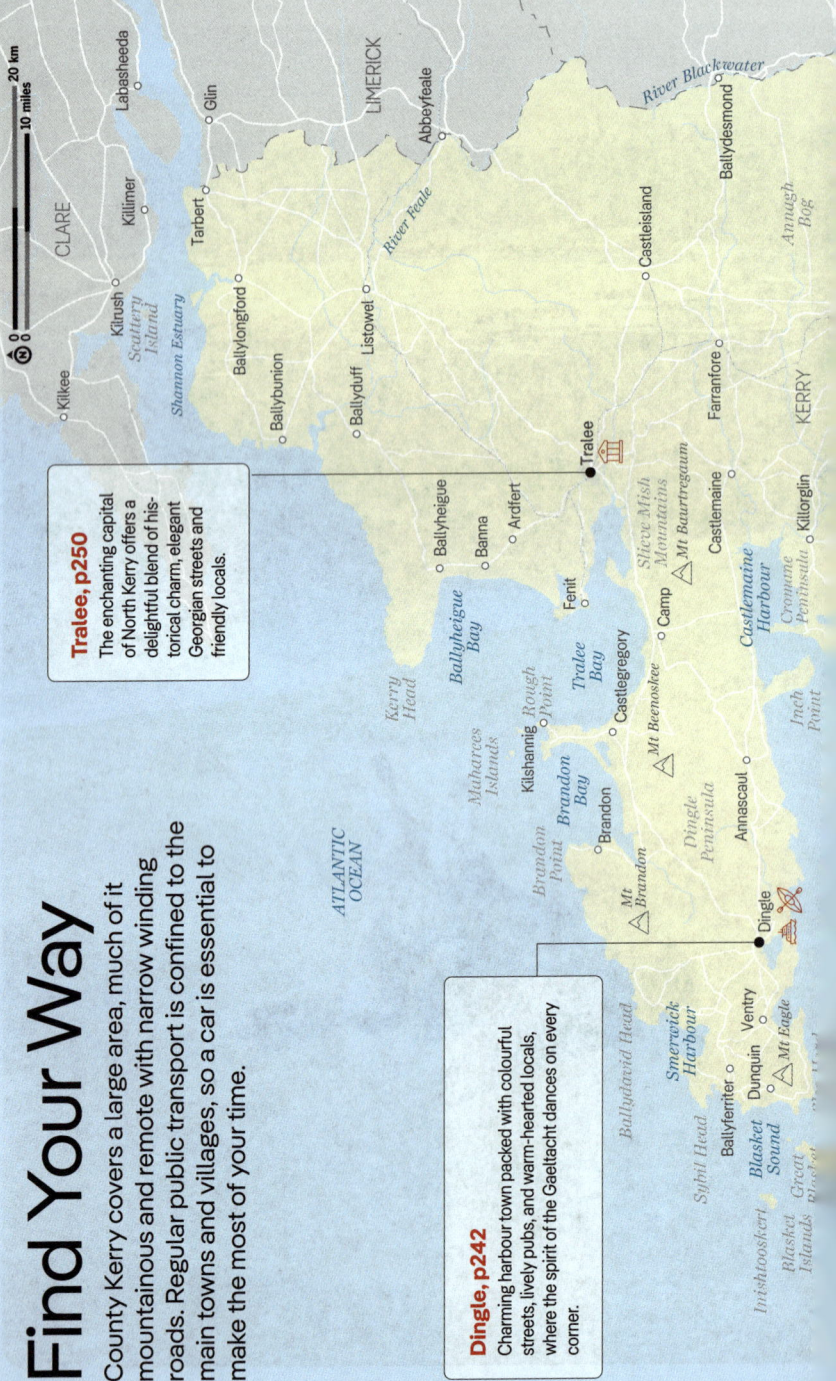

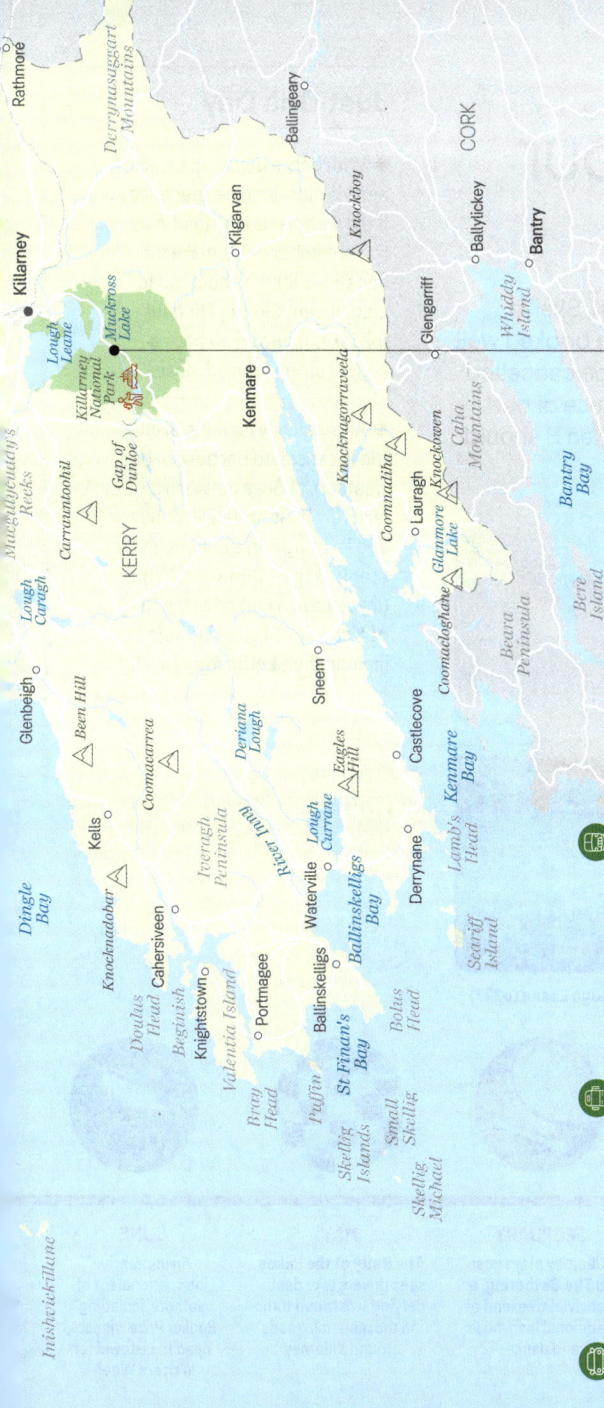

Killarney National Park, p224

Majestic mountains, pristine lakes and ancient forests intertwine, inspiring a deep connection with nature's captivating beauty.

THE GUIDE

KERRY

BUS

Regular bus services ply the main road from Killarney to Tralee and Listowel, with local minibuses serving the Ring of Kerry and Dingle peninsula. A bus from Killarney to Dingle runs in July and August only.

TRAIN

Rail is more useful for getting to Kerry from Dublin or Cork rather than getting around the county. That said, there are around eight trains a day between Killarney and Tralee, with a journey time around 40 minutes.

CAR

You'll want your own wheels for exploring County Kerry, especially for the classic Ring of Kerry, Skellig Ring and Slea Head driving tours. Find car rental outlets in Killarney and at Kerry airport, 17km north of Killarney on the N22.

221

THE GUIDE

KERRY

Plan Your Time

Kerry's top attraction, Skellig Michael, needs to be booked well in advance but can be cancelled at short notice because of bad weather, so have a Plan B should the worst happen.

Lough Leane (p227)

Just One Day

● With only a day to spare, aim for Kerry's most iconic experiences. If the weather is kind (mid-May to September only), make the once-in-a-lifetime boat trip to magnificent **Skellig Michael** (p236), but be sure to book a couple of weeks in advance.

● Alternatively (or if the Skellig trip is cancelled because of bad weather), choose between a leisurely boat-and-bike (or bus and jaunting car) trip through the scenic **Gap of Dunloe** (p228) or (if you have a car) drive the **Ring of Kerry** (p234), making sure to include the **Skellig Ring** (p241).

Seasonal Highlights

Lots of festivals take place throughout the county during the warmer months, particularly from June to August, when you'll need to book accommodation well ahead.

FEBRUARY
Killarney plays host to **The Gathering**, a convivial weekend of traditional Irish music and dance.

MAY
The **Rally of the Lakes** sees drivers take death-defying twists and turns on the mountain roads around Killarney.

JUNE
An impressive international list of authors, including Booker Prize winners, head to Listowel for **Writers Week**.

222

Three Days to Explore

- Devote a day to one of the iconic trips described in the one-day itinerary and split the other two days between Killarney and Dingle.

- Begin with a wander around **Killarney town** (p226) and then take a jaunting car ride out to **Muckross House** (p226), followed by a boat trip on **Lough Leane** (p227), or, if you haven't already done so, take a driving tour of the **Ring of Kerry** (p234) and the **Skellig Ring** (p241).

- On day three, head to **Dingle town** (p242) for a seafood lunch and an afternoon tour of the **Slea Head Drive** (p247).

More Than a Week

- Spend your first three days exploring **Killarney National Park** (p226), touring the **Gap of Dunloe** (p228) by boat and bike (or jaunting car), and enjoying a driving tour of the **Ring of Kerry** (p234).

- Put a day aside for a boat tour to **Skellig Michael** (p236), a Unesco World Heritage site with awe-inspiring monastic ruins.

- Have a relaxing beach day at **Inch Strand** (p246) on your way to **Dingle town** (p242) for an overnight of seafood and music.

- Follow that with a day or two exploring **Slea Head Drive** (p247) and the **Maharees** (p248) on your way to **Tralee** (p250).

THE GUIDE

KERRY

JULY
Féile Lúghnasa in Cloghane celebrates the ancient Celtic harvest festival with theatre performances and traditional events.

AUGUST
A horse fair, street theatre, concerts and fireworks are part of Killorglin's **Puck Fair**, first recorded in 1603.

OCTOBER
The four-day Killarney-based **Kerry International Film Festival** focuses on emerging talent with a short film competition.

NOVEMBER
Writing of all kinds, from poetry to fiction, in both English and Irish, is celebrated at the **Dingle Literary Festival**.

KILLARNEY NATIONAL PARK

Sprawling over 10,236 wild hectares, the sublime Killarney National Park is an idyllic place to explore. Ross Castle and Muckross House draw the biggest crowds, but it's always possible to escape to the hills where native red deer roam the country's largest area of ancient oak woods and glassy lakes reflect panoramic views of Ireland's highest mountains.

The core of the national park is the Muckross Estate, donated to the state by Arthur Bourn Vincent in 1932. The park was designated a Unesco Biosphere Reserve in 1982. The Killarney Lakes – Lough Leane (the Lower Lake, or 'Lake of Learning'), Muckross (or Middle) Lake and the Upper Lake – make up about a quarter of the park and are surrounded by natural oak and yew woodland. The high crags and moors of Purple Mountain (832m) to the west and Knockrower (552m) to the south overlook the lakes.

TOP TIP

Check the calendar before planning a visit to Killarney. During several annual events, such as the Rally of the Lakes (early May) and Ireland BikeFest (early June), campsites and accommodation are packed, and local roads (including the N71 Killarney-Kenmare route) may be temporarily closed.

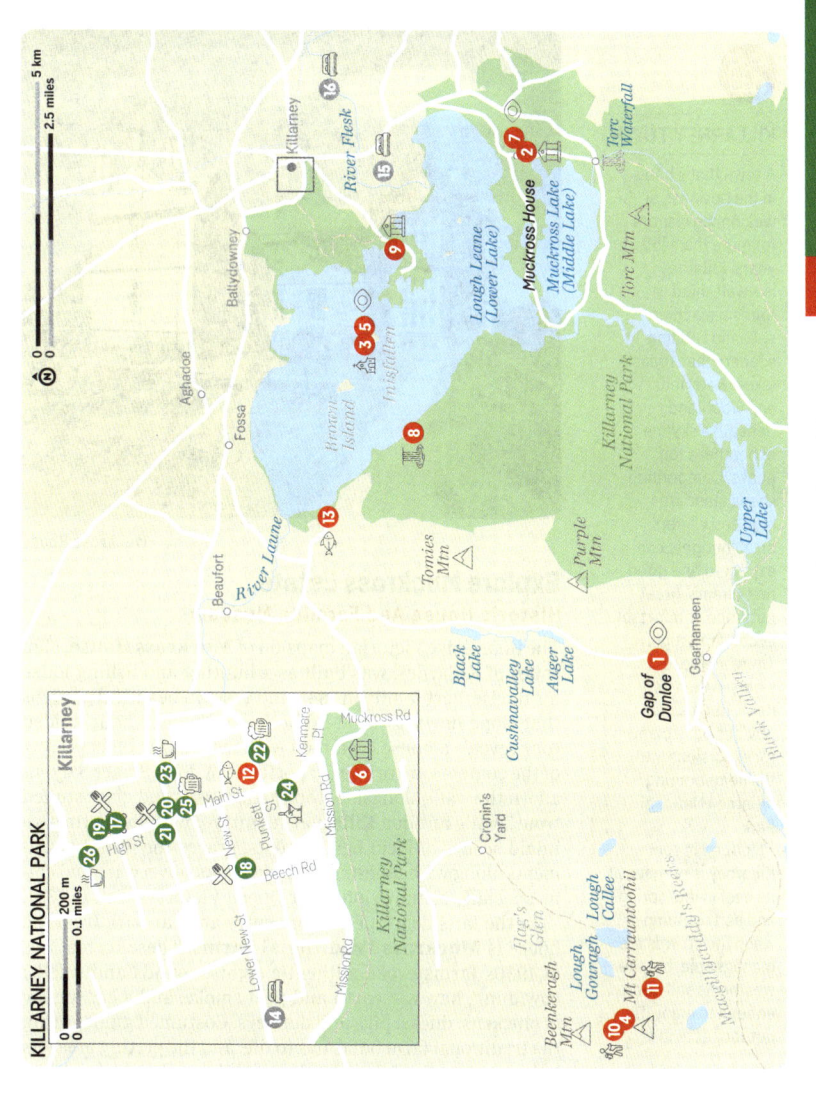

HIGHLIGHTS
1. Gap of Dunloe
2. Muckross House

SIGHTS
3. Augustinian Priory
4. Carrauntoohil
5. Inisfallen
6. Killarney House
7. Muckross Traditional Farms
8. O'Sullivan's Cascade
9. Ross Castle

ACTIVITIES
10. Brother O'Shea's Gully
11. Devil's Ladder
12. O'Neill's
13. Sweeney's

SLEEPING
14. Black Sheep Hostel
15. Cahernane House Hotel
16. Crystal Springs

EATING
17. Brícín
18. Celtic Whiskey Bar & Larder
19. Harrow
20. Murphy Brownes
21. Treyvaud's

DRINKING & NIGHTLIFE
22. Courtney's
23. Curious Cat Café
24. Killarney Grand
25. O'Connor's
26. Petit Délice

KILLARNEY TOWN

A town that's been in the business of welcoming visitors for more than 250 years, Killarney is a well-oiled tourism machine set amid sublime scenery that spans lakes, waterfalls and woodland beneath a skyline of heather-clad peaks. Competition keeps standards high and visitors on all budgets can expect to find good restaurants, great pubs and comfortable accommodation. There are no real sights in the town itself, but it's the obvious base camp for excursions into the neighbouring Killarney National Park.

Mobbed in summer, Killarney is perhaps at its best in late spring and early autumn when the crowds are manageable, but the weather is still good enough to enjoy its outdoor activities.

Muckross House

Explore Muckross Estate
Historic House And Farming Museum

The impressive Victorian mansion of **Muckross House**, 5km south of Killarney, was built as a hunting and fishing lodge for the Herbert family in 1843 and is set in beautiful gardens that slope down to the Middle Lake. The one-hour guided tour reveals a house crammed with fascinating objects (70% of the contents are original); portraits by John Singer Sargent adorn the walls alongside trophy stag heads and giant stuffed trout, while antique Killarney furniture, with its distinctive inlaid scenes of local beauty spots, graces the grand apartments along with tapestries, Persian rugs, silverware and china specially commissioned for Queen Victoria's visit in 1861.

On the far side of the visitor centre and car park from the house is **Muckross Traditional Farms**. These recreations of 1930s farms evoke authentic sights, sounds and smells: cow dung, hay, wet earth and peat smoke, and a cacophony of chickens, ducks, pigs and donkeys. Costumed guides bring the traditional farm buildings to life, and the petting area lets kids get close to piglets, lambs, ducklings and chicks. Allow at least two hours to do the self-guided tour justice. A free shuttle loops around the site.

WHERE TO STAY IN KILLARNEY

Black Sheep Hostel
Traveller-designed hostel with custom-made bunks and built-in lockers. Minimum stay required on weekends May to October. €

Crystal Springs
Wonderfully relaxing B&B with a glass-enclosed breakfast room overlooking the River Flesk. Two-night minimum. €€

Cahernane House Hotel
Magnificent manor dating from 1877, with antique-furnished rooms (some with claw-foot bath or Jacuzzi). €€€

Take a Ride in a Jaunting Car
Horse-Drawn Buggies

Killarney's traditional horse-drawn jaunting cars provide tours from Killarney town to Ross Castle and Muckross Estate, complete with amusing commentary from the driver (known as a 'jarvey'). The cost varies depending on distance; cars can fit up to four people. The main pickup point, nicknamed 'the Ha Ha' or 'the Block', is on Kenmare Pl in Killarney. Jaunting cars also ply the road through the Gap of Dunloe between Lord Brandon's Cottage and Kate Kearney's Cottage.

Expect to pay around €15 to €20 per person for a tour from Killarney to Ross Castle and back. There are no set prices, so haggle for longer tours.

The tradition of touring Killarney's sights in a horse-drawn buggy took off in the 1860s following Queen Victoria's widely reported visit to the area in 1861; many of the family businesses that run tours today can trace their lineage back to that decade.

Cast a Line on Killarney's Lakes
Gone Fishing

The **River Laune**, which flows from Lough Leane to the sea, is one of Ireland's best salmon rivers. The season runs from 17 January to 30 September, with the best fishing from late July onward. Both a permit and a state rod licence are required. You can also fish for salmon in the Killarney lakes (no permit needed, but a state rod licence is still required).

Fishing for brown trout in the lakes of Killarney National Park is free (no permit needed), and the season runs from 15 February to 12 October. Fishing from the bank is allowed, but the best sport is to be had from a boat with an outboard motor, which you can hire at Ross Castle or at **Sweeney's**, at the west end of Lough Leane (up to three people per boat). There is also good fishing for rainbow trout at Barfinnihy Lake, 25km southwest of Killarney on the minor from Moll's Gap towards Sneem.

O'Neill's in Killarney provides information, rents rods and tackle, and sells permits and licences.

BEST PLACES TO EAT IN KILLARNEY TOWN

Curious Cat Cafe
This quirky little cafe serves big breakfasts, US-deli-style sandwiches, buffalo wings and good coffee. €

Murphy Brownes
Elegant and candlelit but pleasantly informal, with a crowd-pleasing menu of Irish and international favourites. €€

Harrow
A refined dining experience with a menu that focuses on prime Irish beef steak and the best local seafood. Dinner only. €€€

Celtic Whiskey Bar & Larder
Buzzing gastropub serving some of the tastiest food in town, ranging from cheese and charcuterie platters to aged fillet steaks. €€

WHERE TO EAT IN KILLARNEY

Treyvaud's
Has a good reputation for subtle dishes that merge traditional Irish produce with European influences. €€

Petit Délice
Rustic, always busy and authentically French cafe-patisserie. €

Brícín
This Celtic-themed restaurant doubles as the town museum; the house speciality is boxty (potato pancake). €€

BOAT & CYCLING TOUR

The Gap of Dunloe by Boat & Bike

A boat trip through the lakes followed by a bike ride through the mountain scenery of the Gap of Dunloe is the classic Killarney experience. Your hostel, hotel or campsite can arrange it for you, including boat tickets and bike hire, or you can book online. The total distance cycled is 23km. Allowing time for stops and an hour for lunch, you should be back in Killarney by 3.30pm.

1 Reen Pier

Boats depart from Reen Pier near Ross Castle at 11am, with bikes propped in the bow. The 1½-hour cruise alone justifies the price. Ask your boater about the highest and lowest water levels seen in the lakes and sit back to enjoy the stories.

The Cruise: You glide past Inisfallen island with its ruined monastery and then turn south to sail under pretty Brickeen Bridge and reach the Meeting of the Waters.

2 Old Weir Bridge

The boat then surges up a rocky channel beneath the Old Weir Bridge. After prolonged dry weather, when lake levels are low, passengers may have to get out and walk a short distance while the boat gets hauled up this shallow, fast-flowing section.

The Cruise: The Long Range is next, a winding channel that is half-lake, half-river. It uncoils beneath the crags of Eagle's Nest mountain

Augher Lake, Gap of Dunloe

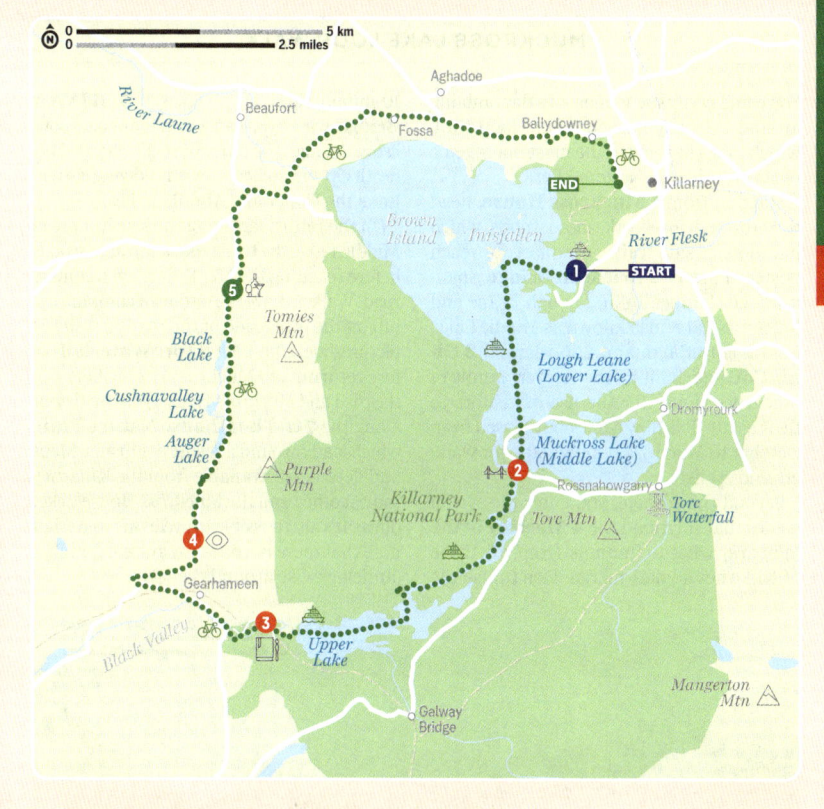

(golden eagles once nested here) before entering the long, narrow Upper Lake.

3 Lord Brandon's Cottage

You disembark at Lord Brandon's Cottage, a 19th-century hunting lodge surrounded by lush, green water meadows. It has a simple open-air cafe and public toilets. The cycling section begins here.

The Ride: The bike section begins with a 4.5km climb to the head of the Gap. It's a steady uphill, but not too steep, and there's no shame in getting off and pushing for a bit.

4 Head of the Gap

At the summit, known as the Head of the Gap, you're rewarded with stunning views in both directions, back down to the Upper Lake and forward into the narrow pass of the Gap itself.

The Ride: Enjoy a 6.5km downhill run to Kate Kearney's Cottage, passing through the Turnpike Boulders and crossing the Wishing Bridge, both good photo opportunities.

5 Kate Kearney's Cottage

This 19th-century pub at the northern end of the Gap of Dunloe is a welcome watering hole, serving cold beers and tasty pub grub. Kitchen hours can be reduced at short notice, so call ahead if you're counting on dining here. The bar hosts live Irish music every night in summer.

The Ride: Follow signs for Killarney along minor roads to the N71 and then a cycle path that hugs the side of the road before veering off through the golf course to end near the town centre opposite St Mary's Cathedral.

MUCKROSS LAKE LOOP WALK

You could easily spend most of a day ambling around this waymarked 9.5km loop trail, which takes in some of the most photogenic parts of Killarney National Park.

Starting from **1 Muckross House**, head west through lovely lakeshore woods, which have lots of side trails to explore, to reach postcard-pretty **2 Brickeen Bridge**, spanning the channel linking Lough Leane and Muckross Lake, also known as Middle Lake. Continue to the quaint 200-year-old **3 Dinis Cottage**, built by the Herbert family of Muckross House for the use of visitors to their estate. It is now a tearoom (closed from October to March), a popular stop for walkers and cyclists.

Beyond the cottage, you enter the sylvan glades that surround the **4 Meeting of the Waters**, where channels from all three of Killarney's lakes merge. Don't miss the 10-minute side trail (no bikes) to **5 Old Weir Bridge**, where you can watch tour boats powering through the narrow, rocky channel beneath its twin arches. A swiftly flowing current links the Upper and Middle Lakes.

On the return leg along the south shore of Middle Lake, the trail passes through woods before reaching the N71 Killarney–Kenmare road. Walkers have the option of climbing uphill on the other side of the road to visit the picturesque, 20m-high **6 Torc Waterfall** before returning to Muckross House. Between the road and Muckross House, you can detour along the **7 Old Boathouse Nature Trail**, which leads around a scenic peninsula. Maps and details are available from the Killarney tourist office and the Muckross House ticket office. It's also possible to cycle this route, but note that there is a one-way system for bikes (anticlockwise around the lake).

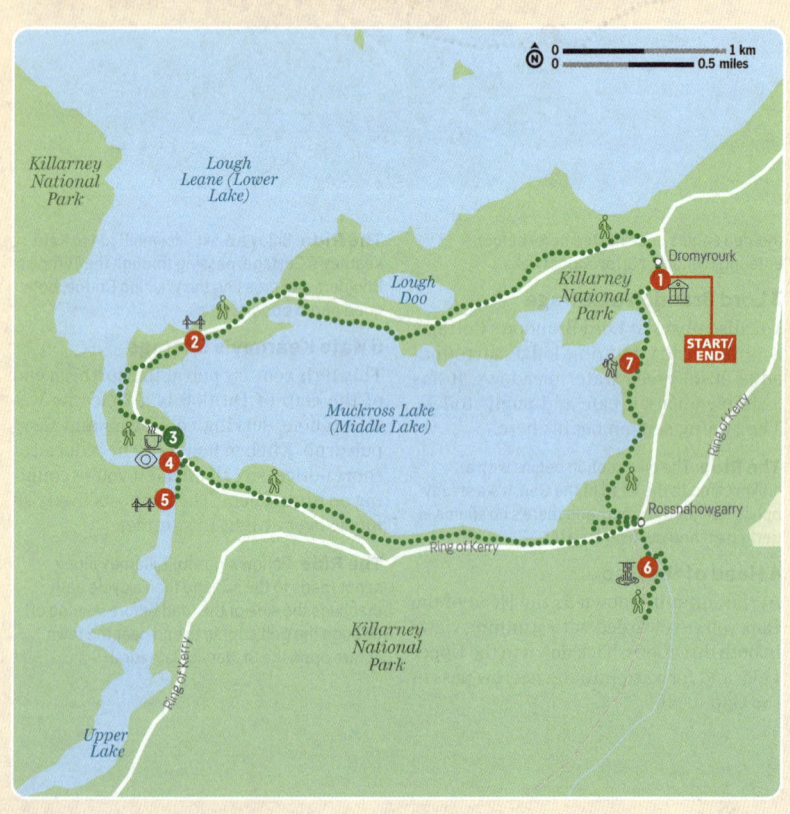

Carrauntoohil (p232)

Enjoy a Picnic with a Panorama
Ornamental Gardens With Mountain Views

Dating from the early 18th century, **Killarney House** was originally the stable block of a much larger French-chateau-style mansion that was built for the landowning Browne family in the 1720s. Most of the chateau was demolished in the 1870s when the family moved to nearby Knockreer House, and when that was destroyed by fire in 1913, the stables were remodelled as a family residence and then abandoned in the 1950s.

The house lay empty and unused for half a century, but it was restored in 2016 and now houses the **Killarney National Park visitor centre**. Free guided tours of the house take place every half-hour.

However, the true glory of Killarney House lies in the vast **ornamental gardens**, which sweep majestically towards a gorgeous view of the Kerry mountains. Pack a picnic and stroll across the huge lawns past colourful flower beds and choose a peaceful spot where you can soak up the view.

Take to the Water on Lough Leane
Scenic Boat Trips

Lough Leane, or the Lower Lake, is the largest of Killarney's lakes and the ideal place to explore by boat. The easiest and most comfortable option is a one-hour waterbus tour with **Killarney Lake Tours**, which departs four times a day from

INISFALLEN

Inisfallen is the largest of the islands in Lough Leane, visible from Ross Castle. In the 7th century, St Finian the Leper founded the earliest monastery here, but little now remains. The extensive ruins of a 12th-century **Augustinian priory** and an oratory with a carved Romanesque doorway stand on the site of St Finian's original. Inisfallen's fame dates from the early 13th century when the Annals of Inisfallen were written here. Now in the Bodleian Library at Oxford, England, they remain a vital source of information on early Munster history and gave the lake its Gaelic name, Lough Léin (Lake of Learning).

You can hire a skippered motorboat from Reen Pier for the 10-minute trip to the island.

WHERE TO DRINK IN KILLARNEY

O'Connor's
Live music plays every night at this tiny traditional pub, one of Killarney's most popular haunts.

Courtney's
Inconspicuous on the outside, this cavernous 19th-century pub bursts at the seams with regular Irish music sessions.

Killarney Grand
The various bars and clubs at this local institution host traditional live music, rock bands and a disco from 11pm.

WHY I LOVE KILLARNEY NATIONAL PARK

Neil Wilson, writer

I've been visiting Killarney for 15 years and never get tired of it. There's always something new to do, whether it's ticking off the 900m summits in the Macgillycuddy's Reeks mountain range, cycling the Gap of Dunloe (or walking it or riding through it in a jaunting car) or trying out the latest restaurants in town. But it's also about doing the same things over again. The boat trip from Ross Castle to Lord Brandon's Cottage crams more interest into its 90 minutes than anywhere I know. No matter how many times I do it, it never gets old.

---

the jetty in front of Ross Castle. You'll cruise past Inisfallen's ruined island **monastery** (no landing) and then on to the roadless west shore of the lake to view **O'Sullivan's Cascade** and Purple Mountain, returning via **Brickeen Bridge**. If you like, you can arrange to be picked up at your accommodation and taken to the jetty by jaunting car.

If you want to land on **Inisfallen Island** to explore the ruined priory, you need to hire one of the many boats departing from **Reen Pier**, just north of Ross Castle, or you could take a three-hour guided kayak tour of the lake with **Outdoors Ireland**, taking in limestone caves and wooded inlets as well as landing on Inisfallen.

Climb Ireland's Highest Peak
Challenging Hillwalk

Macgillycuddy's Reeks is Ireland's highest mountain range, and towering **Carrauntoohil** (1040m) is the country's highest summit. There are several routes up, though even the most straightforward requires good hillwalking and navigation skills, while others are serious scrambling or rock-climbing routes.

The traditional route to the summit is via the **Devil's Ladder**, a gruelling trudge up a badly eroded gully path southwest of the loughs in Hag's Glen, which is unpleasantly loose. An alternative route ascends via **Brother O'Shea's Gully** (rock scrambling and good route-finding ability required), a steep and challenging route through spectacular mountain scenery. The easiest descent is via the **Zig-Zags** to the east of the Devil's Ladder.

Experienced hillwalkers can follow the directions in Adrian Hendorff's guidebook, *The Dingle, Iveragh & Beara Peninsulas: A Walking Guide*. If you're in the slightest bit unsure, hire a guide. **Kerry Climbing** and **Hidden Ireland Adventures** both offer guided ascents of Carrauntoohil year-round, weather permitting (booking is essential).

Climbing Carrauntoohil should never be attempted without a map and compass (and the skills to use them), proper hillwalking boots, waterproofs, and spare food and water. Use Harvey's 1:30,000 *Macgillycuddy's Reeks Superwalker* map or the 1:25,000 Ordnance Survey Adventure Series map *Macgillycuddy's Reeks & Killarney National Park*.

GETTING AROUND

Bicycles are ideal for exploring the scattered sights of the Killarney region, many of which are best reached by two wheels or on foot. Many of Killarney's hostels, campsites and hotels offer bike hire. Alternatively, try Killarney Rent A Bike at O'Sullivan Cycles, which has three locations (on Muckross Rd, Beech Rd and College St).

Beyond Killarney National Park

Sea legs at the ready – the boat trip to stunning Skellig Michael is not to be missed.

The Iveragh (pronounced *eev*-raa) Peninsula to the southwest of Killarney National Park is one of the most scenic parts of Ireland, circumnavigated by the famous Ring of Kerry driving route. The smaller but equally scenic Skellig Ring, which spins off the loop at Waterville, is less travelled but every bit as spectacular. Out in the Atlantic, jagged Skellig Michael keeps its lonely vigil.

If you want to get further off the beaten track, explore the interior of the peninsula – on foot along the eastern section of the Kerry Way from Killarney to Glenbeigh, or by car or bike on the minor roads that cut through the hills, notably the Ballaghisheen Pass between Killorglin and Waterville.

TOP TIP

You can drive the Ring of Kerry in one day, but the more time you take, the more you'll enjoy it.

Skellig Michael (p236)

ROAD TRIP

Ring of Kerry

This famous circuit of the Iveragh Peninsula winds past pretty villages, pristine beaches, craggy mountains and sparkling loughs, with ever-changing views of the island-dotted Atlantic. The 170km route starts and finishes in Killarney. While most of the way is two-lane, there are some narrow sections, notably between Killarney and Moll's Gap. Tour buses travel the Ring anticlockwise; getting stuck behind them is tedious, so the route below is described clockwise.

1 Moll's Gap

The summit of the pass to the south of Killarney is known as Moll's Gap, which is worth a stop for the great views towards the Gap of Dunloe and for breakfast at **Avoca Cafe** (closed November to March).

The Drive: The N71 road descends through a series of swooping bends to Kenmare.

2 Kenmare

Kenmare (pronounced ken-*mair*) is a picturesque small town without the shamrocks-and-shillelaghs tourist tat of Killarney. Its neat triangle of streets is lined with craft shops, art galleries, cafes and good-quality restaurants.

The Drive: From Kenmare town centre, retrace your route north, but turn left on the N70 towards Cahersiveen.

3 Sneem

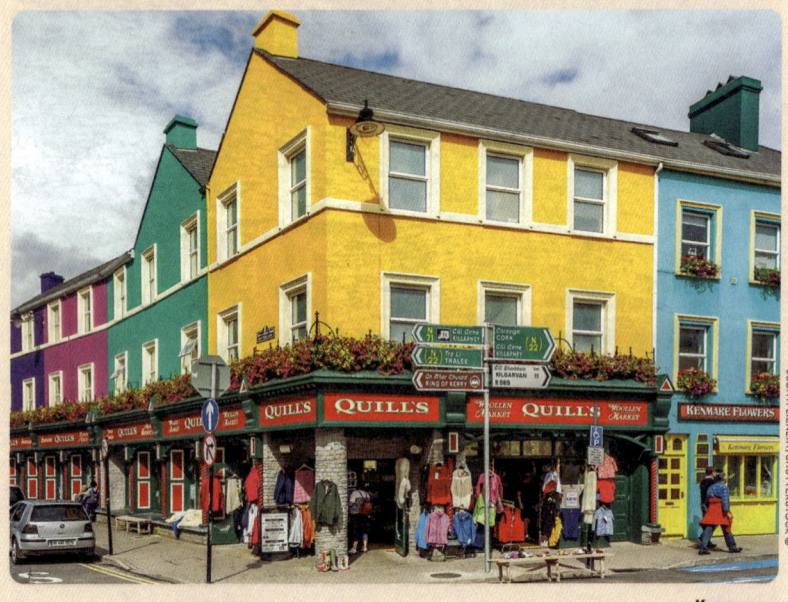

The pretty village of Sneem is split by a river, with separate village squares on either side and a picturesque waterfall tumbling below the old stone bridge between the two. It's a good place to stretch your legs. If you visit on a Tuesday, you'll catch the local farmers market.

The Drive: Beyond Sneem, the coastal scenery ramps into overdrive as the road winds over the hill to Caherdaniel.

4 Caherdaniel

A short detour from the main road at Caherdaniel leads to Derrynane Beach, one of the most beautiful in Kerry, with scalloped coves of golden sand set between grassy dunes and whaleback outcrops of wave-smoothed rock.

The Drive: The N70 now climbs high above the sea, passing Beenarourke viewpoint, with grandstand views over scattered islands, before descending to Waterville.

5 Waterville

Waterville is an old-fashioned seaside resort strung along the N70 at the head of Ballinskelligs Bay, famous for its golf and the fact that silent-movie star Charlie Chaplin holidayed here in the 1960s.

The Drive: Continue north on the N70 to Cahersiveen.

6 Cahersiveen

Cahersiveen (pronounced caar-suh-*veen*) is the main town on the Ring, home to the Old Barracks heritage centre and some excellent places to eat.

The Drive: Follow the N70 for 30km to Kerry Bog Village.

7 Kerry Bog Village

This museum recreates a 19th-century bog village, typical of the small communities that carved out a precarious living in the harsh environment of Ireland's ubiquitous peat bogs. You'll see the thatched homes of the turfcutter, blacksmith, thatcher and labourer, as well as a dairy, and meet Kerry bog ponies.

The Drive: Continue on the N70 to Killorglin and then turn right on the N72 to return to Killarney.

235

TOP SIGHT
Skellig Islands

The jagged, 217m-high rock of Skellig Michael rises dramatically out of the sea 12km off the coast of County Kerry, topped with the remains of an improbable 1400-year-old early Christian monastery. The remote island famously featured as Luke Skywalker's Jedi temple in two Star Wars movies, attracting a whole new audience to the Skelligs' dramatic beauty.

DON'T MISS
- Little Skellig
- Skellig Michael
- The Steps
- Beehive Cells
- Oratories
- The Hermitage

Skellig Michael

Skellig Michael (Michael's Rock; like St Michael's Mount in Cornwall and Mont St Michel in Normandy) is the larger of the two Skellig Islands and a Unesco World Heritage site. Influenced by the Coptic Church (founded by St Anthony in the deserts of Egypt and Libya), the monks' determined quest for ultimate solitude led them to this remote, windblown edge of Europe. Not much is known about the life of the monastery, but there are records of Viking raids in 812 and 823 CE.

Although the site was expanded in the 12th century, the monks abandoned the rock soon afterwards. In the 1820s, two lighthouses were built on the island, along with the road that runs around the base.

The Landing
The landing point for visitors is at a tiny jetty on the northeast side of the island, from where you make your way along the lighthouse road, past a helipad to the cluster of sheds where the Office of Public Works (OPW) guides are based. You will get a safety briefing before you are allowed to climb up to the monastery.

The Steps
Three ancient staircases lead to the top of Skellig Michael, but only the one on the southeast side is currently in use. There are 618 steps cut into the steep face of the rock, with no handrails, save for a short length of chain low down. The steps ascend to the dip between the twin summits, known as Christ's Saddle, where you can catch your breath before the final climb to the monastery gate, 180m above sea level.

The Monastery
The 6th-century monastery is a miracle of masonry, set on platforms built on the vertiginous slope using nothing more than drystone walls and earth. Within the perimeter wall are six beehive cells, where the monks once lived, two domed oratories where they prayed and chanted, a cemetery, and a small 10th-century church. You can also see the monks' south-facing vegetable garden and their cistern for collecting rainwater.

The Hermitage
The Hermitage is a small structure near the summit of Skellig Michael's south peak, opposite the monastery; it is not open to visitors. Probably dating from the 9th century, the tiny oratory (just 2.3m by 1.2m) was possibly used as a retreat by individual monks for solitary prayer.

Getting There
Boat trips to the Skelligs usually run from mid-May to September (dates are announced each year by the OPW, which looks after the site), weather permitting. Boats depart from Portmagee, Ballinskelligs and Caherdaniel. The number of daily visitors is limited, with boats licensed to carry no more than 12 passengers each, so it's wise to book well ahead. The trip costs around €145 per person.

Morning departure times depend on tide and weather, and the trip lasts around five hours in total with 2½ hours on the island, which is the bare minimum to visit the monastery, look at the birds and have a picnic.

PRACTICALITIES
Scan this QR code for prices and opening hours:

LITTLE SKELLIG
The bird sanctuary of Little Skellig is a long, low and jagged rock 2km northeast of Skellig Michael. From a distance, it can look as if it's shrouded in a swirling snowstorm; close up, you realise you're looking at a colony of 23,000 pairs of breeding gannets, the second-largest breeding colony in the world. Tour boats circle the island on the way to Skellig Michael so you can see the birds, and you may spot seals as well.

TOP TIPS
- The 12km sea crossing can be rough; it may be worth taking anti-seasickness pills.
- Bring all the food and water you will need for the day.
- Wear good walking shoes or boots, and bring warm and waterproof clothing. It is always colder and breezier on the sea crossing than you think it will be.
- Toilets were finally installed on the island in 2021.
- If you just want to see the islands up close and without having to clamber out of the boat, consider a 'no landing' cruise with operators such as Skellig Experience on Valentia Island.

I LIVE HERE: WHERE TO GO IN CAHERSIVEEN

Charlotte Sharpe and her team run Mannix Point campsite (facebook.com/campinginkerry). Here she shares some local favourites.

Across from our campsite, you can see **Valentia Island**, easy to visit via the nearby ferry. Take the scenic walk up to **Bray Head**, from where you can (allegedly!) see America. You can definitely see the world-renowned **Skellig Michael**, and a trip there is a life-changing experience. Around Cahersiveen, we have some great walks, and it's also a cyclist's dream. You can visit historical monuments like **Ballycarbery Castle** and the **ring forts**. Restaurant-wise, we are spoiled for choice, from pizza in the **Oratory** and fish and chips in **Eva's** to delicious seafood at **The Point**, and many more.

Valentia Island Lighthouse (p240)

Discover the Back Roads by Bike
Heritage Centre And Ancient Forts

The peaceful back roads to the northwest of Cahersiveen are ideal for exploring by bike. **Casey Cycles** in the town will rent you a touring bike or an e-bike. Start your exploration down towards the river at the **Old Barracks Heritage Centre**. This eccentric Bavarian-castle-style building was built as a Royal Irish Constabulary barracks in response to the Fenian Rising of 1867 and now houses fascinating exhibitions on the Rising and the life and works of local hero Daniel O'Connell, who campaigned for Catholic emancipation and Irish independence in the early 19th century.

Cross the bridge and follow signs for 'Stone Forts'. After 2km, you'll come to two extraordinary stone ring forts situated 600m apart, reached from a shared parking area. **Cahergal**, the larger and more impressive, dates from the 10th century and has stairways on the inside walls, a *clochán* (a circular stone building shaped like a beehive) and the remains of a roundhouse. The smaller, 9th-century **Leacanabuaile** contains the outlines of four houses. Both have a commanding position overlooking Ballycarbery Castle and Valentia Harbour, with superb views of the Kerry mountains.

Round off your explorations by continuing to **White Strand**, one of the best beaches in the area.

WHERE TO STAY BEYOND KILLARNEY NATIONAL PARK

Mannix Point Camping & Caravan Park
This award-winning waterfront campsite near Cahersiveen is one of Ireland's finest, with stunning sunsets over Valentia Island. €

Parknasilla Resort & Spa
Luxury hotel 3km southeast of Sneem has been wowing guests (including George Bernard Shaw) since 1895. €€€

Olde Forge Guesthouse
Views of Kenmare Bay and the Beara Peninsula unfold from the garden terrace of this Caherdaniel B&B. €€

Combine Coastal Beauty with Captivating Heritage
Historic House And Blue Flag Beach

Derrynane House, 2.5km west of the main N70 road at Caherdaniel, was the home of Maurice 'Hunting Cap' O'Connell, a notorious local smuggler who grew rich on trade with France and Spain. He was the uncle of Daniel O'Connell, the 19th-century campaigner for Catholic emancipation who grew up here in his uncle's care and inherited the property in 1825 when it became his private retreat. The house is furnished with O'Connell memorabilia, including the impressive triumphal chariot in which he lapped Dublin after his release from prison in 1844.

The surrounding **gardens**, warmed by the Gulf Stream, nurture subtropical species including 4m-high tree ferns, gunnera ('giant rhubarb') and other South American plants. A network of walking trails leads through the woods towards the beach. Kids can pick up a copy of the **Derrynane Fairy Trail** leaflet at the cafe and track down two dozen 'fairy houses' hidden among the trees.

Just south of the house is **Derrynane Beach**, one of the most beautiful in Kerry, with wave-worn rock outcrops nestled amid acres of golden sand fringed by grass-covered dunes. From the car park at Derrynane House, you can walk 1km along the beach to explore **Abbey Island** and its picturesque cemetery. Look inside the ruined chapel to find the tomb of Daniel O'Connell's wife, Mary.

Explore an Island at the Edge of the Atlantic
Intriguing History And Heritage

Valentia Island is a beautiful and under-visited corner of Kerry with a rich and fascinating history. Its Latin-sounding name is actually an anglicised version of the Irish Béal Inse, meaning 'the mouth of the island', a reference to the natural harbour entrance. The island is laced with narrow roads and lends itself to leisurely exploration by bike, though you could take in the main sights in a day by car. You can reach the island via the bridge at Portmagee or the five-minute car ferry crossing at Knightstown, the island's only village.

A couple of sights explain Valentia's role as the eastern terminus of the first transatlantic telegraph cable (the other end was at Heart's Content in Newfoundland, Canada), established in

STAR WARS SIGHTS

Star Wars aficionados will want to make a pilgrimage to the dizzyingly steep, starkly beautiful monastic island of **Skellig Michael**, which made its dramatic big-screen debut in 2015's *Star Wars: The Force Awakens* and reprised its role as Luke Skywalker's Jedi temple in 2017's *Star Wars: The Last Jedi*. Superfans can even travel to the island with a boat-tour company called **Force Awakens**.

Other *Star Wars* filming locations in Kerry include **Sybil Head** (Ceann Sibeal) on the Dingle Peninsula, 4.5km northwest of Ballyferriter. Elsewhere in Ireland, shooting took place around Loop Head Lighthouse (p297) in County Clare, Brow Head in County Cork and Hell's Hole near Malin Head in County Donegal.

WHERE TO EAT BEYOND KILLARNEY NATIONAL PARK

QC's Seafood Restaurant
Serves the finest seafood on the Ring, locally sourced from the owner's fishing fleet; dinner only, closed Mondays. €€

Skellig Seafront Cafe
Superb coffee and breakfasts while you wait for the boat to Skellig Michael at Portmagee. €

No 35 Kenmare
Exposed timber beams and an open fire set the stage for creative cuisine featuring all-Irish produce. €€€

CROMANE PENINSULA

Unless you know it's here, you wouldn't chance upon Cromane, 9km west of Killorglin, signposted off the N70. The village sits at the base of a narrow shingle spit, with open fields giving way to spectacular water vistas and multihued sunsets. Some of the area's best seafood is served at **Jacks' Coastguard Restaurant**, set in a 19th-century coastguard station.

Southwest of Cromane is **Dooks Golf Club**, one of the oldest links golf courses in Ireland, opened in 1889. A little further along the road, an unsignposted lane (look for the green postbox) leads to **Dooks Beach**, a little-visited gem at the mouth of the River Caragh, with gorgeous views of the Kerry and Dingle mountains.

1866. The **Valentia Transatlantic Cable Station** in Knightstown (closed Mondays and Tuesdays and from November to March) chronicles the epic struggle that saw the birth of global telecommunications and is currently campaigning for Unesco World Heritage status. Also in Knightstown, **Valentia Island Heritage Centre** is an intriguing local museum with a treasure trove of artefacts that tell the tale of the island's history more eloquently than any textbook.

Further flung attractions include **Valentia Island Lighthouse** (closed November to March), set in a 17th-century military fort at the northern tip of the island. You can visit the lightkeeper's house and climb to the top of the lighthouse tower. **Skellig Experience** (closed from December to February) is just across the bridge from Portmagee at the southern end, with exhibits on local history, wildlife and the life of the Skellig Michael monks.

The local landowner has transformed the island's highest point, **Geokaun** (266m), into a network of easy walking trails and viewpoints, with a breathtaking outlook over the Fogher Cliffs. It's possible to drive all the way to the top, so visitors with limited mobility don't miss out on the views. At quieter times, the site is unstaffed, and entry is via an automatic barrier (payment with coins only).

Get a Taste for Seaweed
Beach Foraging Walks

Believe it or not, seaweed has been an important resource throughout Irish history as agricultural fertiliser, medicinal compounds and even a source of food. John Fitzgerald of **Atlantic Irish Seaweed** leads 2½-hour 'seaweed discovery workshops' involving a guided walk along the Derrynane foreshore at low tide, foraging for edible seaweed (instruction on identification and sustainable harvesting is provided), followed by a tasting session of seaweed-based dishes and drinks. Workshops are tide and weather dependent, and booking is essential – check the website (atlanticirishseaweed.com) and Facebook page (facebook.com/Atlanticirishseaweed) for info.

Discover Kenmare Bay on Horseback
Pony Trekking

Whether you're an experienced equestrian or a complete beginner, you can saddle up at **Dromquinna Stables**, 4.5km west of Kenmare on the N70. The trek leaders will pair you with a suitable mount before setting off for a two-hour trot

---

WHERE TO EAT BEYOND KILLARNEY NATIONAL PARK

Smugglers Inn
Gourmet creations incorporating fresh seafood served in a sea-view conservatory just outside Waterville. €€€

Driftwood Surf Cafe
St Finian's Bay on the Skellig Ring is the setting for gourmet fish and chips with a view. €€

Moorings
Nautical-themed Portmagee restaurant specialising in locally landed seafood. €€

Kells Bay House and Gardens

along the shores of Kenmare Bay or up into the hills with grand views over the Beara and Iveragh peninsulas. They also offer 30- or 60-minute lessons and a Saturday pony club for kids, where they can learn horse grooming, tacking and riding.

Take to the Treetops Above a Miniature Rainforest
Exotic Gardens

Built in 1837 as a hunting lodge and estate, **Kells Bay House and Gardens**, 13km northeast of Cahersiveen, is now home to the largest collection of tree ferns in the northern hemisphere, a miniature primeval rainforest that thrives in the mild, humid microclimate of coastal County Kerry. Head gardener Billy Alexander won a gold medal at the 2021 Chelsea Flower Show for his display of Kells Bay ferns.

The exotic gardens sprawl over 17 hectares and incorporate a waterfall, a beach and varied walking trails decorated with dinosaurs carved from fallen trees. Ireland's longest rope bridge, the 33.5m **Skywalk**, sways precariously 11m above the River Delligeenagh, which swirls through the property.

Walled kitchen gardens provide ingredients for the gardens' unexpectedly authentic **Sala Thai** restaurant. There's also luxury B&B accommodation in Kells House.

SKELLIG RING

This 18km loop off the main Ring of Kerry offers an escape from the crowds (the road is too narrow for tour buses, lorries and motorhomes). The wild, scenic drive links Waterville to Portmagee via a Gaeltacht (Irish-speaking) area centred on **Ballinskelligs**, where you'll find a good beach.

Over the hill is **St Finian's**, an even prettier beach with the nearby temptations of **Skellig Chocolate Factory**. Another steep hill leads to the viewpoint at **Coomanaspic**, where you can look over Valentia Island to the hills of the Dingle Peninsula.

On the way down to Portmagee, don't miss the **Kerry Cliffs**, a pay-to-enter walking trail along the top of spectacular 300m-high sea cliffs, with superb views of Skellig Michael and Puffin Island.

GETTING AROUND

Numerous tour companies and hostels in Killarney offer daily coach tours of the Ring of Kerry, lasting from around 9.30am to 5pm. Operators include Killarney Executive Tour, Corcoran's Coach Tours, Deros Tours and Wild Kerry Day Tours. Different tours have different stops, so if you want to see a particular sight, check the itineraries.

Year-round, Bus Éireann service 279A runs daily between Killarney and Waterville via Killorglin and Cahersiveen. Local Link Kerry minibuses run four times a day between Kenmare and Waterville via Sneem and Caherdaniel.

DINGLE

Framed by its fishing port, the Dingle Peninsula's charming little 'capital' manages to be quaint without even trying. Some pubs double as shops, so you can enjoy Guinness and a singalong among hats, hardware, horseshoes and wellies. It has long drawn runaways from across the world, making it a cosmopolitan and creative place. In summer, its hilly streets can be clogged with visitors, but in other seasons, its authentic charms are yours for the savouring.

Dingle is one of those towns whose very fabric is its main attraction. Wander up and down the streets and back alleys, stroll along the seafront, and pop into shops, pubs, and art and craft galleries to see what you find.

Although Dingle is one of Ireland's largest Gaeltacht towns, the locals have voted to retain the name Dingle rather than go by the officially sanctioned – and signposted – Gaelic name of An Daingean.

TOP TIP

Dingle is famed for its independent shops. You'll find local artists' galleries jostling for space with fashion boutiques, jewellery makers, textile weavers, milliners, candlemakers and ceramicists. There's also a specialist cheese shop, a second-hand vinyl record shop, and a couple of excellent bookshops.

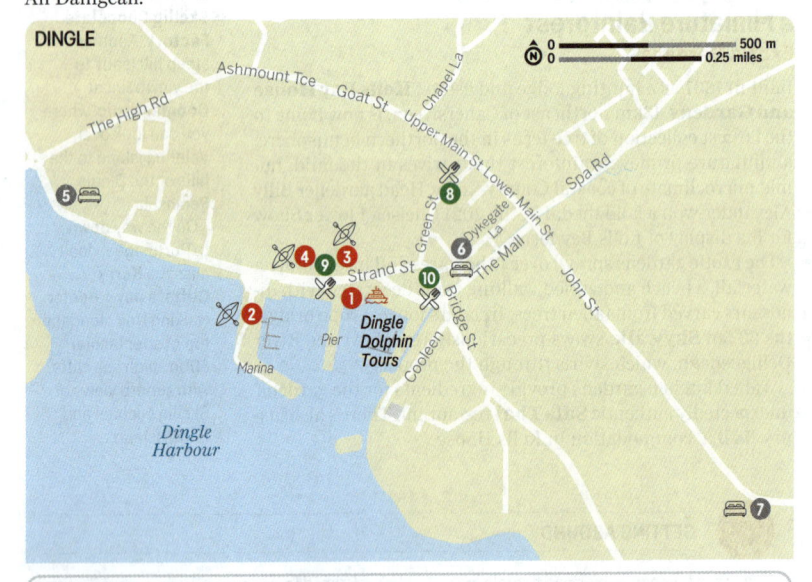

HIGHLIGHTS
1. Dingle Dolphin Tours

SIGHTS
2. Dingle Traditional Rowing
3. Irish Adventure
4. Wild SUP Tours

EATING
5. Castlewood House
6. Hideout Hostel
7. Pax House
8. Fish Box
9. Out of the Blue
10. Reel Dingle Fish Co

Dingle

Board a Harbour Cruise in Memory of Fungie
Sea Cliffs And Wildlife

For more than three decades, the classic Dingle experience was a boat trip to see Fungie, a solitary bottlenose dolphin with an unusual affinity for human company, who took up residence in Dingle harbour in 1983. He was a daily fixture in the life of the village, waiting to greet boat trips every morning and entertaining visitors with his playful repertoire of acrobatic antics until October 2020 when, sadly, he appeared no more.

But Fungie's huge influence on Dingle's tourism trade means that his memory lingers on in many ways. There's the **bronze dolphin sculpture** outside the Dingle tourist information office and a **mural** depicting Fungie on the gable of the Dingle lighthouse keeper's cottage overlooking the harbour entrance (the keeper was the first person to spot Fungie in 1983). If you take one of the ever-popular **harbour cruises**, the commentary still points out Fungie's favourite spots: the beach near the lighthouse where he would accompany human swimmers and the cave outside the harbour known as 'Fungie's Bedroom', where he was observed sleeping during his lifetime.

BEST SEAFOOD IN DINGLE

Fish Box
Expect fast, friendly and efficient service and an inventive seafood menu at this informal but hugely popular eatery. €€

Out of the Blue
One of Dingle's top restaurants, devoted to fresh local seafood – and only seafood. If staff don't like the day's catch, they don't open, and they resolutely don't serve chips. €€€

Reel Dingle Fish Co
Locals queue along the street to get hold of the freshly cooked local haddock (or cod, or monkfish, or hake, or mackerel...) and chips at this tiny outlet. €

WHERE TO STAY IN DINGLE

Castlewood House
Dingle's top hotel, a haven of country-house quiet and sophistication 10 minutes stroll from the town centre. €€€

Pax House
Luxury B&B with outstanding sea views from the glass-framed terrace and balconies opening from some rooms. €€

Hideout Hostel
Central location with top-notch facilities, including two lounges, bike storage and a well-equipped kitchen. €

Fungie also leaves a legacy of ecotourism and increased awareness of the marine environment. The standard one-hour harbour cruise operated by **Dingle Dolphin Tours** offers the chance to spot seals and perhaps some wild dolphins, but it is worth doing for the sea cliff scenery alone. The highlight comes when the skipper (sea conditions permitting) backs the boat gingerly into **Thunder Cove**, a yawning cleft in the cliffs.

Take to the Water in Dingle Harbour
Sample A Range Of Watersports

The sheltered waters of Dingle Harbour make it an ideal location for beginners to try their hand at a range of watersports. **Irish Adventures** runs half-day sea-kayaking trips where you learn basic skills and explore the caves and arches in the sea cliffs at the harbour mouth.

Alternatively, you could try stand-up paddleboarding with **Wild SUP Tours**, which operates half- and full-day SUP safaris around the harbour, as well as a nighttime SUP adventure on a freshwater lake beneath the stars in the heart of the Kerry Dark Sky Reserve.

Dingle Traditional Rowing offers the chance to wield an oar aboard a *naomhòg* (pronounced nuh-*vogue*), the Kerry name for a *currach,* a traditional Irish boat made from a wooden frame covered with tarred canvas (originally animal hides). They were used by the Blasket islanders for fishing and are now maintained and raced by local enthusiasts. Book a one-hour session in Dingle Harbour (minimum of two people) to learn how to row one.

Go Face to Face with a Shark
Discover Dingle's Marine Aquarium

Dingle Oceanworld makes a good rainy-day alternative to a wildlife cruise. Psychedelic fish glide through tanks that recreate such environments as Lake Malawi, the River Congo and the piranha-filled Amazon. Get up close to huge reef sharks and stingrays at the shark tank and stroke a thornback ray at the touch pool. Water pumped from the harbour fills the Ocean Tunnel tank, where you can spot native Irish species, such as dogfish, mullet, plaice, conger eels and the spectacularly ugly wreckfish.

DINGLE FOOD FESTIVAL

Held over three days at the end of September, this fabulous foodie fest features a 'taste trail' with sampling at dozens of locations around town, plus a market, cooking demonstrations, workshops and a foraging walk. There are also beer, cider, whiskey and wine tastings, a bake-off competition and street entertainment, as well as children's events.

Past workshops have included an introduction to beekeeping, a druid's guide to medicinal plants, cheese and wine pairing, cocktail mixing, cake decorating and how to grow herbs in your own kitchen.

GETTING AROUND

Dingle town is easily covered on foot. If you want to venture further afield, bike-hire places include Dingle Electric Bike Experience and Paddy's Bike Shop.

On-street parking is free throughout town, but it's hard to find a spot. There are large pay-and-display car parks on Green St and at the harbour, where you can park all day for a couple of euros.

Dingle Cabs operates a local taxi service and can arrange Kerry, Cork and Shannon airport transfers, as well as private guided tours of the Dingle Peninsula.

Beyond Dingle

Have your phone or camera at the ready – this is where Dingle's scenery goes into overdrive.

One of the highlights of the Wild Atlantic Way, the Dingle Peninsula (Corca Dhuibhne) to the west of Dingle town culminates in the Irish mainland's westernmost point at Dunmore Head. In the shadow of sacred Mt Brandon, a maze of fuchsia-fringed *boreens* (country lanes) weaves together an ancient landscape of prehistoric ring forts and beehive huts; early Christian chapels, crosses and holy wells; picturesque hamlets; and abandoned villages.

But it's where the land meets the ocean around Slea Head Dr – whether in a welter of surf-pounded rocks or where the waves lap quietly in secluded, sandy coves – that the Dingle Peninsula's beauty truly reveals itself.

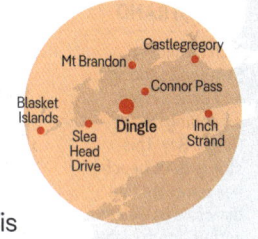

TOP TIP

The road around Slea Head Dr gets pretty narrow and twisty in places, best avoided if you have a caravan or motorhome.

Coumeenoole beach (p247), Slea Head

INCH STRAND

Inch Strand is a 5km-long sand spit and dune system extending into Dingle Bay. This stupendous beach has attracted film directors as well as surfers, land-yachters and anglers – it has appeared in the movies *Ryan's Daughter* (1970), *Excalibur* (1981), and *Far and Away* (1992), among others.

The dunes are a great spot for windswept walks, birdwatching and bathing. The west-facing Blue Flag beach (lifeguarded in summer) is also a hot surfing spot; waves average 1m to 3m. Learn to ride them with **Offshore Surf School** or watch others surf from the terrace at **Sammy's Bar**.

Cars are allowed on the beach, but don't end up providing others with nonstop laughs by getting stuck.

Great Blasket Island

Islands on the Edge of Europe
Boat Trip To The Blaskets

The **Blasket Islands** (Na Blascaodaí) off the tip of the Dingle Peninsula are the most westerly part of Ireland and one of the westernmost points in Europe (after Iceland, the Azores and Rockall). All of the islands were lived on at one time or another; there is evidence of the largest, **Great Blasket** (An Blascaod Mór), being inhabited during the Iron Age and early Christian times. But no more – the last islanders abandoned their homes in 1953, moving to the mainland or North America after they and the government agreed that it was no longer viable to live in such harsh and isolated conditions.

The rich history and cultural life of the islands are celebrated in the **Blasket Centre** at Dunquin, a wonderful interpretative centre housed in a striking modern building with a long white hall ending in a picture window looking directly at the islands. Great Blasket's rich community of storytellers and musicians is profiled along with its literary visitors, such as playwright JM Synge, author of *The Playboy of the Western World*. The more prosaic practicalities of island life are covered by exhibits on boatbuilding and fishing.

WHERE TO STAY BEYOND DINGLE TOWN

Campaíl Teach An Aragail
Situated 450m west of Gallarus Oratory, this campground is just a 1km stroll from beautiful Wine Strand beach. €

Inch Beach House
This bright and cheerful B&B is all about sea views; higher-priced rooms face directly over beautiful Inch Strand. €€

Old Pier B&B
With a view across Smerwick Harbour to the Three Sisters, this B&B enjoys the perfect sunset location. €€

DISCOVER THE SLEA HEAD DRIVE

Starting and finishing in Dingle town, Slea Head Drive runs around the tip of the Dingle Peninsula passing through the villages of Ventry, Dunquin and Ballyferriter. It's home to a host of superbly preserved structures from the ancient past including beehive huts, ring forts, inscribed stones and early Christian sites. Driving clockwise offers the best views. Although it's a mere 47km in length, doing this drive justice requires a full day.

The first stop, 5.5km beyond Ventry, is **1 Dunbeg Fort**, a dramatic example of an Iron Age promontory fortification perched atop a sheer sea cliff. Inside the fort's four outer stone walls are the remains of a house and a beehive hut, as well as an underground passage. Another 800m further on is **2 Fahan Beehive Huts**, a gathering of five stone structures dating from 500 CE, including two that are fully intact. The road is at its narrowest, just a ledge blasted out of the steep rock face, as it rounds **3 Slea Head** itself with views of Dunmore Head (the westernmost point of the Irish mainland) and Great Blasket Island. A car park on the left gives access to the picturesque cove of **4 Coumeenoole Beach**, from where you can easily hike out to Dunmore Head, the westernmost point of the Irish mainland (2km round trip).

The road continues more easily through Dunquin, with stunning views in both directions from the **5 Clogher Head viewpoint** before reaching **6 Músaem Chorca Dhuibhne** (West Kerry Museum), with displays on the history, geology, archaeology and ecology of the peninsula. The route then passes the beautiful 1200-year-old **7 Gallarus Oratory** before returning over the hill to Dingle town.

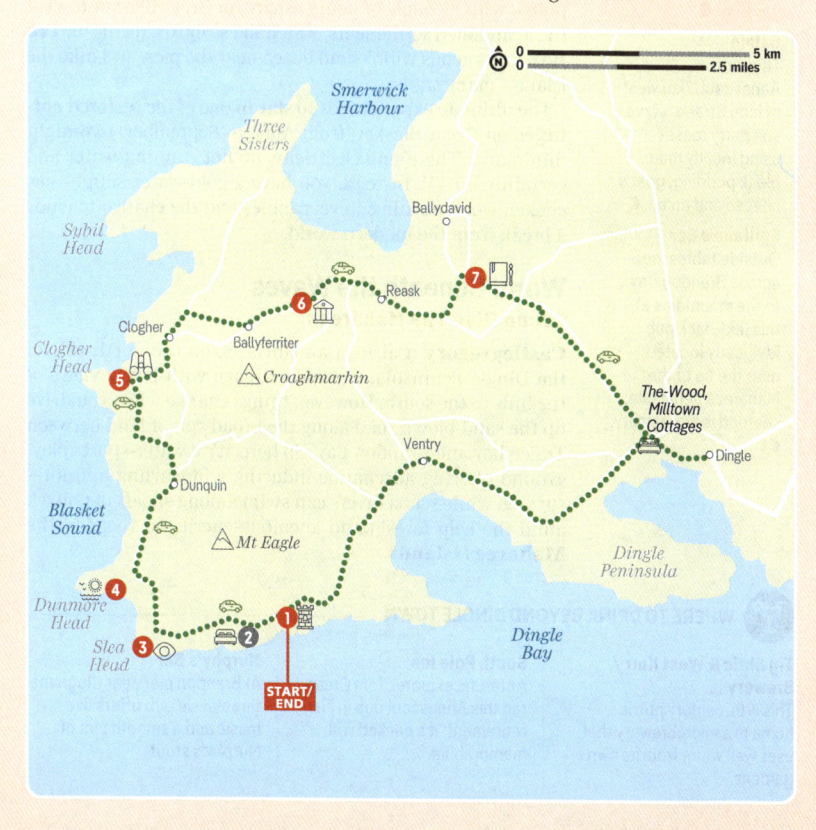

BEST PLACES TO EAT BEYOND DINGLE TOWN

Louis Mulcahy Cafe
The bright, contemporary cafe at Louis Mulcahy Pottery, a popular stop on Slea Head Dr, serves fresh homemade fare with local produce and herbs from its own gardens. €

Báinín
This cafe in Annascaul, 7km west of Inch Strand, serves specialty toasties using locally made black pudding, goat's cheese and onion. €

Spillane's Bar
Outside tables look across Brandon Bay to the mountains at this laid-back pub idyllically located near the tip of the Maharees peninsula; seafood is a speciality. €€

Dahlia anemone, Maharees Islands

Several operators run full-day **boat trips** to explore the sea cliffs and coves around the islands and look for whales and dolphins, with a couple of hours ashore on Great Blasket to visit the abandoned settlements, watch the seabirds, picnic on **Trá Bán** (a gorgeous white-sand beach near the pier) and hike the island's many trails.

The ultimate experience is to stay in one of the restored **cottages** on Great Blasket (from April to September, two-night minimum). There's no electricity, no hot running water and certainly no TV. Instead, you have a cold-water supply, gas cooker, wood-burning stove, candles and the chance to enjoy a break from the modern world.

World Beneath the Waves
Scuba Dive The Maharees

Castlegregory (Caislean an Ghriare), on the north side of the Dingle Peninsula, is a quiet village with lovely views of the hills to the south. However, things change when you drive up the sand-blown road along the broad spit of land between Tralee Bay and Brandon Bay. Up here, it's a water-sports playground offering adrenaline-inducing windsurfing and kitesurfing, while scuba divers can swim among shoals of pollack amid the kelp forests and anemone-encrusted rocks of the **Maharees Islands**.

WHERE TO DRINK BEYOND DINGLE TOWN

Tig Bhric & West Kerry Brewery
This 19th-century pub is home to a microbrewery that uses well water from its own gardens.

South Pole Inn
Antarctic explorer Tom Crean ran this Annascaul pub in his retirement; it's packed with memorabilia.

Murphy's Bar
At Brandon pier near Cloghane, this classic pub offers live music and a smooth pint of Murphy's stout.

Along with Brandon Point and the Blasket Islands, the Maharees offer some of the best scuba-diving in Ireland. For qualified divers, **Waterworld**, based at Fahamore, runs daily boat trips to the best dive sites as well as half-day Try-a-Dive packages for beginners.

Walk in the Footsteps of Saints
Early Christian Ruins

A waymarked 18km walking trail, the **Saint's Road** (*Cosàn na Naomh*) follows the route of an ancient pilgrim path from the beach at Ventry to Ballybrack (An Baile Breac) at the foot of Mt Brandon. A shorter variation is to walk the 3km between the Dingle Peninsula's two main early Christian sites of Gallarus and Kilmalkedar.

Gallarus Oratory, 8km northwest of Dingle town, is one of Ireland's most beautiful ancient buildings, its smoothly constructed dry-stone walls in the shape of an upturned boat. It has withstood the elements in this lonely spot beneath the brown hills for some 1200 years.

Kilmalkedar Church, 3km northeast of Gallarus, has a beautiful setting with sweeping views over Smerwick Harbour. Built in the 12th century on the site of a 7th-century monastery founded by St Maolcethair, it's a superb example of Irish Romanesque architecture. Its round-arched west door is decorated with chevron patterns and a carved human head. In the graveyard, you'll find an Ogham stone and a carved stone sundial.

Brave the Heights of the Connor Pass
Scenic Drive Or Bike Ride

Topping out at 456m, the R560 road across the Connor Pass from Dingle town to Cloghane is Ireland's highest public road. On a foggy day, you'll see nothing but the tarmac in front of you, but in fine weather, it offers phenomenal views of Dingle Harbour to the south and Mt Brandon to the north. The road is in good shape despite being narrow, steep and twisting on the north side. Large signs portend doom for buses and trucks; caravans are forbidden.

The pass is a classic challenge for cyclists. It's best to start in Dingle town, from where the road climbs 400m over 7km. The climb from the north is more brutal and has the added problem of being single track at the final, steepest section, so you'll be holding up traffic.

MT BRANDON

Mt Brandon (Cnoc Bréanainn; 952m) stands in splendid isolation to the north of Dingle, bounded by spectacular cliffs and glacial lakes to the northeast and falling steeply into the sea to the northwest. The easiest way to the summit is via the old pilgrim path from the car park at Ballybrack on its south side, signposted off the R549 11km north of Dingle town.

From the car park, the path leads arrow-straight towards the top, passing numbered wooden crucifixes marking the 14 Stations of the Cross, before deviating to the right for a single zigzag before the summit, which is marked by a huge cairn and a 15th cross. Descend by the same route for a total of 8.5km; allow three hours.

GETTING AROUND

Your own wheels are best for exploring. If you're not pushed for time, it's possible to explore the peninsula west of Dingle town by bike. Several places rent them out.

Local Link Kerry operates minibus services from Dingle town to Ventry, Ballyferriter and Dunquin three to six times a day, and from Tralee to Castlegregory, Clochane and Brandon Point twice a week.

TRALEE

Although it's the biggest town in County Kerry, Tralee is down to earth and more engaged with the business of everyday life than the tourist trade. Nonetheless, a fascinating museum and a historic working windmill make it well worth a stop.

Founded by the Normans in 1216, Tralee has a long history of rebellion. In the 16th century, the last ruling earl of the Desmonds was captured and executed here. His head was sent to Elizabeth I, who spiked it on London Bridge. The Desmonds' castle once stood at the junction of Denny St and the Mall, but any trace of medieval Tralee that survived the Desmond Wars was razed during the Cromwellian period.

Elegant Denny St and Day Pl are the oldest parts of town, with 18th-century Georgian buildings, while the Square, just south of the Mall, is a contemporary open space.

TOP TIP

Tralee is home to Siamsa Tíre, the National Folk Theatre of Ireland. The name (pronounced shee-*am*-sa *tee*-ruh) is Irish for 'mirth and music of the land', and the theatre company specialises in recreating dynamic aspects of Gaelic culture through song, dance, drama and mime. There are several shows a week year-round.

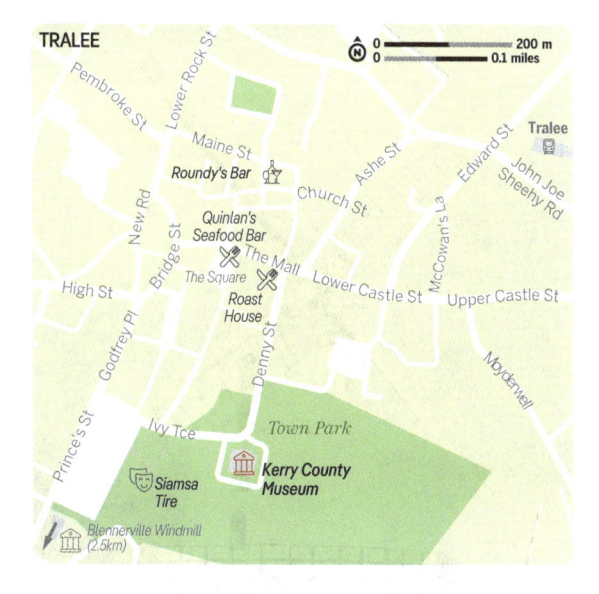

Meet Tralee's Local Heroes
History Brought To Life

Kerry County Museum does an admirable job of interpreting the lives and achievements of local heroes Sir Roger Casement and Tom Crean. In doomed preparations for the 1916 Easter Rising, Casement was famously landed from a German submarine on Banna Strand north of Tralee. Crean was an explorer who accompanied both Robert Falcon Scott and Ernest Shackleton on epic Antarctic expeditions. In the basement, the Medieval Experience recreates life (smells and all) in Tralee in 1450.

A Rose by Any Other Name
International Beauty Contest

The country's biggest beauty pageant – the **Rose of Tralee International Festival**, held in August – divides the nation between those who see it as a celebration of Irishness and critics who deride it as an embarrassing throwback to outdated attitudes. Founded in 1959, the festival sees wannabe 'Roses' plucked from all over Ireland and from Irish communities throughout the world compete for the coveted crown. More than just a beauty contest, though, it's a five-day-long festival bookended by a gala ball and a 'midnight madness' parade led by the newly crowned Rose of Tralee, followed by a fireworks display.

Rose of Tralee

BEST PLACES TO EAT & DRINK IN TRALEE

Roast House
Breakfasts of pancakes with bacon and lunches of barbecue pulled-pork sandwiches: you might have to wait for a table at this ever-popular eatery. €€

Quinlan's Seafood Bar
Quinlan's has its own fishing boats, so you know everything is fresh. The fish and chips are great; alternatives include Dingle Bay squid with sweet chilli sauce. €

Roundy's Bar
Converted from a terrace house (with a tree still growing in the interior courtyard), this hip little bar has cool tunes, regular DJs and live bands.

Blennerville Windmill

Tour a Working Windmill
History And Engineering

Blennerville, 3.4km southwest of Tralee's centre on the N86 to Dingle, used to be the city's chief port, though the harbour has long since silted up. A relic of that time, **Blennerville Windmill** is a 220-year-old structure that has been fully restored and is now the largest working windmill in Ireland. Its modern visitor centre houses exhibitions on flour milling, as well as on the thousands of emigrants who boarded 'coffin ships' from what was then Kerry's largest embarkation point.

GETTING AROUND

Tralee's compact town centre is easily covered on foot. You can walk to Blennerville in 45 minutes via the Canal Walk, which begins at the south end of Basin Rd, or cycle there in 15 minutes. Rent a bike from O'Halloran Cycles in the town centre.

If you're travelling by car, use the main pay-and-display car park on Prince's St. From here, it's only a couple minutes' walk to the Kerry County Museum and the town centre beyond.

Beyond Tralee

Explore endless beaches with mountain views, a world-class golf course and a bucolic book-lover's town.

Consisting mainly of flat farmland – all those cows grazing the lush green pastures provide the milk that goes to make Ireland's famous Kerrygold butter – northern Kerry's landscapes can't compare to the spectacular Ring of Kerry or the Dingle Peninsula. But there are some interesting places that merit a stop.

Banna Strand is one of Ireland's finest beaches, and the little village of Ardfert boasts an impressive ruined cathedral. The seaside resort of Ballybunion is home to a world-class golf club and scenic clifftop walk. The elegant town of Listowel has more literary connections than most Irish towns outside Dublin, and it hosts the country's oldest literary and arts festival.

TOP TIP

Normally sleepy Listowel is at its liveliest during the Writers Week festival at the end of May.

Ballybunion

Ardfert Cathedral

Sunbathe & Swim With a View
Blue Flag Beach

A favourite weekend getaway for Tralee residents, **Banna Strand** is one of the biggest and best Blue Flag beaches in Ireland, a 10km stretch of fine golden sand backed by 10m-high dunes, with fantastic views southwest to Mt Brandon and the Dingle hills. A **monument** 500m south of the main car park marks the spot where the Irish revolutionary leader Roger Casement was landed from a German U-boat shortly before the 1916 Easter Rising.

The beach is 13km northwest of Tralee, signposted off the R551 Ballyheigue road. Signs lead to the main car park, which is often crowded, but there's another, more secluded (unsurfaced) parking area in the dunes 300m southwest of the Casement monument, which gives access to the much quieter south end of the beach.

Romanesque Ruins
Medieval Architecture

The impressive remains of 13th-century **Ardfert Cathedral** are notable for the beautiful and delicate stone carvings on its Romanesque door and window arches. Set into one of the interior walls is an effigy, said to be of St Brendan the Navigator, who was educated in Ardfert and founded a monastery

---

BEST RESTAURANTS BEYOND TRALEE

Oyster Tavern
Pan-fried Kerry Head crab claws, Dingle Bay prawn scampi and lobster in season star at this classy restaurant in Spa, 7km west of Tralee. €€

West End Bar & Bistro
'Fresh or nothing' is the motto of this local icon in the village of Fenit, 13km west of Tralee. The fifth-generation-run bar serves a mouth-watering lineup of seafood. €€

Lizzy's Little Kitchen
This busy Listowel cafe is a top spot for lunch, whether squeezed around one of the tables or perched at the window counter. €

WHERE TO STAY BEYOND TRALEE

Cliff House Hotel
Lovely family-run hotel in Ballybunion, with great sea views from the conservatory-style breakfast room. €€€

Listowel Arms Hotel
Listowel's principal hotel is a Georgian building that balances grandeur with country charm. €€

Teach de Broc
Framed by flowers, this low-rise boutique B&B next to the golf club has 14 spacious rooms that are thoughtfully appointed. €€

here. Other elaborate medieval grave slabs can be seen in the visitor centre. Ardfert is 9km northwest of Tralee on the Ballyheigue road.

Tee Off at Ballybunion Golf Club
Famous Links Course

The beach town of Ballybunion is best known for its eponymous golf club. A statue of a club-swinging Bill Clinton in the middle of town commemorates his visit to the course in 1998. (He played it again in 2001.) **Ballybunion Golf Club** is renowned as one of the finest links courses in the world. Weekends and bank holidays are reserved for members, but visitors can book tee times to play the par 71, 1893-established Old Course on weekday mornings or the par-72 Cashen Course on weekday mornings and afternoons.

Watch Sunset from the Clifftops
Ballybunion Cliff Walk

Ballybunion faces west into the Atlantic and is famed for its glorious sunsets. The best place to soak up the view is from the **Cliff Walk**, a signposted trail that follows the clifftop to the north of the town, starting opposite the Cliff House Hotel and finishing at the beautiful cliff-bound cove of **Nuns Beach**, named for the convent above it.

Overlooking the town's main beach are the restored remains of **Ballybunion Castle** (aka Fitzmaurice Castle), the 16th-century seat of the Fitzmaurices, with views to the Dingle Peninsula and Loop Head, County Clare.

Literary Listowel
Writers Town And Festival

Listowel's tidy Georgian streets are arranged around an attractive main square with a 12th-century Norman castle overlooking the River Feale. This place has more literary credentials than your average provincial town, with connections to half a dozen of Ireland's best-known writers. The **Kerry Writers Museum**, next to the castle, celebrates Listowel's observers of Irish life with rooms devoted to local greats, such as John B Keane and Bryan MacMahon, with simple, haunting tableaux narrating their lives and recordings of them reading their work. During **Writers Week** in late May, bibliophiles flock to Listowel for five days of readings, poetry, music, drama, seminars, storytelling and other events.

CRAG CAVE

This cave was discovered in 1983 when problems with water pollution led to a search for the source of the local river. In 1989, 300m of the 4km-long cave were opened to the public; admission is by 30-minute guided tour involving 72 steps. The remarkable rock formations include a stalagmite shaped (to some) like a statue of the Madonna. There are play areas for kids, a restaurant and a gift shop. The cave is signposted 18km east of Tralee.

GETTING AROUND

Three buses a day run from Tralee to Listowel and continue to Ballybunion, but to explore properly, including Banna Strand and Ardfert, you'll need a car.

If you are continuing north from Kerry to visit County Clare, an hourly car ferry goes from Tarbert to Killimer that saves a 134km detour via Limerick.

Above: Celtic cross, Rock of Cashel (p268); right: Galtee Mountains (p274)

LIMERICK & TIPPERARY

HEARTLANDS, HISTORY AND CULTURE

From marching ditties to rhyming verse, the names Tipperary and Limerick are part of the Western lexicon, but both counties are relatively unexplored by visitors.

Culture and history abound in this region, with castles and abbeys, mountain valleys and quaint undiscovered towns aplenty. Limerick is bordered by the mouth of the mighty River Shannon, Ireland's longest, and the coast to the north. Swelling uplands and mountains separate Limerick from Cork to the south and Tipperary to the east.

County Limerick is closely tied to its namesake city, which has a history as dramatic as Ireland's. In a nation of hard knocks, it has had more than its fair share. The city's streets have tangible links to the past and a gritty, honest vibrancy, while treasures abound in its lush, green countryside.

In contrast, Tipperary town is minor. But amid the county's rolling hills, rich farmland and deep valleys bordered by soaring mountains, it's a peaceful place that's perfect for following a river to its source or climbing a stile to reach a lonely ruin. The Gaelic Athletic Association (GAA) was founded in the town of Thurles, and Tipperary is known as the home of hurling, though both counties have a strong devotion to traditional Irish sports and rugby. Visiting a pub full of supporters on match day is an experience to remember.

In both counties, ancient Celtic sites, medieval abbeys and other relics endure in solitude, awaiting discovery. And even Limerick and Tipperary's best-known sights retain a rough, inspiring dignity.

THE MAIN AREAS

LIMERICK CITY
A buzzing city rich in history. **p260**

CASHEL
A pretty town, a majestic castle and lush countryside. **p266**

THE GALTEES & GLEN OF AHERLOW
Stunning scenery, road trips and hillwalking. **p274**

Find Your Way

Limerick and Tipperary straddle the centre of the lower Midlands, spanning east to the mouth of the Shannon and west to the Atlantic. It takes about two hours to drive between the furthermost edges of these counties.

Cashel, p266
This idyllic town is home to one of the most famous historical sites in Ireland, the Rock of Cashel.

The Galtees & Glen of Aherlow, p274
Nestled between the hills and grassland, the Glen of Aherlow offers scenic drives and hillwalks.

Limerick City, p260
Ireland's third-largest city has an impressive castle on the mouth of the country's longest river.

CAR
As in most places in Ireland, having your own car is the most convenient way to explore, especially if you want to get off the beaten path and into the heartlands of these counties.

BUS & TRAIN
Limerick city is well connected to surrounding towns by bus, but in Tipperary, bus services are limited at times. The train connects both counties. Bus Éireann and Irish Rail serve both regions.

Limerick city (p260)

Plan Your Time

Cities, towns and castles abound from the green hills of the Galtees to the Shannon Estuary, and the heartlands of Ireland give a real insight into the country's culture.

One Day Only

Get to **Cashel** (p266) early to check out the impressive **Rock of Cashel** (p268) looming over the town below. After a morning at the Rock, enjoy a luxurious lunch at **Mikey Ryan's** (p267). Hit the road for **Cahir** (p271) to check out its **castle** and the **Swiss cottage**. Take the scenic drive through the **Glen of Aherlow** (p275) on your way back toward Cashel.

Five Days to Explore

Spend one day in **Limerick city** (p260) before heading to the **Foynes Flying Boat Museum** (p265) and the charming village of **Adare** (p264). Spend your third day in the **Glen of Aherlow** (p274) and **Cahir** (p271) and dedicate another day to **Cashel** (p266). Visit **Thurles** (p272) and go on to **Upperchurch** (p273) to hit the trails. On a Thursday, grab a pint at **Jim O' the Mills** (p273).

Seasonal Highlights

SPRING
Flowers are blooming, and the walking trails in the Galtees are starting to thaw out. Daffodils dot the countryside during St Patrick's Day parades.

SUMMER
Expect longer days and better weather for exploring, as well as lots of local festivals and GAA matches.

AUTUMN
The weather is pleasant as the early evenings start to darken and woodland trees turn wonderful shades of orange and brown.

WINTER
Dark evenings make winter an ideal time to enjoy roaring fires and live music in local pubs. Some attractions may be closed. Christmas lights twinkle.

LIMERICK CITY

The Vikings founded Limerick, Ireland's third-largest city and a gateway to the Wild Atlantic Way, in 922 CE, and its important role in Irish history is evident in its medieval city streets, Norman history and ancient Irish monuments.

Limerick was crowned Ireland's first City of Culture in 2014, and the subsequent investment saw a rejuvenated waterfront complete with a stylish boardwalk. It feels far removed from Frank McCourt's bleak portrayal in his autobiographical novel *Angela's Ashes*, for which he won the Pulitzer Prize. The city has a mighty castle, a spectacular arched stone bridge across the river and a burgeoning arts scene, and is often buzzing with hurling and rugby fans watching matches in the lively local pubs.

Limerick has a decent range of quality accommodation and many excellent eateries that focus on fresh Irish produce. Aim to stay near the city centre for the convenience and the nightlife.

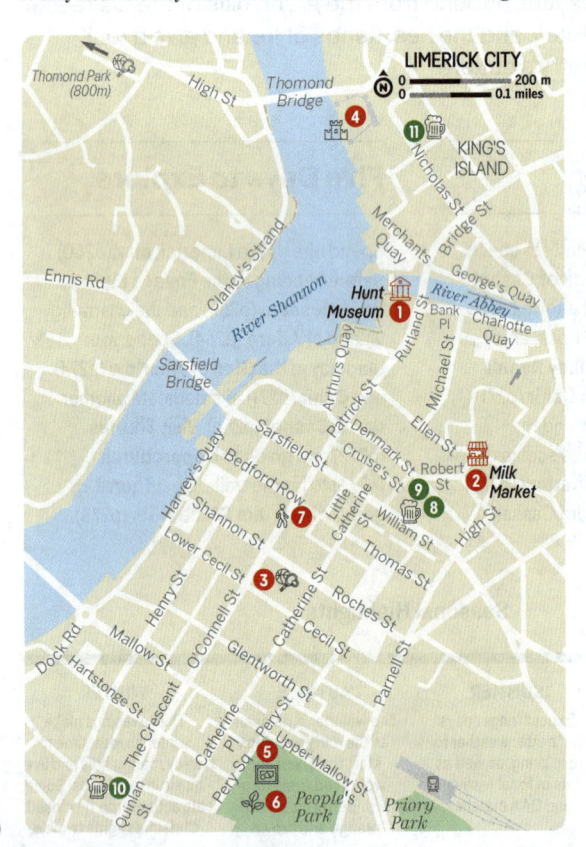

TOP TIP

Limerick city's main places of interest are clustered north of the city centre on King's Island and to the south in the Georgian area. For the best city views, walk from the city centre to King John's Castle, cross Sarsfield Bridge and follow the riverside walk north to Thomond Bridge.

HIGHLIGHTS
1. Hunt Museum
2. Milk Market

SIGHTS
3. International Rugby Experience
4. King John's Castle
5. Limerick City Gallery of Art
6. People's Park

SIGHTS
7. Angela's Ashes Walking Tour

DRINKING & NIGHTLIFE
8. Flannery's Bar
9. Nancy Blake's
10. South's
11. Treaty City Brewery

Milk Market

Spend a Day in Limerick
Architecture And Heritage

Limerick city is home to some of the finest examples of Georgian architecture in Western Europe. Housed in the 18th-century former Custom House, the **Hunt Museum** is unusual compared to Limerick's other Georgian buildings, as the exterior is limestone rather than red brick, designed by Italian architect Davis Ducart in Palladian style. Inside, marvel at artefacts from ancient Greece and Rome as well as art by masters like Pablo Picasso.

If it's a Saturday morning, walk 500m south to the **Milk Market**, the oldest weekly market in the country, which takes place in Limerick's old market buildings. Pick from organic produce and artisan foods including local fruits and vegetables, preserves, baked goods and farmhouse cheeses; browse the flower and craft stalls; or grab a bite at one of the hot-food tables.

Continue south to **People's Park**, a lovely wooded spot at the heart of Georgian Limerick. The **Limerick City Gallery of Art** adjoins the peaceful park. Among its permanent collection of paintings from the last 300 years are works by Sean Keating and Jack B Yeats.

FRANK MCCOURT'S LIMERICK

Since the 1990s, no name has been so closely intertwined with Limerick as Frank McCourt (1930–2009). His autobiographical novel *Angela's Ashes* was a surprise sensation in 1996, winning him the Pulitzer Prize. The book was later made into a film.

When the book was published, the reaction in Limerick was mixed, with some claiming it portrayed the city in a negative light. Today, however, McCourt's legacy is celebrated. The city's tourist office has information about sights related to the book, and you can join *Angela's Ashes* walking tours and drink in South's, one of the pubs McCourt mentions in the book.

WHERE TO DRINK IN LIMERICK CITY

Nancy Blake's
A cosy pub with sawdust on the floor and peat on the fire. The covered beer garden often has live music or sports on TV.

Flannery's Bar
Large and lively pub in a former soap factory, with more than 100 varieties of Irish whiskey and a roof terrace.

South's
Author Frank McCourt had his first pint here. Check out the fantastically reproduced neoclassical interior.

Stroll back north along the quays before arriving at **King John's Castle**, one of the best-preserved Norman castles in Europe. A multimedia experience provides an excellent potted history of Ireland in general, and Limerick in particular.

Afterwards, follow in the footsteps of award-winning author Frank McCourt on a guided **Angela's Ashes Walking Tour**. Book your spot at the tourist office near the castle.

Local Craft Beer Experience
Hops And History

Housed in two renovated 18th-century buildings in the heart of Limerick's Medieval Quarter, **Treaty City Brewery** produces some of the finest craft beers in the country. Join an hour-long tour to learn about the city's rich brewing tradition and discover how the brewers use locally sourced hops and malts to develop unique beers, such as the signature Harris Pale Ale with citrusy and floral flavours.

Limerick in Action
Adventure Activities And Rugby

Experience the city from a watery perspective with **Limerick Adventures** (limerickadventures.com), which offers tours by kayak, SUP or sailboat on the River Shannon. Tours start behind the Hunt Museum and take you past many of Limerick's sights. For those who prefer to keep their feet dry but not necessarily on the ground, the company also offers an abseiling experience at King John's Castle, in which the brave can descend the walls of the fortress by rope.

Rugby fans should visit **Thomond Park**, the home ground of Munster Rugby. On weekdays, you can join a guided stadium tour that takes you to places usually only accessible to players and officials, including the home dressing room, the tunnel and the touchline.

The **International Rugby Experience** on O'Connell St also makes you feel like you're on the pitch – but you're the star of the show. Upon entry, you swipe your ticket at a turnstile and hear the distinctive roar of a match-day crowd. A door opens, and you leave the dressing room like a player heading for the pitch. Giant projections cover every wall, and the voice of local rugby legend Paul O'Connell booms through the sound system.

TRACING IRISH ANCESTRY

An estimated 50 to 80 million people around the world have Irish heritage, and genealogical centres in Limerick and Tipperary can help you get in touch with your roots. Contact the centres in advance to arrange a consultation.

Limerick Genealogy
Professional genealogical research service in Dooradoyle.

Tipperary Family History Research
At the Excel Heritage Centre in Tipperary town.

Tipperary South Genealogy Centre
A comprehensive family-history research service in the Brú Ború Heritage Centre in Cashel.

GETTING AROUND

Limerick city is compact enough to get around on foot or by bike. There's a bike-share scheme, with 23 stations around town and costing €3 for three days with a €150 deposit for visitors. The first 30 minutes of each hire is free.

Buses are frequent and reliable with many stops around the city centre.,

Beyond Limerick City

Get out of the city to explore postcard-perfect villages surrounded by lush countryside and the Shannon Estuary.

Limerick's low-lying farmland is framed on its southern and eastern boundaries by swelling uplands and mountains. Travellers often overlook County Limerick because it's set between Clare and Kerry, two counties home to more famous Irish landmarks, but it's worth lingering here.

Slow down and meander along the scenic River Shannon and its estuary or get your adrenaline pumping on a mountain biking trip and soak in the beauty of the Ballyhoura Mountains. Lose yourself in the charming streets of Adare, renowned for its thatched cottages.

In this part of the country, you can immerse yourself in the outdoors, get away from the crowds and connect with locals.

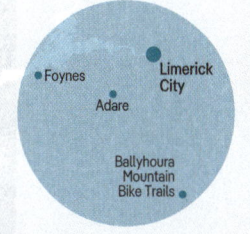

TOP TIP

Adare is famous for its fine dining, but you'll need to reserve in advance for Friday or Saturday dinners.

Thatched cottage, Adare

Ballyhoura Mountain Bike Trails

Ambling Around Adare
Ireland's Prettiest Village

Just a 30-minute drive from Limerick city, the heritage town of **Adare** on the banks of the River Maigue is a picture-perfect village, often touted as one of Ireland's most beautiful. With its blend of history, natural beauty and warm hospitality, Adare is a true experience of Ireland's old-world charm, though it's no secret – the village gets busy at weekends and in summer.

Learn more about the history of the area at the **Adare Heritage Centre** through interactive exhibits, displays and informative guides. Experience medieval Adare with a visit to the 13th-century **Desmond Castle** and the ruins of a **Franciscan Friary**, founded in 1464 and, despite its appearance, one of the most structurally complete Franciscan foundations in Ireland.

Take a tranquil stroll along the banks of the River Maigue in Adare's **Riverside Park**. Enjoy the scenic views and bring a picnic for lunch. If you're a golfer, tee off at the world-class **Adare Manor Golf Resort**. This championship course set amidst rolling parkland offers a challenging and scenic 18 holes.

ADARE MANOR

Built in the mid-19th century for the Earl of Dunraven, this magnificent manor house now houses a luxury hotel. After extensive renovations in 2017, it sports a bedroom wing and a huge ballroom to complement an already elegant property dripping in class and filled with antique furniture.

For a slightly more affordable experience, the manor's superb Oakroom Restaurant and lavish afternoon tea are open to nonguests.

WHERE TO STAY IN ADARE

Dunraven Arms
A family-run place built in 1792 with old-fashioned charm, four-poster beds, open fires and a great restaurant. €€

Berkeley Lodge
Great location with six homely and antique-styled rooms, each in a different colour. Fantastic breakfasts. €

Adare Country House
Relaxed B&B with stylishly decorated rooms a short walk from town. Parking provided. €€

Flying Boats in Foynes
Plane Spotting And Aviation History

From 1939 to 1945, the village of **Foynes** was the landing place for the flying boats that linked North America with the British Isles. The first commercial passenger flight between New York and Europe landed here in 1939 and used the River Shannon as a runway.

The one-of-a-kind **Foynes Flying Boat Museum** houses the world's only full-size replica of a Boeing 314 Flying Boat. Experience how these transatlantic seaplanes were the height of luxury at the time. The site is also home to the **Irish Coffee Centre** where you can book a group Irish coffee masterclass and learn about the history of the world-famous beverage.

Adventure on Two Wheels & Two Legs
Ballyhoura's Mountain Biking And Walking Trails

Strap on your helmet and embark on a thrilling adventure through the rugged beauty of the Ballyhoura Mountains. Spanning a whopping 98km, the **Ballyhoura Mountain Bike Trails** offer an extensive network of routes that cater to all levels of skill and bravery. With challenging singletracks, heart-pounding descents, rock gardens and exciting jumps, it's a mountain biker's paradise.

The area is divided into five loops, with trails from 6km to 52km that range from family-friendly gentle slopes suitable for beginners to more demanding sections designed to test the mettle of even the most experienced riders. In fact, these trails are so good that Oisin O'Callaghan, the 2020 U21 Downhill Mountain Biking World Champion, still rides them when he's home. Feel the rush of navigating the twists and turns as you pedal your way through dense forests and open mountain terrain while taking in breathtaking views.

If you don't have a bike, don't worry – you can rent everything you need for a thrilling ride from **Ballyhoura Mountain Bike Centre**. Guides can lead you through the trails, adding to your experience with their insider tips and stories.

If you'd rather explore the area on two legs, the **Ballyhoura Way** is a 90km waymarked trail with terrain mainly consisting of tarmac roads, forestry tracks, open moorland and field paths. There are plenty of facilities and services near the route's seven trailheads.

THE BIRTHPLACE OF THE IRISH COFFEE

The creation of Irish coffee is attributed to Joe Sheridan, a chef at Foynes Port, which in the 1940s was one of the biggest civilian airports in Europe. One winter's evening in 1943, a flight had to turn back to Foynes Airbase midway through its journey. Feeling sorry for the cold and weary passengers, Sheridan whipped up something warm for them to drink.

The story goes that a silence descended as everyone tasted his invention. According to Sheridan, the perfect Irish coffee should include cream as rich as an Irish brogue, coffee as strong as a friendly hand, sugar as sweet as the tongue of a rogue and whiskey as smooth as the wit of the land.

GETTING AROUND

Hourly Bus Éireann services link Limerick city with Adare and Foynes. To get to Ballyhoura, you'll need your own wheels.

CASHEL

'Cashel of the Kings' was once the seat of the high kings of the province of Munster, which includes Counties Limerick and Tipperary. Cashel town has a long history entwined with folklore, and the main draw is the iconic Rock of Cashel, which stands on a limestone bluff overlooking the Golden Vale below. The iconic religious buildings that crown its blustery summit seem to emerge from the craggy landscape. The bustling and pretty little town itself rewards rambles around its charming streets, and dairy farming is still a way of life in the surrounding communities.

Set on a backdrop of lush countryside, this heritage-filled town has a lot to offer visitors. Fascinating historical sights, local artisanal producers, delightful shops, cute cafes and luxurious accommodation options await. Apart from the Rock, Cashel is best-known in Ireland and beyond for award-winning Cashel Blue farmhouse cheese, Ireland's first-ever blue cheese, still handmade locally.

TOP TIP

The Rock of Cashel is open year-round, but it gets busy in summer. Big tour buses usually arrive around 10.30am, so if you want a quieter visit, go when the site opens at 9am or wait until later in the afternoon.

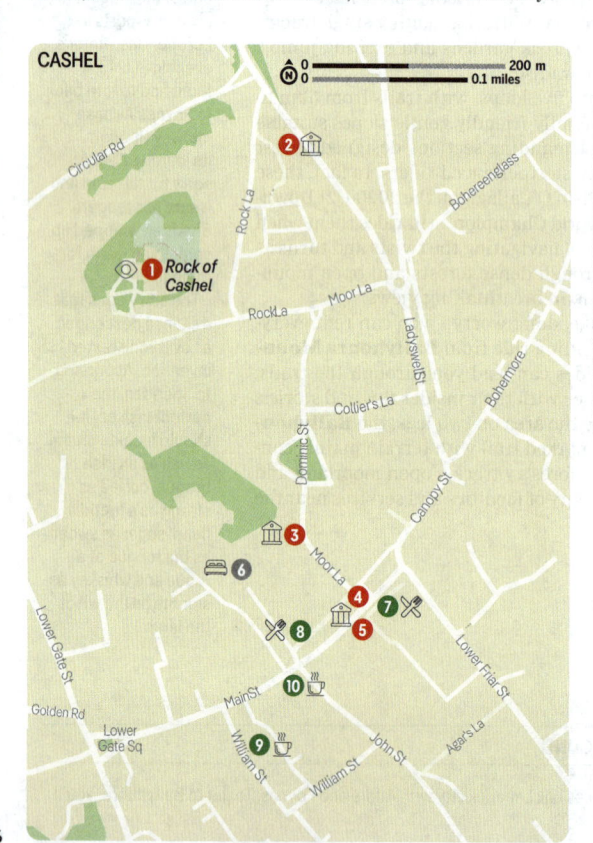

HIGHLIGHTS
1 Rock of Cashel

SIGHTS
2 Brú Ború Heritage Centre
3 Cashel Folk Village
4 Cashel Heritage Centre
5 Kearney's Castle

SLEEPING
6 Cashel Palace Hotel

EATING
7 Bake House
8 Mikey Ryan's

DRINKING & NIGHTLIFE
9 65 Degree Coffee Bar
10 GBowes & Co

Mikey Ryan's

Cashel Beyond the Rock
Check Out The Charming Town

Cashel town can be easily explored in a half-day. On Main St, the **Cashel Heritage Centre** is also the tourist information office, so it makes a great first port of call. Displays inside include a scale model of Cashel in the 1640s with audio commentary. It also houses a large craft shop stocking locally produced items, including Rossa pottery and Fearney Castle ceramics.

Opposite the Heritage Centre is the 15th-century **Kearney's Castle**. Once the home of the Kearney family, it's a historical landmark and might be the oldest standing domestic building in Cashel.

Across the road is the **Cashel Palace Hotel**, originally built in 1732 and restored and reopened in 2022 as a five-star hotel. It's a great spot for a luxurious afternoon tea or strolling the perfectly manicured gardens with amazing views of the Rock.

Nearby, the **Cashel Folk Village** displays some of Ireland's finest thatched buildings. Original artefacts and monuments are spread over three different museums that cover events in Irish history, such as the 1916 Easter Rising. Keep an eye out for the old-style tinkers caravan, a rounded wooden wagon, and antlers of the now-extinct giant Irish elk.

Brú Ború Heritage Centre offers insights into Irish traditional music, dance and song with its Sounds of History cultural exhibition. Located in chambers 7m underground at the base of the Rock, the exhibition tells the story of Ireland from ancient times to the present day. The centre also runs shows nightly in summer except on Sundays and Mondays.

BEST PLACES TO EAT IN CASHEL

65 Degree Coffee Bar
Amazing artisanal coffee as well as baked goods, smoothies and açaí bowls. €

Mikey Ryan's
Gastropub serving up fresh seasonal dishes with quality ingredients. Check out the secret garden. €€

Bowes & Co
Great breakfast and lunch options, from pancakes to soups. Friendly service and good coffee. €

Bake House
A longstanding local favourite that's great for baked goods and a full Irish breakfast. €

GETTING AROUND

Cashel town is easily explored on foot. It takes about 10 minutes to reach the Rock of Cashel from the town centre. Parking in town is cheaper and less crowded than the car park below the Rock.

TOP SIGHT

Rock of Cashel

The Rock of Cashel is one of Ireland's most spectacular historic sites: a prominent green hill, banded with limestone outcrops, rising from a grassy plain and bristling with ancient fortifications. Sturdy walls circle an enclosure containing a round tower, a 13th-century Gothic cathedral and the finest 12th-century Romanesque chapel in Ireland, home to some of the land's oldest frescoes.

PRACTICALITIES

Scan this QR code for prices and opening hours:

DON'T MISS

Frescoes in Cormac's Chapel

Round Tower

Cathedral

St Patrick's Cross

Hall of the Vicars Choral

View from the Rock

Hore Abbey

Cormac's Chapel

Construction of the chapel of King Cormac Mac Carthaigh began in 1127, and it was consecrated in 1134. It's Ireland's earliest surviving Romanesque church. Inside the main door on the left is the sarcophagus said to house King Cormac, dating from between 1125 and 1150.

Cormac's Chapel contains the only surviving Romanesque frescoes in Ireland, which are still undergoing preservation. Gold-headed saints, sapphire blues and robes of blood red are faint but visibly there. The wall paintings in the chancel form the earliest known decoration of its kind and date from the mid-12th century. Some paintings record scenes from the early life of Christ.

Round Tower

The Round Tower is the tallest of the site's buildings and might date from 1101. It was built using a drystone technique, though some spots have now been filled in with mortar for safety reasons. Standing 28m tall, the doorway to this ancient edifice is 3.5m above the ground.

Cathedral

Constructed between 1235 and 1270, the cathedral was built in the shape of a cross. A huge square tower with a turret on the southwestern corner soars above. Scattered throughout are monuments, a 16th-century altar tomb, coats of arms, and stone heads on capitals and corbels.

Hall of the Vicars Choral

Head upstairs from the ticket office to see the restored 15th-century choristers' kitchen and dining hall, complete with period furniture, tapestries, and paintings beneath a fine carved oak roof and gallery.

St Patrick's Cross

In the castle courtyard, this cross is a replica of the eroded original from the Hall of the Vicars Choral, an impressive 12th-century crutched cross depicting a crucifixion scene on one face and animals on the other. The grounds of the complex also include an extensive graveyard with numerous Celtic high crosses marking some of the graves.

Enclosing Walls & Corner Tower

Constructed from lime mortar around the 15th century and originally incorporating five gates, stone walls enclose the entire site. It's thought the surviving corner tower was used as a watchtower. Amble around to enjoy the views of the surrounding countryside and the Devil's Bit to the north.

Hore Abbey

Looking over the valley from the Rock of Cashel, you can see Hore Abbey. Founded in the 1270s by a Benedictine order, the hauntingly beautiful abbey now lies in ruins. Its nooks and crannies and weather-ravaged old gravestones are peaceful to visit. Watch where you step because the field is used for grazing cattle.

There's no entry fee, and you can reach the abbey by walking 10 minutes downhill to the west from the Rock of Cashel or parking next to the Abbey on the small access road.

LEGENDS OF THE ROCK

About 30km north is Devil's Bit Mountain. Local folklore says that the Rock came to be when the devil came down from the sky and bit off a chunk of the mountain and spat it out towards Cashel, where it landed, forming the hill on which the complex sits. According to mythology, St Patrick came here to convert King Aenghus to Christianity.

TOP TIPS

- Access to Cormac's Chapel is by guided tour only. The last tour is at 3.45pm daily. Tickets are limited and can be purchased on-site only.
- Allow an hour and a half to visit, including the Cormac's Chapel tour.
- It's a short walk up a steep incline from the car park to the entrance.
- Good vantage points of the Rock are on the road into Cashel from the Dublin Rd roundabout or from the R660 road to Holycross.
- The best photo opportunities are from the nearby ruins of Hore Abbey, 1km west.

Beyond Cashel

Enjoy rolling green hills, walking trails, woodlands, ancient abbeys and castles found beyond Cashel. A warm welcome awaits in the Tipperary heartlands.

Because it's much less explored than other parts of the country, the area around Cashel is an experience of authentic Ireland. Friendly locals welcome you with 'well' rather than 'hello'.

The town of Cahir has a beautiful castle, and an ornate Swiss cottage, and has been a filming location for several films. Don't miss the farmers market on Saturdays, where you can browse some of the county's finest produce.

To the north, learn about traditional Irish sports in Thurles, where the GAA was founded. Some of the most authentic Irish pubs await, and their traditional music sessions are put on more for locals than tourists. Welcome to the heart of Tipperary.

TOP TIP

One of Ireland's most famous pubs, Jim O' the Mills, opens only on Thursdays – time your trip right.

Mitchelstown Cave

Cahir Castle

Exploring Cahir
Riverside Castle And A Swiss Cottage

At the eastern tip of the Galtee Mountains, 15km south of Cashel, **Cahir** (An Cathair; pronounced 'care') is a compact and attractive town that encircles sublime **Cahir Castle**. The building enjoys a river-island site with massive walls, towers and a keep, mullioned windows, original fireplaces and a dungeon. It's been used as a filming location multiple times, including in Ridley Scott's 2021 film *The Last Duel*. Inside, you can climb the keep.

Walking paths follow the verdant banks of the River Suir, one of Ireland's finest trout-fishing streams. At the end of the walkway along the river is Cahir's other major attraction, the **Swiss Cottage**. This ornate thatched cottage is surrounded by roses, lavender and honeysuckle. A lavish example of Regency Picturesque, the cottage was built in 1810 as a retreat for Richard Butler, 12th Baron Caher, and his wife.

Go Caving in Mitchelstown
An Unexpected Underground Attraction

Hollowed out of a narrow band of limestone along the southern side of the Galtee Mountains, the **Mitchelstown Cave** has nearly 3km of passages, with spectacular chambers full of textbook formations with names such as the Pipe Organ, Tower of Babel, House of Commons and Eagle's Wing. It's not

'WE'LL WINE YOU, DINE YOU & BURY YOU'

A classic multifunctional Irish country pub, **McCarthy's** in the village of Fethard proclaims itself as a bar, restaurant and undertaker. This well-known old-world pub has bucketloads of character. Closely spaced wooden booths and tables are wedged among a thicket of 19th-century bric-a-brac under a wood-panelled ceiling. In fact, the interior remains unchanged since Richard McCarthy opened for business in 1850. There's a shop at the front, a pub at the back and a still operational undertaker's at the side.

They do good pub grub, and sometimes there's live music. All the major beer brands are on tap, as well as the only beer produced in County Tipperary, from the White Gypsy Brewery in Templemore.

WHERE TO EAT IN CAHIR

Galileo
This modern Italian restaurant serves authentic pizza and pasta. Closed Monday to Wednesday. €€

Lava Rock Restaurant
Award-winning cafe with great coffee and cakes as well as lunches – simple food done well. €€

Shamrock Lounge
Old-fashioned pub dishing up big portions of 'Irish mammy dinners' like bacon and cabbage. €

overly developed for tourists, and visitors still buy their tickets as they have done since 1833 from the farmhouse near the cave entrance. Guided tours take about 30 minutes.

Flitter Through Fethard
Medieval Ruins In Horse Country

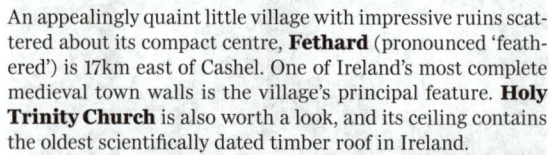

An appealingly quaint little village with impressive ruins scattered about its compact centre, **Fethard** (pronounced 'feathered') is 17km east of Cashel. One of Ireland's most complete medieval town walls is the village's principal feature. **Holy Trinity Church** is also worth a look, and its ceiling contains the oldest scientifically dated timber roof in Ireland.

Housed in Fethard's 17th-century town hall, the **Horse Country Experience** traces the role of the horse in Irish history and culture, from military steeds and plough horses to horse racing and stud farms. In summer, twice-weekly guided tours go to nearby **Coolmore Stud**, the headquarters of the world's largest breeding operation of thoroughbred racehorses.

Thurles' Ties to Gaelic Games
The Birthplace Of The Gaa

Trace the roots of Gaelic games in **Thurles**, the town where the Gaelic Athletic Association was founded. In the Hayes Hotel in 1884, seven founding members established the 'Gaelic Association for the Cultivation and Preservation of National Pastimes', which later became the GAA. Thanks to this heritage, **Semple Stadium** is the largest sporting arena outside of Dublin's Croke Park.

Thurles' tourist office also houses the **Lár na Páirce Museum**, an interpretative centre explaining the history of the GAA. It has an impressive collection of hurleys, jerseys, trophies and medals. The museum can also arrange tours of Semple Stadium.

View the Rock from Devil's Bit
An Easy Heartlands Hike

At 478m, the **Devil's Bit** is a unique hill to climb, and there's an obvious gap in the mountain between an outcrop of rock and a small plateau. Its name comes from a local legend that says that the devil took a bite out of the mountain, creating the large gap. The devil broke his tooth when he bit down and spat out the piece of mountain, which is the mound upon which the famous Rock of Cashel stands. Interestingly, the Devil's Bit is made of sandstone, while the Rock of Cashel is limestone.

BEST PUBS IN THURLES

Brennan's
One of the last remaining family-run 'old man pubs' in town. Owner Pat is a gentleman.

The County
A local favourite that's popular for watching GAA. Expect live contemporary music at the weekend.

De Burcas
A quirky hole in the wall with an open fire. The small snug feels like someone's living room.

The Monks (O'Gormans)
Listen to trad music sessions every Wednesday at this family-run pub with a community atmosphere.

WHERE TO DRINK COFFEE IN THURLES

Deja Brew
Excellent coffee and tasty treats like energy balls with views of the town square.

Hey Day CoffeeHouse
Great coffee with vegan treats and outdoor seating at the end of the square.

Sos Beag
Meaning 'little break', this is a great place for coffee and a sandwich. Outdoor seating is available.

Devil's Bit

The moderately difficult 5km trail takes about two hours return. A large graffiti-covered cross marks the summit. On a clear day, you'll have panoramic views of eight counties.

A good pair of trainers should suffice unless it has been raining heavily, which makes sections of the trail slippery. On the drive back, stop at **The Cottage** in Loughmore to refuel. This quaint cooperative-run cafe and teashop sells delicious house-made scones, baked goods and hearty Irish meals, and it doubles as the village shop.

Hillside Trails & a One-Night-Only Pub
Scenic Walks, Pints And Craic

About 30km north of Cashel, the village of **Upperchurch** is nestled snugly in the rolling hills of Slieve Felim. It's a paradise for walkers, and on a clear day, from the summit of Black Hill, five surrounding counties are visible. Numerous archaeological sites are dotted around the area, with wedge tombs and standing stones dating from the early Bronze Age and the earlier Neolithic period. Three national looped walks go from here, ranging from 1km to 12km, including the rewarding 8km **Eamonn an Chnoic Loop**.

If it's a Thursday, you can grab a pint in one of the best pubs in Ireland. Open just one night a week, **Jim O' the Mills** is in the owner's home, and the living room transforms into a pub with full-on music sessions. Your choice of drink may not be guaranteed, but with the toe-tapping music and great craic, you're not likely to notice.

WHERE TO VISIT IN MID TIPPERARY

Jane Ryan, manager of the Thurles Tourist Office, shares her favourite spots in Mid Tipperary. (*@thurles-touristoffice*)

Thurles
If you dropped a pin halfway between Dublin and Cork, you would land in Thurles. Famous as the birthplace of the GAA, the area makes a perfect base for anyone wanting to experience authentic Ireland.

Jim O' the Mills
Hidden in the hills of nearby Upperchurch and serving pints from their family home, Jim O' the Mills is a pub that offers a memorable and uniquely Irish experience. Jim's opens only on a Thursday night, yet it still attracts trad musicians from across the country and the world who come to session together.

GETTING AROUND

Thurles is easily reached by train from Cork and Dublin, but to really experience this part of Tipperary, it's best to have your own car. Parking is usually paid for in larger towns.

THE GALTEES & GLEN OF AHERLOW

The Galtees are Ireland's highest inland mountains, stretching over 20km and marking a dramatic natural border between eastern County Limerick and Tipperary. Proudly towering over the surrounding countryside with sheep dotting their slopes, the Galtees offer a range of hiking routes with fantastic views when the weather plays ball.

One of Ireland's hidden delights and among the most scenic spots in Tipperary, the Glen of Aherlow is a lush valley where the River Aherlow runs between the Galtee Mountains and the wooded ridge of Slievenamuck. Historically, it was an important pass between Limerick and Tipperary. Nowadays the region is a walker's paradise, offering a variety of low-level loop walks, lake strolls and more advanced mountain hikes. If hillwalking isn't your thing, there's also fantastic fishing, horse riding and cycling in the region. The area is home to two championship-designed golf courses, so you can tee off with a stunning backdrop.

TOP TIP

As with most mountain areas, the weather changes quickly, so check the forecast before you go hiking or road-tripping to make sure you get the best views. If it's not a clear day, don't do the hike up Galtymore, as there are sheer drops near the summit.

Galtee Mountains

GALTEES & GLEN OF AHERLOW

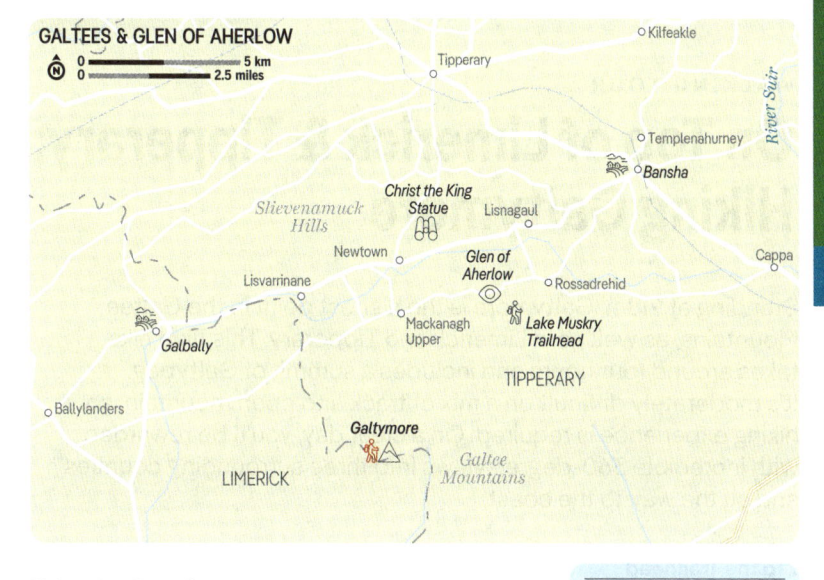

Take the Scenic Route
Walking And Meandering Road Trips

The Glen of Aherlow has eight looped walks on Slievenamuck and two linear walks in the Galtees. One of Aherlow's most popular hikes goes to **Lake Muskry**, a small but scenic lough in a glacier-carved hollow around 490m high in the Galtees. From the tiny village of Rossadrehid on the southern edge of the glen, a narrow road leads uphill to a parking area with an information board. The walk starts here. It follows a rough but easily followed path with green waymarks. Allow three to four hours for the 11km return trip.

If you've had enough of exploring on foot, meander along the roads of the glen by car. Follow the ubiquitous brown signs for the **Glen of Aherlow Drive**, a leisurely 20km scenic drive through the glen from the village of **Bansha** west to **Galbally**. Expect spectacular views of the mountains surrounded by the lush countryside. The roads are narrow in parts, and the tight hairpin corner at the statue of **Christ the King** offers the best views across the glen towards the Galtees. The statue was erected by local volunteers during the Holy Year of 1950, and it's become a symbol for the Glen of Aherlow.

UP THE SUIR WITH A PADDLE

For a different way to experience this enchanting region, get off your feet (or out of the car) and onto the water. Cahir-based **Suir Valley Adventures** offers kayaking trips and lessons on the serene waters of the River Suir. Paddle through lush landscapes in *Fionnuala*, a Celtic longboat, or go it alone in a kayak. Guides have intimate knowledge of the river.

It's a great way to experience part of the **Suir Blueway Tipperary**, a 53km kayak and canoe trail from Cahir to Carrick-on-Suir. Book a two-hour class or a half- or full day of activities.

GETTING AROUND

A car is your best bet for getting around this region. The Local Link Tipperary bus from Cahir to Tipperary town and Cashel stops in Bansha. It takes about 15 minutes and goes three times a day, excluding weekends. From here, you can explore the hills on foot.

WALKING TOUR

On Top of Limerick & Tipperary: Hiking Galtymore

Standing at 918m, Galtymore is the highest point in the Galtee Mountains, as well as in Limerick and Tipperary. This 11km hike takes around four hours and includes a summit of Galtybeg. It's moderately difficult on a mix of track and open mountain, so hiking experience is required. On a clear day, you'll be rewarded with incredible 360-degree views into three surrounding counties and all the way to the coast.

1 To the Trailhead
From the M7 motorway, take exit 12 for Kilbeheny. Drive north on the R639 for 5km. Turn left at the crossroads. A brown sign that reads 'Slí Chnoc Mór na nGaiblte/Galtymore climb' marks the junction. Drive 3km to the end of this road, where there's a small car park.

The Hike: From the car park, take the Black Rd path leading northward. After 100m, you pass through a gate. Continue for about 2.5km.

2 Abbeyshrule Aero Club Monument
The path widens and continues under beech trees. As the path begins to flatten to your right, you'll see a stone monument erected in memory of four

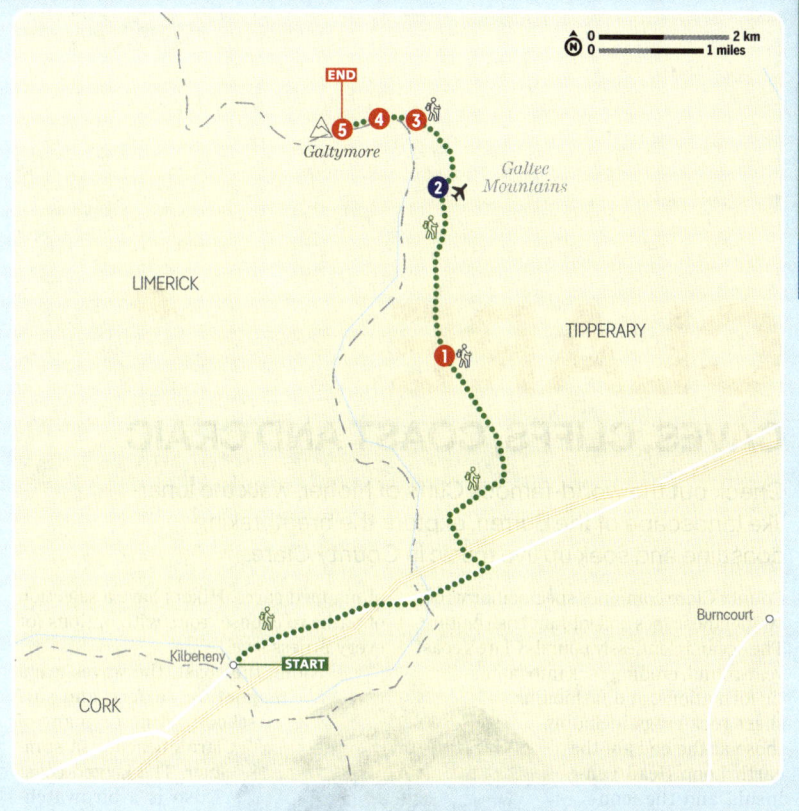

Abbeyshrule Aero Club members who died when their small aircraft crashed close to this spot in 1976.

The Hike: Follow the path as it rises gently uphill and through a second gate. The path continues uphill, and ahead to the left, you will be able to see Galtymore Mountain.

3 A Split to Galtybeg

After about 100m, you reach a stone cairn on your left, where the trail splits in two. Galtymore is straight ahead, and Galtybeg is to your right. Before the path peters out, turn right and walk towards Galtybeg on a wide section of stony ground. Before the gradient of the ground increases, turn left and aim for the Col, the low point between Galtymore and Galtybeg. Follow the indistinct tracks running along the lower slopes of Galtybeg towards the Col.

The Hike: The path cuts back right and then flattens again as you reach a Y junction.

4 The Col to Galtymore's Summit

In wet weather, the ground is particularly boggy, and in poor visibility, the tracks may be hard to find. From the Col, you will see the cliffs on the north face of Galtymore. There is a steep drop down to the corrie lake, Lough Diheen, below. The path runs close to the cliffs, so take care.

The Hike: From the Col, follow the curve of the ground along the top of a gully running up from Lough Diheen and then follow a well-worn path up towards Galtymore.

5 Galtymore's Summit

After 11km from the car park trailhead, you'll see a white Celtic cross that marks the summit of Galtymore. Panoramic views are your reward. Descend along the same route you came up.

277

CLARE

CAVES, CLIFFS, COAST AND CRAIC

Check out the world-famous Cliffs of Moher, walk the lunar-like landscape of the Burren, explore the breathtaking coastline and soak up live music in County Clare.

County Clare combines spectacular windswept landscapes and vibrant Irish culture. The ocean relentlessly pounds Clare's coast year-round, eroding rock into fantastic formations, and fashioning sheer rock crags including those at the ends-of-the-earth Loop Head Peninsula and the iconic Cliffs of Moher. These world-famous cliffs attract tens of thousands of visitors from all over the world to County Clare each year.

Stretching down to the shore – and out as far as the Aran Islands, which are linked to the town of Doolin by ferry – is the moonscape-like bare limestone expanse of the Burren. This karst limestone landscape has ancient megalithic tombs and more than 160km of mapped caves. Hikers have a selection of paths to choose from, with options for every fitness level.

Along the coast, the waves are a magnet for surfers, and surf schools set up on many of Clare's beaches in summer. The jagged coast also is a birdwatcher's paradise, and dolphins jump around in the dark blue waters. Stand in awe of towering sea stacks and natural arches to feel the full power of the Atlantic Ocean.

If the land is hard, Clare's soul certainly isn't. Traditional Irish culture and music flourish here, and it's not just a show for tourists. In larger towns and even the tiniest of villages, you'll find pubs with trad music sessions year-round.

THE MAIN AREAS

THE BURREN
Lunar landscape of limestone.
p282

CLIFFS OF MOHER
Awe-inspiring 214m-high sheer cliffs. **p289**

LOOP HEAD PENINSULA
Spectacular scenery and walks.
p295

Above: Cliffs of Moher (p289); left: The Burren (p282)

Find Your Way

Ennis is the county's transport hub, with bus and train services to Galway and Limerick cities, where you can connect to the rest of the country. Clare has tons of walking trails for explorers on foot.

The Burren, p282

This starkly beautiful landscape has plentiful trails, caves and ancient tombs that are best explored on foot.

Cliffs of Moher, p289

Towering above the churning Atlantic waters, these sheer cliffs are home to an abundance of incredible birdlife.

Loop Head Peninsula, p295

Stay in a former lighthouse keeper's cottage and soak up the dramatic views at the edge of Ireland.

CAR

You need a car to reach many of the trailheads, spectacular beaches and small villages. With your own wheels, you can cover a fair amount of ground and explore the many unnamed back roads.

BUS

Bus Éireann (buseireann.ie) links all the main towns in the region at least once each day, and larger towns see multiple buses a day. However, public transport doesn't reach some smaller villages, and some services are reduced on Sundays.

Fanore Beach (p284)

Plan Your Time

Outdoorsy types will love rambling through the Burren and taking in jaw-dropping views on epic coastal hikes. Come evening, settle back in a pub for a pint and some of the best trad music in the country.

One Day Only

Head to the **Cliffs of Moher** (p289) early to beat the crowds. Continue to **Poulnabrone Dolmen** (p288) and stop into **Ballyvaughan** (p284) for lunch. Your next stop is the **Aillwee Cave** (p283) for an afternoon tour, squeezing in a stop at **Hazel Mountain Chocolate** (p287) for a sugar hit. Drive to **Doolin** (p284) for a toe-tapping evening of trad in the pub.

Five Days to Explore

From Doolin, dig deeper into the stark beauty of the **Burren** (p282) on one of the many marked **walking trails** (p286). Enjoy lunch at **Burren Perfumery** (p287) before heading to **Lahinch** (p293) for sunset pints. The next day, head south to **Kilkee** (p296) and walk along the cliffs. Explore the landscapes and villages on the **Loop Head Peninsula** (p295) by car or e-bike.

Seasonal Highlights

SPRING
Enjoy spots of post-winter colour in the Burren, which bursts with wildflowers, particularly in May.

SUMMER
Clare is busy with visitors, but summer is the ideal time for boat trips and beach time.

AUTUMN
Catch gorgeous sunsets along the Clare coast, especially from the Cliffs of Moher, the Loop Head Peninsula and Doolin Pier.

WINTER
Winter swells bring the best waves for surfers. Warm up from outdoor explorations by a pub fire.

THE BURREN

Stretching across northern County Clare, the rocky, windswept Burren region is a unique striated lunar-like landscape of barren grey limestone that was shaped beneath ancient seas and then forced high and dry by a great geological cataclysm. It covers 250 sq km of exposed limestone and 560 sq km in total.

Springtime wildflowers give the Burren brilliant, if ephemeral, colour amid its stark beauty. Villages throughout the region include the music hub of Doolin on the west coast and charming Ballyvaughan in the north, on the shores of Galway Bay.

South of Ballyvaughan, a series of severe bends twists up Corkscrew Hill (180m), which was built as part of a Great Famine relief scheme in the 1840s. Nearby photogenic prehistoric sites include Poulnabrone Dolmen.

Walking is one of the best ways to experience the Burren's unique geology. If you're planning to hike, pack your rain gear and a good pair of boots.

TOP TIP

Good bases for exploring the Burren include Ballyvaughan, Doolin and Lisdoonvarna. These towns have the greatest number of accommodation and eating options. Although many places accept credit cards, take out cash when you can because ATMs in the region are scarce. There's a decent-sized shop in Ballyvaughan.

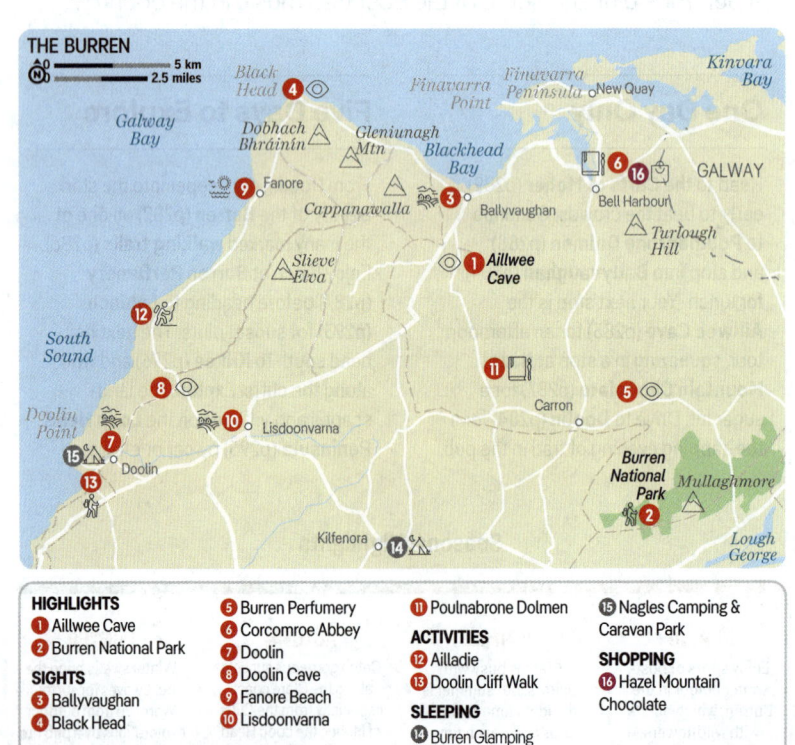

HIGHLIGHTS
1. Aillwee Cave
2. Burren National Park

SIGHTS
3. Ballyvaughan
4. Black Head
5. Burren Perfumery
6. Corcomroe Abbey
7. Doolin
8. Doolin Cave
9. Fanore Beach
10. Lisdoonvarna
11. Poulnabrone Dolmen

ACTIVITIES
12. Ailladie
13. Doolin Cliff Walk

SLEEPING
14. Burren Glamping
15. Nagles Camping & Caravan Park

SHOPPING
16. Hazel Mountain Chocolate

Ailwee Cave

Into the Depths of Aillwee Cave
Ireland's Most Famous Cavern

Formed by rainwater flowing through cracks in the limestone, **Aillwee Cave** is thought to be more than one million years old. The cave remained hidden until it was discovered by a farmer in 1940, who kept the secret to himself until 1973. But once word was out, the entire cave was mapped just four years later. Visitors today can see an underground waterfall, stalactites, stalagmites and bear bones.

To visit Aillwee Cave, you must book a 45-minute guided tour. Wear sturdy shoes or boots and bring a jacket, even if it's warm outside – the temperature inside the cave is a constant 10°C. Children are allowed on the tour, which follows a 1km circular route with five stops. Aillwee Cave also has a cafe and a shop selling local Burren Gold cheese.

Also located here is the fantastic **Bird of Prey Centre**, where you can meet falcons, hawks, owls and eagles. See the raptors in motion during the flying demonstrations that take place throughout the day. You can also book a **Hawk Walk**, a one-hour tour that takes you through hazel woodlands with an experienced falconer. During the walk, the roles are reversed as you become the bird handler and find out exactly what the art of falconry is all about.

BURREN BEAR BONES

Hundreds of animal bones were found in Aillwee Cave in 1976 as it was being developed into a tourist site. More than 20 bear bones were identified, including a skull, and the bear became a symbol of Aillwee Cave.

Radiocarbon dating revealed that the bear skull is 10,400 years old, dating back to the Early Mesolithic period. Only about 1000 people lived in Ireland at this time, and these nomadic hunter-gatherers moved around in search of food. The remains of this bear indicate that the Burren would have been heavily forested during this period, as it could not have survived on the Burren landscape of today.

WHERE TO EAT & DRINK IN BALLYVAUGHAN

Monks
This spot has been a big hit with seafood fans for more than 40 years. €€

L'Arco
Amazing Italian fare prepared by Italian chefs using locally sourced ingredients. €€

O'Loclainn's
Offers more than 70 whiskeys, plenty of craic and as warm a welcome as you could imagine.

ROCK CLIMBING AT AILLADIE

Ailladie (Aill an Daill in Irish, meaning 'Blind Man's Cliff') is an 800m-long limestone sea cliff with a variety of climbing routes that range in height from 8m to about 30m.

Situated below the R477 between Lisdoonvarna to Ballyvaughan, Ailladie isn't visible from the road. To reach the wall, head about 11km north of Lisdoonvarna and continue 1.5km further to reach the coast. Park in the lay-by, and, as you approach from the north, a grassy slope brings you to the Dancing Ledges, a nontidal area with more than 90 different climbing routes.

About 5km north of Aillwee Cave, the town of **Ballyvaughan** makes an ideal base for exploring the northern Burren. It has a picturesque location between the rocky hills and Galway Bay's translucent waters. The town is home to fantastic restaurants and a decent selection of accommodation.

Where the Burren Meets the Atlantic
Surfing The Waves

Fanore (Fan Óir, meaning the 'Golden Slope') is less a village and more a stretch of coastline with buildings scattered along the scenic R477, which hugs the barren coast as it curves past the Aran Islands into Galway Bay.

Scenery aside, **Fanore Beach** and the chance to swim and surf might draw you here. With an extensive backdrop of grass-covered dunes, this Blue Flag–rated beach is patrolled by lifeguards in summer and is a surfing hotspot. **Aloha Surf School** offers classes for all ages and abilities.

At low tide, Fanore Beach's golden sands have exposed limestone outcrops. Take a closer look and you'll see an abundance of fossils of corals, brachiopods and crinoids formed in a shallow tropical sea more than 330 million years ago.

Love in Lisdoonvarna
Meet Your Match

The little town of **Lisdoonvarna** makes a good base for exploring the Burren, and it's the home of a quirky annual festival. Lisdoonvarna was once a centre for *basadóiri* (matchmakers) who, for a fee, would fix up a person with a spouse. Most of the (mainly male) hopefuls would hit the town in September, feet shuffling, cap in hand, after the hay was in. Today, the **Lisdoonvarna Matchmaking Festival** is billed as Europe's largest singles' festival, with music, dancing and partying on September weekends.

For centuries, people have been visiting Lisdoonvarna's mineral springs, and at the town's southern end is a **spa well** with a sulphur spring and a Victorian pumphouse in a wooded setting. The iron, sulphur, magnesium and iodine in the water are believed to be good for rheumatic and glandular complaints.

Live Music & More in Doolin
Ireland's Trad Capital

Doolin is hugely popular as a centre of Irish traditional music. The craic is mighty, the pubs are hopping, and the conversation, as well as the stout, is always flowing. Impromptu

---

WHERE TO STAY IN BALLYVAUGHAN

Wild Burren Cottages
These whitewashed cottages with thatched roofs have stunning coastal views. €€

Burren Atlantic Hotel
Individually styled boutique rooms and self-catering accommodation, plus a spa, gym and tennis court. €€

Hyland Burren Hotel
A family-owned hotel with comfortable rooms, a great restaurant and often live music in the bar. €€

TO THE ARAN ISLANDS

From Doolin Pier, ferries run to Inisheer (p327) in 15 minutes, to Inishmaan (p328) in 25 minutes and to Inishmore (p326) in 35 minutes. You can return via the Cliffs of Moher to take in views on your way back to the mainland.

Doolin

music sessions are almost guaranteed to break out nightly in its famed pubs.

Gus O'Connor's is a sprawling pub dating from 1832 and has a rollicking atmosphere when the music is in full swing. On some summer nights, you won't squeeze inside. Some of the best food in town is served here, including a vegan menu and delicious desserts.

Blackie O'Connell is one of the best uilleann pipe (Irish bagpipe) musicians in the country, and he plays sets in **McGann's** on Tuesday nights. This spot also serves up a tasty seafood chowder. Every Monday, the Wild Atlantic Session kicks off in **Fitz's**, guaranteeing a toe-tapping, Guinness-supping good time. **McDermott's** is a fourth-generation-owned pub where musicians often make an appearance.

The village hosts the annual **Doolin Folk Festival** every June, which has become a firm favourite on the Irish summer festival scene.

Located 6km northeast of the Cliffs of Moher in a landscape riddled with caves and laced with walking paths, Doolin is also a jumping-off point for cliff cruises and ferries to the Aran Islands. The 13km **Doolin Cliff Walk** is the best way to immerse yourself in the area's staggering natural beauty. The trail is relatively flat until you hit the halfway mark. As you work a little harder, you're rewarded with breathtaking views that get better and better with every step. The walk continues

BEST PLACES TO STAY IN DOOLIN

Hotel Doolin
This boutique hotel is situated in the heart of the village with comfortable, modern rooms and amazing breakfast options to set you up for the day. €€

Pipers Rest
These elegant guesthouse rooms on the main street are just a short walk from the pubs in town. €

West Haven House
Run by Cormac and Liz Shannon, the West Haven House opened in 2019 and is already a go-to for visitors. €

WHERE TO EAT IN DOOLIN

Russell's Fishshop
Dig into locally sourced seafood, from fresh lobster rolls and fish and chips to a stellar fish curry. €

McDermott's
Family-run since 1887, this traditional pub has a fantastic menu and tasty house-made apple crumble. €

Oar Doolin
Rustic fine dining with a relaxed vibe; wonderful food and great service. €€

WHY I LOVE THE BURREN

Brian Barry, writer

The Burren is a fascinating region with amazing opportunities to get outdoors and enjoy the natural beauty. From incredible hiking trails and beautiful beaches to the spectacular views of the coast and the karst limestone landscape, the Burren never fails to impress.

The little villages have great pubs, and there's always a trad session somewhere. The locals always make you feel welcome. I love that you can always find a quiet spot to yourself in the Burren to soak it all in.

Burren National Park

along the clifftop before eventually ending at O'Brien's Tower (p291). From the Cliffs of Moher Visitor Centre (p290), you can take a shuttle bus back to Doolin. Count on four or five hours for the walk.

Doolin Cave has Europe's largest free-hanging stalactite, at a staggering 7.3m. A 45-minute tour takes you inside the cave, where guides explain the cave's history.

Hiking in the Burren
Walk The Limestone Landscape

The Burren is a walker's paradise and is best explored on foot. Hikers can take on seven colour-coded marked walking trails in **Burren National Park**, which range from a 30-minute ramble to a three-hour trek.

The looped **Nature Trail** (1.5km, White Route) takes you through beautiful hazel and ash woodlands before passing through hay meadows and along the iconic limestone topography of the Burren. Enjoy spectacular views of Lough Gealáin and the mountain of Mullaghmore in the distance.

Suitable for all ages and fitness levels, the **Knockaunroe Turlough Trail** (1.3km, Orange Route) covers a range of terrain, from turlough, hazel and ash woodlands to flower-rich grasslands, and it offers a stunning look at the Mullaghmore peak.

The highlights of the looped **Slieve Carran** walk (2.5km, Brown Route) are the stone oratory, cave and holy well associated with St Colman, who was a hermit here from 597 to 604.

LONGER HIKES IN THE BURREN

Mullaghmore Return
The 6.5km Green Route takes you to the summit of Mullaghmore along the shores of Lough Gealáin.

Mullaghmore Traverse
A challenging but rewarding 6km trail (Red Route) through remote upland areas of the Burren.

Mullaghmore Loop
With a 140m elevation gain, the Blue Route is the longest and most difficult of the waymarked walks.

The cave is known locally as Colman's Bed. Colman's Well is believed to cure eye ailments, and the little chapel dates from the 10th century.

The 2km **Slieve Carran** trail (Yellow Route) is mostly flat, but it follows rocky terrain, rewarding you with abundant wildflowers. The Burren is home to 23 of Ireland's 30 orchid species, many of which can be found in the grasslands along this trail in the Slieve Carran Nature Reserve.

Burren Sweet Treats
Choc Stop

Watch chocolate being made in small batches using rare cacao beans and raw sugar at **Hazel Mountain Chocolate**, a heavenly smelling cottage-housed chocolate factory in a picturesque hillside location. The dishes at the on-site organic cafe are sustainably produced using flavours from the region, such as sea salt, elderberries, honey, juniper berries and wildflower petals. Refuel with great coffee, tasty cakes and amazing chocolate.

Scents of the Burren
Stop And Smell

The region's wildflowers are the inspiration for the subtle scents at the wonderful **Burren Perfumery**, which creates scented items such as perfumes, candles and soaps that are beautifully packaged in handmade paper. A 10-minute audiovisual presentation details the area's diverse flora, including many fragrant orchids that grow between the rocks. You're free to wander its flower and herb gardens, which provide ingredients for dishes and herbal teas served at its tearoom.

Caves of Wonders
Down Underground

Caving, also called potholing, is a lot of fun and allows you to explore the underground world of the Burren. With more than 200 caves in the region, including the country's longest at 15km, the Burren has countless opportunities to explore its amazing cave networks.

Caving for a day can allow you to see stalactites, stalagmites and underground waterfalls. Access the caves using ladders and ropes and squeeze through narrow gaps to get further inside. **Burren Outdoor Education and Training Centre** (burrenoec.com) and **Epic Ireland** (epicireland.com) run caving trips.

BURREN WILDFLOWERS

No matter when you visit the Burren, wildflowers are in bloom. This stunning region supports a diverse range of flowers, with more than 70% of Ireland's 900 native species, as well as many of the country's native orchid species. A bizarre mix of Arctic, alpine, subtropical and Mediterranean plants grow side by side, made possible by the high light-density heat reflected from the limestone landscape, the moist air from the Gulf Stream and grazing cattle that remove grass and weeds that would otherwise become dominant.

Spring, particularly May, is the best time to see the Burren's wildflowers in bloom.

WHERE TO CAMP IN THE BURREN

Nagles Camping & Caravan Park
Just 100m from Doolin Pier, with 85 serviced hard stands and green camping on 1.6 hectares. €

O'Connor's Riverside Camping & Caravan Park
Friendly family-run spot in Doolin with a beautiful location overlooking the River Aille. €

Burren Glamping
Stay in a converted horse truck with a wood-burning stove on a sustainable farm in Kilfenora. €€

BEST PHOTO SPOTS IN THE BURREN

Photographer and tour guide **Sean Nee** shares his favourite locations in the Burren for photography. @seanneephoto

Black Head
This area of limestone slabs and hand-stacked stone walls stretches down to the coast of Galway Bay. The rock formations and windswept plants are striking in black and white.

Polnabrone Dolmen
This ancient portal tomb is a must-visit. With low light pollution, it's a great place to practise long exposures.

Corcomroe Abbey
This 13th-century abbey is hauntingly beautiful, and it has some of the finest decorative stone carvings of any Irish monument. Climb the hill behind the abbey in spring to take macro photos of the wild orchids and gentians.

Poulnabrone Dolmen

Portal to Another Time
Ireland's Oldest Megalithic Monument

Also known as the Portal Tomb, **Poulnabrone Dolmen** is one of Ireland's most photographed ancient monuments. Built more than 5000 years ago, the otherworldly dolmen (a large slab perched on stone uprights) stands amid a swath of rocky pavements; the capstone weighs 5 tonnes. The site is 9km south of Ballyvaughan and visible from the R480; there's a large free parking area and excellent displays. It's not known exactly what these dolmens were used for, but it's widely believed that they were territorial markers, burial sites, or places of ceremony or ritual.

Archaeological digs in the 1980s led to the discovery of the remains of 33 people, as well as a number of bone objects buried with the bodies. From the excavations, archaeologists learned that the site was in continuous use for more than 600 years.

GETTING AROUND

It's easiest to explore all the nooks and crannies of the Burren with your own car. Cycling is an excellent way of getting off the main roads; ask about rentals at your accommodation.

Bus Éireann stops at key Burren destinations, including Ballyvaughan, Doolin, Fanore and Lisdoonvarna. The Burren National Park Bus is a free service that operates daily between May and August from Corrofin to the trailheads of each of the park's walks.

CLIFFS
OF MOHER

○ DUBLIN

Cliffs of Moher

In good visibility, the Cliffs of Moher are staggeringly beautiful. The entirely vertical cliffs rise to a height of 214m, their edge abruptly falling away into a ceaselessly churning Atlantic. In a progression of vast heads, the dark sandstone and siltstone strata march in a rigid formation. Views stretch to the Aran Islands and the hills of Connemara. Sunsets here see the sky turn a kaleidoscope of amber, amethyst, rose pink and deep garnet red.

One of Ireland's blockbuster sights, the Cliffs of Moher has a high-tech visitor centre, a 19th-century lookout tower and a wealth of walking trails. Visiting by boat can bring the best views. The cliffs' fame guarantees a steady stream of visitors, which can surge in summer. But the tireless Atlantic winds and expansive walking options help thin out the crowds. You're rewarded with epic views if you walk even a short way north or south along the cliffs.

TOP TIP

To escape the crowds, gear up for a hike. Many visitors gather at the main viewing platform; walking south takes you to a puffin-viewing spot. A challenging hiking trail runs from Doolin, which takes 2½ hours minimum to walk. If you're fit and have the right kit, you'll love it.

THE GUIDE

CLARE CLIFFS OF MOHER

CLIFFS OF MOHER

0 — 2 km
0 — 1 miles

Doolin Point
Doolin Ferry
Doolin
South Sound
O'Brien's Tower
Cliffs of Moher Visitor Centre
Cliffs of Moher
Hag's Head
Liscannor
Liscannor Bay

WATCHING FOR WILDLIFE

The Cliffs of Moher are one of the most important bird-breeding sites in Ireland and a huge draw for birdwatchers. More than 20 species of nesting birds call the cliffs home, including razorbills, fulmars, kittiwakes and guillemots. Early May to late August is the best time to see birds here, including the largest colony of puffins in mainland Ireland.

In the waters, look for migrating minke and humpback whales in autumn. Dolphins and porpoises can often be seen too, but spotting them from the clifftop can be difficult – a boat trip increases your chances. Basking sharks feed on zooplankton around the base of the cliffs from April to early August.

Cliffs of Moher by boat

Getting Oriented at the Visitor Centre
Start Your Cliffs Visit

Covered in turf and cut into the hillside, the state-of-the-art **Cliffs of Moher Visitor Centre** has engaging exhibitions that span two floors and cover the fauna, flora, geology and climate of the cliffs. Hear stories from the guides about the formation of the cliffs, the traditions of busking and local characters. At the back of the circular exhibition area is the 'Ledge Experience', a virtual-reality film that takes you flying over the cliffs and diving into the ocean below before returning to the clifftop for a bird's-eye view.

The visitor centre has two (pricey) cafes. The steeply slanting picture windows set into the hillside at **Cliffs View** offer broad views of the big-draw bluffs. **Puffin's Nest** is a crowded and tiny sandwich and coffee pit stop.

Best Hikes at the Cliffs of Moher
Get Your Boots On

South of the cliffs, the epic **Hag's Head** hike connects the village of Liscannor (p293) with the Cliffs of Moher. Hag's Head is a dramatic place from which to view the cliffs, and few

---

UNIQUE WAYS TO SEE THE CLIFFS OF MOHER

Before the Visitor Centre Opens
Cycle or arrive on foot before the visitor centre opens to enjoy an epic sunrise.

Catch the Sunset
When the day-trippers have gone, the cliffs are quiet and peaceful.

Walk the Cliffs
Go beyond the main viewing platform to leave the crowds behind.

venture this way, even though the views are uninhibited. At the tip of Hag's Head is a huge sea arch, and another arch visible to the north. The old signal tower on the head was erected in case Napoleon tried to attack the western coast of Ireland. From Hag's Head, you can continue on to Liscannor for a total walk of just under 12km (about 3½ hours).

To the north, you can follow the trail to Doolin (p294), via the 1835 stone observation post **O'Brien's Tower**, ending at the village 8km later (count on 2½ hours). The tower marks the highest point of the cliffs, and you can clatter up the spiral iron staircase to the rooftop viewing platform of this historic stone tower for the best photo op. On a clear day, you can see the Aran Islands just off the coast, and in the distance, you can often spot the Twelve Pins in Connemara on the opposite side of Galway Bay.

The entire 20km-long Liscannor to Doolin walking path via the cliffs is signposted as the **Cliffs of Moher Coastal Walk**; it's likely to take about five hours.

The hiking trails around the Cliffs of Moher are strenuous, encompassing narrow, exposed cliff paths with steep ascents and descents. Proper boots and kit are a must.

Seeing the Cliffs from the Sea
An Atlantic Angle

The sheer Cliffs of Moher are at their most spectacular when seen from the sea at their feet. Boat trips with **Doolin Ferry** (doolinferry.com) leave from Doolin Pier and take you on a cruise beneath the cliffs. Along the way, you learn about the history, geology and wildlife of the area.

Boat trips typically last about 45 minutes. Book in advance to ensure you have a spot onboard.

Big-Wave Surfing
Spectacular Surge

Beneath the Cliffs of Moher is **Aileen's**, one of the best big-wave surfing spots in the world. In the right conditions, this monster wave can reach heights of more than 15m, attracting some of the most notable names in big-wave surfing.

If you're visiting in winter and a big swell hits, you can watch the action unfold from the top of the cliffs, which create a natural theatre to see elite surfers ride the waves.

THE TRADITION OF BUSKING

Each year, 12 busking licences are given out for the pitches set up at the Cliffs of Moher. Local musicians have been busking here for generations, and this tradition continues today.

Listening to live music while looking out at the open ocean and mind-blowing vistas is a special experience. Along with the crashing waves below, the birds swooping through the air and the wind whistling along the cliff face, these buskers complete the special soundtrack to the world-famous cliffs.

GETTING AROUND

Bus 350 runs from Galway to Ennis, stopping at the Cliffs of Moher, with six trips per day from June to mid-September.

The visitor centre offers a free lift service to O'Brien's Tower using golf buggies for visitors with mobility needs.

Numerous private tour operators run tours to the cliffs from as far afield as Galway, Dublin and Cork.

Beyond the Cliffs of Moher

Surf, golf or kick back in the pubs, enjoying live music, great food and lively villages along the Clare coast.

Around the Cliffs of Moher are fun villages where trad music is on tap and creamy pints are waiting to be sipped. Beautiful stretches of sand, stunning coastal scenery and amazing food are on offer, and your best days in the county's west may be spent on the smallest roads you can find.

South of the plunging Cliffs of Moher, the land flattens, with vistas that sweep across pastures and dunes to the horizon. Some of Ireland's finest surf rolls into shore near the low-key beach towns along the coast, and some visitors simply spend their days chilling out on the sand during the summer months, enjoying magnificent sunsets on Ireland's west coast.

TOP TIP

The weather on the Irish coast can change quickly, so have a good wind- and rainproof layer with you.

Lahinch

Lahinch Golf Club

Layover in Liscannor
West Coast Pit Stop

The small seaside village of **Liscannor** (Lios Ceannúir) looks out over Liscannor Bay southeast towards Lahinch and has given its name to a type of local slate-like rippled stone used for floors, walls and even roofs. It doesn't have any sights as such, but it's a pretty spot to stop. It has some great pubs, amazing seafood and a choice of places to stay. **Vaughan's Anchor Inn** is a landmark, with nautical-memorabilia-covered walls and fresh seafood dishes.

It's reported that Ireland has more than 3000 holy wells, and at least 15 of them are dedicated to St Bridget. The **St Bridget's Well** located between the Cliffs of Moher and Liscannor is arguably the most famous. Said to have healing powers, it's set in an open grotto on the side of the road. Inside the passage to the well are thousands of prayers, rosaries, candles and mementoes left by visitors.

Sands & Greens of Lahinch
Surfing, Golfing And Pubs

On protected Liscannor Bay, **Lahinch** (Leacht Uí Chonchubhair; often spelt 'Lehinch' on road signs) has long owed its living to beach-seeking summer tourists and visitors to the venerable **Lahinch Golf Club**, which dates from the 19th

BEST PUBS IN LISCANNOR & LAHINCH

Egans
Whether you're sitting around the winter fire or enjoying the outdoor summer seating, this live-music hotspot in Liscannor always delivers.

Joseph McHugh's
This lively pub in Liscannor hosts regular music nights and serves fresh seafood, plus some veggie options.

P Frawley's Bar
This family-run pub has more than 150 years of history, a wide selection of whiskey and brilliant live music.

Kenny's Bar
A fourth-generation family business with phenomenal live music during its Tuesday White Horse Sessions.

WHERE TO STAY IN LISCANNOR & LAHINCH

Atlantic View
Rooms have a country-cottage feel at this primrose-yellow B&B set in farmland 5km north of Liscannor. €

Cliffs of Moher Hotel
At the southern end of the Cliffs of Moher Coastal Walk. Some balconies have views over Liscannor Bay. €€

Atlantic Hotel
Grand old hotel in Lahinch with mini-chandeliers and leather-topped desks in the rooms. €€

BEST PUBS IN MILTOWN MALBAY

Friel's Pub
This old-style charmer complete with an open fire has walls crammed with photos and books, plus regular trad sessions.

Michael A's Bar
Have a pint by the fire during the winter or sit out and enjoy the beer garden during the warmer months at this popular watering hole.

Hillery's
Opened in 1891, Miltown Malbay's oldest pub has stained-glass windows and framed photos on the walls. Live trad sessions take place every weekend year-round and most nights in summer.

---

century and remains one of the country's finest. First marked out through the dunes in 1892 by British Army officers of the Black Watch Regiment, Lahinch's renowned par-72 Old Course was designed by Old Tom Morris in 1894 and reworked by Alister MacKenzie in the 1920s and again by Martin Hawtree in 1999. The flatter par-70 Castle Course overlooks ruined Dough Castle. Goats have roamed the fairways since the early 20th century, when their ancestors belonged to a local caddie. They act as a barometer of sorts: when they're out in the dunes, conditions are favourable, but if you see them around the clubhouse, adverse weather is likely on its way.

Like swells after a storm, Clare's **surfing** scene keeps getting bigger and better. On weekends in Lahinch, the exposed beach break, with both left-hand and right-hand waves, attracts hundreds of surfers. Conditions are excellent for much of the year, with the bay's cliffs funnelling regular and reliable sets. Beginners will find the northern end gentler. Watch out for rocks and rips. Surf schools and stores, such as **Ben's Surf Clinic** and **Green Room**, cluster near the seafront, offering lessons and board rental. At low tide, the crescent-shaped bay stretches for more than 2km and is a beautiful spot for a ramble in the sand.

Lahinch has accommodation for all budgets, although much of it closes from November to Easter.

Milling Around Miltown Malbay
Music And More

Miltown Malbay has a thriving music scene and hosts the annual **Willie Clancy Summer School**, one of Ireland's great traditional music events. This tribute to native son Willie Clancy, one of Ireland's greatest pipers, is one of the best traditional music festivals in the country.

The town was a favoured resort for well-to-do Victorians, though it isn't actually on the sea: the beach is 2km southwest at **Spanish Point**. With dazzling views of the setting sun, this lovely beach also offers excellent walks north of the point amid the low cliffs, vast ledges of stone, rock pools, coves and isolated beaches.

Spanish Point

GETTING AROUND

Bus Éireann services stop in Lahinch and Liscannor en route to the Cliffs of Moher, Doolin, Ennis and Galway.

LOOP HEAD PENINSULA

A sliver of land between the Shannon Estuary and the pounding Atlantic, windblown Loop Head Peninsula has an ends-of-the-earth feel. As you approach along the R487, the sea begins to appear on both flanks as the land tapers to a narrow shelf. On a clear day, the lighthouse-capped headland at Loop Head (Ceann Léime), Clare's southernmost point, has staggering views to Counties Kerry and Galway. The often-deserted wilds of the head are perfect for exploration, but be extra careful near the cliff edge.

On the northern side of the cliff near the point, a dramatic crevice has been cleaved into the coastal cliffs where you'll first hear and then see a teeming bird-breeding area. Guillemots, choughs and razorbills are among the squawkers nesting in the rocky niches.

A long hiking trail runs along the cliffs to the peninsula's main town, Kilkee. A handful of other tiny settlements dot the peninsula.

TOP TIP

May is a great time to visit as wildflowers bloom, seabirds nest in the cliffs and dolphins begin to calve. Kilkee has plenty of guesthouses and B&Bs, though during high season, rates can soar and you may have a problem finding a vacancy if you haven't booked ahead. Closures are common in winter.

HIGHLIGHTS
1. Loop Head Lighthouse

SIGHTS
2. Bridges of Ross
3. Carrigaholt
4. Carrigaholt Castle
5. EIRE Sign
6. Glasheen Beach
7. Kilbaha
8. Kilbaha Gallery
9. Kilkee
10. Kilkee Beach
11. White Strand

ACTIVITIES
see 4 Carrigaholt Sea Angling
see 4 Dolphinwatch
12. ilkee Cliff Walk

SLEEPING
13. An Sean Teach
14. Glencarrig B&B
see 1 Loop Head Lighthouse Keeper's Cottage

EATING
15. Diamond Rocks Cafe

KILKEE THALAS-SOTHERAPY CENTRE

In the heart of Kilkee, the family-run **Kilkee Thalassotherapy Centre** offers a range of treatments, including seaweed body wraps, massages and natural seaweed baths. If you've been out adventuring and need some relaxation time, this spa is the place to do it. Choose one of the many treatments to feel refreshed and rejuvenated for the next leg of your journey.

Kilkee Thalassotherapy Centre is located just 100m from the stunning horseshoe-shaped sands of Kilkee Beach.

Kilkee Cliffs

On the Cliffs of Kilkee
Walking The Coast

The Loop Head Peninsula's main town, **Kilkee** (Cill Chaoi), sits on a sweeping semicircular bay with high cliffs on the northern end and weathered rocks to the south. Kilkee first became popular in Victorian times when rich Limerick families built seaside retreats here. Its wide golden beach gets thronged in warmer months. The waters are highly tidal, with wide-open sandy expanses replaced by pounding waves in just a few hours.

St George's Head, to the north, has good cliff walks and scenery. West of the bay, the **Kilkee Cliff Walk** begins at the **Diamond Rocks Cafe**, where you can fuel up on the huge terrace at the water's edge. This walk treats you to magnificent views of the cliffs, sea stacks, caves and the full force of the Atlantic Ocean below. Look out for **Duggerna Rocks**, which form an unusual natural amphitheatre, and natural swimming pools known as the **Pollock Holes**. There's also a huge sea cave.

To make this route into a loop, follow the Kilkee Cliff Walk from Diamond Rocks Cafe until you reach the road. Instead

WHERE TO STAY IN KILKEE

Bay View Hotel
Family-run since the 1880s, this hotel is often touted as one of the best in Clare. €€

Kilkee Bay Hotel
Bright, spacious rooms near the beach and the cliff walk; serves an excellent Irish breakfast. €€

Royal Marine Hotel & Apartments
The 22 rooms and nine well-appointed self-catering apartments have spectacular views of Kilkee Beach. €€

of turning back, take a left and follow the country road back towards town until you see Kilkee Bay in front of you. Turn left and follow the path back to Diamond Rocks Cafe to end with a rewarding meal in the sunshine.

Around the Bend on Loop Head Drive
The Road Less Travelled

Following 80km of dramatic scenery, the **Loop Head Drive** can be completed in a day or broken up across several days.

Start in the Loop Head Peninsula's main town, Kilkee, which has plenty of dining options and places to stay.

From Kilkee, follow the road south to the **Bridges of Ross**. Once upon a time, there were three sea arches here but, nowadays, just one remains standing, and it's worth a visit. The viewing point is a five-minute walk from the car park. This spot is a haven for birdwatchers, and thousands of seabirds pass through in late summer and early autumn as they migrate south.

Continue on to the Loop Head Lighthouse. The scenery along this stretch is spectacular and includes Bishop's Island, St Kee's Well, the Candle Stick and nonstop clifftop views. Once you reach the lighthouse, grab a coffee at the on-site cafe and take a tour before carrying on through farmland towards the village of **Kilbaha**.

Views of the ocean are magnificent as you continue towards **Carrigaholt**, and if you're lucky, you might see dolphins in the waters below. Carrigaholt is a picturesque town on the shores of the River Moyarta. Stop to see Carrigaholt Castle (p298), wander around town and enjoy some local pubs.

From Carrigaholt, follow the road through the small villages of Doonaha and Querrin until you meet the N67. Turning left brings you back to Kilkee.

Live Like a Lighthouse Keeper
Shining Bright At Night

On a 90m-high cliff, the 23m-tall working **Loop Head Lighthouse**, complete with a Fresnel lens, rises up above Loop Head, perched on the edge of a dramatic headland. Guided tours (included in admission) take you up the tower and onto the balcony for panoramic views. In fine weather, you can see as far as the Blasket Islands and Connemara. There's been a lighthouse here since 1670, and the present structure dates from 1854. It was converted to electricity in 1871 and automated in 1991.

KILBAHA GALLERY

Browse an impressive collection of contemporary paintings, mixed media works, ceramics, textiles, bronze sculptures and more at **Kilbaha Gallery**. Run by co-owners Ailish and Liz, Kilbaha Gallery shows off their love for art, and they take private and public commissions from inception to final product. Painters and sculptors work on-site, and there's also a bronze foundry.

WHERE TO STAY & EAT AROUND THE LOOP HEAD PENINSULA

An Sean Teach
This well-appointed guesthouse offers ocean views from its quiet, peaceful location west of Kilbaha. €

Glencarrig B&B
Overlooking the Shannon Estuary on the outskirts of Carrigaholt, this farmhouse B&B is a treat. €

Keating's of Kilbaha
Overlooking Kilbaha Bay, Keating's serves freshly caught local fish with a stunning view. €

For a truly unique experience, stay at the former **Loop Head Lighthouse Keeper's Cottage**, which gives you a real feel for what life was once like out here. Managed by the Irish Landmark Trust (irishlandmark.com), the 19th-century cottage sleeps five and has no TV or wi-fi – all the better for enjoying the radio, books, board games and the warming wood stove.

Loop Head Walks
Hike The Magnificent Coastline

The **Loop Head Walk** is one of the most westerly trails in Ireland and should not be missed. Following the route brings you along one of the most dramatic and awe-inspiring headlands in the country, through the moors and across the clifftop. The 2km path takes about 1½ hours to complete.

Beginning in Loop Head car park, stay west of the lighthouse. The trail then passes the World War II lookout posts before rising to reward you with jaw-dropping views of the cliffs and the crashing waves of the Atlantic below.

For a more challenging walk, try the longer **Kilbaha Loop**. This 15km trail takes about five hours and meanders along exposed coastline, so wear warm layers and sturdy walking shoes. Starting at the lighthouse, follow the coastline south to Kilbaha before looping back via the stunning sea cliffs, taking in **Diarmuid and Gráinne's Rock** and the World War II **EIRE sign**. Originally constructed in 1943 and one of 85 EIRE signs around the coastline of Ireland, it was essentially an early GPS system to allow pilots to know where they were when flying over neutral Ireland. Each one was numbered; the Loop Head sign is number 45.

Legends of Carrigaholt Castle
Historical Hauntings

Built in 1480 by the McMahon family, the five-storey **Carrigaholt Castle** is one of the best preserved in the country. The structure was abandoned in the 19th century, and though the ruins are open to visitors, venturing inside is not possible.

On the edge of the Shannon Estuary, the castle offers magical photo opportunities, especially as the sun hits it in the late afternoon. Local legend says that the castle is haunted, and some say ghosts have been seen conducting military exercises around the castle as far back as 1875. Inside the castle is a room that was sealed off more than 100 years ago to protect the locals from the evil that lies within. An exorcist is believed to have tried to rid the castle of the evil entity in the 1920s but was found dead the next morning, supposedly having died of fright.

BEST BEACHES ON THE LOOP HEAD PENINSULA

Kilkee Beach
This crescent-shaped golden sandy beach in the seaside village of Kilkee has calm waters for swimming and is a popular hangout.

Glasheen Beach
With a decent-sized car park and a few stone picnic tables, this quiet little beach is great for families and offers amazing views while you chill in the sunshine.

White Strand
A five-minute drive from Carrigaholt, White Strand is a beautiful sandy beach at low tide, but at high tide, it's rocky, so keep an eye on tide times.

WHERE TO DRINK IN CARRIGAHOLT

Keane's Bar & Grocery
Nearly 200 years old, Keane's is an authentic pub with a grocery store attached.

Morrissey's Village Pub
Fresh, creamy pints and a warm welcome await at this local favourite.

Long Dock
With regular live music, this cosy but lively family-run pub is worth stopping into for a pint.

Carrigaholt Castle

Deep-Sea Fishing Trips
Angling In The Atlantic

Whether you're a fishing novice or an experienced angler, the waters off the Loop Head Peninsula are a great place to try your luck. These Atlantic waters have an abundance of fish species, including pollock, haddock, whiting, congers, cod, coalfish, and rarer species such as hake, stone bass, and anglerfish.

Porbeagles and blue sharks are also found in the waters here, as well as skates that can be taken off the bottom. To arrange a trip, contact Kilbaha-based **Fishing Adventures Ireland** or **Carrigaholt Sea Angling**.

DOLPHIN SPOTTING

Some 200 resident bottlenose dolphins frolic in the Shannon Estuary, and they're best encountered on a two-hour cruise with **Dolphinwatch** (dolphinwatch.ie). You might also see minke and fin whales in autumn. Sailings depend on tides and weather conditions. Dolphinwatch also runs Loop Head sunset cruises and geology tours.

GETTING AROUND

Regular buses serve Kilkee, and you can reach the Loop Head Lighthouse on TFI Local Link bus 339, which serves the lighthouse twice a day from Kilkee and Kilrush (p301).

If you want to feel the raw energy of the Loop Head Peninsula, rent an e-bike and cycle down the narrow country lanes. Loop Head E-Bikes in Carrigaholt can set you up with everything you need for a day of pedal-powered adventure.

Beyond the Loop Head Peninsula

Away from the Atlantic coast and the rugged Burren, Clare rolls through low-lying green countryside with gentle hills.

County Clare's eastern boundary is the River Shannon and the long, inland waterway of Lough Derg, which stretches 48km from Portumna in County Galway to just south of Killaloe. Lakeside villages here seem a world away from the rugged, evocative west of Clare, but it's a picturesque landscape of water, woods and panoramic views.

Southeastern Clare, where the Shannon swells into its broad estuary, is largely farmland. Shannon Airport is one of Ireland's busiest and has numerous flights to Europe, the UK and North America (with US pre-clearance facilities).

This area's towns have accommodation options, cafes and pubs, but outside of these spots, options are more limited. Ennis is easily accessible, as is Limerick city.

TOP TIP

Ennis makes an ideal base for exploring the county: you can reach any part of Clare in under two hours.

Kilrush

The Waters of Kilrush
Exploring An Island And The Estuary

Overlooking the Shannon Estuary and the hills of Kerry to the south, the lively town of **Kilrush** (Cill Rois) has a strikingly wide main street that reflects its origins as a port and market town in the 19th century.

From the west coast's biggest marina at Kilrush Creek, ferries run 3km offshore to **Scattery Island**, home to magnificent early Christian ruins. This uninhabited, windswept and treeless island was the site of a Christian settlement founded by St Senan in the 6th century. Its 36m-high round tower, the best preserved in Ireland, has its entrance at ground level instead of the usual position high above the foundation. The evocative ruins of six medieval churches include the 9th-century **Cathedral of St Mary**. You can also visit a lighthouse and an artillery battery, built during the Napoleonic wars, at the southern end of the island.

Cruises also depart from Kilrush Marina to view bottlenose dolphins living in the estuary, which is an important calving region for the mammals. Two-hour boat rides on the Shannon with **Dolphin Discovery** offer plenty of opportunities to spot marine life.

Ennis Past & Present
County Clare's Charming Commercial Hub

Ennis (Inis) lies on the banks of the fast-moving River Fergus. The town's medieval origins are recalled by its irregular, narrow streets, but the most important surviving historical site is **Ennis Friary**, founded in the 13th century by the O'Briens, kings of Thomond, who also built a castle here in the 13th century.

In May, singers and dancers come out for **Fleadh Nua**, a lively eight-day trad-music festival.

Fleadh Nua

BEST PLACES TO STAY IN ENNIS

Old Ground Hotel
Entered through a lobby of polished floorboards, cornice work, antiques and open fires, this prestigious landmark dates from the 1800s. €€€

Newpark House
A vine-covered country house dating from 1750, elegant Newpark House sits 3km northeast of the centre off the R352 on 20-hectare woodland grounds. Its six rooms feature plush furnishings, antiques and lots of polished wood. €€

Temple Gate Hotel
The soaring cathedral-ceilinged lobby at this central hotel was once part of the 19th-century Sisters of Mercy convent. €€

GETTING AROUND

Ennis is the county's transport hub. Bus Éireann services operate from the bus station beside the train station. Connect in Galway or Limerick for Dublin.

Irish Rail serves Limerick, where you can make connections to places further afield, including Dublin. The line to Galway takes in some superb Burren scenery.

Aboe: Galway Bay (p308); right: Inisheer Lighthouse (p327)

GALWAY
FESTIVALS, RUGGED LANDSCAPES AND WINDSWEPT ISLANDS

Contrasting lively Galway city with the rugged wilderness of Connemara, remote islands, beautiful beaches and postcard-perfect villages, this county showcases the essence of Ireland.

County Galway's exuberant namesake city, called 'Dublin of the west', is the halfway point of the weaving 2500km Wild Atlantic Way and a swirl of colourful shop-lined streets filled with buskers and performance artists, enticing old pubs that hum with trad music sessions throughout the year, and a sophisticated food scene that celebrates local produce. Known as the festival capital of Ireland, bohemian Galway city hosts some 120 festivals a year.

Some of Ireland's most picturesque scenery fans out from Galway's city limits, particularly along the breathtaking Connemara Peninsula. Tiny roads wander along a coastline studded with islands, dazzling white sandy beaches and intriguing villages; the interior shelters heath-strewn boglands, glassy lakes, looming mountains and isolated valleys. Stone walls and sheep are always on the horizon, and road-tripping along the winding roads is an unforgettable experience. A few places have featured on the silver screen, such as in *The Quiet Man* and *Marley and Me*. In the county's east, towns with medieval remains give way to rolling farmland.

Galway doesn't stop giving at its western coastline. Offshore lie the beautiful Aran Islands. Desolate, windswept yet entrancing, the trio of rugged islands offer a glimpse into Irish life of centuries past.

The county, Ireland's second-largest, gets its nickname of 'Hooker County' from a traditional fishing boat called the Galway hooker.

THE MAIN AREAS

GALWAY CITY
Artsy and music-loving foodie city.
p308

CONNEMARA NATIONAL PARK
Ruggedly beautiful landscapes, mountains and road trips. **p318**

ARAN ISLANDS
Deserted beaches, coastal cliffs and ancient forts. **p324**

CLIFDEN
Picturesque, lively and pub-filled town.
p329

Connemara National Park, p318

Wild and remote, Connemara offers dramatic scenery at every turn. The coastline doesn't disappoint with its dazzling white-sand beaches.

Galway City, p308

Arty and bohemian Galway has brightly coloured pubs heaving with live music, a vibrant food scene and festivals aplenty.

Clifden, p329

At the foot of the Twelve Pins Mountains and overlooking the Atlantic, Clifden is one of Galway's most picturesque towns.

Aran Islands, p324

For many visitors, the rugged Aran Islands represent the character of 'auld Ireland'. Inishmore contains one of Ireland's most important prehistoric stone forts.

FERRY

Aran Island Ferries sail year-round from Rossaveal, 38km west of Galway city, linked by shuttle bus. Ferries depart Galway Harbour from April to September. Inishbofin Ferry departs from Cleggan daily and year-round. Crossings are subject to favourable weather conditions.

BUS & TRAIN

Bus Éireann and Irish Rail operate in the region, and Galway city is well connected with other major towns by both bus and train. Bus Éireann has limited services in most of Connemara. Minibuses operate on the Aran Islands from May to September.

CAR

Driving is the best way to explore all that Galway has to offer, getting you to remote spots that are difficult to access by public transport. Fuel up in larger towns when you can.

Find Your Way

Stretching from the eastern hidden heartlands to the Atlantic Ocean and Galway Bay, Galway is sprawling. It takes about two hours to drive from the easternmost town of Ballinasloe to Roundstone on the Connemara coast.

305

Plan Your Time

Galway's attractions are many and varied. Spend some time soaking up the buzz of the city but don't miss out on the mountain scenery of Connemara and the rugged Aran Islands.

Kylemore Abbey (p332)

One Day in Galway

● Check out the landmarks of **Galway city** (p308) on a DIY **walking tour** (p311) and then experience the vibrant food scene with **Galway Food Tours** (p312).

● Take a seaside stroll to **Salthill** (p314) and grab lunch at **Blackrock Cottage** (p314). Pack your swimmers to do as the locals do and jump off the Blackrock Diving Tower or take a tour of Micil Distillery.

● For a casual local dinner, grab fish and chips at **McDonagh's** (p312). Pub crawl through trad music sessions in the **Latin Quarter** (p310), ending the night in **Róisín Dubh** or **Monroe's Tavern** (p310).

Seasonal Highlights

While Galway city is buzzing year-round, April to October offers the best weather, and places in rural parts of the county are open for visitors. July and August are the busiest.

MARCH
Most towns have **St Patrick's Day** parades. Galway city's St Patrick's Day Festival has live music and traditional dance workshops.

MAY
A Taste of Galway celebrates the county's food and drink scene with street food, cheese-making demonstrations and beer masterclasses.

JULY
The **Galway International Arts Festival** features theatre, music, comedy, visual arts, dance and literary events from global and homegrown artists.

Three Days to Travel Around

● After a day in Galway city, hit the road north via Oughterard for an epic road trip through **Connemara National Park** (p318).

● Spend the night in **Clifden** (p329), and the next day, drive south to Rossaveal to catch a ferry to the **Aran Islands** (p324). If you only have time for one island, make it **Inishmore** (p326), where you can visit Dún Aonghasa, Ireland's oldest prehistoric fort. Between mid-March and the end of October, interisland ferries allow you to visit all three islands in a day. Back on the mainland, stop off at **Spiddal** (p317) to admire the crafts made by local artists.

If You Have a Week

● Spend a few nights in **Galway city** (p308) and enjoy the nightlife. Catch a ferry to the **Aran Islands** (p324), staying a night on **Inishmore** (p326), where coastal walks and clifftop fortresses await.

● Island hop your way back to **Clifden** (p329), a great base for exploring **Connemara National Park** (p318) by car, bike or on foot.

● To the east, visit Ireland's only fjord, **Killary Harbour** (p323), and the photogenic **Kylemore Abbey** (p322).

● Stop by historic monuments, ruined castles and secluded beaches on the **Sky Road scenic drive** (p334) and finish your trip through Galway with a sunset over the Atlantic Ocean.

AUGUST
The week-long **Galway Races** is Ireland's longest horse-racing meet. There's good food, music and fashion, and the craic is mighty.

SEPTEMBER
Wash down oysters with pints of Guinness to the sounds of live music at the **Galway International Oyster and Seafood Festival**.

OCTOBER
A festival of all things equine takes place at **Ballinasloe Fair**, and the **Galway Comedy Festival** is on in the city.

DECEMBER
The enchanting **Galway Christmas Market** runs from mid-November to Christmas in the city.

GALWAY CITY

Galway (Gaillimh) is one of Ireland's most engaging cities. Brightly painted pubs heave with live music, and the faint hum of fiddles, banjos and bodhráns (hand-held goatskin drums) drifts out of its numerous pubs, particularly in the cobbled streets of the Latin Quarter. Restaurants and cafes offer front-row seats for observing buskers and street theatre. The large student population brings out a lively contemporary music scene.

Remnants of the medieval town walls lie between shops selling handcrafted Claddagh rings, books and musical instruments, bridges arch over the salmon-stuffed River Corrib, and a long promenade leads to the seaside suburb of Salthill, on Galway Bay, the source of the area's famous oysters.

Cosmopolitan culinary options abound that make use of the best local and Irish produce. The city hosts a vast array of festivals and cultural events throughout the year, making it a great spot to visit at any time.

TOP TIP

Accommodation can get booked up fast at weekends and during the Galway Races and the various festivals the city hosts, so it's wise to book ahead. Eyre Sq is a great base as it's close to the Latin Quarter, and it offers a range of options to suit all budgets.

Galway Cathedral (p311)

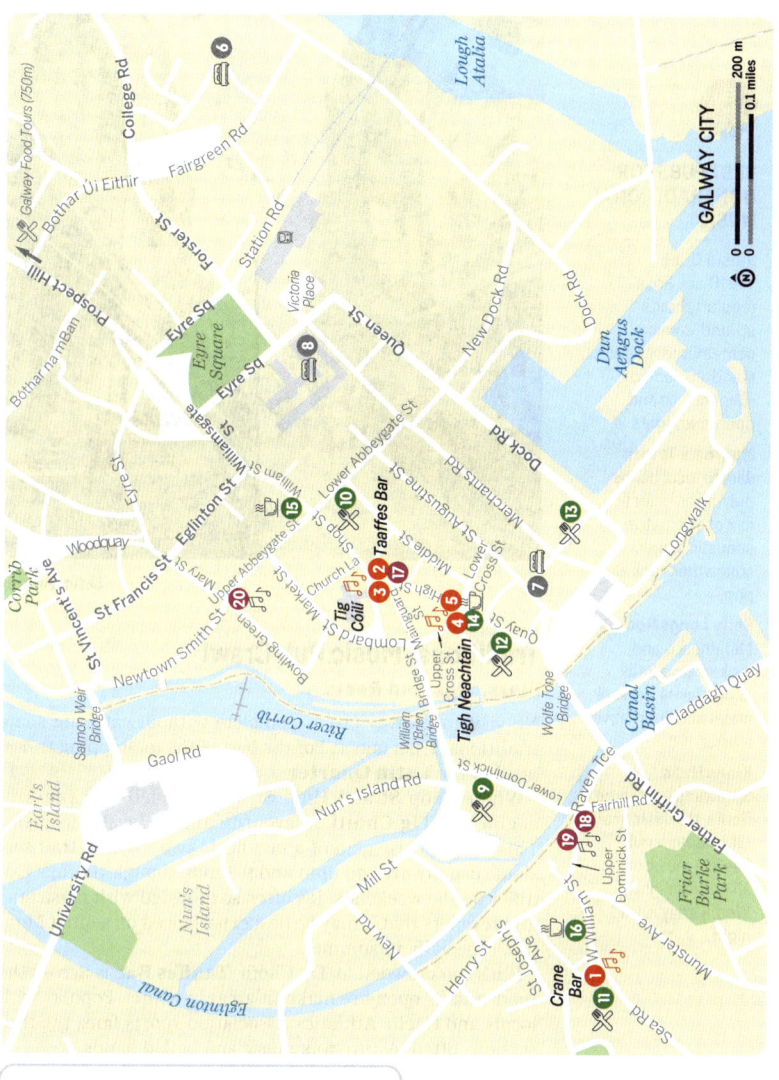

HIGHLIGHTS
1. Crane Bar
2. Taaffes Bar
3. Tig Chóilí
4. Tigh Neachtain

SIGHTS
5. Latin Quarter

SLEEPING
6. Galmont Hotel & Spa
7. House Hotel
8. Kinlay Hostel

EATING
9. Aniar Restaurant
10. Dough Bros
11. Kai
12. McDonagh's
13. Rúibín

DRINKING & NIGHTLIFE
14. Coffeewerk + Press
15. Espresso 44
16. Urban Grind

ENTERTAINMENT
17. Kings Head
18. Monroe's
19. Róisín Dubh
20. Sally Longs Rock Bar

THE GUIDE

GALWAY GALWAY CITY

309

BEST PUBS FOR NONTRADITIONAL MUSIC

Róisín Dubh
The 'Black Rose' regularly hosts up-and-coming contemporary bands, stand-up comedy, silent discos and open-mic nights.

Monroe's Tavern
Jam to local bands playing an eclectic mix of alternative, acoustic singer/songwriter, rock and pop.

Sally Longs Rock Bar
Metalheads and rockers love Sally Longs for its live rock, metal and alternative music.

Kings Head
Sprawling over three floors, this historical 13th-century pub has live music of all genres nightly. Wednesday is trad night.

Latin Quarter

Traditional Music Pub Crawl
Pints, Jigs And Reels

No visit to Galway city is complete without catching some traditional Irish music. For the best of the toe-tapping tunes, head to the **Latin Quarter**.

Where Shop St and High St merge, you'll find the fire-engine-red **Tig Chóilí**, a favourite among local musicians. This atmospheric gem of a pub hosts two evening trad sessions, usually around 6pm and 9.30pm, though timings can differ on the weekends. It's often so crowded with musicians and revellers that it may be best experienced on a quiet Monday, especially in summer.

If it's too crowded at Tig Chóilí, **Taaffes Bar** is across the road, and its open fire makes it great in winter. Popular with locals and Gaelic Athletics Association sports fans, the trad sessions often feature folk music and ballad bands.

Heading down to Quay St where it meets Cross St, you'll find family-run **Tigh Neachtain** (pronounced 'tee-g knock-tin'), founded in 1894. This pub is at the heart of the Galway

Continues on p312

WHERE TO STAY IN GALWAY

Kinlay Hostel
Centrally located hostel just off Eyre Sq, a stroll away from Shop St's traditional pubs. €

House Hotel
Boutique hotel in a converted warehouse with an amazing location in the Latin Quarter. €€

Galmont Hotel & Spa
With scenic Galway Bay views, this luxury city centre hotel features a pool and underground parking. €€€

A WALKING TOUR OF GALWAY'S LANDMARKS

Soak up student vibes at one of Ireland's most prestigious universities, the **1 National University of Ireland**, home to Galway's famous stone Quadrangle. It's a short walk to **2 Galway Cathedral**, one of the city's most iconic buildings with its prominent dome dominating the skyline. Highlights include intricate mosaics and stonework emblazoned with stained glass. To the east of the cathedral is the **3 Salmon Weir Bridge**, a picturesque arched stone bridge that's a great spot for taking photos of the cathedral. In summer, look out for salmon swimming upstream.

Walk east for about 200m to the grey columns of the **4 Town Hall and Courthouse**, now used as a theatre. Go 500m south to **5 Eyre Sq**, a tranquil setting for a pit stop. Grab lunch in **6 O'Connell's** award-winning beer garden. Continue west to admire the Gothic **7 Lynch's Castle**, now a bank but once home to Galway's most powerful family. Nearby is **8 Nora Barnacle's House**, the house of the wife of James Joyce. Walk east to **9 St Nicholas Church**, one of Ireland's oldest parish churches. If it's the weekend, the Galway Market will be in full swing next door at Church Lane. Wander down the Latin Quarter's **10 Kirwan's Lane**, one of the city's finest medieval laneways.

Make your way to the archaeological ruins of the **11 Hall of the Red Earl**, the oldest building excavated in Galway. Head south to the **12 Spanish Arch**, remains of the old medieval wall. Lastly, cross over the Wolfe Tone Bridge for great views of the beautifully coloured homes of the Long Walk from across the water at **13 Nimmo's Pier**. Keep your eyes peeled for the resident dolphin, Nimmo.

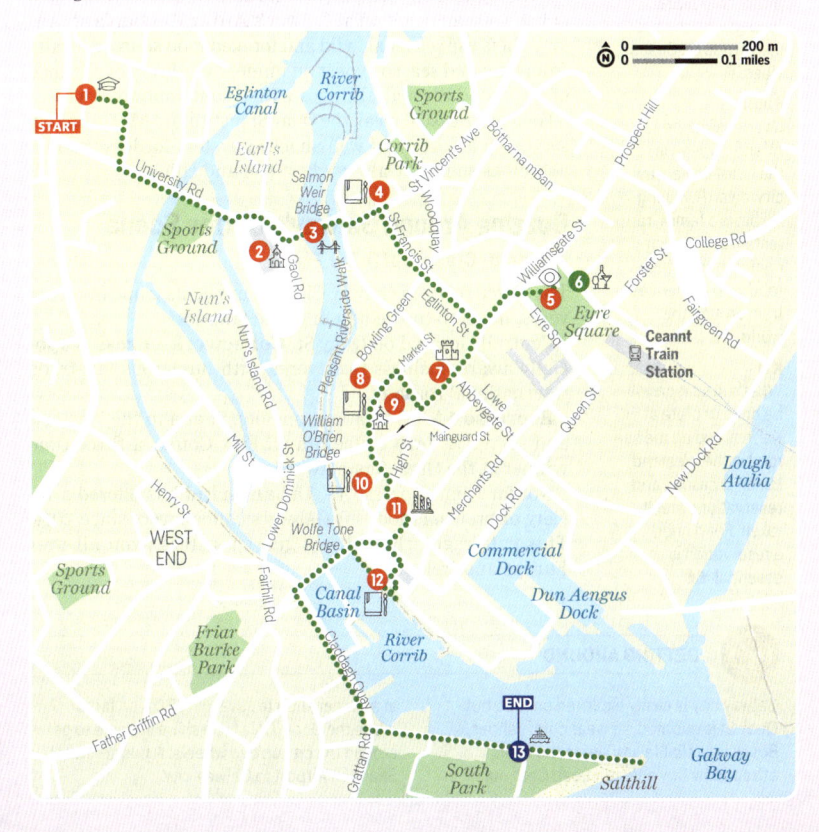

FOODIE SPOTS IN GALWAY CITY

Paula Stakelum, Global Director of Chocolate and Patisserie for Red Carnation Hotels, shares her favourite foodie spots in Galway city. (instagram.com/Paula_pastry)

Dough Bros
Voted Ireland's best pizzeria in 2022, Dough Bros serves Neapolitan-style wood-fired pizza topped with the best Irish produce. Casual vibes. €

Rúibín
Overlooking the Atlantic Ocean in the heart of Galway city, award-winning Rúibín is a family-run restaurant serving contemporary Irish food with influences from around the world. €€

Kai
What's in season will be on your plate at Kai, nestled on the sea road in the Westend. Lunch is casual, and reservations aren't taken. For dinner, a reservation is essential. €€

Continues from p310

music scene and has hosted some of the most talented Irish traditional musicians on the planet, including Sharon Shannon and Brendan O'Regan. As well as the music sessions, great pub food and excellent pints of Guinness await.

Heading away from the Latin Quarter, cross the Wolfe Tone Bridge to the Westend, where the **Crane Bar** holds traditional Irish music sessions nightly in the downstairs pub. It offers amazing traditional music with a community feel, and sessions include singer/songwriters as well as roots music.

Galway's Gastronomic Delights
Sublime Seafood And Michelin-Star Cooking

From Michelin-star dining to the freshest fish and chips, Galway's food scene runs the gamut. To experience the best of Galway's culinary delights in a short time, book an outing with **Galway Food Tours** to sample everything from local oysters and craft beers to artisan cheese and chocolate. Day tours include six food and drink stops, and you'll leave with a goodie bag. The company also offers whiskey tours, as well as food tours by bike.

If indulging in a Michelin Star meal has been on your bucket list, you can tick it off at Galway's **Aniar Restaurant**. Aniar's chefs use seasonal, wild and foraged food sourced locally from land and sea, so expect an immersive dining experience of Irish food through the ages with a contemporary twist.

For a more casual meal, the Quay St institution **McDonagh's** serves up a portion of well-shucked oysters for less than €7 as well as some of Galway's best fish and chips.

Buzzing Around Galway's Coffee Scene
A World-Class Caffeine Fix

The coffee scene in Galway City has upped its game in recent years, much to the delight of coffee fanatics.

Centrally located on Quay St, **Coffeewerk + Press** is a socially aware business that works with numerous fair-trade international roasters.

Espresso 44 has locations on Shop St and in the Westend and serves its own coffee brand, Fixx Coffee, a three-time winner at the Great Taste Awards.

Not far from Espresso 44, **Urban Grind** has offered a variety of brew methods for Galway's coffee lovers since 2014. This cafe regularly features guest roasters from all over Europe and Ireland.

GETTING AROUND

Galway city is easily explored on foot, but Quay St is cobbled, so wear comfy shoes. Buses are reliable and run to the main attractions. Buy a Visitor Leap Card online or at a corner shop to save up to 30% on fares.

Use the Coca-Cola bike-share scheme to get around the city on two wheels. A bus connects Shannon Airport to Galway city.

Beyond Galway City

West of Galway city, quaint seaside towns and villages await. Find glassy lakes and ancient castles to the north and east.

Sleepy seaside suburbs and villages spread west of Galway. Salthill is within walking distance of Galway city, and not much farther on to the west, you'll find yourself in the Galway Gaeltacht (Irish-speaking area), regarded as the cultural heartland of Gaeilge, where the old traditions and heritage of the Irish are at their strongest.

The dramatic island-strewn coastline of Galway Bay is a stark contrast to the county's interior of bog and stone walls. To the south is oyster country in the fishing villages of Clarinbridge and Kilcolgan. To the north, there's superb angling at Oughterard on Lough Corrib's shores as well as scenic road trips. Castles populate towns steeped in historical and literary connections to the east.

TOP TIP

Coastal Salthill, Spiddal or Oranmore make good alternative bases for visiting Galway city.

Oranmore Castle (p315)

SALTHILL WITH KIDS ON RAINY DAYS

The beach keeps kids entertained, but even in summer in Ireland, parents need options for rainy days. Salthill offers the typical amusements along the promenade at **Seapoint Leisure**. There's a dedicated pool table area, a bank of pinball machines and a myriad of teddy cranes in the modern indoor weatherproof arcade.

Atlantaquaria is Ireland's largest native-species aquarium, and houses more than 150 freshwater and sea-dwelling creatures from local waters and more from further afield. Talks, tours and feeding sessions take place daily.

Opposite the beach, **Leisureland** has a pool with a 65m water slide and an inflatable obstacle course. The 25m swimming pool and state-of-the-art gym keep adults busy.

Blackrock Diving Tower

A Day at Seaside Salthill
Swims, Strolls And Sunsets

Within walking distance of the bustle of Galway city or easily reached by bus, **Salthill** offers a quintessential Irish seaside town experience. With distillery tours, coastal walks, tasty treats and amusements, it makes a great alternative for a laid-back stay near Galway city.

Leap into the sea from **Blackrock Diving Tower**, being mindful of the weather, as it can get wild and dangerous on stormy days. Refuel with coffee at **Jungle Beach Break Cafe** to thaw out and warm up. If cold water exposure isn't your thing, take a stroll along **Salthill Beach**. There are rocky outcrops in parts, so wear sturdy shoes rather than flip-flops.

To the north of the D'arcy roundabout on Upper Salthill Rd, **Micil Distillery** is the first legal poitín distillery to open in Galway for more than 100 years. Take a tour to gain unique insights and taste Ireland's moonshine.

WHERE TO EAT IN SALTHILL

Blackrock Cottage
Contemporary Irish cuisine with beautiful views at the end of the promenade. Try the smoothie bowls. €

Gourmet Food Parlour
The first branch outside Dublin serves up flavourful brunches, dinner, tapas and cocktails. €

Pear Tree Cafe & Wine Bar
Cracking coffee and brilliant brunches and sandwiches by day and biodynamic wines in the evening. €

The walk between Galway and Salthill is popular with locals. As you head towards Galway, you'll arrive at the **Claddagh**, the area made famous by Ireland's Claddagh ring (p317) – a piece of jewellery that's a symbol of love, friendship and loyalty – and **Nimmo's Pier** with views of Galway Harbour. Stop to admire the lovingly restored thatched **Katie's Claddagh Cottage**. Walking back to Salthill, you'll stroll along the 3km **Seapoint Promenade**, Ireland's longest, passing the midpoint of the Wild Atlantic Way. Catch the sun setting over Galway Bay.

Round off a day of exploring in **O'Connor's Famous Pub**, where Ed Sheeran filmed the video to *Galway Girl*. With no food or TVs, it's a proper Irish pub experience, full of bric-a-brac on the walls and ceiling.

Eastern Galway's Cultural Heritage
Haunted Castles And Historical Sites

South and east of Galway city lie pretty fishing villages and a multitude of lesser-visited castles and historical ruins. **Oranmore** is in close proximity to Galway city, and its tranquil setting on the bay makes it a good alternative base. After a coffee stop in **Espresso 44**, visit the enchanting and owner-occupied **Oranmore Castle**. Supposedly haunted, it was featured on an episode of the American paranormal reality television series *Scariest Places on Earth*.

Continue south and stop for a seafood lunch at **Moran's Oyster Cottage**, an atmospheric thatched pub and restaurant in a quiet cove in **Kilcolgan**.

At the southeastern corner of Galway Bay is the colourful village of **Kinvara**, with a charming stone harbour and Dunguaire Castle sitting by the water's edge. The 16th-century tower was once a meeting point for writers WB Yeats, Bernard Shaw and JM Synge.

The extensive ruins at the monastic site of **Kilmacduagh**, 6km southwest of Gort, include a well-preserved 34m-high round tower and remains of a small 14th-century cathedral. Northeast of Gort is **Thoor Ballylee**. Once the summer home of Yeats, its 16th-century Norman tower was the inspiration for one of his best-known works, *The Tower*.

About 30km north on the motorway takes you to the 'Fields of Athenry'. You'll hear this Irish folk song sung as the Munster Rugby team's anthem at Limerick's Thomond Park (p262), but **Athenry** is in County Galway. It's one of the best-preserved medieval towns in Ireland and features magnificent **Athenry Castle**.

CLARINBRIDGE OYSTER FESTIVAL

Established in 1954, the Clarinbridge Oyster Festival is a quieter alternative to the Galway Oyster Festival, with great food, Guinness, music and entertainment on the banks of the River Clarinbridge.

The oysters actually come from Dunbulcan Bay, west of Clarinbridge village, where they're protected from harsh Atlantic storms. Almost 3 sq km of beds lie in an ideal mixture of freshwater and seawater vital for growing perfect oysters, which take three to five years to develop. More than 100,000 oysters are eaten during the weekend-long celebration. With what many consider to be the best oysters in the world, this is a culinary experience to remember.

WHERE TO EAT SEAFOOD BEYOND GALWAY CITY

O'Grady's On the Pier
Simply prepared fresh seafood with great service at this nautical-themed seafront restaurant in Barna. €€

Hooked
Traditional fish and chips with contemporary flair and ever-changing daily specials in Barna. €€

Paddy Burkes Bar & Restaurant
A traditional pub in Clarinbridge that serves oysters, seafood platters, and fish and chips. €€

Driving Around Lough Corrib
Ireland's Second-Largest Freshwater Lake

Turn off the main roads to experience one of Galway's lesser-known but stunningly scenic drives, a loop of **Lough Corrib**. You'll pass through lesser-visited but still idyllic beauty spots, with a quick detour into neighbouring County Mayo.

Leave Galway on the N59 for the busy market town of **Oughterard**, one of Ireland's principal angling centres. Just before town, take a quick detour to visit the mighty **Aughnanure Castle**, renowned for its unusual double bawn (area surrounded by walls outside the main castle). Linger in town for a coffee or lunch at family-run **Conneely's Cafe** or detour for a spot of fishing or a cruise on the lake. **Corrib Cruises** runs day cruises out to the largest island on Lough Corrib, **Inchagoill**, a lonely place dotted with ancient monastic ruins.

As you drive towards Clifden and into Connemara, the landscape changes dramatically, with lush green fields giving way to barren mountains and boglands. About 7.5km west of Oughterard off the N59 is **The Quiet Man Bridge**, a picturesque drystone double-arched bridge featured in the iconic 1950s film. Continue to Maam Cross and turn north onto the R336, enjoying the stunning mountain views in all directions. At Maam Bridge, turn east onto the R345 and hug the shores of Lough Corrib.

Continue through the lively village of Cornamona, taking in more beautiful vistas until you reach the village of Clonbur. Cross the border into County Mayo to reach **Cong** village, the setting for the film *The Quiet Man*. Superfans can check out **The Quiet Man Museum**, and an interesting forest walk leads to the 78 steps of the **Guinness Tower**.

From Cong, pass through Cross and Glencorrib. The ruins of **Ross Errilly Friary** are considered to be the most complete Franciscan monastic ruins in Ireland. Get there from Headford, another angling centre and a busy town. From Headford, go south on the N84 to get back to Galway city.

Into the West: the Gaeltacht
Linguaphile Delights And Irish Arts

West of Galway city is the Galway Gaeltacht, the country's largest Irish-speaking area. Stretching along the coastline of Galway Bay from the Claddagh, home of the famous ring, into the Connemara Mountains, this region is home to stunning scenery ringed by stone walls and sprinkled with sheep

---

ORANMORE'S AWARD-WINNING CRAFT BEER

Just outside of Oranmore, **Galway Hooker Craft Brewing Co** produces the original Irish Pale Ale, Ireland's most popular style of craft beer. Named after the iconic small wooden sailing boats from the county, Galway Hooker operates from a state-of-the-art facility. It's Ireland's third-oldest craft brewery and the oldest brewery in the province of Connacht, though it was established only in 2006.

Galway Hooker has won numerous awards for its flavour profile, and drinkers can find its beers in pubs, restaurants and shops around the country. It started guided tours in 2023, allowing visitors to get a behind-the-scenes look.

WHERE TO DRINK COFFEE IN OUGHTERARD

Calendar Coffee
Serving locally roasted, seasonally sourced flavourful coffee; 2km south of Oughterard.

My Little Flower Coffee
Brews Calendar Coffee's roast right in town and serves delicious cakes too.

Keogh's Bar & Coffee Shop
Local pub serving a decent cup of coffee, though the Irish coffee is the best.

Ross Errilly Friary

and quaint villages. It's rich with heritage and folklore, and Irish culture and traditions are still very much alive.

Though it's only 18km away from Galway city, **Spiddal** (An Spidéal), one of the most vibrant Gaeltacht towns in the country, feels vastly removed from the buzz of urban life. **Spiddal Craft Village** is an Irish handicrafts haven where in-house artisans design, create and sell their unique wares. Studios in the Craft Village house artists' workshops, where basket weaving, acrylic painting, stained glass, pottery, screen printing and Celtic jewellery are created.

CLADDAGH RINGS

Proudly adorning fingers around the world, the Claddagh ring is traditionally a symbol of love. The two open hands represent friendship and hold a heart that signifies love. They're topped by a crown of loyalty. Traditionally, your relationship status would indicate how the ring is worn.

Single
On your right hand, with the point of the heart facing your fingers and away from your heart.

In a relationship
On your right hand, with the point of the heart pointing at your wrist and heart.

Engaged
On your left hand, with the point of the heart facing your fingers.

Married
On your left hand, with the point of the heart facing your wrist.

GETTING AROUND

The best way to explore at your leisure is with your own wheels. Main roads are well marked, but be careful of narrow bends and wandering sheep on smaller roads.

Frequent bus services operate from the suburbs of Salthill, Spiddal and Oranmore to Galway. A train line connects Athenry and Gort to each other and to Galway city.

CONNEMARA NATIONAL PARK

One of Ireland's six national parks, Connemara shows off the country's wild, rugged and raw landscape at its best. The national park is part of the larger region of Connemara and the Connemara peninsula. From Galway city, a slow, shore-side route passes hidden beaches and seaside hamlets. West of Spiddal, the scenery becomes increasingly dramatic, with parched fields rolling to fissured bays.

Once all privately owned and part of the Kylemore Estate, the land was donated in 1980, and the national park opened to the public. It encompasses 20 sq km of scenic mountains, bogs, heaths, grasslands and woodlands. The Maumturk Mountains and the peaks of the Twelve Bens range include networks of scenic hiking and biking trails.

Connemara National Park is home to rare plant species, wild deer and Connemara ponies, Ireland's only native breed. Everywhere you look, the land is laced with stone walls.

TOP TIP

Connemara doesn't have any formal campgrounds inside the national park, but if you want to camp or are planning a multiday hiking trip, you can wild-camp as long as you obey the camping exclusion zone and follow the Wild Camping Code (nationalparks.ie/connemara/things-to-do).

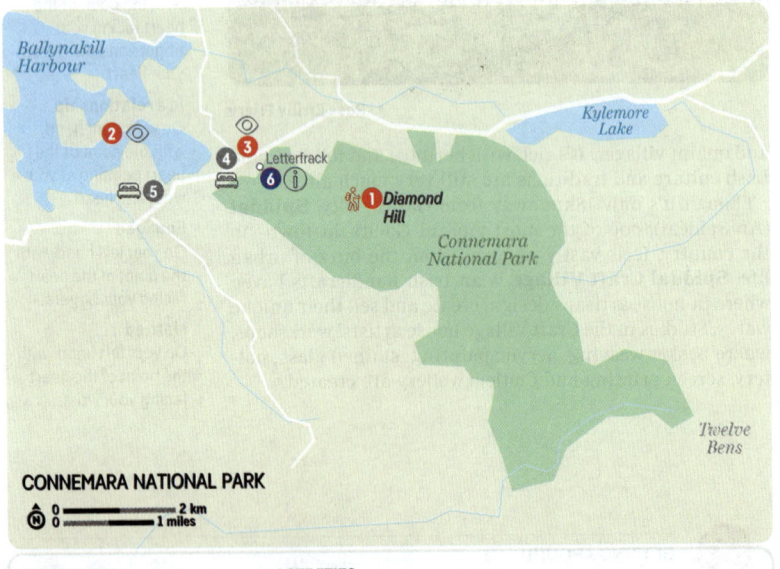

HIGHLIGHTS
1. Diamond Hill

SIGHTS
2. DK Connemara Oysters

ACTIVITIES
3. Connemara Wild Escapes

Sleeping
4. Connemara National Park Hostel & B&B

5. Rosleague Manor

INFORMATION
6. Connemara National Park Visitor Centre

Connemara National Park

A Walk in the Park
Trails Through Connemara

Connemara's big draw is hillwalking, which is the best way to immerse yourself in the region as you can't drive through the boundaries of the national park itself. Some short family-friendly walks offer a great introduction to Connemara, such as the looped 1km **Ellis Wood Nature Trail** and **Sruffaun-boy Trail**, a 1.8-km loop trail that gives great views of the lake.

Park rangers lead free guided walks from the **Connemara National Park Visitor Centre** in Letterfrack. Some walks have themes, such as flora and fauna, history, and children's activities. The visitor centre is inside a historical building that dates from 1890 and once belonged to the Letterfrack Industrial School. Pick up free maps with suggested trails and check out the small exhibits that describe the peatland landscape and conservation efforts. There's a nice cafe, as well as a playground and indoor and outdoor picnic facilities.

Poking out of the earth into a point, **Diamond Hill** (442m) gets its name from its shape and the type of stone it's made from. When the sun shines, Diamond Hill's quartzite sparkles and shimmers in the sun. The hike up is well worth the effort,

LORD OF THE RINGS INSPIRATION

Connemara National Park is said to have inspired JRR Tolkien's *Lord of the Rings* series. During his time as an English professor at Oxford University's Merton College, Tolkien spent five summers as an external examiner at University College Galway (now National University of Ireland Galway) between 1949 and 1959. During his visits to Galway, he took frequent trips to the Burren and Connemara. Perhaps these stark otherworldly landscapes inspired his imagination when conjuring up the Shire and Mordor.

WHERE TO STAY IN CONNEMARA NATIONAL PARK

Connemara National Park Hostel and B&B
Affordable, charming and great value; choose between spacious dorms or private en-suite rooms. €

Oyster Cottage
Luxurious cottage at DK Connemara Oysters with panoramic views of the Atlantic and Connemara's hills. €€

Rosleague Manor
Richly coloured rooms furnished with antiques and original art, overlooking Ballynakill Harbour and the Twelve Bens. €€€

WHY I LOVE CONNEMARA

Noelle Kelly, writer

As Oscar Wilde put it, Connemara is home to a 'savage beauty'. For me, the region's dramatic scenery truly encompasses what rural Ireland is all about. With bleak bogs, mountain peaks, grand castles, thatched cottages, and stone bridges and walls, the area is varied in physical beauty while maintaining a deep connection with traditional Irish culture.

I first visited as a teenager, and it was my first experience of such a rugged Irish landscape. Dotted with lost sheep, beautiful beaches and stunning scenery around every turn, Connemara never fails to take my breath away whenever I return.

---

and you're rewarded with panoramic mountain and coastal views from the summit. On a clear day, Inishbofin and Kylemore Abbey (p322) are visible, as well as the majestic Twelve Bens, Mweelrea and Tully Mountains.

Hikers have two trail options on Diamond Hill. The easiest of the two is the 3km **Lower Diamond Hill Walk** (allow 1½ hours for the return trip). You don't get the same amazing views as you would from the summit, but you're still rewarded with breathtaking views of the surrounding Connemara coastline and islands. The 7km **Upper Diamond Hill Trail** takes about three hours. Both trails start at the Connemara National Park Visitor Centre and are well-marked. While you don't need to be a seasoned hillwalker to reach the summit, the trail is somewhat challenging. Gravel footpaths and wooden boardwalks make the journey over the bog and to the top enjoyable, as your feet stay dry. Check the weather before you set off and be prepared for all seasons with adequate layers and the proper footwear. Towards the summit, the trail can be quite steep and is exposed to the elements.

The visitor centre is a great place to enjoy coffee, soups and sandwiches before getting started, or reward yourself with a delicious homemade scone after your hike while looking back up at the summit of Diamond Hill.

Connemara Wild Escapes is a Letterfrack-based outfit offering guided hikes, horse riding, cycling and kayaking to get you into the wilderness of Connemara.

Farm-Fresh Oysters
On The Half Shell

Learn about oyster farming at **DK Connemara Oysters**, based in Letterfrack. Take the one-hour tour to understand the process from seed to plate, from turning bags in the bay to grading and packing. Afterwards, there's an oyster-shucking demonstration. If you're feeling adventurous, you can shuck your own and sample the oysters. It's a brilliant activity for a rainy day, and it's family-friendly for children older than six.

Oysters

GETTING AROUND

Driving is the most convenient option to get around at your own leisure, and there's free parking at the visitor centre. Buses connect Galway city and Clifden with Letterfrack. Once you're there, you can walk around the national park.

Beyond Connemara National Park

Connemara's gateway town of Letterfrack is a great place to explore Kylemore Abbey, Leenane and Killary Harbour.

The north coast of Connemara is awash with gorgeous beaches, raw mountain vistas and stark views out to the moody sea. Ever in the shadows of the Maumturks and Mweelrea, Connacht's highest peak in neighbouring County Mayo, this small corner of Galway offers incredible natural beauty. The coast hooks deeply inland at Killary Harbour, Ireland's only fjord. A short distance south, see Kylemore's 19th-century abbey, whose stunning neogothic architecture and solid granite walls make it one of the most popular places to visit in the county.

Bypass the N59 for a series of small roads that follow the twists and turns along the coast, promising more off-the-beaten-path experiences and adventures on both land and sea.

TOP TIP

If you're travelling on a budget, you can see Kylemore Abbey for free from the car park on a clear day.

Killary Harbour (p323)

BEYOND CONNEMARA NATIONAL PARK **GALWAY**

THE GUIDE

OYSTERS EVERYWHERE

In the south of Galway, catch September's **Clarinbridge Oyster Festival** (p315) and stop for lunch in **Moran's Oyster Cottage** (p315) in Kilcolgan, an atmospheric thatched pub and restaurant set in a quiet cove overlooking Dunbulcaun Bay, where the oysters are reared.

BEST BEACHES IN NORTH CONNEMARA

Glassilaun Beach
Connemara or the Caribbean? A magnificent crescent of sand awaits between Renvyle and Killary.

Lettergesh
This beautiful long sandy beach with mountain views to the north was a filming location for *The Quiet Man*.

Renvyle Beach (White Strand)
Pure white sand, crystal clear waters and a hillock in the middle for panoramic vistas.

Church, Kylemore Abbey

Postcard-Perfect Kylemore Abbey
Neogothic Architecture

Photogenically perched on the shores of Pollacapall Lough, 4km east of Letterfrack, the crenellated 19th-century neogothic fantasy **Kylemore Abbey** looks like a scene from a fairy tale. Mitchell Henry, the son of a wealthy Manchester cotton merchant of Irish origin, originally built this 19th-century structure, then called Kylemore Castle. Benedictine nuns have been living here since 1920, and it was the first Benedictine abbey in Ireland.

Kylemore Abbey features a neogothic **church** and a **mausoleum** where Mitchell Henry and his wife, Margaret, are interred. In 1874, Margaret contracted dysentery on holiday

WHERE TO EAT IN LEENANE

Leenane Hotel
Try regional specialities such as fresh Killary Bay salmon or a rack of Connemara Mountain lamb. €€

Purple Door Cafe
Great breakfast and lunch stop that dishes out soup, sandwiches, delicious coffee and cakes until 4pm. €

Misunderstood Heron
Award-winning seasonal food truck serving tasty vegan and vegetarian options and fantastic coffee. €

322

in Egypt and died 16 days later. Distraught, Mitchell had his wife's body embalmed and brought back to Connemara, and built a cathedral-in-miniature in her memory. The architecture of this sandstone church building is remarkable, and it replaces the typical grotesque Gothic features such as gargoyles with delicate flowers, birds and angels. The Victorian-era walled gardens are a pleasant 20-minute stroll or a free shuttle bus ride from the visitor centre, along the edge of Maladrolaun Lake. There's also a tea house near the gardens and a craft shop and restaurant within the complex.

Allow at least two hours to explore Kylemore Abbey and the gardens. If you simply want to snap a photo of Kylemore Abbey from afar, you'll only need a quick 10-minute stop. One of the best viewpoints of the abbey and that postcard-perfect picture is actually from the car park.

Adventures in Killary Harbour

Activities On Land And Water

Slicing 16km inland and more than 45m deep in the centre, **Killary Harbour** is strikingly scenic and often referred to as Ireland's only fjord. The small village of **Leenane** sits on its shores, nestled between the Mweelrea, Devil's Mother and Maamturk Mountains, and the approach is spectacular from all directions. *The Field*, a famous Irish film directed by Jim Sheridan and starring Richard Harris, Tom Berenger and Sean Bean, was filmed mainly in Leenane and around Killary Harbour.

Killary is the place to tackle adventurous activities on land and water. **Killary Adventure Company** offers kayaking, archery, coasteering, gorge walking, clay pigeon shooting, high-ropes courses and an obstacle course through the Connemara bog.

At **Killary Sheep Farm**, you can experience life on a traditional Connemara farm with Tom Nee, who puts on impressive displays of sheep herding with his sheepdogs, as well as demonstrations of sheepshearing and bog cutting. You might even get the opportunity to feed baby lambs.

Three kilometres west of Leenane, **Killary Fjord Boat Tours** offers 90-minute cruises of the harbour from Nancy's Point. Keep your eyes peeled for dolphins. You also pass a mussel farm and stop at a salmon farm.

North of Leenane, you can go chasing waterfalls and scout a film location. Low and wide **Aasleagh Falls** are framed by a series of rapids and pools. One of the most memorable scenes in *The Field* involved a fight with the American, which was filmed here.

BEST ROAD TRIPS BEYOND CONNEMARA NATIONAL PARK

Inagh Valley to Killary Harbour
See mountains and picturesque lakes south of Killary Harbour on the R344.

Leenane to Drummin
Wind spectacularly along the N59 and the northern side of Killary Fjord through the Doolough Valley with spectacular views of the Twelve Bens.

Lough Corrib Loop
Loop Ireland's second-largest lake (p316) along the N84, R334 and R346 with picturesque villages, historical ruins and stunning vistas.

ARAN ISLANDS

THE GUIDE | ARAN ISLANDS GALWAY

Windswept, rugged, remote and desolate, the three tiny Aran Islands give a feeling of being transported back in time. Inishmore (Inis Mór), Inishmaan (Inis Meáin) and Inisheer (Inis Oírr) are an extension of the unique limestone landscape of the Burren in County Clare and actually geographically closer, but are in County Galway's boundaries.

Thought to be inhabited since the 5th century, the islands are home to ancient forts, religious ruins, staggering cliffs smashed by Atlantic surf, deserted beaches and raw natural beauty. Their isolation meant that islanders maintained a traditional lifestyle well into the 20th century, and Irish (Gaelic) is still the main language spoken on the islands today, though most islanders speak English too.

For a memorable experience of Irish culture and scenery in its purest, it's worth the quick, although sometimes rough, crossing to visit at least one of the three Aran Islands in Galway Bay.

TOP TIP

Some businesses do not accept cards or have minimum-spend policies. ATMs are hard to find, so bring cash with you. Be prepared for four seasons in a day and wear layers. Irish weather is changeable in general but even more so on the islands.

Horse, Inisheer (p327)

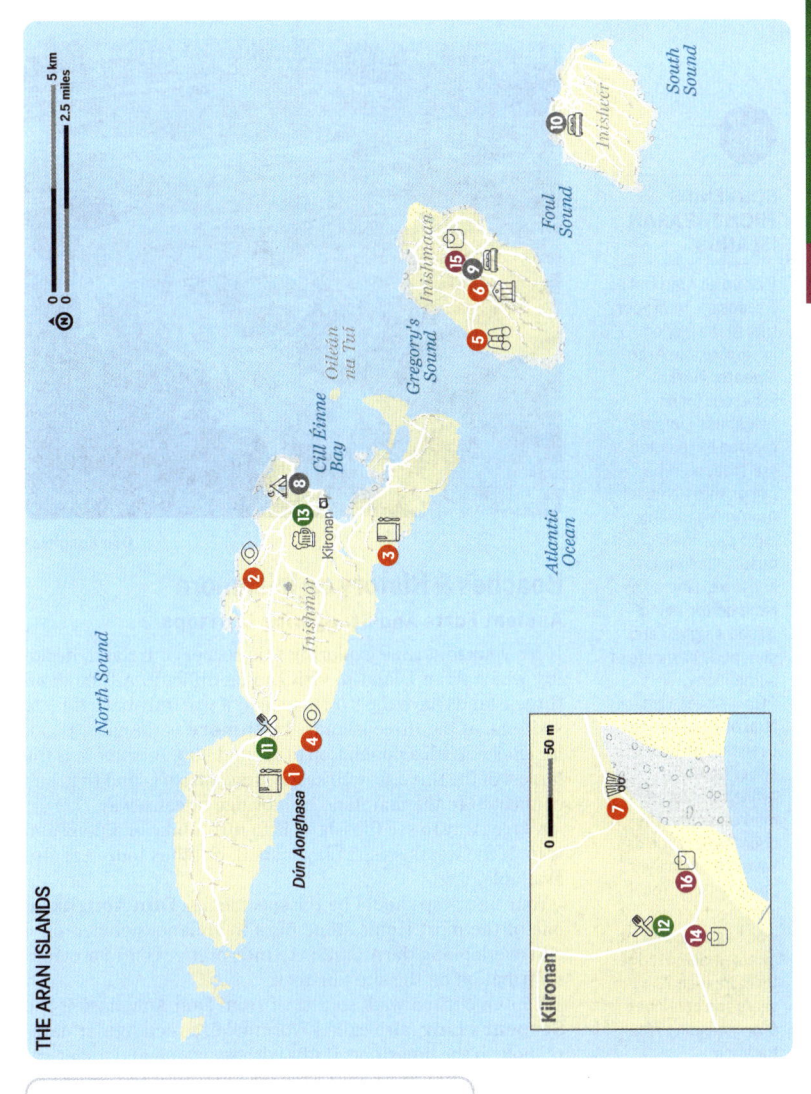

THE ARAN ISLANDS

HIGHLIGHTS
1. Dún Aonghasa

SIGHTS
2. Aran Goats Cheese
3. Dún Dúchathair
4. Serpent's Lair
5. Synge's Chair
6. Teach Synge

ACTIVITIES
7. Dive Academy Scuba Diving School

SLEEPING
8. Aran Islands Camping & Glamping
9. Inis Meáin
10. South Aran House

EATING
11. Teach Nan Phaidí
12. The Bar

DRINKING & NIGHTLIFE
13. Joe Watty's Bar & Restaurant

SHOPPING
14. Aran Sweater Market
15. Inis Meáin Knitting Company
16. Man of Aran Fudge

Aran sweater detail

THE GUIDE

GALWAY ARAN ISLANDS

SOUVENIRS FROM THE ARAN ISLANDS

Pick up an Aran knit as a keepsake from your trip. At the pier on Inishmore, the **Aran Sweater Market** is famous for its handmade jumpers, created by talented craftspeople who live on the island. All Aran knit garments must pass the highest quality standards and are examined by hand before being issued a signed and stamped certificate of authenticity.

On Inisheer, visit **Man of Aran Fudge**. Even though these sweet treats are available at farmers markets across the country, here you can savour them in their home setting. You'll also meet Tomás, who has been making award-winning fudge for more than 20 years and continues a longstanding family tradition.

Dún Aonghasa

Beaches & History on Inishmore
Ancient Forts And Staggering Clifftops

If it's your first time exploring this corner of Ireland, deciding which Aran Island to visit can be difficult. Although all three islands have their own appeal, if you only have time to visit one of the three islands, **Inishmore** is the most popular choice. With a population of around 900, Inishmore is the largest of the three, as well as the largest Irish island that isn't connected to the mainland by a bridge or causeway.

A great way to see the island is to hire a bike or a pony and trap. If the weather isn't playing ball, minibus tours are also available.

Your first stop should be the spectacular **Dún Aonghasa**, one of the most iconic stone forts in Ireland, perched on a cliff overlooking the Atlantic. An interpretive centre provides information on the site's history.

A 750m clifftop walk southeast from Dún Aonghasa is the **Serpent's Lair** (also called Wormhole), a rectangular natural hole in the limestone. It fills with seawater, and underwater tunnels that lead out to the ocean. Admire another historical fortress at **Dún Dúchathair**, the Black Fort. Dating from the Iron Age or early medieval period, it stands guard over Inishmore from a clifftop promontory.

WHERE TO EAT ON INISHMORE

Joe Watty's Bar & Restaurant
Listen to live trad music while you dine on delicious seafood. Book ahead for dinner. €€

The Bar
Fresh seafood and pub grub in a former priest's house. The outside patio overlooks the harbour. €€

Teach Nan Phaidi
Traditional Irish dishes with a few modern twists served in an old thatched cottage. €

WALKING AROUND INISHEER, THE SMALLEST ARAN ISLAND

In about five hours with stops for sightseeing, you can walk around Inisheer's 11km shoreline. From the **1 Inisheer ferry pier**, walk west along the narrow road parallel to the shore and go straight onto the small fishing pier at the northwest corner of the island. Continue along the road with the shingle shore on one side and a dense patchwork of fields enclosed by stone walls on the other.

About 1km from the sharp junction, turn left at the painted sign. About 100m along the paved lane is the **2 Sacred Well (Well of Enda)**. Continue southwest as the path becomes a rough track. After about 600m, head roughly south across the limestone pavement and strips of grass to the shore. Follow the gently sloping rock platform around the southwestern headland, Ceann na Faochnaí, and walk east to the **3 Inisheer Lighthouse** near Fardurris Point.

Stay with the coast, turning northeast. You'll see the wreck of the **4 Plassy** in the distance. Head north, following the track, which then becomes a sealed road at the northern end of **5 Lough More**. Continue following the road along the northern shore of the island, past the **6 airstrip**. Detour to **7 Teampall Chaoimháin**, the burial site of St Caomhán, the patron saint of the Aran Islands. The ruins date from the 10th century. Soak in the incredible views from nearby **8 O'Brien's Castle**. Check out **9 Cnoc Rathnaí**, a remarkably intact Bronze Age burial mound dating from 1500 BCE. It was submerged in sand and rediscovered in the 19th century.

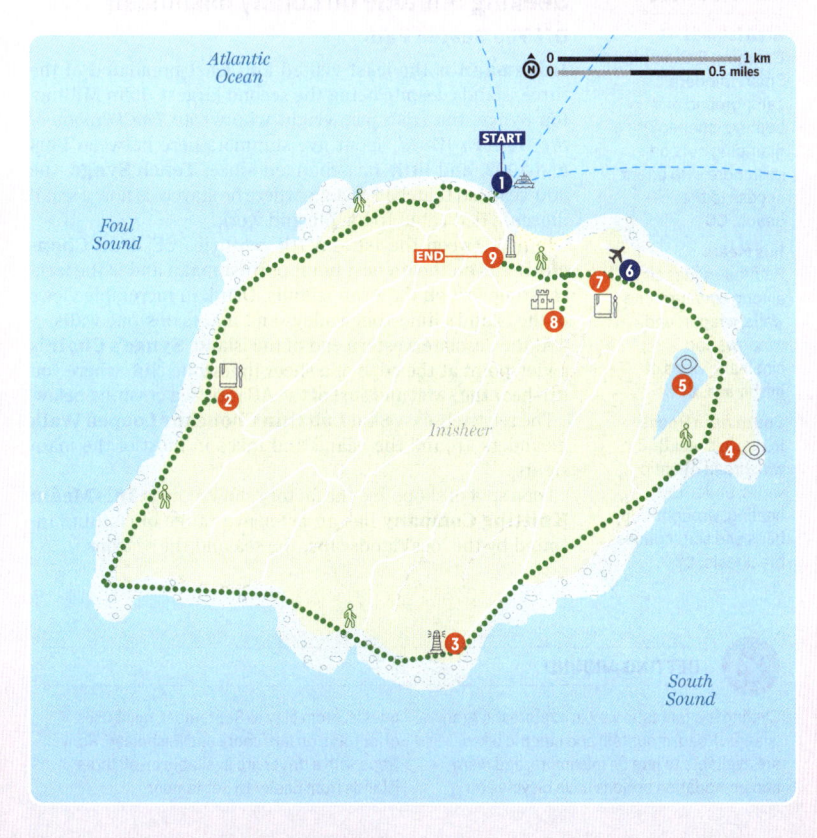

Sample Award-Winning Cheese
Goat's Milk Delight

At **Aran Goats Cheese**, Gabriel will introduce you to his herd of Nubian and Saanen goats that graze on the unique pastures of Inishmore, which gives the cheese its delicious creamy, salty flavour. You'll be taken through the whole process of how this award-winning cheese is made before sampling and experiencing the range for yourself.

Scuba Diving in the Atlantic
Under The Sea

With crystal-clear waters and vibrant underwater life, the Aran Islands have gained a reputation for being one of the best places to dive in Europe. **Dive Academy Scuba Diving School** on Inishmore offers PADI scuba courses for kids and adults, plus guided dive trips for certified divers. The Gulf Stream warms these waters and brings nutrients, resulting in varied and rich marine life, such as sea anemones, coral, dolphins, seals and dogfish.

Seeking Solitude on Lonely Inishmaan
Off The Beaten Path

Inishmaan is the least visited and least populated of the three islands despite being the second largest. John Millington Synge, the Irish playwright who wrote *The Playboy of the Western World*, spent five summers here between 1898 and 1902, and little has changed since. **Teach Synge**, the 300-year-old thatched cottage where he stayed, is now a small museum dedicated to his life and work.

Built between the 1st and 7th centuries CE, **Dún Chonchúir** sits on the highest point of Inishmaan and is the largest stone fort on the Aran Islands. Drink in incredible views of the island's limestone valleys and mazes of stone walls.

At the desolate western end of the island, **Synge's Chair** is a viewpoint at the edge of a sheer limestone cliff, where you can hear the swell and surf of the Atlantic sea crashing below.

The relatively easy 8km **Lúb Dún Chonchúr Looped Walk** meanders around the island and takes in most of the main sights.

For a spot of shopping, the factory showroom at **Inis Meáin Knitting Company** has an extensive range of clothing inspired by the local landscape, the sea and the seasons.

BEST PLACES TO STAY ON THE ARAN ISLANDS

Aran Islands Camping & Glamping
Smart, modern campground and beehive-shaped glamping huts on Inishmore with direct access to the beach. €€

Inis Meáin
Boutique suites sit among curving stone walls, wraparound windows and cinematic views of Inishmaan. €€€

South Aran House
Rustic Inisheer B&B with broad Atlantic views, underfloor heating, wrought-iron beds and scrumptious breakfasts. €€

GETTING AROUND

Cycling is a fantastic way to explore the Aran Islands. Road, mountain and electric bikes are available to hire on Inishmore, and many accommodation options have bicycles for guests. From May to September, minibuses offer tours on Inishmore and Inishmaan. Pony traps with a driver are available on all three islands from Easter to September.

CLIFDEN

A colourful and bustling market town in the heart of the Connemara region, Clifden has a stunning location at the foot of the Twelve Bens Mountains overlooking the Atlantic Ocean, making it one of the most picturesque towns in Ireland. As the region's largest town, Clifden is often referred to as the capital of Connemara.

The town is home to lots of lively pubs, a wide choice of dining options, a weekly farmers market, a strong cultural and artistic scene, and warm Irish hospitality. With a captivating blend of natural beauty and welcoming locals, Clifden is a great place to stay for a few days for a somewhat cosmopolitan respite from exploring the more rural regions of Connemara.

Clifden has a wide range of accommodation across all budgets, and restaurants and pubs cluster in Clifden's town centre. Many of Clifden's pubs have live music, especially in the summer months.

TOP TIP

This is pony country, and rides along the beaches are popular. The area's famous ponies are exhibited at Clifden's showgrounds during the annual Connemara Pony Show (p331) in August. Other events during the show include Irish dancing. Book your accommodation in advance if you're planning to visit in the summer.

CLIFDEN

HIGHLIGHTS
1. Lavelle Art Gallery
2. Whitethorn Gallery

SIGHTS
3. Clifden Castle
4. Connemara Heritage & History Centre
5. Market Square

ACTIVITIES
6. Errislannan Manor

SLEEPING
7. Abbeyglen Castle Hotel
8. Ben View House
9. Clifden Eco Beach Camping

EATING
10. Mannions Seafood Bar & Restaurant
11. Mitchell's
12. Off the Square

DRINKING & NIGHTLIFE
13. Anchor Bar
14. EJ Kings
15. Guys Bar
16. Lowry's Bar
17. MC McGraths
18. Upstairs Downstairs Cafe

SHOPPING
19. Clifden Bookshop
20. Conn O'Mara

Mannion's Seafood Bar and Restaurant

🍴 BEST PLACES TO EAT IN CLIFDEN

Off The Square
Locally sourced seafood and local lamb and sirloin beef feature at this busy bistro. €€

Mitchell's
Enjoy a hearty feed at this award-winning restaurant inside one of the oldest terraced buildings in town. €€

Mannion's Seafood Bar & Restaurant
This longstanding family-run restaurant serves mouthwatering foods and has traditional Irish music. €€

Clifden's Cosmopolitan Vibes
Castles, Strolls And Shopping

Kickstart a day in Clifden with coffee and brunch at **Upstairs Downstairs Cafe**. Afterwards, browse for books in the tiny **Clifden Bookshop** next door, dropping into **Whitethorn Gallery** and **Lavelle Art Gallery** and drifting in and out of the many gift shops in town, like **Conn O'Mara**.

On Fridays, savour delicious crêpes from Le Crepe Wagon at the farmers market on **Market Sq**. Browse the offerings from Connemara with everything from organic vegetables, herbs, bread, pies and even clothes on offer. If it's not Friday, head to **12 Pins Coffee** for a caffeine and cake fix.

Walk to Clifden Bay and along Beach Rd, taking in views of the harbour and the Twelve Bens. With its seafront setting, the **Anchor Bar** at Clifden Boat Club is the perfect place for a rest and a drink before heading back to town.

If you don't want to get back to town just yet, turn left on your way back to visit the spectacular ruins of the Gothic-style

🛏 WHERE TO STAY IN & AROUND CLIFDEN

Clifden Eco Beach Camping
Ireland's first climate-neutral campground has well-maintained facilities near the beach, 10km northwest of Clifden. €

Abbeyglen Castle Hotel
Complete with turrets and straight out of a fairy tale amid landscaped grounds on Sky Rd. €€€

Ben View House
Great-value, welcoming, family-run B&B in a 19th-century townhouse in the heart of town. €€

Clifden Castle. Overlooking the bay, this historical landmark dates from 1812. Admire the ancient stonework, magnificent pillars and beautifully crafted archways. If you want to save it for another day, it's just a 2km wander or cycle from Clifden.

Soak Up Connemara's Heritage
History, Traditions And Farm Animals

For an immersion in traditional Connemara culture, the award-winning, family-run **Connemara Heritage and History Centre** is 6km from Clifden. The restored pre-Famine cottage of Dan O'Hara is the main draw and illustrates the life of a typical 19th-century Connemara tenant farmer. There's a multilingual audiovisual and history presentation that tells O'Hara's life story, from his eviction from the farm to his emigration to New York. The centre also shows the history of Connemara from the prehistoric to the present.

Explore reconstructed *crannógs* (artificial islands), a ring fort and an early Christian oratory, and get up close with Connemara ponies, sheep, chickens and donkeys. Enjoy spectacular views of the Roundstone Bog from the hilltop above as it stretches towards the Atlantic Ocean. Guided tours are by old-style carriage and can include turf-cutting demonstrations, sheep herding and even a full-day walking tour of this 4-sq-km estate on request. There's a large craft shop, restaurant and a free car park on-site.

Equine Experiences in Clifden
Horse Riding And Connemara Pony Show

Errislannan Manor is a stately old manor estate with gardens, woodlands, a trout lake and an equestrian centre that breeds Connemara ponies. On the Connemara coast 6.5km south of Clifden, the property offers the chance to get up close and personal with the famous Connemara ponies with guided horseback tours through the grounds and into Connemara's moors and mountains.

Clifden puts on the **Connemara Pony Show** every August, which attracts visitors from near and far. The highlight of the festival is the biggest showcase of Connemara ponies in the world, which stand out for their versatility, resilience and gentle nature. Compared to other types of ponies, the compact build, intelligence and adaptability of Connemara ponies make them prized for equestrian activities.

At the show, ponies compete in in-hand classes, ridden classes, working hunter classes and a puissance (high jump) competition. There's also a dog show, a domestic arts show and Irish dancing.

BEST PUBS IN CLIFDEN

Lowry's Bar
Iconic pub voted the best in Ireland at the National Hospitality Awards. There's traditional music nightly in summer.

EJ Kings
A good spot for live music, EJ Kings regularly hosts local musicians and is popular with tourists and locals.

MC McGraths
Enjoy a creamy pint in one of the oldest family-owned bars in Clifden.

Guys Bar
Expect turf fires, pub grub, small intimate snugs and corners, and live trad music.

GETTING AROUND

Clifden is easily explored on foot, and cycling is also a good option. Hire a bike from All Things Connemara or Mannion's Bikes.

Beyond Clifden

Epic road trips, coastal cycles, boglands, achingly beautiful beaches and more island hopping reward visitors outside of Clifden.

The Irish name for Clifden is An Clochán, which means stepping stone, and it's a fitting description because the town is often used as a stepping stone for exploring the wider region.

Beyond Clifden, some of Ireland's most breathtaking and secluded beaches await. The area is also home to some of the region's best cycle trails as well as epic scenic road trips, such as the aptly named Sky Road. The walking trails of Connemara National Park are easily accessible, or you can walk across the sand to Omey Island at low tide. Stay a while in this lesser-explored part of Galway and you'll be rewarded with sleepy seaside villages and stunning views around every turn.

TOP TIP

On the Sky Road scenic drive, set off clockwise from the southern side for the best views, which peak at sunset.

Roundstone

Dog's Bay

Connemara on Two Wheels
Coastal Cycling Routes

With its dramatic setting between the rugged peaks of the Twelve Bens and the rolling waves of the Atlantic, the area surrounding Clifden is a cycling hub. A range of routes guide cyclists to spectacular scenery. Hire a bike in Clifden from **All Things Connemara** and **Mannion's Bikes** and then set off on a cycle.

The **Cleggan Loop** is a 33km trip north to the rocky coast around the charming fishing village of **Cleggan**, following the fringes of Streamstown Bay. The route passes **Omey Island**, and you can visit this beautiful island on foot when the tide is out. Climb to the top of **Cleggan Head** to admire the views of the village below as well as Inishbofin, Inishturk, Clare Island and the ever-present Twelve Bens. From Cleggan, a mountain road climbs gradually through a forested area before a speedy descent back down to town.

The **Ballyconneely and Roundstone Loop** is a 40km ride that takes cyclists through the natural wilderness of Derrygimlagh and Roundstone bogs. You'll pass the site of the crash-landing of the first transatlantic flight by Alcock and Brown in 1919 and the old Marconi transatlantic wireless station. Further on towards Ballyconneely, **Coral Strand** makes a lovely photo stop. At **Roundstone**, one of the oldest fishing villages in Ireland, pause to enjoy the catch of the day directly from the busy harbour. Pedal to the stunning beaches of **Gurteen** and **Dog's Bay** with their pristine white sands and azure waters. The coast road has fine views and gentle gradients.

FEEL LIKE A CASTAWAY AT OMEY ISLAND

Following the coast northwest of Clifden brings you to the tiny village of Claddaghduff. Turning west by the Catholic church, you will come out on Omey Strand. You can drive or walk across the sand to tiny Omey Island at low tide and go for a swim or a stroll on its white sandy beaches.

Though the island is now uninhabited, it has a handful of abandoned houses. Tide times are displayed on the noticeboard in the car park. Don't be tempted to cross between half tide and high tide or if there's water on the route. Time your visit so you can return before half or high tide.

GETTING AROUND

The area around Clifden is best explored by car or bike. Bikes can be rented in Clifden from All Things Connemara and Mannion's Bikes.

ROAD TRIP
Driving the Sky Road Loop

Starting and ending in Clifden, this 16km route traces a dizzying loop to the township of Kingston and back, taking in rugged, stunningly beautiful coastal scenery. Without stopping, the drive would take only 30 minutes, but it's best to allow about 2½ hours to soak up the spectacular scenery and stop along the way. The Sky Road separates into the lower and upper road routes. For the best views, take the upper road.

1 Clifden

The journey for the Sky Road begins in the vibrant lively town of Clifden. For this drive, you'll need your own wheels.

The Drive: A little more than 1km up the hill from Clifden, you'll see a signpost that points you in the direction of John D'Arcy Monument Hill. Pull over and get to the monument on foot.

2 John D'Arcy Monument

Founded in the 19th century, Clifden is a relatively new town by Irish standards and was founded by John D'Arcy. Following D'Arcy's death in 1839, this monument was erected in his memory at the peak of the hill that overlooks the western end of town. There are expansive views of the Connemara landscape of mountains, bogs and coast. It's one of the best spots to snap photographs of Clifden.

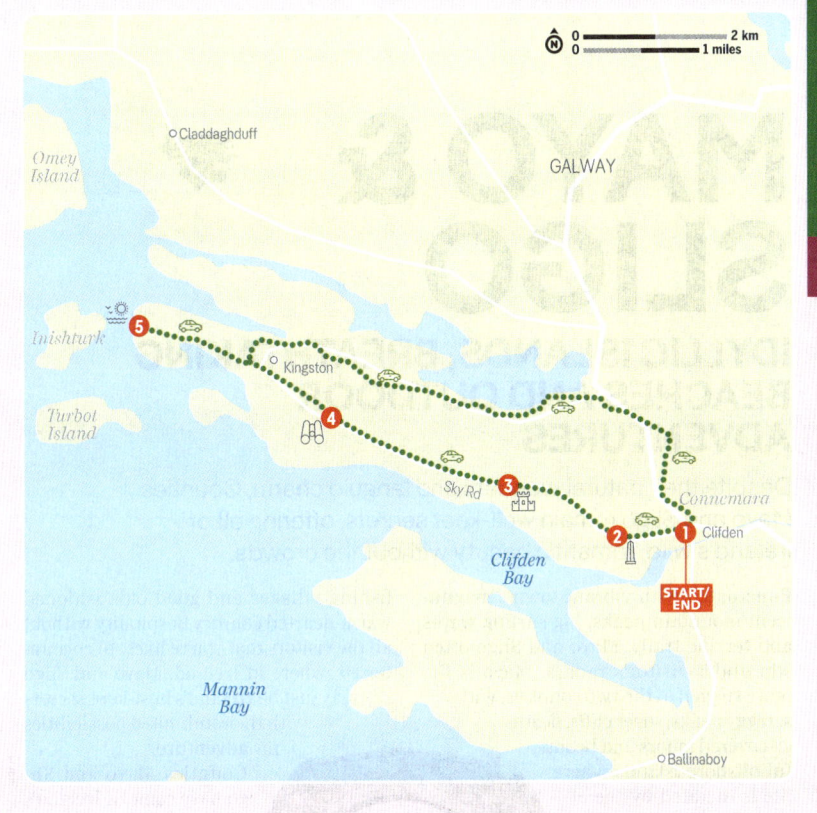

The Drive: Continue northwest on Sky Rd for about 2km to reach Clifden Castle. You'll see a wide opening on your left that includes a turn to the south along another road to a small car park. An arched gateway leads to the castle.

3 Clifden Castle

The D'Arcy family built this castle, now derelict and roofless, as their family home. It looks older than it actually is, and it was constructed in Gothic Revival style in 1818. It faces Clifden Bay, which makes for a picturesque photo.

The Drive: Back on Sky Rd, continue northwest for 2.7km.

4 Sky Road Viewpoint

This viewpoint, marked by one of the wrought-iron Wild Atlantic Way signs, is the pinnacle of the road trip and the best spot to take photos. There's a car park with some picnic tables, making it a perfect place for a snack with a view.

The Drive: Follow Sky Rd through the township of Kingstown, reaching the coast after 3km.

5 Eyrephort Beach

Visitors to quiet and secluded Eyrephort Beach are rewarded with far-reaching views of the nearby offshore islands of Inishturk and Turbot, as well as the Connemara countryside and the Atlantic Ocean. This beautiful beach is a little off the beaten track, providing a welcome seaside reprieve. Remnants of Viking history, including a grave, sword and shield, have been discovered here. Make your way back to Clifden to finish the Sky Road loop. The northern side of the peninsula is less dramatic.

MAYO & SLIGO

IDYLLIC ISLANDS, BREATHTAKING BEACHES AND OUTDOOR ADVENTURES

Despite their natural wonders and languid charm, Counties Mayo and Sligo remain well-kept secrets, offering all of Ireland's wild, romantic beauty without the crowds.

Punctuated with vibrant towns, magnificent mountain peaks, big surfing waves and terrific trails, Mayo and Sligo often slip under visitor's radars. Mayo is the more rugged of the two counties, with scraggy peaks, sheer cliffs, heather-covered moors and beautiful offshore islands where life is dictated by the elements. Sligo is more pastoral, and its lush fields, fish-filled lakes and flat-topped mountains inspired William Butler Yeats to compose some of Ireland's most ardent verse.

Both counties boast grand stretches of golden sands and legendary breaks that lure the surfing cognoscenti from around the globe. Visit and you'll find all this plus an improbable bounty of prehistoric sites, elegant Georgian towns, abandoned manor houses, charming fishing villages and good old-fashioned warm-hearted country hospitality without all the visitors that you're likely to encounter elsewhere in Ireland. Mayo and Sligo may just be Ireland's best-kept secrets with their unlimited possibilities for adventure.

Counties Mayo and Sligo have some of Ireland's most outstanding accommodation options, from waterside castles to spotless B&Bs, remote island getaways and cheerfully run guesthouses, all set within some of the finest landscapes in the country. Glorious seafood is the staple here as you wind your way along the shore, but beyond seafood chowder, lobster and mussels, there's a host of inventive delights from locally sourced ingredients and culinary magic. You certainly won't go hungry.

THE MAIN AREAS

WESTPORT
Picturesque, pretty and plenty of craic.
p342

ACHILL ISLAND
Remote, wild and untouched.
p349

ENNISCRONE
Beaches, dunes and seaweed baths.
p358

MULLAGHMORE
Raw, rugged Atlantic views.
p366

Above: Achill Island (p349); left: Great Western Greenway (p347)

Find Your Way

While some of the major towns are connected by public transport, driving is the best way to get out into the magic of this remote region. Cyclists and hikers will find plenty of paths to explore.

Achill Island, p349
Home to breathtaking cliffs, challenging hikes and jaw-dropping beaches, Achill Island is remote, unspoilt and a world unto itself.

Westport, p342
This picturesque spot is one of Ireland's few planned towns with great restaurants, pubs and brilliant live music.

Enniscrone, p358
Set along a seemingly endless stretch of sand that's backed by extensive dunes, Enniscrone is perfect for adventure or relaxation.

Mullaghmore, p366
The iconic mountain of Benbulben and the wild Atlantic Ocean make a wonderful backdrop for exploring the Mullaghmore headland.

CAR
Hiring a car gives you the freedom to reach out-of-the-way places and set your own agenda. Petrol stations are easy to find, and parking is generally easy. Drive with care on the winding country roads.

BUS & TRAIN
The train is of limited usefulness, principally servicing Westport, Ballina and Sligo town. Extensive Bus Éireann (buseireann. ie) services take in most destinations within Mayo and Sligo and other counties in the region and beyond.

Keem Bay (p351)

Plan Your Time

Remote destinations and the region's small country roads mean that travel can be slow going. Plan your time carefully to make the most of your trip. Some places shut down in winter.

One Day Only

Kickstart your day with views of Clew Bay from the **Wild Atlantic Sauna** (p346) at Old Head Beach. Take a surf lesson with the pros at **Surf Mayo** (p346) in Louisburgh and have a meal in town before taking a road trip to see the spectacular **Doolough Valley** (p346). Loop back to your base in **Westport** (p342) for a pint and trad music at **Matt Molloy's** (p343).

Three Days To Explore

Get an early start from **Westport** (p342) and drive to **Achill Island** (p349) to spend time at the beach before making your way to **Wild Nephin National Park** (p355) for a walk. The following day, head north to **Céide Fields** (p364), see the sea stacks at **Dun Briste** (p364) and recover your energy at **Kilcullen's Seaweed Baths** (p359). Catch the sunset from **Enniscrone Beach** (p359).

Seasonal Highlights

SPRING
The narrow, winding lanes come to life with springtime blooms of white, yellow and purple wildflowers.

SUMMER
The towns and villages have fully awakened from their winter slumber and put on a host of festivals.

AUTUMN
Purple heather transitions to shades of rusty red in Wild Nephin National Park; admire it from the hiking trails.

WINTER
Cold weather brings the big waves, and surfers get in on the action all along the coast.

Dun Briste (p364)

WESTPORT

Bright and vibrant even in the depths of winter, Westport is a photogenic Georgian town with tree-lined streets, riverside walkways and a great vibe. It sits on the edge of spectacular Clew Bay with some beautiful beaches nearby and the impressive peak of Croagh Patrick on its doorstep. Westport Quay, the town's harbour, is a picturesque spot with shops and cafes.

With an excellent choice of accommodation, fine restaurants and pubs renowned for their music, it's a hugely popular place, but one that has never sold its soul to tourism. Westport is packed with superb restaurants and cafes: just wander along Bridge St and the little alleyways off it to make some tasty discoveries.

Westport is Mayo's nightlife hub and is thronged with pubs, many of them with regular live music. The town's central location makes it a convenient and enjoyable base for exploring the county.

TOP TIP

The area around Westport is superb for cycling, with gentle coastal routes or more challenging mountain trails to test your legs, all within a short distance of town. The Great Western Greenway, a 42km cycling route between Westport and Achill, begins 500m from the centre of town off the N59.

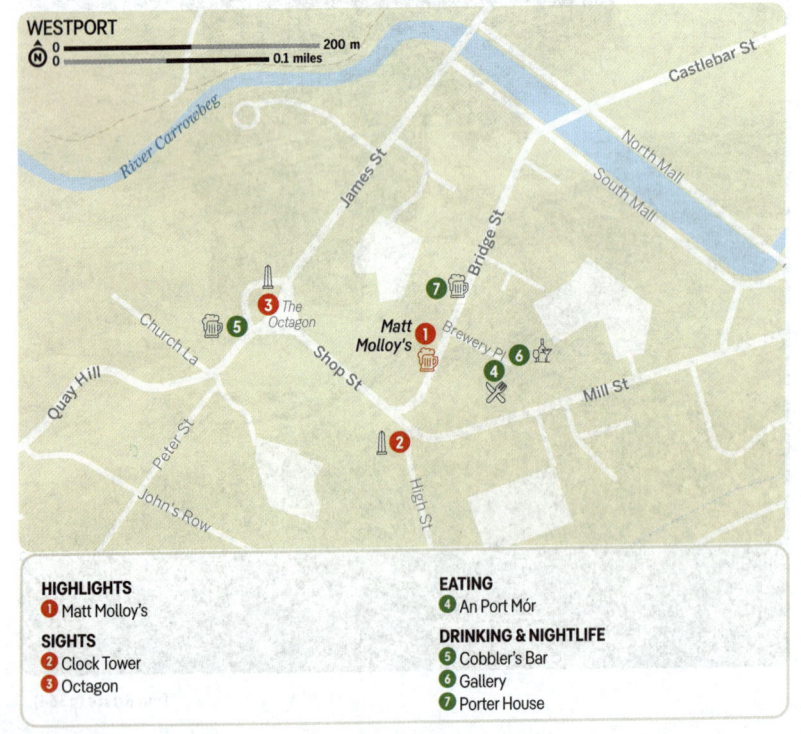

HIGHLIGHTS
1. Matt Molloy's

SIGHTS
2. Clock Tower
3. Octagon

EATING
4. An Port Mór

DRINKING & NIGHTLIFE
5. Cobbler's Bar
6. Gallery
7. Porter House

Wandering Westport
Learning The Landmarks

Strolling around Westport and soaking up the vibes is an experience in itself. It's one of the few planned towns in Ireland, laid out in the Georgian architectural style. Walk the tree-lined promenade of the River Carrowbeg and snap photos of the stone bridges that cross the water.

In the centre of Westport, at the corner of Bridge and Shop Sts, the 1947 art deco-style **Clock Tower** is a popular meeting point for locals. Wander down the little side streets off Bridge St to find even more gems.

On the corner of Shop and James Sts is the **Octagon** monument, a local landmark built in 1845.

Listen to Trad Music
Tap Your Toes

Westport has tons of pubs, and many put on live music regularly. **Matt Molloy**, the fife player from the Chieftains, runs an old-school pub that bears his name, and Mayo's musical heritage comes vividly to life seven nights a week. The intimate setting has plenty of little nooks and crannies, and Molloy himself makes an appearance from time to time. The atmosphere is electric when things get going. When the fire is roaring and the music is playing in the back bar, there's nowhere better to be.

Originally a shoe repair shop, the **Cobbler's Bar** now attracts some of the best local musicians for regular trad sessions every Thursday and Sunday night. With live music seven nights a week and afternoon sessions on Fridays, Saturdays and Sundays, the award-winning **Porter House** is a great place for music and pints.

Matt Molloy's

BEST PLACES TO TREAT YOURSELF IN WESTPORT

An Port Mór
This little restaurant packs a big punch. Its menu features gutsy flavours, excellent meats and much-lauded seafood (try the excellent Clew Bay scallops). Just about everything is procured from the region. €€

Gallery
Ireland's first natural wine bar, this unpretentious spot is also part record store and part secondhand bookshop.

Pantry & Corkscrew
The heart of Mayo's slow-food movement comes from this kitchen, which works culinary magic with seasonal, local and organic produce. €€

GETTING AROUND

Westport is compact, and it's easy to get around on foot. Rent a bike to venture further afield. The town has a train station with regular services to Dublin. Bus Éireann services head to nearby towns and Galway.

Beyond Westport

Ireland's holy mountain, the surrounding hills and stunning Clew Bay offer plenty of opportunities for outdoor adventures.

Get stuck into country life outside of Westport. Learn about rural Ireland at a fascinating national museum, take on the scenic drive through Doolough Valley – one of the most beautiful routes in the country – or venture out to Clare Island to get away from it all.

The town of Louisburgh has fantastic cafes, and you can learn to surf from its beaches. This region is also home to one of Ireland's most iconic mountain peaks and has grim reminders of Famine tragedies.

For many travellers, the great outdoors is the draw around Westport, with plenty of opportunities for hiking, cycling, swimming or just chilling out at the beach.

TOP TIP

If you plan to hike in the area, be aware that lowland walking routes are marked, but mountain trails are not.

Doolough Valley (p346)

National Museum of Ireland – Country Life

A Look into Country Life
Rural History And Heritage

Northeast of the town of Castlebar, the **National Museum of Ireland – Country Life** is the only branch of Ireland's national museum outside of Dublin. The extensive and engrossing displays of this riverside museum delve into Ireland's fascinating rural traditions and skills. It's set in a modern, photogenic facility that overlooks a lake in the lush grounds of 19th-century Turlough Manor. The museum explores everything from the role of the potato to boat building, herbal cures and traditional clothes.

Before you visit, check the programme of events, which often includes activities and walks to further breathe life into the experience.

The lovely **Turlough Round Tower** is visible from the grounds. Stretching up 23m and featuring a single lofty window, this 11th-century structure crowns a hilltop beside a ruined 18th-century church.

DOOLOUGH TRAGEDY

On 30 March 1849, in the midst of the Famine, hundreds of starving men, women and children set off from Louisburgh for Delphi Lodge, where they had heard they would be reassessed for Famine relief. There was no food for them upon their arrival, so they walked back to Louisburgh. The weather was freezing and bitter and the people so malnourished and weak that many died.

Marked today by a grim memorial cross in the Doolough Valley that serves as its epitaph, the Doolough Tragedy still casts a black shadow across the sublime landscape. Every year, a Famine Walk to Louisburgh from Delphi commemorates the disaster.

WHERE TO GET A DRINK BEYOND WESTPORT

Cronin's Sheebeen
This traditional pub in Rosbeg champions local producers and ingredients.

Tavern Bar & Restaurant
Known for its extensive menu; located near the base of Croagh Patrick, making it the perfect post-hike pub.

Staunton's Pub
Serving for more than 100 years, this historic family-run pub in Lecanvey has wonderful food.

THE PIRATE QUEEN

The life of Grace O'Malley (Gráinne ní Mháille or Granuaile, c 1530–1603) reads like fantasy adventure fiction. Twice widowed and twice imprisoned for acts of piracy, she was a fearsome presence in the troubled landscape of 16th-century Ireland.

Born into a powerful seafaring family that controlled most of the Mayo coastline and traded internationally, the independent Grace soon decided she should join the family business.

Legend has it that while still a child, she asked her father if she could join a trip to Spain but was refused on the grounds that seafaring was not for girls. She promptly shaved off her hair, dressed in boys' clothing, returned to the ship and announced that she was ready to sail.

Driving through Doolough Valley
Jaw-Dropping Road Trip

The R335 from Leenane in County Galway to Westport is one of Ireland's most beautiful scenic routes. Largely untouched by housing, cut turf or even stone walls, the desolate **Doolough Valley** is a sublime journey, the steep sides of the surrounding mountains simply sliding into the steely grey waters of Doo Lough as sheep graze placidly on the hills – they occasionally park themselves in the middle of the road too.

This is also one of Ireland's most poignant spots – the site of the Doolough Tragedy – a Famine catastrophe that occurred in 1849.

Choose a dry and clear day to tackle the road as curtains of rain can greatly diminish the views. If you have time, wander down the side roads to the north and west of the valley to reach glorious, often-deserted beaches.

Learn to Surf in Louisburgh
Ride Mayo's Waves

With 1168km of beaches, cliffs and inlets, Mayo has the longest coastline in Ireland and is a popular destination for surfers. The friendly vibe in **Louisburgh** makes the town a great place to learn to surf. Run by local surfers, **Surf Mayo** was the first dedicated surf school in the county and offers lessons at Carrowniskey Strand.

Afterwards, head to the **Wild Atlantic Sauna** at Old Head Beach to relax in the heat while enjoying stunning views of Clew Bay.

Cruise to Clare Island
Ruins And Pirate History

Clew Bay is dotted with some 365 islands, the largest of which is mountainous **Clare Island**, 5km offshore but half a world away. Dominated by rocky Mt Knockmore (462m), its varied terrain is terrific for walking and climbing, and swimming can be enjoyed at its safe, sandy beaches. The island is also one of the dwindling number of places where you can find choughs (resembling blackbirds but with red beaks).

Clare Island has the windswept ruins of the 13th-century **Clare Island Abbey** and **Granuaile's Castle**, both associated with the pirate queen Grace O'Malley. The abbey's chancel roof is dotted with faded fragments of murals dating from around 1500. Look out too for the tomb reputed to be that of Grace O'Malley, where a stone inscribed with her family motto formidably declares: 'Invincible on land and sea'.

WHERE TO STAY ON CLARE ISLAND

Clare Island Guesthouse
Boutique accommodation in a heritage property offering guests an opportunity to get away from it all. €€

O'Grady's
A short hop from Clare Island's Blue Flag beach, this luxury self-catering accommodation is the perfect base. €€

Clare Island Campsite
Conveniently located near the pier and beach with showers, toilets and a drinking water tap. No reservations. €

Great Western Greenway

The island is also a great place to retreat from the world and reflect on the beauty of Ireland. Among the many stirring hikes, there's a self-guided **archaeological walk**, which goes past Bronze Age mounds from 1000 BCE, or you can climb Mt Knockmore. Spectacular views enthral visitors. End your day of exploring by sampling the world's first whiskey aged at sea, at **Clare Island Whiskey**.

Clare Island Ferries and **O'Malley Ferries** run boats from Roonagh Quay, 8km west of Louisburgh to Clare Harbour. There are around eight sailings daily in July and August, and two to four sailings daily the rest of the year. The journey takes about 20 minutes.

You can often pick up a taxi at the harbour and rent bikes; your accommodation may also be able to arrange transport.

Cycle the Great Western Greenway
On Your Bike

Following the route of the old Westport-Achill Railway (which ran from 1895 to 1937), the **Great Western Greenway** (greenway.ie) is a terrific reason to cycle through this part of Mayo. The 44km trail, which travels via Newport and Mulranny, penetrates gorgeous countryside and waterfront scenery, consisting of three main sections, none of which require more than moderate effort.

Count on spending a full day cycling this route, factoring in photo stops along the way, but it's also possible to cycle sections and arrange for a bike hire company to pick you up at a designated spot. You can easily rent bicycles all along the

WHY I LOVE LIVING IN MAYO

Mayo-based surf instructor **Edwina Horgan** shares why she loves living in the rural landscape of County Mayo.

'Mayo is a place of raw, rugged beauty, full of amazing places to explore. I have been living in Mayo for more than half my life, surfing, hiking and exploring the wild landscape. Mayo has some great small towns and villages to go for a night out and catch live music from trad to rock and roll and bluegrass. Westport and Louisburgh have great food options, from date-night restaurants to casual cafe-style dining and coffee on every corner. The community here is strong, the welcomes are warm, and the goodbyes are long.'

WHERE TO EAT IN NEWPORT

Kelly's Kitchen
Enjoy award-winning Irish breakfasts, coffee and delicious baking. €

Grainne Uaile
Gastropub with an extensive menu and trad sessions; enjoy a pint with views of Clew Bay from the outdoor seats. €€

Port Chipper
Grab fish and chips from this local favourite. It's mainly takeaway, but there are a few seats outside. €

Croagh Patrick

NATIONAL FAMINE MEMORIAL

Sitting at the foot of Croagh Patrick is the National Famine Memorial, a spine-chilling sculpture of a three-masted ghost ship wreathed in swirling skeletons, commemorating the lives lost on so-called 'coffin ships' people got on to escape the Famine.

Emigrants fleeing Ireland in search of a better life endured horrendous cramped and unhygienic conditions as they crossed the Atlantic. The sculpture was created by Dublin artist John Behan.

Great Western Greenway. **Westport Bike Hire** on James St in Westport (p342) can set you up with everything you need for this epic adventure.

Climbing Croagh Patrick
Ireland's Holy Mountain

St Patrick couldn't have picked a better spot for a pilgrimage than conical **Croagh Patrick** (also known as 'the Reek'). On a clear day, the tough two-hour climb rewards with stunning views over Clew Bay and its sandy islets.

It was on Croagh Patrick that Ireland's patron saint fasted for 40 days and nights and where he reputedly banished venomous snakes. Climbing the 764m holy mountain is an act of penance for thousands of believers on the last Sunday of July (Reek Sunday). The truly contrite take the ancient 35km pilgrim's route, **Tóchar Phádraig** (Patrick's Causeway), from Ballintubber Abbey and ascend the mountain barefoot. The 7km trail taken by the less repentant begins from the signed car park in the west end of **Murrisk**. The steep trail is rocky in parts, and it gets crowded on sunny weekends. At the summit, you'll find a 1905 whitewashed church and a 9th-century oratory fountain. Views are sublime. The average return trip takes three to four hours. Murrisk is 8km west of Westport.

GETTING AROUND

You need a car to get around the more remote areas of this region. Bike hire is available in Westport for adventures outside of town.

ACHILL ISLAND

Ireland's largest offshore island, Achill (An Caol) is linked to the mainland by a short bridge. Despite the accessibility, there's plenty of remote-island feel: soaring cliffs, rocky headlands, sheltered sandy beaches, broad expanses of blanket bog and rolling mountains. You can surf the swells on the island's magnificent Blue Flag beaches while kitesurfers and windsurfers harness the power of the wind. The island also has its share of history, having been a frequent refuge during Ireland's various rebellions.

Achill is at its most dramatic in winter, when high winds and lashing seas make it seem downright inhospitable. The year-round population, though, remains as welcoming as ever. In summer, heather, rhododendrons and wildflowers bloom, splashing the island with colour.

The village of Keel is the island's main centre of activity, which is a relative term. Shops and services also cluster at the end of the bridge onto the island, at Achill Sound.

TOP TIP

Instead of following the main road (R319) from Mulranny to Achill Island, take the signposted Ocean Rd, which curves clockwise around the Corraun Peninsula. The narrow road passes an odd fortified tower, and as it hugs the isolated southern edge, the views across Clew Bay and out to sea are stunning.

Carrowgarve, Achill Island

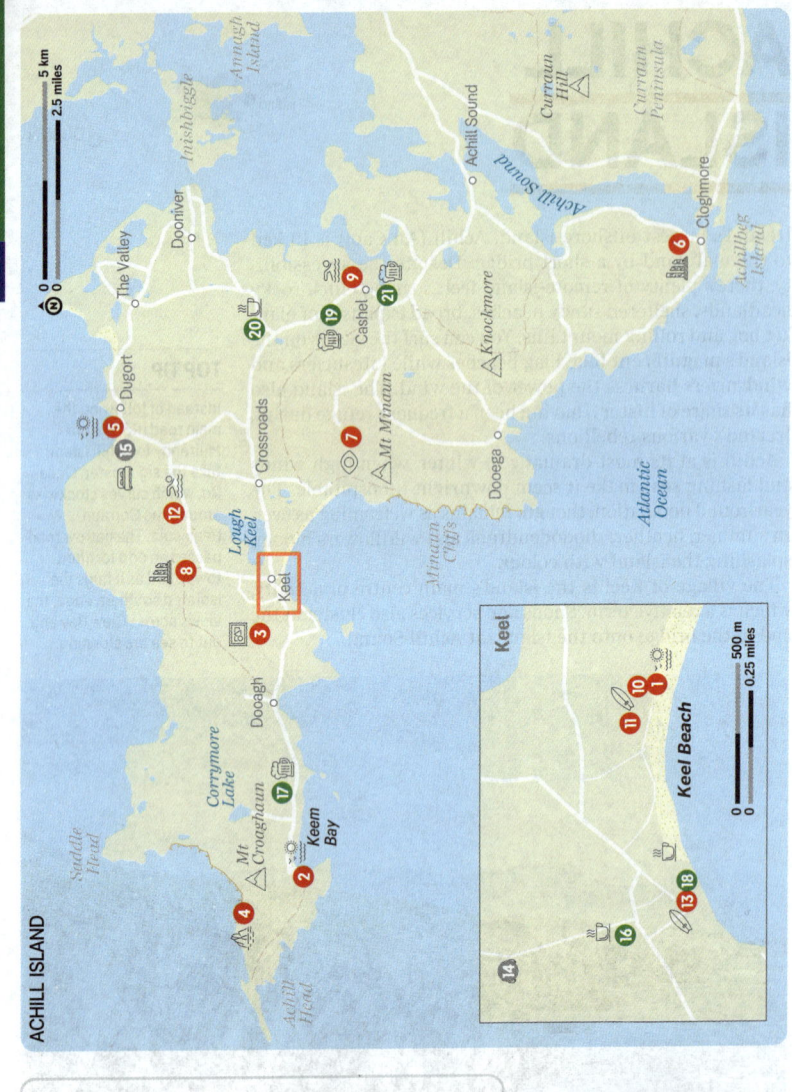

ACHILL ISLAND

HIGHLIGHTS
1. Keel Beach
2. Keem Bay

SIGHTS
3. Achill-henge
4. Croaghaun Cliffs
5. Dugort Beach
6. Grace O'Malley's Castle
7. Minaun Heights
8. Slievemore

ACTIVITIES & COURSES
9. Achill Outdoor Education & Training Centre
10. Achill Surf School & Adventure Centre
11. Blackfield Surf School
12. Pure Magic
13. Soundwave Surf School

SLEEPING
14. Ferndale
15. Luxury Bed & Breakfast
15. Strand Hotel

DRINKING & NIGHTLIFE
16. Beehive Crafts & Gifts
17. Gielty's
18. Lili Bán
19. Lynott's
20. Salt Dock
21. Ted's

Achill Island

Keem Bay

Best Beaches on Achill Island

Bay Of Beauty

Tucked away at the far west of the island, **Keem Bay** is Achill's most remote Blue Flag beach. Grassy slopes lead down to the beach, and the crescent of golden sand sits at the foot of steep cliffs, hemmed in by rock on three sides. The perfectly clear turquoise water and fine white sand make this a firm favourite with visitors, and spiralling down to this perfect cove feels like finding the pot of gold at the end of an Irish rainbow.

It's a stunning drive here from Keel, 8km to the east, taking in expansive views across the water as the road climbs beside steep cliffs. The 4km-long **Keel Beach** (also known as Trawmore Beach) is arguably the best-known stretch of sand on Achill, with great pubs, cafes and restaurants; a large car park; and surf schools. It sits in the shadow of the magnificent Minaun Cliffs (p352), and this long flat stretch of sand is a haven for watersports. Sunbathers have plenty of space to chill out in summer, and it's the perfect place for a ramble, with incredible views of the cliffs to soak in along the way.

On the northern side of the island at the base of Slievemore Mountain, small **Dugort Beach** offers excellent mountain views from the sheltered golden sands.

JOHN LENNON & CLEW BAY

Clew Bay is said to have 365 islands, one for every day of the year. The views of the bay from the surrounding area are spectacular, and in fact, the location is stunning enough to have caught the eye of musician John Lennon, who purchased 38-hectare Dorinish Island in 1967 and planned to build a house for himself and his wife, Yoko Ono.

In 1970, he sold the island to a hippie commune that built a summer camp before it was finally sold to a farmer in 1984, who still grazes sheep here.

WHERE TO STAY ON ACHILL ISLAND

Ferndale Luxury Bed & Breakfast
Adults-only accommodation with themed rooms, ocean views and great breakfasts. €€

Pure Magic
An ideal base for outdoor enthusiasts. Chill out in the hammock and enjoy stellar cooking. €€

Strand Hotel
A stone's throw from Dugort Beach, this hotel has a bar, restaurant and spacious rooms. €€

On the Water
Adventures And Watersports

Achill has many scalloped bays tame enough for swimming, but more adrenalin-fuelled activities are possible too. Keel Lake has shallow flat waters and great wind, providing the ideal location for kitesurfing, windsurfing, wing foil and paddleboarding lessons with **Pure Magic**. **Achill Outdoor Education and Training Centre** has been open since 1971, offering a range of activities including kayaking, sailing, windsurfing and coasteering.

Budding surfers have several schools to choose from. **Soundwave Surf School** has surf lessons, stand-up paddleboarding, guided walks and regular music events. **Blackfield Surf School** specialises in small, personal surf and SUP lessons at Keel Beach. **Achill Surf School and Adventure Centre** runs the activities gamut, from orienteering and climbing to surfing and sea kayaking, guaranteeing a great time in the outdoors.

Such Great Heights
The Best Views Of Achill

In the centre of Achill Island is **Minaun Heights**, where you can soak up incredible views of the island. As you drive up the narrow, winding road to the small car park, the views get more impressive the higher you climb.

Hop out at the car park and take a short ramble to the summit at 466m to enjoy views of Achill Island, Clare Island and Blacksod Bay. On a clear day, the vistas are incredible, but even when there are clouds, the sun peeks through.

Hiking Achill Island
Ireland's Highest Sea Cliffs

Achill Island is a wonderful place for hiking, and the views are terrific. Ramblers can climb **Mt Slievemore** (671m) or take on the longer climb up **Mt Croaghaun** (664m). This route goes over the mighty 687m-tall **Croaghaun Cliffs**, the highest sea cliffs in Ireland; allow two hours. The starting point for the trail to Croaghaun is from the car park at Keem Bay.

Island Ghost Town
Left To The Elements

The bleak remains of more than 80 houses in the deserted village of **Slievemore** at the foot of Mt Slievemore are slowly being reduced to rock piles, a poignant reminder of the island's

---

BANSHEES OF INISHERIN FILMING LOCATIONS

Cloughmore
The crew constructed JJ Devine's pub on the southeast corner of the island.

Purteen Harbour
Between the villages of Pollagh and Keel, the harbour hosted a specially built portside street scene, including O'Riordan's shop and a post office.

Keem Bay
The private building was the home of Colm Doherty.

Corrymore Lake
Mrs McCormick's cottage was here, and it was also the setting for one of the film's major tragedies.

St Thomas' Church
The mass scenes were filmed at this 19th-century church.

WHERE TO DRINK ON ACHILL ISLAND

Gielty's
The most westerly pub in Europe, this third-generation-run spot has great music and wonderful food.

Lynott's
With a thatch roof and stone walls, Lynott's is hailed as the smallest pub in Ireland.

Ted's
Established in 1951 and still family-run, Ted's has regular music sessions, great food and outdoor seating.

Grace O'Malley's Castle

past hardships and a vanished way of life. Research into why the village was abandoned is ongoing; some historians think that the Famine helped prompt villagers to emigrate or move closer to the sea and its alternative food sources. The adjacent graveyard compounds the desolation.

Castle of the Pirate Queen
Grace O'Malley's Stronghold

The 12m-high, 15th-century **Grace O'Malley's Castle** rising beside the shore at Kildownet is associated with Ireland's famous pirate queen. Entering through a steel turnstile is an eerie experience – it reveals a tall hollow shell with slits for windows and a square hole in the roof.

Pondering Achill-henge
A Mysterious Structure

Built by property developer Joe McNamara in 2011 without planning permission, **Achill-henge** is somewhat of a controversial structure. Nobody knows why it was built, with some saying it was a political statement and others maintaining it's a tourist attraction.

Achill-henge consists of 30 concrete columns topped by a ring of stone. Roscommon-based street artist Joe Caslin transformed the site into a temporary art installation with 30 3.5m-tall drawings as part of his 'Our Nation's Sons' project.

BEST CAFES ON ACHILL ISLAND

Beehive Crafts & Gifts
Get culture along with your cake at Beehive – the popular cafe doubles as a crafts shop. It's just a stone's throw from Keel Beach and has a decent choice for a coffee, soup of the day, panini or house-baked goodies. €

Salt Dock
This cool coffee truck in Bunacurry serves delicious sweet bites and locally roasted Carrow Coffee. €

Lílí Bán
Enjoy locally roasted coffee and tasty treats, including vegan options, with views of Keem Bay from this delightful coffee shack. €

GETTING AROUND

Dooagh-based Achill Bikes can hook you up with everything you need to explore the island by pedal power. Bus 450 runs a few times a day from Westport to Dooagh.

Beyond Achill Island

Get stuck into Wild Nephin National Park, stargaze, and explore the rugged, wild and remote west Mayo coastline.

Home to some of the darkest and clearest skies in the world, Wild Nephin National Park is a paradise for stargazers, set far from any urban light pollution. By day, take in views of the expansive blanket bog and immerse yourself in the wild landscapes with spectacular views of Achill Island and the churning Atlantic Ocean.

To the northwest, the thinly populated Gaeltacht (Irish-speaking) Mullet Peninsula dangles some 30km into the Atlantic and feels more cut off than many islands, with a similar sense of loneliness. You'll find pristine beaches along its sheltered eastern shore and lots of sheep – often fully blocking the road. The main settlement is the town of Belmullet (Béal an Mhuirthead).

TOP TIP

Wild camping is allowed in Wild Nephin National Park, but a permit is required to light a fire.

Wild Nephin National Park

Wild Nephin National Park

Exploring Wild Nephin National Park
Untouched Landscapes

The huge and scenic **Wild Nephin National Park** – comprising some of Europe's greatest areas of blanket bog – is home to magnificent natural diversity, including otters, mountain hares, native red deer, peregrine falcons, corncrakes and whooper swans. A short nature trail with interpretation panels leads from the visitor centre across the bog, revealing superbly sublime views of the surrounding mountains. Staff can recommend more ambitious hikes, and there are displays on whaling and the ubiquitous purple heather.

The views of Achill Island, mountains and shore do their best to upstage the food in the appealingly airy **Ginger & Wild** cafe in the park's visitor centre, but the quiches, soups, scones and cakes more than hold their own.

By night, Wild Nephin becomes **Mayo Dark Sky Park**, Ireland's first International Dark Sky Park. It's a must-visit for stargazers or anyone who wants to appreciate pristine night skies. Extending across more than 150 sq km, this area has almost zero light pollution, allowing the skies above to truly shine.

Three night-sky **viewing points** are located at easy-to-access locations throughout the park. The park hosts the annual three-day **Mayo Dark Sky Festival**, which puts on

WEST COAST GOLF COURSES

Mulranny
Opened in 1896, this small nine-hole natural links course offers golfers incredible views of Clew Bay.

Castlebar Golf Club
In a picturesque parkland setting with tree-lined fairways and the occasional pond, this golf course has hosted the All-Ireland Cups and Shields, and it's a joy to play.

Westport Golf Club
This championship venue has hosted the Irish Amateur Close and Irish PGA Championships, and has unbeatable views of Croagh Patrick.

WHERE TO STAY IN MULRANNY

Mulranny Park Hotel
This fabulous four-star hotel offers a leisure club complete with a heated pool and hot tub. €€€

McLoughlin's of Mulranny
Expansive views of Clew Bay reveal themselves from the back of this welcoming, comfortable accommodation. €€

Moynish House
Family-run B&B on Clew Bay with a fully licensed bar; only a 10-minute drive from Achill. €€

family-friendly events to celebrate the nightscapes, allowing you to learn more about astronomy as well as the park's heritage and environment. With rocket-making displays, storytelling workshops, educational talks and plenty of activities that the whole family can enjoy, this festival is always a big hit.

If you're not camping in the park, your best accommodation option is overnighting in Newport or on Achill Island. It's most convenient to visit the park by car. The entrance is signposted along the N59 between Mulranny and Bangor Erris.

Walking the Claggan Mountain Coastal Trail
Boardwalk Across Boglands

With beautiful uninterrupted panoramic views of Wild Nephin National Park, Achill Island and Claggan Mountain, the flat 2km **Claggan Mountain Coastal Trail** takes you along a breathtaking boardwalk that leads into Wild Nephin, allowing you to cross the expansive boglands with ease. This vibrant landscape of flowering bogland is sandwiched between the villages of Mulranny and Ballycroy.

Ferry to Inishbiggle
Tiny Island Big On Beauty

Inishbiggle (Inis Bigil) is a small 2.6-sq-km landmass between Achill Island and mainland Ireland. Once home to more than 100 people, the island has only about 20 residents now.

The Bullsmouth Channel that separates this beautiful island from the mainland has one of the strongest currents in Europe, often making it inaccessible in the winter. During the summer months, the family-run **Inishbiggle Ferry Service** runs regular boats from Ballycroy, taking about 10 minutes to cross the channel. Visitors are treated to stunning views of West Mayo.

The island has lovely walking trails and puts on the annual **Inishbiggle Festival** at the end of July.

Walking the Letterkeen Loops
Mountain Views From The Trail

Accessible from a well-signposted road outside the town of Newport, the **Letterkeen Walking Loops** are colour-coded with different options to choose from.

The shortest walk is the 6km **Bothy Loop**. The blue and purple loops follow the same trail for about 3km before branching out. All three of these trails require a reasonable level of fitness. The purple loop is the most challenging, as it's rough

---

ERRIS HEAD LOOP WALK

Designated as a special area of conservation, Erris Head is home to diverse flora and nesting fulmars and guillemots. Gannets fish in the water, and you might spot seals, dolphins and porpoises.

The Erris Head Loop Walk is about 5km and follows a gradual incline along the headland; allow two hours. This straightforward walk treats you to mind-blowing Atlantic views. Eagle Island and its famed lighthouse come into view about halfway along the trail.

The ground can be boggy, so wear sturdy boots and pack your raincoat, as the weather can change quickly.

WHERE TO EAT BEYOND ACHILL ISLAND

Denny's Ferry Bar & Store
Historic pub in Rossport with outdoor seating, live music most weekends, and great pints and food. €€

Lúnasa
On the square in Belmullet, this cute shop has a tearoom that serves delicious dishes. €

Talbot Seafood Bar & Barony Restaurant
This popular casual spot in Belmullet is dedicated to using fresh local produce. €

Blacksod Lighthouse

underfoot and includes a climb. The full 12km **Letterkeen Loop** is a strenuous path that takes about three hours to complete. The incredible mountain scenery is worth every step, and Newport has some great pubs where you can celebrate your completion of the circuit.

Taking on the Bangor Trail
Kilometres Of Solitude

If you're an experienced hillwalker and looking for a challenge, the 39km waymarked **Bangor Trail** is a great choice. Beginning in Newport, the trail takes you along a range of terrains, including bog tracks, open countryside, country roads and across rivers.

Immerse yourself in solitude and enjoy the isolation of nature. The trail follows a path designed to move livestock that might date from the Iron Age, and pre-Famine ruins can be seen at certain points. Keep an eye out for deer, frogs, grouse and hares. Because you cross bogland and rivers, waterproof boots and good rain gear are essential.

Watching the Water at Dún na mBó
The Power Of The Atlantic

On the northwestern edge of the Mullet Peninsula is the impressive blowhole of **Dún na mBó**. When wild Atlantic swells charge against the cliff, water is quickly funnelled upwards, exploding through the blowhole in magnificent fashion. A sculpture that mimics old-style megaliths and fortresses surrounds the blowhole.

LIGHTHOUSES OF ERRIS

The Erris region is home to four lighthouses, at Blacksod, Eagle Island, Blackrock and Ballyglass. That might seem like an excessive number of lighthouses in a span of just 25km, but when you see the jagged, rocky shoreline, you might come to understand why these beacons are so important.

Léim Siar in Belmullet provides bike hire, allowing you to pack your lunch and head off on a two-wheeled adventure to take in views of all four lighthouses. The lights of all of the lighthouses can also be seen on a clear night from the hill at Alt, Bunnahowen.

GETTING AROUND

A free shuttle bus operates in June, July and August, connecting Bangor Erris and Westport with multiple stops along the way. Otherwise, the best way to explore the area is by car.

ENNISCRONE

In County Sligo, this low-key holiday town facing Killala Bay is all about the ocean and the glorious views and sunsets. The 5km-long Enniscrone Beach is the main reason to visit. This beautiful beach – which seemingly goes on forever – pulls in surfers, walkers, sunseekers and sandcastle builders, and is one of the best on Ireland's west coast. Book a surf lesson with 7th Wave Surf School or head off on a coastal walk to take in the views. Cars can drive straight onto the beach, and a lifeguard is normally on duty from June to September. The beach is backed by expansive sand dunes that are rich with flora and fauna.

Enniscrone is equipped with several excellent B&Bs and guesthouses, and seafood rightly features strongly on the menus of the cafes, bars and restaurants dotted along Main St.

TOP TIP

Summer is the busiest time of the year in Enniscrone, so book your accommodation in advance if you're planning to visit this time of year. After a day of activity on the beach or in the surrounding area, try a seaweed bath to unwind, relax and recharge.

HIGHLIGHTS
1 Enniscrone Beach
2 Kilcullen's Seaweed Baths

ACTIVITIES
3 Enniscrone Pier
4 Enniscrone Pitch & Putt

EATING
5 Gilroy's Bar & Áit Eile Restaurant
6 Ocean Bar
7 Pizzeria La Piazzetta

Soak in a Seaweed Bath
Take The Plunge

Enniscrone is famous for its traditional seaweed baths, which are some of the most atmospheric in the country. **Kilcullen's Seaweed Baths**, an Edwardian bathhouse, has buckets of character, with original fittings including vast porcelain baths, solid brass taps and panelled wood cabinets.

Settle into a large porcelain tub, soak in the hot seawater and let the nutrients in the seaweed do their work. Towels are provided, and private rooms are available. There's no better way to treat yourself after a day of adventuring, hiking or hanging out at the beach.

Play Pitch & Putt
Par For The Course

Enniscrone is home to one of the oldest and best pitch and putt courses in the west of Ireland. The par-3 **Enniscrone Pitch & Putt course** is open seven days a week and is a fun family activity. The entrance to the course is off Main St.

Walk the Enniscrone Coast
Sea-Filled Scenes

The 2km coastal loop that starts from **Enniscrone Pier** offers beautiful views and takes most walkers about 40 minutes to complete.

From Enniscrone Pier, follow the flat trail, taking in stunning views of Killala Bay and the surrounding coastal scenery. At the end of the path, turn right and follow the road back to the pier where you started. Alternatively, you can take the same coastal path back to the pier, allowing you to soak up vistas of Enniscrone Beach and Mayo's Nephin Mountains in the distance.

Kilcullen's Seaweed Baths

BEST PLACES TO EAT IN ENNISCRONE

Pizzeria La Piazzetta
This fantastic Italian restaurant on Main St serves gourmet pizzas, pasta and tasty risotto alongside a great selection of wines. €€

Gilroy's Bar & Áit Eile Restaurant
Don't miss this award-winning restaurant when you're in town. The menu uses locally sourced produce and fresh seafood, and is a guaranteed winner every time. €€

Ocean Bar
Inside Ocean Sands Hotel, this restaurant has a variety of lunch and dinner options with magnificent views of Enniscrone Beach. €€

GETTING AROUND

Enniscrone is a compact town, so getting around on foot is easy. Bus 458 runs from Sligo town. The nearest train station is in Ballina, 15km away.

Beyond Enniscrone

From ancient stone-walled fields to jaw-dropping coastal vistas and spectacular beaches, the area around Enniscrone is simply breathtaking.

Following County Mayo's wild shore rewards you with some of the finest views in Ireland and a bunch of amazing beaches too. It's a scenic journey from Enniscrone, no matter which way you're headed. Travellers have opportunities to fish, surf, hike and explore castles and other historic buildings.

Along the coast, you won't have much difficulty finding a place for the night, with many accommodation options set in a gorgeous landscape of unblemished rural beauty with sweeping views over the sea. Natural features such as the sea stacks of Dun Briste remind you of the power of the crashing Atlantic.

This wild corner of Ireland is full of life and will blow you away at every turn.

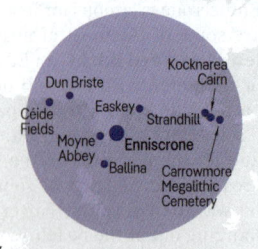

TOP TIP

The roads in this area are twisting and narrow, so if you're driving, go slow and allow plenty of time.

Belleek Castle

Ballina

Attractions In & Around Ballina
Festivals, Castles And Mills

County Mayo's third-largest town, **Ballina**, is synonymous with salmon. If you find yourself here during fishing season, you'll be joined by droves of green-garbed waders, poles in hand, heading for the River Moy – which pumps right through the heart of town. The popular five-day **Ballina Salmon Festival** has been a summer fixture for more than 50 years and includes parades, dances, an art show and fishing competitions.

North of town, **Belleek Castle** was built between 1825 and 1831 on the site of a medieval abbey. The castle was bought in the 1960s by fossil collector Marshall Doran, who gave it an eclectic and eccentric interior, some of it nautical (including the Spanish Armada bar). Tours visit the Banquet Hall and Doran's collection of fossils, weaponry and armour. To fully get in the castle mood, check in for the night, as the grand place also serves as a hotel; there's also a fine restaurant. The surrounding **Belleek Woods** are one of the largest urban forests in Europe, with several marked trails for walkers and cyclists.

Midway between Ballina and Castlebar, **Foxford Wool-**

BEST PLACES TO STAY IN BALLINA

Mount Falcon Estate
Hidden away on 40 hectares between Lough Conn and the River Moy lies this 1870s mansion, whose rooms ooze old-world grandeur. The tranquil tempo is endlessly relaxing. €€€

Ballina Manor Hotel
Enjoy mountain and river views a short stroll from the town centre on the banks of the River Moy. €€

Great National Hotel Ballina
This four-star hotel has a range of elegant rooms and a fantastic leisure centre with a pool, sauna and gym. €€

WHERE TO EAT IN BALLINA

Crockets Quay
This restaurant on the banks of the River Moy does well-executed pub grub. €€

Poacher Restaurant
Cosy, intimate restaurant serving up imaginative seasonally led menus with superb attention to detail. €€

Luskin's Bistro
This family-run restaurant has gained a reputation as one of the top restaurants in Mayo. €€

Knocknarea Cairn

SPLIT ROCK OF EASKEY

Sitting in a field off the R297 road near Easkey is Split Rock. This massive boulder measures 6m long and 2.5m tall. The rock was moved north from the Ox Mountains on the west coast of Sligo by retreating glaciers at the end of the last Ice Age.

It's known locally as Fionn's Stone because legend has it that Fionn MacCumhaill (aka Finn McCool), a warrior in Irish mythology, was involved in a giants' stone-throwing competition. Angry that his throw didn't reach the ocean, he leapt down and struck the rock with his sword.

Locals believe that if you walk through the crack in the rock three times, it will close on you.

en Mill was founded in 1892 and set up to ease post-Famine suffering and provide much-needed work. It remained open until 1987, during which time its woven goods achieved great acclaim. Now operated by locals, it employs a fraction of the hundreds who previously worked here. Free 20-minute tours detail the history, manufacturing and craftsmanship that these woollen mills are known for. The shop sells scarves, blankets, throws and other items made in the mill.

On Your Board in Easkey
Sligo's Surf Capital

Easkey Beach is one of Europe's best year-round surfing destinations, and the cool little town is a good addition to any itinerary, whether or not you brought your board. Head to the beach for a surf lesson, walk the 2km stretch of golden sand, go for a swim in the crystal-clear waters or sit back and enjoy a spectacular west coast sunset.

Take a walk along the windswept cobbles of **Easkey Pier** to take in stunning views of the rugged coastline, Benbulben Mountain in the distance and the spectacular Slieve League

WHERE TO EAT IN STRANDHILL

Strand Bar
This long-established family-run pub and restaurant is popular for its wonderful food, including stonebaked pizzas. €€

Dunes Bar
With a menu of grub from burgers to nachos, Dunes is the perfect post-surf spot. €€

Stoked
Wows diners with its tapas and international cuisine, encouraging sharing and tasting as much as possible. €€

Cliffs further north on a clear day. To the edge of the pier is **Roslee Castle**, built in 1207. Perched on the edge of the Atlantic, the ruins make a great photo and a brilliant vantage point to watch the local surfers in action.

Surfing Strandhill
Atlantic Waves

The great Atlantic rollers that sweep the shore of **Strandhill** make this long, red-gold beach a magnet for surfers. This northwest-facing beach picks up just about any type of swell from north to southwest, resulting in one of the most consistent beach breaks in the entire country. These conditions have produced some of the best surfers in Ireland.

Strandhill Surf School and **Perfect Day Surf & SUP School** offer rentals and lessons.

Legends & History of Knocknarea Cairn
The Possible Grave Of Queen Maeve

Sligo's ultimate rock pile sits atop a magical mountain hike. **Knocknarea Cairn** is popularly believed to be the grave of legendary Queen Maeve (Queen Mab in Welsh and English folk tales), who is said to be buried upright in the cairn, holding a spear and facing her adversaries in Ulster. The 40,000 tonnes of stone have never been excavated, despite speculation that a tomb on the scale of the one at Newgrange (p439) lies buried below.

The cairn is perched high atop a limestone plateau (328m), and a 1.2km trek up the mountain reveals spectacular views. From the top, you can gaze out over Benbulben, Rosses Point and the Atlantic Ocean beyond.

WB Yeats was enthralled by the myth and lore of Knocknarea, and its magic wormed its way into his verse. In *Red Hanrahan's Song* about Ireland, he writes: 'The wind has bundled up the clouds high over Knocknarea, And thrown the thunder on the stones for all that Maeve can say'.

Having got to the mountaintop, signs urge you not to climb the cairn itself. An estimated 100,000 walkers visit the site each year, and an increase in the number of people clambering over the stacked stones is causing erosion to this historic structure.

The site is 2km northwest of Carrowmore. Strandhill or Sligo town make good bases. The parking area is off the R292.

CARROWMORE MEGALITHIC CEMETERY

One of the largest Stone Age cemeteries in Europe, **Carrowmore** is a must-see attraction in Sligo. Some 30 monuments, including passage tombs, stone circles and dolmens, adorn the rolling hills of this haunting site, which is thought to predate Newgrange in County Meath by 700 years. Along with Carrowkeel, Loughcrew and Brú na Bóinne, Carrowmore dates back 6000 years and is considered one of the 'big four' important megalithic sites in Ireland.

To get here, follow the R292 southwest from Sligo town for 4km, and follow the signs.

WHERE TO STAY IN SLIGO TOWN

Sligo Park Hotel
Landscaped grounds, mature trees and an array of facilities help lend this modern hotel a country-club air. €€

Glasshouse Hotel
You can't miss this cool hotel in the centre of town, its sharp glass facade jutting skyward. €€

Riverside Hotel
From its central location on the riverbank, guests have easy access to everything in town. €€

Ruins of Moyne Abbey
Historic Franciscan Friary

Overlooking the mouth of the River Moy 3km east of Killala is **Moyne Abbey**, complete with a tower, church and cloisters. This Gothic-style abbey was built in 1462, and the Franciscan order thrived here for more than 130 years. In 1590, the English governor of Connacht set the friary alight in an effort to destroy the wealth of a local family. Cromwellian soldiers later desecrated the altar and killed the friars.

This site is off the beaten path, and there is no dedicated parking. Park with care on the roadside nearby and cross through fields to access this stunning ruin.

Sculpted by the Sea
An Atlantic Creation

An astonishing sea stack lashed by foaming ocean water, **Dun Briste** is Mayo's top natural sight, measuring 45m tall, 63m long and 23m wide. Legend attests that St Patrick drove all the vipers from Ireland onto the stack on Downpatrick Head, leaving the mainland snake-free. Try to choose a clear day for a visit to amplify the visuals.

The sea stack was shorn from the mainland in 1393 by a severe storm that left poor unfortunates stranded upon it (and later rescued). Indeed, the remains of buildings survive on the stack to this day. A viewing area has been constructed by a huge blowhole set back slightly from the cliff edge. It has numerous plaques detailing the history and folklore of the area. During storms, seawater is dramatically blasted through the blowhole.

You can drive most of the way up to the sea edge, but then you'll need to walk the last 400m or so.

Stone Age Monuments at Céide Fields
Peering Into The Past

Set on a clifftop high above the Atlantic Ocean, **Céide Fields** contain some of the world's most extensive Stone Age monuments. So far stone-walled fields, houses and megalithic tombs – about half a million tonnes of stone – have been found, the legacy of a farming community nearly 6000 years old. The visitor centre, in a glass pyramid overlooking the site, gives a fascinating glimpse into these times. Take a guided tour of

---

BEST COASTAL WALKS

Aughris Head
An invigorating 5km walk traces the cliffs around this remote headland, where dolphins and seals can often be seen swimming into the bay. Birdwatchers should look out for kittiwakes, fulmars, guillemots, shags, storm petrels and curlews.

Raghly Cliff Walk
This 2.7km route begins at Raghly Beach car park. Walk south, keeping the coast to your right, and continue to the blowhole and spectacular sea cliff views.

Killaspugbrone Coastal Walk
This 6.8km walk is completely flat and begins in Strandhill. Follow the purple markers.

BEST OFF-THE-BEATEN-TRACK BEACHES

Dunmoran Strand
A sandy secret in a rural area surrounded by dunes. A 2.5km hiking trail leads to Aughris Head.

Carrowmore Beach
Sometimes called Kilcummin Back Strand, this beach is at the end of a narrow road that runs along the cliffside.

Ross Beach
Near Killala town, this cute beach is great for families, safe for swimming and rarely crowded.

Moyne Abbey

the site to fully appreciate the findings. As much of the tour is outside, be sure to wear appropriate footwear and clothing.

The nearest village is beautifully sited **Ballycastle**, consisting of a sole sloping street. Sleeping and eating options are limited, but an excellent choice is the **Stella Maris** a few kilometres west of town. With a turret at each end and a long glass-fronted veranda in between, Stella Maris is a charismatic sight. Dating from 1853, it was originally a British Coast Guard station and later a convent. Today, upmarket rooms combine antiques, stylish modern furnishings and killer views of a lonely stretch of coast.

Mary makes everyone feel welcome at charming **Mary's Cottage Kitchen** on Main St, with good coffee, fresh-baked goods, lunch items, chocolate treats and a back garden. **Healy's Bar** is a sky-blue-painted family-run pub offering live music and a beer garden.

KILLALA

The town of **Killala** is pretty enough, but it's really renowned for its glorious namesake bay nearby. It's claimed that the ever-busy St Patrick founded Killala, and the Church of Ireland church sits on the site of the first Christian church in Ireland.

About 10km north, **Lackan Strand** is a stunning and vast expanse of golden sand – it's particularly beautiful as the sun goes down. There's good surf here and plenty of places to get lost in. Follow the R314 about 4.5km northwest from Killala and then turn at the signpost for Kilcummin.

GETTING AROUND

Driving is the best way to get around this rural part of Ireland. Many sights are not connected by public transport.

MULLAGHMORE

The sweeping arc of sand and the safe shallow waters make the pretty fishing village of Mullaghmore a popular family destination. It's a place of incredible natural beauty and world-class surf, which has helped put Ireland on the international big-wave surfing map. When big winter swells push in from the North Atlantic, they create waves that can tower more than 18m, giving 'Mully' the reputation as one of the heaviest, coldest and most unpredictable big-wave spots in the world.

Even if you're not here to watch the Atlantic wave action, you can enjoy all that the area has to offer. The golden sands of horseshoe-shaped Mullaghmore Beach stretch out for 3km, and the sheltered bay backed by expansive sand dunes is ideal for walkers. Hikers can take on the scenic Mullaghmore Head Loop, or you can head into the pubs for live music.

TOP TIP

Abandoned in 1948, Inishmurray Island is 7km from the mainland and has early Christian remains and pagan relics, including three well-preserved churches, beehive cells and open-air altars. There's no regular boat service; organise a boat trip from the harbour. Landing on the island is weather dependent, so enquire early.

Mullaghmore Head

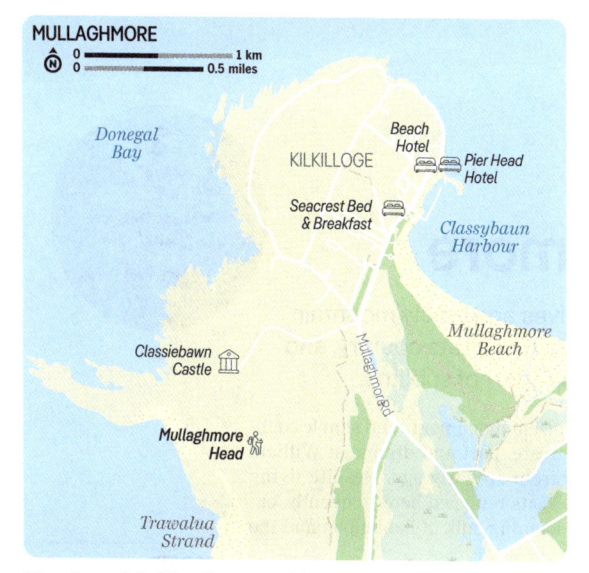

Explore Mullaghmore Head
Wander The Wild Headland
Starting in the village, the **Mullaghmore Head Loop** is a fantastic walk that follows the road that hugs the coast. Birdwatchers should keep an eye out for oystercatchers, gannets, fulmars and Manx shearwaters. Walkers are treated to stunning views of Classiebawn Castle, Donegal Bay, Slieve League and Sligo's iconic Benbulben Mountain. Allow an hour and a half to complete the loop.

Alternatively, you can drive the loop, taking in panoramic views of Counties Sligo, Donegal and Leitrim along the way.

Get a Glimpse of Classiebawn Castle
A Scenic Setting
Built in 1874, photogenic **Classiebawn Castle** sits proudly on Mullaghmore Head and has gained international acclaim after it was featured on the TV show *The Crown*. Set on 1215 hectares of land, the neogothic turreted pile is privately owned and not open to the public, but views of it against a dramatic backdrop of mountains and sea make for a terrific sight.

It was built for Lord Palmerston in 1856 and was later home to the ill-fated Lord Mountbatten, who was killed near here in 1979 when the IRA rigged his boat, the *Shadow V*, with explosives. Also killed in the blast were Lady Doreen Brabourne – the 83-year-old mother-in-law of Lord Mountbatten's daughter – and his 14-year-old grandson Nicholas Knatchbull. A simple cross and a plaque serve as a memorial.

BEST PLACES TO STAY IN MULLAGHMORE

Beach Hotel
Serving as a hub in Mullaghmore since it opened in the 1950s, this brilliant hotel is located in the heart of town and near the beach. €

Pier Head Hotel
The 40 rooms feature bright colour schemes, and the best have extensive ocean or harbour views. Other draws include a sweeping rooftop terrace, a hot tub, spa and indoor pool. €€

Seacrest Bed & Breakfast
Host John ensures a warm welcome, cooks a great breakfast and is full of local knowledge. €€

GETTING AROUND
In summer, bus 982 links Sligo town and Mullaghmore. Getting around the village and Mullaghmore Head is possible on foot. If you want to venture further afield, you are best off with your own vehicle.

Beyond Mullaghmore

Evocative coastal drives and lonely mountain paths highlight the heart of Yeats country, and the scenery is nothing short of sublime.

County Sligo's lush hills, ancient monuments and simple country life inspired Nobel laureate, poet and dramatist William Butler Yeats (1865–1939) from an early age. Despite living almost all his life abroad, Yeats returned here frequently, enamoured of the lakes, the looming hulk of Benbulben and the idyllic pastoral setting.

Northern Sligo still captivates travellers today, and you can visit important places in Yeats' life and work. His memorial in the village church in Drumcliff rests in the shadow of forbidding and iconic Benbulben Mountain, which you can hike up or around.

Elsewhere, watch sheepdogs at work and explore some of the most important megalithic sites in Europe.

TOP TIP

Sligo has a number of festivals that celebrate Yeats, including Tread Softly and Yeats International Summer School.

Sligo town centre

Sligo Abbey

Learning about Sligo Town
History And Heritage

Pedestrian streets lined with inviting shopfronts, stone bridges spanning the River Garavogue, and trad sessions spilling from pubs contrast with contemporary art and glass towers rising from prominent corners of compact **Sligo town**. It makes a fantastic, low-key and easily manageable base for exploring Yeats country.

Founded in 1252, **Sligo Abbey** is the town's most well-known landmark. This handsome Dominican friary burned down in the 15th century and was later rebuilt. Friends in high places saved the abbey from the worst ravages of the Elizabethan era and rescued the sole sculpted altar to survive the Reformation.

BEST PLACES TO EAT IN SLIGO TOWN

Eala Bhán
This lively restaurant on the banks of the River Garavogue offers excellent seafood and steak dishes, as well as veggie and vegan choices. €€€

Hargadons
You'll have a hard time leaving this superb 1868 inn with its winning blend of old-world fittings and gastropub style. The great-value food is renowned, transforming local ingredients such as oysters with continental flair. €€

Hooked
The menu reflects this restaurant's dedication to local food, serving an array of all-day options with the help of nearby producers. €€

WHERE TO DRINK IN SLIGO TOWN

Snug Bar
This cosy little bar has great live music and is touted to have the best pint of Guinness in town.

Fureys
A lively spot with a great atmosphere and a good chance of a live music session breaking out.

Thomas Connolly
Operating since 1780, Thomas Connolly offers more than 160 whiskies and a large selection of gins.

WB Yeats' grave

GLENIFF MILL

Because of an abundance of water and the possibility of a workable mine on Tievebaun Mountain, Gleniff Mill was built near the entrance to its namesake valley, within walking distance of Ballintrillick village. Today, only the foundations of the mill can be seen, and a hiking trail begins where the mill used to be, continuing along the banks of the roaring river that used to drive the mill's waterwheel.

Following the river, the 1.5km path continues until it meets the dam. Keep an eye out for wildlife along the way.

The Burial Place of WB Yeats
'Cast A Cold Eye On Life, On Death'

Benbulben's beauty was not lost on WB Yeats, one of the greatest poets of the 20th century. Before he died in Menton, France, in 1939, he had requested: 'If I die here, bury me up there on the mountain, and then after a year or so, dig me up and bring me privately to Sligo.' His wishes were apparently followed in 1948, when what was thought to be his body was interred in the churchyard at **Drumcliff**, where his great-grandfather had been rector, though doubts later emerged as whether those were actually Yeats' bones that had been reburied.

The poet's epitaph is from Yeats' poem 'Under Ben Bulben':
'Cast a cold eye
On life, on death.
Horseman, pass by!'

Walking Around Benbulben
Mountains And Forests

A stolid greenish-grey eminence visible all along Sligo's northern coast, **Benbulben** (525m), often written Ben Bulben, resembles a table covered by a pleated cloth: its limestone plateau is uncommonly flat, and its near-vertical sides are scored by earthen ribs.

Walking the peaks is not for the uninitiated, but the relatively flat **Benbulben Loop**, also known as the Gortarowey Walk, is a more accessible trail. In the shadow of the iconic mountain, the 5.5km circular walk runs through protected lands with spruce and fir trees.

Watch Sheepdogs at Work
Paw PATROL

Ireland is home to approximately six million sheep, and with so many sheep to manage, farmers rely on the help of their intelligent and well-trained sheepdogs. In Streedagh, expert trainer Martin Feeney of **Atlantic Sheepdogs** showcases these dogs' incredible abilities in their working environment.

Feeney, who has represented Ireland for 20 years on the international stage with his dogs, puts on an hour-long show for visitors. You'll see the dogs seamlessly move sheep around the fields and learn about how the dogs are trained. If you visit in summer, you might have an opportunity to see sheepshearing in action.

Court Tomb of Creevykeel
Neolithic Necropolis

The neatly stacked piles of rocks at **Creevykeel Court Tomb** stretch some 50m along and sketch a shape similar to a lobster's claw. They outline what is one of Ireland's finest court tombs and enclose several burial chambers. The structure dates from around 4000 BCE to 2500 BCE, with chambers being added over time. Once in the unroofed oval court, smaller visitors can duck under the stone-shielded entrance to reach the site's core.

Excavation work has uncovered polished stone axes, Neolithic pottery, clay balls, flint knives and cremation burials. The site is free to enter.

Creevykeel Court Tomb

GETTING AROUND

Much of County Sligo is explorable by bus, but for more flexibility, hire a car. Bus Eireann operates several routes from Sligo town that service the wider area. Europcar, Enterprise and car-hire companies have offices south of Sligo town on Old Dublin Rd.

Above: Fairy Bridges (p399); right: Doe Castle (p383)

DONEGAL
IRELAND'S UNMISSABLE FORGOTTEN COUNTY

Towering cliffs, spectacular beaches, remote wilderness and wild coastal views await visitors to Donegal.

County Donegal is the wild child of Ireland and home to some of its most ravishingly sublime scenery and beautiful beaches. It's a county of extremes: at times desolate and battered by brutal weather, yet also a land of unspoilt splendour where stark peaks and sweeping beaches bask in glorious sunshine, and port-side restaurants serve fine food. Donegal shares a small border with County Leitrim to the south, isolating it from the rest of the Republic of Ireland.

Donegal's rugged interior, with its remote mountain passes and shimmering lakes, is only marginally outdone by the long and labyrinthine coastline with windswept peninsulas and isolated pubs. Proudly independent, one-third of Donegal is official Gaeltacht territory, with Irish as the lingua franca.

After its northern start in Derry, the Wild Atlantic Way really begins to strut its stuff here, as the county's untamed craggy coastline truly puts the 'wild' into the Way. Donegal is well supplied with outstanding places to stay. The only problem is you may not want to check out. You'll find everything from simple B&Bs and guesthouses to historic heritage hotels, grand country houses and well-equipped hostels, many immersed in glorious scenery.

The local food scene is flourishing, and the long Donegal coastline offers a veritable seafood feast. The fantastic seafood is matched by excellent restaurants specialising in modern Irish cuisine, gastropub fare and international menus.

THE MAIN AREAS

GLENVEAGH NATIONAL PARK
Adventure awaits in the Derryveagh Mountains. **p376**

MALIN HEAD
Explore Ireland's most northerly point. **p385**

SLIEVE LEAGUE CLIFFS
Europe's highest accessible sea cliffs. **p392**

Find Your Way

Buses link major towns, but by far the best approach is to hire a car and hit the roads and byroads. Alternatively, hire a bicycle and tackle Donegal's demanding terrain.

Glenveagh National Park, p376

Experience the wild beauty of the Derryveagh Mountains, learn about the history of Glenveagh Castle and admire the spectacular gardens.

Slieve League Cliffs, p392

Take in awe-inspiring views of Europe's tallest accessible sea cliffs, tackle one of the trails or view them from the ocean below.

Malin Head, p385

Visit Ireland's most northerly point, take in dramatic coastal scenery while walking an alpaca and see the magnificent northern lights.

FERRY

Ferry services run to many of Donegal's islands and also link up some of the peninsulas. Check the weather ahead of time and book in advance to avoid disruptions to your plans.

CAR

Driving is the best way to get around Donegal. With your own wheels, you can move at your own pace, cover more ground and access the off-the-beaten-track destinations that public transport can't reach.

Malin Head (p385)

Plan Your Time

A lot of the activities and destinations in Donegal take time to reach, travel between and explore, so it's wise to have a plan of action to maximise your time.

Pressed For Time

Base yourself in **Donegal town** (p397) and start your morning with a tour of Donegal Castle. Head to the **Slieve League Cliffs** (p392) for a hike or a boat trip and finish the day watching the sunset from **Malin Beg** (p394). Leave early the next morning for **Glenveagh National Park** (p376) via the **Glengesh Pass** (p397), stopping in **Ardara** (p396) on the way.

Five Days To Explore

Follow the itinerary to the left and then visit **Arranmore Island** (p384). In the morning, go to **Tory Island** (p382) and then drive the Wild Atlantic Way Route to **Doe Castle** (p383). Stay in Letterkenny for the night. **Grianán of Aileách** (p389) is your first stop the next morning before exploring the **Inishowen Peninsula** (p391) and making your way north to **Malin Head** (p385).

SEASONAL HIGHLIGHTS

SPRING
March is one of the best times of the year to see the **northern lights**.

SUMMER
Festival-goers are spoilt for choice. Check out **Sea Sessions** in June and the **Ardara Bluegrass Festival** in July.

AUTUMN
The **leaves change colour** in the hills of Donegal, and as the season winds down, you'll likely have the trails to yourself.

WINTER
Surfers hit the **big waves**, and the power of the Atlantic is incredible to experience.

GLENVEAGH NATIONAL PARK

◆ DUBLIN

Ireland's second-largest national park, Glenveagh is a sublime panoply of lakes overlooked by brooding mountains, with valleys scooped from the land and scattered with both forest and swaths of bog that offer an enticing, unspoilt landscape coupled with wonderful options for hiking. Its wealth of wildlife includes the golden eagle, which was hunted to extinction here in the 19th century but reintroduced in 2001, and the country's largest herd of red deer.

Such serenity came at a heavy price. The land was once farmed by 244 tenants, who were forcibly evicted by landowner John George Adair in the winter of 1861 following what he called a 'conspiracy', but really because their presence obstructed his vision for the valley. Adair put the final touches on his paradise by building the spectacular lakeside Glenveagh Castle, while his wife introduced the park's definitive red deer and rhododendrons.

TOP TIP

With so much to do in Glenveagh National Park, it's wise to give yourself a full day to explore. Break up the day with lunch at the tearooms at the castle or the visitor's centre cafe. The best nearby accommodation options are in the villages of Letterkenny and Churchill.

Lough Veagh (p379)

Dark Side of the Rooms
A Tour Of Glenveagh Castle

Modelled on Scotland's Balmoral Castle, **Glenveagh Castle** is a characterful building with a dark history. John George Adair was a Scottish-Irish businessman and landowner who made his fortune by acquiring estates that went bankrupt after the Famine. He began construction on this castle in 1867, completing the building in 1873. He died suddenly in 1885, leaving the estate to his wife, Cornelia, who laid the stunning gardens.

After Cornelia passed away in 1921, Arthur Kingsley Porter, a professor at Harvard University, purchased the castle. However, he went missing on a trip to Inishbofin under mysterious circumstances and was never found (presumed drowned but later rumoured to have been spotted in Paris). In 1937, an Irish-American named Henry McIlhenny bought the castle. After restoring it and redeveloping the gardens, he sold the estate to the Irish government in 1975.

Learn about the fascinating history of this castle and hear stories about its previous owners on a 45-minute guided tour. The most eye-catching of the flamboyantly decorat-

WHY I LOVE GLENVEAGH NATIONAL PARK

Brian Barry, writer

The raw, wild rugged beauty of this national park is incredible, and it's home to a diverse range of wildlife. Whether you're strolling along the shores of the lake, walking the trails around the castle or wild camping, you can truly feel and appreciate the peace and tranquillity that Glenveagh has to offer. You can always find a place to yourself in this remote and isolated area and admire the magnificent scenery that surrounds you.

WHERE TO EAT IN GLENVEAGH NATIONAL PARK

Synge & Byrne
Great place to fuel up in the visitor centre at the entrance to the park. €

Glenveagh Tea Rooms
Soup, sandwiches and treats in the courtyard at the back of Glenveagh Castle. €

Take a Picnic
Bring food with you and dine alfresco. Just be sure to leave no trace. €

Glenveagh Castle

VISITOR CENTRE

At the entrance to the park off the R251, 23km northwest of Letterkenny, the **Glenveagh National Park Visitor Centre** has a 20-minute video on the ecology of the park and the infamous Adairs, as well as informative displays on both subjects. Reception sells the necessary midge repellent, as vital as walking boots in summer and waterproofs in winter. Facilities include a large car park, toilets, baby-changing spaces and a restaurant.

ed rooms are in the round tower, including the tartan-and-antler-encrusted **music room** and the **blue room** where guests Greta Garbo and Ella Fitzgerald once stayed.

The exotic gardens are similarly spectacular, boasting terraces, an Italian garden, a walled kitchen garden and the Belgian Walk, built by Belgian soldiers who stayed here during WWI. The gardens' cultured charm is in marked contrast to the wildly beautiful landscape that enfolds the area.

Hiking in Glenveagh National Park
Walks For Every Fitness Level

One of the best ways to appreciate this vast and varied park is simply by wandering around the majestic sweep of its forbidding golden landscape.

The park features nature trails along lakes and through woods and blanket bog, and a short walk leads to a viewing point behind Glenveagh Castle. Get advice and study maps

---

WHERE TO STAY NEAR GLENVEAGH NATIONAL PARK

Letterkenny
The nearest major settlement is Letterkenny, 23km away, which has plenty of accommodation options.

Churchill
Located in the quiet Irish countryside, this quaint village is the perfect place for hikers to relax.

Camping in Glenveagh National Park
There are no serviced campsites, but hikers on multiday treks are allowed to camp.

at the visitor centre. The park's six marked trails are well signposted. The walks vary in length and difficulty, and experienced hikers can find more challenging routes beyond the marked trails.

Beginning at the visitor centre, the 2km **Lakeside Walk** follows the shores of Lough Veagh to Glenveagh Castle. Native broadland trees are plentiful along the trail, and the terrain is mostly flat. It's a great alternative to taking the shuttle bus to the castle.

The 2km looped **Derrylahan Nature Trail** takes you through more remote areas of the park where you are treated to bogland views and meander through forests of Scots pine. The path is a gravel track that covers both flat and steep ground.

For a half-day hike, the 8km **Glen Walk** (Bridle Path) is worthwhile. This walk takes you a little further off the beaten path into the Derryveagh Mountains, rewarding you with spectacular views of the valley below. The beginning of the route is on a flat gravel path before it climbs for the last 3km or so. You need to arrange a pick-up at the other end or return the same way.

Your best chance of spotting red deer in their natural habitat is on the 7km **Lough Inshagh Trail**. Like the Bridle Path, this is not a looped walk, so you need to arrange for pick-up or drop-off at Lackanoo car park or return via the same trail. The terrain is a little more challenging, but the scenery is worth every step, and you can get an appreciation for just how vast Glenveagh National Park is.

Although the 1km **View Point Trail** is on the short side, it's one of the steepest routes. The trail begins outside of the castle gardens and follows a stony path to a viewpoint high above the castle. From the top, the views of the surrounding mountains, the lake and the castle below are incredible.

Glenveagh National Park

GLENVEAGH'S RED DEER

Glenveagh National Park is home to the biggest herd of red deer in Ireland, and they are the park's largest and most famous animals. The park services protect the herd, but the deer roam freely through the landscape. Although red deer are native to Ireland, the herd was expanded with stock brought in from Scotland in the 17th century. Red deer are located in almost all areas of the national park, with higher concentrations in the uplands. As these are wild animals, they can be difficult to spot. During the rutting season from mid-September to mid-November, the male deer bugle to prospective mates and are more active overall, making sightings more common.

GETTING AROUND

Driving is the best way to reach and explore Glenveagh National Park. By public transport, take the Local Link bus 271 from Burtonport to Letterkenny, which passes through the Glenveagh car park.

A shuttle bus goes from the visitor centre to the castle every 15 minutes from 10am. Bike hire is also available.

Beyond Glenveagh National Park

- Tory Island
- Doe Castle
- Carrickfinn Beach
- Mt Errigal
- Arranmore Island
- Glenveagh National Park

Surrounding Glenveagh National Park are stunning beaches, remote islands and historic sites that should not be overlooked.

Adventures await outside Glenveagh National Park, including challenging hikes, offshore islands and jaw-dropping beaches.

Few places in Ireland are more savagely beautiful than northwestern County Donegal. The rocky Gaeltacht (Irish-speaking) area between Dungloe and Crolly is known as the Rosses (Na Rossa) and is scattered with shimmering lakes, grey-pink granite outcrops and golden-sand beaches pounded by Atlantic surf. The islands of Arranmore and Tory are fascinating to those eager for a glimpse of a more traditional way of life.

One of the most beautiful beaches in Donegal is backed by impressive dunes where wildflowers bloom, and Doe Castle, home of the MacSweeneys, is one of the county's most unique castles.

TOP TIP

Northwestern Donegal is well-equipped with hotels and B&Bs, and wherever you go, you'll find somewhere to hang your hat for the night.

Carrickfinn Beach (p383)

Mt Errigal

Reach New Heights
Climb Donegal's Highest Mountain

The pinkish-grey quartzite peak of **Mt Errigal** (751m) dominates the landscape of northwestern Donegal, appearing conical from some angles, but from others like a ragged shark's fin ripping through the heather bogs. Its name comes from the Gaelic *earagail*, meaning 'oratory', as its shape brings to mind a preacher's pulpit. This mountain is the highest point in County Donegal and the steepest of the Seven Sisters range. Its looming presence and isolated position immediately command your attention and seem to dare walkers to attempt the strenuous but satisfying climb to its pyramid-shaped summit.

If you're keen to take on the challenge, pay close attention to the weather: it can be a dangerous climb on windy or wet days, when the mountain is shrouded in cloud and visibility is minimal. Hikers tackle the twin summits throughout the year, and the south-face route is the most popular approach as it is less steep. From the car park to the summit, the route is 4.5km return and takes approximately three hours, following the same route up and back.

MULTIDAY HIKE: SLÍ AN EARAGAIL

With a total ascent of 720m, the multiday Slí an Earagail loop covers 77km of coastal paths, woodland tracks, bog roads and quiet country lanes. Relatively flat overall, this trail is a looped section of the much longer Slí Dhún na nGall route that passes through west Donegal's Gaeltacht areas.

Walkers will have the peak of Mt Errigal in their eyeline regularly but are also treated to stunning coastal and island views. The walk takes three to five days to complete, and there are plenty of places to stop along the way. Find supplies and accommodation in the villages of Gweedore, Bunbeg, Falcarragh and Derrybeg.

WHERE TO STAY & EAT NEAR ERRIGAL

Errigal Hostel
At the foot of Errigal Mountain, this excellent purpose-built hostel has superb facilities. €

Glen Heights B&B
The rooms are bright and inviting, and the Donegal charm is in full swing. €€

Dunlewey Centre
This amalgam of craft shop, museum, activity centre and concert venue also has a restaurant. €

Tory Island

KING OF TORY TRADITION

Tory Island was home to the last remaining kingship in Ireland. Since the 6th century – and possibly even longer – a king has overseen the island. Throughout the 1800s, the king came from a particular lineage, but this tradition eventually faded away.

The King of Tory Island acted as an ambassador for the island, greeting people as they arrived on the ferry from the mainland. Dublin-born Patsy Dan Rogers, who moved to Tory Island at age 4, was the last King of Tory. Since his passing in 2018, the title has remained vacant. A self-described 'primitive' artist, musician and storyteller, Rogers would entertain all who arrived on the shores of Tory Island.

For experienced climbers, the approach via the north-face route follows two steep ridges. Expect grade 1 scrambling on the first ridge section. The route becomes steeper and more exposed on the second section, Tower Ridge, involving grade 3 scrambling. Most climbers require a rope and climbing gear to ascend safely. Previous mountain and scrambling experience is advised for this route.

Heading to Tory Island
Home Of Ireland's Last Kingship

Ireland's most remote inhabited island, the distant crag of **Tory Island** (Oileán Thóraí) has taken its fair share of batterings, blasted by sea winds and stung by salt spray. Although it's only 11km north of the mainland, the rough sea has long consolidated the island's staunch independence and strengthened its sense of remoteness.

The island has its own dialect of Irish and even had an elected 'king' until 2018, who acted as community spokesperson and welcomed visitors to the island. Over the decades, Tory Island's inhabitants earned a reputation for distilling and smuggling contraband poitín. However, the island is perhaps best known for its 'naive' (or outsider) artists, many of whom have attracted the attention of international collectors.

The island has just one pebbly beach and two recognisable villages: **West Town** (An Baile Thiar), home to most of the island's facilities, and **East Town** (An Baile Thoir).

WHERE TO STAY & EAT ON TORY ISLAND

Tory Island Hotel
The island's sole hotel is a friendly place with comfortable bedrooms inside a sunny yellow building. €€

An Cluib
This cosy little pub not far from the ferry serves traditional pub grub. €€

Tory Shop
Put together a picnic from this shop near the harbour. €

To explore the island, take a walk along the 4km **Tory Island Loop trail** to experience that edge-of-the-world feeling. Divers can head underwater to the wreck of HMS *Wasp* 15m below the surface, and the clear waters offer excellent conditions. There's a dive centre at the **Tory Island Hotel**.

Passenger ferries run to Tory Island from Magheroarty (Machaire Uí Rabhartaigh; 45 minutes). Sailing times vary according to weather and tides, and it's not uncommon for travellers to be stranded on the island in bad weather. Bring waterproof clothes as it can be a wild ride.

As you disembark from the ferry, look for the 12th-century **Tau Cross**, an odd, T-shaped cruciform that suggests the possibility of seafaring exchanges with early Coptic Christians from Egypt. Not far from the Tau Cross, the 6th- or 7th-century **Cloigtheach Bell Tower** has a circumference of nearly 16m and a round-headed doorway high above the ground.

To make the most of your visit, plan an overnight stay and experience the island once the day trippers have left.

White Sand Strand
A Beautiful Beach

Backed by Donegal Airport, which has been voted the world's most scenic airport every year since 2020, **Carrickfinn Beach** is a gorgeous stretch of undeveloped beach. Enjoy a long walk across this expansive stretch of white sand or ramble through the extensive dunes where beautiful wildflowers bloom in the warmer months.

Thanks to the impressive size of this beach, you can always find a peaceful spot to sit and soak up the sunshine, even in the busier summer months. The crystal-clear waters are great for swimming, and lifeguards are on duty from June to September.

Castle by the Bay
Stronghold Of The Macsweeney Doe Clan

Sitting inside beautiful Sheephaven Bay is 15th-century **Doe Castle**, the stronghold of the MacSweeneys. It's a deeply picturesque spot: a low, water-fringed promontory with a moat hewn out of the rock. The best way to appreciate the castle's charm is to wander the peaceful grounds, admiring its slender tower and crenellated battlements. The castle and grounds are free to enter, and guided tours are available in the summer. The castle was originally built by the O'Donnells in the 15th century, and the Scottish MacSweeney Doe clan took

---

WORLD'S MOST SCENIC AIRPORT

Donegal Airport might not be the biggest or the busiest airport in the world – it has flights to Dublin and Glasgow, Scotland, only – but for three years in a row since 2020, it has won the accolade of World's Most Scenic Airport in a survey by PrivateFly, a private jet charter company.

The airport's 1.5km runway runs straight down the middle of a narrow headland flanked on either side by white sand. Once you're airborne, the view over the surrounding coastline and the countless islands below is mind-blowing, giving Donegal Airport every chance of winning this title again and again.

WHERE TO STAY ON ARRANMORE ISLAND

Arranmore Holiday Village
These self-catering cottages are 1km from the ferry pier. €€

Arranmore Lighthouse
Spend a night in a lighthouse with amazing views for a memorable visit. €€€

The Cove
Just a few hundred metres from the ferry is this cosy, great-value B&B. €€

over the site in 1440, maintaining ownership for almost 200 years until it fell into English hands.

Doe Castle became a national monument in 1934. After falling into disrepair, it was restored by the Irish government's Office of Public Works. The MacSweeney grave slab inside the tower house dates from 1544, while the tower is thought to have been built in 1420. Guided tours take you through the castle's rooms and the grounds, giving you a unique perspective of its history.

Life on Arranmore Island
A Long History Of Habitation

Ringed by dramatic cliffs, cavernous sea caves and clean sandy beaches, **Arranmore Island** (Árainn Mhór) lies just 5km from the mainland. Measuring just 9km by 5km, the tiny island has been inhabited since the early Iron Age (800 BCE), and a prehistoric promontory fort can be seen near the southeastern corner. Today, it's Ireland's second-largest inhabited island with a population of 469.

The west and north are wild and rugged, with few houses to disturb the sense of isolation. The island is a walker's paradise with a selection of coastal and inland trails to choose from. The 14km **Arranmore Island Loop** treats hikers to jaw-dropping views of the coast as it brings you into the rugged island interior and along its inhabited southern and eastern sides.

Scuba divers can head underwater with **Dive Arranmore**, and anyone can join a 'sea safari' to look for seals and other marine life. Try surfing, rowing or kayaking with **Cumman na mBád** and check out the famous **Arranmore Island Steps** that are carved directly into the stone.

Access to the island is via the **Arranmore Island Ferry**, which departs from the Gaeltacht (Irish-speaking) fishing village of **Burtonport**. The journey takes about 15 to 20 minutes. Cycling is a fun way to explore the island, and there's a bike-hire company close to the pier.

Arranmore Island

BEST PUBS ON ARRANMORE ISLAND

Early's Bar
This family-run traditional Irish pub that's steeped in history offers great Guinness, stonebaked pizzas and plenty of craic.

Phil Bans Pub
This cosy pub guarantees a great night with a warm welcome, a friendly atmosphere and regular live music to get your feet tapping.

Neily's Bar
With a deck out back for the summer months and a fire in the winter, this little pub is always worth stopping into for a pint.

GETTING AROUND

Buses connect some of the towns in northwestern Donegal, but the best way to get around is by car.

MALIN HEAD

The rolling swells never stop coming across the sea at Malin Head, the northern extreme of Ireland. It's a name familiar to sailors and meteorological buffs, as Malin Head is one of the weather stations mentioned in BBC Radio's daily shipping forecast. You can almost imagine you can see Iceland (you can't) as you peer out through sometimes perfectly crystal blue but ever-blustery skies, which can change from sun to squall at the drop of a sou'wester. The rolling grasslands are dotted with suitably thick-coated donkeys, cows and well-wrapped-up hikers.

Explore the dramatic beaches, check out some of Europe's largest dunes and walk along the country's northerly point with an alpaca. Photographers and stargazers might be able to witness the northern lights, as low light pollution and clear skies create the perfect theatre for this mind-blowing light show.

Donegal might be known as the 'forgotten county', but Malin Head is an unforgettable destination.

TOP TIP

Basking sharks, the world's second-largest fish, live in the waters around Malin Head. Weighing more than 4 tonnes and growing up to 12m long, these magnificent creatures are commonly seen from April to August, with sightings peaking in May and June.

MALIN HEAD

HIGHLIGHTS
1. Malin Head Trail

ACTIVITIES
2. Wild Alpaca Way

SLEEPING
3. Malin Head View B&B
4. Seaview Tavern
5. Whitestrand B&B

DRINKING & NIGHTLIFE
6. Farren's Bar

INISHOWEN 100

This superb driving and cycling route gets its name from the 100 glorious miles of scenic coastal and mountain scenery that it covers. While driving the route is most popular, it is also a favourite with cyclists, although a good level of fitness and experience is required, as there are some very steep ascents along the way. This standalone route is well-signposted and can be started or finished at any point along the trail, including Malin Head.

Hiking Malin Head Trail
Spectacular Coastal Views

Get a feel for the rugged, unspoilt beauty of the most northerly tip of mainland Ireland on the **Malin Head Trail** from Banba's Crown to Hell's Hole. This clifftop walk gives you unbeatable views of the cliffs and the wild coastline beyond. Brown signs mark the way.

On the northernmost tip of Malin Head, called **Banba's Crown**, stands a cumbersome 1805 tower that was built by the British admiralty and later used as a Lloyds signal station. Around it are concrete huts that were used by the Irish army in WWII as lookout posts. To the west from the fort-side car park, a path leads 700m to **Hell's Hole**, a chasm where the incoming waters crash against the rock forms.

The view to the west takes in the Inishowen Hills, Dunaff Head, low-lying Fanad Head with its lighthouse, the twin 'horns' of Horn Head and the twin bumps of Tory Island. In the far distance, to the left of Fanad's lighthouse, are the Muckish and Errigal Mountains. To the east lie raised beach terraces, and offshore you can see the lighthouse on the remote island of Inishtrahull. On a few nights a year, you can even see the northern lights.

The Malin Head Trail is a linear walk of approximately 650m one way, which takes about 30 minutes to hike.

WHERE TO STAY ON MALIN HEAD

Seaview Tavern
Enjoy sea views from the comfortable rooms in one of the most picturesque areas of the Inishowen Peninsula. €€

Whitestrand B&B
Friendly owner Mary is a wealth of knowledge on the area and offers a fantastic Irish breakfast. €

Malin Head View B&B
All guest rooms have stunning sea views, and the location is ideal for exploring the area. €€

Tower, Banba's Crown

Have a Drink at Farren's Bar
Family Run For Six Generations

Fancy a pint in Ireland's most northerly pub? Established in 1825, this old-style bar has been in the Farren family for six generations and is still a family-run business.

Enjoy a warm welcome and take a seat by the fire while you wait for your Guinness to settle. It's located just 2km from Ireland's most northerly point. Farren's Bar has a 23-hour licence and is the perfect spot to relax after a day's adventure.

On the Trail with Wild Alpaca Way
New Hiking Buddies

If you're in search of a new hiking companion, check out **Wild Alpaca Way**, a family-run business at Knockmanny Bens that gives you the opportunity to walk through spectacular scenery with an alpaca for company.

You're partnered with your very own alpaca before heading off on a stroll that takes a little over an hour. Guided by your alpaca, you can take in jaw-dropping views of Malin Head all the way to the Isle of Doagh and beyond.

THE *STAR WARS* CONNECTION

Malin Head was used as a filming location for *Star Wars: The Last Jedi*, and a replica Millennium Falcon was constructed at the country's most northerly point. While the Millennium Falcon is no longer there, fans can visit the spot where it used to sit.

If you plan your visit right, you can attend the annual **May The Fourth Be With You Festival**, which takes place on 4 May. You can even have your photo taken at one of the signs for the R2D2, previously the R242, renamed in honour of the film being shot here.

GETTING AROUND

You'll need a car to get to and around Malin Head.

THE GUIDE

Beyond Malin Head

Ancient sites and ruined castles abound on the Inishowen Peninsula, as do traditional thatched cottages that haven't yet been turned into holiday homes.

Northeastern Donegal is the perfect territory for exploring along coastal roads to headland tips, sheltered bays and out-of-the-way coves. This is where the wildness of Donegal finds its true fullness on its scenic and windswept peninsulas, where the views go on forever.

Surrounded by vast sea loughs and open ocean, Inishowen (meaning 'Island of Eoghain', the chieftain who also gave his name to County Tyrone) attracts a lot of birdlife. The variety is tremendous, with well over 200 resident and migrant species, including well-travelled avian visitors from Iceland, Greenland and North America. Irregular Atlantic winds mean rare and exotic species also blow in from time to time. A wealth of sights await exploration.

TOP TIP

This region has a considerable choice of restaurants, so there's no need to pack supplies unless you're heading off the beaten track.

Grianán of Aileách

Gap of Mamore

Mind the Gap
Scenic Drive Around Buncrana

Arguably one of the best driving routes in Donegal, the **Gap of Mamore** rises 263m above sea level and provides mind-blowing views of Lough Swilly, the Fanad Peninsula and the northern end of the Inishowen Peninsula, as it twists between Buncrana and Clonmany. Drive cautiously on this twisting, steep, narrow section of road, which is beloved by motorists as well as walkers and cyclists.

Buncrana is a busy but appealing town with its fair share of pubs and a long sandy beach on the shores of Lough Swilly.

Step Back in Time at Grianán of Aileách
Notable Neolithic Monument

The amphitheatre-like stone fort of **Grianán of Aileách** encircles the top of Grianán Hill like a halo with eye-popping views of surrounding loughs. On clear days, you can see as far as Derry. The fort may have existed at least 2000 years ago, but it's thought that the site itself goes back to pre-Celtic times as a temple to the god Dagda. Between the

---

BEST PLACES TO EAT ON THE INISHOWEN PENINSULA

Ballyliffin local **Eamonn Grant** shares his top Inishowen Peninsula restaurants.

Ballyliffin Hotel
This is my second home and a must-visit when in the area. The chef uses as much local produce as possible.

Kealys Seafood Bar
It's across from Greencastle Harbour, so you know the seafood can't get much fresher. Foyle oysters and fresh Atlantic fish are the stars.

Harbour Inn
Offers a bistro-style menu so everyone's tastes are catered for. The hard part is having to choose what to eat, from chicken bang bang to fillet steaks, Atlantic salmon and creamy mushroom risotto.

WHERE TO STAY IN BUNCRANA

Inishowen Gateway Hotel
This hotel a few steps from Buncrana Beach has a 20m pool and a wellness spa. €€

Lake of Shadows Hotel
This elegant boutique seaside hotel is great value, and the restaurant is excellent. €€

Harbour Inn
Family-run inn on the hillside overlooking the beautiful beaches around Lough Swilly. €

THE GUIDE | DONEGAL BEYOND MALIN HEAD

Fort Dunree

5th and 12th centuries, it was the seat of the O'Neills, before being demolished by Murtogh O'Brien, king of Munster. Most of what you see now is a reconstruction built between 1874 and 1878.

The fort is 18km south of Buncrana, and it's free to enter.

Set Sail to Inishtrahull Island
History And Wildlife

Some 11km out to sea from Malin Head is the tiny, uninhabited and little-known island of **Inishtrahull**. In 1928, the island's residents were subjected to a mandatory evacuation, and although no ferry runs to the island, it's possible to visit on a full-day boat trip with **Amazing Grace Yacht Charters**, which departs from Bunagee. You might see basking sharks, dolphins and grey seals as you make your way to the island.

A two-hour guided tour shows what island life used to be like in this remote settlement. The lighthouses, old buildings, graveyard and school are all part of the itinerary. The island is designated as a Special Area of Conservation and a Special Protection Area by the National Parks and Wildlife Service, so expect to see an abundance of sea life and birdlife.

BEST PLACES TO GET COFFEE

Caffe Banba
This welcoming family-run cafe in Carndonagh is Ireland's most northerly bakery.

Inish Brew
Enjoy tasty treats, fresh scones and delicious coffee overlooking Trawbreaga Bay in Drumaville.

Cúl a'Tí
Amazing coffee in Culdaff; the food menu focuses on locally grown produce and fresh seafood.

Coffee Cup
This coffee shop at Fort Dunree might be Ireland's most scenic.

Gap Coffee Co
This coffee shop in Bridge End on the Wild Atlantic Way serves a range of salads and sandwiches.

WHERE TO STAY IN BALLYLIFFIN

Ballyliffin Lodge & Spa
This grand hotel has rooms looking out onto sublime ocean views. Treat yourself at the state-of-the-art spa. €€

Ballyliffin House & Spa
This family-run boutique hotel offers spacious rooms and excellent customer service. €€

Ballyliffin Hotel
Bright rooms, relaxed surroundings and excellent food in the centre of town. €€

Golf on the Inishowen Peninsula
Tee Off

With two championship courses, **Ballyliffin Golf Club** is among the best places to play a round of golf in Donegal. The scenery is so beautiful that it can distract even the most focused golfer. It hosted the 2018 Irish Open, and the village of **Ballyliffin** has an upmarket atmosphere with some good hotels and restaurants.

Enjoy spectacular views of Lough Foyle on the well-maintained 18-hole course at **Greencastle Golf Club**. Set amongst the staggering natural beauty of the Inishowen Peninsula, it's one of the most challenging courses in Donegal.

Sample the World's Best Chowder at Nancy's Barn
Chowder Champions

Fans of seafood chowder should make a stop at **Nancy's Barn** in Ballyliffin. Having won the title of All-Ireland Chowder Champion at the annual chowder cook-off in Kinsale, chef Kieran Doherty stepped up to compete against bowls from across the pond.

The New England Great Chowder Cook-Off in the United States is the longest-running event of its kind and is the pinnacle of success in the world of chowder. Nancy's Barn was the first overseas contestant to take part. After making nearly 950 litres of chowder, the Irish team emerged victorious.

Military History at Fort Dunree
Defensive Fortification And Museum

Fort Dunree is the best preserved and most dramatic of six forts built by the British on Lough Swilly following the 1798 uprising of the United Irishmen, which was supported by France when fears of a French invasion were at fever pitch.

The original fort, built in 1813, houses a military museum, while the surrounding headland is littered with WWI and WWII remains you can explore. There are several good waymarked walks. The Saldanha Suite houses a wildlife discovery room.

The winding fjord of **Lough Swilly** is one of Ireland's great natural harbours and has played its part in many historical dramas, from Viking invasions and the Flight of the Earls to the 1798 Rising and WWI.

Huge naval guns were added to Fort Dunree in the late 19th century, and during WWI, the lough was used as a marshalling area for Atlantic convoys, and as an anchorage for the Royal Navy's Grand Fleet. Unusually, it remained in British hands after the partition of Ireland in 1922 and was only handed over to the Republic of Ireland in 1938.

WALKS IN THE URRIS HILLS

The Urris Hills, a rugged ridge of resistant quartzite, provide grandstand views of the Inishowen coast and the distant hills of Muckish, Errigal and Glenveagh. A network of waymarked walking trails ranges from 2km to 11km in length. Starting points are at Butler's Bridge and the car park at the north end of the Gap of Mamore.

Starting at Glen House in Clonmany, an easy 800m trail leads to the cascading 10m-high Glenevin Waterfall, with benches and picnic tables along the way. From Clonmany, follow the road signed to Tullagh Bay, cross the river and bear right at an intersection. Butler's Bridge and the waterfall car park are about 1km further on.

GETTING AROUND

You'll want to be in a car to reach the Inishowen Peninsula, though there are a few sporadic bus services.

SLIEVE LEAGUE CLIFFS

The Cliffs of Moher get more publicity, but the Slieve League Cliffs (Sliabh Liag) are higher – and free to visit. In fact, these spectacular sea cliffs are among the highest in Europe, plunging some 600m to the ceaselessly churning sea. Feeling the energy of the ocean, watching the water crash up on the rocks and taking in the jaw-dropping panoramic views is simply incredible.

Standing on top of these cliffs is a true edge-of-the-world experience, and you can admire the cliffs from dry land or head out on the water. Walkers have a range of trails to choose from, and you can head out on a boat trip for a different perspective of these immense cliffs and maybe even take a dip in the waters below.

From the village of Teelin, a road through the stark landscape leads to the lower car park beside a gate in the road.

TOP TIP

The **Slieve League Visitor Centre** is a great source of information on walks and activities in the area. It also has exhibits about the cliffs, geology and local history. If you don't want to walk, you can buy tickets for the shuttle bus to the Bunglass Viewpoint.

Slieve League Cliffs

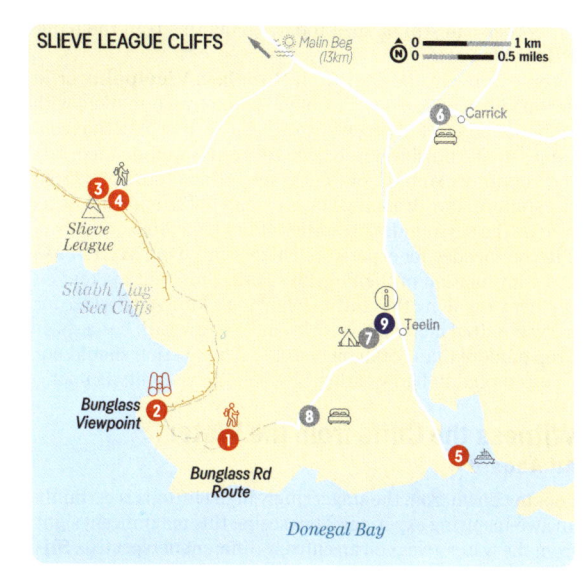

SLIEVE LEAGUE CLIFFS

HIGHLIGHTS
1. Bunglass Rd Route
2. Bunglass Viewpoint

ACTIVITIES & TOURS
3. One Man's Pass
4. Pilgrim's Path
5. Sliabh Liag Boat Trips

SLEEPING
6. Hegarty's Slieve League Lodge
7. Sliabh Liag Camping
8. Slieve League B&B

INFORMATION
9. Slieve League Visitor Centre

BASE JUMP AT SLIEVE LEAGUE

In 2020, Greg McEntee completed the first recorded BASE jump from the top of the Slieve League Cliffs. He jumped from the tallest and steepest section at the top of the cliffs known as the Eagles Nest (Nead an Iolar), the only part of the cliffs deemed steep enough to allow a parachute to open.

Leaping off the clifftop, McEntee landed on the storm beach just inside the Giant's Table and Chair rock formation. This highly technical jump was the first of its kind at the cliffs.

Hiking the Slieve League Cliffs
Lace Up Your Boots

Getting into the wilderness is the best way to experience the remote, rugged landscape of the Slieve League Cliffs. Hikers can take three main paths, which are steep in sections and require appropriate footwear and clothing. The scenery along the trails is mind-blowing, and although the hikes can be challenging, the rewards are worth every step. The cliffs are subject to high winds and fog. Before attempting these hikes, check the weather to ensure the conditions are appropriate.

The **Bunglass Road route** is a busy but more accessible option, which doesn't mean the views are any less spectacular. Beginning at the lower car park, the trail climbs steeply for about 45 minutes before reaching Bunglass Point, the most popular vantage point of the cliffs. You can also begin this walk from the village of Teelin.

During the 17th and 18th centuries, Catholic worship was outlawed in Ireland. However, instead of converting to the English Anglican Church, many Catholics travelled in secret to remote 'mass rocks' that served as makeshift churches. Slieve League was one of these places, and the remains of its

WHERE TO STAY NEAR THE SLIEVE LEAGUE CLIFFS

Hegarty's Slieve League Lodge
Fantastic family-run hostel in Carrick with a range of room types available. €

Slieve League B&B
This great B&B in Teelin has a lounge with a fireplace and can arrange bike hire. €€

Sliabh Liag Camping
Family- and pet-friendly campsite at the foot of the cliffs has hot showers and electric hookups. €

mass rock can still be seen today, giving this trail the name **Pilgrim's Path**.

You can begin the trail from **Bunglass Viewpoint** or in Teelin village. The beginning of the 4.7km trail is marked with stone steps before giving way to a steep narrow path that continues up the hillside. From here, the trail is well-defined, taking you to the summit of Cnockrawer (Cnoc Ramhar). From the summit, jaw-dropping views extend to the cliffs below, as well as the surrounding counties of Leitrim, Sligo and Mayo.

Recommended for experienced hikers only, **One Man's Pass** is a continuation of the Pilgrim's Path. This route takes you further west along the clifftop following a knife-edge ridge for a few hundred metres. The rocky and narrow path has a sheer drop of more than 550m on one side. This section should not be attempted in bad weather or when the visibility is poor.

Witness the Cliffs from the Water
All Aboard

Looking down from the staggeringly high clifftops is certainly an awe-inspiring experience, but seeing this magnificent sight from the water gives you an entirely different perspective. **Sliabh Liag Boat Trips** is located at Teelin Harbour and operates two 12-person boats on multiple sailings per day, which last nearly two hours.

On board, you'll learn about the history and legends of the area. If you're on board the *Nuala Star*, the company's flagship vessel, you can even jump in for a quick dip in the Atlantic Ocean, and if you're lucky, you might spot dolphins during your tour.

Malin Beg: Donegal's Finest White-Sand Beach
Dig Your Toes In

Surrounded by tall horseshoe-shaped cliffs, **Malin Beg** is one of the most off-the-beaten-path stretches of sand in the country. To access the beach, you need to make the drive and then descend 174 steps to reach the stunning white sand.

The crystal-clear waters are perfect for swimming, and the sunsets are divine. Malin Beg is also known as Silver Strand because of its impossibly white sand, and you would be forgiven for thinking you had boarded a plane to the Caribbean.

WILDLIFE TO LOOK OUT FOR

Seabirds
The cliffs attract thousands of birds to the sheer ledges where they nest. Common gulls, herring gulls, guillemots, puffins and a host of other birds are regularly spotted here.

Basking Sharks
The second-largest fish in the world clocks in at 12m long and 4 tonnes in weight. Basking sharks can often be seen from mid-April to August at the cliffs.

Dolphins
Keep your eyes peeled to spot bottlenose dolphins, which are often seen swimming and playing in the water below the cliffs.

GETTING AROUND

Vehicle access to the cliffs is limited, but you can park at the visitor centre, and a shuttle bus goes to the viewpoint. On public transport, take the Local Link 293 bus from Donegal town to Carrick and then walk 25 minutes to the visitor centre.

Beyond the Slieve League Cliffs

As you continue along the coast from the cliffs, County Donegal's scenery-o-meter is still set on high.

Donegal Bay and the surrounding areas are home to some true gems in this part of the country. Walkers will be blown away by the multiday Bluestack Way route, and the Glengesh Pass drive takes you into true isolation. Around here, you can truly get off the beaten track, escape the crowds and have waterfalls and waves all to yourself.

The picturesque town of Ardara has some excellent pubs where a trad session is always on the cards, and you can also see the traditional handloom in action. In Donegal town, the castle is a must for history buffs.

Finding a good hotel or B&B in southwestern Donegal is not a problem, though some close out of season.

TOP TIP

Southwestern Donegal is pretty well stocked with restaurants, but it's a good idea to buy supplies for more remote areas.

Glengesh Pass (p397)

ASSARANCA WATERFALL

Located 8km outside of Ardara is one of the most beautiful waterfalls in Donegal and arguably one of the most picturesque in Ireland. The cascading water flows down the side of the mountain right next to the roadside, making access a breeze.

There's plenty of parking available next to the waterfall, and the views over the coast behind you are magical. The idyllic and tranquil setting is the perfect place to sit back, relax and enjoy the sounds of nature.

Eddie Doherty Handwoven Tweed

Admire Ardara
Trad Music And Handweavers

Gateway to the switchbacks of the Glengesh Pass, the heritage town of **Ardara** (pronounced arda-rah; Ard an Rátha in Irish) is the heart of Donegal's tweed and knitwear industry. You can visit the weavers at work and see the region's most traditional crafts in action. Stop by **Eddie Doherty Handwoven Tweed** to catch Doherty himself hand-weaving on a traditional loom. He'll cheerfully explain every step of the process.

Ardara has a lot of decent accommodation choices and makes for an excellent base for exploring the surrounding region. Many of the town's pubs host regular traditional-music sessions; just stroll down the main drag until you hear the good cheer pouring out the door.

WHERE TO EAT IN ARDARA

Nancy's Bar
Superb seafood and chowder, including fresh oysters at an old-fashioned pub. €

Sheila's Coffee & Cream
Little cafe with hot dishes such as beef and Guinness stew and enticing desserts. €

Doherty's Bar
Come for the pints, stay for the music and enjoy great pizza. €

Driving the Glengesh Pass
Meander Through Remote Countryside

On a narrow road between Ardara and Glencolumbcille, the magnificent **Glengesh Pass** (Glean Géis; meaning 'Glen of the Swans') is one of Donegal's most scenic driving routes. It was scoured out aeons ago by implacably vast glacial forces and is approached down several switchbacks that lead towards thatched cottages and a swath of pastoral beauty. Pull over at the viewpoints to take in the whole epic scenario spilling out before you.

History in Donegal Town
Story-Filled Castle

Pretty and compact, **Donegal town** occupies a photogenic spot at the mouth of Donegal Bay. With a backdrop of the Blue Stack Mountains, a handsome and well-preserved castle, and a good choice of places to eat and sleep, it makes an excellent base for exploring the popular coastline nearby.

On the banks of the River Eske, Donegal town was a stamping ground of the O'Donnells, the great chieftains who ruled the northwest from the 15th to 17th centuries. Today, despite being the county's namesake, it's neither its largest town (that's the much larger Letterkenny) nor the county town (that's the even smaller town of Lifford).

Guarding a picturesque bend of the river, the well-preserved 15th-century **Donegal Castle** is an imperious monument to Irish and English might. Built by the O'Donnells in 1474, it served as the seat of their formidable power until 1607, when the English decided to rid themselves of pesky Irish chieftains once and for all. Rory O'Donnell was no pushover, though, torching his own castle before fleeing to France in the infamous Flight of the Earls. The castle was rebuilt in 1623 by Sir Basil Brooke, along with the adjacent three-storey Jacobean house. Further restoration in the 1990s kicked things into shape; don't miss the magnificent upstairs **Great Hall** with its vast and ornate fireplace, French tapestries and Persian rugs. Afterwards, corkscrew down the spiral staircase to the storeroom. Guided tours run hourly.

BEST PLACES TO STAY IN DONEGAL TOWN

Abbey Hotel
Convenient option on the Diamond at the heart of town; good bar and restaurant too. €€

Central Hotel
This affordable hotel has a swimming pool and is a stone's throw from Donegal Castle, the pubs and all the action in town. €€

Gateway Lodge
Refurbished modern rooms close to the town centre of Donegal town. €

WHERE TO EAT SEAFOOD IN KILLYBEGS

Killybegs Seafood Shack
This spot on the pier is said to have the best fish and chips in Ireland. €

Anderson's Boathouse Restaurant
Overlooking the harbour, this excellent restaurant serves fresh seafood and other dishes. €€

Marina Cafe
Reasonable prices, house-made tartar sauce and fresh fish make Marina Cafe a big hit. €

BEST SWIMMING IN BUNDORAN

Local adventure guide **Ronan Shaw** shares his favourite sea swimming spots in Bundoran (instagram.com/ronan.bosco.shaw).

Nuns Pool
This natural rock pool deepened by a seaward wall is excellent year-round, with enough depth to swim but still shallow enough to stand.

Thru Penny Pool
Below the main seafront walk, this shallow, sandy-bottomed spot is exposed to waves often. Below the south end of Rougey Walk, you have the diving board with higher cliff jumps off the rock on either side.

Blue Stack Way

Hike the Blue Stack Way
Ramble Through Remote Wilderness

The 65km **Blue Stack Way** is a challenging but rewarding trek, traversing the Blue Stack Mountains and giving hikers breathtaking views along the way. It connects Donegal town with Ardara along the shores of Lough Eske and the River Owenroe and through the foothills of the Blue Stack Mountains and moorlands.

It takes three days to complete the Blue Stack Way, and you can start at either end, though most people begin in Donegal town. Accommodation is available in Ardara, Donegal town, Glenties and the village of Drimarone, 3.5km off the main trail.

If you're not up for the long hike, **Lough Eske** is an easy scenic diversion from Donegal town, offering picturesque lake views.

WHERE TO EAT IN DONEGAL TOWN

Olde Castle Bar
This ever-busy pub off the Diamond serves some of the area's best food. €€

Simple Simons
Serves fresh and nutritious food, including veggie and vegan options. €

Blueberry Tea Room
A perennial and cosy local favourite, this cafe serves simple, honest food in hearty portions. €

Hit the Waves in Bundoran
Ireland's Premier Surf Town

Blinking amusement arcades, fairground rides and fast-food diners give **Bundoran** the feel of a cheery beach town, but Donegal's best-known seaside resort has solid waves and attracts a mixed crowd of young families, pensioners and growing legions of surfers. The beach of **Tullan Strand** has rip tides, so swimming can be risky, but the views are stunning, and the surfing is grade A.

Best surfed on mid to high tide, **Rossnowlagh Beach**, 16km north of Bundoran, is an excellent spot for beginners. The waves are much more mellow than in Bundoran, and there's plenty of room to spread out.

Bundoran has several surf schools, each of which rents out gear and has its own basic hostel-style accommodation. All offer deals on surf and accommodation packages.

If you'd rather stay on dry land, the scenic 2.5km **Roguey Cliff Walk** connects Bundoran's town centre with Tullan Strand. It passes a series of sea stacks known as the **Fairy Bridges**, once believed by locals to be haunted. The path begins at Promenade Rd, just east of the river.

Every July, the town hosts **Sea Sessions**, three days of surfing, skating, music and partying to kick off the summer season.

BEST CAFES IN BUNDORAN

Buoys & Gulls
This vibrant cafe has amazing ocean views, tasty flat whites, and a range of treats and toasties. €

Foam
With a minimalist, Scandinavian-inspired interior, this speciality coffee shop stands out. The menu includes seasonal dishes and vegan options, and it's the perfect place to start your day or refuel between surfing sessions. €

Hardy Baker
Great coffee, fresh-baked goodies, breakfasts and lunch seven days a week. €

Bundoran

GETTING AROUND

Driving is the easiest way to get around this area, but there are also several Local Link bus routes. Donegal town is the hub for many of these services.

THE MIDLANDS

THE IRISH HEARTLAND

Rolling countryside, archaeological treasures and stately homes: this region is a flavour of Ireland off the main tourist beat – and all the better for it.

If you're in search of a genuine slice of rural Irish life, you'll find it here in the country's heart. Often bypassed by visitors moving through the country from Dublin and the east to the wildness of the western coastlines, the Midlands region brims with verdant pastoral landscapes, stately homes, archaeological treasures, sacred monastic sites, lakeside vistas and sleepy towns where the locals are genuinely glad to see you. This is no exaggeration: that mythical Irish friendliness you've read about? You'll find it in abundance in the smaller cities and towns of Ireland's core.

Getting lost along the twisting back roads of counties Laois, Leitrim, Longford, Offaly, Roscommon and Westmeath is an unhurried pleasure, and you're virtually guaranteed to happen upon a local village shop, pub, garage or post office that's scarcely changed in decades. Mobile phone coverage can be patchy in parts, and internet connection is occasionally rudimentary, but there are fewer tour buses and souvenir stalls hawking tourist tat. Instead, you'll find an unvarnished version of Irish life and culture, albeit with some swanky hotels and wonderful country house restaurants.

The River Shannon dominates the Midlands, meandering through fields and forests, drawing boaters and anglers in shoals. Stylish hotels and gourmet restaurants continue to spring up along its banks, making it a wonderfully scenic and surprisingly cosmopolitan way to travel.

THE MAIN AREAS

CLONMACNOISE
Stunning early Christian settlement.
p404

STROKESTOWN
Noteworthy Famine museum.
p415

BELVEDERE HOUSE & GARDENS
Magnificent Georgian mansion.
p425

Above: Slieve Bloom Mountains (p414); left: Celtic Cross, Clonmacnoise (p404)

Find Your Way

The Midlands covers six counties – Laois, Leitrim, Longford, Offaly, Roscommon and Westmeath – which make up Ireland's belly. These places are often forsaken by mass tourism, and public transport can be patchy.

Strokestown, p415

This handsome Georgian town is home to a moving museum dedicated to Ireland's biggest disaster, the Great Famine.

Belvedere House & Gardens, p425

Wander the magnificent corridors and gardens of this beautiful Georgian mansion and marvel at its spiteful history.

Clonmacnoise, p404

Contemplate the lost land of saints and scholars at Ireland's finest monastic site.

CAR

Your own wheels are the most convenient way to get around this area of Ireland. The M4 and M6 motorways cross the region from east to west, and single-lane secondary roads get you everywhere else.

BUS & TRAIN

The major towns have train stations with services to destinations including Dublin, while buses serve the region from surrounding counties. Ireland West Airport Knock in County Mayo is useful for accessing the north Midlands from the UK.

Shannon River

Plan Your Time

Journey through Irish history from ancient days to more modern times before exploring mountains and bogland, all fuelled by fine food and whiskey.

Pressed for Time

Visit the monastic ruins of **Clonmacnoise** (p404) before heading west to Boyle to explore **Strokestown Park House** (p417) and the **National Famine Museum** (p416). Take in the prehistoric sites at **Corlea** (p412) and then travel east towards Mullingar to discover **Belvedere House** (p425) and take a hike in the beautiful **Fore Valley** (p428), home to the little-visited ruins of a 7th-century monastic site.

Midlands in a Week

After visiting **Strokestown** (p415), take a cruise along the **Shannon-Erne Waterway** (p422). Explore the battlements of **Athlone Castle** (p410) and have a drink in **Sean's Bar** (p410), Ireland's oldest pub, before indulging in some lakeland activities on **Lough Ree** (p410). Head south into County Laois and walk in the **Slieve Bloom Mountains** (p413) before stopping into Abbeyleix for a drink or two in **Morrissey's** (p413).

Seasonal Highlights

SPRING
Early May is a nice time to visit Strokestown, which hosts a three-day **International Poetry Festival** over the bank holiday weekend.

SUMMER
Boyle gets artsy for 10 days in July during the **Arts Festival**, featuring music, theatre, storytelling and exhibitions of contemporary Irish art.

AUTUMN
Ireland's answer to Glastonbury, **Electric Picnic** takes place in the estate of Stradbally Hall in County Laois in the first week of September.

WINTER
Belvedere House's version of a Christmas market is the **Food & Design Festival** in early December, which features locally made handicrafts and lots of food.

CLONMACNOISE

Clonmacnoise ● DUBLIN

Location, location, location: St Ciarán couldn't have picked a finer setting for his monastery, founded in the 6th century and overlooking a bend in the mighty Shannon. What he couldn't have known, though, was that in the centuries that followed, his get-away-from-it-all monastery would grow to become one of Ireland's holiest and most significant monastic sites, drawing in scholars from all over Europe.

All that ecclesiastical glamour, however, attracted the attention of the Vikings, who raided the site nine times between 837 and 953 CE, each time making off with a variety of treasures.

What was left is packed together within the confines of a walled field and includes the ruins of a cathedral, two round towers, three high crosses, nine churches and a graveyard with more than 700 early Christian tombstones. Overlooking the site to the west are the ruins of a 13th-century Norman castle.

TOP TIP

The site isn't large, but there's plenty to see, so put a couple of hours aside for your visit. If you want to avoid summer crowds, it's a good idea to visit early or late in the day. The tiny country lanes nearby can get clogged with coaches.

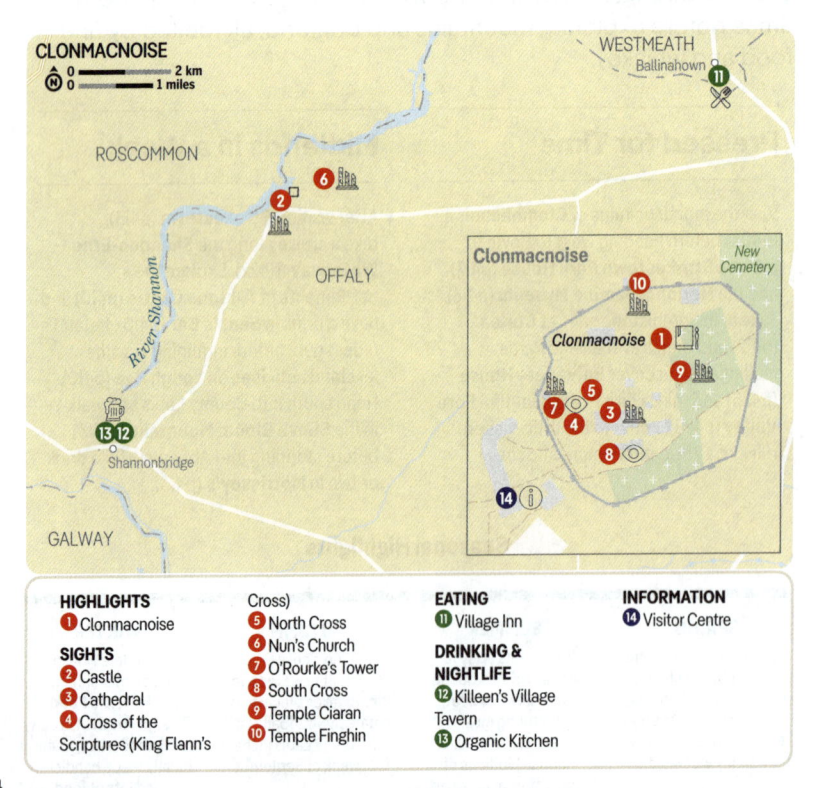

HIGHLIGHTS
1. Clonmacnoise

SIGHTS
2. Castle
3. Cathedral
4. Cross of the Scriptures (King Flann's Cross)
5. North Cross
6. Nun's Church
7. O'Rourke's Tower
8. South Cross
9. Temple Ciaran
10. Temple Finghin

EATING
11. Village Inn

DRINKING & NIGHTLIFE
12. Killeen's Village Tavern
13. Organic Kitchen

INFORMATION
14. Visitor Centre

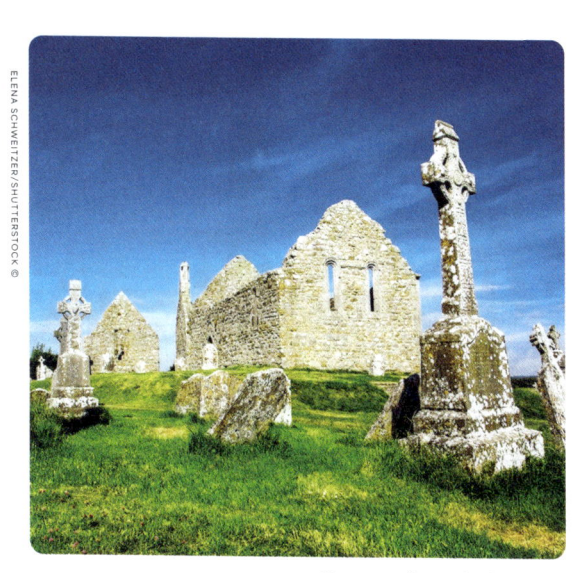

Clonmacnoise Cathedral (p406)

Temples, Towers & Cathedrals
A Centre Of Christian Learning

That throwaway line about Ireland being the 'land of saints and scholars'? It was coined because of places like **Clonmacnoise**, and though it might be ruined now, it doesn't take much imagination to see it as it was just more than 1000 years ago, full of eager students from all over Europe who came to learn the art of illuminating manuscripts from some of the most respected monks in Christendom.

Access to Clonmacnoise is via the excellent **visitor centre**, made up of three connected conical huts that echo the dwellings that would have housed those who lived here. If early monastic history escapes you, don't worry: the 20-minute audiovisual show is a terrific primer to the importance of the place.

Among the artefacts in the museum are the original high crosses (replicas have been put in their former locations outside), and there's a real sense of drama as you descend to the foot of the imposing **Cross of the Scriptures (King Flann's Cross)**, one of Ireland's finest. It's very distinctive, with unique upward-tilting arms and richly decorated panels depicting the Crucifixion, the Last Judgment, the arrest of Jesus and Christ in the tomb.

Only the shaft of the richly decorated **North Cross**, which dates from around 800 CE, remains, while the equally adorned

A BRIEF HISTORY

When St Ciarán founded this monastery in 548, it was the most important crossroads in the country, the intersection of the north-south River Shannon and the east-west Esker Riada (Highway of the Kings).

The giant ecclesiastical city had a humble beginning, and Ciarán died just seven months after building his first church.

The monks lived in small huts surrounding the monastery. The site was burned and pillaged on numerous occasions by both the Vikings and the Irish. After the 12th century, it fell into decline, and by the 15th century, it was home solely to an impoverished bishop. In 1552, the English garrison from Athlone reduced the site to a ruin.

WHERE TO EAT NEAR CLONMACNOISE

Killeens Village Tavern
Old-world pub in Shannonbridge serving good pub grub from steak sandwiches to fish and chips. €€

Organic Kitchen
Fallon's pub in Shannonbridge has a concession serving organic burgers sourced from nearby Clanwood Organic Farm. €€

Village Inn
Elegant restaurant in Ballynahown serving well-made classics from steak to a weekly fish special. Open dinner only. €€

O'Rourke's Tower, Clonmacnoise

CLONMACNOISE FROM THE SEA

More than 1000 years ago, the Vikings were repeat (and unwelcome) visitors to Clonmacnoise, sailing up the Shannon in their longboats to sack and pillage their way through the monastic city.

Although these days the most popular way to visit Clonmacnoise is by road, one of the nicest ways to approach is by boat, and with **Viking Tours** (vikingtoursireland. ie) you can do so in a replica ship.

The 90-minute trip departs from the dock by Athlone Castle and brings you downriver, where you disembark for a visit to the site, minus the sacking and the pillaging. Along the way, you'll get a quick history lesson, as well as the chance to spot wildlife.

South Cross has mostly abstract carvings, with swirls and spirals on one side and a Crucifixion scene on the other.

The site itself is impressive, but it helps to imagine it as a busy settlement where every building is complete. The largest building is the **cathedral**, originally built in 909 but significantly altered and remodelled over the centuries. Its most interesting feature is the intricate 15th-century Gothic doorway, designed so a whisper carries from one side of the door to the other – it was so lepers could confess their sins without infecting the priests.

The two round towers are the 19.3m-high **O'Rourke's Tower** and, on the northern edge of the site, a tower connected to **Temple Finghin**. The former is the oldest of the two: lightning blasted the top off O'Rourke's Tower in 1135, and the stones were used in the construction of the latter, which dates from around 1160.

The small churches at Clonmacnoise are called temples, a derivation of the Irish word *teampall* (church). Tiny **Temple Ciaran** is reputed to be the burial place of St Ciarán.

About 500m east of the site itself, beyond the modern graveyard, is the secluded **Nun's Church** with wonderful Romanesque arches and minute carvings. One has been interpreted as Ireland's earliest sheila-na-gig, a carved female figure in an acrobatic pose with feet tucked behind the ears.

West of the site, on the ridge near the car park, is a motte with the oddly shaped ruins of a 13th-century **castle** – also known as Clonmacnoise Castle – built by John de Grey, bishop of Norwich, to watch over the Shannon.

GETTING AROUND

Tour buses descend on Clonmacnoise between April and September. If you're travelling independently, you need your own car or a bike. The site is 25km south of Athlone on the N62 and R444. The nearest village is Shannonbridge, 7km southwest.

Beyond Clonmacnoise

Bogland, battlements and archaeological remains sit cheek by jowl with busy towns and beautiful mansions.

Beyond magnificent Clonmacnoise, green and watery County Offaly has vast swathes of bogland, and its main town, Birr, has a fabulous castle as well as one of Europe's largest and most famous telescopes. County Laois has some pretty villages and the dramatic Slieve Bloom Mountains, as well as the beautiful Emo Court, one of Ireland's grandest buildings.

To the north, Westmeath's county town of Athlone is a good base for wider exploration, especially of Lough Ree, which cuts across the border into County Roscommon. North of here is Longford, where the big attractions are archaeological: the Iron Age Corlea Trackway and an impressive portal tomb, Aughnacliffe Dolmen, are worth seeking out.

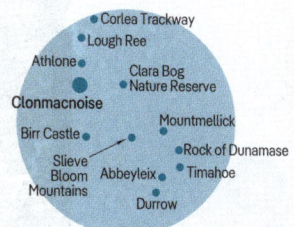

TOP TIP

Many museums and attractions are closed or have greatly reduced hours from November to March.

Birr Castle (p408)

THE WORLD'S MOST HAUNTED CASTLE

Around 12km southeast of Birr on the R421 is **Leap Castle**, reputedly one of the most haunted castles in Europe. Originally the residence of the O'Carroll family, the 1514-built castle was the scene of many dreadful deeds and is famous for its eerie apparitions. Its most renowned inhabitant is the 'smelly ghost', a spirit that apparently leaves a lingering odour after sightings. Another apparition is the self-explanatory 'red lady'. It's open for visitors – if you dare.

Birr Castle gardens

Battlements of Birr
Science And Splendour

It's easy to spend half a day exploring the attractions and gardens of **Birr Castle** demesne. The castle dates from 1620 and is a private home, but from May to August, you can visit the main living quarters on tours, which must be booked in advance. Most of the present building dates from around 1620, with alterations made in the early 19th century.

The 50-hectare castle grounds are famous for their magnificent **gardens** set around a large artificial lake. The gardens are home to more than 1000 species of plants from all over the world, so there's invariably something in bloom. Look for one of the world's tallest box hedges (which has made the *Guinness Book of Records*), planted in the 1780s and now standing 12m high, and the romantic Hornbeam cloister. There are waterfalls, wildflower meadows and a pergola festooned with a wisteria planted in 1936.

The Parsons clan, who have owned the castle since 1620, are a remarkable family of pioneering Irish scientists, and their

WHERE TO STAY IN OFFALY

Kinnitty Castle Hotel
Stunning neogothic castle with 37 superbly atmospheric rooms, all with period furnishings. €€

Maltings Guesthouse
In Birr, large pine-furnished rooms in a 19th-century malt storehouse once used by Guinness. €

Walcot B&B
Georgian townhouse set back from the road amid sprawling formal gardens across from Birr Castle. €€

work is documented in the historic **science centre**. Exhibits include the massive telescope built by William Parsons in 1845. The 'leviathan of Parsonstown', as it was known, was the largest telescope in the world for 75 years and attracted a wide variety of scientists and astronomers. It was used to make innumerable discoveries, including the spiral galaxies. After the death of William's son, the telescope slowly fell to bits. It has been completely restored, however, and may be viewed in all its glory in the gardens.

William Parsons' wife, Mary Ross, was a keen photographer, and her darkroom was reputed to be one of the first of its kind in the world. You can now view a replica. Other highlights are a children's **adventure playground**, complete with a playhouse, hobbit huts and trampolines, and the excellent **Courtyard Cafe** (open daily from March to October; weekends only November and December), which showcases local produce.

Offaly's Boglands
The Beauty Of The Bog

Clara Bog is one of the few great expanses of classic bogland in Western Europe to escape being stripped for fuel. Deceptively flat and seemingly lifeless, it offers a fascinating window into the natural world. At the magical **Clara Bog Nature Reserve**, a preserved 464-hectare raised bog landscape, you'll hear water coursing, birds chirping and insects buzzing, but the most memorable impression is the sense of quiet. A 1km loop boardwalk leads from a parking area 2km south of Clara village (7.5km southeast of the M6; where there's also a visitor centre).

Look for tiny wildflowers growing amid the pillowy soft peat and enjoy the sweeping views of distant green hills and the soft Offaly light on boggy pools of water.

Much of County Offaly's once extensive boglands were stripped of peat for electricity generation during the 20th century. Now Lough Boora, 17km north of Kinnitty, is the focus of a scheme for bog restoration. More than 50km of walking and cycling trails cross the **Lough Boora Parklands,** with excellent birdwatching, fishing, rare flora and a Mesolithic site. Maps are available at the visitor centre, which has a cafe and adjacent bike hire.

Ireland's diversifying renewable energy portfolio, including its growing number of wind farms, will further help in the recovery of the boglands.

TULLAMORE DEW

The big draw in Offaly's busy county town is the **Tullamore Dew Visitor Centre**, located in an 1829 canal-side warehouse. This famous whiskey producer's behind-the-scenes tour includes a welcome Irish coffee, the chance to try some whiskey blending and 'dip the dog' – where you sample whiskey straight from the cask – before finishing with more tastings.

BEST PUBS IN OFFALY

JJ Houghs Singing Pub
This 250-year-old vine-clad pub in Banagher is renowned for its nightly singing sessions.

Chestnut
Dating from 1823, the Chestnut in Birr also has regular traditional sessions.

Craughwell's
Stop for a pint at this pub in Birr, known for its rollicking trad-music sessions and impromptu singalongs.

A Mighty Fort
An 800-Year-Old Norman Castle

The one-time garrison town of Athlone straddles the River Shannon, with the west bank an enchanting jumble of twisting streets, colourfully painted houses, historic pubs and antique shops. Overshadowing them is the hulking **Athlone Castle,** a Norman fortification built in 1210.

The ancient river ford at Athlone was an important crossroads on the Shannon and the cause of many squabbles over the centuries, but the construction of the castle by the Normans put paid to any dispute and asserted their dominance over the region.

But all good things must come to an end and in 1690 the Jacobite town survived a siege by Protestant forces, but it fell a year later – under a devastating bombardment of 12,000 cannonballs – to William of Orange's troops. The castle was soon remodelled, and further major alterations took place over the following centuries. A lightning strike in 1697, however, ignited the castle's magazine, causing 260 barrels of gunpowder to explode, destroying much of the town in the process. Inside, modern displays bring to life the tumultuous history of the town and detail life here through the ages.

Inside this low 13th-century riverside castle, modern displays bring to life the tumultuous history of the town and detail life here through the ages. The highlight is the cacophonous **Siege Experience,** which takes place in a circular panoramic gallery.

On the river opposite the castle is the **Luan Gallery,** a contemporary art space with rotating exhibitions by top Irish artists. Also facing the castle is the colossal neoclassical **Church of St Peter & Paul**. Designed by Irish architect Ralph Byrne and completed in 1939, its stained-glass windows portray images of St Peter, St Paul, St Patrick, the Last Judgement and Purgatory, all created by Richard King in the Harry Clarke Workshop.

Loughs, Laughs & Lost Villages
History And Fun By A Lake

Monks once inhabited many of the 50-plus islands within **Lough Ree**, and their ecclesiastical treasures drew Vikings like bears to honey-laced beehives. These days, it lures visitors for sailing, trout and pike fishing, and birdwatching. Migratory birds that nest here include Bewick's swans, whooper swans, golden plovers and curlews.

Poet, playwright and novelist Oliver Goldsmith (1728–74), author of *The Vicar of Wakefield*, is closely associated with

---

A PINT OF HISTORY

You might not guess it from the front, but **Sean's Bar** on Main St in Athlone dates from 900 CE, making it Ireland's oldest watering hole – look for the Guinness Records certificate. An inn was established here by Luain Mac Luighdeach, whose other services included helping travellers cross the Shannon at Áth Mór, 'the Great Ford.'

The settlement that grew up here became known as Áth Luain (Ford of Luan), from which we get the name Athlone. Peat fires warm the low-ceilinged interior, which has uneven floors (to help flood waters run back down to the river), sawdust and curios. Live music plays in the riverside beer garden most nights in summer.

WHERE TO EAT IN ATHLONE

Dead Centre Brewing
A working brewery (which you can tour) that also serves excellent gastropub-style grub. €€

Fatted Calf
New York–style bistro that spotlights locally sourced meat; the daily steak special is superb. €€

Hatters Lane Bistro
Hollywood-themed bistro serving tasty meat and seafood dishes, such as hake in Dublin Bay prawn bisque. €€

Church of St Peter & Paul, Athlone

the area running alongside the eastern shore of Lough Ree. Known as Goldsmith Country, the region is beautifully captured in his writings.

On the County Roscommon (western) side of the lough is **Baysports**, Ireland's largest inflatable waterpark. Think giant slides, castles and towers for all ages – it's incredibly popular in summer.

To the north is the deserted medieval village of **Rindoon**, arguably the most atmospheric spot along the entire lake. Founded in the 1200s and abandoned in the 14th century, the deserted village incorporates the overgrown remains of long medieval walls, a castle, an old hospital, a church and a mill. In spring, when the bluebells are out in the woods, it's a real picture.

Rindoon sits on a peninsula that juts into the west side of Lough Ree, 4.5km east of Lecarrow and is accessible by foot, bicycle or boat. From the car park, it's a 700m walk southeast to the ruins.

CYCLE THE GREENWAY

The **Old Rail Trail Greenway** runs for 43km from the centre of Athlone to Mullingar, along a converted stretch of the Midlands Great Western Railway line. The mostly flat trail is a cinch to ride: the countryside is beautiful, and the trail takes you under stone arched bridges and past restored station houses.

You can rent bikes from Buckley Cycles in the heart of Athlone. Alternatively, you can get on one of the bike-share Moby Bikes scattered throughout Athlone, but the terms of the rental agreement are that you can't leave the bike anywhere so that precludes even locking it up safely and heading off for a wander.

WHERE TO STAY AROUND LOUGH REE

Wineport Lodge
Modern-rustic lodge facing Killinure Lough. On-site amenities include a spa and fine-dining restaurant. €€€

Glasson Lakehouse
Modern, spacious and stylish resort with a spa, heated outdoor pool and 18-hole-championship golf course. €€€

Hodson Bay Hotel
Huge lake-facing resort hotel. Activities centre Baysports is directly in front of it for lakeside fun. €€

Corlea Trackway

IRELAND'S PRETTIEST ESTATE

The neoclassical, copper-domed **Emo Court**, 8km south of Portarlington, was designed in 1790 by James Gandon, architect of Dublin's Custom House. Originally the country seat of the first Earl of Portarlington, it later became a Jesuit novitiate. Admission is by a compulsory 40-minute guided tour.

Studded with Greek statues, the extensive grounds contain more than 1000 different trees, including huge sequoias. Enjoy refreshments at the cafe or a leisurely picnic before a scenic stroll through the woodlands to Emo Lake.

Rent boats for up to three people from **Lough Ree Boat & Bike Hire** in Lecarrow, near Rindoon. The outfit also rents bikes (including helmets and locks) for a spin around the lough.

A Road to the Past
A 2000-Year-Old Archaeological Marvel

One of Ireland's archaeological highlights is the extraordinary **Corlea Trackway**, an Iron Age bog road built in 148 BCE. Moving around the mossy, often waterlogged boglands of the Midlands was not an easy task, so settlers laid a wooden track across the terrain. It was known locally as the Danes' road, even though it predated the first Vikings by at least some 800 years. For a wider historical context, the road was laid around the same time as the Siege of Carthage during the Punic Wars in North Africa.

WHERE TO STAY IN LAOIS

Roundwood House
An 18th-century Palladian villa in secluded woods with 10 bedrooms and two self-catering cottages. €€

Castle Durrow
Stately 18th-century Castle Durrow has activities including tennis, archery, clay pigeon shooting and fishing. €€€

Ballyfin House
Regency mansion at the foot of the Slieve Bloom Mountains with luxuries including personal butlers. €€€

An 18m stretch of the pavement-like oak track – the largest of its kind in Europe – has been preserved in a humidified hall at the site's **visitor centre**, which screens a 17-minute educational film. A highly informative one-hour guided tour details the bog's unique flora and fauna, and explains how the track was discovered and methods used to preserve it. Objects found beneath the track also point to similar tracks discovered in other parts of Europe.

The centre is just off the N55 in Keenagh, County Longford, 30km north of Athlone.

Mountains & Mansions
The Quiet Beauty Of County Laois

There's a mildly anonymous quality to Laois (pronounced 'leash'), which is often overlooked as drivers zoom past. Away from the main roads, though, this hidden corner of Ireland has some wonderful sights. About 6km east of the county town, Portlaoise, is the **Rock of Dunamase**, a craggy limestone outcrop rising 45m out of the flat plains. It was first settled in the Bronze Age, but the ruins at the top date from the 12th century. You'll need some imagination to envisage the site as it was before it was destroyed by Cromwell's henchmen in 1650, but the views from the summit are breathtaking.

Laois' villages are also worth seeking out. About 12km southeast of Portlaoise is the tiny charming village of **Timahoe**, home to a tilting 30m-tall, 12th-century round tower with an elaborately carved Romanesque doorway 5m above the ground.

Not far from here is **Abbeyleix** (pronounced 'abbey-leeks'), as fine an example of a planned 18th-century town as you'll find in Ireland. It's also home to one of our favourite pubs in Ireland, **Morrissey's**, which opened in 1775 as a grocer's and hasn't changed much since.

The neat rows of houses, pubs and cafes surround a manicured village green in **Durrow**. On the western side stands the imposing gateway to the 18th-century **Castle Durrow**, a stately 18th-century building that is now a fancy country-house hotel.

A quiet Georgian town located on the River Owenass, **Mountmellick** was renowned for its linen production in the 19th century. It owes much of its history to its Quaker settlers and its place on the Grand Canal, a story well told in the town **museum**. You can

WALKING GUIDES

Slieve Bloom Walking Club's website (slievebloom.ie) has comprehensive information and 17 downloadable looped walking routes ranging from 4km to 75km. It organises three- to four-hour guided walks (departure points vary), as well as an annual three-day walking festival in early May, which has been going strong since 1994.

Rock of Dunamase

WHERE TO DRINK IN LAOIS

Poole's Bar
Traditional bar in Rosenallis with regular music sessions.

Kavanagh's
A great bar in the middle of Portlaoise that specialises in live music.

Moloney's
This Mountmellick institution is a lovely spot for a quiet pint during the day, but music fills it at night.

Slieve Bloom Mountains

> ### FEEL THE ELECTRICITY
>
> Ireland's answer to Glastonbury is on a much smaller scale but draws numbers with equal fervour. **Electric Picnic**, which takes place at Stradbally Hall 11km east of Portlaoise, is a spirited three-day open-air arts and music festival. It draws all kinds of names, from the likes of Björk, the Chemical Brothers and the Arctic Monkeys to emerging performers including Fred Again, Robyn and Fontaines DC. Tickets sell out months in advance, and most people camp, creating a vast communal party.

also pick up a guide to a 4km **heritage trail** that guides you around the town.

Rising out of the plains are the dramatic **Slieve Bloom Mountains**, whose upper slopes are protected by the 2300-hectare **Slieve Bloom Nature Reserve**, which tops out at 527m. The area has some excellent walking options, from gentle ambles between Glenbarrow and Rosenallis to sections of the **Slieve Bloom Way**, an 84km-long signposted trail that does a complete circuit of the mountains, taking in most major points of interest. Along with good walking suggestions, the National Parks & Wildlife Service website (npws.ie) has info about the flora and fauna, including herbs and wildflowers.

GETTING AROUND

Trains run through the main towns, including Athlone, Tullamore and Portlaoise. Buses link many of the towns throughout Offaly and Laois, but services are limited. You're better off using your own wheels.

STROKESTOWN

As you arrive in Strokestown, you're left in little doubt as to the whole point of the town, which was to service the considerable needs of the local estate owners. The Mahon family received the land as a gift from King Charles II in 1666, and they eventually added a huge Palladian mansion. Around the same time, the town was built with the proviso that it included Europe's widest street (later surpassed by O'Connell St in Dublin), making it one of the few planned towns in Ireland.

While Strokestown is sleepy enough, it is notable for its historic estate (home of the Mahon family for 300 years) and unmissable Famine Museum, which allows you to explore up close the contrasting parallel lives of the haves and have-nots in 18th- and 19th-century Ireland.

Add in the nearby ancient Celtic site of Rathcroghan and you can easily spend a day exploring the area.

TOP TIP

Dining and sleeping options in Strokestown are quite limited, making this much more of a day-trip destination. Roscommon town is 19km southwest and has a better selection, but if you fancy overnighting in Strokestown, the Percy French Hotel has decent rooms and the best restaurant in town, with decent veggie dishes.

Strokestown Park House (p417)

STROKESTOWN

THE MAHON FAMILY

The history of Strokestown is effectively the history of the Mahon family. The founder of the estate, Captain Nicholas Mahon, was gifted the land for services rendered during the Cromwellian invasion of 1649, but he and his successors were deemed to be pretty generous landlords. Thomas Mahon (1701–82) built the mansion you see today and oversaw the construction of the town for the workers on the estate.

By the time Denis Mahon took over, the estate was in huge debt, which resulted in the evictions that eventually led to his murder. The last Mahon to live in the house was Olive Pakenham-Mahon, who left in 1981.

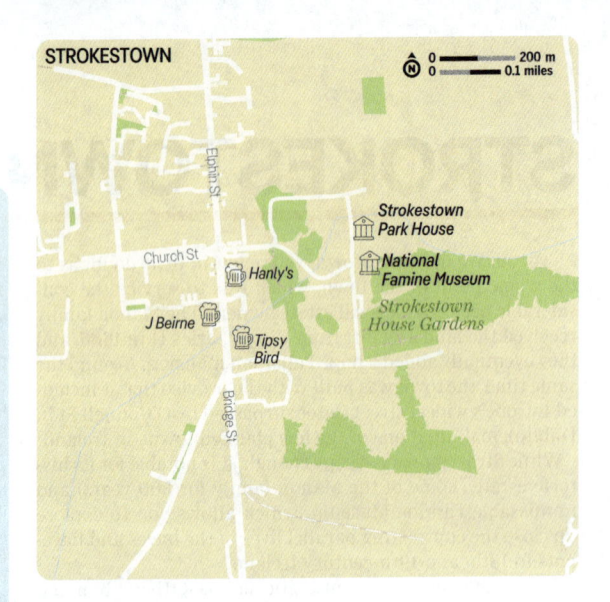

The Spectre of Hunger
Examining Ireland's Greatest Disaster

'Our families are really and truly suffering in our presence and we cannot much longer withstand their cries for food. We have no food for them, our potatoes are rotten and we have no grain'. This haunting testimony is part of the Cloonahee Petition, dated 22 August 1846 and just one of the documents on display at the **National Famine Museum** in the Stable Yard of Strokestown Park. The story of those who died and those who were forced to leave is told in concise, harrowing detail at this extraordinary museum.

As well as some genuinely touching artefacts, the museum uses modern techniques to tell the story of the Famine, including projections, soundscapes and voiceovers, but the whole effort is underpinned by thousands of documents from the time.

Mahon's role in the Famine was more than that of an observer. He evicted around 3000 of his tenants for nonpayment, 500 of whom died on the overcrowded 'coffin ships' he chartered to transport them away from Ireland. Two hundred perished in quarantine in Québec (the cheapest route). Perhaps unsurprisingly, Mahon was murdered by three of his tenants

WHERE TO DRINK IN STROKESTOWN

J Beirne
A quintessential traditional pub, with a grocer and petrol pumps outside.

Hanly's
This classic pub in the middle of town specialises in craft beer.

Tipsy Bird
Known locally as Squids, this pub has music sessions most nights.

in 1847, two of whom were publicly hanged in Roscommon. The gun they used is on display.

You can visit the museum on a self-guided tour or join one of the thrice-daily tours, which also include a visit to Strokestown Park House.

The National Famine Museum hosts an annual **Famine Summer School** over a weekend in June, featuring talks, films, exhibitions, live music and theatre, which explore the legacy of the Famine.

A Grand Demesne
Layers Of 19th-Century Ireland

At the end of Strokestown's handsome main avenue, triple Gothic arches lead to **Strokestown Park House**. Ireland has plenty of fine Palladian mansions, but this one, designed by Richard Cassels in 1730, is as much a time capsule of 18th-century privilege as it is an example of Georgian extravagance.

The hour-long guided tour covers the grand rooms of the main house as well as a galleried kitchen with original ovens dating from 1740, a schoolroom with an exercise book of neatly written dictation from 1934 (and, according to her red pen, deemed disgraceful by the governess), and a toy room complete with 19th-century toys and funhouse mirrors. Guides peel back the layers of the social structure of the time and reveal the tensions among the landlords, middlemen and tenants, which exacerbated the effects of the potato blight that directly caused the Famine.

Over the centuries, the estate (originally 120 sq km) decreased in size along with the family's fortunes. When it was eventually sold in 1979 by Olive Pakenham-Mahon, it had been whittled down to (a still vast) 120 hectares. Thankfully for visitors, the estate was bought as a complete lot, so virtually all its remaining contents are intact. The walled garden (a good indicator of the family's wealth) contains the longest herbaceous border in Ireland.

In the old granary of the estate are the fine Woodland Cafe and Shop. You can buy replicas of some of the documents found in the exhibition, including the Clonahee Petition.

Drawing room, Strokestown Park House

A TRADITION OF HOSPITALITY

On the River Shannon's western bank about 13km east of Strokestown, **Keenan's Hotel** is a small hotel, pub and restaurant that has been in the same family since 1838. The 12 stylish sage- and olive-toned guest rooms are wonderful (Bono has stayed a few times), while the food in the restaurant is sensational: think Roscommon lamb shanks with sweet potato mash, Longford sirloin with sautéed mushrooms, Leitrim goat's cheese tart with wild herbs and beetroot, and Shannon-caught trout with parsnip purée.

GETTING AROUND

Although a regular bus service runs to Strokestown from Dublin via Longford, you're better off with your own transport.

Beyond Strokestown

Archaeological wonderlands, boat trips and adventure playgrounds are an easy drive from Strokestown.

Studded with megalithic tombs, ring forts and mounds, Roscommon is shrouded in myth and history. To the west is Europe's most important Celtic site, while north of here is the county town of Boyle. About 25km northwest of Boyle is Ireland's only coal mine – the tour down its 400m shaft is way more interesting than it sounds.

A few kilometres east of Boyle but over the border in County Leitrim is one of the great adventure playgrounds in Ireland, home to a huge lake surrounded by trails and a forest that you can walk along the top of, as well as Carrick-on-Shannon, a centre for boating trips along Ireland's longest river and a hugely popular weekend destination.

TOP TIP

Lough Key Forest Park is home to a series of walking trails that range from the short and gentle to the longer and more arduous, including a 20km trail that takes you as far as Cloondara in County Longford, which is also popular with cyclists.

Rathcroghan Mound

Oweynagat Cave

Royal Ancients
Europe's Most Important Celtic Site

If you're interested in Irish prehistory, then **Rathcroghan** (**Cruachan Aí**), on the edge of the village of Tulsk, is an archaeological motherlode and Europe's most important collection of Celtic monuments. Scattered across a 6km-wide area are 240-odd sites that cover an impressive 5000 years of human history.

The whole place could be straight out of an Indiana Jones adventure: a combination of extraordinarily important archaeological sites and some of the juiciest stories in Irish mythology, from battles between mighty bulls to the gates of hell.

Start at the excellent **visitor centre**, which has diagrams, photographs, informative panels and maps that explain the significance of the sites. Staff can let you know when access to the monuments is possible; some are privately owned. Most are along a 6km stretch of the N5 to the west. **Rathmore** and **Rathcroghan Mound** both have public access and parking.

Oweynagat Cave (Cave of the Cats), believed to be the entrance to the Celtic otherworld, is also nearby. The area around it is most closely associated with the pagan harvest

SAMHAIN

The harvest festival of Samhain was a precarious time for the ancient Celts, who believed that the spirits of the underworld would wander through the gates of hell to walk amongst them. To ward off unwelcome visitors, they would disguise themselves as ghosts, carve ghoulish grins into turnips and go door to door collecting fuel for bonfires and loaves of bread to leave for the spirits.

Fast-forward a few thousand years and you've got Halloween, with pumpkins taking the place of turnips and sugary treats taking the place of bread. Curiously, Samhain has plenty of similarities to Day of the Dead celebrations, which came out of Aztec and Toltec traditions.

WHERE TO STAY IN ROSCOMMON

Clonalis House
Elegant Georgian mansion in Castlerea with rooms in the main house and four self-catering cottages. €€€

Lough Key House
Beautifully restored Georgian country house in Boyle with six individually decorated guest rooms. €€

Kilronan House
West of Arigna Mines, this luxury castle hotel is one of Ireland's finest. €€€

Boyle Abbey

THE KINGS OF BOYLE

The history of Boyle is the history of the King family, former residents of the grand King House. In 1603, Staffordshire-born John King was granted land in Roscommon with the aim of 'reducing the Irish to obedience'. Over the next 150 years, through canny marriages and cold-blooded conquests, his descendants made their name and fortune, becoming one of the largest landowning families in Ireland. The town of Boyle subsequently grew around their estate but suffered badly during the Famine years.

festival of Samhain, which gave us the modern celebration of Halloween. As it's located on private land, a guide has to accompany anyone who enters the cave; arrange this at the visitor centre.

Historic Boyle
Scenic Town With Pedigree

A quiet town at the foot of the Curlew Mountains, **Boyle** is a worthwhile stop. On the banks of the River Boyle is the finely preserved (and reputedly haunted) **Boyle Abbey**, founded in 1161 by Cistercians and featuring a mix of architectural styles, including Romanesque and Gothic.

Sinister-looking mannequins at the **King House Historic & Cultural Centre** tell the turbulent history of the Connacht kings, the town of Boyle and the King family, including a grim tale of tenant eviction during the Famine. Kids can try on replica Irish cloaks, breeches and leather shoes; write with a quill; and build a vaulted ceiling from specially designed blocks. One room is devoted to Hollywood star Maureen O'Sullivan (1911–98), who was born nearby on Main St.

WHERE TO EAT IN ROSCOMMON

Drumanilra Farm Kitchen
A farmshop-restaurant in Boyle where all products come from the family's organic farm on Lough Key. €

Regan's Gastro Pub and Restaurant
Elegant gastropub in the middle of Roscommon town serving pasta and meat and fish dishes. €€

Rogue & Co Cafe
Gorgeous cafe in Roscommon town that serves tasty breakfasts, exquisite sandwiches and good wine. €€

The mansion's courtyard has a cafe and a large shop selling local crafts, and it's also the location of a weekly **farmers market**.

About 3km out of town is the impressive **Drumanone Dolmen**, a portal tomb built before 2000 BCE that's one of Ireland's largest. To reach it from Boyle's town centre, follow Patrick St west and then the R294 for 3km until you pass under a railway arch. Keep going for another 400m and you'll see a small abandoned building on your right. Stop here and climb up the hill and over the railway line. Take care and shut the gates.

Adventure Playground
Fun And Beauty In One Place

Ireland's best-known adventure playground is the 350-hectare **Lough Key Forest Park**, 4km east of Boyle. Sprinkled with small islands, it shelters picturesque ruins, including a 12th-century abbey on tiny **Trinity Island** and a 19th-century castle on **Castle Island**. It's a favourite with families for its wishing chair, bog gardens, fairy bridge and viewing tower. Marked walking trails wind through the park.

The park was once part of the Rockingham estate, owned by the King family from the 17th century until 1957. Rockingham House, designed by architect John Nash, was destroyed by a fire in the same year. All that remains are some stables, outbuildings and eerie tunnels leading to the lake that were built to hide the servants from view.

There is an informative visitor centre, and the **Lough Key Experience** incorporates a panoramic, 300m-long treetop canopy walk that rises 9m above the woodland floor, with sweeping lake views. Other attractions include the **Boda Borg Challenge** (minimum of three people), a series of rooms filled with activities and puzzles (great for sudden bursts of rain), and an **outdoor adventure playground**. You can also rent e-bikes and Segways to use on dedicated trails throughout the park.

Going Underground
Explore A Genuine Mine

Ireland's first and last coal mine, operational from the 1600s to 1990, is remembered at the **Arigna Mining Experience**, set in the hills above Lough Allen, 23km northeast of Boyle. The highlight is the 50-minute underground tour, which takes you 400m down to the coal face and includes a

WATER ACTIVITIES ON LOUGH KEY

You can hire row boats from **Lough Key Boats** (loughkeyboats.com) or take an hour-long boat tour aboard the 40-seater *Trinity MV*, with four departures daily during operating hours from the dock in Lough Key Forest Park. Alternatively, you can also book a private charter aboard the outfit's 10-seater powerboat, which comes with a driver/guide and includes a visit to Trinity Island.

If you fancy some fishing, the Boyle-based guides at **Angling Services Ireland** (anglingservice-sireland.com) know where all the pike (year-round), perch and trout (January to September) are. Guided day trips also include tuition for fishers looking to improve their technique or who want to learn to use modern electronics, such as sonar and mapping units.

WHERE TO STAY IN CARRICK-ON-SHANNON

Bush Hotel
Family-run hotel from the 18th century; Michael Collins stayed in Room 1 in 1917. €€

Drumhierney Woodland Hideaway
Eco-friendly alpine-style lodges spread around 40 hectares of dense woodland 7km north of Carrick. €€€

Lough Rynn
Magnificent 19th-century castle amid 120 hectares with nature trails and a walled garden. €€€

simulated mini-explosion. Tours are led by ex-miners who really bring home the gruelling working conditions and dangers. There's also an exhibition dedicated to the miners and the equipment they used, plus a short video.

Wear warm clothing and sturdy shoes, as it can be cold and muddy.

Covering 128km of north Roscommon, east Sligo and mid-Leitrim, the **Miners Way and Historical Trail** is a series of well-signposted tracks and hill passes following the routes taken by miners on their way to work. The trail usually takes around five days to complete; a brochure with maps is available from local tourist offices.

Cruising the Waters
Carrick-On-Shannon's Best-Known Activity

Carrick-on-Shannon has thrived as a boating centre since the completion of the Shannon-Erne Waterway in 1994, which linked Ireland's largest river with the two lakes that make up Lough Erne in Northern Ireland.

A number of companies do a roaring trade for cruises on the Shannon, covering short hops to multiday journeys. With so much activity on the water, the town has become a hugely popular weekend destination, with a good choice of accommodation and restaurants, and a great music and arts scene.

The Centre of Ireland
Castles And Priories

The county town of **Roscommon** is very much a place of local business and commerce, but it has a small, stately centre and some significant and picturesque abbey and castle ruins that make it worth exploring. It's also the geographic centre of the island.

The impressive ruins of the town's Norman **castle** stand alone in a field to the north of town, beautifully framed by the landscaped lawns and small lake of the town park. Built in 1269, the castle was almost immediately destroyed by Irish forces, and its turbulent history continued until the final surrender to Cromwell's forces in 1652, which took down the fortifications. A conflagration in 1690 sealed the castle's fate.

Set in a former Presbyterian church (1863), the volunteer-run **Roscommon County Museum** has an idiosyncratic collection, including an inscribed 9th-century slab from St Coman's monastery and a superb medieval sheila-na-gig (carved female figure with exaggerated

---

PICKING A CRUISE

For shorter cruises, **Moon River** (moonriver.ie) is your best bet. The 110-seat boat *Moon River* runs one-hour cruises on the Shannon, which is a great way to have the Shannon experience without having to commit to a longer excursion. Boats set off one to four times a day, depending on the season. Check online or the information board at the quay for times.

If you want to make cruising more of a holiday, **Emerald Star** (emeraldstar.ie) has a huge range of boats, from budget options to luxury eight-berth cruisers. **Carrick Craft** (cruise-ireland.com) has two- to 10-berth cruisers, with 23 different types of boats to choose from. The minimum rental for both Emerald Star and Carrick Craft is three nights.

WHERE TO EAT IN CARRICK-ON-SHANNON

Oarsman
This 18th-century gastropub specialises in craft beer and carefully prepped dishes like slow-braised lamb belly. €€

Honestly Farm Kitchen
Ethical carnivore, vegetarian and plant-based cuisine in a glass space that once housed a KFC. €€

Red Bank
Artwork adorns the walls of this elegant space, but the real treat is in the tented dining space at the back. €€

Roscommon Castle

genitalia). The unusual stained-glass Star of David window, representing the Trinity, above the door is another draw. Don't leave without hearing the story of Lady Betty, the 18th-century hanging woman. The museum is also the town's unofficial tourist office.

At the south end of town, the remains of a 13th-century **Dominican priory** are almost hidden behind a primary school. It merits a quick visit for its unusual 15th-century carving of eight *gallógli* ('gallowglasses' or mercenary soldiers) wielding seven swords and an axe.

Ireland by Canal
Cruising The Grand And Royal Canals

You can drive into the Midlands or get public transport, but by far the most enjoyable way of travelling through the middle of Ireland is aboard a cruiser on the Royal and the Grand, the 18th-century canals that cut a swathe through the country from Dublin.

EAT, DRINK & REST

Set back from the square in its own courtyard, the 19th-century **Gleeson's Townhouse & Restaurant** has 25 individually decorated rooms ranging from simple affairs with pine furniture and buttercup-yellow walls to more extravagant rooms with floral wallpaper, cushions and curtains. Local grass-fed lamb is the speciality of Gleeson's elegant restaurant, particularly the stew with rosemary and thyme.

The shop has an array of sweet and savoury pastries, premade salads, cured meats, cheese and wine that are ideal to take for a picnic during your explorations of the county's ancient sites.

WHERE TO EAT & DRINK ALONG THE ROYAL CANAL

Nanny Quinns
Yellow-fronted bar in Thomastown, County Westmeath, that also serves good pub grub. €€

The Bridge House
A lively pub on the eastern side of Mullingar that has an all-day menu. €€

Rustic Inn
This Abbeyshrule watering hole is a beaut; a snug little country bar with a terrific restaurant. €€

HOW LEITRIM BEWITCHED A DUBLIN YOGA TEACHER

Noeleen Tyrrell (@*noeleentyrrell_yoga*) is a yoga teacher living in Leitrim. Though the county gets relatively few visitors, she thinks it might be the friendliest place in Ireland.

'When I first moved to the county from Dublin, a friend from the US sent me a letter not knowing my address. But they knew the car I was driving, so the envelope read: Noeleen Tyrrell, the Red Mini, Dromahair. And it arrived!

From that moment, I was smitten. I'm still here almost 30 years later, and not a lot has changed. The wildness of the countryside, hedges unkempt and spilling with wild roses and columbine, a lake or mountain around every turn: this is Leitrim.'

Grand Canal

The **Grand Canal** threads its way from Dublin through Tullamore to join the River Shannon at Shannonbridge, a total of 132km. The canal passes through relatively unpopulated countryside, with bogs, pretty villages and 44 finely crafted locks lining the journey.

The 145km-long **Royal Canal** follows Kildare's northern border, flowing over a massive aqueduct near Leixlip, before it joins the River Shannon at Cloondara in County Longford, with 46 locks en route, including a supposedly haunted bridge at the 13th lock, near Maynooth in County Kildare.

You can hire narrow boats at several locations along the canals, which is an excellent way to journey through the waterways. **Barrowline Cruisers** and **Canalways** are major firms with multiple locations. You can also find rental firms in the boating centres of Banagher and Carrick-on-Shannon.

If you're a first-timer, don't worry: all companies provide training at the outset as well as safety equipment, including lifejackets. Licences are not required. Support is also provided en route should you have any difficulty. Remember that most companies require the barge to be returned to the base from which it was hired.

GETTING AROUND

Buses link the main towns including Carrick-on-Shannon, and Boyle and Roscommon town have train stations, but your own wheels are the easiest means of transport.

BELVEDERE HOUSE & GARDENS

In a country stacked with gorgeous Georgian mansions, Belvedere House isn't just one of the most impressive examples of the style, but it's a pile that also comes with its fair share of rattling skeletons. Even today, more than 250 years after the events that cemented its place in local lore, the house's potted history makes it one of the most compelling stops along Ireland's Georgian trail as well as one of the Midlands' blockbuster attractions.

Another huge part of the attraction is its location by the shores of beautiful Lough Ennell, proof that the 18th-century landed gentry really did have their pick of the best places to build their homes.

Surrounding the house are 65 hectares of gardens, parkland and woodland trails. There's a cafe, exhibition centre with regular events and children's playground if the young ones get bored of the house's rich history.

TOP TIP

Check out Belvedere House's regular calendar of events, which run from farmers markets to summertime concerts. Christmas is especially festive with a strong Narnia theme; there's also a green-robed Victorian Santa dispensing gifts and playing games with visiting children.

Belvedere House 425

BELVEDERE'S ADVENTURER OWNER

Belvedere's last owner, Charles Howard Bury, was easily its most adventurous. He fought with distinction in WWI, but only after he hunted and killed a man-eating tiger in India that had devoured 21 men.

He led an expedition in 1921 to see if Everest could be climbed, where he found footprints that were declared to be those of the Abominable Snowman.

He bought Belvedere House and lived there with a younger actor, Rex Bart Beaumont, aka 'Sexy Rexy,' and a pet bear called Agu that he wrestled daily in the gardens. Bury died in 1963, leaving Beaumont to eventually sell the house to the Irish state in 1980.

Jealous Wall, Belvedere House

A Georgian Masterpiece
Sadness And Splendour

In 1740, Robert Rochfort, the 1st Earl of Belvedere, engaged the services of noted architect Richard Cassels to build him a hunting lodge, or 'bolt hole,' by the shores of Lough Ennell. The result was the immense Belvedere House with semicircular bow ends and windows and rococo ceilings with some of the finest stucco work in Ireland (added around 1760 by French artist Barthelemij Cramilion) in the upper rooms. Downstairs is one of the most beautiful dining rooms in the country, with plenty of Irish oak and a huge fireplace lined with Italian Carrara marble.

The gardens, with their Victorian glasshouse, walled garden and lakeshore setting, make for wonderful rambling.

While the house and grounds have a stately grandeur, Robert's legacy is one of cruelty and horror. He suspected that his wife Mary, whom he largely neglected after she bore him a daughter instead of the son he so desperately wanted, was having an affair with his brother Arthur. She was placed under house arrest at Gaulstown House, Rochfort's ancestral home, where she remained for 31 years, slowly going insane while Robert moved permanently into Belvedere House.

Meanwhile, Rochfort's other brother, George, built his home nearby, a fine mansion called Tudenham, which annoyed Robert so much that he ordered Ireland's largest folly to be built so that it would block the view. The ready-made 'ruin' later became known as the Jealous Wall.

When Robert died in 1774, Mary was finally released from her arrest, whereupon she is said to have asked, 'Is the tyrant dead?'

GETTING AROUND

Belvedere House is 7.5km south of Mullingar, which is where the nearest buses and trains go. The best way to get here is by car.

Beyond Belvedere House & Gardens

Exploring the rest of Westmeath brings you to some ancient sites and a stunning valley.

Belvedere House is only a few kilometres south of the regional service town of Mullingar, which has few sights of its own but is a busy transport hub for the area and a good jumping-off point for exploring the wider region. Restored sections of the Royal Canal extend in either direction from the town.

The area around Mullingar is a pastoral landscape of cattle farms and lakes, and its attractions are relatively low-key and unexplored. To the north is mostly lakeland, but just beyond the unassumingly handsome town of Castlepollard is a wonderful monastic site at the foot of a beautiful valley.

South of Mullingar is Kilbeggan, best known for its historic distillery.

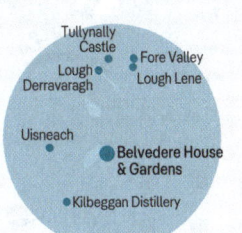

TOP TIP

Most hotels in Westmeath are clustered in and around Athlone and Mullingar, with B&Bs dotted around the county.

Benedictine priory, Fore Valley (p429) 427

Tullynally Castle

Peace in the Valley
Monastic Ruins And Beautiful Scenery

Little explored but worth every effort to see, the emerald-green **Fore Valley** is 5km east of Castlepollard near the shores of Lough Lene. This stunning spot is home to atmospheric monastic ruins with nary a visitor to enjoy them, and it's all the better for the peace and quiet.

In 630 CE, St Fechin founded a monastery just outside the village of Fore. There's nothing left of this early settlement, but three later buildings in the valley are closely associated with 'seven wonders' said to have occurred here. The oldest of the three buildings is **St Fechin's Church**, containing an early 13th-century chancel and baptismal font. Over the Cyclopean entrance is a huge lintel stone carved with a Greek cross and thought to weigh about 2.5 tonnes. It's said to have been put into place by St Fechin's devotions – the wonder of the stone raised by prayer.

WHY I LOVE THE FORE VALLEY

Fionn Davenport, writer

My parents introduced me to the Fore Valley when I was a young child, and I remember how beautiful and quiet it was and how it all just seemed to exist without any kind of fanfare. As Irish tourism developed apace in the decades that followed, the Fore Valley stayed pretty much as it was when I was a kid. There's a trail now and a coffee shop, but otherwise, it's just as it was when my parents first brought me.

WHERE TO STAY IN MULLINGAR

Annebrook House Hotel
Right in the town centre, accommodation is in an annex with 26 contemporary rooms. €€

Greville Arms Hotel
Dating from 1884, this grande-dame hotel has 40 spacious rooms; James Joyce was a frequent guest. €€

Railway House
Family-run B&B in the middle of town. Rooms are basic but clean and tidy. €

A path runs from the church to the attractive little **anchorite cell** which dates from the 15th century and was lived in by a succession of hermits. The **Fore Abbey Coffee Shop** in the village holds the key, as well as a handy walking map outlining the stops on the 3km trail that loops around the valley.

On the other side of the road near the car park is **St Fechin's Well**, filled with water that will not boil. Cynics should beware of testing this claim, as it's said that if you try it, doom will come to your family. Nearby is a branch from the three-branched tree that will not burn; the coins pressed into it are a more contemporary superstition.

Further over the plain are the extensive remains of a **13th-century Benedictine priory**, the Monastery of the Quaking Scraw, miraculous because it was built on what once was a bog.

The last two wonders are the mill without a race and the water that flows uphill. The mill site is marked, and legend has it that St Fechin caused water to flow uphill, towards the mill, by throwing his crosier against a rock near Lough Lene, 1.3km to the southeast.

Around Mullingar
Lakes And Distilleries

The best-known of the lakes north of Mullingar is 8km-long **Lough Derravaragh**, associated with the legend of the children of Lír, who were turned into swans here by their jealous stepmother. Each winter, the legend is recalled by thousands of snow-white migratory swans that flock here from as far away as Russia and Siberia.

About 10km to the east is **Lough Lene**, a 500-hectare lake dotted with ancient burial sites, old ruins and ringforts. The eastern end of the lake is known as the Cut and is a popular swimming spot; there's a pebble beach and parking. The turnoff is just north of the village of Collinstown.

In between the two lakes and just outside Castlepollard is the imposing Gothic Revival **Tullynally Castle**, the seat of the Pakenham family. Although the castle is closed to visitors, its 12 hectares of gardens and parkland are an enchanting place to roam.

South of Mullingar is tiny **Kilbeggan**, home to Ireland's oldest licensed distillery – take the tour.

WITH THE ANCIENTS

Between Mullingar and Athlone on the R390 is **Uisneach**, the centre of Ireland during Neolithic times when sea levels were lower. (The centre today is 46km to the west.) Ancient constructions found so far include earthworks that may have been a royal palace, a possible fort and holy wells. The 2-sq-km site is mostly privately owned, so the only way to visit is by an informative two-hour tour.

GETTING AROUND

A car should be your main transport mode for getting around County Westmeath, though the bus connections are reasonably good. Both Athlone and Mullingar have train stations.

Above: Trim Castle (p450); right: Slane Castle coat of arms (p444)

MEATH, LOUTH, MONAGHAN & CAVAN

THE STORY OF IRELAND

Visit the fertile fields that bear traces of Irish history from prehistoric times and those that bore the bloody battles that defined modern Ireland.

Irish civilisation was born in the fields of Meath and Louth, where the earliest settlers made their homes. Although this area is now largely part of the ever-widening Dublin commuter belt, the earliest inhabitants' legacies endure at the mystical tombs at Brú na Bóinne and Loughcrew – both of which predate the Pyramids of Giza in Egypt – and on the Hill of Tara, the seat of Ireland's high kings and the gateway to the Celtic otherworld.

By the banks of the quiet River Boyne is a monument to the most decisive battle in Irish history. In 1690, the Protestant forces of William of Orange defeated the Catholic army of James II, defining the course of Irish history for the next 300 years and counting.

Following St Patrick's arrival, the faithful built abbeys, high crosses and round towers to protect their treasured manuscripts from Viking raids. Magnificent ruins at Mellifont and Monasterboice recall a time when Ireland was known as the 'land of saints and scholars'.

To the northwest, the undulating hills and fish-filled lakes of Counties Cavan and Monaghan are wild and remote, making them the ideal location for splendid walking trails amid rugged scenery and unspoilt landscapes, scenes that inspired one of Ireland's greatest modern poets, Patrick Kavanagh, and whose legacy is maintained at one of the best interpretative centres in the country.

THE MAIN AREAS

BRÚ NA BÓINNE
Stunning Neolithic complex.
p436

TRIM CASTLE
A classic medieval fortification.
p450

COUNTY CAVAN
The lakeland county.
p454

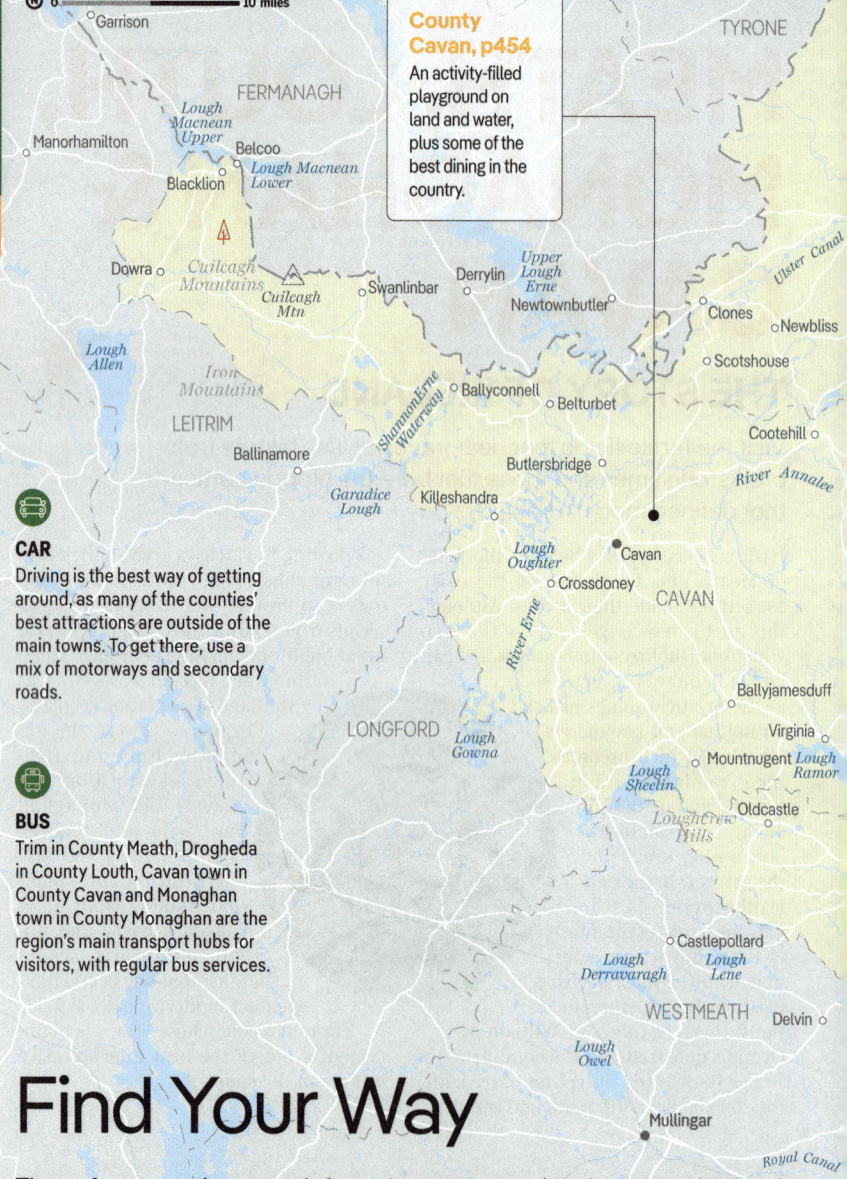

County Cavan, p454
An activity-filled playground on land and water, plus some of the best dining in the country.

CAR
Driving is the best way of getting around, as many of the counties' best attractions are outside of the main towns. To get there, use a mix of motorways and secondary roads.

BUS
Trim in County Meath, Drogheda in County Louth, Cavan town in County Cavan and Monaghan town in County Monaghan are the region's main transport hubs for visitors, with regular bus services.

Find Your Way

These four counties stretch from the northeast right into the middle of the country, skirting the border with Northern Ireland. Transport links are excellent in Meath and into Louth, but get slightly thinner the more inland you go, so getting around by car is a better bet.

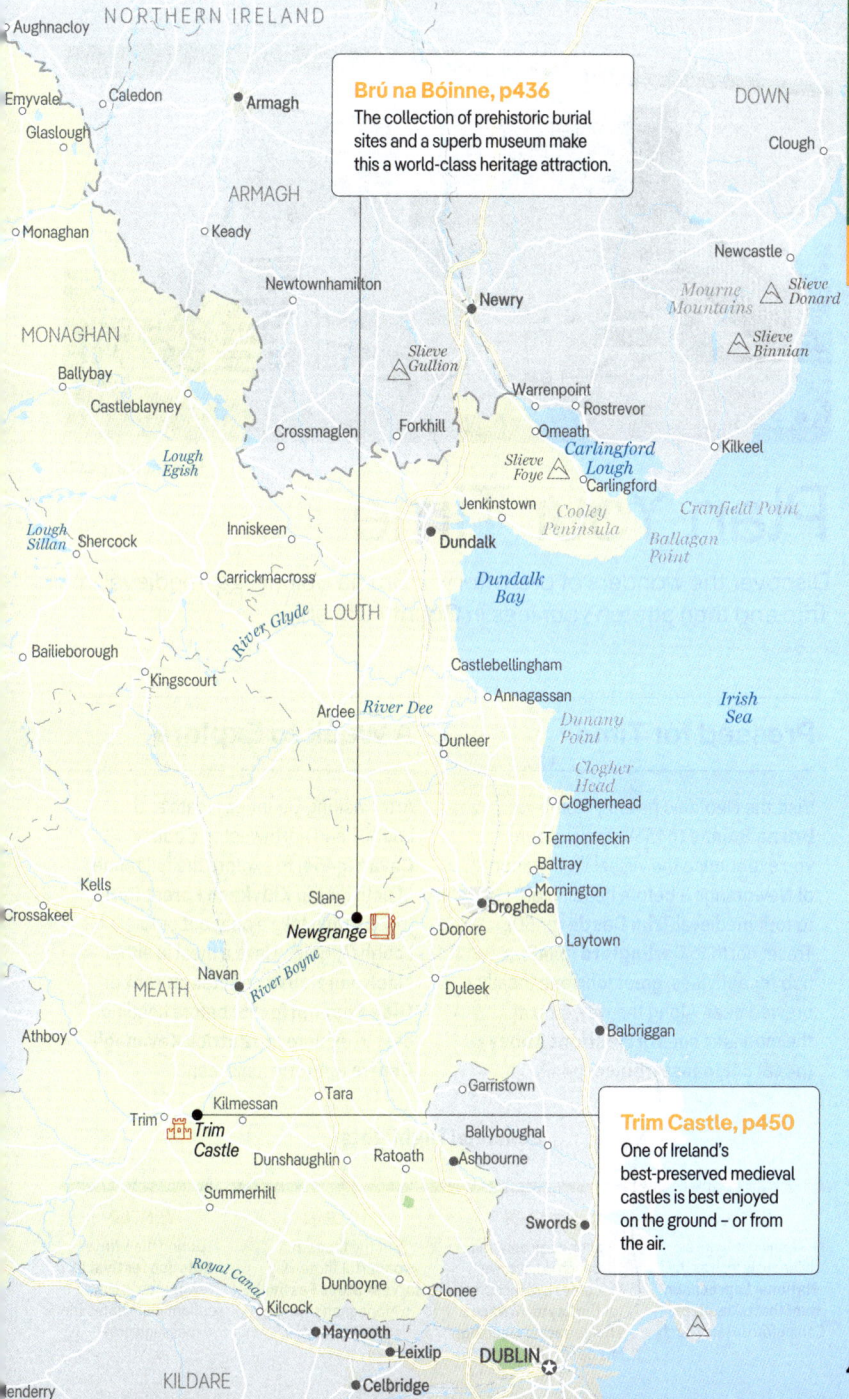

Brú na Bóinne, p436

The collection of prehistoric burial sites and a superb museum make this a world-class heritage attraction.

Trim Castle, p450

One of Ireland's best-preserved medieval castles is best enjoyed on the ground – or from the air.

THE GUIDE

MEATH, LOUTH, MONAGHAN & CAVAN

433

Newgrange (p439)

Plan Your Time

Discover the wonders of prehistory at Brú na Bóinne, get medieval in Trim and then stretch your legs in County Cavan.

Pressed for Time

Visit the Neolithic passage tombs at **Brú na Bóinne** (p436) – making sure you experience the virtual illumination of Newgrange – before heading off to tour medieval **Trim Castle** (p450). Travel north to **Carlingford** (p449), a hub for activities, great food and locally brewed beer. Along the way, stop at the monastic sites of **Mellifont Abbey** (p446) or **Monasterboice** (p447).

A Week to Explore

After visiting Counties Meath and Louth, head northwest to **County Cavan** (p454) to explore the full range of activities in **Killykeen Forest Park** (p455), then take a boat out onto Lough Oughter. Have a meal in either **MacNean House and Restaurant** or **Olde Post Inn** (p455) before heading east to explore the **Patrick Kavanagh Centre** (p458) in Inniskeen.

Seasonal Highlights

SPRING
Nothing is quite as hilariously Irish as the **National Leprechaun Hunt** that takes place in Carlingford in late March.

SUMMER
For one day only, the beach in Laytown becomes a racecourse for the **Laytown Races**, a horse-racing meet that has been run since 1868.

AUTUMN
Get the blues at a wonderful three-day **Harvest Blues Festival** in Monaghan town in early September.

WINTER
During the **Winter Solstice festival** at Newgrange, a shaft of sunlight illuminates the passage grave.

High cross, Monasterboice (p447)

BRÚ NA BÓINNE

Halfway between the busy town of Drogheda and the quieter village of Slane, the vast Neolithic necropolis known as Brú na Bóinne (Boyne Palace) is one of the most extraordinary sites in Europe. A thousand years older than Stonehenge, it's a powerful testament to the mind-boggling achievements of prehistoric humankind.

The complex, a Unesco World Heritage Site, was built to house the remains of those in the top social tier, and its tombs were the largest artificial structures in Ireland until the construction of the Anglo-Norman castles 4000 years later. The area consists of many different sites; the three principal ones are Newgrange, Knowth and Dowth.

Over the centuries, the tombs decayed, were covered by grass and trees, and were plundered by everybody from Vikings to Victorian treasure hunters, whose carved initials can be seen on the great stones of Newgrange.

TOP TIP

Brú na Bóinne can get very crowded. As there are only 750 tour slots, you may not be guaranteed a visit to either of the passage tombs. Tickets are sold on a first-come, first-served basis (no advance booking). Arrive early in the morning or visit midweek.

Knowth (p440)

BRÚ NA BÓINNE

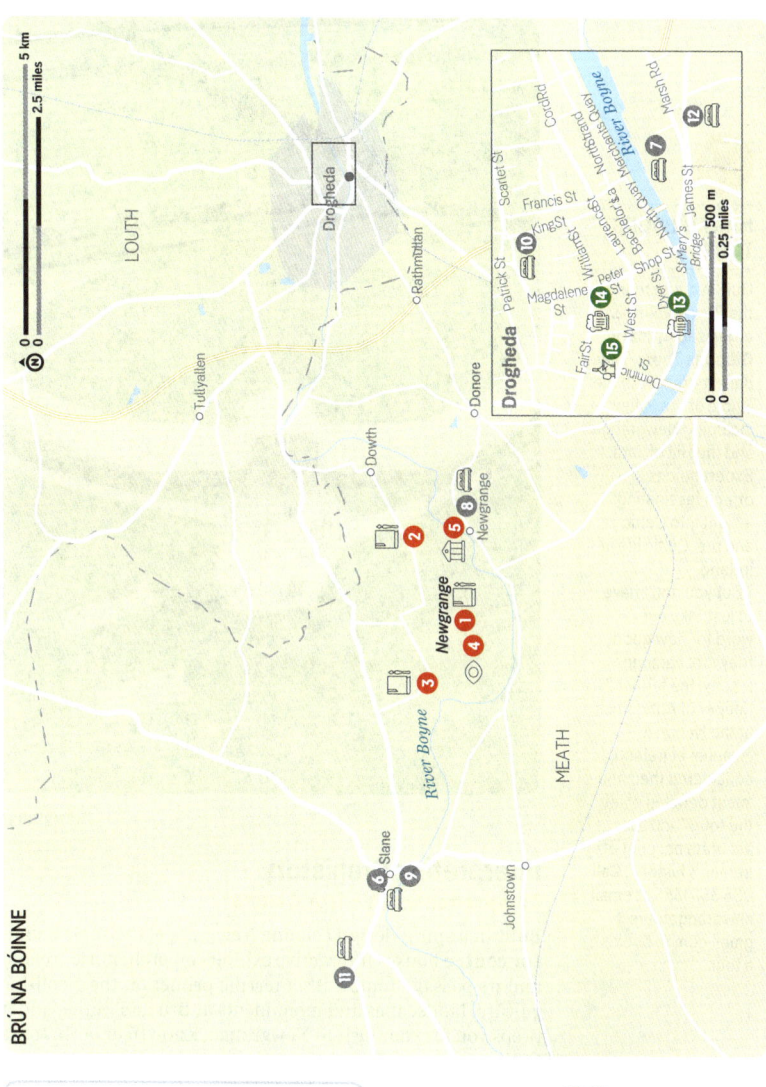

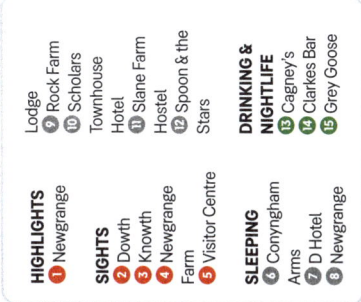

Drogheda

HIGHLIGHTS
1. Newgrange

SIGHTS
2. Dowth
3. Knowth
4. Newgrange Farm
5. Visitor Centre

SLEEPING
6. Conyngham Arms
7. D Hotel
8. Newgrange Lodge
9. Rock Farm Scholars Townhouse
10.
11. Slane Farm Hostel
12. Spoon & the Stars

DRINKING & NIGHTLIFE
13. Cagney's
14. Clarkes Bar
15. Grey Goose

Woodhenge, Knowth (p440)

MARY GIBBONS TOURS

Our favourite tour of the Boyne Valley is organised by **Mary Gibbons Tours**. These daily tours take in the whole of the valley, including Newgrange and the Hill of Tara. Expert guides offer a fascinating insight into Celtic and pre-Celtic life in Ireland.

But you don't have to just take our word for how good they are: Eamonn P Kelly, the former Keeper of Antiquities at the National Museum of Ireland, considered them the 'most detailed of all the tours' and 'an accurate account of Ireland's history'. Call 086 355 1355 or email newgrangetours@gmail.com to book a tour.

Newgrange

Interpreting Prehistory
Comprehensive Visitor Centre

Built in a spiral design echoing Newgrange, the superb **visitor centre** houses interactive exhibits on prehistoric Ireland and its passage tombs. It's a terrific primer on the Neolithic culture, landscapes and monuments at Brú na Bóinne, and it preps you for your visit to Newgrange, Knowth or both; tours to the sites leave from here.

The centre has regional tourism info, an excellent cafe, plus a bookshop and souvenir shop. Upstairs, a glassed-in observation mezzanine looks out over Newgrange.

WHERE TO STAY NEAR NEWGRANGE

Conyngham Arms
Wonderfully restored 18th-century coaching inn with 15 rooms, a beautiful garden and an excellent restaurant. €€

Rock Farm
Yurts and huts on an organic farm along the River Boyne. The state-of-the-art kitchen includes a pizza oven. €

Slane Farm Hostel
These 18th-century stables have been converted into a wonderful hostel that's part of a working dairy farm. €

A Grave Matter

Europe's Most Remarkable Passage Tomb

A startling 80m in diameter and 13m high, **Newgrange**'s white round stone walls, topped by a grass dome, look eerily futuristic. Underneath lies the finest Stone Age passage tomb in Ireland. Dating from around 3200 BCE, it predates Egypt's Pyramids of Giza by some six centuries.

The tomb's precise alignment with the sun at the time of the winter solstice suggests it was also designed to act as a calendar. However, no one is quite sure of its original purpose. The most common theories are that it was a burial place for kings or a centre for ritual.

Newgrange's name derives from 'new granary', and the tomb did serve as a repository for wheat and grain at one stage. But a more popular belief is that it comes from the Irish for 'Cave of Gráinne', a reference to a popular Celtic myth. *The Pursuit of Diarmuid and Gráinne* tells of the illicit love between the woman betrothed to Fionn MacCumhaill (or Finn McCool), leader of the Fianna, and Diarmuid, one of his most trusted lieutenants. When Diarmuid was fatally wounded, his body was brought to Newgrange by the god Aengus in a vain attempt to save him, and the despairing Gráinne followed him into the cave, where she remained long after he died. This suspiciously Arthurian tale (substitute Lancelot and Guinevere for Diarmuid and Gráinne) is undoubtedly a myth, but it's still a pretty good story. Newgrange also plays another role in Celtic mythology as the site where the hero Cúchulainn was conceived.

Over time, Newgrange deteriorated and at one stage was even used as a quarry. The site was extensively restored in 1962 and again in 1975.

A superbly carved kerbstone with double and triple spirals guards the tomb's main entrance, but the area has been reconstructed so that visitors don't have to clamber in over it. Above the entrance is a slit, or roof-box, which lets light in. Another beautifully decorated kerbstone stands at the exact opposite side of the mound. Some experts say that a ring of standing stones encircled the mound, forming a great circle about 100m in diameter, but only 12 of these stones remain, with traces of others below ground level.

Holding the whole structure together are the 97 boulders of the kerb ring, designed to stop the mound from collapsing outwards. Eleven of these are decorated with motifs similar to those on the main entrance stone, although only three have extensive carvings.

NEWGRANGE WINTER SOLSTICE

At 8.20am on the winter solstice (between 18 and 23 December), the rising sun's rays shine through the roof-box above the entrance, creep slowly down the long passage and illuminate the tomb chamber for 17 minutes. There is little doubt that this is one of the country's most memorable, even mystical, experiences.

There's a simulated winter sunrise for every group taken into the mound. To be in with a chance of witnessing the real thing on one of six mornings around the solstice, join the 30,000 others in the free lottery, where 50 names are drawn in late September. Fill out the form at the Brú na Bóinne Visitor Centre or email brunaboinne@opw.ie.

WHERE TO DRINK IN & AROUND DROGHEDA

Grey Goose
Huge downstairs bar in Drogheda; the upstairs cocktail lounge has leather sofas and music at weekends.

Clarkes Bar
Wonderful 1900 boozer out of a time capsule. The unrestored wooden interior features snugs and leaded-glass doors.

Cagney's
A classy spot for wines by the glass, whiskeys and more than 300 gins, including locally distilled Listoke 1777.

SECRET DOWTH

The third of Brú na Bóinne's passage graves is **Dowth**, similar in size to Newgrange – about 63m in diameter – but slightly taller at 14m high. Because of safety issues, Dowth's tombs are closed to visitors, though you can visit the mound (and its resident grazing sheep) from the L1607 road between Newgrange and Drogheda.

It has suffered badly at the hands of everyone from road builders and treasure hunters to amateur archaeologists, who scooped out the centre of the tumulus in the 19th century. For a time, Dowth even had a tearoom ignobly perched on its summit.

The white quartzite that encases the tomb was originally obtained from Wicklow, 70km south. In an age before horse and wheel, it was transported by sea and then up the River Boyne. More than 200,000 tonnes of earth and stone also went into the mound.

You can walk down the narrow 19m passage, lined with 43 stone uprights (some of them engraved), which leads into the tomb chamber about a third of the way into the colossal mound. The chamber has three recesses, and in these are large basin stones that held human bones. As well as the remains, the basins would have contained funeral offerings of beads and pendants, but these were stolen long before the archaeologists arrived.

Above, the massive stones support a 6m-high corbel-vaulted roof. A complex drainage system means that not a drop of water has penetrated the interior in 40 centuries.

To Know Knowth
The Largest Burial Mound

It might not have the same instant appeal as Newgrange, but the burial mound at **Knowth** is larger and more complex and has the greatest collection of passage-grave art ever uncovered in Western Europe. Early excavations cleared a passage leading to the central chamber, which at 34m is much longer than the one at Newgrange. In 1968, a 40m passage was unearthed on the opposite side of the mound.

Human activity at Knowth continued for thousands of years after its construction, which accounts for the site's complexity. The Beaker folk, so-called because they buried their dead with drinking vessels, occupied the site in the Early Bronze Age (c 1800 BCE), as did the Celts in the Iron Age (c 500 BCE). Remnants of bronze and iron workings from these periods have been discovered.

Around 800 to 900 CE, it was turned into a *ráth* (earthen ring fort), a stronghold of the powerful O'Neill clan. In 965, it was the seat of Cormac MacMaelmithic, later Ireland's high king, and in the 12th century, the Normans built a motte and a bailey (a raised mound with a walled keep) here. The site was finally abandoned around 1400.

MORE PASSAGE TOMBS

Ireland has at least 230 known passage tombs, with the best-known at **Loughcrew** (p445), and at **Carrowkeel** and **Carrowmore** (p363) in County Sligo.

WHERE TO STAY IN DROGHEDA

D Hotel
Minimalist rooms at this slick riverside hotel are bathed in light and decked out in designer furniture and cool gadgets. €€

Scholars Townhouse Hotel
This former monastery is now the best hotel in Drogheda, with 16 smallish but beautifully appointed rooms. €€

Spoon & the Stars
Rory and Hannah's well-run budget accommodation blends vintage and contemporary furnishings. €

Knowth

Farm Life
Family-Friendly Animal Encounter

When you've reached your limit with Neolithic passage graves, the 135-hectare working **Newgrange Farm** is a great option, especially for kids who've had quite enough of prehistoric runes. This family-run operation allows visitors to feed the ducks, lambs and goats; milk a cow; pet a rabbit; and take a tractor ride. Children's play areas include a straw maze and toy tractors, and there are indoor and outdoor picnic areas, and a cafe.

Sunday at 3pm is a very special time when the 'sheep derby' is run, with teddy bear 'jockeys' tied to the animals' backs. Visiting children are made owners of individual sheep for the race.

Follow the signs on the N51.

NEWGRANGE LODGE

Footsteps east of the Brú na Bóinne Visitor Centre, **Newgrange Lodge** is a converted farmhouse with 23 rooms ranging from dorms with four to 10 beds to hotel-standard doubles with private bathrooms.

Enjoy breakfast in buffet or continental style, or sit down with a full Irish, but whichever you opt for, try the excellent homemade bread. Superb facilities include a self-catering kitchen, two outdoor patios, a lounge with an open fire, board games, books and free bikes. There's also 24-hour front desk service, laundry and free parking. Rates include continental breakfast with homemade scones.

GETTING AROUND

Trains on the Dublin–Belfast line stop in Drogheda. County Meath has numerous Bus Éireann (buseireann.ie) services, but to get off the beaten track, your own wheels are best. Tour companies hit the main sights, and most depart from Dublin.

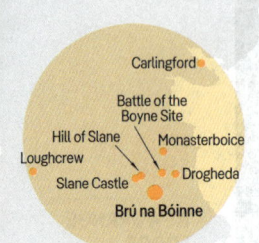

Beyond Brú na Bóinne

The region surrounding the Boyne Valley is a shallow bowl packed with history and heritage.

The Neolithic ruins at Brú na Bóinne might grab all the headlines, but the surrounding region is dripping with history, including more passage graves ignored by most visitors. Other highlights include two beautiful monastic sites dating from the Middle Ages, an 18th-century castle that is still in use as a residence and as the setting for an annual mega-concert, and a site by the River Boyne that in 1690 bore witness to the most significant battle in recent Irish history.

At the northern end of County Louth is the pretty medieval town of Carlingford, while east of Brú na Bóinne is Drogheda, whose citizens bore the terrible brunt of Cromwell's invasion in 1649.

TOP TIP

Thefts have been reported in the parking spots at Monasterboice and other historic sites. Don't leave anything of value visible.

Battle of the Boyne reenactment

Battle of the Boyne visitor centre, Oldbridge House

The Location of the Battle of the Boyne
A Most Decisive Encounter

Arguably the most consequential battle in Irish history took place at this site by the banks of the River Boyne in 1690, about 6km northeast of Brú na Bóinne and 6km west of Drogheda. On 1 July 1690, on a path of farmland now marked as the **Battle of the Boyne Site**, more than 60,000 soldiers of the armies of King James II and his nephew and son-in-law King William of Orange clashed swords (and cannons and guns).

Although the four-hour battle was not especially bloody (casualties topped out at 2250), it was the culmination of an almighty struggle for supremacy between the supporters of the Catholic James and the Protestant William, who had deposed his uncle as king of England two years earlier. By the battle's end, William had prevailed, and James eventually conceded defeat and slinked off to France.

The history is well told in the **visitor centre**, located in Oldbridge House, where you can watch a short film about the battle, see original and replica weaponry of the time, and explore a laser battlefield model. Self-guided walks through the parkland and battle site allow time to ponder the events that saw Protestant interests remain in Ireland. Costumed reenactments take place in summer.

TAKE TO THE WATER

One of the most peaceful ways to explore the Boyne Valley is to row a traditional oak and spruce eight-seater *currach*, a rowing boat made of a framework of laths covered with tarred canvas. Tours with **Boyne Boats** (boyneboats.ie) head along the Boyne Navigation canal network past the Battle of the Boyne Site, with commentary relaying its history as well as stories relating to *Game of Thrones*, in which the boats starred.

WHERE TO EAT AROUND DROGHEDA

Fisherman's Catch
Freshly caught seafood served at a family-owned business in Clogherhead. €

Glyde Inn
This 18th-century pub in Annagassan dishes up locally caught seafood. €€

Gilna's Cottage Inn
Busy restaurant in Laytown offering classic pub grub upstairs from a popular bar. €€

Slane Castle

Castles, Concerts & Whiskey
18th-Century Performance Venue

Still the private residence of Henry Conyngham, Earl of Mountcharles, 18th-century **Slane Castle** is best known for its massive outdoor concerts featuring rock-royalty names. Past performers include U2, the Rolling Stones, Bruce Springsteen and, in 2023, Harry Styles.

Built in Gothic Revival style by James Wyatt in 1785, the building was later altered by Francis Johnson for George IV's visits to Lady Conyngham, allegedly his mistress. Guided castle tours lasting 45 minutes include the neogothic ballroom, completed in 1821, and the Kings Room.

Tours and tastings are also available at its stable-housed **whiskey distillery**, which produces triple-cask-matured whiskey. There's also a superb restaurant and a bar.

St Patrick's Fire
The Holiest Of Hills

About 1km north of Slane village is the **Hill of Slane**, a fairly plain-looking mound that stands out only for its association with a thick slice of Celto-Christian mythology. According to

---

THE LEDWIDGE MUSEUM

This quaint cottage, 1km east of Slane on the N51, was the birthplace of poet Francis Ledwidge (1887–1917). A keen political activist, Ledwidge was thwarted in his efforts to set up a local Gaelic League branch but found an outlet in verse. He died on the battlefield at Ypres in World War I, having survived Gallipoli and Serbia.

The museum provides an insight into Ledwidge's works, and the cottage itself is a humbling example of how farm labourers lived in the 19th century.

WHERE TO EAT IN DROGHEDA

Stockwell Artisan Foods Cafe
Stock up on sandwiches, soups and salads at this popular cafe and deli. €

D'Vine
Convivial cellar bistro that does everything from Mediterranean tapas dishes to gourmet burgers. €€

Scholars Townhouse Hotel
The award-winning restaurant at this lovely hotel is the best in town. €€

legend, St Patrick lit a paschal (Easter) fire here in 433 to proclaim Christianity throughout the land. The story goes that Patrick's paschal fire infuriated Laoghaire, the pagan high king of Ireland, who had expressly ordered that no fire be lit within sight of the Hill of Tara. He was restrained by his far-sighted druids, who warned that 'the man who had kindled the flame would surpass kings and princes'. Laoghaire went to meet Patrick, and all but one of the king's attendants, a man called Erc, greeted Patrick with scorn.

Undeterred, Patrick plucked a shamrock from the ground, using its three leaves to explain the paradox of the Holy Trinity: the union of the Father, the Son and the Holy Spirit in one. Laoghaire wasn't convinced, but he agreed to let Patrick continue his missionary work. Patrick's success that day, apart from keeping his own life and giving Ireland one of its enduring national symbols, was good old Erc, who was baptised and later became the first bishop of Slane. To this day, the local parish priest lights a fire here on Holy Saturday.

On a clear day, climb the evocative ancient stone steps of the tower to enjoy magnificent views of the Hill of Tara, the Boyne Valley and seven Irish counties.

Tombs of Loughcrew
Low-Profile Neolithic Complex

Brú na Bóinne gets most of the attention, but the Stone Age passage graves strewn about the Loughcrew Hills, along the R154 near Oldcastle, are just as old and equally as significant. They're well off the beaten track and attract relatively few visitors, which means you can enjoy this moody and evocative place in peace.

Like Brú na Bóinne, the graves were built around 3000 BCE, but unlike their better-known and better-excavated peers, the Loughcrew tombs were used at least until 750 BCE.

Although the area has 32 tombs, most are on private land and inaccessible to the public. It is possible, however, to visit **Cairn T** at Carnbane East, a steep but scenic 15-minute climb from the car park. The cairn is 35m in diameter, with numerous carved stones. One of its outlying kerbstones, the Hag's Chair, is covered in gouged holes, circles and other markings.

Light pierces the chamber on the spring and autumn equinoxes, when Heritage Ireland guides are in attendance; guides are also here in summer. Otherwise, pick up the key to enter the passageway from the cafe at Loughcrew Gardens. Bring a torch.

You can also book a tour (including tea, coffee and scones) through the **Loughcrew Megalithic Centre**. Centred on a

CHEESE CENTRAL

Renowned **Sheridans Cheesemongers** (sheridanscheesemongers.com) has its warehouses and HQ in Pottlereagh, County Meath, about 12km east of Loughcrew on the border with County Cavan. A former train station now houses a cavernous barn-style shop crammed with cheeses from across Europe. Irish varieties include Cashel Blue, Durrus, Gubbeen and smoked Knockanore. It also sells chutneys, crackers, freshly baked bread, charcuterie, smoked fish, wines and its own cookbooks.

A small market showcasing local farmers and other producers is set up on Saturdays.

WHERE TO EAT IN DROGHEDA

Black Bull
Cosy pub doing solidly good standards, such as chargrilled steaks, burgers, and fish and chips. €€

Salthouse Brasserie
Solid breakfasts and lunch options, freshly squeezed orange juice and good coffee. €

Aisha's Cafe & Bistro
Mediterranean dishes from falafel to pizza as well as a great kids' menu. €€

collection of thatched cottages, the centre encompasses a museum detailing the megalithic wonders hereabouts, as well as a cafe, a hostel, glamping yurts and a craft shop with stunning photography of the area, including cairns that aren't accessible to the public. Special equinox events take place here. It runs tours of Cairn T by arrangement.

Into Drogheda
A Town With History

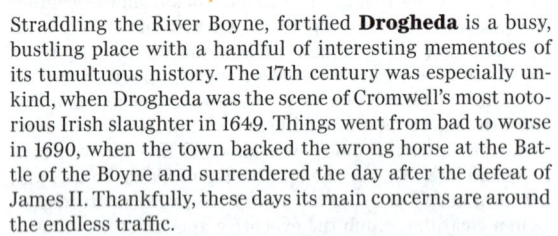

Straddling the River Boyne, fortified **Drogheda** is a busy, bustling place with a handful of interesting mementoes of its tumultuous history. The 17th century was especially unkind, when Drogheda was the scene of Cromwell's most notorious Irish slaughter in 1649. Things went from bad to worse in 1690, when the town backed the wrong horse at the Battle of the Boyne and surrendered the day after the defeat of James II. Thankfully, these days its main concerns are around the endless traffic.

In the heart of Drogheda is **St Peter's Roman Catholic Church**, whose main draw is the shrivelled head of St Oliver Plunkett (1629–81), kept in a glittering brass and glass case in the north transept. He was an innocent victim of the hysterical Popish Plot, a made-up conspiracy that Catholics were trying to kill Charles II after the Restoration.

The town's other church, **St Peter's Protestant Church**, is the building whose spire was burned by Cromwell's men, resulting in the death of 100 people seeking sanctuary inside.

Overlooking Drogheda is the **Millmount Museum and Tower**, whose highlights include a room devoted to Cromwell's brutal siege of the town and the Battle of the Boyne. The pretty, cobbled basement is full of gadgets and kitchen utensils from bygone times. The tower has great views over the town.

Marvelous Monastic Ruins
Ireland's First Cistercian Abbey

In its Anglo-Norman prime, **Mellifont Abbey**, 1.5km off the main Drogheda–Collon road (R168), was the Cistercians' first and most magnificent centre in Ireland. Highly evocative and well worth exploring, the ruins still reflect the site's former splendour. Mellifont's most recognisable building and one of the country's finest examples of Cistercian architecture is the 13th-century **lavabo**, the monks' octagonal washing room.

In the mid-12th century, Irish monastic orders had grown a little too fond of the good life and were not averse to a bit of

---

HERITAGE CARD

If you're planning to visit several archaeological and historic sites, invest in a **Heritage Card** (heritageireland.ie), which provides unlimited access to more than 45 different attractions, including the Battle of the Boyne Site, Brú na Bóinne and the Hill of Tara. Free admission also covers guided tours. The card is valid for one year and is available at all participating sites, as well as at tourist offices in major towns and cities. The card costs €40 for adults and €90 for a family of four adults and two children, so it's worth totting up how much you plan on visiting before investing in one.

WHERE TO EAT NEAR SLANE

Browne's Bar
The bar in Slane Castle serves locally sourced dishes and a high-end evening menu in the Gandon Room. €€

Conyngham Arms
Upmarket pub grub in the gastropub at the back of the eponymous hotel. €€

Tankardstown House
This spectacular manor house 10km northwest of Slane serves casual lunches and refined evening meals. €€€

Mellifont Abbey

corruption. In 1142, an exasperated Malachy, bishop of Down, invited a group of hardcore monks from Clairvaux, France, to set up shop in a remote location, where they would act as a sobering influence on the local clergy. Unsurprisingly, the Irish monks didn't get on with their French guests, and the latter soon left for home. Still, the construction of Mellifont continued, and within 10 years, nine more Cistercian monasteries were established. Mellifont was eventually the mother house for 21 lesser monasteries, and at one point, as many as 400 monks lived here. In 1556, after the Dissolution of the Monasteries, a fortified Tudor manor house was built on the site.

There's good picnicking next to the rushing stream. The visitor centre describes monastic life in detail.

Monasterboice: A Most Ancient Site
Early Christian Ruins

Crowing ravens lend an eerie atmosphere to **Monasterboice**, an intriguing monastic site down a leafy lane in sweeping farmland. Here you'll find a cemetery, two ancient church ruins, one of the finest and tallest round towers in Ireland, and two of the most important high crosses.

AT THE RACES

It's a singular event in the Irish horse racing calendar: for one day in early September, bookies, punters and jockeys assemble on the beach for the **Laytown Races**, the only organised race run on sand. It was first held in 1868 and was organised as a side event to coincide with a sailing regatta. By the turn of the 20th century, however, the race overtook the regatta in terms of importance, and today the meet attracts more than 5000 racing aficionados. Until 1995, the race could be as long as 5km, but these days, it's run over no more than six furlongs (1.2km).

Laytown is 11.5km southeast of Drogheda, just off the M1 motorway.

Note that horse racing is of concern to animal welfare activists due to concerns around the horses' safety.

WHERE TO STAY AROUND CARLINGFORD

Carlingford House
This stately 1844 manor house achieves the perfect balance of old-world character and contemporary comfort. €€

Ghan House
An 18th-century Georgian house with 12 exquisitely decorated rooms. The restaurant is superb. €€€

Belvedere House
An excellent deal, this lovely B&B has seven modern and cosy rooms with antique furniture. €€

Carlingford Adventure Centre

FRESH OUT OF THE OVEN

Brothers John and Ollie O'Neill know a thing or two about baking bread. They are the fifth generation of bakers in the family-owned **O'Neills Bakery** in Annagassan village, where breads, cakes and buns are sold warm from the ovens (one of which is more than a century old). They don't use any preservatives, and all of their breads are made from a recipe handed down by their great-grandfather. If you knock at the door around the side of the building, one of the bakers will let you in, and you can choose from their wide selection of breads, tasty cakes and fluffy rolls.

The original monastic settlement is said to have been founded in the 5th or 6th century by St Buithe, a follower of St Patrick, although the site probably had pre-Christian significance. St Buithe's name somehow got converted to Boyne, and the river is named after him. An invading Viking force took over the settlement in 968, only to be comprehensively expelled by Donal, the Irish high king of Tara, who killed at least 300 Vikings in the process.

The high crosses of Monasterboice are superb examples of Celtic art. The crosses had an important didactic use, bringing the gospels alive for the uneducated, and they were probably brightly painted originally, although all traces of colour have long disappeared.

The cross near the entrance is known as **Muiredach's Cross**, named after a 10th-century abbot. The western face relates to the New Testament, and from the bottom, it depicts the arrest of Christ, Doubting Thomas, Christ giving a key to St Peter, the Crucifixion, and Moses praying with Aaron and Hur.

WHERE TO EAT AROUND CARLINGFORD

Ghan House
Classic multicourse menus (no à la carte) make this the best spot in the area. €€€

Bay Tree
Simple, stylishly presented dishes made from seasonal locally sourced ingredients. €€

PJ O'Hare's
Hearty main courses at this popular pub include pies and tapas-style dishes. €€

The **West Cross** is near the round tower and stands 6.5m high, making it one of the tallest high crosses in Ireland. It's much more weathered, especially at the base, and only a dozen or so of its 50 panels are still legible. The more distinguishable ones on the eastern face include David killing a lion and a bear.

A third, simpler cross in the northeastern corner of the compound is believed to have been smashed by Cromwell's forces and has only a few straightforward carvings. This cross makes a great evening silhouette photo, with the round tower in the background.

The **round tower**, minus its cap, is more than 30m tall and stands in a corner of the complex. Records suggest the tower's interior went up in flames in 1097, destroying many valuable manuscripts and other treasures. It's closed to the public.

The site is just off the M1 motorway, about 8km north of Drogheda. Come early or late in the day to avoid the crowds.

Loughs & Medieval Villages
Exploring The Serene Cooley Peninsula

Forested slopes and multihued hills rise above the dark waters of Carlingford Lough, cleaving the picturesque **Cooley Peninsula**. Country lanes wind their scenic way down to deserted stony beaches, while sweeping views stretch north across the water (and border) to the majestic Mourne Mountains.

Amid the medieval ruins and whitewashed houses, the vibrant medieval village of **Carlingford** buzzes with pubs, restaurants and boutiques. Spread around town are the ruins of an 11th-century **castle** and **Dominican friary**, while the photogenic **Tholsel** is the only surviving gate to the original town.

Carlingford is a good centre for all kinds of activities, from sailing and SUP to rock climbing. Check out the **Carlingford Adventure Centre** for details.

About 8km southwest of Carlingford on the R173 is the **Carlingford Brewing Company**, where tours start with a sample and then take you through the brewing process and finish with three more tastings. The post-tour lunch of pizzas wood-fired in-house is a great way to wrap up. Its four brews are named for Carlingford landmarks: Tholsel Blonde, Taaffe's Red, Friary Pale Ale and King John's Stout. Live jazz and blues musicians often play in the evenings.

FITZPATRICK'S

Overflowing inside and out with bric-a-brac – milk cans, lanterns, antlers, church pews, crockery, street signs, barrels, bellows, banknotes and even tables dangling upside down from the ceiling – **Fitzpatrick's** is a locally patronised treasure with fantastic craic. The pub grub is superb; book ahead for lunch or dinner.

The flower-filled, umbrella-shaded beer gardens and petting zoo with resident braying donkeys are positively hopping on sunny days.

Traditional Irish music strikes up frequently in the evening. There are menus for kids and babies.

GETTING AROUND

Buses link Carlingford with Dundalk, which is the nearest major town. Otherwise, you'll need your own wheels. A car ferry travels between Greenore near Carlingford and Greencastle, County Down, Northern Ireland.

TRIM CASTLE

These days, Trim is a fairly ordinary dormitory town on the edge of the wider Dublin conurbation, but it was one of Ireland's most significant medieval settlements, and the primary evidence of that rises high above the town centre. It's hard to imagine nowadays, but a measure of Trim's importance was that Elizabeth I considered building Trinity College here. One student who studied in Trim (at Talbot Castle and St Mary's Abbey) was Dublin-born Arthur Wellesley (1769–1852), the first Duke of Wellington.

Beyond the magnificent castle, Trim's history is everywhere, from atmospheric ruins to streets lined with tiny workers' cottages. There's a handful of good hotels and B&Bs, while Castle St has the best concentration of restaurants. If you're looking for a way to spend an evening, pubs are situated on both banks of the River Boyne. Look out for Brú Brewery's craft beers, made in Trim.

TOP TIP

Trim's tourist office is in the old town hall building next to the castle. It has a handy tourist trail map covering all the local sights. It also has a cafe and genealogy centre. To explore your ancestry, make an appointment in advance.

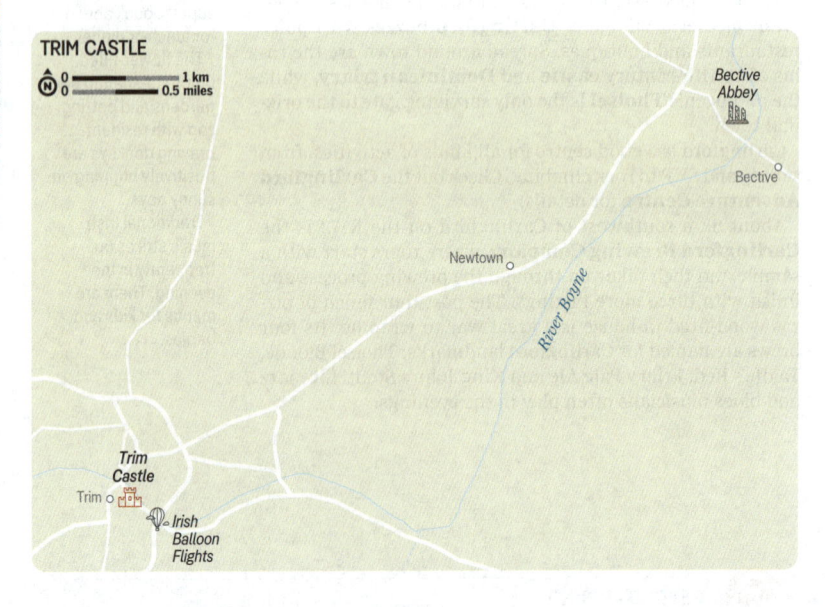

The Ultimate Fortification
Ireland's Mightiest Norman Castle

If you need proof that medieval castles were built to last, the monumental three-storey keep of **Trim Castle** is it. It was Ireland's largest fortification, founded by Hugh de Lacy in 1173, destroyed within a year by Ruaidrí Ua Conchobair (Ireland's last high king), rebuilt around 1200 and hardly modified since. The cruciform-shaped tower is massive. Its 20 sides were protected by a ditch, curtain wall and water-filled moat that made it virtually impregnable.

The castle is often referred to as King John's Castle, after a 1210 visit by King John (of Robin Hood fame). In 1399, Richard II stayed here just before he was deposed by Henry Bolingbroke, later Henry IV. Richard famously left Henry's two sons at Trim Castle when he returned to negotiate with their father; one of those was Prince Hal, the future Henry V.

The engaging tour takes you to the battlements at the top, from where you can imagine being a 17th-century defender fighting off Cromwell's attacks. (It didn't go well, as Cromwell took the castle in 1649.)

Besides playing a central role in a chunk of British and Irish history, Trim Castle stood in for both Edinburgh Castle and the Tower of London in 1996's *Braveheart*.

Cistercian Remains
A Beautifully Preserved Abbey

Trim's medieval past is also evidenced by the extraordinarily preserved yet little-visited ruins of Cistercian **Bective Abbey**. Founded by Murchadh O'Melaghin, King of Meath, in 1147, the abbey was confiscated by Henry VIII between 1536 and 1541 to fund his military campaign. The evocative ruins are free to visit and are open around the clock.

Bective Abbey

TRIM FROM ABOVE

Float over patchwork fields, ruins, castles and churches aboard a hot-air balloon with Trim-based **Irish Balloon Flights** (balloons.ie). The meeting point is the car park of the Knightsbrook Hotel on Dublin Rd, 2.5km southeast of Trim's centre. Schedules and launch locations vary according to weather conditions. Flights last an hour, followed by champagne or soft drinks. Kids must be eight or older.

GETTING AROUND

Bus Éireann links Trim with Dublin (1¼ hours, hourly) and Drogheda (1¼ hours, hourly).

Beyond Trim Castle

Not far from Trim is a site of ancient significance and another rooted very much in modern entertainment.

The area around Trim is a mix of rolling fields and farmland between villages and townlands whose lifeblood are the ballooning residential estates built to house a growing population.

A few kilometres east of Trim is one of Ireland's most sacred sites, Tara, home of druids and Celtic high kings. But it too has been threatened by the needs of expanding suburbs, with a motorway running alongside its eastern edges.

To the south, in between the blossoming towns of Dunshaughlin and Ratoath, is Emerald Park, Ireland's version of the USA's Six Flags or the UK's Alton Towers amusement parks, albeit on a much smaller scale. Despite its size, it's immensely popular and fun.

TOP TIP

Atop Cormac's House is the Stone of Destiny, said to be the inauguration stone of the high kings.

Hill of Tara

Mount of the Hostages

Sacred Tara
Ireland's Most Important Ancient Site

Free to visit and always open, the **Hill of Tara** is Ireland's most sacred stretch of turf, occupying a place at the heart of Irish history, legend and folklore. It was the home of the mystical druids, the priest-rulers of ancient Ireland who practised their particular form of Celtic paganism under the watchful gaze of the all-powerful goddess Maeve (Medbh). Later it was the ceremonial capital of the high kings, all 142 of them, who ruled until the arrival of Christianity in the 5th century. It is also one of the most important ancient sites in Europe, with a Stone Age passage tomb and prehistoric burial mounds that date back 5000 years.

Although its historic and folkloric significance is immense, little remains other than humps and mounds on the hill. The small **visitor centre** has a 20-minute film explaining the site, but you'll need a good imagination to visualise how it might have looked at its zenith.

Tara's Protestant church grounds and graveyard spill onto the remains of the **Rath of the Synods**, a triple-ringed fort where some of St Patrick's early meetings (synods) supposedly took place. South of the church is the Royal Enclosure, a large oval Iron Age hill fort, 315m in diameter and surrounded by a bank and ditch cut through solid rock under the soil. Inside are several smaller earthworks: the **Mound of the Hostages** (the oldest part of Tara; closed to the public); **Royal Seat**, a ring fort with a house site; and **Cormac's House**, a barrow (burial mound) in the side of the circular bank.

EMERALD PARK

Just off the M2 motorway, Emerald Park is an incredibly popular amusement park that includes Europe's largest wooden inverted roller coaster (named after legendary hero Cúchulainn), a 5D cinema (yes, 5D), a high-speed spinning Rotator and the stomach-churning Air Race ride. Flight School and Dino Ride are family-friendly coasters, while the Viking Voyage is a water flume ride.

There's also a zoo, rock climbing, a zip line and a fantastic playground.

You might still hear the park referred to as Tayto Park because until 2023 its title sponsor was the producer of the much-loved Irish potato crisp.

GETTING AROUND

Tara's eastern edge pushes up against the M3 motorway. If you're visiting Tara by bus (there is an hourly service from Dublin and Drogheda to Trim), ask the driver to drop you off at Tara Cross.

COUNTY CAVAN

County Cavan is a remote paradise for lovers of outdoor pursuits, especially of the watery variety. Boaters and anglers will find a slice of heaven in the 'Lake Country' (Cavan's nickname) and supposedly there's a lake for every day of the year (including leap years). Among the lakes is a gentle landscape of meandering streams, bogs and drumlins. Spectacular walking trails wind through the wild Cuilcagh Mountains, which are the source of the 300km River Shannon.

The area has an intricate history. Magh Sleacht, a plain near the border village of Ballyconnell, was an important druidic centre in the 5th century when St Patrick was busy converting the pagan Irish to Christianity, and the area is still littered with tombs, standing stones and stone circles dating from this time.

Cavan's lakes create a tangled knot of narrow, twisting roads. Take your time and enjoy the views that appear unexpectedly around each bend.

TOP TIP

While Cavan town has places to stay, more charming options are located in smaller villages and rural areas. In these villages, you'll also find extraordinary culinary experiences, as they're home to fantastic restaurants run by some of the best chefs in Ireland.

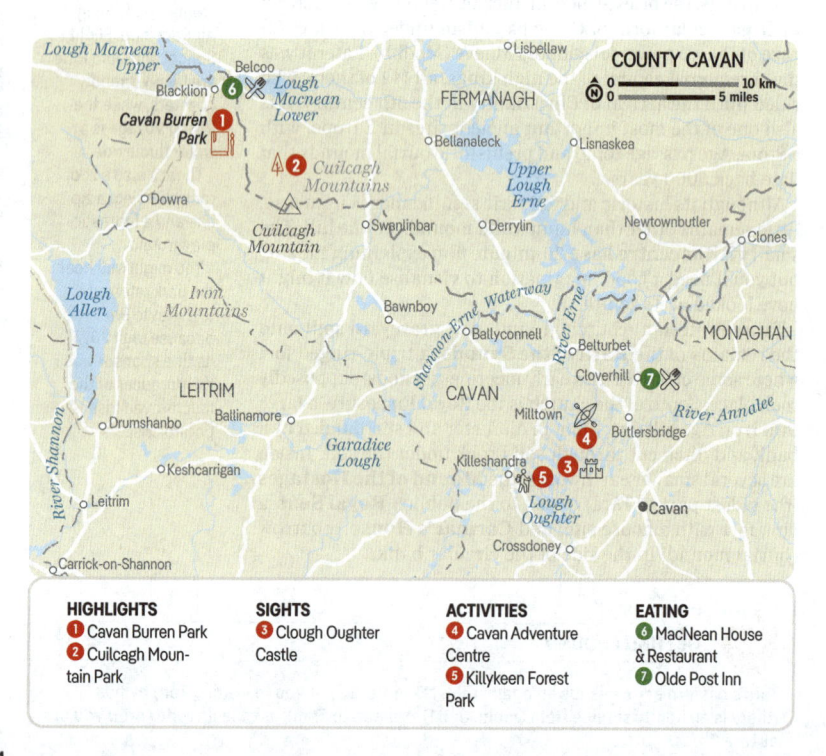

HIGHLIGHTS
1. Cavan Burren Park
2. Cuilcagh Mountain Park

SIGHTS
3. Clough Oughter Castle

ACTIVITIES
4. Cavan Adventure Centre
5. Killykeen Forest Park

EATING
6. MacNean House & Restaurant
7. Olde Post Inn

Cuilcagh Mountain Park

> **MARBLE ARCH CAVES**
>
> The Cuilcagh Mountain Park visitor centre and the park's most high-profile attraction, the Marble Arch Caves, lie over the border from Blacklion in County Fermanagh (p557).

Borderline Wonders
A Trans-National Geopark

The border between the Republic and Northern Ireland runs along the ridge of Cuilcagh Mountain, the distinctive tabletop summit of **Cuilcagh Mountain Park**, the world's first cross-border geopark. Its lower slopes are protected peatland habitats, while the upper slopes have dramatic sweeping cliffs.

Just 3km south of Blacklion, within the Cuilcagh Mountain Park and traversed by the **Cavan Way** walking route, the otherworldly **Cavan Burren Park** is the main draw. This megalithic site was identified in the 1870s but farmed until the 1950s and only established as an official site in 2014. Highlights include a promontory fort circa 500 BCE and the Giant's Grave wedge tomb from 2500 BCE. An unstaffed information shed has interpretive panels.

Forests & Loughs
A Watery Wonderland

Sprawling over 240 hectares, **Killykeen Forest Park**, 12km northwest of Cavan, has various nature trails that lead through the woods and along the shore of Lough Oughter, which is popular with anglers.

Many of the low overgrown islands in the lake were *crannógs* (fortified, artificial islands). The most spectacular is home to **Clough Oughter Castle**, a 13th-century circular tower perched on a tiny speck of land. It was used as a lonely prison and then as a stronghold by rebel leader Owen Roe O'Neill before being destroyed by Cromwell's army in 1653. The castle lies out of reach over the water, but you can get there by canoe on a trip organised by **Cavan Adventure Centre**. The outfit rents out canoes and kayaks and runs tours of the local waterways, including Killykeen Forest Park.

CAVAN CUISINE

County Cavan has two of the best dining experiences in all of Ireland.

Award-winning TV chef Neven Maguire grew up in Blacklion, right on the border with Northern Ireland. He has turned his gorgeous village house into the superb **MacNean House and Restaurant**, where bookings must be made months in advance to sample his exemplary cuisine.

The lovely little village of Cloverhill, 4km north of Butlersbridge, is best known for the award-winning **Olde Post Inn**, a gastronomic restaurant housed in an 1884 former post office. Acclaimed chef Gearoid Lynch's contemporary cuisine is based on traditional ingredients, such as monkfish, salmon, duck and lamb, and vegetarian and gluten-free options are available.

> **GETTING AROUND**
>
> Cavan town is the main hub for buses. The county is not served by train.

Beyond County Cavan

Celebrate the life and poetry of Patrick Kavanagh and admire the delicate lace of Carrickmacross.

County Cavan's neighbour to the east is Monaghan, whose undulating landscape is known for its tiny rounded hills that resemble bubbles in badly pasted wallpaper. Known as drumlins, these bumps are the result of debris left by retreating glaciers during the last Ice Age. But to many Irish, Monaghan is synonymous with the poet Patrick Kavanagh, whose work was influenced by the landscape and is celebrated in a wonderful centre in his birthplace of Iniskeen.

In the early 19th century, lacemaking became an important facet of the local economy. Carrickmacross was one of the key centres of the industry, and you can still see the fine needlework on display.

TOP TIP

Monaghan town has the biggest concentration of places to eat, and the farmers market takes place on Friday.

Patrick Kavanagh memorial, Iniskeen

Inniskeen

The Life of the Poet
Centre Dedicated To Patrick Kavanagh

About 12km northeast of Carrickmacross, the small village of **Inniskeen** is typical of so many rural settlements in this part of Ireland. However, this largely farming community is forever associated with the life and work of its best-known son, the poet Patrick Kavanagh (1904-67), who was born and raised here.

Kavanagh's long work *The Great Hunger* (1942) blasted away the earlier clichés of Anglo-Irish verse and revealed Ireland's poor farming communities as half-starved, broken-backed and sexually repressed. One of his most famous poems, 'Stony Grey Soil' (1943), sticks to the theme and expresses frustration and anger at the Monaghan landscape that 'burgled his bank of youth' and 'clogged the feet of [his] boyhood'.

ON RAGLAN ROAD

One of Kavanagh's best-known poems, 'On Raglan Road' (1946), is an ode to his then-girlfriend Hilda and is centred on the first time he saw her on Dublin's Raglan Rd.

Kavanagh was friendly with Luke Kelly, a member of the popular folk group The Dubliners, and one night over drinks, Kelly suggested putting the poem to the tune of a traditional Irish air, 'The Dawning of the Day'. The result is one of the most beautiful and popular ballads of the Irish folk lexicon, performed by countless singers including Van Morrison, Mark Knopfler, Billy Bragg and Sinéad O'Connor; Kelly's original is still the best.

WHERE TO STAY IN MONAGHAN

Castle Leslie
Magnificent Victorian pile 11km northeast of Monaghan town, with 20 characterful rooms. €€€

Hilton Park
A gorgeous 18th-century country-house retreat with six spacious rooms, all with original furnishings. €€€

Shirley Arms
Good family-run hotel in the centre of Carrickmacross with contemporary rooms. €€

Carrickmacross lace

MONAGHAN BLUES

For more than a quarter of a century, the annual **Harvest Blues Festival** (harvestblues.ie) has put Monaghan town on the musical map. The best festival of its genre is a four-day, three-night extravaganza that takes place in early September in venues throughout the town and on a variety of stages. The mix of local, national and international acts includes some of the top soul and blues artists around, including the perennially popular Derry-born Rob Strong.

Previous performers have included Mud Morganfield (Muddy Waters' son), Duke Robillard and Gerry McEvoy – a longtime member of Rory Gallagher's band. In 2023, star performers were Canadian Anthony Gomes and The Soul Movers from Argentina.

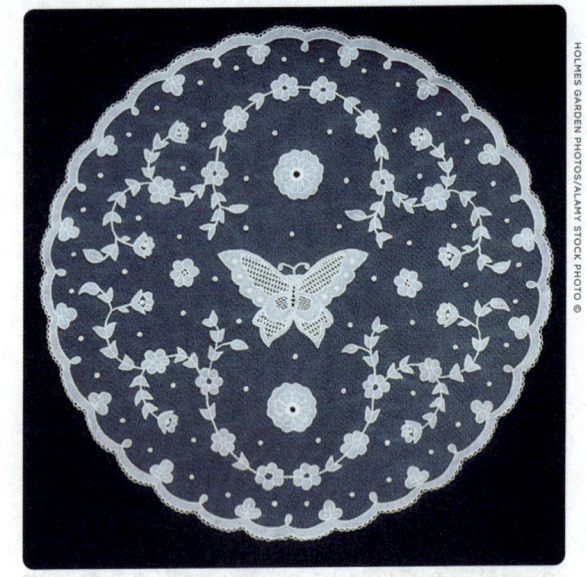

The village's old parish church where Kavanagh was baptised is now the **Patrick Kavanagh Centre**, whose staff have a passion for his life and work that is contagious. Download a self-guided literary tour of the village and the picturesque surrounding countryside (5.6km in all) from the website (patrickkavanaghcentre.com). The centre hosts events including a Writers' Weekend in late July/early August.

Delicate Lace
The Home Of Lacemaking

Carrickmacross was first settled by early English and Scottish Planters, and its broad main street is flanked by elegant Georgian houses with gorgeous poster-paint-coloured facades. It's most famous as the home of delicate Carrickmacross lace, an industry revived in 1871 by the St Louis nuns.

In the town's former cattle yards, a local cooperative runs the thimble-sized **Carrickmacross Lace Gallery**, where you can see lacemaking demonstrations and check out exquisite designs. Designs are appliquéd on organza using thick thread and close stitches and then embellished with a variety of point stitches, guipure, pops and the lace's distinctive loop edge. Lacemakers take commissions, and you can purchase delicate pieces made into fridge magnets, bookmarks and more.

Unassuming Monaghan
Low-Key County Town

It may be the county town, but Monaghan's residents live their lives utterly unaffected by tourism. It's an enjoyable place to wander and admire the elegant 18th- and 19th-century limestone buildings. Many buildings have gently rounded corners, an unusual architectural feature in Ireland.

More than 70,000 artefacts from the Stone Age to modern times are housed at the excellent **Monaghan County Museum**. Its crowning glory is the 14th-century Cross of Clogher, an oak altar cross encased in decorative bronze panels. Other impressive finds include the Lisdrumturk and Altartate Cauldrons, medieval *crannóg* artefacts, and some frightening knuckle-dusters and cudgels relating to the border with the North.

About 3km southwest of town is **Rossmore Forest Park**, once part of the barony of Rossmore. The park has three looped walks and the remains of the 19th-century castle once owned by the Rossmores. Look out for giant redwoods, a yew avenue and Iron Age tombs. It's also home to badgers, foxes, pygmy shrews, hedgehogs, otters and five of Ireland's seven bat species.

Monaghan town

GETTING AROUND

Monaghan town and Carrickmacross are well served by bus, but elsewhere, you'll need your own wheels. No trains go to County Monaghan.

BELFAST
CHARACTERFUL PORT CITY

A former industrial boom town scarred by sectarian conflict, Belfast has transformed into a modern city with a thriving cultural life and arts scene.

With the recent marking of the 25-year anniversary of the Good Friday Agreement of 1998, it was possible to see just how much Belfast has changed over the intervening decades. Though political tensions remain, the years of paramilitary campaigns and sectarian violence have been left in the past.

The ethnic makeup of Belfast is also changing. The 2021 census showed ethnic minorities now make up 7% of Belfast's population of 345,000, an increase from 3% in 2011. Nearly half (49%) of Belfast's population was raised Catholic, while those raised Protestant account for 36%. The nationalist party Sinn Féin is now the largest party in both the Belfast City Council and the Northern Ireland Assembly. However, there is a growing middle ground of voters who identify as neither unionist or nationalist.

The trauma of the Troubles has left scars, but an atmosphere of determined optimism has prevailed, allowing space for culture and the arts to thrive. In 2021 Belfast was named a Unesco City of Music in recognition of its musical heritage. The 1792 Belfast Harp Festival was perhaps the most important event in the history of Irish music, since it served to document traditional harp music that might otherwise have been lost. Years later, the violence and sectarianism of everyday life in 1970s Belfast were fertile ground for an emerging punk rock music scene, which provided an outlet for undercurrents of rage and disaffection in the city. The story of Belfast's punk scene is told in the 2013 film *Good Vibrations*. The city also has a packed programme of arts festivals throughout the year, including the Belfast International Arts Festival in October.

Over recent years, Belfast has also emerged as a major film and TV production destination. Titanic Studios was used to film HBO's blockbuster series *Game of Thrones*. Since then, the filming of further TV series and movies has helped rebrand Belfast as a 21st-century city and provided a boost to the local economy.

But history is rarely far from mind in Belfast. The murals of West Belfast reflect issues of national identity at the root of the conflict. Meanwhile, no visitor to Belfast leaves without learning something about the *Titanic*.

THE MAIN AREAS

CITY CENTRE
Shopping and architecture.
p466

CATHEDRAL QUARTER
Culture and nightlife. **p474**

TITANIC QUARTER & EAST BELFAST
Historic shipyards. **p481**

QUEEN'S QUARTER & SOUTH BELFAST
Leafy campus and riverside nature.
p488

WEST & NORTH BELFAST
Community culture and hilltop walks. **p495**

Above: Custom House (p476); left: Domed ceiling, Belfast City Hall (p468)

BELFAST | THE GUIDE

Find Your Way

With the landmarks of the hills to the north and west and the iconic yellow gantry cranes to the east, Belfast is small and easy to navigate. The city centre, Cathedral Quarter and Titanic Quarter are best tackled on foot, while buses and trains link the centre with neighbourhoods further afield.

FROM THE AIRPORT

Belfast has two airports. Most flights arrive in Belfast International, 30km northwest of the city centre and a 40-minute journey by bus or car. George Best City Airport is a smaller airport 6km and around 10 minutes' drive east of the city centre.

Belfast Lough

Holywood

River Lagan

🏛 Titanic Belfast

Shore Rd

Bussel Rd

Cave Hill Country Park

⛰ Cave Hill

ANTRIM

Antrim Rd

West & North Belfast

p495

Crumlin Rd

0 — 1 mile
0 — 2 km

462

THE GUIDE

BELFAST

Cathedral Quarter p474

City Centre p466

Queen's Quarter & South Belfast p488

Titanic Quarter & East Belfast p481

BICYCLE

The city's cycle network includes a number of traffic-free stretches. Cycling is quick and convenient, but frequent rain showers can put a dampener on things. Bikes can be rented through the city's bike-share scheme Belfast Bikes.

TRAIN

Trains are a useful way to reach certain suburbs to the north, south and east of the city centre, and for day trips to the coast. The beach at Holywood, County Down, is a 10-minute train ride east from Belfast city centre.

BUS

Metro and Glider buses fan out across the city from the central hub at Donegall Sq. During the day, buses are a convenient way to get around, but most routes do not operate between around 11pm and 6am.

463

Plan Your Days

Check the weather forecast, then plan a day of indoor market grazing and museum visits, or long walks through the Cathedral Quarter, city centre or Titanic Quarter.

St George's Market (p473)

Day 1

Morning
- If it's Friday, Saturday or Sunday, head to **St George's Market** (p473), where you can browse the stalls and eat breakfast or brunch on the go.

Afternoon
- Next, see more Victorian architecture on a city centre **walking tour** (p472), timing your wander to take in a guided tour of **City Hall** (p468). Finish with a pint of Guinness or a gin and tonic in the **Crown Liquor Saloon** (p469).

Evening
- Book tickets in advance to catch a performance at the **Grand Opera House** (p469) before splashing out on a meal at Michelin-starred **OX** (p493) or **Deanes EIPIC** (p493).

You'll Also Want to...
Get out of the city centre and into the neighbourhoods to discover local beauty spots and learn more about Belfast's history.

TAKE A RIVERSIDE WALK
Follow the River Lagan south through the nature-rich **towpath** (p493), with ancient oak trees, butterfly-filled meadows and wildflowers.

EAT AN ULSTER FRY
Head to **Maggie Mays** (p493) to try a traditional local breakfast of eggs, bacon, sausages, potato bread and more.

EXPLORE THE BELFAST HILLS
For breathtaking views, tackle the ascent up **Cave Hill** (p500) or take a hike at **Divis** and **Black Mountain**.

Day 2

Morning
- Start the day at **Titanic Belfast** (p483). Allow several hours to view the multimedia exhibition and to explore *SS Nomadic*.

Afternoon
- Have lunch at **Drawing Office Two** (p487), then take a walk around **Titanic Quarter** (p486), finishing with a tour and tasting at **Titanic Distillers** (p485).

Evening
- Head to Cathedral Quarter for a cocktail (p480) followed by dinner at **Muddlers Club** (p478) or a pizza in the beer garden at the **Sunflower** (p480). Check listings or ask around to find live music, comedy or storytelling events in the neighbourhood.

Day 3

Morning
- Have breakfast at **Established Coffee** (p479) or **Neighbourhood Cafe** (p479) before exploring the street art of the **Cathedral Quarter** (p478) and the **Entries** (p471). Spend the rest of the morning browsing **independent stores** (p473).

Afternoon
- Take the bus to Queen's Quarter and head straight to **Ulster Museum** (p491) to view the treasure-filled galleries. Then take a walk through **Botanic Gardens** (p490), stopping to look inside the Palm House and Tropical Ravine greenhouses.

Evening
- Have dinner in Queen's Quarter at **Bo Tree Kitchen** (p494) or **A Peculiar Tea** (p493), then join students on the dance floor at the **Limelight** (p494).

VISIT A NOTORIOUS FORMER JAIL
Crumlin Road Gaol (p498) is a window into Belfast's dark history, from the Victorian era through to the Troubles.

CYCLE THE TOWPATH OR GREENWAY
Hire a bike and explore the countryside via the off-road cycle paths at **Lagan Towpath** (p493) and **Comber Greenway** (p487).

SEE THE MURALS OF WEST BELFAST
Belfast's political and sectarian divisions are reflected in the murals painted to declare allegiances and stake-out territory; see them in **West Belfast** (p499).

SAMPLE BELFAST'S BEST BEER
Head to East Belfast to try the lagers and ales at **Boundary Brewing** (p487), then explore **Banana Block** (p487).

CITY CENTRE

SHOPPING AND ARCHITECTURE

By day, the city centre bustles with shoppers and office workers. High-street chains and sleek malls dominate the shopping district here, but there are also independent stores selling quality arts and crafts and secondhand goods. At night, the area's bars and restaurants fill with drinkers and diners; options range from market-stall snacks to Michelin-starred fine dining.

The neighbourhood's architecture tells the story of its past. Grand Victorian buildings are the legacy of the prosperous shipbuilding and linen-trading days: the Crown Liquor Saloon, Grand Opera House, St George's Market and City Hall were all built during that time. Blocks constructed in the 1970s and 1980s bear witness to the damage done by bombs during the Troubles, but the ambitious architecture of new buildings such as the Grand Central Hotel speaks of a new period of optimism in the city.

TOP TIP

For views of the city centre and beyond, head to the dome in Victoria Square shopping mall. The free viewing platform offers an outlook through the glazed dome to the Belfast skyline, including landmarks such as the Albert Clock, City Hall, Samson and Goliath (the iconic yellow Harland & Wolff gantry cranes) and the Belfast hills.

City Hall (p468)

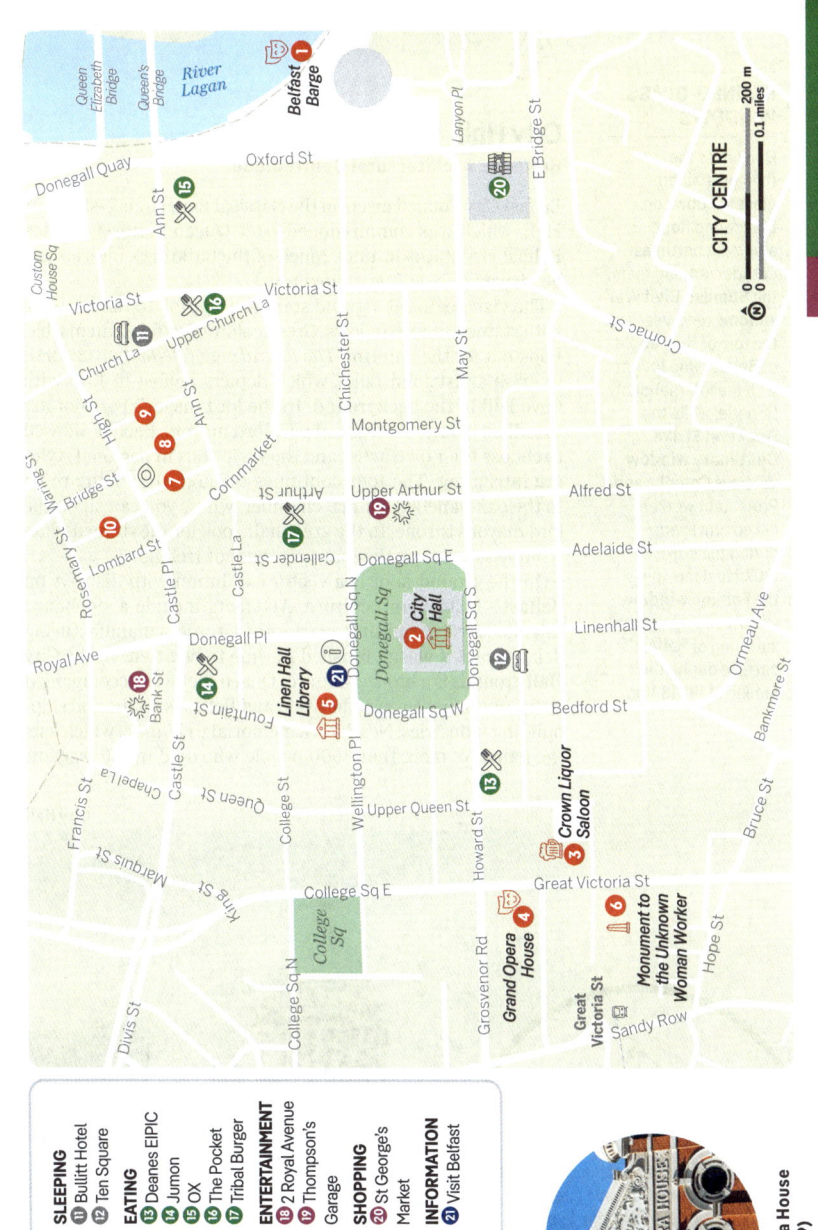

BELFAST CITY CENTRE

HIGHLIGHTS
1. Belfast Barge
2. City Hall
3. Crown Liquor Saloon
4. Grand Opera House
5. Linen Hall Library
6. Monument to the Unknown Woman Worker

SIGHTS
7. Crown Entry
8. Joy's Entry
9. Pottinger's Entry
10. Winecellar Entry

SLEEPING
11. Bullitt Hotel
12. Ten Square

EATING
13. Deanes EIPIC
14. Jumon
15. OX
16. The Pocket
17. Tribal Burger

ENTERTAINMENT
18. 2 Royal Avenue
19. Thompson's Garage

SHOPPING
20. St George's Market

INFORMATION
21. Visit Belfast

Grand Opera House (p469)

STAINED-GLASS WINDOWS

Don't miss the themed stained-glass windows on the ground floor, along the northeast corridor. Among them, the **Spanish Civil War window** recognises the role of the people of Belfast who fought with the International Brigade, while the **Dockers' Strike Centenary window** portrays Catholic and Protestant workers linked arm in arm during the strike of 1907. Most moving is the **Famine window**, which remembers the suffering of Belfast's citizens during the famine of the 1840s.

City Hall
Belfast's Architectural Centrepiece

Belfast City Council meets in the classical Renaissance-style City Hall, which was commissioned after Queen Victoria granted Belfast city status in 1888. Much of the building's interior can be viewed during free guided tours.

The visit begins at a grand staircase leading to the rotunda, with stained-glass windows, Greek columns and Italian marble. Look out for the painting *The Founding of Belfast, 1613* (1951) by Irish artist John Luke, which depicts Belfast in 1613 with Cave Hill in the background. In the lord mayor's corridor are the idiosyncratic portraits of past lord mayors. Each is allowed to choose their own artist and the variations in personal styles are intriguing. The tour continues through the robing room to the oak-panelled council chamber, where you can sit on the lord mayor's throne. In the great hall, look for the stained-glass windows depicting the four provinces of Ireland.

On the ground floor is a visitor exhibition with displays on Belfast's history and culture. Artefacts include a sideboard intended for the captain's quarters of *Titanic*; a manufacturing delay meant it wasn't finished in time to be fitted. In the City Hall grounds is a bronze statue of Queen Victoria, accompanied by figures representing education and Belfast's textile and ship-building industries. Nearby is a memorial to *Titanic*, which lists the names of more than 1500 people who died in the tragedy.

City Hall

VICTORIAN BELFAST

City Hall was just one of many buildings to go up during Belfast's late-19th-century industrial boom. Explore more Victorian architecture in the city centre on a walking tour (p472).

Crown Liquor Saloon
Flamboyantly Decorated Gin Palace

Not only is the **Crown** a historical monument and famous Belfast landmark, but it is also a pub in which you can admire the intricate interior as you drink. Located opposite the train station and Grand Opera House, the Crown was refurbished in the late 19th century to appeal to commuters and theatregoers.

The exterior is decorated with ornate tiles and has a mosaic of a crown on the pavement at the bar's entrance. The interior is a maximalist expression of coloured glass, marble, ceramics, mirrors and mahogany.

Along one side of the pub is a long bar, and on the other is a row of wooden snugs, complete with panelled doors that bolt closed for privacy. These cosy booths still have gunmetal plates, originally used for striking matches, and bells that once allowed drinkers to order without leaving their seats. Atmospheric gas-lamp lighting and a decorative carved ceiling add to the sense of history.

Crown Liquor Saloon

Grand Opera House
Elaborate Victorian Theatre

Built in 1895, the **Grand Opera House** is one of Belfast's great Victorian landmarks. The best way to experience the building's grandeur is to attend a performance; the Opera House hosts visiting drama, ballet, opera, dance and musical companies, but you'll need to buy tickets in advance (goh.co.uk).

Otherwise the theatre's interior can be seen on a guided tour. These take in the inner workings of the theatre and offer a glimpse backstage, as well as an opportunity to view the swirling wood and plaster work, fancy gilt work, painted ceiling panels and carved elephant heads of the interior.

Grand Opera House

Monument to the Unknown Woman Worker

Monument to the Unknown Woman Worker

Monument to the Unknown Woman Worker
Public Art Expressing Female Solidarity

Outside Great Northern Mall on Great Victoria St, look for a bronze sculpture of two women, which is easily missed amid the throng of passersby. Created in 1992, the piece by Louise Walsh references inequalities for women in the home and workplace. Look closely to see details such as a typewriter on the stomach and a telephone on the chest of one woman, denoting women in the workforce, and a baby's bottle and laundry basket on the body of the other, representing domestic labour.

Belfast Barge
Floating Arts Centre

Moored at Lanyon Quay on the River Lagan, this **barge** hosts a range of events, from cinema clubs and family days to comedy nights and concerts. The venue is operated by the charity Lagan Legacy, which was set up to preserve artefacts rescued from Belfast's shipyards as they were being demolished. Below deck, the barge houses a museum that tells the story of the city's maritime and industrial history, and is an archive for photographs and audiovisual recordings of the personal stories of Belfast's former dockers and shipbuilders.

Linen Hall Library

Linen Hall Library
Belfast's Oldest Library

The **Linen Hall Library** was established in 1788 by members of the United Irishmen, and moved to its current location in a former linen warehouse a decade later. It houses an important Irish, local studies and political collection, including most of what has been written about Northern Irish politics since the 1960s.

Inside, take a look at the Troubled Images exhibition, a collection of iconic political posters that tells the story of Northern Ireland's sectarian conflict and peace process in the late 20th century. These visual representations show how the political landscape and attitudes towards armed conflict evolved in the 1970s, '80s and '90s.

White's Tavern

MORE IN CITY CENTRE

Explore the Entries
Narrow Alleyways

Amid the city centre bustle, don't miss these narrow alleyways. They were once commercial and residential thoroughfares connecting Ann St and Waring St with High St, where the River Farset flowed. Since 1848, the river has been contained by underground tunnels. As part of the **Belfast Entries Project**, a number of street artists were commissioned to brighten the alleyways with pieces reflecting the area's people, culture and history.

On **Pottinger's Entry** is the Morning Star, a family-run pub dating from 1810. Outside, look for street art by Nomad Clan depicting pelicans as seen on the Pottinger family crest. On **Winecellar Entry** is White's Tavern, Belfast's oldest tavern. Nearby is a piece by street artist Emic inspired by the poem 'Belfast Confetti' by Ciaran Carson. **Joy's Entry** is named after Francis Joy, who founded the *Belfast News Letter* in 1737; look for the statue of his grandson Henry Joy McCracken, the United Irishman who was jailed here in 1798. **Crown Entry** is where the Society of United Irishmen was founded in 1791 by Wolfe Tone; street art here depicts a salmon, a reference to the River Farset.

OLAUDAH EQUIANO & THE UNITED IRISHMEN

At the High St end of Joy's Entry, a piece by street artist Dreph depicts Olaudah Equiano, a Black abolitionist who visited Belfast and met with the United Irishmen. Born in Africa, Equiano was kidnapped and enslaved as a child. After purchasing his freedom in London he became a writer and abolitionist. In 1791 he travelled to Ireland to oversee the production and promotion of his book in which he shared his experiences of slavery.

While in Belfast, Equiano stayed with Samuel Neilson, one of the founders of the Society of United Irishmen and their newspaper the *Northern Star*, which took an abolitionist stance. Influenced by ideas of the French Revolution, the United Irishmen sought religious equality and separation from England.

WHERE TO EAT IN THE CITY CENTRE

Tribal Burger
Industrial-style joint selling burgers, wings and shakes; there's a second branch on Botanic Ave. **£**

The Pocket
In the Flatiron building, the Pocket serves coffee and brunch dishes, including an excellent Ulster Fry. **£**

Jumon
Vegan and vegetarian southeast Asian fusion dishes (ramon, jackfruit curry, dumplings) and cocktails. **££**

VIEW VICTORIAN BELFAST

Many of Belfast's grandest buildings date back to the Victorian era, when industry was booming and the town was bestowed with city status. This walking tour takes in some of the city centre's finest Victorian architecture. Start at the elegant, red-brick **1 St George's Market** (p473), built in 1896, and peek inside to see the glazed roof and wrought-iron columns.

From here, walk west along May St and turn right onto Victoria St to reach **2 Bittles Bar**, housed in an unusual 19th-century triangular building. Outside is the **3 Jaffe Memorial Fountain**, a gilded, cast-iron drinking fountain (now dry) that was erected in 1874 by Belfast's only Jewish mayor, Otto Jaffe. Retrace your steps south along Victoria St and turn right onto Chichester St to reach the **4 Garrick**, a pub that's been in operation since 1870. Stop to admire the wood panelling and Victorian tiles inside. Continue west along Chichester St to pass more Victorian architecture, including the **5 Robinson & Cleaver Building**, built in 1874 to house an upmarket department store. First established in 1788, the **6 Linen Hall Library** (p470) is now housed in a former Victorian linen warehouse. Opposite is **7 City Hall** (p468), fronted by a dour statue of Queen Victoria herself. Walk south through the grounds and continue south along Bedford St to reach the **8 Ulster Hall**, a concert venue that opened in 1862.

Walk west along Franklin St and Amelia St, then turn right on Great Victoria St. You are now outside the **9 Crown Liquor Saloon** (p449), a magnificent Victorian gin palace decorated with ornate tiles. On the other side of Great Victoria St is the **10 Grand Opera House** (p449), opened in 1895.

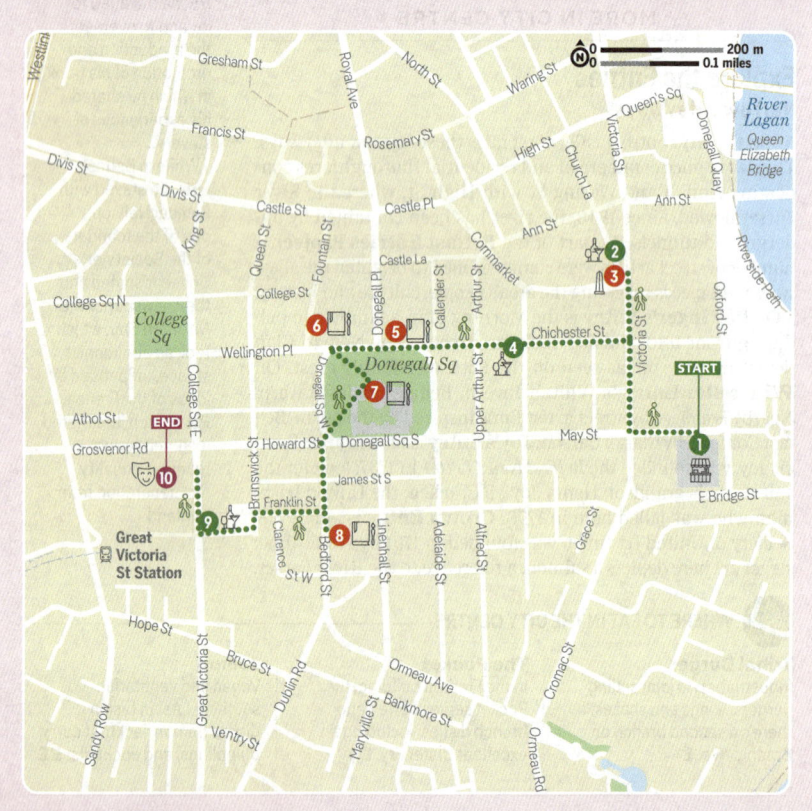

A Morning at St George's Market
Local Food And Crafts

Spending a morning browsing and snacking at **St George's Market** is the perfect way to sample local produce and to shop for artisan crafts and souvenirs. The Victorian-era building hosts three different markets on Friday, Saturday and Sunday mornings and early afternoons (vendors pack up by around 2pm on Friday and 3pm at weekends), though many of the same stalls are open on all three days.

Friday's variety market includes plenty of fresh fish and shellfish from Kilkeel and Portavogie in County Down, as well as locally grown fruit and vegetables, clothes, books and antiques. Saturday's food and craft market has more stalls selling prepared dishes like tapas, curries and vegan pastries, as well as artisan goods such as hand-poured candles and jewellery. Sunday's craft and antiques market has a mix of stalls from the Friday and Saturday markets.

The vendors are mostly the craftspeople, bakers, fishers and farmers who have grown, caught or created what they are selling, and they are happy to chat about their wares. Look out for meat from **Hillstown Farm**, prebiotic foods from **Amberline Preserves** and mushrooms from **Sporeshore**. The egg, bacon and sausage-filled soda farls at the **Belfast Bap Co** are a popular hangover cure, while **Ann's Pantry** sells typical local buns and tray bakes, including fifteens (a sweet snack made with marshmallows, digestive biscuits and coconut). For traditional sweets like rock, honeycomb and nougat, check out **Aunt's Sandra's Candy Factory**. Wash it all down with a flat white from **Drop Hopper Coffee**, or a cup of **Suki Tea**.

Live music adds to the market's buzz; for a calmer, less-stimulating atmosphere, visit during the market quiet hours from 9am to 10am on Friday and Saturday, and 10am to 11am on Sunday. Look out for special themed markets to celebrate Christmas and Halloween.

There has been a market on this site since 1604, making St George's Ireland's oldest continually operating market. The current building dates from 1896.

A TASTE OF BELFAST

From fine dining to market grazing, it's easy to eat well in Belfast. For an entertaining introduction, with plenty of samples, book the Belfast Food Tour with Taste & Tour.

To sample local Irish stew (a comforting bowl of meat and potatoes) or seafood chowder (a creamy broth filled with the flavours of the sea), try White's Tavern (p471). Guinness bread is another local speciality; look for it at St George's Market (p473). For an Ulster Fry (a greasy plate of bacon, eggs, potato bread and more) head to Maggie Mays (p493).

Belfast's history is told through local drinks and animated films during Belfast by the Glass at the Spirit Circle at the National (p480).

WHERE TO STAY IN THE CITY CENTRE & CATHEDRAL QUARTER

Bullitt Hotel
Designed with modern convenience in mind, rooms at the Bullitt have comfy beds and fast wi-fi. **££**

Ten Square
Service is first rate, and rooms are decorated with contemporary art at this stylish Donegall Sq hotel. **££**

Merchant Hotel
Luxury hotel occupying the palatial former Ulster Bank head office in the Cathedral Quarter, with opulent furnishings and a spa. **£££**

CATHEDRAL QUARTER

CULTURE AND NIGHTLIFE

At the heart of Belfast's nightlife are the pubs, bars and clubs of the Cathedral Quarter, a small artsy neighbourhood named for St Anne's Cathedral that is home to recording studios, media companies and dynamic arts venues. Cobbled Hill St comes alive at night; on long summer evenings, the party spills out onto the street, as revellers gather on Commercial Ct, surrounded by colourful street art and a canopy of hanging umbrellas. One of the most successful bands to emerge from Belfast in recent years is Snow Patrol, who played some of their first gigs at the Duke of York pub. On the surrounding blocks are several traditional pubs with regular live music, while the city's gay bars are clustered around Union St in the north of the Cathedral Quarter.

In May the Cathedral Quarter Arts Festival brings music, drama, poetry, street theatre and art to the neighbourhood.

TOP TIP

The Cathedral Quarter is the area around St Anne's Cathedral that merges into the city centre. There is a more commercial feel to the city centre, while the Cathedral Quarter is more artsy and alternative, but it's easy to walk between places and explore both neighbourhoods on the same day, since the whole area is relatively compact.

St Anne's Cathedral (p476)

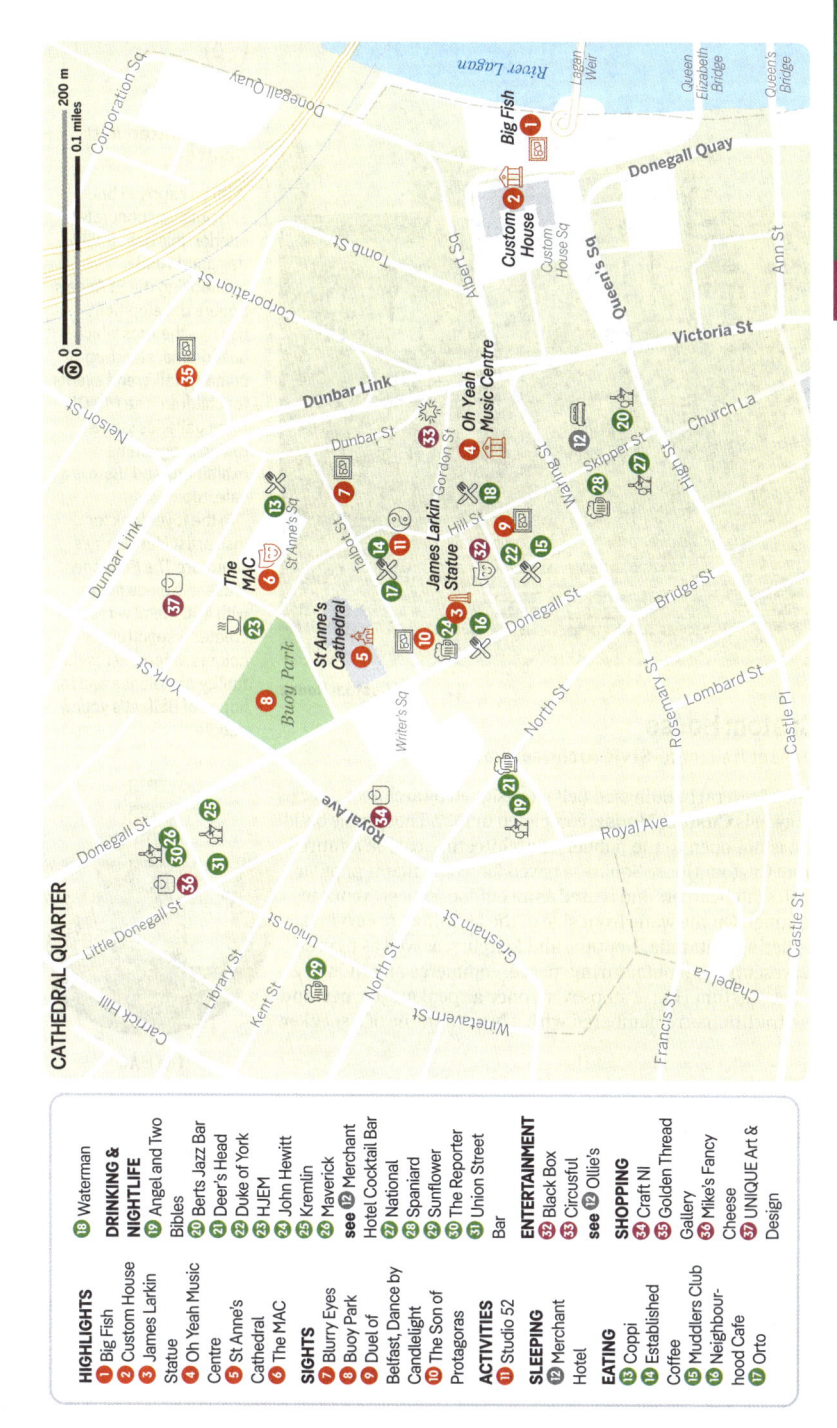

CATHEDRAL QUARTER

HIGHLIGHTS
1. Big Fish
2. Custom House
3. James Larkin Statue
4. Oh Yeah Music Centre
5. St Anne's Cathedral
6. The MAC

SIGHTS
7. Blurry Eyes
8. Buoy Park
9. Duel of Belfast, Dance by Candlelight
10. The Son of Protagoras

ACTIVITIES
11. Studio 52

SLEEPING
12. Merchant Hotel

EATING
13. Coppi
14. Established Coffee
15. Muddlers Club
16. Neighbourhood Cafe
17. Orto
18. Waterman

DRINKING & NIGHTLIFE
19. Angel and Two Bibles
20. Berts Jazz Bar
21. Deer's Head
22. Duke of York
23. HJEM
24. John Hewitt
25. Kremlin
26. Maverick
see 12 Merchant Hotel Cocktail Bar
27. National
28. Spaniard
29. Sunflower
30. The Reporter
31. Union Street Bar

ENTERTAINMENT
32. Black Box
33. Circusful
see 12 Ollie's

SHOPPING
34. Craft NI
35. Golden Thread Gallery
36. Mike's Fancy Cheese
37. UNIQUE Art & Design

Custom House
Elegant Italianate-Style Architecture

One of several buildings in Belfast designed by architect Charles Lanyon is **Custom House**, completed in 1857. Though the building is not open to the public, its architecture can be admired from Custom House Square, a paved forecourt that is popular with skateboarders and is used as an outdoor concert venue in summer. On the waterfront side of the building are carvings depicting Britannia, Neptune and Mercury, as well as figures representing manufacturing, peace, commerce and industry.

The Custom House steps were once a speakers' corner, and the tradition is remembered with a bronze statue of a speaker.

Custom House

The MAC
Metropolitan Arts Centre

With an exposed brick and polished concrete interior, this beautifully designed venue overlooking the St Anne's Square development has two theatres which host drama, stand-up comedy, talks, and events for children. The **MAC**'s three galleries stage a rolling programme of exhibitions and there is a cafe, too.

In the foyer look for Irish artist Mark Garry's sculpture *The Permanent Present*, a piece made with 400 metal wires that creates a spectrum of colours. It represents the futility of violence and the hopes of Belfast's young people.

The MAC

St Anne's Cathedral
Anglican Cathedral With A Striking Spire

St Anne's is the Church of Ireland cathedral for which the neighbourhood is named. The building's most striking feature is its titanium-clad spire, which can also be seen inside the cathedral, where it extends from the nave to emerge through a glass platform in the roof, rising 80m high. The **baptistery** is notable for its Romanesque-style ceiling mosaic of the Creation.

Don't miss the **Titanic pall** (a cloth draped over a coffin), a textile embroidered with some 1500 crosses in memory of those who died in the tragedy. The piece was created in 2012 to mark the centenary of the disaster; the indigo blue colour evokes the night sky under which the ship went down.

James Larkin Statue
Tribute To A Trade Unionist

At the gable end of the Irish Congress of Trade Unions building, on Donegall St Pl, a life-sized bronze statue of James Larkin (1874–1947) recognises the role of the social activist in the promotion of workers' rights. Liverpool-born Larkin, who is depicted with his arms raised and his mouth open as if addressing the masses, is particularly known for his role as an organiser of the Dockers Strike of 1907.

Oh Yeah Music Centre

Big Fish
Ceramic-Tiled Salmon

The 10m-long salmon on Belfast's regenerated Laganside Waterfront is covered with a mosaic of tiles that tell the story of Belfast. The piece was created in 1999 by local artist John Kindness, who selected various motifs to depict the city. Look for detailed architectural drawings of the Grand Opera House and the Albert Clock, the leaning memorial clock tower located nearby. Images of politicians John Hume and David Trimble, and U2's Bono are a reference to a concert held to promote the Good Friday Agreement of 1998. The underbelly of the **fish** is decorated with images of parasites.

Big Fish

Oh Yeah Music Centre
Social Enterprise Supporting Belfast's Musicians

Housed in a converted whiskey warehouse, the **Oh Yeah Music Centre** is a social enterprise that provides rehearsal spaces for musicians as well as home to an exhibition on Northern Ireland's music history. The memorabilia on display includes items related to punk bands the Undertones and Stiff Little Fingers, and from Terri Hooley's Good Vibrations record store. Look out for a vintage sign from Cyprus Avenue, the east Belfast street made famous by Van Morrison. Another prized item is the Fender guitar used by Snow Patrol's Gary Lightbody to write the hit 'Chasing Cars'. Conversations between Snow Patrol and members of the Belfast music industry were the impetus for the launch of the Oh Yeah Music Centre project in 2005.

THE GUIDE

CATHEDRAL QUARTER BELFAST

BELFAST'S LIVE MUSIC SCENE

Dolores of Creative Tours Belfast shares her favourite places to hear live music (@ *creativetoursbelfast*).

Cathedral Quarter
Some of Belfast's best gigs are held at the Black Box (p480), the Oh Yeah Music Centre (p477) and the Sunflower (p480).

American Bar
This old-style pub in Sailortown (north Belfast) with memorabilia on the walls is little changed from the days when its clients were the local dockers. Downstairs it holds folk music sessions and a Saturday afternoon blues club. Upstairs is an intimate venue that hosts local singer-songwriters.

2 Royal Avenue
It's worth checking what's on at this new cultural space in the city centre.

Duncairn
This special venue in north Belfast is a former church, with great acoustics.

Mike's Fancy Cheese

MORE IN CATHEDRAL QUARTER

Discover the Neighbourhood's Street Art
Painted Walls

Belfast is known for its sectarian murals, often painted on gable ends to stake out territory and declare political allegiances. But in the Cathedral Quarter, the culture of painting walls has been reset with the emergence of a non-sectarian street art scene. Much of the neighbourhood's street art was commissioned as part of the annual **Hit the North** festival, started in 2013 by a local arts organisation.

Some of the world's leading street artists have left their mark in the neighbourhood. Walk along Hill St to see a number of pieces, including Irish artist Conor Harrington's *Duel of Belfast, Dance by Candlelight*. It depicts two historical

WHERE TO EAT DINNER IN THE CATHEDRAL QUARTER

Coppi
Italian restaurant serving comforting bowls of pasta, like porcini mushroom ravioli with duck ragu. ££

Waterman
This bright Hill St bistro serves contemporary European dishes; there's a cookery school upstairs. ££

Muddlers Club
Book ahead to sample the seasonal tasting menu of beautifully presented plates at this exceptional restaurant. £££

figures fighting over a dead animal, while a third man looks on, a comment on colonialism. Nearby, just off Talbot St, *The Son of Protagoras* by MTO shows a dove of peace that has been killed by two arrows bearing the symbolism of the Catholic and Protestant churches. A block east, *Blurry Eyes* by Dan Kitchener is a mural of a rainy-night city scene that looks even better when the wall is wet after a downpour. Cross Royal Ave and walk along Kent St and Union St to see more than 50 different pieces. To find out more about the artists and what their work represents, check out the annotated map on the Seedhead Arts website (seedheadarts.com). Seedhead Arts also offers street art walking tours; some of the guides are street artists themselves.

Catch a Live Music Session
Trad, Jazz, Folk And Pop

The Cathedral Quarter is Belfast's best neighbourhood for live music. For authentic trad sessions, head to the **John Hewitt** on Thursday nights and Sunday afternoons, when local musicians gather around a table to play. Another safe bet for live music is the **Sunflower**, where there is something scheduled every day of the week, from open mic nights to jazz and blues, folk music, and Sunday evening trad sessions.

At the Merchant Hotel, **Berts Jazz Bar** has nightly jazz performances in an elegant setting. To hear crooners belting out the usual crowd-pleasers, head to the **Duke of York**, a traditional pub crammed with memorabilia with live music at weekends. Outside on Commercial Ct, a canopy of colourful umbrellas covers the cobbled courtyard; it takes on a street-party atmosphere in warm weather. At weekends there are usually live performers in a number of bars on and around **Hill St**, so take a stroll and follow your ears.

Sample Mike's Fancy Cheese
The Best Irish Dairies

Cheese lovers should be sure to visit Mike's Fancy Cheese, a specialist shop selling some 50 varieties sourced from Irish dairies. Many cheeses are from small boutique producers, such as Carraignamuc and Sobhriste raw milk cheeses from the Lost Valley Dairy in Cork. Pick up some Abernethy butter (a slow-churned butter produced in County Down), a loaf of sourdough and a jar of Belfast-made chutney to make the ultimate cheese sandwich.

LGBTIQ+ NIGHTLIFE

Belfast's LGBTIQ+ scene is centred around Union St in the Cathedral Quarter. Events to look out for include **Pride** in July or August, and the **Outburst Queer Arts Festival** in November.

For nightlife, head to the **Kremlin**, a long-standing Soviet-kitsch-themed bar guarded by a statue of Lenin, with a cocktail bar and club area. Nearby is the **Maverick**, a friendly bar that hosts a range of events including open mic nights and comedy shows. Upstairs, **Boombox** nightclub is known for its excellent drag acts. **The Reporter** is an old-style pub that celebrates Belfast with local memorabilia and drinks. Lastly, **Union Street Bar** runs quizzes and events including Dragged Out Saturdays cabaret nights; it also serves food.

WHERE TO EAT BRUNCH IN THE CATHEDRAL QUARTER

Established Coffee
Airy, industrial-style cafe which roasts its own beans and serves coffee and brunch. **£**

Neighbourhood Cafe
Head here for speciality coffee and dishes like mushroom toast, Turkish eggs and buttermilk pancakes. **£**

Orto
A pastry or wood-fired pizza from this all-day pizza bar could hit the spot. **£**

Buy Local Art
Paintings, Prints, Ceramics And Textiles

The Cathedral Quarter is the perfect place to pick up an original piece by a local artist. Before you shop, get inspired by the work on display in the contemporary visual arts space **Golden Thread Gallery**. At Ulster University, **UNIQUE Art and Design** sells pieces by students, alumni and other local designer makers; you might bag a piece by an up-and-coming star. Nearby, **Craft NI** is a shop and gallery space displaying the work of more than 40 local designer makers in a range of media, from textiles and ceramics to wood and glass.

Try Something Different
Alternative Activities

If you've always wanted to learn circus skills or speak at a storytelling event, the Cathedral Quarter could be the place to do it. On Hill St, **Black Box** is an innovative arts centre with a dynamic programme of magic nights, comedy shows, art exhibitions and live music. Try your hand at drawing at Black Box's **Real Sketchy** event, or submit a piece of themed writing for a chance to take the stage at the venue's monthly **Tenx9** storytelling night. Black Box also runs club nights for adults with learning disabilities, and has a gig buddies scheme to make its events more accessible.

Nearby on Gordon St, **Circusful** is a circus school offering classes in skills such as trapeze and aerial apparatus for children and adults. Back on Hill St, **Studio 52** offers vinyasa flow yoga classes as well as themed workshops such as yoga accompanied by Irish poetry and live guitar music. If **skateboarding** is your thing, you can join the young people who practise their skills at **Buoy Park** and Custom House Sq.

BEST PUBS IN THE CATHEDRAL QUARTER

Deer's Head
Refurbished saloon bar and brewpub, where the stouts, lagers and ales are brewed onsite.

Spaniard
This atmospheric pub is stocked with a variety of rums and is often crammed with customers.

Sunflower
Pass through the security cage (preserved as a relic of Belfast's social history) to reach a bar stocked with local spirits and craft beers. The beer garden has a wood-fired pizza oven.

INDEPENDENT SHOPS

Adjoining the Cathedral Quarter, the city centre has a number of independent, family-run and specialist shops, where you can shop for everything from musical instruments to handcrafted jewellery. From Friday to Sunday, don't miss **St George's Market** (p473).

WHERE TO GET A COCKTAIL IN THE CATHEDRAL QUARTER

Angel and Two Bibles
A speakeasy-style cocktail bar offering extensive Old and New Testament–themed drinks lists.

Merchant Hotel Cocktail Bar
Table service and complimentary bar snacks make a cocktail at the Merchant a luxury experience.

National
The renovated former National Bank building is a grand setting for cocktails and club nights.

TITANIC QUARTER & EAST BELFAST

HISTORIC SHIPYARDS

These days *Titanic* is so closely connected to Belfast's identity that there is a neighbourhood named after it: the shipyards where *Titanic* was constructed are now part of the redeveloped Titanic Quarter. At its centre is Titanic Belfast, a state-of-the-art multimedia museum that has become the city's number-one tourist draw. Around it are several other sites with links to the *Titanic*, as well as Titanic Studios, the studios at the centre of Belfast's burgeoning film industry.

The residential neighbourhoods of East Belfast where the shipyard workers once lived are now home to a growing creative community and a cooperative brewery. East Belfast is also a tangible presence in many of Van Morrison's songs, which have nostalgic references to the neighbourhood where he grew up; sites include the Hollow from 'Brown Eyed Girl' and Cyprus Avenue. Nearby is the landmark building known as Stormont, where the Northern Ireland Assembly meets.

TOP TIP

If you enjoy cycling, consider exploring the Titanic Quarter by bike. Travelling on two wheels makes it quick and easy to cover ground in the flat, open spaces of the former dockyards, and cycling routes are largely traffic free. The city's bike-share programme Belfast Bikes has a docking station at the Odyssey Complex.

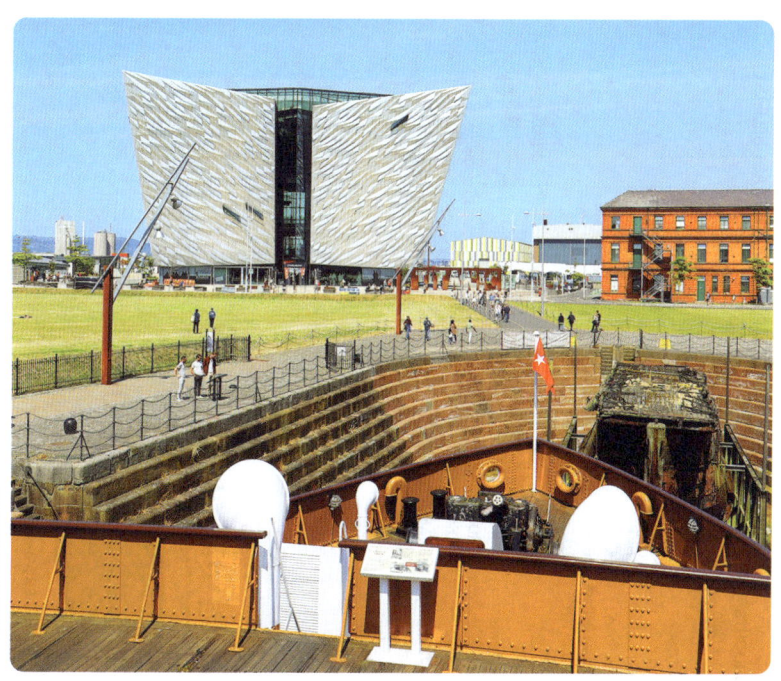

Titanic Belfast (p483)

TITANIC QUARTER & EAST BELFAST

HIGHLIGHTS
1. Dock Cafe
2. HMS Caroline
3. Odyssey Complex
4. SS Nomadic
5. The Strand
6. Titanic Belfast
7. Titanic Distillers

SIGHTS
8. CS Lewis Square
see 3 W5

ACTIVITIES
9. Vertigo Indoor Skydiving

EATING
10. Cyprus Avenue
see 13 Flout!

DRINKING & NIGHTLIFE
11. Boundary Brewing
12. Drawing Office Two
see 11 Root & Branch

SHOPPING
13. Banana Block

TRANSPORT
14. Comber Greenway

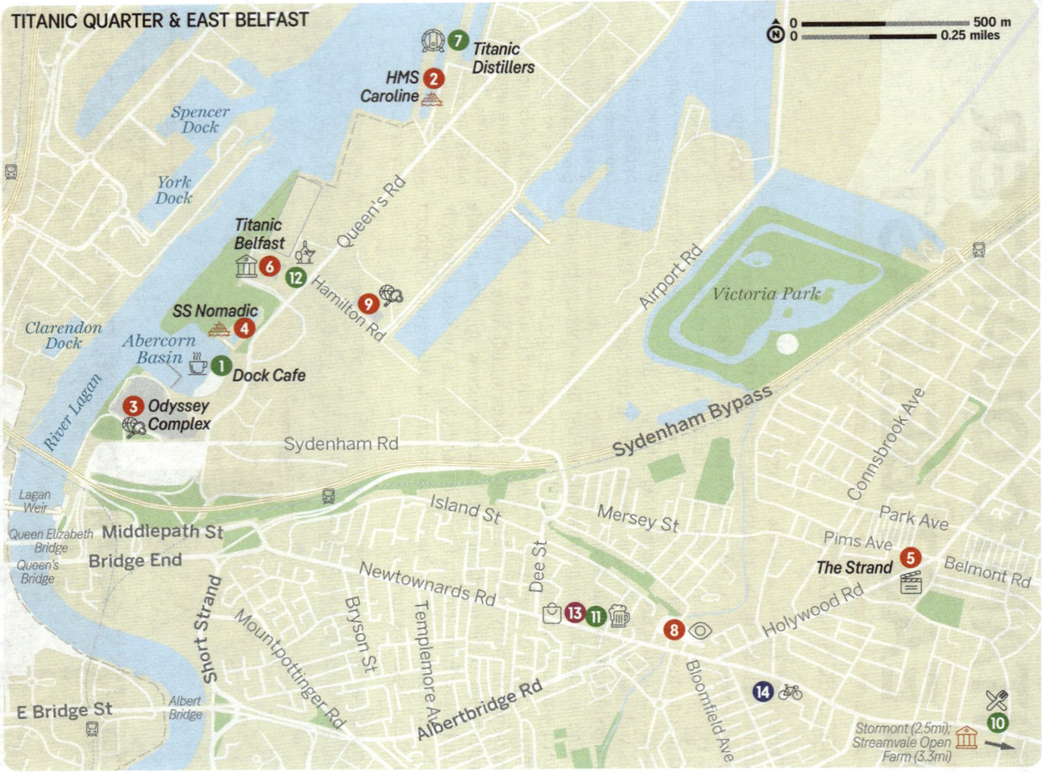

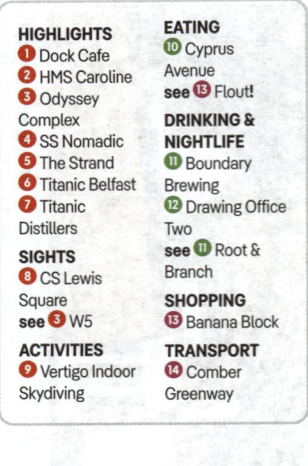

SS Nomadic

482

Titanic Belfast
The Story Of The Infamous Ship

Standing at the head of the slipway where *Titanic* was built is the gleaming angular edifice of **Titanic Belfast**, a multimedia exhibition that charts the history of the world's most famous ocean liner.

The story starts in Boomtown Belfast, which depicts the city's turn-of-the-century rise to an industrial powerhouse. The exhibits recreate the experience of walking down a 1911 Belfast street, with animated projections and soundtracks, to reach the gates of Harland & Wolff shipyard. From here a shipyard ride descends from the gantry, with a soundtrack of workers' chatter and the hammering of rivets. Next the exhibit recreates the excitement of *Titanic's* launch, then shows the ship's interior, with replica passenger cabins and a screen simulation tour of the ship. Life aboard the ship is recreated with a walk on deck; look for touching family letters dispatched before the ship got into trouble, and a first-class dinner menu.

The sinking of *Titanic* is represented by the sounds of Morse code, the final messages sent to nearby ships and the stories of survivors. The domino effect exhibit shows how a series of factors interacted to cause the disaster. Finally, the Ship of Dreams gallery has a suspended scale model of the ship and a number of artefacts, including a *Titanic* deckchair recovered from the surface and a violin belonging to the musician Wallace Hartley.

Titanic Belfast

SS NOMADIC

Next to Titanic Belfast is the **Nomadic,** the last remaining vessel of the White Star Line. Built in Belfast in 1911, the little steamship ferried 1st- and 2nd-class passengers between Cherbourg Harbour and ocean liners that were too big to dock at the French port. On 10 April 1912, it delivered 172 passengers to *Titanic.*

Nomadic was requisitioned during both world wars and ended up as a floating restaurant in Paris. In 2006, it was rescued from a breaker's yard and brought to Belfast for restoration.

TITANIC QUARTER

There are several sites related to *Titanic* in the area, including Thompson dry dock and pump house, now **Titanic Distillery** (p485). Explore the neighbourhood on a **walking tour** (p486).

HMS Caroline
WWI Royal Navy Cruiser

The UK's last surviving WWI Royal Navy cruiser has been converted into a floating museum at Alexandra Dock. Audio tours take in the captain's quarters, officers' cabins, marine mess, sick bay and galley kitchen, with interactive exhibits and a film dramatisation of **HMS *Caroline's*** role in the 1916 Battle of Jutland. The engine room has been preserved as it was when it was an active warship. There are also interactive displays that simulate firing a torpedo and steering the ship.

HMS Caroline

The Strand
Iconic Art Deco Cinema

This art deco movie theatre first opened in 1935, during the golden age of cinema when Belfast was home to around 40 picture houses. Though it has gone through various guises over the intervening years, it is now back in operation as a cinema, showing a variety of classic films and current releases. It also serves as a community arts space, hosting creative workshops for adults and children. Check the schedule for special events, such as comedy nights. The Strand is on Holywood Rd, a 10-minute bus ride east of the city centre; the building's architecture alone makes it worth the trip.

The Strand

Dock Cafe
Rest And Recharge In Titanic Quarter

The tea, coffee and snacks at this **cafe** are offered in return for a voluntary donation in the honesty box; there is no pressure to pay, and it is also fine to bring your own food and drinks to consume inside. Staffed by volunteers, the cafe is a large, bright space full of mismatched donated furniture and decorated with local art and memorabilia. Outdoor tables have views of the surrounding sights in Titanic Quarter, Cave Hill and the docks.

Towards the back of the cafe, look for the childhood bedroom door of Thomas Andrew, the chief naval architect who oversaw the design and construction of *Titanic*. There is also a 'prayer garden' plant-filled space for reflection.

Odyssey Complex
Riverside Sports And Entertainment Complex

In Titanic Quarter, the **Odyssey Complex** is a sports and entertainment complex containing a cinema and W5, a hands-on science centre for children aged three to 11, with themed educational spaces and interactive exhibits. Here kids can play a tune on a laser harp and explore the immersive vortex light tunnel. Also at the complex is the SSE arena, home to Belfast Giants ice-hockey team. The Giants have won the UK's Elite Ice Hockey League multiple times; the season is from September to April.

Odyssey Complex

Stormont
Northern Ireland's Parliament Building

Stormont's white neoclassical facade is one of Belfast's most iconic. Built in 1932 to house the Northern Ireland parliament, the building occupies a dramatic hilltop position reached by a 1.5km tree-lined avenue. Following the Good Friday Agreement of 1998, **Stormont** became home to the Northern Ireland Assembly, the devolved legislative body. Free guided tours of the Great Hall, Assembly and Senate Chambers give an informative overview of the power-sharing political system and the Good Friday Agreement on which it is based.

Walking trails through the grounds pass through woodland areas and by several sculptures. Don't miss the bronze cast of the piece *Reconciliation* by Josefina De Vasconcellos; three further casts are located in Berlin, Coventry and Hiroshima.

Stormont

Titanic Distillers
Whiskey Distillery In A Former Pump House

Whiskey and *Titanic* history collide at this distillery housed in the pump house at Thompson Dock, where the ship was fitted out. The pump house has been beautifully restored, with much of the old machinery preserved in place next to new copper stills and mash tuns. See around the building, learn about the distilling process and taste whiskeys on guided tours, which set Belfast's first working distillery for 90 years in its historical context; the city was once a major whiskey producer. The distillers also offer guided dock tours of the huge dry dock built to accommodate *Titanic*.

485

DISCOVER TITANIC QUARTER

Start at **1 Lagan Weir** and cross the footbridge to Queen's Quay. Turn left and follow the riverbank path to **2 Odyssey Complex**. You are now on Queen's Island, formed in 1841 using material that was dredged up to create a shipping channel. Follow the path to Abercorn Basin, a working marina, and continue to **3 Titanic Kit**, a bronze sculpture that depicts the ship in the form of a toy model kit.

Next, cross the footbridge to reach Hamilton Dock and **4 SS Nomadic** (p483). The silhouette statues on the dockside relate to the *Nomadic*, which ferried *Titanic*'s passengers from Cherbourg harbour to the ship. They represent a Belfast shipyard worker, a French sailor and Charlie Chaplin, once a *Nomadic* passenger. Cross the footbridge to the 1867 **5 pump house**, which contained the machinery used to drain Hamilton Dock. Now the gleaming, angular structure of **6 Titanic Belfast** comes into full view. To the right of the Titanic Belfast building are the drawing offices where *Titanic* was designed, now the **7 Titanic Hotel**.

Behind Titanic Belfast are the **8 slipways** from which *Titanic* and its sister ship *Olympic* were launched. Walk to the far end of the slipways to get a sense of the ships' size. From here there is a good view of the yellow Harland & Wolff cranes, known as Samson and Goliath.

Continue along the waterside to the **9 Great Light**, a former lighthouse lens, and on to Alexandra Dock, home to naval vessel **10 HMS Caroline** (p484). Behind it is the pump house used to drain the water from Thompson Dry Dock, where *Titanic* was fitted out. The building is now **11 Titanic Distillery** (p485).

MORE IN TITANIC QUARTER & EAST BELFAST

Explore East Belfast
Public Art And Local Enterprise

Newtownards Rd is the location of a cluster of exciting local enterprises, neighbourhood arts projects and community spaces, a 15-minute bus trip east of the city centre.

Start your exploration at **CS Lewis Square**, where public art celebrates one of Belfast's most famous authors. Irish artist Maurice Harron created seven bronze statues related to *The Lion, the Witch and the Wardrobe*.

Three blocks west, at the Portview Trade Centre, is **Boundary Brewing**, a cooperative that produces highly rated ales and lagers onsite. Head to the tap room to sample the range, or book ahead for brewery tours. Coffee roaster **Root & Branch** also has its roastery and espresso bar here; pop in for coffee or to pick up some beans.

At the same complex, **Banana Block** is an innovative commercial and community events space in a former linen mill. Outlets include cheesemakers **Velo Cheese**, mushroom specialists **Hearty Growers** and the record shop **Sound Advice**. Look out for events including yoga classes, drag brunches and mushroom workshops.

Cycle the Comber Greenway
East Belfast By Bike

The Comber Greenway is an 11km path along a former railway line to the village of Comber in County Down. The traffic-free greenway begins at the car park at Ravenscroft Ave near Holywood Rd in East Belfast, but you can follow the Sustrans route along quiet residential streets from the city centre or Titanic Quarter. The flat tarmacked path leads east through the city, passing close to Stormont (p485) before emerging into the countryside. At the end of the greenway, you can extend your cycle to explore the shores of Strangford Lough.

Comber Greenway

BEST FOR KIDS

W5
This hands-on, interactive science discovery centre is at the Odyssey Complex (p485).

Colin Glen
Woodland area in West Belfast with ziplines, rope courses and a Gruffalo trail.

Vertigo Indoor Skydiving
This centre in Titanic Quarter replicates the thrill of falling from a plane inside a wind tunnel.

Streamvale Open Farm
Kids can feed animals and take tractor rides at this farm on the outskirts of East Belfast.

WHERE TO EAT IN TITANIC QUARTER & EAST BELFAST

Flout!
This pizzeria on Newtownards Rd is highly regarded by critics and punters alike; arrive early. **£**

Cyprus Avenue
Family-friendly Ballyhackamore bistro that's open for breakfast, lunch and dinner. **££**

Drawing Office Two
The former Harland & Wolff drawing offices at Titanic Hotel are now an airy bar and restaurant. **££**

QUEEN'S QUARTER & SOUTH BELFAST

LEAFY CAMPUS AND RIVERSIDE NATURE

South of the city centre are the leafy streets and student bars of the Queen's Quarter, which takes its name from Queen's University. Academic life extends beyond the campus to the neighbouring Ulster Museum, located in **Botanic Gardens**, Belfast's prettiest park. Nearby are coffee shops, independent bookstores and boutiques.

This is Belfast's most ethnically diverse area; in addition to international students, it is where many members of the city's growing Chinese, South Asian and other minority communities live. In August Belfast Mela celebrates global cultures with a festival of music and dance held in Botanic Gardens.

Further south, Cutter's Wharf is one of several access points for the Lagan Towpath. Located at the centre of a designated Area of Outstanding Natural Beauty, the towpath passes through a variety of wetlands, tree-fringed riverside meadows and mixed woodlands and is a tranquil place for walking and cycling.

TOP TIP

For a scenic walk or bike ride from Queen's Quarter to the city centre, take the riverside path. Stroll or cycle through Botanic Gardens to reach Stranmillis Embankment and then follow the pedestrian and cycle path north for 3km along the west bank of the Lagan to reach Queen's Bridge, just east of the city centre.

Lagan Towpath (p493)

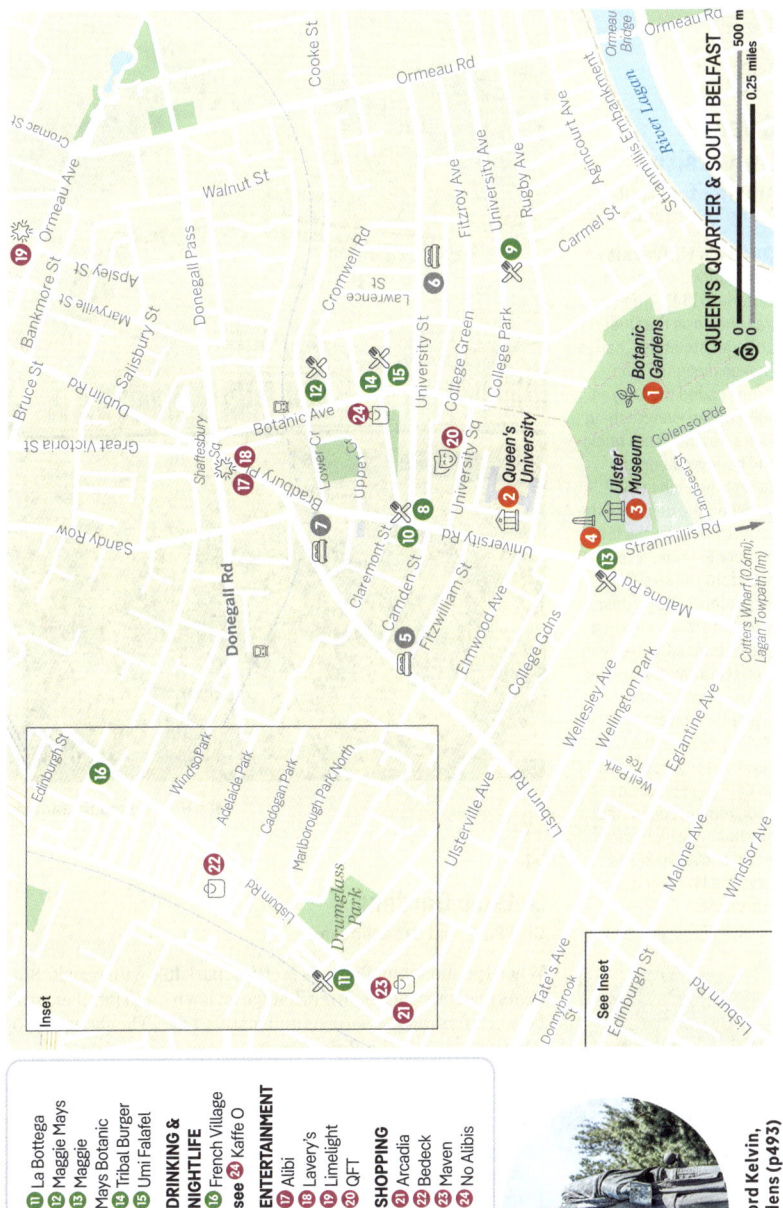

QUEEN'S QUARTER & SOUTH BELFAST

HIGHLIGHTS
1. Botanic Gardens
2. Queen's University
3. Ulster Museum

SIGHTS
4. Lord Kelvin Statue

SLEEPING
5. Botanical Backpackers
6. Global Village
7. Vagabonds

EATING
8. A Peculiar Tea
9. Bo Tree Kitchen
10. Holohan's Pantry
11. La Bottega
12. Maggie Mays
13. Maggie Mays Botanic
14. Tribal Burger
15. Umi Falafel

DRINKING & NIGHTLIFE
16. French Village
    see 24 Kaffe O

ENTERTAINMENT
17. Alibi
18. Lavery's
19. Limelight
20. QFT

SHOPPING
21. Arcadia
22. Bedeck
23. Maven
24. No Alibis

Statue of Lord Kelvin, Botanic Gardens (p493)

Queen's University
Architecture And Campus Grounds

Queen's University was founded by Queen Victoria in 1845, when it was known as the Queen's College. Architect Charles Lanyon designed what is now called the Lanyon building, an eye-catching Tudor Revival in red brick and honey-coloured sandstone built in 1849; he based the design of the central tower on the 15th-century Founder's Tower at Oxford University's Magdalen College. Just inside the main entrance is a Welcome Centre, with tourist information, maps and a souvenir shop. Inside the university's McClay Library, the CS Lewis reading room has an engraved wooden door, reminiscent of the one behind which Narnia was discovered in *The Lion, the Witch and the Wardrobe*.

Palm House, Botanic Gardens

Queen's University

Botanic Gardens
City Park And Greenhouses

When the sun is out, Belfast's prettiest park fills with people. Students read on benches, lovers lounge on lawns, and families stroll between fragrant flowerbeds and mature trees. The showpiece of this city oasis is the **Palm House**, a cast iron and curvilinear glass greenhouse designed by Charles Lanyon. The gardens were founded in 1828 at a time when plant hunting was all the rage, and it was soon decided that a glasshouse was needed for the exotic species gathered from around the globe. Work began on the structure in 1839, but the birdcage dome was not added until 1852. Look out for details such as rosettes in the structure's ironwork.

A second greenhouse, the redbrick **Tropical Ravine**, was added in 1889 to house tropical ferns, orchids, lilies and banana plants in a sunken glen. Inside, a raised walkway overlooks some 190 plant species housed in temperate and tropical zones. Notable plants include a Japanese fibre banana tree dating from 1904 and tree ferns thought to be 150 years old.

Ulster Museum
Five Floors Of Galleries

In a bright modern building in Botanic Gardens, the **Ulster Museum** is packed with fascinating treasures in galleries spread over five floors. Start in the art galleries at the top of the building and spiral down through the levels. In the nature galleries, don't miss the Snapshot of an Ancient Sea Floor, a fossilised portion of a 200-million-year-old seabed with jumbled ammonite shells and petrified driftwood.

One history gallery displays **Takabuti**, an Egyptian mummy dating from around 660 BCE that was brought to Belfast and unwrapped in 1835. Another highlight is the **Armada Room**, which houses treasures recovered from the wreck of the *Girona*, a Spanish galleon that sank off the north Antrim coast in 1588. In the Early People's Gallery, look for the bronze Bann Disc, a superb example of Celtic design from the Iron Age.

On the ground floor an overview of local history from 1500 onward includes exhibits on the formation of the Society of United Irishmen and the Rebellion of 1798 against British rule in Ireland. Look for a letter from Theobald Wolfe Tone, and the death mask of James Hope (1764–1847), a local linen weaver who fought in the Rebellions of 1798 and 1803.

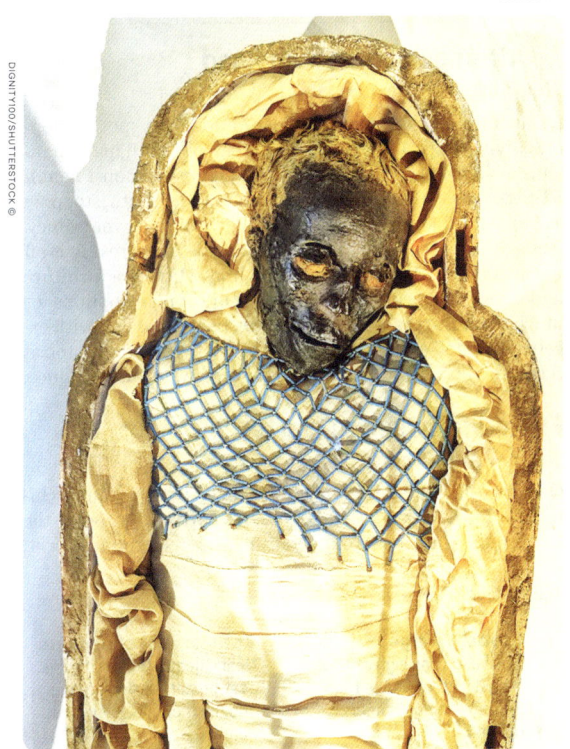

Takabuti

THE TROUBLES & BEYOND

On the ground floor of the museum, this gallery explores Northern Ireland's emergence from years of conflict through a series of objects related to the Troubles. The idea behind the display is that the nuances of how the period is differently understood and remembered are best represented through a diverse range of memorabilia. One evocative item is a bomb disposal robot; such robots were developed in 1972 to allow bombs to be disarmed remotely.

WHY I LOVE BELFAST

Isabel Albiston, writer

Belfast's excellent restaurants and dynamic arts scene are just part of the reason why I love my hometown. From live bands to storytelling events, there's always something interesting going on, and it seems like no sooner has one festival ended than a new one begins.

The political tensions that make headlines are rarely a part of everyday life, and are often defused by the characteristic dark humour that defines the city. What's more, the stunning coastlines of Counties Antrim and Down are mere minutes away, while the Lagan Towpath makes it easy to connect with nature without leaving the city.

Queen's University

MORE IN QUEEN'S QUARTER & SOUTH BELFAST

An Afternoon on Lisburn Road
Shopping, Coffee And Lunch

Lisburn Rd makes a pleasant destination for a spot of shopping, with stops for coffee and lunch, and perhaps a manicure or haircut. Start at the deli and coffee shop **French Village** for a coffee and a pastry, then wander south, stopping at any boutiques or health food stores that take your fancy. **Bedeck** is worth a look for its range of homewares. Just off Lisburn Rd on Maryville Ave, don't miss **Maven**, a furniture and design shop run by two sisters. One of many options for lunch is **La Bottega**, an Italian cafe, bistro and deli with excellent cannoli and Italian pastries. Finally, be sure to stop at **Arcadia**, an independent deli crammed with local produce.

Exploring Queen's Quarter
Culture And Greenery

Queen's Quarter is a leafy neighbourhood with elegant architecture and a bookish vibe. At **Queen's University** (p490) the Lanyon Building is surrounded by manicured grounds. Next,

BEST HOSTELS IN QUEEN'S QUARTER

Vagabonds
Within walking distance of the city centre, Vagabonds has dorms, private rooms and common areas for socialising. £

Global Village
This hostel has high ceilings, period features, an outdoor area and a bright cheery decor. £

Botanical Backpackers
Near Queen's University, this cosy hostel has dorm rooms and the friendly feeling of a home. £

enter **Botanic Gardens** (p490) through the Stranmillis Rd gate to see the **Lord Kelvin statue**, which celebrates the Belfast-born physicist who invented the Kelvin scale, a measure of temperatures from absolute zero. Spend some time exploring **Ulster Museum** (p491), then stroll through the gardens; be sure to take a look at the birdcage-domed **Palm House** and redbrick **Tropical Ravine** greenhouses. Leave the park through the Botanic Ave gates and take a walk north, stopping where you please for coffee (try **Kaffe O**) or lunch (try **Maggie Mays Botanic**, **Tribal Burger**, or **Umi Falafel**). Browse the shelves of independent bookstore **No Alibis**, or catch a film at the arthouse cinema **QFT**.

Riverside Adventures on the Lagan Towpath
Wildlife-Rich Waterways

The River Lagan was once used to transport linen from the mills near Lisburn to Belfast for export. These days the wetlands, riverside meadows and mixed woodland on its banks are a haven for wildlife. One of the best ways to explore the area is by bike, following the Sustrans **Route 9** traffic-free path south along the riverbank from Belfast to Lisburn (20km), from where you can catch a train back to Belfast. It is also possible to explore shorter sections of the towpath by bike or on foot.

Just south of Cutter's Wharf at Stranmillis, the Lagan Towpath extends south from the **Lagan Gateway** pedestrian and cycle bridge. From here, the towpath winds along the west bank of the Lagan. Cross the bridge at **Mickey Taylor's lock** to explore **Moreland's Meadow**, an island created by the canal that allowed barges to avoid the bend in the river. On the east bank of the river is **Belvoir Forest,** where the **Belvoir Oak** tree is an estimated 500 years old.

Return to the towpath and continue south to reach **McLeave's Lock**. Here the old lock and stone bridge remain intact, and the lock-keeper's cottage has been preserved as a small museum. Nearby is **Lock Keeper's Inn**, a cafe with tables overlooking the river.

Beyond Clement Wilson park is **Shaw's Bridge**, a 300-year-old stone bridge. Cross over to follow the path along the east bank to **Minnowburn,** an area of meadowland and woodland. Trails lead through tall beech trees and up to **Terrace Hill Garden**, with views across the river to **Malone House**. The tables here are a picturesque spot for a picnic.

Further along the east bank of the Lagan, south of Minnowburn car park, a signposted pedestrian trail leads through

WILDLIFE-SPOTTING IN SOUTH BELFAST

Kingfisher
These bright blue and orange birds can sometimes be spotted diving for fish in the River Lagan.

Grey heron
Elegant birds often seen fishing near Moreland's Meadow.

Common otter
These shy mammals are known to live in and around the River Lagan; look for their tracks.

Speckled wood butterfly
Head to sun-dappled areas of woodland to see these butterflies.

Common seal
Seals are often seen in Belfast harbour; they have also been spotted upstream in the River Lagan.

WHERE TO SPLASH OUT ON FINE DINING IN BELFAST

A Peculiar Tea
In Queen's Quarter, Chef Gemma Austen creates imaginative tasting menus and playfully themed afternoon teas. **£££**

OX
In a pared-back contemporary space by the River Lagan, OX offers creative seasonal tasting menus. **£££**

Deanes EIPIC
Chef Alex Greene displays originality and flair in his tasting menus at this city centre restaurant. **£££**

BELFAST'S BEST CLUB NIGHTS

Limelight
South of the city centre, this longstanding venue hosts gigs and club nights; tunes range from hip-hop to techno to pop anthems.

Ollie's
Dance with a sophisticated crowd in the former bank vaults of what is now the Merchant Hotel.

Thompson's Garage
When the city centre pubs close, revellers stumble over to Thompsons to keep the party going.

Lavery's
In Queen's Quarter, Lavery's transforms into a nightclub at weekends.

Alibi
Opposite Lavery's, Alibi hosts international DJs and fire dancers.

Giant's Ring

undulating farmland to **Giant's Ring** (also accessible by road). Built in around 2000 BCE during the late Neolithic or early Bronze Age period, this prehistoric ceremonial earthwork is nearly 200m in diameter and has a stone passage grave in the centre. The views west towards the Belfast hills are particularly beautiful in the golden early evening light.

Back at the river, continue south to Gilchrist Bridge and cross back to the west bank. From here, the river snakes south through open farmland to reach **Sir Thomas and Lady Dixon Park**. Take time to explore the walled garden, meadow and woodland trails, and the spectacular **Rose Garden**, in bloom from mid-July. From the park, it's a further 8km to Lisburn.

Belfast City Bike Tours offers 'bike and brew tours' along the towpath to **Hilden Brewery** in Lisburn, returning to Belfast by train; the company also offers bike rental. The area around Shaw's Bridge is a popular spot for kayaking, canoeing and SUP; try Belfast Boat Club for paddlesports.

Local life on Ormeau Road
Discovering Neighbourhood Haunts

To experience local life in South Belfast, spend a few hours exploring the independent shops, cafes and restaurants of Ormeau Rd. Join the dog walkers, families and joggers in **Ormeau Park**, then head south along Ormeau Rd. For specialist wines, craft beers and spirits, pop into **The Vineyard**. Try **General Merchants** (p500) for lunch or **Stove Bistro** for dinner. For something sweet, head to **Al Gelato**.

WHERE TO EAT IN QUEEN'S QUARTER

Maggie Mays
Popular with students, Maggie Mays serves comfort food and all-day breakfasts, including Ulster Fries. **£**

Bo Tree Kitchen
Authentic Thai curries, stir fries and street food made with herbs and spices imported from Thailand. **£**

Holohan's Pantry
This Irish restaurant is a good place to try boxty, a traditional savoury potato pancake. **£££**

WEST & NORTH BELFAST

COMMUNITY CULTURE AND HILLTOP WALKS

West and North Belfast are largely residential areas extending as far as the Belfast hills, where walking trails offer fabulous views of the city and beyond. Though scarred by decades of civil unrest during the Troubles, West Belfast is a compelling place to visit. Here, a series of murals charts the history of the conflict and current political themes.

West Belfast developed with the linen mills that propelled the city into late-19th-century prosperity. It was an area of low-cost, working-class housing, and even in the Victorian era was divided along religious lines. These sectarian divisions became yet more entrenched from the early 1970s, as paramilitary groups ramped up their campaigns of armed conflict. But despite the area's violent past, there is a spirit of optimism and hope for the future. These days the area is safe and visitors are welcome; in August, the Féile an Phobail festival celebrates West Belfast's community and culture.

TOP TIP

One visible sign of ongoing divisions are the so-called peace lines that still separate some of Belfast's Catholic and Protestant communities. The longest section divides Falls Rd and the Shankill in West Belfast; its steel gates are generally open during the day. It is best to avoid the area at night and during times of heightened political tension.

Féile an Phobail festival

WEST & NORTH BELFAST

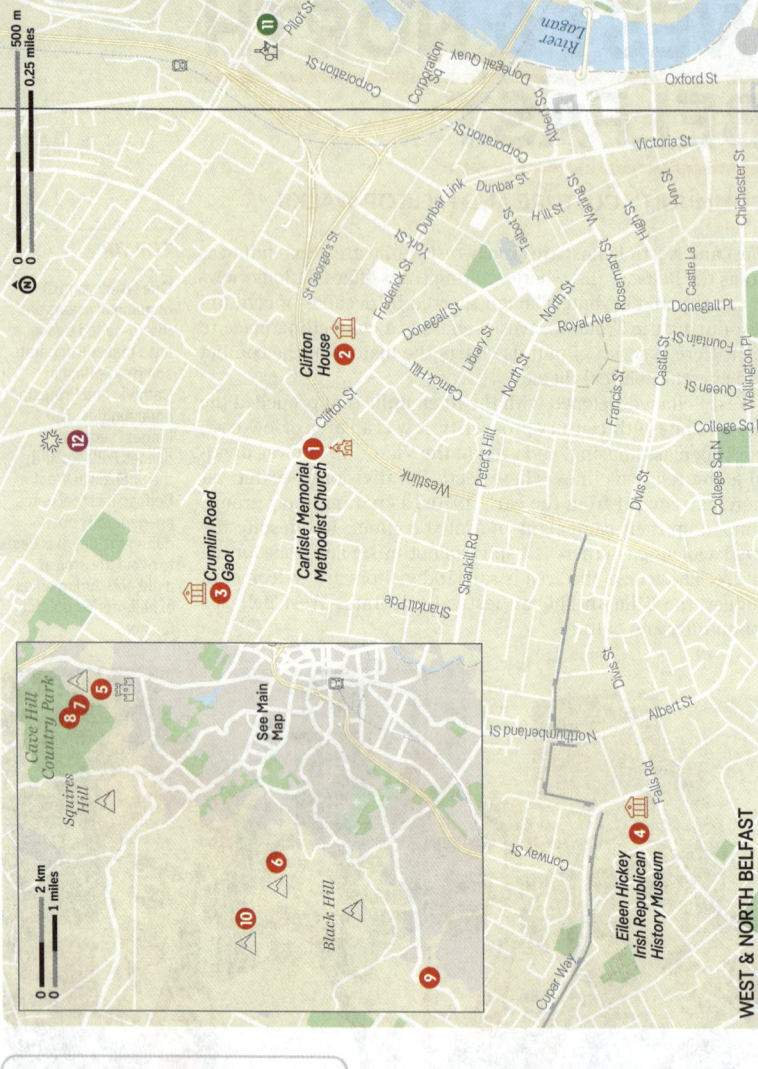

HIGHLIGHTS
1. Carlisle Memorial Methodist Church
2. Clifton House
3. Crumlin Road Gaol
4. Eileen Hickey Irish Republican History Museum

SIGHTS
5. Belfast Castle
6. Black Mountain
7. Cave Hill
8. Cave Hill Country Park
9. Colin Glen
10. Divis

DRINKING & NIGHTLIFE
11. American Bar

ENTERTAINMENT
12. Duncairn

Belfast Castle (p500)

Carlisle Memorial Methodist Church
Former Church Turned Events Space

This striking Gothic Revival building was built in 1875 as a memorial to the children of local merchant James Carlisle. It was once one of Belfast's most important Methodist churches, but its inner-city location in an area affected by sectarian conflict led to a declining congregation. The church closed in the early 1980s, after which it fell into disuse. Recent structural renovation work has brought the building back to life, and it is now used as a stripped-back and atmospheric events space.

Carlisle Memorial Methodist Church

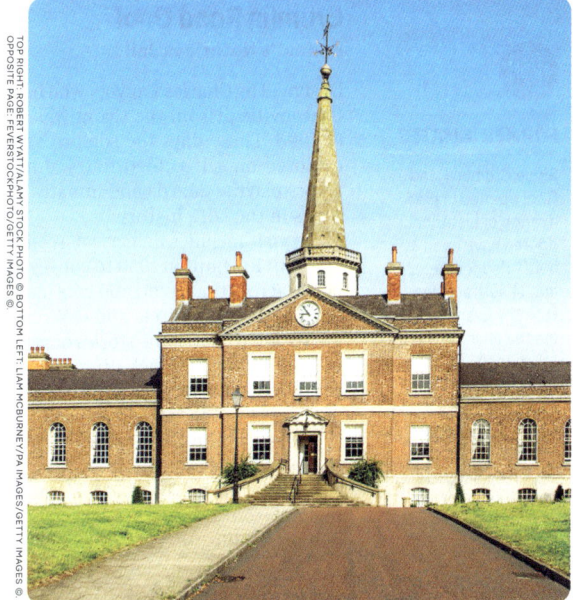

Clifton House

Eileen Hickey Irish Republican History Museum
History Of The Republican Struggle

At the Conway Mill complex, this museum houses artefacts related to the Republican struggle. The collection was started by **Eileen Hickey**, who was imprisoned at the Armagh Gaol from 1973 to 1977. At the entrance to the museum is a recreation of the Armagh Gaol cell in which Hickey was held, including her bed, personal photographs and an original cell door. The main exhibition space has handicrafts made by Republican prisoners, such as harps and intricate model caravans. Other items include rubber and plastic bullets, and a collection of weapons.

Clifton House
Georgian Poorhouse

Opened in 1774, **Clifton House** is Belfast's finest surviving Georgian building, with a pointed clock tower and ornamental gates. It was originally built as a poorhouse by the Belfast Charitable Society, with the involvement of Robert Joy (United Irishman Henry Joy McCracken's uncle). The building is open to the public twice a week for guided tours.

Nearby on Henry Pl is Clifton Cemetery. Here the McCracken family grave marks the final resting place of Henry Joy McCracken and his sister, the abolitionist, philanthropist and social reformer Mary Ann McCracken. Clifton House offers guided tours of the graveyard and walking tours of places related to Mary Ann McCracken.

Crumlin Road Gaol
Belfast's Notorious Jail

Designed by Charles Lanyon, who based his plans on London's Pentonville prison, the Crum was a working jail from 1846 to 1996. These days the sombre Victorian buildings can be explored on self-guided tours, during which holograms of actors playing guards and inmates tell stories from different times in the jail's history.

The visit includes an eerie descent into the tunnel beneath Crumlin Rd, built in 1850 to convey prisoners from the courthouse across the street, and continues through to the echoing halls of the Gaol Circle and C-Wing. Here the cramped cells are set up to convey the stories of prisoners from different eras in the jail's history, including a young woman held in 1846, a child jailed during the Victorian era, and political prisoners who served time in the Crum during the 1970s and 1980s. The most chilling of all is the execution chamber; the jail was the scene of the executions of 17 men between 1854 and 1961.

At weekends book ahead for tours guided by an actor playing a prison guard, who tells colourful stories of jailbreaks and prison life.

> **FORMER INMATES**
>
> Since Crumlin Road Gaol opened in 1846, a range of historical figures have been held prisoner there. In 1914 suffragettes Dorothy Evans and Madge Muir were taken to the Crum for possession of explosives after a series of arson attacks.
>
> In 1924 Éamon de Valera, then leader of Sinn Féin, was imprisoned for illegally entering Northern Ireland; he was held in solitary confinement for a month. And in 1966, Ian Paisley served time in the Crum for unlawful assembly; his supporters rioted outside in protest.

Crumlin Road Gaol

A WANDER THROUGH WEST BELFAST

Falls Rd is the main thoroughfare of Republican West Belfast, also known as the Gaeltacht (Irish-speaking) Quarter. Start at the **1 Solidarity Wall** on Divis St. The collection of murals here express Republican sympathies with the Palestinian and Basque peoples among others; one mural pays tribute to abolitionist Frederick Douglass, an advocate of the Irish independence movement in the 19th century.

Walk west along Divis St, which becomes Falls Rd, and turn right onto N Howard St to reach the **2 Peace Line** separating Catholic and Protestant communities; the gate here is closed at night. Return to Falls Rd.

Continue west, then turn right onto Conway St to reach **3 Conway Mill**, a restored 19th-century flax mill that now houses artists' studios and work spaces for local enterprises. At the same complex is the Eileen Hickey Irish Republican History Museum (p497).

Back on Falls Rd, walk west, passing **4 Falls Road Carnegie Library**; don't miss the angel carvings at the entrance. Next, look for the **5 mural of Bobby Sands**, who led the 1981 hunger strikes in which he and nine others died. The mural bears Sands' own words: 'Our revenge will be the laughter of our children'.

Walk west along Falls Rd, passing Dunville Park and Royal Victoria Hospital, to reach **6 Cultúrlann McAdam Ó Fiaich**. Housed in a red-brick former Presbyterian church, this Irish language and cultural centre is the focus for West Belfast community activity. There is a shop selling Irish-language books and a cafe here, too. To return to the city centre, take the G1 bus east along Falls Rd.

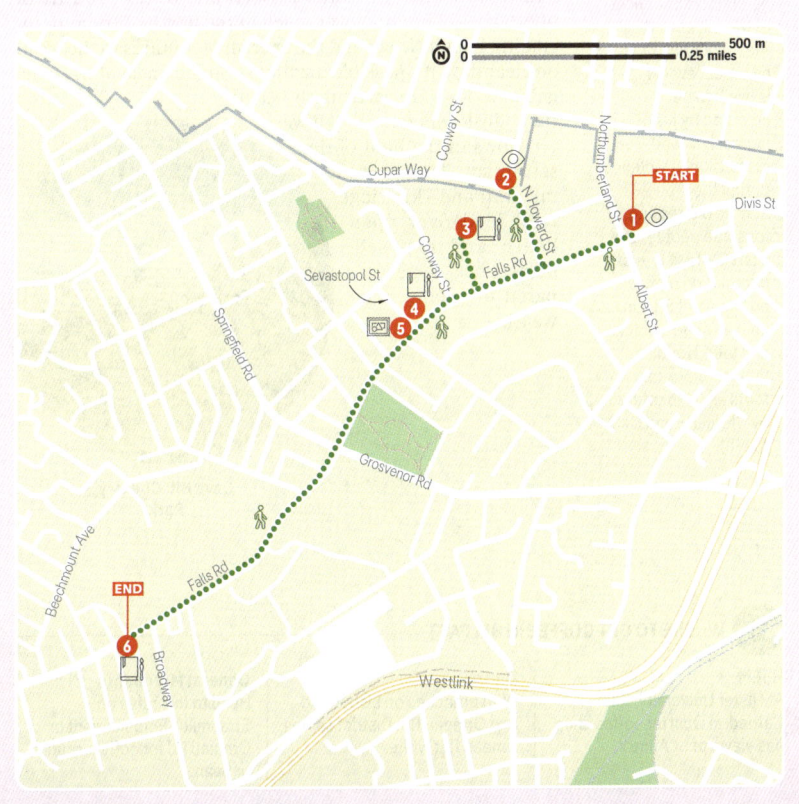

Adventures in the Belfast Hills
Nature And Panoramic Views

Forming the city's western and northern limits, the Belfast hills offer natural beauty and spectacular views.

Cave Hill is a North Belfast landmark and the site of **Belfast Castle** (1870). Evidence suggests that people lived on Cave Hill as far back as the Stone Age and the remains of a Bronze Age settlement have been discovered; the castle has displays on the hill's history and a cafe with tables in the pretty gardens.

From Belfast Castle car park, walking and mountain-biking trails traverse **Cave Hill Country Park**. The 7km Cave Hill walking trail emerges through woodland to cross heath and meadowland, with views across Belfast Lough. In spring the air is perfumed with the scent of gorse and wildflowers, and full of colourful butterflies. Scramble up to take a closer look at the caves for which the hill is named on the ascent to McArt's Fort at the summit. Here members of the United Irishmen looked down over the city in 1795 and pledged to fight for Irish independence. Pause to take in the views across the city to the docks and south to the Mourne Mountains; the coast of Scotland is often visible, too.

In West Belfast, the trails at **Divis** and **Black Mountain** offer views extending over much of the north of Ireland, including Lough Neagh and the Sperrin Mountains to the west; on clear days it's possible to glimpse Sliabh Sneacht in Donegal. The views are particularly beautiful at dusk, when the lough water glows in the light of the setting sun. The 5km summit trail and 7km ridge trail lead over open heath and exposed blanket bog; come prepared for changeable weather.

Cave Hill Country Park

BLACK TAXI TOURS

Black taxi tours of West Belfast's murals are offered by a number of taxi companies and local cabbies. These can vary in quality and content, but in general they are an intimate and entertaining way to see the sights.

Be aware that these tours often reflect the personal experiences of the driver, and the recounting of historical events is likely to be coloured by his or her background. The discussion of violence during the Troubles may be distressing for some people. The **Visit Belfast** tourist information office on Donegall Sq can help arrange a black taxi tour. Troubles-themed black taxi tours are also offered by Crumlin Road Gaol (p498).

WHERE TO GET COFFEE IN BELFAST

HJEM
At Ulster University, this Cathedral Quarter coffee shop has views of St Anne's.

District
With branches on Lisburn Rd and Ormeau Rd, District serves a mean flat white.

General Merchants
Head to the cafes on Stranmillis Embankment or Ormeau Rd for coffee, brunch or beans.

Belfast Castle

Above: Navan Fort (p523); right: Tollymore Forest Park gates (p514)

DOWN & ARMAGH

COASTLINE, MOUNTAINS AND LEGENDS

Follow in St Patrick's footsteps, from the site of his first church to his grave, passing scenic coastal landscapes and mountains steeped in legend.

Close to Belfast, the upmarket commuter villages of County Down have a cosmopolitan vibe and some excellent restaurants. Menus name-check local ingredients like Comber potatoes, Kilkeel crab and Mourne lamb.

Further south, the Mourne Mountains occupy one of the most beautiful corners of the North, with a distinctive landscape of grey granite, yellow gorse and whitewashed cottages. The lower slopes of the hills are latticed with a neat patchwork of drystone walls cobbled together from huge, rounded granite boulders. The area is now part of the Mourne Gullion Strangford Unesco global geopark, and the Mournes, Strangford Lough and the Ring of Gullion are all designated areas of outstanding natural beauty.

The recognition of the geological and cultural significance of the Ring of Gullion is long overdue. This area of South Armagh, which during the Troubles was known for its army watchtowers and IRA roadblocks, is now celebrated for its natural beauty and Celtic heritage.

And while the conveniences of modern life are never far away in Down and Armagh, the area has some fascinating historical sites to discover, including Neolithic passage tombs and dolmen and an enigmatic Iron Age monument at Navan Fort. There are a number of sites related to St Patrick's missions in the area, while several grand country house estates offer a window into more recent history.

THE MAIN AREAS

NEWCASTLE
Where the Mournes meet the sea.
p508

ARMAGH
Ireland's ecclesiastical capital.
p520

Find Your Way

Down and Armagh are small with good roads, making car journeys easy and quick. It's possible to make day trips from Belfast, but it's worth staying overnight on the coast or in the hills.

Armagh City, p520
Discover a library of historic texts, two cathedrals named for St Patrick, elegant Georgian architecture and a mysterious Iron Age monument.

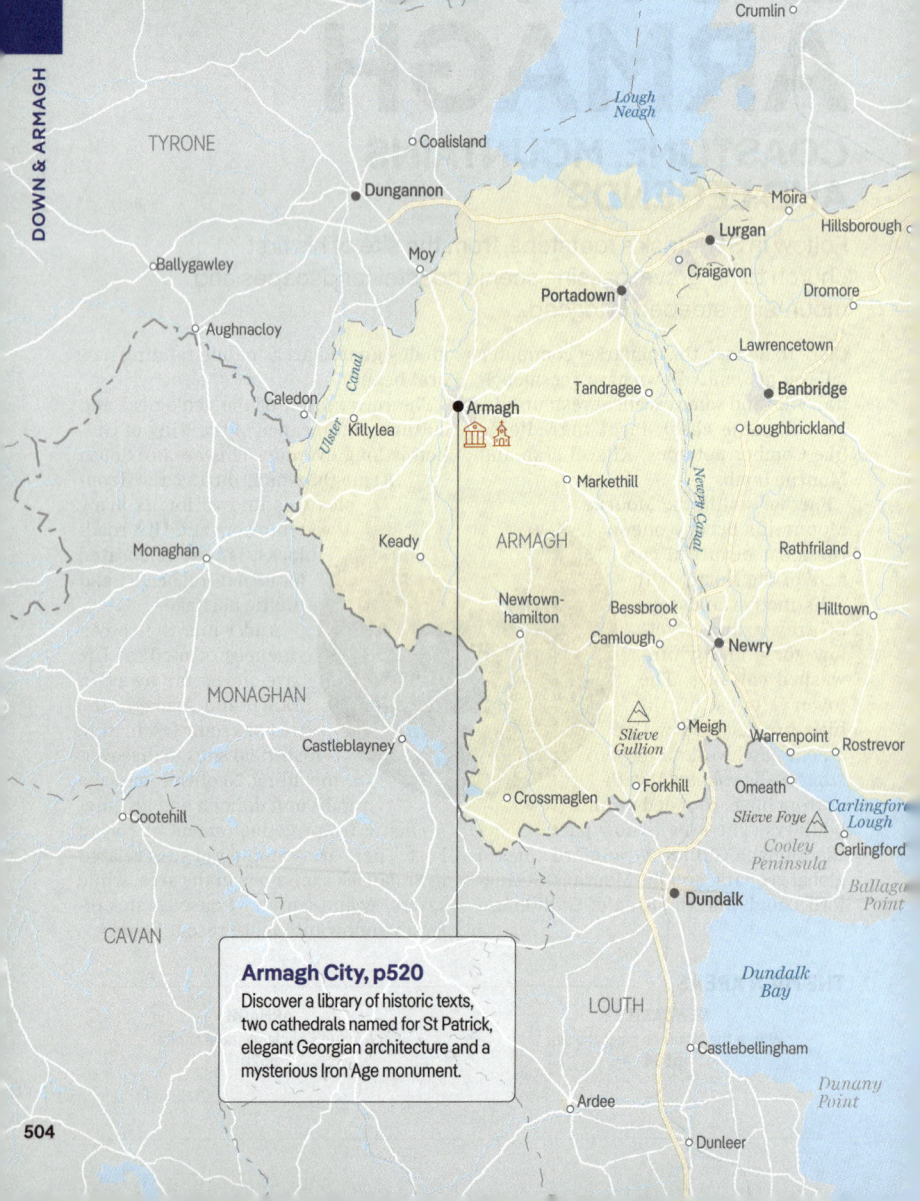

THE GUIDE

DOWN & ARMAGH

Newcastle, p508
The seaside town at the foot of the Mournes has a sandy beach and trails through forests and into the hills.

CAR
The easiest way to get around Down and Armagh is by car, especially in rural areas where public transport is infrequent. Most places in the two counties are less than an hour by car from Belfast.

BICYCLE
Several designated cycle routes pass through the two counties: route 99 connects Belfast to Newcastle via the Ards Peninsula, and route 9 follows the towpath from Belfast to Newry, linking up with route 91 to Armagh.

Ards Peninsula (p518)

Plan Your Time

With a wealth of walking and cycling trails to discover, allow time to explore at a slower pace, with plenty of stops at beauty spots along the way.

Pressed for Time

Head to Newcastle and hit the hills, climbing **Slieve Donard** (p510), walking in **Tollymore** (p514) or exploring the **Mournes** by bike (p511). Next, spend a day at Strangford Lough, visiting **Castle Ward** (p517) and then taking the ferry to the **Ards Peninsula** (p518). The next morning, drive to **Armagh** (p520), stopping at **Slieve Gullion** (p525) on the way. Spend the afternoon exploring the city's historic buildings.

Five Days to Explore

Allow several days to explore the Mournes, including the hiking and mountain-biking trails at **Kilbroney Park** (p515). Time your visit to catch a trad or folk session in a pub in **Rostrevor** (p515). After exploring the **Ards Peninsula** (p518), head to the **North Down coast** (p519) to visit the museums and dine out. Next, make your way to Armagh for a tour of **Navan Fort** (p523).

Seasonal Highlights

SPRING
St Patrick's Day is celebrated with a festival in Armagh and a parade in Downpatrick. In May, Blues on the Bay is held in Warrenpoint.

SUMMER
Warm weather brings families to the beach and walkers to the hills. In July, folk musicians gather in Rostrevor for the Fiddler's Green Festival (p515).

AUTUMN
Thousands of brent geese begin to arrive at Strangford Lough. The apple harvest is celebrated with a food and cider festival in Armagh.

WINTER
Christmas markets are held at Castle Ward and Hillsborough Castle. On colder days, the Mournes are coated with snow.

Kilbroney Park (p515)

NEWCASTLE

Located in a spectacular coastal setting at the foot of the Mournes, Newcastle is a pleasing combination of cheery seaside town with ice cream shops and games arcades, faded Victorian holiday resort, and vibrant community centre. At the northern end of town, the Royal County Down Golf Course has topped lists of the best and most beautiful courses in the world; it sits next to the landmark red-brick Slieve Donard hotel. From here, contemporary sculptures dot the 1km-long seafront promenade.

The town's main attraction is the beach, which stretches northeast to a nature reserve. The little harbour at the south end of town once served the stone boats that exported Mourne granite from the quarries of Slieve Donard. Wherever you are in Newcastle, the Mourne Mountains dominate the horizon, inviting walkers to scale their rolling peaks. From town, trails lead along former smuggling tracks into the hills.

TOP TIP

The summertime Mourne Rambler bus runs a circular route from Newcastle around the Mournes, stopping at Tollymore Forest Park, Silent Valley, Carrick Little (for Slieve Binnian) and Bloody Bridge. Alternatively, the Mourne Shuttle Service runs a timetabled route linking several walkers' car parks, allowing for linear hiking routes; reserve ahead (07516 412 076).

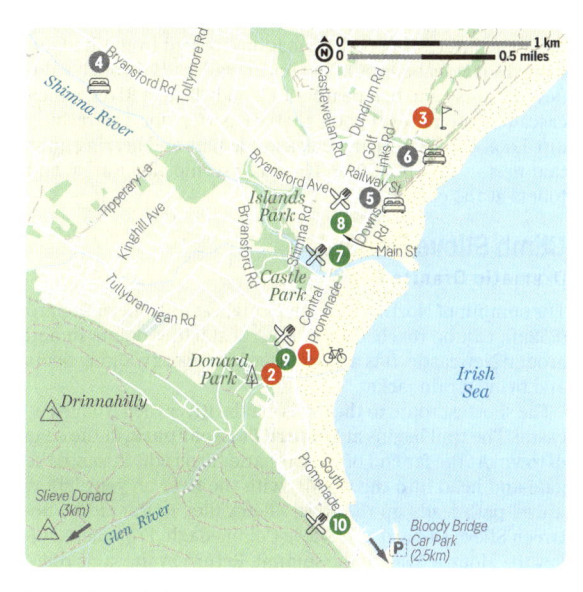

SIGHTS
1. Bike Mourne
2. Donard Park Car Park
3. Royal County Down Golf Club

SLEEPING
4. Enniskeen Country House Hotel
5. Hutt Hostel
6. Slieve Donard Resort & Spa

EATING
7. Brunel's Restaurant
8. Cafe Mauds
9. Great Jones
10. Niki's Kitchen Cafe
11. Olive Bizarre

Beaches & Coastal Walks
Exploring The Seafront

Newcastle's beaches, coastal paths and promenades make for wonderful walks in the shadow of the Mournes.

At the northern end of town, the **Royal County Down Golf Club** is a links course set amid flowering heather and gorse on the coast. Visitors can play on certain days of the week, but you'll need to book several months in advance.

South of the golf course is the redbrick facade of the **Slieve Donard Resort & Spa**. In the grounds, a sculpture pays tribute to the poet and songwriter Percy French, who wrote 'The Mountains of Mourne'. The piece is inscribed with lyrics from the song, a letter to a loved one expressing one man's longing to return to the place where 'the mountains of Mourne sweep down to the sea'.

From the hotel, a promenade extends south, with Newcastle beach to the east, the Mournes to the south, and the shops, arcades and cafes of Newcastle town to the west; look out for another monument to Percy French and several other sculptures along the way. Near the footbridge across the Shimna River, stop for an ice cream at **Cafe Mauds** (p510).

Drive or cycle 5km south of town to **Bloody Bridge car park** to access the coastal path. The rugged coastline here

WHY I LOVE NEWCASTLE & THE MOURNES

Isabel Albiston, writer

Though I have known the area since I was a child, I always catch my breath at the first glimpse of the Mournes on the drive into Newcastle. The combination of sparkling sea, sandy beaches and rolling mountains is truly beautiful, but more than that, it feels welcoming, as if the Mournes are waiting to embrace me. It's a place that will always hold fond memories for me, of splashing in the river with friends and walking in the hills. There is a freshness in the air that makes me feel renewed.

WHERE TO STAY IN NEWCASTLE

Hutt Hostel
In a renovated Victorian townhouse by the beach, this hostel has shared dorms and excellent amenities. £

Enniskeen Country House Hotel
This traditional 19th-century manor house hotel, 2km northwest of town, has mountain and sea views. ££

Slieve Donard Resort & Spa
This magnificent red-brick hotel by the beach has been a local landmark since 1898. £££

has some interesting rock formations formed from tilted upturned shale seabeds. A 1.6km linear trail leads through wildflowers, gorse and bell heather to Bloody Bridge River, which cascades into natural pools that are perfect for a refreshing dip. Look out for fulmars, black guillemots and herring gulls that nest in the cliffs here. There is a scenic picnic area, and toilets at the car park.

Climb Slieve Donard
Dramatic Granite Peak

The summit of Northern Ireland's highest hill, Slieve Donard (852m), can be reached from several starting points in and around Newcastle. It is a fairly steep hike; wear walking boots and bring a rain jacket.

The shortest route to the top is via the River Glen from Newcastle. The trail begins at **Donard Park car park**, at the edge of town. At the far end of the car park, turn right through the gate and head into the woods, with the river on your left. A gravel path leads up the River Glen valley to the saddle between Slieve Donard and Slieve Commedagh. From here, follow the Mourne Wall to the summit. Return by the same route (round-trip 9km; allow at least three hours). An alternative route to the summit starts at Bloody Bridge on the coast and follows the river up to the Mourne Wall (round-trip 10km). Walk NI (walkni.com) has detailed descriptions of both routes.

On a clear day, the view from the top extends to the hills of Donegal, the Wicklow Mountains, the coast of Scotland, the Isle of Man and even the hills of Snowdonia in Wales. At the summit, look for the prehistoric Great Cairn, a passage tomb dating from around 3000 BCE. About 200m northeast, overlooking Newcastle, is the Bronze Age Lesser Cairn. The mountain is named for St Donard, who retreated here to pray in early Christian times; he is believed to have used the cairns as a hermitage until his death in 506 CE.

Slieve Donard

BEST PLACES TO EAT IN NEWCASTLE

Niki's Kitchen Cafe
Popular cafe serving breakfasts, lunchtime soups and sandwiches, and teatime tray bakes and scones. £

Olive Bizarre
Come here for coffee, cakes, brunch and lunch, including vegan options. £

Cafe Mauds
When the sun comes out, head to Mauds for a cone or an ice cream sundae. ££

Great Jones
This restaurant serves generous portions of holiday favourites, like fish and chips, steaks and burgers. ££

Brunel's Restaurant
Beautifully presented plates and creative combinations of local produce; excellent desserts, too. £££

GETTING AROUND

Newcastle is small enough to explore on foot. Cycling is a handy way to reach nearby beaches and walking trails; Bike Mourne rents bikes and e-bikes from its shop in town. There are regular buses to Belfast and Newry. In the summer, the Mourne Rambler bus loops through the mountains.

CYCLE AROUND THE MOURNES

This 46km loop along quiet roads takes in some of the Mournes' most beautiful scenery; allow three to four hours. Bike Mourne in Newcastle rents e-bikes (book ahead).

From Newcastle, head south along Central Promenade, passing the harbour. From here, Kilkeel Rd hugs the coast as it steadily climbs; inhale sea breezes as you pedal. Stop at **1 Bloody Bridge car park** to take a detour on foot along the coastal path to Bloody Bridge River. Get back on your bike and continue south along the coast. In Glasdrumman village, turn right onto Quarter Rd. From here the road gently climbs into the foothills of the Mournes, passing grazing sheep as you cycle towards rolling mountain peaks.

Follow the bend in the road left onto Head Rd. Soon you'll reach **2 Carrick Little car park**, the start point for hikes up Slieve Binnian. If you're ready for coffee or lunch, turn right up the track to **3 Carrick Cottage Cafe**.

Back on Head Rd, continue west to reach the entrance to **4 Silent Valley Reservoir**, where the River Kilkeel was dammed in 1933 to supply Belfast and County Down with water. Cycle up to the water's edge to take in the views.

Return to Head Rd and continue west, then turn right onto Moyad Rd. From here, there are views of Carlingford Lough to the south. Cycle through the peaceful mountain terrain, passing **5 Spelga Dam**; pull over at the roadside viewpoint for a better look.

At the fork, turn right onto Slievenaman Rd and continue to **6 Tollymore Forest Park**. If you still have power in your legs, enter the park for a hike or a cycle along the riverbanks and forest trails. Return to Newcastle via Bryansford Rd.

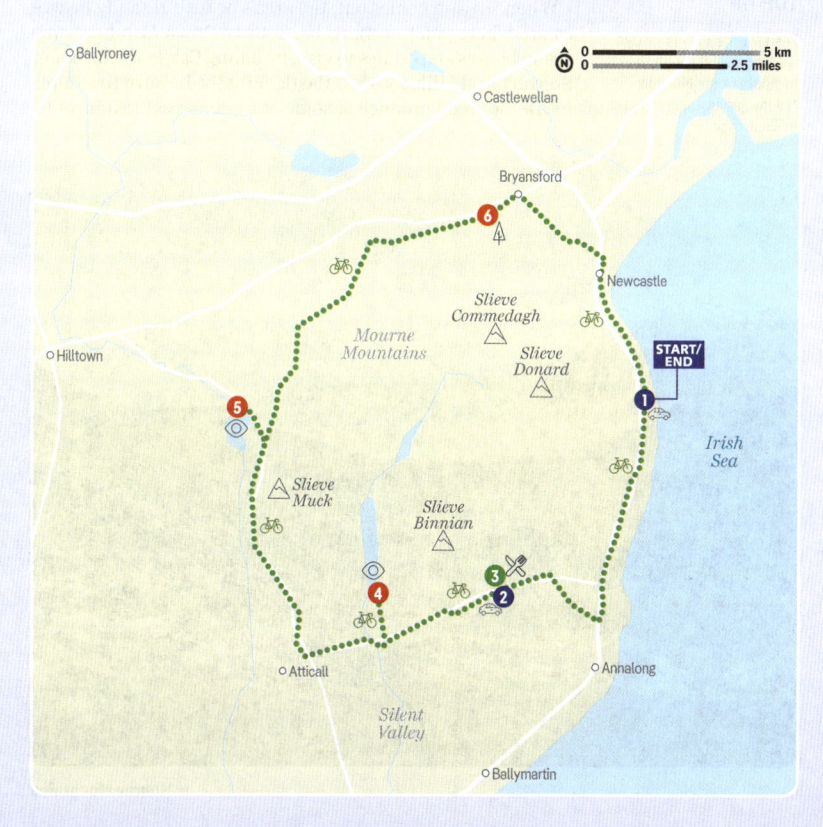

Beyond Newcastle

From walks in the Mourne Mountains to birdwatching at Strangford Lough, you'll want to spend some time exploring County Down.

There is no shortage of attractions in the area beyond Newcastle. Options for activities abound, from walks along the drystone Mourne Wall to horse riding at Castlewellan to kayaking in Strangford Lough, an area rich in wildlife. Some of Ireland's best mountain-biking trails traverse the wooded hillsides of Kilbroney Park; afterwards, stop for a pint in Rostrevor, a village known for its folk music festival.

When the sun comes out, the area's beautiful sandy beaches are where you'll want to be. County Down also has some grand houses and estates to visit, including Castle Ward, Mount Stewart and Hillsborough Castle. Finally, be sure to sample locally sourced produce at some of Ulster's best restaurants.

TOP TIP

The Mourne Way is a 40km walking trail through the foothills of the Mourne Mountains from Newcastle to Rostrevor.

Mourne Mountains

BIKE RIDES IN THE MOURNES

As well as cycling at Tollymore, you can hire a bike and hit the mountain-biking trails at **Castlewellan** (p514) and Kilbroney Park (p515), or explore further into the Mournes along quiet roads on a circular route from Newcastle (p511).

Dundrum Castle

Take in the Views in Dundrum
Castle Ruins, Seafood And Nature

The village of Dundrum is worth visiting for its Norman castle, fresh seafood and spectacular coastal nature reserve. It's located 6km north of Newcastle; the Newcastle to Belfast bus stops here.

First explore the ruins of **Dundrum Castle**, founded in 1177 by Anglo-Norman knight John de Courcy. Enter the grassy castle complex for wonderful views across to the Mournes from de Lacey's keep.

Dundrum Bay is famous for its oysters and mussels. Stop for lunch at **Mourne Seafood Bar** (p514) or the **Buck's Head Inn** (p514), or pick up food to go from **Scopers** (p514).

Next take a walk across the grassy sand dunes of **Murlough National Nature Reserve**. The reserve is a 1.5km walk south of Dundrum via Keel Point Rd. Traversed by a network of boardwalks and paths, the dune system here is home to 22 species of butterflies, including the marsh fritillary. Beyond the dunes lies a 6km-long golden sand beach. Walking trails lead through woodland, over the dunes and along the strand.

THE KINGDOM OF MOURNE

The crescent of low-lying land on the southern side of the mountains is known as the Kingdom of Mourne. Cut off for centuries (the main overland route passed north of the hills), it developed a distinctive landscape and culture. Until the coast road was built in the early 19th century, the only access was on foot or by sea.

Smuggling provided a source of income in the 18th century. Boats carrying French spirits would land at night and packhorses would carry the casks through the hills to the inland road, avoiding the excise men at Newcastle. The Brandy Pad, a former smugglers' path from Bloody Bridge to Tollymore Forest (p514), is a popular walking route today.

WHERE TO STAY IN THE MOURNE MOUNTAINS

Mourne Lodge
Homely hostel with dorms and private rooms, a kitchen and a cosy living room. **£**

Meelmore Lodge
Perfectly located for mountain walks, Meelmore Lodge has dorms, private rooms and a campsite. **£**

Leitrim Lodge Farm Pods
These glamping pods have a double bed and two bunks, making them a good choice for families. **£££**

COUNTY DOWN FOOD TIPS

Caroline Wilson, founder of the Belfast Food Tour, shares her tips. (instagram.com/tasteandtour)

Scopers
This hot food bar in Dundrum is not your usual takeaway. Think stuffed courgette flowers, mussel floss chips, salt and chilli squid and venison burgers. Take it to eat on the beach.

Fodder
If eating local, seasonal produce in a tepee is your thing, don't miss Fodder, a working farm near Downpatrick. There's a cafe, farm shop, foraging classes and 2km of trails through the woodland on which their cows graze.

Noble
This tiny restaurant near the sea in Holywood is a must: wonderful wine, freshly landed crab, Portavogie prawns and a Parmesan and truffle risotto I want to swim in.

Legananny Dolmen

Woodland Walks at Tollymore Forest Park
Stepping Stones And Forest Trails

This scenic forest park, 3km west of Newcastle, offers lovely walks and bike rides along the River Shimna and across the Mournes' northern slopes. At the river there is a hermitage, five stone bridges and stepping stones to explore. Longer trails lead further into the hills through fragrant pine forest, emerging onto the mountain slopes with views out to the coast. There are picnic tables, and charcoal barbecues are permitted. You can also pitch a tent at the campground here.

Stone Age Monument in the Dromara Hills
Dolmen With Mountain Views

On the western slopes of Slieve Croob (532m), the **Legananny Dolmen** is a Stone Age megalith single-chamber portal tomb, dating from 2500 BC to 2000 BC. Its granite capstone balances delicately atop the three slim upright stones, while its elevated position gives it an impressive view of the Mournes.

The dolmen is 17km northwest of Newcastle, in the Dromara hills, and reachable by car or bicycle. On the way from Newcastle, make a stop at **Castlewellan Forest Park**, 10km south of the dolmen, which has lakeside walks and mountain-bike trails (there is bike hire available here, too). It's also possible to explore the forest on horseback on a guided ride with **Mount Pleasant Equestrian Centre**.

WHERE TO EAT & DRINK IN DUNDRUM

Garden House Cafe
At Seaforde Gardens and Butterfly House, this cafe serves coffee, snacks and home-baked cakes. £

Mourne Seafood Bar
This informal spot serves oysters, seafood chowder, crab, langoustines and daily specials, all sourced locally. ££

Buck's Head Inn
Welcoming pub and restaurant serving local seafood and other mains; look for the pink facade. ££

Cycle or Hike Through the Real-Life Narnia
Forest That Inspired Cs Lewis

Near the village of Rostrevor, the forested hills of **Kilbroney Park** can be explored on foot, by bike or by car. Although the journey from Newcastle to Rostrevor is a little shorter via inland roads (30km), it's worth taking the scenic coastal route via Kilkeel (37km, about 35 minutes' drive) for the sea views.

There is a sense of magic to the place; CS Lewis once said that the part of Rostrevor that overlooks Carlingford Lough was his idea of Narnia. Dip your toe into the enchanted forest with a walk along the 1.2km **Fairy Glen Walk**, which follows the Kilbroney River from the village, connecting with other trails further into the park. Continue east to reach the 1km **Narnia Trail**, a children's woodland path dotted with characters from *The Lion, the Witch and the Wardrobe*.

The main Kilbroney trailhead and car park is 1km east of the village. Here there's a cafe and campsite; mountain-bike hire and an uplift service is offered by **Bike Mourne** (book ahead). The mountain-biking trails here include a 27km red trail and a 19km black trail; they are considered to be among Ireland's best. For a scenic, 4km circular hike, try the waymarked **Cloughmore Trail**. It follows the Glen River up to the Cloughmore Stone, a 30-tonne granite boulder inscribed with Victorian-era graffiti, from where there are superb views over the lough. It's also possible to reach the stone by car via the forest drive; it's a 10-minute walk from the upper car park.

Discover the Newry Canal Towpath
Waterside Cycle Or Hike

The Newry Canal towpath meanders through peaceful rolling countryside from Portadown to Newry (32km). Both towns are on the Belfast to Dublin train line, so it's possible to cycle or walk one way and get the train back. Newry is 40 minutes by car from Newcastle.

The canalside Hollie Berrie at the Tearooms in Scarva is a good place to stop for lunch. Just south of Scarva, the towpath passes Lough Shark, where it's possible to spot an array of wildlife, including whooper swans in winter.

In Newry, take a detour to visit **Bagenal's Castle**, the town's oldest surviving building which houses the Newry and Mourne Museum.

FOLK & TRAD MUSIC IN ROSTREVOR

In July, folk musicians gather in Rostrevor for the weeklong **Fiddler's Green Festival**, with a packed schedule of concerts and events. But you can also catch live folk and trad music in Rostrevor most nights throughout the year.

The **Rostrevor Inn** hosts songs and stories nights on Wednesdays, as well as trad sessions at weekends and regular folk music nights.

On Tuesdays, head to the **Corner House** to hear trad sessions performed by the Corner House Clan.

The **Kilbroney** is another village pub with regular live music. Nearby, the **Old Killowen Inn** hosts impromptu trad music and set sessions at weekends.

Listen out for the song 'The Town of Rostrevor' by late folk singer Tommy Makem.

WHERE TO STAY ON THE NORTH DOWN COAST

Cairn Bay Lodge
Family-run guesthouse in an Edwardian home in Bangor, with creative decor and sea views. **££**

Ennislare House
Near Bangor train station, this guesthouse is in a Victorian townhouse with spacious rooms. **££**

Crawfordsburn Old Inn
In operation since 1614, this historic inn has a bar with log fires and luxurious rooms. **£££**

Behind the Scenes of *Game of Thrones*
Official Studio Tour

Fans of *Game of Thrones* can learn how the blockbuster HBO series was made on a behind-the-scenes tour of Linen Mill Studios, where much of the series was filmed. A shuttle bus runs to the studio from the Boulevard shopping mall near Banbridge, 30 minutes' drive from Newcastle.

The high-tech self-guided tours recreate the drama of the series from the offset, with smoke and blasts of cold air as screens open to reveal Westeros. There are plenty of original props, costumes and scenery to see: highlights include the Winterfell great hall, the Dragonstone map table, the map courtyard at King's Landing and the throne room.

Displays explain how the show was produced, including examples of the art department's storyboards and models, and filmed interviews with costume designers. The behind-the-scenes look at the prosthetic department includes the eerie Hall of Faces, for which the team made 600 unique face masks. *Game of Thrones* fans should allow several hours to tour the exhibition.

FILMING LOCATIONS

Some key scenes set in Winterfell were filmed on location at Castle Ward. Other County Down filming locations include Tollymore Forest Park (p514) and Inch Abbey near Downpatrick (p517).

Visit Royal Hillsborough
British Monarch's Northern Ireland Residence

The village of Hillsborough, 19km south of Belfast and 39km (40 minutes' drive) north of Newcastle, was awarded royal status and a name change in 2021. **Hillsborough Castle**, the official home of the Secretary of State for Northern Ireland and a royal residence, is open to the public for guided tours.

Hillsborough Castle is not a castle but a late-18th-century mansion house; it was bought by the British government in 1925. Book a tour to see the throne room, state drawing room and dining room, and Lady Grey's study where, in 2003, Tony Blair and President George W Bush held talks on invading Iraq. Don't miss the castle gardens; highlights include the lime-tree walk and the restored, 18th-century walled garden. Look out for events in the castle grounds, such as concerts, food festivals and gardening workshops.

The castle was built as the family home of the wealthy Hill family, who had previously lived in the **fort** that now sits at the edge of **Hillsborough forest park**. From the pedestrian entrance to the castle, cross Main St and go through the gates next to the Plough Inn to view the fort (the interior is closed to the public), then take a walk around the lake

BEST PLACES TO EAT & DRINK IN HILLSBOROUGH

Round House Bakery
Pick up a loaf of artisan sourdough or a pastry at this village bakery. **£**

Plough Inn
This pub has a maze of wood-panelled nooks and crannies; it offers bistro and restaurant meals. **££**

Parson's Nose
A snug downstairs bar leads to a bright restaurant serving refined pub food and pizza. **££**

The Hillside
This homely pub serves real ale and mulled wine beside the fireplace in winter. **££**

WHERE TO EAT ON THE NORTH DOWN COAST

Guillemot Kitchen Cafe
Opposite Bangor marina, this cafe does all-day breakfasts, gourmet sandwiches, soups, salads and homemade cakes. **£**

The Bay Tree
Holywood cafe and restaurant with a pretty outdoor courtyard; it's known for its cinnamon scones. **£**

Fontana
This Holywood restaurant serves local lobster, aged steak and homemade bread; there's a kids menu, too. **£££**

in the forest park. Finally, relax with a drink in one of the village's excellent pubs.

Learn the Life Story of St Patrick
Downpatrick's Cathedral And Sights

St Patrick's mission to spread Christianity in Ireland began and ended in Downpatrick, 20km northeast of Newcastle, where there are a number of sights connected to the saint.

Begin at the **St Patrick Centre**, where a multimedia exhibition tells the life story of Ireland's patron saint in his own words. From here, a path leads uphill to **Down Cathedral**. In the churchyard, look for a slab of Mourne granite placed here in 1900 to mark the traditional site of **St Patrick's grave**.

Next, take a look inside the cathedral; don't miss the stained-glass window depicting scenes from St Patrick's life. The cathedral's elevated pipe organ is considered one of Ireland's finest; if you're lucky you might catch a recital by one of the skilled organists who travel to Downpatrick for the pleasure of playing it. Walk up English St to the **Down County Museum** to see the 10th-century Downpatrick High Cross.

In a secluded glen 3km east of Downpatrick are **Struell Wells**, where St Patrick is believed to have spent the night immersed in what is now the drinking well. Between the bathhouses and the ruined chapel stands the eye well, whose waters are said to cure eye ailments.

Continue 4km north to reach **Saul Church**, a replica 10th-century church and round tower built in 1932 to mark the 1500th anniversary of St Patrick's arrival. It is located at the site where St Patrick is said to have founded his first church in 432.

To the east is **Slieve Patrick** (120m), a hill with stations of the cross along the path to a 10m-high statue of St Patrick at the summit.

Discover Castle Ward
Country House And Grounds

This country house estate overlooking Strangford Lough, 40 minutes' drive northeast of Newcastle, has all kinds of historic buildings, gardens, woodland areas and meadows to explore, connected by a series of walking and cycling trails.

Start with a tour of **Castle Ward House**, a remarkable building of two halves. The front facade was designed in a neoclassical style, to suit the architectural tastes of Lord Bangor, while the rear facade is Gothic, to suit his wife. The differing styles continue inside; don't miss the incredible fan

ON THE TRAIL OF ST PATRICK

Downpatrick is the final stop on **St Patrick's Way**, a 132km signposted pilgrim walk from Armagh City, linking sites related to St Patrick. Starting at Navan Fort (p523), the walk passes along the Newry canal towpath (p515) from Scarva to Newry, then on to Rostrevor (p515) and across the Mourne Mountains to Newcastle on the way to Downpatrick. You can pick up a free Pilgrim's Passport at the Navan Centre and tourist offices and collect stamps along the way.

If walking doesn't appeal, pick up a map for the St Patrick's Trail, which highlights St Patrick-related and other Christian sights on a driving route from Armagh to Bangor.

WHERE TO EAT & STAY ON ARDS PENINSULA

Pier 36
In Donaghadee, Pier 36 is a pub and restaurant (try the scampi) with B&B rooms. **££**

Portaferry Hotel
This elegant seafront hotel and restaurant is in a converted row of 18th-century terrace houses. **££**

Saltwater Brig
Located on the shoreline near Kircubbin, this pub and restaurant has a huge beer garden. **££**

Ulster Folk and Transport Museum

STRANGFORD LOUGH WILDLIFE

Strangford Lough is a designated marine nature reserve that's home to porpoises, seals and otters, as well as flocks of nesting seabirds. One of the great birdwatching spectacles of Ireland is the autumn arrival of vast flocks of light-bellied brent geese (75% of the world population). Around 30,000 geese come here during winter, as well as knots and redshanks. It's also possible to see peregrines, merlins and the short-eared owl.

One of the best places to bird-spot is **Castle Espie Wetland Centre**, on the western shore of Strangford Lough. The grounds are dotted with birdwatching hides and are great for fledgling naturalists, with family bird-feeding sessions and an adventure playground.

vaulting of Lady Bangor's Gothic boudoir.

The estate was used as a filming location for *Game of Thrones*; pick up a map to see where key scenes were filmed. At the shore, **Clearsky Adventure Centre** rents bikes, kayaks and canoes, and offers *Game of Thrones*–inspired archery sessions at Winterfell Castle. It also rents tents for overnight stays at **Castle Ward Caravan Park**.

Explore the Ards Peninsula
Sea Life And Stately Homes

The Ards Peninsula is the finger of land to the east of Strangford Lough that almost touches the thumb of the Lecale Peninsula at the Portaferry Narrows. A car ferry connects the village of Strangford, 40 minutes' drive northeast of Newcastle, with Portaferry on the Ards Peninsula.

Portaferry is a neat huddle of streets around a medieval tower house, which looks across the Narrows to a matching tower in Strangford. Its top attraction is **Exploris**, an aquarium with marine life from Strangford Lough and a sanctuary where seals are nursed to health and rereleased into the wild. From Portaferry, take a walk along minor coastal roads north for 2.5km to Ballyhenry Island or south for 6km to the nature reserve at Ballyquintin Point. Both are good for birdwatching and seal spotting.

WHERE TO STAY IN & AROUND DOWNPATRICK

Castle Ward Caravan Park
Castle Ward Estate has a campsite with pitches for tents and caravans, and basic glamping huts. **£**

Denvir's Hotel & Pub
This old coaching inn in Downpatrick dates from 1642; it has six rooms with period features. **££**

Cuan Boutique Hotel
In the village of Strangford, the Cuan has luxurious rooms and a restaurant serving local seafood. **£££**

Head north to reach Greyabbey (20km). Stop here to take a look at the remains of the Cistercian abbey, founded in 1193 by Affreca, wife of Anglo-Norman knight John de Courcy. Don't miss the herb garden, full of medicinal plants once cultivated by the monks.

Continue north for 3km to reach **Mount Stewart**, a magnificent 18th-century stately home. Take a tour to learn the story of the house and its contents; treasures include the painting of racehorse *Hambletonian* (1800) by George Stubbs, one of the most important paintings in Ireland. The house overlooks formal gardens filled with subtropical plants and eccentric topiary. Walking trails through the grounds lead around a lake and to a woodland hide for spotting red squirrels. Don't miss the 18th-century Temple of the Winds, a classical Greek–style summer house built on a high point above the lough.

Day Tripping on the North Down Coast
Museums, Beaches And Cafes

The Bangor to Belfast train line makes it easy to visit the north Down coast on a day trip from Belfast. Bangor is 1 hour's drive north of Newcastle.

First, stop for a meal or snack in **Holywood**, which has excellent cafes and restaurants. From here the coastal path leads east to Bangor (14km) and beyond. Walk along the coastal path (3.2km) or take the train east to Cultra to visit the **Ulster Folk and Transport Museum**. Allow time to explore the historic terraced houses, schools, churches, farmhouses, forges and mills that have been transported from locations around the country and rebuilt at the Folk Museum. The adjacent Transport Museum has steam locomotives, trams, buses and cars.

Get back on the train to Helen's Bay, where you can swim in the sea or walk east along the coastal path to **Crawfordsburn Country Park** (if you're driving, park at Crawfordsburn). Take a detour to walk through the forest here; a 5km trail leads past a railway viaduct and up to meadows with spectacular coastal views.

From here, continue along the coast to take the train from Carnalea to the terminus in Bangor. At **Bangor Castle**, pop into the **North Down Museum** (look out for the sugar-cube model of Bangor Castle) and then explore the beautiful Victorian **Walled Garden**; concerts and events are held here in summer.

BEST FOR KIDS IN COUNTY DOWN

Ulster Folk Museum
See reconstructed period buildings and farm animals at this open-air museum.

Pickie Fun Park
Swan-shaped pedal boats and mini golf by the sea in Bangor.

Ark Open Farm
This farm near Newtownards has animals to pet, a fairy-tale forest and tractor rides.

Castle Espie
Kids can see ducklings and play on zip wires, rope swings and in treehouses.

Exploris Aquarium
Discover the marine life of Strangford Lough, as well as tropical fish, sharks and a crocodile.

GETTING AROUND

Buses link Newcastle with Newry, Belfast and Downpatrick. You'll need to change buses in Belfast to get to Hillsborough, and change in Newry or Belfast to get to Banbridge. Change in Kilkeel to get to Rostrevor and in Downpatrick to get to Strangford and Castle Ward. From Strangford, you can catch the ferry to Portaferry and explore the Ards Peninsula by bus, car or bicycle from there. For Bangor and the north Down coast, catch the bus or train from Belfast.

ARMAGH CITY

The reserved and somewhat parochial atmosphere of Armagh city these days belies its importance as a religious centre steeped in history and legend. Excavations at Navan Fort suggest the site was once occupied by royalty or high priests of great importance, who more than 2000 years ago may have brought animals from as far away as Africa. The site is mythologised in the Ulster Cycle of legends as the court of King Conchobar mac Nessa, uncle of the great warrior Cúchulainn. Little wonder then that in the 5th century, St Patrick chose a nearby hill as the site of his first church, at the location of what is now St Patrick's Church of Ireland Cathedral.

Armagh remains the ecclesiastical capital of Ireland, the seat of both the Anglican and Roman Catholic archbishops of Armagh. Their two cathedrals look across at each other from their respective hilltops.

TOP TIP

Check to see if your visit coincides with one of Armagh's festivals and events. In March, the St Patrick's Festival includes music, drama, film and dance performances. At Navan Fort, Celtic traditions are marked with events for the summer solstice in June and Lughnasa in August.

St Patrick's Roman Catholic Cathedral (p522)

HIGHLIGHTS
① Armagh Courthouse
② Armagh Gaol
③ Armagh Observatory
④ Armagh Robinson Library
⑤ Charlemont Place
⑥ No 5 Vicar's Hill
⑦ St Patrick's Church of Ireland Cathedral
⑧ St Patrick's Roman Catholic Cathedral
⑨ The Mall

SLEEPING
⑩ Armagh City Hotel

EATING
⑪ 4C Coffee House & Kitchen
⑫ Uluru Bar & Grill

Armagh's Historic Buildings
Centre Of Religion And Learning

Armagh's compact city centre is packed with historically and architecturally significant buildings, many of them built during Richard Robinson's time as Archbishop of Armagh from 1765 to 1794.

Start at the **Armagh Robinson Library**, founded by Archbishop Robinson in 1771. It houses the Archbishop's personal library, including a 1st edition of *Gulliver's Travels*, published in 1726 and annotated by Jonathan Swift himself. Nearby you can see ancient coins and early Christian artefacts from Robinson's collection at **No 5 Vicar's Hill**.

Opposite is **St Patrick's Church of Ireland Cathedral**, occupying the site of St Patrick's original stone church. Be-

Armagh Observatory

BEST PLACES TO EAT IN COUNTY ARMAGH

4C Coffee House & Kitchen
This quirky cafe in Armagh city serves breakfast, lunch and cakes; has indoor and outdoor seating. £

Uluru Bar & Grill
An Australian-style restaurant in Armagh city, specialising in chargrilled meats, plus local craft beers and ciders. ££

Groucho's on the Square
Characterful pub and restaurant in Richhill; local ingredients include Armagh pork. ££

Killeavy Castle Estate
In a listed castle in the Ring of Gullion, this hotel has a fine-dining restaurant and a bistro. £££

fore going in, take a look at the stone to the north of the entrance marking the burial place of Brian Ború, the high king of Ireland, who died near Dublin during a battle against the Vikings in 1014. Inside, look for the **Tandragee Man**, a 3000-year-old stone carving believed to represent the Irish king Nuadhe.

Walk down Abbey St and College St to reach the **Mall**, a long grassy park created under the direction of Archbishop Robinson. It's flanked by notable buildings such as **Armagh Courthouse** and **Armagh Gaol**, and Georgian terraces, including **Charlemont Place**.

At the northern end of the Mall, walk up Robinson Dr to reach the **Armagh Observatory**, founded by Archbishop Robinson in 1789 and still a leading astronomical research institute. The observatory building is closed to the public but the grounds contain sundials, a scale model of the solar system and a human orrery showing the positions and orbits of the earth.

Finally, take a walk up to the twin towers of **St Patrick's Roman Catholic Cathedral**, built between 1840 and 1873 in Gothic Revival style. Inside, the walls and ceilings are covered in beautiful coloured mosaics.

WHERE TO STAY IN COUNTY ARMAGH

Bluebell Lane
Stay in a safari tent, a shepherd's hut or a pod near Slieve Gullion. £

Armagh City Hotel
Large, modern hotel in Armagh city with excellent amenities; deluxe rooms have cathedral views. ££

Newforge House
Historic country house in Magheralin; overnight guests can dine in the superb restaurant. ££

History at Navan Fort
Enigmatic Iron Age Monument

Perched atop a drumlin on the outskirts of Armagh city, Navan Fort is Ulster's most important archaeological site. The **Navan Centre** offers scheduled guided tours that place the fort in its historical and mythical context, featuring costumed actors and a re-creation of an Iron Age settlement. A good option for children is the Meet the Warriors tour, with face painting, costumes and storytelling (book ahead). The Legendary Navan Fort tour includes a guided walk around the site.

Navan Fort was probably a site of rituals and ceremonies and was an important centre from around 330 BCE to 330 CE. These days you can climb the grassy mounds and enjoy views towards the cathedrals of Armagh, but it's worth booking a tour or picking up a leaflet from the Navan Centre to better understand the site.

The main circular earthwork enclosure is 250m in diameter, with two smaller earth mounds on the hilltop. The excavation of the larger mound revealed the remains of a structure that intrigued archaeologists. It appears to be a temple with a roof supported by concentric rows of wooden posts, constructed in around 95 BCE. The discovery of the skull of a Barbary ape, believed to have been brought from North Africa in the 2nd century BCE, has led experts to believe that the site might have been the residence of a high priest or king.

Navan Fort

THE LEGENDS OF EMAIN MACHA

Navan Fort appears in early literature as Emain Macha, the court of mythical King Conchobar mac Nessa. The Ulster Cycle is a series of legends set in the heroic age of the distant past, and one of four cycles in Irish mythology.

The central tale, Táin Bó Cúailnge (The Cattle Raid of Cooley), tells the story of a raid by the army of Queen Medbh of Connacht. The hero of the Ulster Cycle tales is Cúchulainn, a great warrior. During the *táin*, the men of Ulster were weakened by a curse after the pregnant goddess Macha was forced to race against a horse-drawn chariot. Only Cúchulainn, who was born outside Ulster, was unaffected by the curse, leaving him to defend Ulster alone.

GETTING AROUND

Armagh's hilly city centre is small enough to explore on foot. There are several buses a day to Belfast and Newry. Navan Fort is 3km west of Armagh city; take bus 73 from the bus centre.

Beyond Armagh City

With tranquil hill walks and peaceful bird-watching spots, County Armagh offers natural beauty without the crowds.

TOP TIP

The 180km signposted Loughshore Trail cycle route encircles Lough Neagh via a series of quiet country roads and traffic-free paths.

The area between Armagh city and the southern shore of Lough Neagh is apple orchard country, where Armagh Bramleys are grown and turned into cider; apple-growing conditions are improved by a slight microclimate effect created by the lough. At the lough, birdlife thrives; the various habitats at Oxford Island offer wonderful wildlife-watching opportunities.

In South Armagh, the Ring of Gullion is an unusual geographical landform that is now part of the Mourne Gullion Strangford Unesco Geopark. At the centre of a circle of hills stands Slieve Gullion, a seemingly magical place linked to several Celtic legends, and the place where the mythical warrior Cúchulainn got his name.

Slieve Gullion

Lakeside Nature Trails at Oxford Island
Birdwatching At Lough Neagh

This peninsula of land on Lough Neagh's southern edge, 30 minutes' drive north of Armagh city, contains a range of habitats, including woodland, wet grassland (meadows that are important breeding grounds for butterflies) and reedy shoreline, which can be explored on walking and cycling trails. There are several birdwatching hides; look out for grey herons, great crested grebes, little grebes, coots and moorhens. Follow the tree trail to see 20 different native species.

Explore the Ring of Gullion
Folk Tales And Hiking Trails

The Ring of Gullion is a string of rugged hills encircling Slieve Gullion (573m) in an unusual 60-million-year-old geological formation known as a ring dyke. Begin exploring at **Slieve Gullion Forest Park**, 30 minutes' drive from Armagh city. Here Slieve Gullion Courtyard (an area with an information point, cafe and car park) is the starting point for Fionn's Giant Adventure, a magical forest trail for children, with hidden fairy doors and play equipment in the trees. From here, follow the scenic drive to a parking and picnic area, from where you can hike to the summit (1.3km).

At the top, look for a Neolithic burial chamber which aligns with the setting sun of the winter solstice; it is Ireland's highest surviving passage tomb. From here there are outstanding views of the outer hills that form the Ring of Gullion. Continue north along the mountain path to reach a small lake; legend has it that Calliagh Berra (who lived in the South Cairn passage tomb) tricked the giant Finn McCool into diving into the bottomless lake to retrieve her ring.

Nearby, at **Bluebell Lane** (p522), you can book a place on a woodturning workshop and make your own Celtic bowl.

BIRDWATCHING SPOTS

Strangford Lough has many wonderful spots for birdwatching; **Castle Espie Wetland Centre** (p518) near Comber has birdwatching hides and binoculars. Fulmars, black guillemots and herring gulls nest in the cliffs at the Mourne Coastal Path near **Bloody Bridge** (p509).

LOUGH NEAGH EELS

The eels of Lough Neagh are believed to have been eaten by locals since the Bronze Age, and are still caught and sold today by members of the Lough Neagh Fishermen's Cooperative.

At Oxford Island Nature Reserve, look for the sculpture *Eel Retreat* by Trudi Entwistle, which captures the motion of eels swimming through water. The eels' remarkable journey from the spawning grounds of the Sargasso Sea to Lough Neagh was the inspiration for Seamus Heaney's poem 'A Lough Neagh Sequence'.

GETTING AROUND

National cycle route 9 links Newry with Slieve Gullion Courtyard via minor roads (15km); it's a 35km drive southeast from Armagh city to the forest park. Oxford Island is also connected to Newry and Belfast via cycle route 9; it's a 30km drive from Armagh city.

DERRY & ANTRIM

HOME TO THE CAUSEWAY COAST

This dramatic coastline of basalt cliffs, hexagonal rocks and sandy beaches is backed by rolling hills and farmland.

Counties Derry and Antrim's remarkable landscape of cliffs, glens and caves form part of the Antrim Plateau: the entire area between Cave Hill in Belfast and the north coast, extending west as far as Binevenagh Mountain, is formed of basalt rock and layers of limestone. The most striking natural features, such as the U-shaped valleys of the Antrim Glens, were formed during the Ice Age, around 20,000 years ago.

As you head north through County Antrim, you may notice that the regional accent has a Scottish lilt. This corner of Ireland has long had strong cultural connections with its closest neighbour (there is just 20km of sea between Antrim's Torr Head and the Scottish Mull of Kintyre). During the 16th century, the Scottish MacDonnell clan took control of several castles on the north coast, including Dunluce.

These days the Causeway Coast is home to a number of independent producers of artisan goods. There are waves to surf, paths to hike and excellent cafes and restaurants to enjoy. Little wonder, then, that the area has become an increasingly popular place to live.

To the west, the walled city of Derry sits alongside a broad sweep of the River Foyle. Though Derry's turbulent history forms part of the city's fabric, it also has a thriving arts and music scene, and hosts some of Ireland's best festivals.

THE MAIN AREAS

DERRY CITY
Historic walled city.
p532

BALLYCASTLE
Gateway to the Causeway Coast.
p543

Above: Blackhead Lighthouse (p554); left: Grey seal, Rathlin Island (p546)

THE GUIDE

DERRY & ANTRIM

Derry City, p532
Walled city on the River Foyle with a fascinating but turbulent history and a thriving cultural scene.

Find Your Way

Derry and Antrim's biggest attractions are located on or near the coast. To see them, follow the coastline from Belfast to Derry, allowing plenty of time for detours and hikes along the way.

Ballycastle, p543

The seaside town of Ballycastle is perfectly located for trips to the Causeway Coast and the Antrim Glens.

CAR & BICYCLE

Having your own wheels is the easiest way to get around. Roads are generally good in both counties. Sustrans cycling route 93 extends all the way from Derry to Larne, including several traffic-free sections.

BUS & TRAIN

Coastal buses are handy for getting back from one-way hikes and avoiding car park fees. Services are limited or nonexistent to out-of-the-way places. The Derry to Coleraine train journey is one of Ireland's most scenic.

THE GUIDE

DERRY & ANTRIM

529

Old Bushmills Distillery (p549)

Plan Your Time

You'll want to hit the Causeway Coast's major sights, but allow time to take walks and spot wildlife in the spaces in between.

Two Days on the Causeway Coast

From Ballycastle, head to the **Carrick-a-Rede Rope Bridge** (p547) and then hike west along the coast to the **Giant's Causeway** (p548). Finish with a tour of the **Old Bushmills Distillery** (p549). The next day, drive west towards Derry, stopping in **Downhill** (p541) on the way. Walk around **Derry's city walls** (p535), then listen to live music in one of the **city's pubs** (p534).

Five-Day Loop from Belfast

Head to the **Gobbins** (p555) and then drive to Ballycastle via the **Antrim Glens** (p532), stopping at Cushendun and Cushendall. Spend the following day on **Rathlin Island** (p546). Next, drive west to Portrush, stopping to see **castles** (p551) and the **Giant's Causeway** (p548). Continue west to **Derry** (p532) for a day. Stop at **Seamus Heaney Home Place** (p539) on the drive back to Belfast.

Seasonal Highlights

SPRING
Wildflowers bloom along the cliffs of the Causeway Coast. In May puffins arrive at Rathlin Island and the Gobbins.

SUMMER
The weather is mild and coastal sights and beaches are busy. The best time for sea bathing and camping.

AUTUMN
Fewer people at popular sites like the Giant's Causeway. In October, Derry celebrates Halloween with concerts and street parties.

WINTER
Bigger swells bring surfers to Portrush, Downhill and Benone. A Christmas craft fair is held at Derry's Guildhall.

Guildhall (p537) from the Derry city walls

DERRY CITY

The artistic and cultural hub of Ireland's northwest, Derry has a complicated history that continues to seep into its present. The city's very name is a source of conflict: while nationalists prefer Derry, many unionists insist on Londonderry. Attempts by the local council to change the city's official name to Derry were foiled by a UK ruling that the city's legal name could only be changed by legislation or royal prerogative. Most people, regardless of political persuasion, call it Derry in everyday speech.

Divisions can also be seen in the city's layout: the Bogside is a Catholic neighbourhood while the Fountain remains a Protestant area. Across the Foyle, the Waterside is home to both Catholics and Protestants.

The city was depicted in the series *Derry Girls* (2018–22). Set in the 1990s, the series uses humour to show everyday life for teenagers during the final years of the Troubles.

TOP TIP

The Derry Urban Greenways are two cycling and walking paths on either side of the River Foyle. From the Peace Bridge, the Foyle Valley Greenway extends south along the west bank, continuing inland to Strabane. The Waterside Greenway runs north from the Peace Bridge along the east bank to Foyle Bridge.

Peace Bridge (p537)

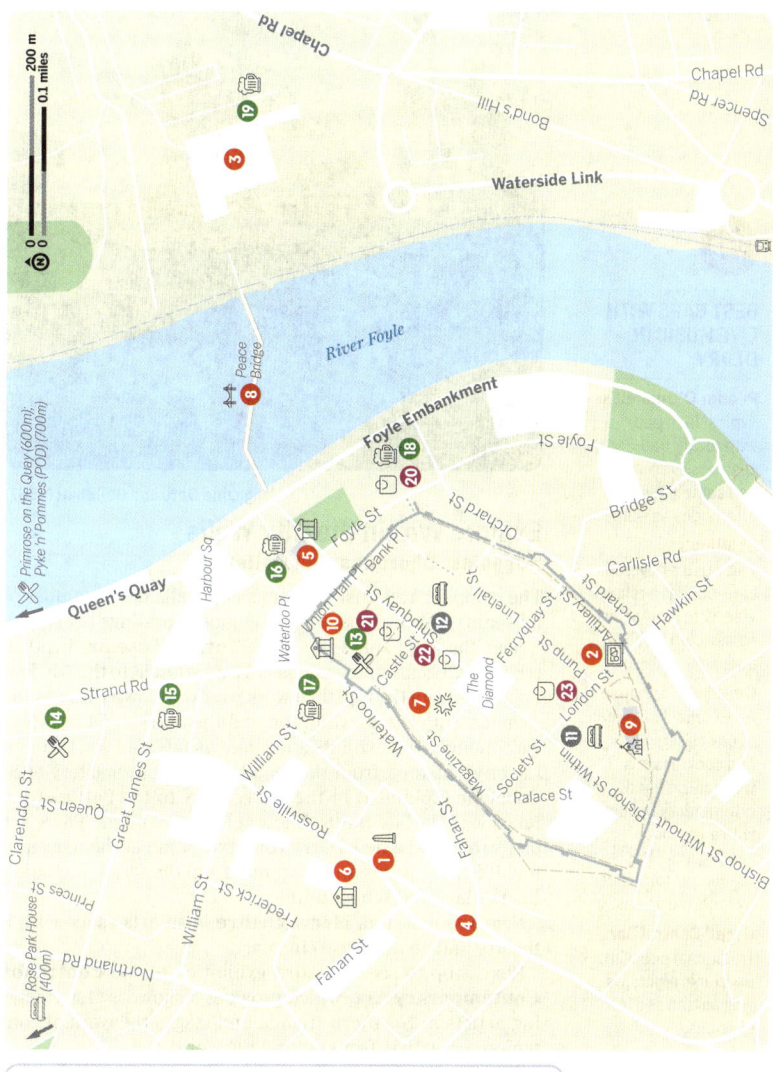

SIGHTS
1. Bloody Sunday Memorial
2. Centre for Contemporary Art
3. Ebrington Square
4. Free Derry Corner
5. Guildhall
6. Museum of Free Derry
7. Nerve Centre
8. Peace Bridge
9. St Columb's Cathedral
10. Tower Museum

SLEEPING
11. Bishop's Gate Hotel
12. Shipquay Hotel

EATING
13. Artis by Phelim O'Hagan
14. Pyke 'n' Pommes (53-55)

DRINKING & NIGHTLIFE
15. Grand Central Bar
16. Guildhall Taphouse
17. Peadar O'Donnell's
18. Sandino's
19. Walled City Brewery

SHOPPING
20. Cool Discs Music
21. Craft Village
22. Derry Designer Makers
23. Smart Swag

Magazine Gate and Guildhall (p537)

BEST BARS WITH LIVE MUSIC IN DERRY

Peadar O'Donnell's
Typical Irish pub with rowdy trad sessions every night and sometimes afternoons as well.

Sandino's
This poster-covered cafe-bar has a relaxed vibe, with regular live music, club nights and gigs.

Guildhall Taphouse
An excellent selection of craft beers and cocktails in a wooden-beamed, 19th-century building, with an outdoor seating area. Hosts regular performances by local musicians.

Grand Central Bar
Traditional pub with open-mic nights, as well as trad and folk sessions.

Explore Within the City Walls
Museums, Churches And Galleries

The compact area inside Derry's city walls has a number of museums, cultural spaces and religious buildings to explore.

Near the Magazine Gate is the **Tower Museum**, inside a replica 16th-century tower house. Head straight to the 5th floor for a view from the top, then work your way down through the Armada Shipwreck exhibition and the Story of Derry. Here well-thought-out exhibits and audiovisuals lead you through the city's history, from the founding of the monastery of St Colmcille (Columba) in the 6th century to the Battle of the Bogside in the late 1960s. Allow at least two hours. There are plans to create a new Derry Girls exhibition at the museum; it will feature props and costumes from the series, including Erin's diary and school uniform.

Near the museum, **Nerve Centre** is an arts space with a theatre and an arthouse cinema.

Next, stop to see the latest exhibition at the **Centre for Contemporary Art**, which provides a showcase for emerging artists in Northern Ireland and stages the work of contemporary artists from around the world.

Finally, take a look inside the Church of Ireland **St Columb's Cathedral**, Derry's oldest surviving building. In the porch look for the original foundation stone of 1633 that records the cathedral's completion. Nearby is a hollow mortar shell fired into the churchyard during the Great Siege of 1688–89.

WHERE TO STAY IN DERRY

Rose Park House
Good-value B&B in the Rosemount neighbourhood, a 15-minute walk west of the city centre. ££

Shipquay Hotel
Boutique hotel in a historic building in the centre of town; look for online deals. £££

Bishop's Gate Hotel
Rooms have period features at this hotel inside Derry's city walls; good bar and restaurant. £££

A WALK AROUND DERRY'S CITY WALLS

The best way to get a feel for Derry's layout and history is to walk the 1.5km circumference of the city's walls. Allow one hour.

Start at the **1 Diamond**, Derry's central square. Head west on Butcher St, where the town's butchers once had their shops, to **2 Butcher's Gate**, and climb the steps to the top of the city walls.

Stroll downhill to **3 Magazine Gate**. Inside the walls is the modern O'Doherty's Tower, housing the Tower Museum; outside the walls stands the Guildhall (p537). The River Foyle used to come up to the northeastern wall here. In the middle is the **4 Shipquay Gate**.

Follow the walls southwest and climb to Newgate Bastion. Pause here to look back at the **5 Derry Girls mural**, depicting the five main characters from the series.

Continue to **6 Ferryquay Gate**, where the apprentice boys barred the gate at the start of the Great Siege of 1688–89. The stretch of wall beyond overlooks the Fountain housing estate, the last significant Protestant community on the western bank of the Foyle.

Continue around the southern stretch of wall to the **7 Double Bastion**, home to Roaring Meg, the most famous of the cannons used during the Siege of Derry. The next section of wall is known as the **8 Grand Parade**, and offers an excellent view of the murals painted by the Bogside Artists.

An empty plinth on **9 Royal Bastion** marks the former site of a monument to the Reverend George Walker, joint governor of the city during the Great Siege; it was blown up by the IRA in 1973. A little further along is the **10 Apprentice Boys' Memorial Hall** and the adjoining Siege Museum.

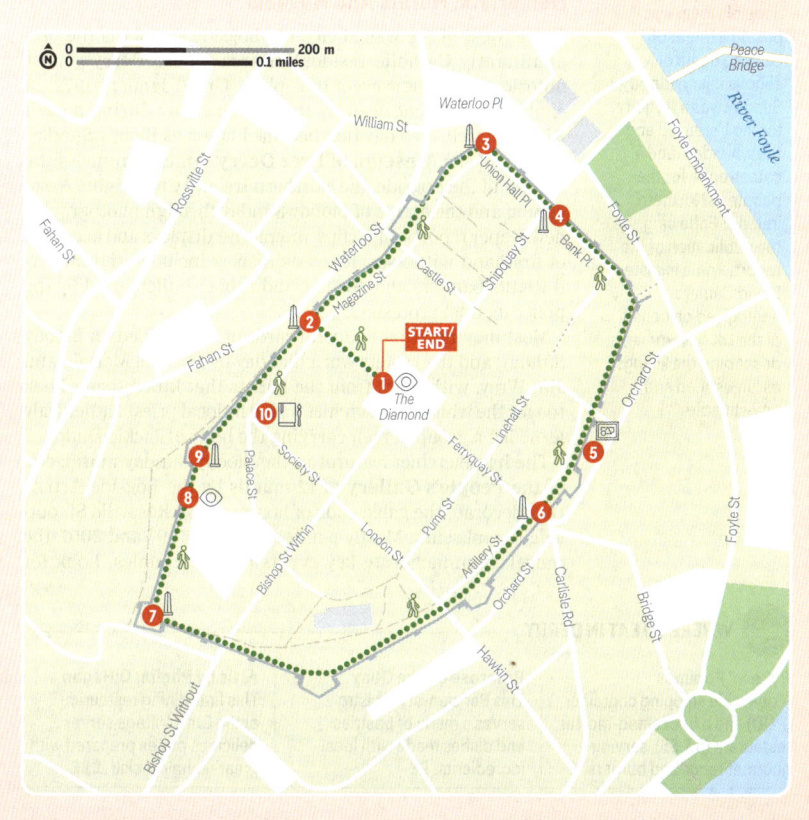

THE BLOODY SUNDAY INQUIRY

Longstanding dissatisfaction with the 1972 Widgery investigation, which had failed to find anyone responsible for the events of Bloody Sunday, led to the Bloody Sunday Inquiry, headed by Lord Saville. Its report was published in 2010.

Lord Saville found that 'The firing by soldiers of 1 PARA on Bloody Sunday caused the deaths of 13 people and injury to a similar number, none of whom was posing a threat of causing death or serious injury. Bloody Sunday was a tragedy for the bereaved and the wounded, and a catastrophe for the people of Northern Ireland.' Following the publication of the report, Prime Minister David Cameron apologised on behalf of the UK government, describing the killings as 'unjustified and unjustifiable'.

Stained-glass window, the Guildhall

Learn the Poignant History of the Bogside
Memorials, Murals And Museum

To the west of the walled city, the Bogside district is the predominantly Catholic residential area where Derry's most notorious and tragic event took place. On 30 January 1972, 13 civilians were shot dead by the British Army during a Civil Rights march, on a day that became known as Bloody Sunday.

Begin at the **Museum of Free Derry**, which chronicles the history of the Bogside, the Northern Ireland Civil Rights Association and the events of Bloody Sunday through photographs, newspaper reports, film clips, interactive displays and accounts of firsthand witnesses. Items on display include original Civil Rights banners and posters, and rubber bullets used by the police against protesters.

Most moving are the funeral cards of those killed on Bloody Sunday, and the jackets worn that day by Michael McDaid and Jim Wray, with holes from the bullets that killed them. Look too for the white handkerchief waved by local priest Father Daly as he led a group of men carrying the body of Jackie Duddy.

The handkerchief features in the Bloody Sunday mural, one of the **People's Gallery** of 12 murals by the Bogside Artists that decorate the gable ends of houses along Rossville St, outside the museum. Mostly painted between 1997 and 2001, the murals commemorate key events in the Troubles. Look for

WHERE TO EAT IN DERRY

Pyke 'n' Pommes
A quayside shipping container (POD) and a bricks-and-mortar restaurant (53-55), serving gourmet tacos and burgers. **£**

Primrose on the Quay
This Parisian-style bistro serves a menu of pastries and dishes made with local ingredients. **££**

Artis by Phelim O'Hagan
This fine-dining restaurant at the Craft Village serves delicious plates prepared with great technical skill. **£££**

Operation Motorman, showing a British soldier breaking down a door with a sledgehammer and *The Petrol Bomber,* a young boy wearing a gas mask and holding a petrol bomb.

The most poignant mural is *The Death of Innocence,* which depicts 14-year-old schoolgirl Annette McGavigan, who was killed in crossfire on 6 September 1971, and was the 100th victim of the Troubles. Her image represents all the children who died in the conflict. The final mural in the sequence, completed in 2004, is the *Peace Mural,* a swirling image of a dove, a symbol of peace and of Derry's patron saint, Columba.

South of the museum, on Rossville St, is **Free Derry Corner**, where the gable end of a house painted with the famous slogan 'You are Now Entering Free Derry' still stands. Nearby, the **Bloody Sunday Memorial** is a simple granite obelisk commemorating those who died.

Look Inside the Guildhall
Architecture And Stained-Glass Windows

Standing just outside the city walls, the neogothic Guildhall was originally built in 1890, then rebuilt after a fire in 1908.

Inside, the highlight is the stained-glass windows, which were presented by the London livery companies. A new window at the entrance will commemorate the victims of Bloody Sunday.

On the 1st floor, look for a display cabinet containing John Hume's Nobel Peace Prize and other awards. The nationalist politician and civil rights activist from Derry was one of the key architects of the Good Friday Agreement in 1998; he and the unionist politician David Trimble were jointly awarded the Nobel Prize the same year.

Cross the Bridge to Ebrington Square
River Views And Craft Beer

The S-shaped pedestrian and cyclist **Peace Bridge** spans the River Foyle, linking the walled city on the west bank to Ebrington Sq on the east.

Access the bridge from the riverbank near Guildhall and cross to the west bank, from where there are views of the Guildhall's clock tower, modelled on London's Big Ben.

Ebrington Square was a 19th-century fort, and later a British Army base; the former parade ground now serves as a public square, performance venue and exhibition space. Walk across the square to **Walled City Brewery**, a craft brewery and gastropub.

BEST SHOPS IN DERRY

Cool Discs Music
Independent record shop with a wide selection of music by Irish artists old and new.

Craft Village
A handful of craft shops sell Derry crystal, handwoven cloth, ceramics, jewellery and other items.

Derry Designer Makers
Sells pieces by a collective of artists and craftspeople, who take turns staffing the shop at the Craft Village.

Smart Swag
Come here for original pieces, like jewellery made from vinyl records, upcycled furniture, screen-printed T-shirts and illustrations of Derry.

GETTING AROUND

Buses and trains arrive at the North West Hub on the Waterside. There is also a large park-and-ride car park here. A greenway links the hub with the city centre (1km) via the Peace Bridge. Buses to Derry City Airport leave from the Foyle St bus centre, stopping at the North West hub on the way.

Derry's main attractions can be reached on foot or by bike; Claudy Cycles offers rentals. It's best to avoid driving within the walled city, where streets are narrow and traffic moves slowly.

Beyond Derry City

To the east of Derry, the coast is lined with broad sandy beaches with surfing breaks and ancient dunes.

There is some outstanding scenery in the areas surrounding Derry. The basalt mountain of Binevenagh dominates the landscape in the Roe Valley and at the coast near Downhill and Benone. The triangle of land at the mouth of Lough Foyle is mostly taken up by a firing range and is also home to a prison. Still, it's worth a visit for its vast sandy beaches. Surfers should head to Benone, Downhill and Portrush.

South of Derry, the newly improved A6 road to Belfast climbs over the Sperrin Mountains at the Glenshane Pass. North of Lough Neagh, the Seamus Heaney Home Place museum and arts centre in the village of Bellaghy is worth a detour.

TOP TIP

The train journey from Derry to Coleraine passes beautiful scenery, travelling right along the coast for much of the way.

Benone Strand (p540)

Seamus Heaney HomePlace

Explore Heaney's Homeland
Landscapes That Inspired Poetry

Nobel Prize–winning poet Seamus Heaney's home town of Bellaghy is the location of **HomePlace**, an exhibition and arts centre dedicated to the poet and his work. Bellaghy is near the main road from Belfast to Derry, and about halfway between the two cities (45 minutes' drive east of Derry and 40 minutes northwest of Belfast).

References in Heaney's poetry to the local landscape, everyday village life and the people who influenced him are highlighted in a creatively laid-out exhibition, which places his work in the context of his home and surroundings. Audio guides allow you to listen to poems read by Heaney himself, bringing his words to life. On display are personal items, including Heaney's duffle coat and his old school bag.

From Home Place, take a walk north along William St to St Mary's Church to visit **Heaney's grave**; his simple gravestone reads 'Walk on air against your better judgement.' Also in the village is *The Turfman* (2009), a sculpture by David Annand that represents the poem 'Digging'.

Follow signs to **Lough Beg** nature reserve, 3km south of Bellaghy, a wildfowl refuge and a landscape described in

BEST FESTIVALS & EVENTS IN DERRY

Derry Halloween
The people of Derry city put on their spookiest fancy dress for this five-day street festival with fireworks, concerts and ghost tours.

City of Derry Jazz
Five days of live jazz at various venues around the city.

Foyle Film Festival
This weeklong event in Derry city is the North's biggest film festival.

North West 200 Motorcycle Race
Ireland's biggest outdoor sporting event is run on a road circuit taking in Portrush, Portstewart and Coleraine.

WHERE TO STAY IN COUNTY DERRY

Benone Tourist Complex
This campsite adjacent to Benone Strand has sites for tents and caravans, as well as basic glamping huts. £

Rick's Causeway Coast Hostel
Neat terrace house in Portstewart with spacious dorms, a living room and a kitchen. £

Cul-Erg House
Family-run B&B near the Portstewart seafront, with an onsite cafe serving homemade cakes. ££

ACTIVITIES AROUND BENONE

Dan Lavery, founder of Long Line Surf School, shares his tips. (instagram.com/longlinesurf)

Surfing
We rent out 8ft longboards at the Sea Shed at Benone, where there are good beginner waves. The surf gets bigger towards Downhill.

Hotbox sauna
Sweat it out in the wood-fired Finnish sauna in a trailer on Benone Strand, then run into the sea.

Stand-up paddleboarding
Paddle down the Roe River, with views of Binevenagh. You might spot kingfishers and otters. Rent gear and access the river at **Swanns Bridge Glamping**.

Beach walks
From Benone you can walk west along the beach for 11km to Magilligan Point. The **Point Bar** there does a good pint of Guinness by the fire.

Mussenden Temple

Heaney's poignant poem 'The Strand at Lough Beg'. A boardwalk leads along the shoreline (the strand) and loops around Longpoint Wood, with views of Church Island. Stop at the post looking out across the water to the distant church spire to hear a recording of Heaney reading his poem, which was written in response to the death of his cousin in a shooting during the Troubles.

Birds to look out for include curlews, redshanks and snipe; listen out for the 'peewit' call of lapwings, too. In autumn, whooper swans arrive from Iceland to spend winter at the lough.

Bask in the Beauty of Binevenagh & Benone
Sandy Beach And Basalt Mountain

Backed by grassy dunes, behind which Binevenagh Mountain looms, the broad sandy beach at Benone is a spectacular spot.

There is parking at **Benone Strand** (45 minutes' drive from Derry). From there you can walk on the beach and take in the wild natural beauty of the often windswept coastline, or hire a surfboard from the Sea Shed Coffee & Surf and get in the water.

From Downhill, 4km east of Benone, the signposted **Binevenagh Scenic Drive** leads up Bishop's Rd to the **Gortmore viewpoint** and picnic area, from where there are views over Lough Foyle to Donegal.

WHERE TO STAY IN COUNTY DERRY

Laurel Villa Guest House
In Magherafelt, this elegant poetry-themed guesthouse displays an impressive collection of Heaney memorabilia. **££**

Strand House
Luxurious B&B near Portstewart strand with welcoming hosts, spacious common areas and excellent breakfasts. **£££**

Burrenmore Nest
At Downhill, these exceptional forest lodges on stilts have hot tubs and views of the trees. **£££**

Discover Downhill Forest & Demesne
Beach, Forest And Clifftop Library

Downhill Strand is at the eastern end of an 11km stretch of beach extending all the way to Magilligan Point. It's a 45-minute drive east of Derry. The nearest train station is Castlerock (3km).

Perched on a grassy cliff overlooking Downhill Strand, **Mussenden Temple** is one of the iconic sights of the northern coastline. It is part of **Downhill Demesne**, the National Trust–owned grounds that from 1774 were the home of the bishop of Derry. The grand manor house he built for himself is now in ruins, but the colonnaded, dome-capped Mussenden Temple – the bishop's private library – remains intact.

Follow trails through the grounds of Downhill Demesne to the **Bishop's Gate**. Exit here and cross the road to enter **Downhill Forest**. Follow the riverside path through the tall trees; look out for the giant Sitka spruce on your left. When the forest path ends at Burrenmore Rd, turn left to see a waterfall and to reach the **Sea Shed** cafe. Return via Burrenmore Rd to emerge onto the main road opposite the main **Lion's Gate** entrance to Downhill Demesne.

Seaside Fun at Portstewart & Portrush
Ice Cream, Beaches And Surfing

There is a holiday atmosphere in the neighbouring seaside towns of Portstewart in County Derry (50 minutes' drive from Derry) and Portrush in County Antrim (55 minutes drive from Derry).

Portstewart Strand is west of town, extending west to the mouth of the River Bann. There are lovely walks here through the ancient dunes. On the town's main promenade, look for **Morelli's**, a local institution, founded by Italian immigrants and serving its own ice cream since 1911. Its sundaes are legendary.

From Portstewart, the **coastal path** leads 10.5km along the coast to the Strand to Whiterocks, 3km east of Portrush.

In summer, **Portrush** bursts with holidaymakers, who spend rainy days in the amusement arcades. **Portrush Strand** is one of Ireland's top surfing centres. Book lessons with **Troggs Surf School** at the East Strand. It also offers surfboard and wetsuit rental, and can provide surf reports and general advice.

BEST PLACES TO EAT IN COUNTY DERRY

Lir
On the banks of the River Bann in Coleraine, Lir offers a tasting menu of sustainable seafood; it's one of the best restaurants in the North. £££

Anglers Rest Benone
This cosy pub serves burgers and bowls of chowder by the fire. ££

Warke's Deli
Stop by for soup or a sandwich, or pick up a hamper to take to the beach. £

Harry's Shack
Located right on Portstewart Strand, Harry's serves local seafood with ocean views. ££

SURF SPOTS

In addition to Benone and Downhill, **Portrush** (p541) is another popular north coast surfing spot; the best beach breaks are at Portrush East Strand. There are several surfboard hire shops and surf schools in the town.

WHERE TO GET COFFEE IN COUNTY DERRY

Sea Shed Downhill
In Downhill Forest, this cafe serves coffee and pastries to satisfy the fussiest coffee connoisseur.

Lost & Found
With branches in Coleraine and Portstewart, Lost & Found is a local favourite for its brunches and flat whites.

3hree Kings
Airy cafe on the Portstewart promenade that serves breakfast and lunch.

BEST CAUSEWAY COAST PRODUCE

Lacada Brewery
A community-owned brewery in Portrush. Try Lacada beers at **Kiwi's Brew Bar** in Portrush.

North Coast Smokehouse
Hand-smoked salmon, trout, salt, black pepper and dulse produced in a small smokehouse near Ballycastle.

Broighter Gold
This cold-pressed rapeseed oil is produced at a family farm in Limavady. Look for it in local shops and delis.

Broughgammon Farm
Farm near Ballycastle that specialises in cabrito (kid goat meat), free-range rose veal and seasonal wild game. Visit the farm shop and cafe.

Portstewart Golf Club

Discover Underwater Wrecks
Diving In The North Atlantic

The waters around Portstewart abound with marine life and shipwrecks, offering fantastic diving. Based in Portstewart, Aquaholics offers dives to nearby sites, including a Skerries cavern with walls covered in soft coral, and the wreck of HMS *Drake* near Rathlin Island.

If you'd rather stay above water, you can book a boat trip along the Causeway Coast, with views of Dunluce Castle, the Skerries and the Giant's Causeway itself. You might spot dolphins and basking sharks on the way.

Golfing on the North Coast
Tee Off By The Atlantic

Portstewart and Portrush are known for their excellent golf courses, which date back to Victorian times.

On the western side of town, **Portstewart Golf Club** has three courses: the Strand par-72 championship links course, the par-68 Riverside course and the par-64 Old Course. It's on the western side of Portstewart, on the road to Portstewart Strand.

But the biggest draw for golfers is **Royal Portrush**. Founded in 1888, Royal Portrush is spectacularly situated alongside the Atlantic at the town's eastern edge. It has two links courses: the Dunluce, with its water's-edge White Rock (5th) and ravine-set Calamity Corner (16th) holes, and the Valley.

Royal Portrush first hosted the Open Championship in 1951. To the delight of local golf fans, the Open returned to Portrush in 2019; it will be held at Royal Portrush again in 2025.

GETTING AROUND

Trains run between Derry and Coleraine, with connections to Portrush, and bus services connect the coastal towns, including Downhill, Portstewart and Portrush. Cycle Route 93 links Derry and Coleraine via inland roads. However, the easiest way to get around is by car.

BALLYCASTLE

Named by the UK's *Sunday Times* as Northern Ireland's best place to live in 2022, Ballycastle is a seaside town with a thriving trad music scene, a broad sandy beach, and views of nearby Rathlin Island and Fair Head. The town's main street has as many small family-run businesses as big-name chain stores, and you'll find more pubs here than might be expected for a town of this size. It's the kind of place where locals know the name of their butcher and the deli counter cheese comes from a nearby farm. In fact, Ursa Minor Bakehouse is known across Ireland for its sourdough bread, while Morton's, the harbourside fish and chip shop, was recently named on a list of the country's best. The town is also known for its famous Ould Lammas Fair, one of Ireland's oldest fairs, which takes place in late August.

TOP TIP

If you want to pack a picnic, the family-owned general store and delicatessen **McLister's** is a good place to pick up supplies, including speciality cheeses. The shop at Ursa Minor Bakehouse has a small selection of deli produce as well as bread and baked goods.

SIGHTS
1 Ballycastle Strand

ACTIVITIES
2 Sea Haven Therapy

SLEEPING
3 An Caisleán Guesthouse
4 Salthouse Hotel

EATING
5 Morton's Fish & Chips
6 Ursa Minor Bakehouse

DRINKING & NIGHTLIFE
7 House of McDonnell

SHOPPING
8 McLister's

Experience the Ould Lammas Fair
Ponies, Dulse And Yellowman

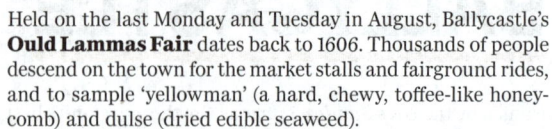

Held on the last Monday and Tuesday in August, Ballycastle's **Ould Lammas Fair** dates back to 1606. Thousands of people descend on the town for the market stalls and fairground rides, and to sample 'yellowman' (a hard, chewy, toffee-like honeycomb) and dulse (dried edible seaweed).

The name Lammas originated from Lughnasadh, a Celtic festival to mark the beginning of the harvest season. The fair includes a livestock market, pony rides, buskers and street performers.

Tap Your Toes to Trad Music
Music And Craic

On Saturday afternoons, join the **Ballycastle Traditional Music Trail** on a guided walk to three Ballycastle pubs, with music and stories along the way. The guides are all musicians with links to the local trad music scene. The trail ends with a trad session at **House of McDonnell**, an authentic local pub that is known for its music.

Take a Seaweed Bath
Relax In Hand-Harvested Seaweed

If hiking on the Causeway Coast has left you feeling tired and achy, head to **Sea Haven Therapy** to immerse yourself in a relaxing natural seaweed bath (good for muscular aches, joint pain and circulation) while enjoying views of Rathlin Island and beyond. You can also book a massage. It's next to the Rathlin Island ferry terminal at Ballycastle Harbour.

Build Sandcastles & Swim in the Sea
Bucket-And-Spade Fun

East of town, **Ballycastle Strand** is a 1.2km-long sandy beach with views of Rathlin Island and Fair Head. There are lifeguards in summer and it is a lovely spot for a swim (though the water here is chilly year-round).

Ould Lammas Fair

BEST PLACES TO EAT & STAY IN BALLYCASTLE

Ursa Minor Bakehouse
Some of Ireland's best sourdough is baked here; the upstairs cafe serves breakfast and lunch. £

Morton's Fish & Chips
Fish and chips don't come fresher: local boats unload their daily catch right alongside this harbourside hut. £

An Caisleán Guesthouse
Well-run B&B located a short walk from the town and beach, with a large guest lounge. ££

Salthouse Hotel
Luxury hotel on the outskirts of town with sea views and a restaurant and spa. £££

GETTING AROUND

Ballycastle town is small enough to cover on foot or by bike. There is a large car park at the harbour.

THE GUIDE

DERRY & ANTRIM BEYOND BALLYCASTLE

Beyond Ballycastle

An extravaganza of sea stacks, beaches, cliffs and caves, the Causeway Coast is one of the most beautiful places in Ireland.

Of all the attractions in Ballycastle's surrounds, the Giant's Causeway is the most famous. For hundreds of years, travellers have come to view the geological marvel of the hexagonal basalt columns; these days visitors continue to arrive by the coachload. Visit the Causeway in the early morning or late evening to avoid the crowds.

But beyond the Causeway, County Antrim has much more to explore, from the world's oldest licensed whiskey distillery to nesting seabird colonies to atmospheric castle ruins. The North Antrim coast offers some of the country's best walks. South of Ballycastle, the Antrim Coast and Glens is a designated Area of Outstanding Natural Beauty, with rolling hills to hike and waterfalls to discover.

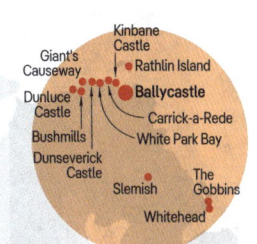

TOP TIP

The seasonal Causeway Rambler service links Coleraine with Ballycastle via Portrush, Dunluce Castle, Bushmills, the Giant's Causeway and Carrick-a-Rede Rope Bridge.

Carrick-a-Rede rope bridge (p547)

545

Guillemots, Rathlin Island

WHY I LOVE RATHLIN ISLAND

Isabel Albiston, writer

The first time I disembarked at Rathlin pier, I noticed that several of the nearby rocks were occupied by sunbathing seals. It felt like the short ferry journey had brought us to a different world. Rathlin's rugged beauty is instantly beguiling, and its size is just right: small enough to get around on foot, but large enough for longer hikes. But for me, the biggest draw is the noisy seabird colony on the western sea stacks, where the birds return to mate each year. Recently, I finally saw a pair of puffins among the squawking seabirds; watching them was just as special as I hoped it would be.

Wildlife-Watching & Windswept Walks on Rathlin Island
Hiking, Birdwatching And Seal Spotting

Rugged, L-shaped Rathlin Island is 6km north of Ballycastle and reachable by ferry (25 to 40 minutes). With the exception of people with disabilities, only island residents can take their car to Rathlin, but bicycles are permitted on the ferry and nowhere on the island is more than 7km (about 1½ hours' walk) from the ferry pier.

From the harbour, cycle, hike or take the Puffin minibus (it waits at the pier for ferries to arrive) to the **Westlight Seabird Centre** (7km) for views of a thriving seabird colony at a nearby sea stack. Every year, thousands of seabirds return here to breed, including puffins, guillemots, razorbills, kittiwakes and fulmars.

Royal Society for the Protection of Birds staff and volunteers can help you identify birds and show you where to look for puffins and their chicks using the centre's telescopes and binoculars. Best times to see puffins are mid-May (when the birds gather on the cliffs), mid-June (when chicks begin hatching) and late July (when puffins prepare to return to sea).

The viewing platforms are at the base of Rathlin's upside-down west lighthouse, which houses the seabird centre. The

---

WHERE TO EAT, DRINK & STAY ON RATHLIN ISLAND

Rathlin Glamping
These glamping pods looking directly at the ocean have attached bathrooms and small kitchenettes. ££

Manor House
Rathlin's 18th-century manor house is now a guesthouse and restaurant, with views across Church Bay. ££

McCuaig's Bar
Rathlin Island's pub and beer garden overlooks the harbour, an idyllic spot for a pint and a meal. ££

building is unusual because the light is at its base and not at its top. Built into the cliff face, it was a feat of engineering when completed in 1919. The lighthouse tower now contains exhibits on Rathlin's marine life and history; don't miss the recreated lighthouse keeper's bedroom.

Head back to the harbour, where you might spot seals. From here, walking routes lead to **Rue Point Lighthouse** (4.5km) and **East Lighthouse** (3km). The routes are also suitable for cycling.

Beneath the East Lighthouse, and only accessible by sea, is the cave where Scottish King Robert the Bruce is said to have been inspired by a spider. Bruce had fled to the island following a defeat in 1306, but after watching the tenacious spider spinning its web, he was encouraged to return to fight for his crown.

In the south of the island, the clifftop **Roonivoolin walking trail** is a good place to spot meadow pipits, rock pipits and wheaters, hear the singing of skylarks and see Irish hares.

Wobble Across to Carrick-a-Rede
Rope Bridge Over The Atlantic

Fishers once slung a rope bridge over the chasm between the sea cliffs and the little island of Carrick-a-Rede to allow them access to migrating salmon; these days a sturdier, 20m-long, 1m-wide bridge of wire rope sways 30m above the rock-strewn water. To cross the bridge, you must book a time slot in advance on the National Trust website. The bridge is 9km west of Ballycastle; the Causeway Rambler bus stops here.

From the car park and ticket office, a 1km coastal trail leads over the cliffs to the bridge, with the Atlantic on the left and windswept farmland on the right; look out for butterflies, rabbits and hares. Soon you'll reach a set of steps, cut into the cliff face, leading down to the rope bridge.

Crossing the bridge is perfectly safe, but frightening if you don't have a head for heights. Dare to look down and you might spot basking sharks, dolphins and porpoises. From the island, views take in Rathlin Island and Fair Head to the east. Peer over the cliffs to spot seabirds including kittiwakes and guillemots.

On the island, look for a whitewashed fisher's cottage, abandoned after dwindling salmon stocks put an end to fishing in 2002.

CAUSEWAY COAST

From Carrick-a-Rede, the Causeway Coast Way continues west all the way to Portstewart. A shorter section takes you as far as the Giant's Causeway (p548).

CAUSEWAY COAST MARINE LIFE

Dolphins sometimes swim alongside boats, and there are plenty of harbour porpoises in the waters of the Causeway Coast. To see harbour seals head to Rathlin Island, where they can be spotted splashing in the water and basking on rocks.

If you go out onto the water there is a good chance of spotting basking sharks, which are filter feeders that swim open-mouthed just beneath the surface. Orca sightings are rare, but these killer whales have been spotted off the coast of Rathlin.

WHERE TO STAY ON THE CAUSEWAY COAST

Sheep Island View Hostel
Independent hostel in Ballintoy with dorms and private rooms. There's a kitchen and laundry. **£**

Portrush Holiday Hostel
Located in a Victorian terrace house near the beach, with cheerily decorated dorms and a large kitchen. **£**

Bushmills Hostel
Modern, purpose-built hostel with dorms and private rooms; has a kitchen, laundry and bike shed. **£**

BEST ACTIVITIES ON THE CAUSEWAY COAST

Rock climbing
The dolerite crag at Fair Head is considered the greatest expanse of climbable rock in Ireland.

Coasteering
Scramble over rocks, jump into the water and swim into sea caves with Causeway Coasteering.

Diving
Explore around the Skerries and discover wrecks near Rathlin Island with Aquaholics (p542).

Surfing
Surf the beach breaks in Portrush (p541), Benone (p540) or Downhill (p541).

Hiking
Walk the Causeway Coast Way (p550), one of the finest coastal walks in the country.

SEABIRD SIGHTINGS

It's possible to spot nesting seabirds, including kittiwakes, fulmars and puffins, from the **Gobbins** cliff path (p555) 30km north of Belfast on the East Antrim coast.

Listen to Sand Hum at White Park Bay
Wildflowers, Butterflies And Rabbits

The 3km-long sweep of sand backed by ancient dunes at White Park Bay is a special spot, located 12km west of Ballycastle. The remains of Neolithic huts have been found here, suggesting the bay was home to some of Ireland's earliest communities.

Access the beach at the western end, driving down a steep lane just north of the A2 Whitepark Rd to reach a National Trust car park. From here, follow the path down to the beach. Listen carefully; the sand here is so fine that when the wind blows it makes a low humming sound. Note that due to strong currents, the sea here is not suitable for swimming.

In the dunes, look out for colourful wildflowers, butterflies and rabbits. From time to time, cows belonging to a local farmer have also been known to wander onto the beach.

Follow in Giant Footsteps
Causeway Of Hexagonal Columns

Equally exhilarating when cloaked in mist as when bathed in sunshine, the Giant's Causeway is one of Ireland's most atmospheric landscape features. Uneven stacks of tightly packed hexagonal columns stand in neat clusters along the water's edge, forming a causeway that inspired the legend that the stones were put in place by a giant. It is a 25-minute drive from Ballycastle.

The geological phenomenon of the rocks and the legends associated with them are explained in the National Trust's **Giant's Causeway Visitor Centre**; it also rents out audio guides to listen to as you explore the rocks.

From the visitor centre, it's a gentle 10- to 15-minute walk downhill to the Causeway itself, where you can walk out onto the stones as the ocean laps around you. The lower coastal path leads east as far as the **Amphitheatre** viewpoint, passing impressive rock formations including **the Organ**, a stack of 60 vertical basalt columns resembling organ pipes.

From here, you can retrace your steps west to the **Shepherd's Steps**, and climb to the clifftop path and walk west to return to the visitor centre, or head east past the Chimney Stacks headland as far as Dunseverick or beyond.

Visiting the Causeway is free of charge but you pay to use the car park on a combined ticket with the visitor centre; parking-only tickets aren't available. In summer it's often necessary to book visitor centre admission and car parking spaces in advance. Alternatively, use the free car park in Bushmills and walk or take the bus up the Causeway; it's 3km by road or 5km via the railway-side path (p551).

WHERE TO STAY ON THE CAUSEWAY COAST

Elephant Rock Hotel
Boutique hotel in a Victorian terrace in Portrush, with sea views and bold interior decor. **£££**

Bushmills Inn Hotel
The Bushmills Inn is an old coaching inn; the luxurious accommodation is in a modern annex. **£££**

Causeway Hotel
Located at the Giant's Causeway, this hotel is ideal for exploring the coast before the crowds arrive. **£££**

Old Bushmills Distillery

Whiskey & Walks in Bushmills
Drams, Shops And Riverside Strolls

The name Bushmills is widely known thanks to the village's famous whiskey, produced at the world's oldest licensed distillery. Bushmills is a 25-minute drive from Ballycastle.

Old Bushmills Distillery occupies a large lot at the southern end of the village; book ahead to join a tour. The whiskey is made with Irish barley and water from St Columb's Rill, a tributary of the River Bush, and matured in a variety of barrels. After the tour, you can try a sample of your choice from Bushmills' range.

In Bushmills village, pop into the **Designerie**, which sells handcrafted ceramics, soaps, art and textiles by Irish designer-makers. There are some fine pieces to be found here, including soft leather bags, glass sculptures and handwoven blankets. Upstairs the Makers House contains the shared studio space of eight local designers, who are happy to discuss their work.

Finally, take a walk or cycle along the **railway-side path** from Bushmills narrow-gauge railway station to the Giant's Causeway. The 5km trail follows the River Bush and passes Runkerry Beach on its way to the Causeway headland.

THE LEGEND OF FINN MCCOOL

The story goes that the Irish giant Finn McCool built the Causeway so he could cross the sea to fight his rival, the Scottish giant Benandonner. When Benandonner pursued Finn back across the Causeway, Finn disguised himself as a baby and hid in a giant cradle. Fearing an encounter with the parents of such a large child, who he assumed to be even bigger, Benandonner fled back to Scotland, ripping up the Causeway as he went.

All that remains are its ends – the Giant's Causeway in Ireland, and the island of Staffa in Scotland, which has similar rock formations.

WHERE TO EAT ON THE CAUSEWAY COAST

Bothy Coffee
Head to White Park Bay for breakfast pancake stacks, sandwiches and cake, plus coffee roasted in-house. **£**

Market Square
This restaurant in Bushmills specialises in burgers, plus other dishes made with local produce. **££**

Tartine at the Distillers Arms
Refined dishes made with local ingredients are on the menu at this Bushmills restaurant. **£££**

HIKE THE CAUSEWAY COAST WAY

The Causeway Coast Way stretches for 53km from Portstewart to Ballycastle, but the most scenic section – the 16.5km between Carrick-a-Rede and the Giant's Causeway – can be walked in a day and is one of the finest coastal walks in Ireland. Allow four hours.

After testing your nerve on the **1 Carrick-a-Rede Rope Bridge** (p547), take the path from Larrybane car park along a clifftop with views of Sheep Island. At Ballintoy church, turn right and follow the road down to **2 Ballintoy Harbour**.

Continue along the shoreline past a series of conical sea stacks and arches, and scramble around the foot of a limestone crag to reach the 2km-long sandy sweep of **3 White Park Bay**. The going here is easiest at low tide, when you can walk on the firm sand. At the far end of the bay, scramble over rocks and boulders at the bottom of a high limestone cliff for 250m (slippery in places) to **4 Portbradden**.

Beyond Portbradden, white limestone gives way to black basalt, and the path threads through a natural tunnel in the rocks before weaving around several rocky coves. At tiny **5 Dunseverick Harbour**, follow a minor road for 200m before descending steps on the right. The path then wanders along the grassy foreshore, rounds a headland and crosses a footbridge above a waterfall before reaching **6 Dunseverick Castle**.

From here, the often narrow clifftop path climbs steadily. Near Benbane Head, the walk's highest and most northerly point, a wooden bench marks the viewpoint known as Hamilton's Seat. Soak up the spectacular panorama of 100m-high sea cliffs, stacks and pinnacles stretching away to the west, before you set off on the final stretch. Descend the **7 Shepherd's Steps** to reach the **8 Giant's Causeway** (p548).

Bushmills Railway
Victorian Railway to the Giant's causeway

Brought from a private line on the shores of Lough Neagh, the narrow-gauge line and diesel locomotive railway follows the route of a 19th-century tourist tramway for 3km from Bushmills to the station below the Giant's Causeway Visitor Centre. Trains run daily in July and August, and at weekends only in June and September.

Clamber over Coastal Castle Ruins
Photogenic Cliffside Ruins

The ruins of three castles along a 25km stretch of the Causeway Coast are evocative of the time when the area was controlled by the powerful MacDonnell clan. Legendary chieftain Sorley Boy MacDonnell seized Dunluce Castle in 1565, his brother Colla MacDonnell built Kinbane Castle in 1547, and Dunseverick Castle was also a stronghold of the MacDonnells from 1560.

The most westerly and most complete of the three castles is **Dunluce Castle**, 5km east of Portrush (which is 30 minutes' drive from Ballycastle). Perched precariously atop sheer basalt cliffs, the ruins are truly atmospheric. A narrow bridge leads from the mainland across a dizzying gap to the main part of the fortress, from where the views are sublime.

After exploring the ruins of the gatehouse, inner and outer ward and the Renaissance-style manor house, don't miss the path that leads down to the **Mermaid's Cave** beneath the castle crag. For spectacular castle views (and photos), stop at Magheracross car park and picnic site, 750m west of Dunluce on the main road.

Next, head east around Causeway Head and pull over in the lay-by to see the ruins of **Dunseverick Castle**, atop steep basalt cliffs. Over the years most of the castle has been lost to the sea.

Continue east to **Kinbane Castle**, which sits on a limestone headland jutting out from the basalt cliffs, with incredible views of Rathlin Island and Scotland. From the car park, there are 140 steep steps down to the shore, from where a rough path and more steps lead up to the ruins. Take care as you clamber around the headland, with nothing but sheer cliff face between you and the crashing waves below. The view back to the shoreline from here is timeless, with few visible signs of 21st-century life.

ST PATRICK'S TIME AT SLEMISH

The man who later became known as St Patrick is believed to have been kidnapped as a 16-year-old boy from his home on the west coast of Roman Britain and taken to Ireland. For the following six years, he herded sheep for a local chieftain on the slopes of Slemish Mountain. In his writings, Patrick described how during this period of isolation and deprivation he would pray throughout the day and night and was visited by a vision of an angel who helped him escape captivity onboard a ship to the European continent.

After returning to Britain, Patrick felt called to go back to Ireland to set up his mission.

WHERE TO STAY IN THE ANTRIM GLENS

Watertop Farm Campsite
Camping pitches on a family-run farm, 10km east of Ballycastle on the road to Cushendun. **£**

Ballyeamon Barn
Near Glenariff Forest Park, this barn has hostel accommodation and hosts regular storytelling and music sessions. **£**

Cullentra House
This modern bungalow sits high above Cushendall village, offering good views of the Antrim coast. **££**

ROAD TRIPS

The Antrim Glens by Road

Scenic roads traverse the northeastern corner of Antrim, a high plateau of black basalt lava overlying beds of white chalk. Along the coast, between Cushendun and Glenarm, the plateau has been dissected by a series of glacier-gouged valleys known as the Glens of Antrim. This driving route from Ballycastle to Glenarm takes in woodland waterfalls and breathtaking cliff-top views. Bring walking boots for hikes on the way.

1 Fair Head

Branching off from the A2 4.5km east of Ballycastle, the single-track **Torr Head Scenic Route** is an alternative route to Cushendun. It's not for the faint-hearted, as it clings to steep slopes high above the sea. The first turnoff from Torr Head Rd leads to Fair Head, where there is a car park and walking trails. The 4km **Perimeter Walk** follows the line of the cliff edge, with views of the famous **Rathlin Wall** climbing site below.

The Drive: Choose between returning to the A2 for a more straightforward drive to Cushendun, or continuing along the precarious and narrow road via Torr Head to the village. Both are scenic drives.

2 Cushendun

This charming village has interesting architecture and caves to explore. Park at **Cushendun Beach** and walk south through the dunes to the village. Take a look at the distinctive Cornish-style

Layd Old Church, Cushendall

cottages, which were designed by Clough Williams-Ellis.

Cross the river and walk east to explore **Cushendun Caves**. In the village, **Corner House** cafe serves lunch, cakes and scones.

The Drive: Follow Knocknacarry Rd south then bear left onto the minor Layde Rd., Continue until you reach Layd Church (signed).

3 Cushendall

The ruins of **Layd Old Church** occupy a picturesque site on the cliffs above Cushendall. It was once part of a Franciscan friary, founded in the 13th century. Near the gate stands an ancient, weathered cross. There are picnic tables here with sea views.

The Drive: Head south through Cushendall town, passing the 1817 Curfew Tower, and follow the coastal road to Waterfoot. From here the A43 runs inland along Glenariff.

4 Glenariff

At the head of the Glenariff Valley is **Glenariff Forest Park**, where the main attraction is Ess-Na-Larach Waterfall, an 800m walk from the visitor centre. You can also walk to the waterfall from the restaurant **Laragh Lodge**, 600m downstream; a good place to stop for lunch.

The Drive: Return to Waterfoot and drive south along the coastal road, right along the water's edge.

5 Glenarm

The village is home to **Glenarm Castle**, the family seat of the McDonnell family. The castle interior can be seen on guided tours; check the website for details. Take a look at the walled garden, with herbaceous borders and water features.

Head through the village to **Glenarm Forest**, where the 3.5km river trail offers great views of the castle.

BEST *GAME OF THRONES* FILMING LOCATIONS

Dark Hedges
Gnarled, entwined beech trees that doubled as the Kingsroad; located 14km southwest of Ballycastle.

Ballintoy Harbour
This Causeway Coast location was Lordsport on the Iron Island of Pyke, where Theon and Yara Greyjoy are reunited.

Cushendun Caves
This is where Melisandre gives birth to a shadow creature.

Larrybane Quarry
Near the Carrick-a-Rede Rope Bridge, this was Renly Baratheon's camp in the Stormlands.

Downhill Strand
This beach in County Derry was used as a filming location for scenes set on Dragonstone Island.

Slemish Mountain

Follow in St Patrick's Footsteps at Slemish Mountain
Views Of The Antrim Hills

The skyline to the east of Ballymena is dominated by the distinctive craggy peak of Slemish (438m). It's a 40km drive north of Belfast and 54km south of Ballycastle (50 minutes' drive).

The hill is one of many sites in the North associated with Ireland's patron saint. The young St Patrick is said to have tended sheep on its slopes (p551).

On St Patrick's Day, hundreds of people make a pilgrimage to its summit; the rest of the year it's a pleasant climb, though steep and slippery in wet weather, rewarded with fine views of Lough Neagh, the Antrim coast and Scotland. There is a toilet block and picnic tables at the car park but no shop or cafe. It's 1.5km to the summit and back; allow one hour.

Wander from Whitehead to Blackhead Lighthouse
Railways And Coastline

The railway town of Whitehead, 1 hour 10 minutes' drive from Ballycastle, is worth visiting for its coastal walks to Blackhead Lighthouse and at the Gobbins (p555), 3km north of Whitehead on Islandmagee.

WHERE TO EAT & DRINK IN THE ANTRIM GLENS

Mary McBride's
In Cushendun, this pub serves bar meals downstairs and more refined plates in the upstairs restaurant. ££

McCollam's
Locally known as Johnny Joe's, this pub is the town's liveliest, with regular trad sessions.

Harry's Restaurant
With its cosy lounge-bar, Harry's is a Cushendall institution; the menu features steaks and seafood. ££

The 3.5km round-trip walk to **Blackhead Lighthouse** begins from Whitehead car park on Old Castle Rd. It follows the shoreline (look out for seals, basking on rocks) then ascends up stone steps to the lighthouse (not open to the public). Steps on the other side take you back down to sea level. Here the highlight is the walkway under the cliffs, from where you can see dark swirling water underfoot.

Whitehead also has a **railway museum** that will appeal to train enthusiasts, with a workshop and foundry, and a locomotive house where you can board the trains. Short steam train trips are offered most weekends in summer; book ahead.

Afterwards, stop for coffee and cake at **Bank House**, a cafe and gift shop housed in a former bank.

Take a Dramatic Cliff Walk at the Gobbins
Cliff-Face Path Over Churning Seas

Tubular bridges, rocky surfaces, tunnels, caves and narrow crevices form a dramatic cliff path at Islandmagee, the slender peninsula that runs parallel to the coastline between Whitehead and Larne. The Gobbins coastal path is accessible on 2½-hour guided tours (book ahead). A good level of fitness, a minimum height of 1.2m and suitable footwear are essential. Islandmagee is 88km south of Ballycastle (about one hour by car) and 30km north of Belfast. Ballycarry train station, on the Belfast to Larne line, is 1.5km west of the Gobbins Visitor Centre.

Tours leave from the visitor centre, from where it's a five-minute bus ride to the path. The most strenuous part of the 5km walk is the return climb up the steep access path; otherwise the path is not physically demanding. Guides explain the history of the Gobbins and highlight geological and natural features of the coastline. As well as spectacular views out to the Irish Sea, you might spot dolphins and puffins on the walk.

Above the Gobbins path, a viewing platform and clifftop path are free to access without booking a tour. Plans are in the works to link up the higher and lower paths to create a circular route, but at research time the project had not yet been given the green light.

At the northern tip of Islandmagee, 10km north of the Gobbins Visitor Centre, is **Brown's Bay**, a sheltered, horseshoe-shaped bay with a sandy beach, with views of the Antrim headlands.

A FEAT OF ENGINEERING

The Gobbins first opened as a tourist attraction in 1902, when the new railway made the area accessible to visitors from Belfast. It was created by local engineer Berkeley Deane Wise, who saw the potential of the Antrim coastline as a tourist attraction.

The path was closed in the 1930s and fell into disrepair; a £7.5 million investment saw the attraction reopen in 2016.

The basalt cliffs at the Gobbins are at the eastern edge of a basalt structure that stretches from Cave Hill in Belfast to Binevenagh in County Derry. The rock was created by volcanic eruptions 65 million years ago, during which time the hexagonal columns of the Giant's Causeway were also formed by quick-cooling pools of lava.

GETTING AROUND

It's possible to get around by bus, which stops at the towns and the villages of the Causeway Coast and Antrim Glens, but it's easier by car. There are trains from Belfast to Portrush, Whitehead and Carrickfergus. Sustrans cycle route 93 takes in glorious coastal scenery on the way from Larne to Coleraine.

Above: White Island (p565); right: Belleek Pottery (p566)

FERMANAGH & TYRONE

ANCIENT LANDSCAPE OF LAKELANDS AND HILLS

Hidden in the loughs and waterways of Fermanagh and the boggy hills of Tyrone are intriguing historical remains and an array of wildlife.

Life in Fermanagh revolves around the water. The summer boat traffic on Lough Erne hearkens back to a time when the waterways were the main thoroughfares across an Ireland covered in thick and treacherous woodland. Islands such as Devenish were chosen as strategically located, accessible sites for monasteries that were the important religious, cultural and political centres of their time. As recently as the 1950s, the islands were home to a substantial community of islanders; these days, they are virtually uninhabited and have become an important habitat for birds, particularly breeding waders. The islands are also used to graze livestock, which are transported in special boats.

Tyrone's three largest towns – Omagh, Dungannon and Cookstown – form a triangle across its centre, but the county's biggest draw lies in the untouched wildness of the Sperrin Mountains, whose southern foothills are scattered with prehistoric sites. The area encompassing Davagh Forest and the Beaghmore Stone Circles is now a designated dark sky park, with an observatory and astronomy-related walking trails. It's a magical place, and there is a sense of timelessness in the views of the Milky Way above the forest treetops in Davagh. It's possible that the intriguing stone circles of Beaghmore were laid out to reflect the sky; it is fitting, then, that the site is once more a place for stargazers to gather.

THE MAIN AREAS

ENNISKILLEN
Island town.
p560

Find Your Way

County Fermanagh is known as the lakelands for a reason: it's about one-third water. Between the loughs, the terrain is rugged and hilly. Small, rural County Tyrone is home to the Sperrin Mountains.

BOAT
Lough Erne's islands can be reached by boat, kayak or canoe. Self-drive motor boats are available for hire (no experience required). Taxi boats and tours also take passengers out onto the water.

BICYCLE & CAR
Scenic cycling routes traverse both counties, but you'll need power in your legs for the hills. Driving is the most convenient way to get around because public transport is patchy outside the main towns.

Enniskillen, p560
The island town has museums and a country house to discover, plus adventures to be had in the surrounding waters.

Enniskillen Castle (p561)

Plan Your Time

You'll want to get out onto the water and explore the loughs and islands, but there are land-based attractions to visit too. Allow time for walks in the hills.

Pressed for Time

Start at **Enniskillen Castle** (p561) and then take a boat trip to **Devenish Island** (p564) to see the remarkable round tower and monastic ruins. The next day, drive to the **Cuilcagh Boardwalk Trail** (p566) and hike to the viewing platform, and then descend down to the **Marble Arch Caves** (p568). Next, drive to **OM Dark Sky Park** (p570) and stay until nightfall to see the stars.

Four Days to Travel Around

Follow the itinerary to the left and then head to **Castle Archdale** (p565), where you can hire a kayak and paddle out to White Island. From Castle Archdale, make a stop at **Caldragh Cemetery** (p566) before returning to Enniskillen, from where you can walk or cycle to **Castle Coole** (p561). The next day, spend the morning at Florence Court and then head to Crom and explore **Upper Lough Erne** (p569).

Seasonal Highlights

SPRING
The **Bluegrass Omagh** music festival takes place at Ulster American Folk Park. Mayfly season begins, the best time for trout fishing on Lough Erne.

SUMMER
July and August are the busiest months at the Fermanagh lakes. The long summer days are ideal for **hillwalking** in the Sperrin Mountains.

AUTUMN
The **FEARmanagh** endurance event involves trail running, cycling and kayaking a 74km course along Lough Erne and up the Magho Cliffs.

WINTER
Long winter nights mean more time for **stargazing** at the OM Dark Sky Park and Observatory.

ENNISKILLEN

Located on the banks of the River Erne between Upper and Lower Lough Erne, Enniskillen is quite literally surrounded by water: the town centre is an island, accessed at either end by bridge. Enniskillen Castle guards the island's western end, its twin-turreted Watergate looming over passing fleets of cabin cruisers. Boating and watersports are a way of life here, and it's easy to get out onto the water in a kayak or a self-drive boat.

Oscar Wilde and Samuel Beckett were pupils at the Portora Royal School, now called Enniskillen Royal Grammar School. Wilde's connection to Enniskillen is celebrated with 150 gold-leaf swallow sculptures, mounted on buildings around town in reference to his story *The Happy Prince*.

The town's name is also prominent in the history of the Troubles. On Remembrance Sunday in 1987, an IRA bomb killed 11 people during a service at Enniskillen's war memorial.

TOP TIP

Enniskillen Castle and Castle Coole are connected by the 4.5km Castle to Castle trail. The signed route is 90% traffic free and is suitable for walking or cycling; it links up with the Kingfisher Trail cycling route, which has great views of the river along the way.

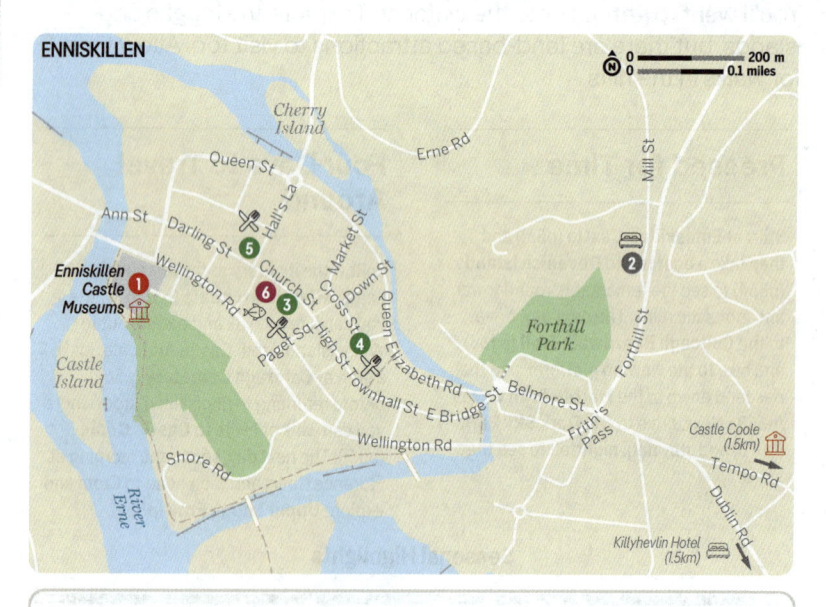

HIGHLIGHTS
1. Enniskillen Castle Museums

SLEEPING
2. Enniskillen Hotel

EATING
3. 28 at the Hollow
4. Dollakis
5. Jolly Sandwich Bar

SHOPPING
6. Home, Field & Stream

Learn about Fermanagh's Past at Enniskillen Castle
Museums In Former Maguire Stronghold

Enniskillen Castle was a former fortress of the 16th-century Maguire chieftains. These days, the **Enniskillen Castle Museums** complex houses the Fermanagh County Museum, with displays on the county's history, archaeology, landscape and wildlife.

Start in the galleries of **Barrack Coach House**. On the ground floor, look for the 1000-year-old 16kg block of bog butter, unearthed by a Fermanagh farmer in 1980. It was probably buried in the bog to preserve it for consumption during winter.

Upstairs, the **Lakelands Gallery** has fascinating displays dedicated to the history of Fermanagh's waterways. It includes local stone heads, fragments of crosses and a model of the Devenish Island round tower. Don't miss the River Erne Horn, a medieval instrument uncovered during the dredging of the river.

The adjacent **art gallery** has pieces by local artists, including TP Flanagan's work *Victim* (1974), painted in response to the death of his friend in a terrorist shooting.

The **Castle Keep**, the oldest part of the complex, has displays on the Maguire chieftains and Fermanagh's military history.

Explore the House & Grounds at Castle Coole
18th-Century Mansion

Castle Coole, a National Trust–owned neoclassical country house, sits on 600 hectares of parkland traversed by walking trails. It's 2.5km southeast of Enniskillen town centre.

The house's double cantilever staircase, Italian marble fireplaces, Regency furniture and basement servants' quarters can be seen on guided tours. When King George IV visited Ireland in 1821, a state bedroom was specially prepared at Castle Coole in anticipation of his visit. Though the king never showed up, the bedroom, draped in red silk and decorated with paintings depicting *A Rake's Progress*, is one of the highlights of the tour.

Castle Coole

BEST PLACES TO EAT & STAY IN ENNISKILLEN

Jolly Sandwich Bar
Divine house-baked cakes and pastries, plus salads and sandwiches. **£**

Dollakis
Family-run Greek restaurant serving small meze plates and daily specials. **££**

28 at the Hollow
Beneath Blakes of the Hollow, chef Glen Wheeler creates innovative fine-dining plates. **£££**

Enniskillen Hotel
This centrally located hotel has budget motel rooms and more stylishly decorated hotel rooms. **££**

Killyhevlin Hotel
Lakeside resort 1.5km south of town with hotel rooms, self-catering lodges, a spa and a restaurant. **£££**

GETTING AROUND

Enniskillen town centre is small enough to explore on foot. Enniskillen Castle has a large car park. Several buses a day go to Belfast and Dublin.

To get out onto the water, hire a kayak or canoe from Blue Green Yonder or a self-drive boat from Erne Boat Hire, both at the Blueways Water Activity Zone, or book a trip with Erne Water Taxi. Erne Tours boat trips to Devenish Island leave from the Round O Jetty.

A STROLL AROUND THE ISLAND TOWN

This walk around Enniskillen's central island gives a taste of local life. Allow around three hours including stops. Start at the **1 Buttermarket**, where the restored buildings of the old marketplace house craft shops and artists' studios. Don't miss Ann McNulty's beautiful ceramics; stop by her pottery studio to see her work.

Walk southeast down Cross St and then turn right onto Water St. On the right, look for a mural of **2 The Happy Prince** from the story by former Enniskillen schoolboy Oscar Wilde, who was inspired to write the tale by the view of Cole's Monument from his dormitory window. It tells of a gold-leafed statue of a prince who asks a swallow to give his gold to the poor. On the left is the town hall, with its 1901 **3 clock tower** watched over by two stone soldiers, representing the town's military history.

Cross Townhall St to the Diamond to see more street art, this time a **4 trad session** featuring the late Fermanagh musician John McManus on the fiddle. Continue northwest on Townhall St. At Charlie's Bar, look for a mural of *Line of Duty* actor **5 Adrian Dunbar**, who was born in Enniskillen; it features his character's catchphrase 'Now we're suckin' diesel'.

Next, stop for a drink in **6 Blakes of the Hollow**, a pub that has barely changed since 1887, with a marble-topped bar, sherry casks and wood panelling. Continue on Townhall St to reach **7 Headhunters Barber Shop and Railway Museum**, which displays a collection of railway memorabilia and is open for haircuts. From here, continue to Castle St and then head south to reach **8 Enniskillen Castle Museums** (p561). Allow at least an hour to view the exhibitions here.

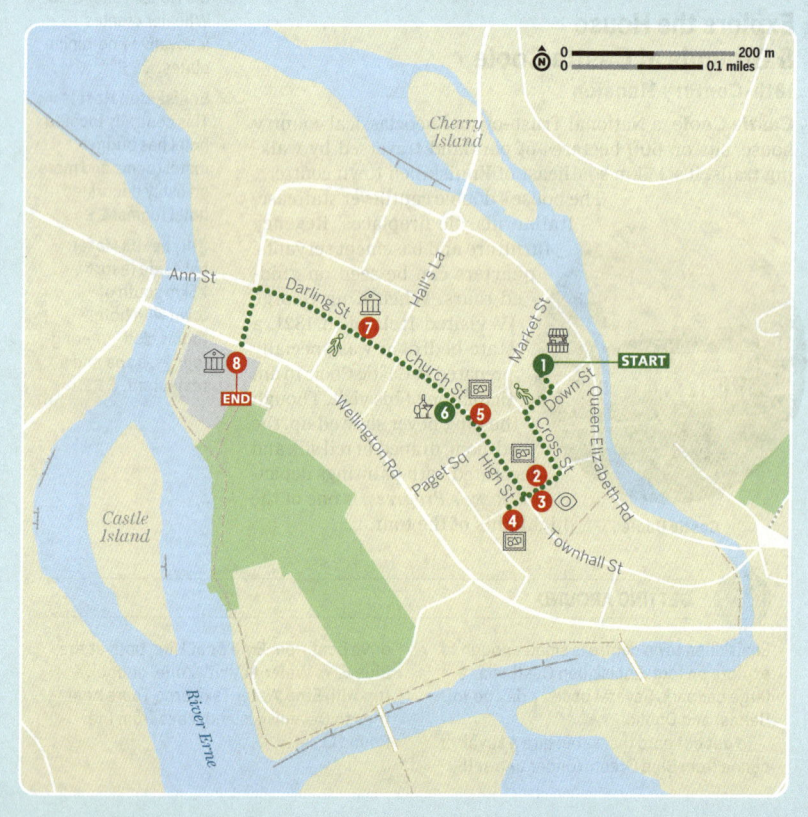

Beyond Enniskillen

The loughs and hills surrounding Enniskillen offer adventures on water and land, with ancient stone figures and wildlife to spot.

The town of Enniskillen is the perfect launchpad for day trips by boat or kayak around the inlets and islands of Lough Erne. This waterway was an important pilgrimage route during early Christian times, and today you can visit the remains of a thriving monastic community on Devenish Island. Less is known about the mysterious stone figures on nearby Boa and White Islands.

Going back further in time, the southern slopes of Tyrone's Sperrin Mountains are dotted with ancient monuments, including the Bronze Age stone circles at Beaghmore, created more than 4000 years ago. But these intriguing stones are recent history in relation to the cave systems and limestone landscapes of the Cuilcagh Mountain Geopark, formed 340 million years ago.

TOP TIP

The Kingfisher Trail is a long-distance cycling trail from Enniskillen. A 115km section of the route loops around Lower Lough Erne.

A PLACE OF PILGRIMAGE

In early Christian times when overland travel was difficult, Lough Erne was an important waterway between the Donegal coast and inland Leitrim. At this time, the lough was the route taken by pilgrims travelling via Devenish Island to Lough Derg in Donegal. There are records of pilgrims from all over Europe staying on the island.

Devenish Island was raided by Vikings in 837 and again in 923, but by the 12th century, Devenish was a large and important community of up to 1000 monks. The stonemasons and builders responsible for the round tower were some of the most skilled craftsmen of their day, and Devenish continued to thrive as a centre of learning and arts until the 16th century.

St Mary's Abbey, Devenish Island

Boat Trip to Devenish Island
Round Tower And Monastery

Located 2.5km north of Enniskillen in Lower Lough Erne, **Devenish Island** is Fermanagh's most important monastic site. Take a boat trip to see the remains of an Augustinian monastery founded in the 6th century by St Molaise, which include a 12th-century round tower in near-perfect condition. Erne Tours and Erne Water Taxi offer guided trips to the island from Enniskillen, or you can make your own way there in a self-drive boat from Erne Boat Hire.

From the jetty, the first building on the left is the remains of **Teampull Mór**, a 13th-century church that had a regular congregation right up to the 17th century. Take time to look at the unusual carved headstones in the graveyard. Inside the church is a medieval stone coffin known as St Molaise's Bed. Local folklore has it that lying in the stone bed and turning over three times will cure ailments, but it's a tight squeeze.

WHERE TO STAY IN COUNTY TYRONE

An Creagán Cottages
Self-catering cottages in an idyllic setting in the foothills of the Sperrins. ££

Sperrinview Glamping
These glamping pods have bathrooms, kitchenettes and large windows looking out to the night sky. ££

Silverbirch Hotel
This large hotel in Omagh has friendly staff, a bar and a restaurant. ££

The next structure you'll pass is the 12th-century **St Molaise's House**, which was built as a shrine to house the saint's remains. Ahead is the magnificent Round Tower, built as a bell tower, a watch tower and a place of refuge. It's not usually open to the public.

The final building is the remains of **St Mary's Abbey**, built in the 12th century. To the south of the abbey is a well-preserved **15th-century cross**. Go around to the back (western side) of the abbey and look for the carved stone head over the arch. Climb up the narrow stone steps of the tower to see the vaulted ceiling and views out over the island.

Back at ground level, walk up to the fence behind the abbey for views of the ruins, the tower and the water; it's a good spot for photos.

The Enigmatic Figures of White Island
Adventure By Kayak

Of all the stone carvings at Lough Erne, the **White Island** figures are the strangest and most evocative. Finding a way to reach the island is all part of the adventure. One option is to hire a kayak and paddle from the Castle Archdale marina, 18km north of Enniskillen on the eastern shore of Lough Erne. Castle Archdale Boat Hire rents kayaks, canoes and motorboats.

From the marina, the paddle out by kayak takes around 30 minutes. Near the jetty at the eastern tip of the island are the ruins of a small 12th-century church, surrounded by grass. Inside are eight extraordinary stone figures, thought to date from the 9th century, lined up along the wall. The age and interpretation of these figures have been the subject of much debate. Look for the figure with a grimacing face with puffy cheeks, thought to represent lust, and the hooded figure with a staff that is likely to be a bishop or abbot.

Once back at Castle Archdale, you can walk or cycle the forest trails. There is pony trekking in the summer.

> **ABOUT THE ISLANDS**
>
> The Lakelands Gallery at Enniskillen Castle Museums (p561) has excellent displays on the monastic settlement at Devenish Island as well as information about the figures on White Island (p565) and Boa Island (p566).

> **ANGLING IN FERMANAGH**
>
> The lakes of Fermanagh are renowned for both coarse and game fishing. In May, anglers compete to reel in the biggest catch during the **Fermanagh Classic Fishing Festival**.
>
> Lough Erne has pike, perch, rudd, bream, roach, salmon and brown trout. The mayfly season usually lasts a month from the second week in May.
>
> To fish in Northern Ireland, you need a rod licence and a permit or day tickets, which can be purchased from **Home, Field & Stream** in Enniskillen. See the government website NI Direct (nidirect.gov.uk) for angling season dates, limits and permit information.

WHERE TO EAT IN COUNTY TYRONE

An Creagán Restaurant
Courtyard restaurant near the Beaghmore Stone Circles serving breakfast, lunch, traybakes and scones. **£**

Brewer's House
This cosy pub in Donaghmore village has open fires and serves creative modern dishes. **££**

Chapter V
In the village of Moy, the chefs at Chapter V use local ingredients to create flavourful dishes. **£££**

Stone Statues of Caldragh Cemetery
Intriguing Figures

At the end of a short country lane off the main road through Boa Island, the atmospheric **Caldragh Cemetery** contains two intriguing stone figures, surrounded by a muddle of gravestones and long grass. **Boa Island** is 35km north of Enniskillen and connected to the mainland by road; get here by car or bike.

The most intriguing of the statues is the larger Dreenan Figure, thought to date from the early Christian period. Nearby is a smaller figure, brought here from Lusty More island. There's no information about the enigmatic figures at the graveyard itself.

Take in the Views from the Cliffs of Magho
Scenic Forest Drive

Lough Navar Forest lies at the western end of Lower Lough Erne, 36km north of Enniskillen. Here the Cliffs of Magho, a 250m-high and 9km-long limestone escarpment, rise above a fringe of bog, heath and native woodland on the southern shore. A 10km scenic drive leads to the **Magho Viewpoint**, and there are plenty of walking trails in the forest.

The panorama from the Magho clifftop is one of the finest in Ireland. It looks out over the shimmering expanse of lough and river to the Blue Stack Mountains, the sparkling waters of Donegal Bay and the sea cliffs of Sliabh Liag.

See How Belleek Pottery is Made
Factory Tour

The world-famous **Belleek Pottery**, founded in 1857, can be found in an imposing grey building in the village of Belleek, 40km northwest of Enniskillen. It has been producing fine Parian china for more than 150 years and is especially noted for its delicate basketware. Pieces are available to buy in the shop. You can see the pottery being made on guided tours of the factory floor, which include the mould-making process and the delicate task of handcrafting flowers.

Climb the Stairway to Heaven
Hike The Cuilcagh Boardwalk Trail

Known as the 'stairway to heaven', the photogenic **Cuilcagh Boardwalk Trail** up its namesake mountain has become one of Fermanagh's most popular walks. It leads 6km to a viewing platform at the edge of the mountain plateau,

---

MYSTERIOUS ORIGINS OF THE CALDRAGH CEMETERY FIGURES

The exact origins and meanings of the figures at Caldragh Cemetery remain unclear. The Dreenan Figure, which has been in the graveyard since at least 1841, was believed for many years to date from the pagan Iron Age and was thought to be 2000 years old. Though it was long referred to as a Janus (multifaced) figure, it is actually two separate figures placed back to back. It is now thought to date from the early Christian period, from 500 to 1000 CE. Experts have proposed that the figure might represent Badhbh, a frightening war goddess in local folklore.

Seamus Heaney wrote the poem 'January God' about the statue, referencing the Roman deity Janus who the figure was then believed to represent.

WHERE TO EAT NEAR UPPER LOUGH ERNE

Little Orchard Tea Room
The cafe at Castle Crom serves soup, sandwiches, house-baked brownies and cakes. **£**

Kissin' Crust
Lisnaskae coffee shop stacked with house-baked pies, quiches and scones; serves lunchtime soup and sandwiches. **£**

Watermill Restaurant
Seasonal Irish fare is given a French twist at chef Pascal Brissaud's lakeside restaurant. **£££**

Cuilcagh Boardwalk Trail

which has breathtaking views of Lough Erne and beyond. The trail begins 500m east of the turnoff to Marble Arch Caves, a 16km drive southwest of Enniskillen.

The first 4km of the trail follow a gravel path through limestone grasslands with grazing sheep. Soon the landscape begins to change to blanket bog, coated with white bog cotton in spring and purple moor grass in late summer. It's here that the boardwalk begins. It was not constructed with the convenience of walkers in mind, but instead to protect the delicate blanket bog beneath it.

The final ascent is via a series of steps over boulders and streams to a platform with a fantastic view of the drumlins of Upper Lough Erne. The trail is 6km each way; allow around three hours.

Beyond the platform, a rough mountain path traverses the summit plateau to reach a Bronze Age cairn. The summit plateau is a breeding ground for golden plovers and is rich in rare plants such as alpine clubmoss. Unless you have a map and compass, it's best to turn back once you reach the end of the boardwalk; mist can roll in quickly, and it's easy to get lost.

GEOLOGY OF THE CUILCAGH LAKELANDS

Because of its important geology, the area around Cuilcagh Mountain forms part of the **Cuilcagh Lakelands Unesco Global Geopark**. The landscape is rich in limestone, which was formed 340 million years ago by layers of lime-rich mud and sea creatures. Cuilcagh Mountain is made from layers of sandstone on top of limestone, and its slopes are coated with blanket bog.

The Geopark's biggest attractions are the Cuilcagh Boardwalk Trail and the nearby Marble Arch Caves. The water in the caves runs down Cuilcagh Mountain, so if you hike the boardwalk trail before descending into the caves, you will be tracing the water's path.

WHERE TO STAY NEAR UPPER LOUGH ERNE

Crom Campsite
Camping and glamping are available in the peaceful grounds of the National Trust's Crom Estate. **£**

Share Discovery Village
Tent pitches, glamping pods and self-catering chalets on the loughshore, plus an indoor pool. **£**

Watermill Lodge
A secluded lakeside setting makes for a peaceful night's rest in these B&B guest rooms. **££**

WILDLIFE WATCHING AT LOUGH ERNE

Birdlife is abundant at Lough Erne. The Royal Society for the Protection of Birds (RSPB) **Lower Lough Erne Islands Reserve** is an important habitat for breeding waders (curlew, snipes, lapwings and redshank), as well as a colony of breeding Sandwich terns. Garden warblers arrive in summer. Look for these birds on the islands and at Castle Caldwell Forest, which is also home to red squirrels.

In Upper Lough Erne, **Crom Estate** is a haven for pine martens, bats and many species of birds. Flocks of whooper swans and goldeneyes overwinter here, great crested grebes nest in the spring, and you'll find Ireland's biggest heronry in a 400-year-old oak grove on the island of **Inishfendra**, just south of Crom Estate.

Florence Court

Discover a Subterranean World
Awe-Inspiring Cave System

To the south of Lower Lough Erne lies a limestone plateau, where Fermanagh's abundant rainwater has carved out a network of subterranean caverns, the largest of which are known as the **Marble Arch Caves**. You can explore 1.5km of show cave passages on a guided tour. Book online in advance at marblearchcaves.co.uk. The caves are a 16km drive or cycle southwest of Enniskillen.

When water levels are high enough, tours begin with a short boat trip along the waters of the underground River Cladagh to Junction Jetty, where three subterranean streams meet up. You then continue on foot to a tunnel leading into the New Chamber and through the Moses Walk, a walled pathway sunk waist-deep into the river. The reflections of the formations in the water are evocative and otherworldly. If the water levels of the river are too low (or too high) for a boat trip, a walking tour is offered instead.

Look out for scheduled 'Earth Yoga' classes, which take place in the show cave.

WHERE TO STAY NEAR LOWER LOUGH ERNE

Castle Archdale Country Park
A popular loughside site with pitches for tents and caravans, as well as glamping pods. **£**

Tully Mill Cottages
These neat self-catering cottages are right by the Florence Court estate; good for families. **££**

Corralea Cottages
Self-catering cottages near Belcoo; facilities include a forest spa, paddle sports equipment and e-bikes. **££**

Explore the Country Estate at Florence Court
Spectacular House And Grounds

Florence Court is a grand baroque country house in a superb setting, surrounded by parkland and woodland and with views of Benaughlin Mountain. It's a 12km drive from Enniskillen.

Take a house tour to see the famous rococo plasterwork and antique Irish furniture. In the drawing room are three large paintings of Fermanagh from the 1730s; Devenish Island looks almost the same today. One of the tour highlights is viewing the downstairs servants' quarters.

Hire a bike to explore the 9km-long red trail through the landscaped grounds and woodland, passing an ancient Irish yew tree. Don't miss the large walled garden and restored kitchen garden, with glasshouses used for growing food.

Paddle around Upper Lough Erne
Woodland, Islands And Wildlife

Upper Lough Erne is not so much a lake as a spectacular watery maze of islands, inlets, reedy bays and meandering backwaters. The area is home to an array of wildlife. Crom is a 30km drive south of Enniskillen.

Hire a kayak or canoe at **Share Discovery Village** to get out onto the water. The route from Share to Crom is a lovely half-day paddle. It takes you past **Inish Rath**, an island with a Hare Krishna temple. On Sundays, visitors are welcome to join the community for worship and lunch. You can also hire a rowing boat or motorboat at Crom.

Allow time to explore on land at **Crom Estate**, a National Trust–managed property with a large area of natural woodland and thriving wildlife. You can walk from the visitor centre to the old castle ruins, a walled garden and gnarled yew trees, enjoying views over the reed-fringed lough. Castle Crom itself is privately owned and closed to the public.

Experience the Story of Emigration from Ulster to America
Open-Air Museum

In the 18th and 19th centuries, more than two million people left Ulster to forge a new life across the Atlantic. Their story is told at the **Ulster American Folk Park**. It's 8km north of Omagh and a 50km drive northeast of Enniskillen.

BEST COUNTY FERMANAGH PRODUCE

Fermanagh Black Bacon
The O'Doherty family's black bacon comes from rare-breed pigs that roam Inish Corkish Island. Buy it from O'Doherty's Fine Meats in Enniskillen.

Bread from Joe the Baker
Order loaves of organic sourdough and pastries online (joethebaker.com) during the week and collect them from Joe at the Bread Table in Enniskillen on Saturday.

Boatyard Gin
Boatyard Distillery on the western bank of Lough Erne uses local botanicals in its gins. Book a tour and get there by boat or road.

WHERE TO STAY NEAR LOWER LOUGH ERNE

Lusty Beg Island
Private island retreat reached by ferry from Boa Island, with self-catering chalets and B&B rooms. **£££**

Finn Lough
Stay in a transparent forest bubble dome at this wonderful complex with an outdoor spa. **£££**

Lough Erne Resort
Luxury hotel and golf resort with extensive grounds on the western shores of the lough. **£££**

Exhibits are split into Ulster cottages and American log cabins, with guides in period costume on hand to bring the stories to life. Original buildings from various parts of Ulster have been dismantled and reerected here, including a blacksmith's forge, a weaver's thatched cottage, a Presbyterian meeting house and a schoolhouse. The two parts of the park are cleverly linked by passing through a mock-up of an emigrant ship. In the American section of the park, you can visit a genuine 18th-century stone cottage and a log house, both shipped across the Atlantic from Pennsylvania, plus many more original buildings.

However, the museum glosses over the impact of emigration from Ulster to America on indigenous people and how immigrants from Ulster were likely to have benefited from the labour of enslaved people and their descendants. As the museum notes, census records show that there were five Black people living and working in the Tennessee plantation house in 1870, five years after slavery was abolished in Tennessee. There are plans to focus more on the stories of such people in the future.

The only building in its original place is the Mellon Homestead, around which the park was built. Thomas Mellon, who was born in the farmhouse in 1813, emigrated to Pennsylvania as a child and went on to become the founder of Mellon Bank. There is usually a costumed guide in the house making soda bread on the griddle; be sure to try it.

Stargaze at OM Dark Sky Park
Visit An Observatory And Go Mountain Biking

In the sparsely populated Sperrin Mountains, the starry night skies above Davagh Forest and the ancient stone circles of Beaghmore are now an official International Dark Sky Park. At Davagh Forest, an **observatory** houses telescopes and an exhibition; it's a 75km drive northeast of Enniskillen.

Book an observatory tour to learn about astronomy, look through telescopes and see the night sky using a virtual reality headset. For a chance to look through the observatory's 355mm LX600 Meade telescope, look out for regular stargazing events. Remember that in June, it stays light until after 10pm, but in December, the sun sets as early as 4pm. The park remains open all night, even when the observatory is closed. There are toilets in the lower car park.

From the observatory, a **solar search walking trail** leads to the **Beaghmore Stone Circles**. Along the way, an

---

BEST ACTIVITIES IN THE SPERRIN MOUNTAINS

Mountain Biking
Hit the trails at Davagh Forest and Gortin Glen Forest Park.

Walking
Climb to the summit of Mullaghcarn from Gortin Glen Forest Park or hike around the Gortin Lakes.

Foraging
Book a guided walk on the grounds of An Creagán to search for berries and herbs, which were used by early settlers for food and medicine.

Stargazing
Visit the observatory in Davagh Forest to look through a telescope at the night sky.

WHERE TO EAT & DRINK NEAR LOWER LOUGH ERNE

Black Cat Cove
This pub in Belleek has antique furniture, an open fire and serves good bar meals. ££

Lodge Bar & Restaurant
You don't have to stay overnight at Lusty Beg Island to eat at the resort's restaurant. ££

The Barn
The menu at Finn Lough's restaurant is arranged by flavour; creative cocktails are a house speciality. £££

Beaghmore Stone Circles

information board for each planet in the solar system is positioned at a distance relative to its distance from the sun in space. Much of the trail is over boardwalk, with views of the rolling hills of the Sperrins along the way.

At **Beaghmore**, the intriguing cluster of seven stone circles dating from the Bronze Age might also be related to astronomy and could have been created to chart lunar, solar and stellar events. It's sometimes possible to see the northern lights from here, too.

During daylight hours, **Davagh Forest** provides some of the best mountain biking in Ireland, ranging from family-friendly green and blue trails along a wooded stream to 16km of red trails leading to the top of Beleevenamore Mountain, with several challenging rock slabs and drop-offs on the descents. Bikes can be rented from Sperrin Bike Hire, located next to Sperrinview Glamping, 3km from the trailhead.

Davagh's **walking trails** give you more time to enjoy this landscape of rolling hills and sweeping forests. A 3km loop trail takes in the forests and red-hued stream.

COUNTY TYRONE'S CELTIC CROSSES

A 6th-century monastic site on the western shores of Lough Neagh is the evocative location of the **Ardboe High Cross**, one of Ireland's best-preserved and most elaborately decorated Celtic stone crosses. The 10th-century cross has 22 carved panels depicting Old and New Testament scenes, including Christ's entry into Jerusalem. It's located 16km east of Cookstown.

The 10th-century Celtic high cross in the village of **Donaghmore**, 4km north of Dungannon, has similar carvings of biblical scenes.

GETTING AROUND

Public transport is patchy in both Fermanagh and Tyrone, and to reach many places, you'll need your own car or bike. Get to the islands of Lough Erne by kayak, canoe or motorboat.

TOOLKIT

TOOLKIT

The chapters in this section cover the most important topics you'll need to know about in Ireland. They're full of nuts-and-bolts information and valuable insights to help you understand and navigate Ireland and get the most out of your trip.

Arriving
p574

Getting Around
p575

Money
p576

Accommodation
p577

Family Travel
p578

Health & Safe Travel
p579

Food, Drink & Nightlife
p580

Responsible Travel
p582

LGBTIQ+ Travel
p584

Accessible Travel
p585

Driving the Wild Atlantic Way
p586

Nuts & Bolts
p587

Language
p588

Rotten Island Lighthouse, Killybegs (p397)
LUKASSEK/SHUTERSTOCK ©

Arriving

TOOLKIT

Dublin is the main point of entry for most travellers to Ireland. Flights arrive at Dublin Airport, 10km north of the city centre, which has two interconnected terminals. There are ATMs, restaurants and convenience stores in the terminal buildings, and buses connect Dublin Airport with towns and cities across Ireland. You can also fly to Belfast, Shannon and Cork.

Duty Free
Duty-free prices are available to people travelling from the Republic of Ireland to countries outside the European Union, including Britain. They are not available for journeys from Northern Ireland to the EU or Britain.

SIM Cards
SIM cards for unlocked phones can be purchased from WHSmith in Terminal 1 Arrivals and the Spar convenience store in Terminal 2 Arrivals. Both terminals have free wi-fi.

Ferry
Car ferries from Liverpool in England, Holyhead in Wales and Cherbourg in France arrive at Dublin ferry port, 5km east of the city centre. Belfast has ferry connections to Scotland and England.

US Preclearance
When travelling from Dublin to the USA, passport and immigration formalities are handled before boarding at US Preclearance; allow extra time. When you arrive in the US, the flight is treated as a domestic arrival.

Public Transport from Airport to City Centre

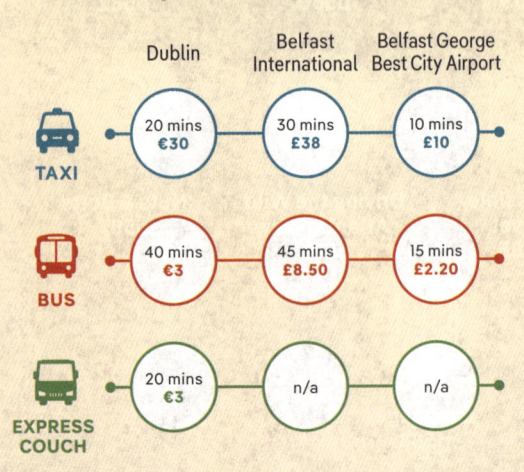

	Dublin	Belfast International	Belfast George Best City Airport
TAXI	20 mins €30	30 mins £38	10 mins £10
BUS	40 mins €3	45 mins £8.50	15 mins £2.20
EXPRESS COACH	20 mins €3	n/a	n/a

POST-BREXIT TRAVEL

Although the UK left the European Union in 2020, the Common Travel Area (CTA) grants free movement between Ireland and the UK to Irish and UK citizens. It means you don't need to show your passport to border agents when travelling between the UK and Ireland, but your airline may require a photo ID.

The Brexit Withdrawal Agreement committed all parties to maintaining a 'soft' border (one with no passport or customs checks) between Northern Ireland and the Republic. You'll know when you've entered the North or the South because the road signs change, but there are no border formalities.

Getting Around

Exploring Ireland's wildest and most beautiful corners is easiest by car. Keep your camera and walking boots handy for impromptu stops along the way.

TOOLKIT

TRAVEL COSTS

Rental
From €15/day

Petrol
Approx €1.60/litre

EV charging
€9–23 for a full charge

Tolls
€1.60–10

Travel Cards

In Dublin, the Leap Visitor Card includes all Dublin Bus, Luas tram, DART and commuter train travel for one, three or seven days. The Irish Explorer rail pass includes five days of unlimited rail travel in the Republic within 15 consecutive days.

Toll Roads

Ireland has 11 toll roads, 10 of which have conventional barrier toll plazas where you pay at the cashier's booth. Dublin's M50 toll plaza is barrier-free; pay online before 8pm the following day (eflow.ie). A peak rate of €10 is charged on weekday mornings and evenings at the Dublin Tunnel.

TIP

Download Transport for Ireland's TFI Live app (transportforireland.ie/available-apps/tfi-live) to plan bus, train and tram trips using real-time departure information.

RURAL ROAD HAZARDS

Ireland's rural roads can be steep, narrow and winding. Single-track roads with blind bends can be challenging, even without the hazard of wandering sheep. If you see an oncoming vehicle, look for a passing place to pull into. The etiquette is for the car nearest to a passing place to reverse; thank the driver with a wave. Be aware, too, that mist can roll in quickly at the coast and on the hills, reducing visibility.

Bus

Private buses compete with Bus Éireann in the Republic and also run where the national buses are irregular or absent. Few bus journeys last longer than five hours. Bus Éireann bookings can be made online (buseireann.ie). Book early to get the lowest fares.

Train

Ireland's rail network is limited, but trains are a quick and comfortable option for certain intercity routes, including Belfast to Dublin and Dublin to Cork. Services are operated by Irish Rail (irishrail.ie) in the Republic and NI Railways (translink.co.uk) in Northern Ireland. For the best fares, book in advance.

Hiring a Car

Cars can be hired in every major town and city, but book in advance, especially during the summer when demand sometimes outstrips supply. Most cars are manual; automatic cars are more expensive. You need to be 25 years old or over to hire a car from most companies.

DRIVING ESSENTIALS

Drive on the left.

50

Speed limits are in kilometres per hour in the Republic and miles per hour in Northern Ireland.

.05

Blood alcohol limit is 0.05%.

Money

CURRENCY:
IRELAND: EURO (€), NORTHERN IRELAND: POUND (£)

Credit Cards

Nearly all businesses take cards. In many cases, card payment is preferred, and some restaurants and tour companies accept payment only by card. Most accommodation, including campsites, requires credit card details or advanced payment to secure a reservation. A few rural guesthouses and campsites accept cash only.

Contactless Payments

Card payments for amounts up to €50 (£100 in Northern Ireland) are usually contactless. You pay by tapping your card on the machine.

Digital Payment

Payments using digital wallets on mobile phones have become increasingly popular in Ireland. They can be used anywhere that accepts contactless card payments.

Taxes & Refunds

Most goods come with a value-added tax (VAT) of 23% (20% in Northern Ireland), which non-EU residents can claim back under the Retail Export Scheme. The scheme is also available in Northern Ireland. The goods must be taken out of the EU within three months of the purchase date.

HOW MUCH FOR...

Surfboard rental
€20

Museum entry
€12

Bike rental
€20

Bus ticket from Dublin to Cork
€12

HOW TO... Save Some Euros

Many attractions offer discounted rates if you buy tickets online in advance. You can also buy visitor passes that include entry to a number of attractions, such as the Dublin Pass. The Heritage Card includes free entry to all Office of Public Works–managed sites; it can be a good deal depending on how many spots you plan to visit.

EXCHANGE RATES

If you are offered a choice of currencies when paying by card, choosing to pay in the local currency nearly always offers a better rate than selecting payment in your home currency.

GET PAID TO LIVE ON AN IRISH ISLAND

In 2023, the Irish government started offering grants of up to €84,000 to people willing to buy a vacant home on one of the country's offshore islands. The government later clarified that the money could be used only to add insulation or make structural repairs to a property that had been empty for more than two years. The scheme applies to islands that are not accessible by bridge; these islands have suffered decades of depopulation. If the idea of a home renovation project on a remote island appeals, a new life on Clare Island could be beckoning.

Accommodation

Lighthouses

A number of Ireland's iconic lighthouses are available to rent as holiday lets. You might have to climb some stairs, but the wild scenery and sea views are unbeatable. The Irish Landmark Trust preserves buildings of special historical interest and rents them as holiday accommodation. Properties include Wicklow Head Lighthouse and lightkeeper's houses at Blackhead Lighthouse in County Antrim and St John's Point in County Donegal.

Castles

If you have a fairy-tale fantasy of staying in a castle, Ireland might be the place to experience it. Some of Ireland's grandest castles are now luxury hotels, including Ashford Castle in County Mayo, Lough Eske Castle in County Donegal and Ballynahinch Castle in County Galway. Castles are usually set in magnificent locations, often with extensive grounds and woodland to explore.

Tree Houses & Bubble Domes

Some of Ireland's most atmospheric accommodations are hidden in the woods. In County Fermanagh, the transparent forest bubble domes offer views of the night sky. Across the country, you'll find beautifully designed tree houses, in which you can spend a night in the woods, such as Burrenmore Nest in County Derry.

Cabin Cruises & Canal Barges

One way to experience Ireland's inland waterways is to hire a live-aboard motorboat or canal barge. A number of companies offer self-drive, liveaboard cabin cruisers for exploring the Shannon-Erne Waterway. You can also rent a narrowboat or barge and cruise the Grand Canal and River Barrow. No previous boating experience is required.

HOW MUCH FOR A NIGHT IN...

Camping pitch
€20

B&B
€120

Castle hotel
€500

Glamping Pods & Yurts

Camping in Ireland always carries the risk of a washout, but swapping your tent for a timber pod raises the comfort level and reduces the risk of leaks. Glamping pods range from basic huts with bunks (bring your own bedding) to cabins with attached bathrooms and kitchenettes. Alternatively, book a stay in a proper bed in a luxurious glamping yurt. These are often spectacularly located, with gorgeous views.

THE HOUSING CRISIS

The relocation of a number of multinational companies to Dublin is one factor that has contributed to a housing crisis in the city. Rents have soared, and housing is scarce. In 2023, the Department of Housing reported that there were more than 9000 homeless people living in Dublin.

In some areas of the country, such as the Dingle Peninsula in County Kerry, a shortage of affordable housing is partly caused by properties being bought up as holiday homes and landlords choosing to rent properties on Airbnb.

Family Travel

From interactive museums to cycling paths, nature trails and beaches, Ireland has plenty to keep kids entertained. The country's small size, mild climate and relative safety make it an easy place for families to explore. You can experience the wildness of the coast and rural hills but still be back in a town within a couple of hours.

Where to Sleep

Nearly all hotels provide cots, but reserve ahead, especially during holiday periods. Many hotels have interconnecting rooms and offer babysitting services. In summer, look for kids' clubs and other activities. Glamping in pods has become increasingly popular in Ireland. Most sleep four to six people and are perfect for families. Some guesthouses do not accept young children, so check before booking.

Seeing the Sights

Most of Ireland's museums, wildlife centres and other visitor attractions cater to kids as much as they do to the adults who accompany them, and they offer reduced-price admission for families. Many visitor experiences feature activities for children, especially during the school holidays, and most attractions have playgrounds and picnic tables. Activity centres offer kids' programs for all ages.

Eating

Restaurants generally have high chairs, children's menus and baby-changing facilities. Fine-dining restaurants might not be suitable for kids. Pubs do not allow under 15s after 9pm. Supermarket meal deals offer good-value lunches (a sandwich, drink and a snack) on the go.

On the Road

Public transport is free for children under five. Child seats are mandatory in rental cars for children under four years old. Car-hire companies can provide them, but you'll need to book in advance.

KID-FRIENDLY PICKS

Beyond the Trees (p129)
Explore treetop walkways, a forest viewing tower and a giant slide at Avondale Forest Park in County Wicklow.

Spike Island (p198)
Visit the former prison island in County Cork.

Irish National Heritage Park (p149)
Learn about 9000 years of Irish history at this open-air museum in Wexford.

Waterford Greenway (p161)
Cycle p161 family-friendly trail from Waterford city to Dungarvan.

W5 (p485)
An interactive science discovery centre in Belfast.

LAND OF GIANTS & FAIRIES

Irish folklore is full of tales of giants and mischievous fairies. Far from being friendly wish-granting creatures, the fairies were troublesome entities that humans took great care not to disturb or annoy. As for the giants of Irish mythology, the Fomorians were sea monsters that were the archenemies of the Tuatha Dé Danann, the ancient tribe of Ireland. Legend has it the Giant's Causeway was built by Finn McCool.

The myths are brought to life at the Giant's Lair trail at Slieve Gullion Forest Park in County Armagh (p525), where an innovative storybook forest trail passes fairy houses and the discarded belongings of a giant.

Health & Safe Travel

INSURANCE

Travel insurance is not required to enter Ireland, but comprehensive insurance is highly recommended to cover theft and loss as well as any medical problems. EU citizens carrying a free European Health Insurance Card (EHIC) are covered for most emergency medical care but not for nonemergencies or emergency repatriation.

Midges

These little biting insects are most active between May and September, particularly in the boggy areas of Connemara and Donegal. They often appear in swarms around dusk. Luckily they don't carry diseases, and the windiness of the Irish climate helps keep them at bay. Locals use Avon's Skin So Soft moisturiser to prevent bites.

Theft & Fraud

Crime levels in Ireland are low, and it is a relatively safe country for travellers. Nearly all crimes against tourists happen in Dublin, and they mostly consist of pickpocketing, bag snatching and theft from cars. Don't leave anything visible through the windows of your car when you park, and try to find secure parking areas.

BEACH SAFETY

Rip currents are the leading hazard for beachgoers. If lifeguards aren't present, ask locals whether the water is suitable for swimming.

SWIM SAFELY

Red and yellow flag
A lifeguarded area; the safest place to swim.

Red flag
Danger. Do not enter the water.

Black and white chequered flag
An area for surfing, kayaking and other non-powered craft. Do not swim here.

Reporting a Crime

The best place to report an incident is the nearest *garda* (police) station, or PSNI station in Northern Ireland. Ask for an incident report, which is usually required for insurance claims and emergency documents. The Irish Tourist Assistance Services (ITAS) provides free help and support to people who are victims of crime while travelling in Ireland.

NORTHERN IRELAND

Sectarian conflict is unlikely to cause problems for travellers these days, but it's a good idea to keep an eye on the news. Avoid any areas where there are riots or clashes with the police. Though rare, this kind of violence does occasionally flare up. However, such clashes do not usually pose a safety threat or cause widespread disruption.

Food, Drink & Nightlife

When to Eat

Breakfast (7-10am) During the week, Irish people usually eat toast, cereal or porridge. Cooked breakfasts are more often eaten at weekends.

Lunch (12.30-2pm) Often soup and a sandwich, or something light.

Dinner (5-9pm) Also called tea, this is the main meal of the day. Sometimes followed by a dessert (pudding) of something sweet like apple pie.

Where to Eat

Cafes The best Irish cafes serve house-made soups, salads, sandwiches, baked potatoes and cakes.

Coffee shops Specialist coffee shops sell lattes, flat whites and drip coffees, plus pastries.

Pubs Most pubs also offer meals, usually generous portions of comfort food like fish and chips.

Restaurants Irish restaurants range from family-friendly bistros to Michelin-starred fine-dining establishments.

Food trucks Sometimes parked in particularly scenic places, food trucks serve everything from lobster rolls to Thai food.

MENU DECODER

Starter An appetiser dish eaten at the start of the meal.

Main course The entree or main dish of the meal.

Dessert A sweet pudding, cake or ice cream eaten at the end of the meal.

Cheese board A plate of cheese and crackers sometimes offered on dessert menus.

Pretheatre menu A fixed-price, two- or three-course menu served in the early evening; often good value for money.

Tasting menu A fixed menu of specially prepared small plates.

Wine pairings A glass of specially selected wine with each course.

Sunday roast Roast beef, chicken or lamb served with roast and mashed potatoes, vegetables and gravy.

Chips Like potato fries but fatter and fluffier. Crisps are potato snacks sold in packets (known as chips in the US).

HOW TO... Order Drinks in a Pub

If you're in a pub with friends, it's usual for people to take turns buying a round of drinks for the group. When it's your turn, announce your intentions by saying 'my round.' Ask everybody in your party what they would like and then order and pay at the bar. If you're with a large group or on a tight budget don't fret, it's not always necessary to get a round, and you can order your own drink.

Draft beer and Guinness are served by the pint and half pint; specify the quantity when you order. In Ireland, a standard measure of spirits is 35.5mL; you can order a single or a double (70mL). Tipping the person behind the bar is not expected, but you may wish to do so, especially if you are ordering a round.

HOW MUCH FOR A...

pint of Guinness
€6

takeaway fish and chips
€12

flat white
€4

glass of wine
€7

gourmet dinner
€70

ice cream cone
€3

Ulster Fry
€10

HOW TO... Pack a Perfect Picnic

The practice of bringing food on an outdoor excursion to eat in scenic surroundings has been popular across Europe since the French Revolution, when French aristocrats fled their homeland and brought their fondness for picnicking with them. In Ireland, picnics have long been an integral part of summer family outings to the beach, the hills or even the local park.

For a typical Irish picnic, you'll need a blanket. This can be laid out on the grass or sand, with the food placed in the middle, or draped over the top of a picnic table. As for the picnic food, these days the options extend far beyond the traditional ham sandwiches on white sliced bread. Instead, look for freshly baked sourdough in an artisan bakery. Next, stop at a deli to pick up Irish cheeses, quiches and pies. Sausage rolls (sausage meat wrapped in flaky pastry) are also ideal for a picnic. Look out for punnets of local strawberries, sometimes sold at the roadside when strawberries are in season. For a truly authentic Irish picnic experience, bring a flask of tea. (It will help keep you warm if the temperature drops.) Most importantly, don't forget to buy several bags of Tayto crisps.

If it starts pouring with rain and you end up eating your sandwiches in the car, take solace in the fact that this is an Irish picnicking tradition.

Gourmet Picnic Hampers

If packing a picnic sounds like too much effort, a number of hotels and guesthouses offer luxury picnic experiences, where they prepare a gourmet hamper for you to bring on an excursion to a nearby beauty spot.

FARM TO TABLE

Farm-to-table and farm-to-fork dining are terms used for restaurants that source their ingredients directly from local farmers, fishing boats and artisan suppliers, with a focus on seasonal and organic produce. At the forefront of the farm-to-table movement in Ireland is Ballymaloe House, a restaurant in County Cork where the daily menu is based on what has been cultivated on-site and at nearby farms. While the restaurant at Ballymaloe House has used house-grown produce since the 1960s, this sustainable practice has been gaining traction in Ireland.

Menus at farm-to-table restaurants are based on whatever seasonal produce is currently available, which usually changes day by day. In addition to being more sustainable, fresh ingredients taste better, so the philosophy of many farm-to-table chefs is to let the flavours shine through in deceptively simple dishes.

Foraging is also undergoing a revival in Ireland. These days, it's common to see foraged herbs on restaurant menus, and several farms offer foraging trips to help identify edible wild berries, mushrooms, elderflower, samphire, wild garlic and sorrel. Edible seaweeds, which have long been foraged on Ireland's shores, have recently become fashionable again for their health benefits.

If you have self-catering accommodation, you can create your own farm-to-table experience by shopping at a farmers market and preparing a meal with the ingredients. To take your farm-to-table cooking skills to the next level, enrol in a course at Ballymaloe Cookery School, Darina Allen's County Cork establishment, where ingredients are sourced from the organic farm and gardens.

Responsible Travel

TOOLKIT

Climate Change & Travel

It's impossible to ignore the impact we have when travelling, and the importance of making changes where we can. Lonely Planet urges all travellers to engage with their travel carbon footprint. There are many carbon calculators online that allow travellers to estimate the carbon emissions generated by their journey; try resurgence.org/resources/carbon-calculator.html. Many airlines and booking sites offer travellers the option of offsetting the impact of greenhouse gas emissions by contributing to climate-friendly initiatives around the world. We continue to offset the carbon footprint of all Lonely Planet staff travel, while recognising this is a mitigation more than a solution.

Save the Seals

Visit the seals and help support the work of Courtown Seal Rescue (p151) in County Wexford. Volunteers rescue and rehabilitate orphaned and injured seals, plant trees, and raise awareness of marine conservation issues.

Delta Sensory Gardens

These accessible gardens in Carlow (p169) include a five senses garden, a musical fountain and a sculpture garden. Proceeds go to the adjacent Delta Centre for adults with disabilities, for whom the gardens were designed.

Buy Local Arts & Crafts

Design Ireland (designireland.ie) highlights the work of independent Irish designers and makers, and the artists also host workshops and demonstrations in their studios. Craft NI (craftni.org) does the same in Northern Ireland and has a shop in Belfast.

Bogland Boardwalks

Boardwalk trails have been constructed to protect areas of delicate blanket bog, including the Cuilcagh Boardwalk Trail (p566) in County Fermanagh. Stick to the path to avoid damaging the bogs.

In Dublin, get your coffee from one of three branches of Mug Shot Café. These cafes are owned and managed by PACE, a social enterprise that creates jobs for people who have experienced prison.

The Irish Wildlife Trust campaigns for the protection of Ireland's wildlife and manages a number of wildlife reserves. Get involved by joining one of the events hosted at branches around the country.

BRIGIT'S GARDEN

This not-for-profit garden in Galway is themed around Celtic festivals. It was established to help people get in touch with nature and learn about Celtic traditions. There is also a focus on herbs and their healing properties.

BURREN ECOTOURISM

The Burren Ecotourism Network (burren.ie) has brought together more than 70 local businesses, including artisan producers and cycling tour providers, to create a community model for sustainable tourism in the Burren and Cliffs of Moher Geopark.

Rewilding

The rewilding movement aims to restore Ireland's native forests. Pick up Eoghan Daltun's book *An Irish Atlantic Rainforest: A Personal Journey into the Magic of Rewilding* to learn about his efforts to rewild an area of the Beara peninsula.

Wind-Powered Hotel

The Salthouse Hotel (p544) in County Antrim has an on-site wind turbine and solar panels that supply renewable energy to both the hotel and the car park EV chargers. Air source heat pumps are used for heating.

Pick up litter with other volunteers on a community beach cleanup organised by Clean Coasts (cleancoasts.org).

Organic Trust (organictrust.ie) has a list of certified organic farm shops and organic produce vendors.

Walkinstown Green Social Enterprises

WALK empowers people with disabilities by providing training, employment and community. Support them by eating at the social enterprise cafe Green Kitchen and Garden Shop in Dublin.

14 million tonnes

The amount of waste produced by people in Ireland each year. The Circular Economy is a set of measures designed to ensure that raw materials remain in use for as long as possible through reuse and recycling.

RESOURCES

sustainabletravelireland.ie
Has a list of tourism providers that meet the criteria of sustainable tourism.

iwt.ie
The Irish Wildlife Trust's website, with information on current campaigns.

LGBTIQ+ Travellers

Ireland is generally welcoming to LGBTIQ+ travellers, and it is unusual to encounter hostility at hotels or other accommodation. Conservative attitudes persist, and Ireland's LGBTIQ+ community continues to face discrimination and harassment, but travellers are not usually the targets. Dublin, Belfast, Galway and Cork have well-established gay scenes, and Pride is celebrated with parties and parades.

Pride

Pride celebrations take place across the country. Ireland's biggest LGBTIQ+ event is Dublin Pride, which kicks off in June and culminates in a huge parade through the capital on the last Saturday of the month. Belfast Pride is held in late July, with more than 150 events across 10 days. A weeklong festival takes place in Cork city in late July and early August, and in Galway in August. Smaller events and parades are held in Wexford in May, Mayo in June, Inishowen in June, Carlow in July, Limerick in July, Derry (Foyle Pride) in August and Waterford in August.

THE SCENE

Dublin has plenty of community-friendly bars and clubs in the city centre; the most well-established is the George. In Belfast, the LGBTIQ+ scene is centred on Union St in the Cathedral Quarter.

In Dublin, stop by Outhouse (outhouse.ie), an LGBTIQ+ resource centre and cafe. It's a great place to meet people and find out what's on. The website has listings for events and organisations across Ireland.

LGBTIQ+ Ireland

In line with a troubling trend across Europe, the number of reported hate crimes against the LGBTIQ+ community in Ireland has risen. Homophobic or transphobic harassment and violence are crimes and can be reported to the police. You can also call the LGBT Helpline on 1800 929 539.

TRANS-FUSION

Held in Dublin in early July, this weeklong arts festival celebrates Ireland's trans community with poetry, storytelling, spoken word, comedy, history and music events. One of the festival's aims is to show how shared performance spaces and the arts can boost self-esteem and lead to positive mental health outcomes.

POLITICS

In 2017, Taoiseach Leo Varadkar became Ireland's first openly gay head of government. He had come out publicly in 2015, in the lead-up to the referendum in which Ireland voted to change the constitution to recognise same-sex marriage. Varadkar has expressed his support for the trans community, acknowledging in a 2022 press interview that it is 'extraordinarily difficult to be trans in Ireland today'.

Béar Féile

This four-day bear event in Dublin features DJs, parties, bear bingo, a bear *céilidh* (session of traditional Irish dance and music) and a Mr Bear Ireland competition. It takes place in March, with events at bars and clubs in the city centre.

Accessible Travel

Ireland still has accessibility issues, but efforts have been made to improve the country's public spaces with ramps, lifts and other facilities and to create a welcoming environment for people who have learning disabilities or are neurodiverse.

Autism-Friendly Town

Clonakilty in West Cork has been named Ireland's first autism-friendly town by the charity AsIAm. The accreditation involved training staff in local businesses, becoming service-dog friendly and introducing quiet spaces.

Airport

Passengers with reduced mobility can request airport assistance. The request should be made at least 48 hours in advance through your airline. You can also prebook assistance at Dublin Airport through the PRM Assist Mobile app (prmassist.com).

Accommodation

All hotels built since 2010 should have lifts, ramps and other facilities. Urban chain hotels are most likely to have fully accessible rooms. Other accommodations such as B&Bs, private rentals and historic hotels may not be accessible.

ACCESSIBLE ATTRACTIONS

The Beyond the Trees (p129) experience at Avondale Forest is fully wheelchair accessible. At the Giant's Causeway (p548), a shuttle bus links the visitor centre with the stones.

Inclusive Beaches

In Northern Ireland, Inclusive Beaches (maemurrayfoundation.org) offers free loans of beach wheelchairs at several locations, including Portstewart Strand in County Derry, which also has accessible parking and disabled toilet and shower facilities.

Beach Wheelchairs

Use the filter option on the website beaches.ie to search for beaches with beach wheelchairs and disabled access in the Republic. The Disability Federation of Ireland (disability-federation.ie) has a list of contacts for reserving beach wheelchairs.

JAM CARD

Designed to be used by people with learning disabilities or autism, the JAM Card (jamcard.org) can be downloaded onto your phone, or you can request a physical card. It is used to discreetly ask 'just a minute' when you need more time.

RESOURCES

Disability Federation of Ireland (disability-federation.ie) advocates for people with disabilities in the Republic of Ireland.

Disability Action (disabilityaction.org) is the equivalent body in Northern Ireland.

Enable Ireland (enableireland.ie) is a national disability services provider for adults and children.

AsIAm (asiam.ie) provides details of autism support groups.

Transport for Ireland (transportforireland.ie) has information on accessibility for public transport users as well as contact information for wheelchair-accessible taxis.

Sensory Rooms

A number of hotels have adapted rooms with projectors and special lighting for people with autism; some also have sensory playrooms for children. Hotels with adapted rooms include the Pillo Hotel in Ashbourne and the Radisson in Sligo.

How to Drive the Wild Atlantic Way

The Wild Atlantic Way is an official, waymarked driving route that extends 2500km along Ireland's western coastline from the Inishowen Peninsula in Donegal to Kinsale in west Cork. Along the way are plenty of places to stop and take in views of jagged cliffs, crescent strands and sheep-studded hills, as well as towns where you can catch a trad session in a pub or eat local seafood.

The Route

The route is split into 14 stages spread across nine counties: Donegal, Leitrim, Sligo, Mayo, Galway, Clare, Limerick, Kerry and Cork. It's marked by signposts featuring a blue wave and the direction of travel (N for north and S for south). You can drive the route in either direction, but if you drive from south to north, you're on the side of the road that's closest to the sea. Highlights along the route are marked with 'discovery point' signs; these are good places to stop along the way.

Cycling

Cycling the Wild Atlantic Way is a challenge. It's hilly, and the roads can be busy with cars, especially in summer. The full route takes six or seven weeks by bike, so most cyclists choose a section of the route to cover. The prevailing wind is southerly, so south to north should be easier (even though the wind can't be relied on to cooperate).

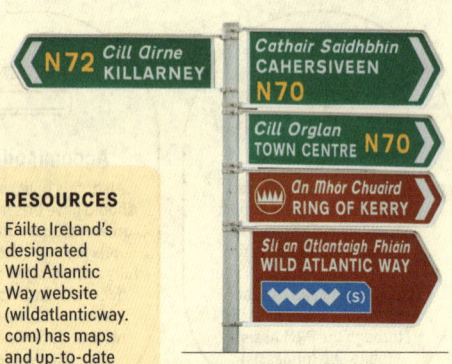

RESOURCES

Fáilte Ireland's designated Wild Atlantic Way website (wildatlanticway.com) has maps and up-to-date information about the route.

WILD ATLANTIC ISLANDS

Along the route, a number of islands make interesting detours. In Donegal, you can catch a trad session and meet a community of artists on Tory Island, or explore the walking trails of wild Arranmore. In County Mayo is Achill Island, which can be reached by a causeway from the mainland. Take your pick of three Aran Islands in Galway, which can be accessed by ferry; each one gives the feeling of living at the edge of the world. At the tip of the Beara Peninsula in Cork is Dursey Island, which can be reached by cable car.

Nuts & Bolts

SMOKING

It is illegal to smoke indoors everywhere except private residences.

TAP WATER

Tap water throughout Ireland is safe to drink. In fact, in some parts of the country, such as Belfast and County Down, the tap water has a particularly pleasant taste.

Mobile Phone Coverage

Mobile phones in Northern Ireland use UK networks. If you have a European SIM card, you might be charged different rates in Northern Ireland and the Republic. Some rural areas do not have mobile phone coverage, so download maps before taking a car journey.

Weights & Measures

The metric system is used except for liquid measures of beer, which comes in pints.

GOOD TO KNOW

Time zone
GMT, GMT+1 late March through October

Country code
353 (Republic); 44 (Northern Ireland)

Emergency number
999

Population
7.2 million

Electricity 230V/50Hz

Type G

PUBLIC HOLIDAYS

New Year's Day
1 January

St Brigid's Day
1st Monday in February (Republic of Ireland only)

St Patrick's Day
17 March

Easter Monday
March/April

Easter Tuesday
March/April (Northern Ireland only)

May Holiday
1st Monday in May (Republic only)

Spring Bank Holiday
Last Monday in May (Northern Ireland only)

June Holiday
1st Monday in June

The Twelfth 12 July (Northern Ireland only)

August Holiday
1st Monday in August (Republic of Ireland only)

Summer Bank Holiday Last Monday in August (Northern Ireland only)

October Holiday
Last Monday in October (Republic of Ireland only)

Christmas Day
25 December

St Stephen's Day (Boxing Day)
26 December

Language

Irish (Gaeilge) is the country's official language. In 2003 the government introduced the Official Languages Act, whereby all official documents, street signs and official titles must be either in Irish or in both Irish and English

Basics

Hello. Dia duit. *deea gwit*
Hello (reply). Dia is Muire (duit). *deeas mwira dit*
Good morning. Maidin mhaith. *mawjin wah*
Good night. Oíche mhaith. *eeheh wah*
Goodbye. Slán leat. *slawn lat*
Yes. Tá. *taw*
It is. Sea. *shah*
No. Níl. *neel*
It isn't. Ní hea. *nee hah*
Thank you (very much). Go raibh (míle) maith agat. *goh rev (meela) mah agut*
Excuse me. Gabh mo leithscéal. *gamoh lesh scale*
I'm sorry. Tá brón orm. *taw brohn oruhm*
I don't understand. Ní thuigim. *nee higgim*
Do you speak Irish? An bhfuil Gaeilge agat? *on vwil gwaylge oguht*
Cad é seo? What is this? *kod ay shoh*
Cad é sin? What is that? *kod ay shin*
I'd like to go to... Ba mhaith liom dul go dtí... *baw wah lohm dull go dee...*
I'd like to buy... Ba mhaith liom... a cheannack *bah wah lohm... a kyanukh...*
another/ one more. ceann eile. *kyown ella*
nice. go deas. *goh dyass*

Signs

Fir. Men. *fear*
Gardaí. Police (plural). *gardee*
Leithreas. Toilet. *lehrass*
Mna. Women. *mnaw*
Oifig An Phoist. Post office. *iffig ohn fwisht*

Days of the Week

Monday. Dé Luaín. *day loon*
Tuesday. Dé Máirt. *day maart*
Wednesday. Dé Ceádaoin. *day kaydeen*
Thursday. Déardaoin. *daredeen*
Friday. Dé hAoine. *day heeneh*
Saturday. Dé Sathairn. *day saherin*
Sunday. Dé Domhnaigh. *day downick*

Today. inniu. *inyuv*
Tomorrow. amárach. *am-oar-uck*
Yesterday. inné. *innay*

Emergencies

Help! Cabhrú. *cowroo*
Go away! Imigh leat. *imig lat*
I'm ill. Tá tinis orm. *Taw tinis urum*
Call ...! Glaoch ar... *Glay-uck air...*
...a doctor an dochtúir. *on ducktoor*
...the police an garda siochana. na gardaí. *on gorda she-uck-awna/ na gardee*

NUMBERS

1 **haon** *hayin*

2 **dó** *doe*

3 **trí** *tree*

4 **ceathaír** *kahirr*

5 **cúig** *cooig*

6 **sé** *shay*

7 **seacht** *shocked*

8 **ocht** *hukt*

9 **naoi** *nay*

10 **deich** *jeh*

DONATIONS TO ENGLISH

Whiskey, galore (from Irish *go leor*), banshee, smithereens (from *smiodar*, meaning "debris"), Tory (from Irish *toraí*, meaning "outlaw")

Cupla Focal

Here are a few phrases os Gaeilge (in Irish) to help you impress the locals:

Tóg é gobogé. Take it easy. *tohg ay gobogay*
Ní féidir é! Impossible! *nee faydir ay*
Ráiméis! Nonsense! *rawmaysh*
Go huafásach! That's terrible! *guh hoofawsokh*
Slainte! Your health!/Cheers! *slawncha*
Táim go maith. I'm fine. *thawm go mah*
Nollaig shona! Happy Christmas! *nuhlig hona*
Go n-éirí an bóthar leat! Bon voyage! *go nairee on bohhar lat*

Gaeltachts

Despite its official status, Irish is really only spoken in pockets of rural Ireland known as the Gaeltacht, the main ones being Cork (Corcaigh), Donegal (Dún na nGall), Galway (Gaillimh), Kerry (Ciarraí) and Mayo (Maigh Eo).

Dialects

Irish has three main dialects: Connaught Irish (in Galway and northern Mayo), Munster Irish (in Cork, Kerry and Waterford) and Ulster Irish (in Donegal). The blue pronunciation guidelines given here are an anglicised version of modern standard Irish, which is essentially an amalgam of the three – if you read them as if they were English, you'll be able to get your point across in Gaeilge without even having to think about the specifics of Irish pronunciation or spelling.

WHO SPEAKS IRISH?

As well as the Gaeltachts listed above, there exists also a number of Neo-Gaeltachts like the Gaeltacht Quarter in Befast, parts of west County Clare and south county Derry.

PRONUNCIATION

Irish divides vowels into long (those with an accent) and short (those without) and also disinguishes between broad (a, á, o, ó, u) and slender (e, é, i and í), which can affect the pronunciation of preceding consonants. Other than a few odd-looking clusters, such as mh and bhf (pronounced both as w), consonants are generally pronounced as they are in English.

The 2022 census reported almost 2 million Irish speakers in the Republic and 6,000 in Northern Ireland according to the 2021 UK census

STORYBOOK

STORYBOOK

Our writers delve deep into different aspects of Irish life.

A History of Ireland in 15 Places
From Celts to Vikings to Revolution; Ireland's complicated history
Isabel Albiston
p592

Meet the Irish
What does it mean to be Irish?
Fionn Davenport
p596

Gaelic Games: More than Sport
A look into hurling and gaelic football
Fionn Davenport
p598

WB Yeats
Yeats and Irish mysticism, Celtic revival and unrequited love
Brian Barry
p601

Ireland's Red Deer
An ancient indigenous deer facing endagerment
Brian Barry
p603

Ceide Fields (p364)

A HISTORY OF IRELAND IN
15 PLACES

Ireland's history has been marked by invasions by the Vikings, the Normans and the English, whose long period of domination of Ireland was met with resistance and rebellion. These 15 places are linked to key moments in Irish history, offering snapshots ranging from Neolithic ceremonies to recent political conflicts. By Isabel Albiston

THE EARLIEST EVIDENCE of humans in Ireland to have been discovered is a butchered bear bone that was found in a cave in County Clare and carbon-dated to 10,500 BCE. In fact, Ireland's prehistoric period is rich and intriguing. Early standing stone arrangements are believed to relate to astrology, and mysterious ceremonial sites align with the sun at key moments in the year. The time before the arrival of the Celtic tribes is associated with the mythical fairy folk of the Tuatha de Dannan.

The beginnings of Christianity in Ireland heralded a period in which the country's earliest monasteries were important centres of learning, though soon these monastic centres would have to fend off attacks from the Vikings. However, Ireland's darkest and most turbulent history relates to its fractured and complicated relationship with its close neighbour, England. Ever since the invasion of the Anglo-Normans in the 12th century, Ireland has suffered under various iterations of English dominance and occupation. Even after Ireland's hard-won independence from Britain, the country was left divided, creating a precarious political situation in the North.

Through it all, Ireland's folk traditions and literary output have thrived, reflecting the themes of rebellion and resistance that run through its history.

1. Céide Fields
WORLD'S OLDEST STONE-WALLED FIELDS
Preserved beneath the blanket bogs of County Mayo are a series of dwelling areas, tombs and fields that date from around 3700 BCE. These stone-walled fields are the oldest and some of the largest such enclosures to have been uncovered in the world. The rectangular plots of this Stone Age farming site indicate a system of community farming, which by this period had replaced hunting in Ireland. In the 1930s, a local teacher came across stone walls buried beneath the bogs, but he failed to pique the interest of the experts he wrote to, and excavation didn't begin until 1969.

For more on the Céide Fields, see page 365

2. Brú na Bóinne
PREHISTORIC PASSAGE TOMBS
Located within a bend in the River Boyne in County Meath are the burial tombs of Newgrange, Knowth and Dowth, which date from around 3200 BCE. The remarkable complex is one of the most important Neolithic sites in the world, and the ceremonial structures also contain a large collection of megalithic art. Newgrange's passage leads to a central chamber that directly aligns with the sunlight of the winter solstice, and it was a place of ritual. In 2020, analysis

of the DNA of a man buried in Newgrange revealed that his parents were closely related, suggesting he could have been royal.

For more on Brú na Bóinne, see page 436

3. Navan Fort
MYSTERIOUS MOUND STEEPED IN LEGEND

Near Armagh city, the intriguing Iron Age monument Navan Fort is believed to have been occupied by royalty or high priests. Excavations suggest that the largest structure was once a temple and probably a site of rituals and ceremonies, but the precise details remain a mystery. Navan Fort is referenced in Irish legends as Emain Macha, the court of a mythical Irish king. The significance of the site as a centre of power and spirituality could be one reason why St Patrick later chose to build his first stone church on a nearby hill, where St Patrick's Cathedral stands today.

For more on Navan Fort, see page 523

4. Slemish Mountain
THE LEGEND OF ST PATRICK

At age 16, Ireland's patron saint was kidnapped from his home in 5th-century Roman Britain and brought to Ireland. It was during his hours of solitude tending sheep on Slemish Mountain in County Antrim that Patrick dreamed of his escape from Ireland on board a ship. After a difficult journey, Patrick made it back to Britain but later felt called by a vision to return to Ireland to spread Christianity. Though Patrick was not the first Christian missionary in Ireland, his mission was hugely influential. St Patrick's death date, 17 March, is celebrated across Ireland with parties and parades.t

For more on Slemish Mountain, see page 544

5. Clonmacnoise
EARLY CHRISTIAN MONASTERY

The monastery established on the banks of the River Shannon by St Ciarán in 548 CE was once an influential centre of learning, attended by monks from all over Europe. It was one of Ireland's earliest monastic settlements, and its strategic location further increased its prominence. The monks were the scholars of their day, as well as skilled builders who designed and constructed the round stone towers found at Clonmacnoise and other monastic sites. After the 12th century, the site was in decline, and what remained was reduced to ruins by the English in 1552.t

For more on Clonmacnoise, see page 404

6. Waterford City
VIKING SETTLEMENT

Vikings settled in what is now Waterford city from as early as 914 CE, naming the town Vadrarjfordr. The Vikings chose the site because of its easily defended location on the River Suir; they established settlements in Dublin and Wexford for the same reason. Today their legacy lives on in Waterford's Viking Triangle, the oldest part of the city, which contains a giant replica Viking chessboard. By the 12th century, the Anglo-Normans had arrived, adding medieval buildings and constructing city walls. These days, Waterford's walls are the canvas for a vibrant street art scene.

For more on Waterford city, see page 155

7. Clare Island
IRELAND'S PIRATE QUEEN

Born into a powerful seafaring family on the Mayo coast, Grace O'Malley (Gráinne Ní Mháille, 1530–1603) took to waylaying cargo vessels at Galway port and demanding payment for safe passage. If they refused, she would have them looted. She soon controlled Mayo's Clew Bay and settled on Clare Island, though she

Celtic cross, Clonmacnoise (p404)

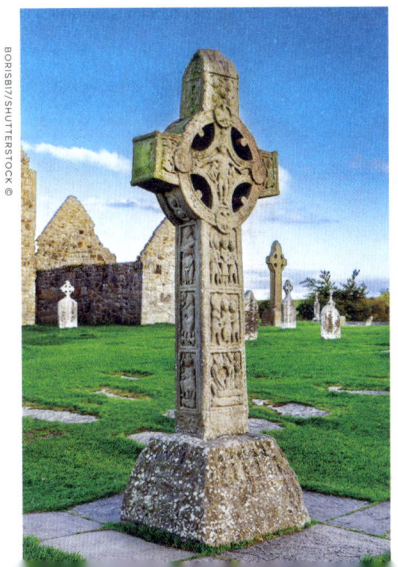

continued marauding around the Irish and Scottish coasts. After O'Malley's piracy caught the attention of the English, she ended up meeting Queen Elizabeth I, who offered her a pardon and a title; O'Malley replied that she was already the Queen of Connacht. She is thought to be buried on Clare Island.

For more on Clare Island, see page 346

8. Donegal Castle
FLIGHT OF THE EARLS

In 1607, after years of fighting against the English in Ulster, the Gaelic earls Hugh O'Neill and Rory O'Donnell boarded a ship in Rathmullan and left Ireland for good, an event known as the Flight of the Earls. It's believed that as an act of defiance against the English, O'Donnell torched his own castle in Donegal before fleeing. The Flight of the Earls marked the end of the rule of Irish chieftains and left Ulster open to English rule and to the policy of Plantation, in which the Gaelic earls' land was confiscated and redistributed to British settlers.

For more on Donegal Castle, see page 397

9. Belfast Entries
THE SOCIETY OF UNITED IRISHMEN

In 1791, Theobald Wolfe Tone was invited to Belfast to attend the inaugural meeting of the Society of United Irish Men at a tavern in Crown Entry. Inspired by the French Revolution, the Society's initial aims were religious equality and parliamentary reform. In the face of British attempts to suppress the Society, it was forced underground and soon planned an armed rebellion with the help of the French. It was ultimately unsuccessful, and the rebels were arrested and the leaders sentenced to execution.

Today, the historic events of the Belfast Entries are referenced in street art in the narrow alleyways.

For more on Belfast Entries, see page 471

10. Dunbrody Famine Ship
FAMINE AND EMIGRATION

As a result of the Great Famine of 1845 to 1851, it's estimated that up to one million people died and some two million emigrated from Ireland. Though the immediate cause was the failure of the potato crop, the British government insisted that food exports from Ireland continue throughout the Famine and left Irish people to starve. New Ross in County Wexford was a departure point for 'coffin ships' that left Ireland for North America. Today, an experience aboard a replica ship tells of the harrowing journey across the Atlantic, which countless passengers didn't survive.

For more on the Dunbrody Famine Ship, see page 154

11. Butter Market
CORK'S FOODIE HERITAGE

An 1855 butter-weighing implement known as the Firkin Crane bears testament to the days when Cork had the largest butter market in the world. It was here, outside the Old Butter Market, that butter was weighed and packed for export. The nearby Cork Butter Museum displays a slab of butter that was buried in the peat bogs, where it remained preserved for 1000 years.

The city's foodie history can also be experienced at the English Market, set up in 1788 by the Protestant or 'English' corporation that then controlled the city; these days it showcases some of Cork's best produce.

For more on the Butter Market, see page 193

12. Sweny's Pharmacy
WHERE LEOPOLD BLOOM BOUGHT SOAP

Of all the writers and poets who have contributed to Ireland's rich literary heritage, James Joyce was arguably the most influential.

Dunbrody Famine Ship (p154)

Sweny's Pharmacy (p74)

His modernist novel *Ulysses* (1922) takes place in Dublin over the course of a single day, 16 June 1904. In it, the protagonist Leopold Bloom visits a number of real-life locations, including Sweny's Pharmacy, where he buys a bar of lemon soap. The pharmacy, which was established in 1847, has been preserved as it was in Joyce's day; today it sells soap and books and hosts literary events. Joyce's *Ulysses* notebooks are displayed in the Museum of Literature Ireland.

For more on Sweny's Pharmacy, see page 74

13. Dublin's General Post Office
1916 EASTER RISING

In an armed uprising that aimed to overthrow British rule, a group of republicans seized Dublin's General Post Office on Easter Monday 1916 and announced the formation of an Irish republic. After less than a week of fighting, the rebels surrendered. But the subsequent execution of the 15 rebellion leaders garnered sympathy for the cause among Irish people, and the Easter Rising was the start of the revolution that led to the War of Independence and the creation of the Irish Free State in 1921. However, six of Ireland's 32 counties would remain part of the UK.

For more on the General Post Office, see page 91

14. The Bogside
BLOODY SUNDAY

A peaceful civil rights protest in Derry ended in the killing of 14 unarmed civilians by British paratroopers on 30 January 1972, on what is known as Bloody Sunday. The shootings occurred in the Bogside neighbourhood, near Free Derry Corner, where the events are commemorated with wall murals and memorials and at the Museum of Free Derry. In 2010, following a years-long inquiry into the day, British Prime Minister David Cameron apologised on behalf of the British government for the 'unjustified and unjustifiable' killings. It was a tragic event that exacerbated the years of violent conflict in Northern Ireland that followed.

For more on the Bogside, see page 536

15. Stormont
END OF THE TROUBLES

On 10 April 1998, the signing of the Good Friday Agreement at Belfast's Stormont parliament building marked the end of 30 years of armed political conflict, known as the Troubles. It included a clause that grants people from Northern Ireland the right to identify as Irish, British or both. The public voted in favour of the Agreement in referendums in the North and South, leading to the establishment of a power-sharing Northern Ireland Assembly at Stormont. However, the complexities of the power-sharing system and political scandals have led to the suspension of the Assembly for extended periods.

For more on Stormont, see page 485

MEET THE IRISH

Charming, affable and quick-witted: the Irish have a very positive reputation. While usually genuine, Irish charm cloaks a deeper, more complex character. Fionn Davenport tries to unravel the Irish psyche.

THE KEY TO understanding the Irish is knowing that we go to great lengths to never appear to take ourselves too seriously, even when we are deadly earnest. We put a premium on self-deprecation and the outward appearance of modesty.

Ireland's best-loved sons and daughters are skilled at marrying excellence with humility, and nothing will endear you more to the Irish than being incredibly good at something while making it clear that success hasn't changed you at all. Olympic gold? That's great, so long as your mother's home-cooked meals are still the best prize of all.

This form of modest self-deprecation is traditionally characterised as an *béal bocht*, or 'putting on the poor mouth' – letting on that you're worse off than you really are. It's an attribute born out of centuries of struggling Irish tenants exaggerating the difficulty of their circumstances to elicit the forbearance of (English) landlords in a system where any material improvement would risk an increase in rent. Times may have changed, but undoing mores hardwired into Ireland's cultural DNA is a slow burn.

Yet recent prosperity and the unique brand of self-awareness of millennials and Gen Z Irish are going a long way towards doing that. Like their peers across the western world, younger Irish have a heightened sense of identity and a clearer sense of their place in the world. Rather than hide their candle under a bushel as previous generations did, they loudly celebrate their strengths and accomplishments. They are also more vocal in support of one another, partly a reaction to constantly grappling with the pitfalls of the digital world's never-ending feedback loop.

The same tensions inform the Irish sense of humour, which is infused with sarcasm, irony and the mastery of the deadpan understatement. Where else would you refer to WWII as 'the Emergency' and 30 years of sectarian violence in Northern Ireland as 'the Troubles'?

Dark humour is stock-in-trade. Whether to deal with poverty and political unrest or a housing crisis that puts starter homes beyond the reach of most young people, finding laughter in grim situations serves as a coping mechanism and transforms potentially debilitating situations into moments of shared resilience. We diminish the power of adversity by laughing at it.

'Slagging' is the Irish art form of teasing. It might seem caustic to unfamiliar ears, but your ability to 'take a slagging' in good spirits is the ultimate test of how grounded you are and a truer measure of the strength of friendship than a cheaply paid compliment. Making humorous light of yourself acts as a social lubricant and a way of connecting with others on an equal footing. You know we love you; just don't expect us to tell you.

People

In 2023, the Republic of Ireland's population was five million, and 1.9 million people live in Northern Ireland. The urban/rural divide is 65/35, and 79% of the population uses social media.

HOME IN MY IRISH SKIN

I was born in Dublin, in a mother-and-child home, as my birth mother got pregnant as a teenager at a time when having a baby out of wedlock was a societal no-no. As luck would have it, I was adopted by an Irish father and an Italian mother, which meant I grew up bilingual and – crucially – spent all of my summers in Italy until I left school.

As a result, I always had a feeling of 'otherness', my sense of Irishness tempered by a strong attachment to my mum's Italian heritage and a disavowal of the narrow-minded Catholicism that dominated Irish society for all of my youth.

In the early 1990s, I joined the Irish diaspora and moved to the US. The country I returned to at the dawn of the millennium was almost unrecognisable from the one I left, its gaze no longer inward but outward, as it sought to remould a more inclusive society. Twenty-five years later, I'm more home than ever.

All Ireland Hurling Championship 2023

GAELIC GAMES:
MORE THAN SPORT

Enshrined in ancient tales, Gaelic games are a unifying community force and essential to Irish culture. By Fionn Davenport

MORE THAN MUSIC and literature – more even than Guinness and perhaps the Irish language itself – Gaelic games encapsulate Irishness like nothing else. They are enmeshed in the fabric of Irish life and act as a useful shorthand for the best qualities of Irish culture. Their governing body, the Gaelic Athletic Association (GAA), is therefore more than a sporting organisation; it is the custodian of the identity, heritage and community spirit of the Irish people.

That's a lot of heavy lifting for some games. There are four of them; the most popular by far is Gaelic football, followed by hurling, camogie (the women's version of hurling) and handball, which is a lot like American handball and is played in various formats, including one-wall, three-wall and four-wall versions. Handball's adherents are passionate but few; in truth, when talking about Gaelic games, most people stick to football, hurling and camogie.

The Rules

Both Gaelic football and hurling are played by two teams of 15 players whose aim is to get the ball through what resembles a rugby goal: two long vertical posts joined by a horizontal bar, below which is a soccer-style goal protected by a goalkeeper. Goals (below the crossbar) are worth three points, whereas a ball placed over the bar between the posts is worth one point. Scores are shown thus: 1-12, meaning one goal and 12 points, giving a total of 15 points.

Gaelic football is played with a round, soccer-size ball, and players are allowed to kick it or handpass it, as in AFL football in Australia. Hurling is played with a flat stick or bat known as a hurley or *camán*. The small leather ball, called a *slíotar*, is hit or carried on the hurley; a well-struck ball can travel over 100m at 150km/h. Both games are played over 70 action-filled minutes.

The Majesty of Hurling

If Gaelic football is the most popular game, hurling is more revered. It's also one of the world's oldest field games and is mentioned in the epic tales of Irish mythology. In the last decades of the 19th century, the newly established GAA gave pride of place to hurling as the most Irish of Irish sports: an ancient game that not only puts a premium on skill and athleticism but also enshrines the values of courage and fair play that resonated deeply with the Gaelic Revival – the intellectual and cultural movement that underpinned Ireland's march towards independence.

STORYBOOK

Gaelic Football

Gaelic football is much younger than hurling, and today's version was developed in the latter half of the 19th century, mostly by blending a variety of rudimentary field games with the newer games of rugby and soccer, resulting in a uniquely Irish style of football. At its core, the GAA sought to instil pride in Irishness at a time when British rule had significantly impacted the cultural landscape, but Gaelic football was as much a nod to modernity as it was a recognition of the growing popularity of 'English' games.

A National Obsession

The games are played at club level throughout the country, and the best players are selected to play for their respective counties.

It's the ultimate ambition of every player to represent their county in an All-Ireland final at Dublin's Croke Park stadium, the climax of a knockout championship that is played first at provincial and then at inter-provincial level.

Almost every county in Ireland plays Gaelic football, with Kerry and then Dublin by far the most successful. The exceptions are Kilkenny, Limerick, Waterford, Clare and Tipperary, where hurling is king and football is an afterthought. A handful of other counties – Cork, Dublin, Galway, Offaly and Wexford – put serious effort into both games.

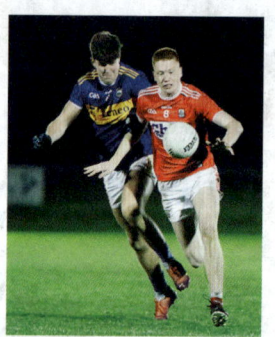

Cork vs Tipperarary, Gaelic football McGrath Cup
D. RIBEIRO/SHUTTERSTOCK ©

Strictly Amateur

Perhaps the most striking feature of Gaelic games is their steadfastly amateur status. Players play for their hometown clubs and, if they're good enough, their county. Even the best players don't receive salaries and often balance rigorous training with full-time jobs or study.

At its best, the amateur ethos fosters a unique sense of purity, camaraderie and grassroots enthusiasm. Clubs become tight-knit communities, and players are deeply connected to local identities, only ever moving from their hometown clubs for work or study (and even then county players will only ever play for their home county).

Unlike most professional sports leagues, the majority of GAA clubs are volunteer-driven. Whether it's a tiny village in County Kerry or a busy Dublin suburb, the local GAA club is the cornerstone of the community, and its busy calendar of events serves to raise funds and reinforce the community connection.

The Politics of Irish Sport

Politically, the GAA has served as a unifying force, albeit with complexities. It was founded as a nationalist institution and many of its members fought for Irish independence: Croke Park's Hogan Stand is named after one of the victims of an atrocity committed by British soldiers in 1920. For much of its existence, players were barred from playing soccer or rugby under penalty of exclusion, but this prohibition was finally lifted in 1971.

Although in Northern Ireland Gaelic games are still played almost exclusively in nationalist communities, efforts have been made to bridge the sectarian divide: one of the most visible results was the 2002 establishment of a Gaelic club for members of the Police Service of Northern Ireland.

The (Slow) March Towards Greater Inclusivity

Women's participation in Gaelic games has seen a recent surge. There are more than 500 camogie clubs throughout Ireland, while Ladies Gaelic Football (to give it its proper name) is one of the fastest-growing participation sports in Europe.

Nevertheless, the Camogie Association and the Ladies' Gaelic Football Association are not officially part of the GAA and struggle to get access to grounds, equipment and training facilities. In 2023 the situation got so bad that players threatened to go on strike unless the three organisations agreed to a charter to improve conditions and pursue talks on full integration.

WB Yeats and Georgie Hyde Lees

WB YEATS

Irish mysticism, a Nobel Prize and thwarted love – it's no wonder William Butler Yeats is one of Ireland's best-known poets.
By Brian Barry

WIDELY REGARDED AS one of the most significant figures of 20th-century literature, WB Yeats was greatly influenced by Ireland's rich cultural heritage and his country's natural beauty – particularly that of his mother's home county of Sligo. Awarded the Nobel Prize in Literature in 1923 largely for his work as a playwright, Yeats went on to write some of his most famous poetry later in his career. It's as a poet rather than as a playwright that he is now best remembered.

Beginnings

William Butler Yeats was born in Dublin in 1865. His mother, Susan, came from a prosperous Sligo family and his father, John, studied law but abandoned his legal career to pursue his ambitions of becoming a landscape and portrait painter. The family moved to London so John could follow his dreams of becoming an artist, but Yeats spent large parts of his boyhood in Sligo, and the county's landscape would have a profound impact on his work.

Irish Mysticism & Identity

Yeats liked to say that by age 24 (in 1889) he'd read 'most, if not all, recorded Irish folk tales'. His writings, whether poetry, prose or plays, celebrated Celtic legends and myths. He firmly believed that the Irish could emerge from English domination and create their own purely Irish identity by revelling in the ancient Celtic myths still commonly recounted across the island. In 1888 Yeats collaborated on the landmark *Fairy and Folk Tales of the Irish Peasantry*. Four years later, he wrote the children's book *Irish Fairy Tales*. In these works he codified many of the most common Irish myths, characters and legends, including fairies, leprechauns and banshees.

The Abbey Theatre

At the turn of the 20th century, Yeats showed an increased interest in theatre and in the summer of 1897 he stayed at the estate of Lady Gregory in County Galway. The Gregory house and estate offered him some sanctuary from the stress of an increasingly public life in both Ireland and Britain. During this stay, he, Lady Gregory and Edward Martin conceived the idea of a Celtic theatre, which would become the Irish Literary Theatre. Seeking to support the resurgence of Irish literature and cultural traditions, the theatre put on its first show in Dublin in May 1899. Yeats continued to be involved in the Abbey Theatre until his death, as both board member and playwright.

Never to Be: Maud Gonne

Maud Gonne was an English heiress and a committed Irish nationalist whom Yeats met in 1889. He quickly became infatuated with Gonne and she would have a lasting influence on his work and life. He proposed to her in 1891 and again in 1899, 1900 and 1901, but she always refused his offers. Much to his dismay, she married Irish nationalist Major John MacBride in 1903. Yeats was distraught at having lost his muse to another man and set about ridiculing MacBride in his letters and poetry. Gonne's marriage was a disaster and eventually she and MacBride separated. Yeats and Gonne later spent one night together, but she wrote to him afterwards to say that their relationship could not continue. She would write further letters highlighting the advantage to artists of remaining chaste. Yeats wrote about his night with Gonne in his poem 'A Man Young and Old'.

Poetry

Yeats' most famous poems demonstrate his deep-rooted love of the Irish landscape as well as his interest in Irish mysticism and his awareness of early-20th-century political turmoil.

'Wild Swans at Coole' (1916–17) lyrically describes the natural world:

Upon the brimming water among the stones
Are nine-and-fifty swans

He then contrasts it with an awareness of human decline:

All's changed since I, hearing at twilight,
The first time on this shore,
The bell-beat of their wings above my head,
Trod with a lighter tread.

Written just after WWI, 'The Second Coming' (1919) blends a Christian sensibility with the horror of global catastrophe:

...what rough beast, its hour come round at last,
Slouches towards Bethlehem to be born?

The later 'Sailing to Byzantium' (1928) is also concerned with age and decline: 'That is no country for old men'. Later still, 'Under Ben Bulben' (1939) sums up the poet's major concerns of Irish mysticism, the Sligo landscape (punctuated by the the mountain of Ben Bulben) and humankind's struggle for spiritual meaning:

Many times man lives and dies
Between his two eternities,
That of race and that of soul,
And ancient Ireland knew it all.

A Nobel Laureate

When Yeats was awarded the Nobel Prize in Literature in December 1923 'for his always inspired poetry, which in a highly artistic form gives expression to the spirit of a whole nation', he was aware of the platform he had been given to highlight Ireland's newfound independence. The symbolic value of an Irish poet winning the prize was enormous. Yeats answered many letters of congratulations with, 'I consider that this honour has come to me less as an individual than as a representative of Irish literature; it is part of Europe's welcome to the Free State.'

A Poet to the Last

In 1939, after a short illness, Yeats died at the age of 73 in the French Riviera town of Roquebrun. In line with his wishes, he was buried in Drumcliff, County Sligo. His grave is marked by a simple gravestone engraved with an epitaph from 'Under Ben Bulben':

Cast a cold Eye
On Life, on Death.
Horseman, pass by.

IRELAND'S RED DEER

Present in Ireland since the Neolithic period, indigenous red deer have been endangered by habitat loss, overhunting and interbreeding with non-native species. By Brian Barry

IRELAND'S MAJESTIC RED deer are thought to have been present in the country since the end of the last ice age. Brought to Ireland by Neolithic people, they roamed freely until habitat destruction and overhunting caused their numbers to decline sharply. At the turn of the 20th century, there were more than 1500 red deer in Killarney, County Kerry, but this number had fallen to as few as 60 by 1960. Populations have steadily increased in recent years thanks to conservation efforts, and between 700 and 800 native red deer now live in the woodlands and mountains around Killarney National Park.

Stags, Hinds & Fawns

As their name suggests, Ireland's native red deer have a rich red coat that changes to a darker greyish brown in winter. Stags can be as tall as 120cm at the shoulder and weigh up to 190kg. Hinds (females) are up to 110cm tall at the shoulder and weigh up to 110kg.

Stags' antlers, with a soft skin covering called velvet, grow from spring until late

Red deer, Killarney National Park

summer. Antlers most commonly have 14 to 16 tines (points), but a dominant male's antlers can have up to 20 tines. Ahead of the autumn rutting season – when stags use their antlers to spar with each other – the velvet dies off (or is scraped off on trees), the stags grow thick manes on their throats, their aggression increases and their neck muscles swell.

Hinds begin breeding at around 18 months old. For two weeks after they're born, fawns will remain hidden when the mother goes out to graze. A young fawn found on its own has not been abandoned and should not be moved or touched.

Outside the breeding season, stags and hinds live separately.

Herd size depends on the deer's habitat. Larger herds form when the deer live in open country, and herds remain smaller in woodland areas. The deer graze year-round but also eat moss, lichen, heather shoots and mat-grass through the winter months.

Young red deer, Killarney National Park

Seeing Deer in the Wild

The best time to see stags is in late September and early October during the rut. The main herds can be found in the lowlands of Killarney National Park in County Kerry and the surrounding Cores, Torc and Mangerton Mountains. These animals are direct descendants of the Scottish red deer that were introduced to Ireland more than 5000 years ago.

Red deer can also be found in County Wicklow in the Glendalough Valley and at Turlough Hill, but these herds have crossbred with Sika deer, a Japanese breed that was introduced to Powerscourt in County Wicklow in 1860 and to Killarney in 1865. There are wild red deer in Connemara in County Galway and Glenveagh National Park in County Donegal, but these deer were introduced from Scotland in the late 19th century.

Protection & Conservation

Red deer are a protected game species in Ireland, and a licence from the National Parks & Wildlife Service is required to hunt them. Stag-hunting season is from 1 September to 31 December, and hinds may be hunted from 1 November to 28 February. The hunting of all red deer in County Kerry, where the last native herd is located, is strictly prohibited.

In the 1980s a number of red deer were transported by helicopter to Inishvickillane, a private island in County Kerry, to prevent interbreeding with Sika deer. The island herd flourished, but because of the harsh Atlantic conditions and limited feeding, the deer are much smaller.

Red deer have had no natural predator since wolves were eradicated from Ireland more than 200 years ago. The biggest threat to Killarney's native red deer is genetic contamination through crossbreeding with Sika deer, though this has not yet been recorded in the national park. It is vital that the genetic purity of Ireland's last remaining indigenous herd of red deer is maintained, so scientists are closely monitoring the situation.

INDEX

A

Abbeyleix 413
abbeys, *see* monastic sites
accessible travel 15, 18, 42, 585
accommodation 577, *see also individual locations*
Achill Island 349-54, **350**
  accommodation 351
  beyond Achill Island 354-7
  drinking 352-3
activities 42-3, 44-5 *see also individual activities*
Adare 264
Ahakista 215
airports 574
  Donegal Airport 383
Allihies 216
alpacas 387
amusement parks
  Emerald Park 453
Antrim 527-55, **528-9**
  accommodation 546, 551
  drinking 546, 554
  food 546, 549, 554
  itineraries 530, 550, 552-3, **550**
  shopping 549
aquariums
  Atlantaquaria 314
  Dingle Oceanworld 244
  Exploris 518
Aran Islands 324-8, **325**
  accommodation 328
  food 326, 328
  itineraries 327, **327**
  shopping 326, 328
architecture 20-21, 103-4
Ardara 396
Armagh 503-25, **504-5**, 520-5
  accommodation 522

  food 522
  itineraries 506
Armagh city 520-3, **521**
  beyond Armagh city 524-5
Arranmore Island 384
Athenry 315

B

Ballina 361-2
Ballycastle 543-4, **543**
  beyond Ballycastle 545-555
  food 544
Baltimore 208
Banshees of Inisherin 352
Bantry 209-11, **209**
  beyond Bantry 212-17
bars 77
base jumping 393
basking sharks 290, 394, 547
beaches 15
  Ballycastle Strand 544
  Ballydonegan Beach 216
  Ballyquin Beach 165
  Banna Strand 254
  Benone Strand 540
  Brittas Bay 133
  Brown's Bay 555
  Carrickfinn Beach 383
  Clonea Strand 163
  Coumeenoole Beach 247
  Councillor's Strand 161
  Curracloe Beach 151
  Cushendun Beach 552
  Derrynane Beach 239
  Dog's Bay 333
  Dugort Beach 351
  Easkey Beach 362-3
  Fanore Beach 284
  Glasheen Beach 298
  Glassilaun Beach 322
  Gurteen 333
  Inch Strand 246
  Keel Beach 351
  Keem Bay 351
  Kilkee Beach 298
  Lackan Strand 365
  Lawlor's Strand 161
  Lettergesh 322
  Malin Beg 394
  Portrush Strand 541

  Portstewart Strand 541
  Renvyle Beach (White Strand) 322
  Rosslare Strand 152
  Rossnowlagh Beach 399
  safety 579
  Salthill Beach 314
  Spanish Point 294
  Trá Bán 248
  Tullan Strand 399
  White Park Bay 548
  White Strand (Cahersiveen) 238
  White Strand (Clare) 298
Belfast 460-501, **462-3**, *see also individual neighbourhoods*
  Belfast city centre 466-73, **467**
  itineraries 464-5, 472, 486, 499, **472**, **486**, **499**
  Queen's Quarter & South Belfast 488-494, **489**
  Titanic Quarter & East Belfast 481-487, **482**
  West & North Belfast 495-501, **496**
Belfast city centre 466-73, **467**
  accommodation 473
  drinking 469, 471
  food 471, 473
Belvedere House & Gardens 425-426
  beyond Belvedere House & Gardens 427-9
Benbulben 370-1
beyond Dublin City Centre 107-13, **108**
  accommodation 110-111
  drinking 113
  food 111, 112-113
big houses, manors & estates 16-17
  Adare Manor 264
  Bantry House 210
  Belvedere House & Gardens 425-6
  Cappoquin House and Gardens 165
  Castle Coole 561
  Castle Ward House 517-18
  Castletown House 138
  Clifton House 497

  Curraghmore Estate 164
  Derrynane House 239
  Downhill Demesne 541
  Dromana House & Gardens 165
  Emo Court 412
  Errislannan Manor 331
  Florence Court 569
  Killruddery House & Gardens 131
  Mount Congreve House and Gardens 159
  Mount Juliet 179
  Mount Stewart 519
  Muckross House 226
  Powerscourt Estate 125
  Powerscourt Townhouse 63
  Puxley Manor 214
  Rothe House and Garden 174
  Russborough House 132
  Strokestown Park House 417
birdwatching 207, 290, 356, 394, 409, 518, 525, 539, 546-7, 568
  Bird of Prey Centre 283
  National Birds of Prey Centre 132-3
Birr 408-9
Blackwater Valley 165
Blarney Castle 200
Blasket Islands 246, 248
boat trips 110, 154, 165, 176, 208, 228-9, 231-2, 243-4, 291, 316, 323, 394, 421, 422, 423-4, 443
Book of Kells 58
books 39
Boyle 420-21
breweries
  Boundary Brewing 487
  Carlingford Brewing Company 449
  Dungarvan Brewing Company 164
  Galway Hooker Craft Brewing Co 316
  Guinness Storehouse 83
  Hilden Brewery 494
  Lacada Brewery 542
  Treaty City Brewery 262
  Walled City Brewery 537

605

INDEX

B–C

Brú na Bóinne 436–41, 592–3, **437**
  accommodation 438, 440, 441
  beyond Brú na Bóinne 442–9
  drinking 439
  food 439
Bundoran 398, 399
Burren, the 282–288, **282**
  accommodation 284–5
  drinking 283, 285
  food 283, 287
bus travel 577

C

Caherdaniel 235
Cahir 271
camping 207, 287, 579
canoeing, see kayaking & canoeing
Cape Clear Island 207
car rental 575
Carlingford 449
Carlow 141, 166–70, **142**
  accommodation 169
  food 169
  itineraries 144
Carlow town 166–7, **166**
  beyond Carlow town 168–70
  shopping 167
Carrauntoohil 232
Carrick-a-Rede 547
Carrickmacross 458
Carrick-on-Shannon 422
Cashel 266–9, **266**
  beyond Cashel 270–3
  food 267
Castlegregory 248–9
castles 16–17
  accommodation 577
  Athenry Castle 315
  Athlone Castle 410
  Aughnanure Castle 316
  Bagenal's Castle 515
  Ballybunion Castle 255
  Bangor Castle 519
  Belfast Castle 500
  Belleek Castle 361
  Birr Castle 408–9
  Blarney Castle 200

Map Pages **000**

606

Cahir Castle 271
Carlow Castle 167
Carrigaholt Castle 298
Classiebawn Castle 367
Clifden Castle 331
Clough Oughter Castle 455
Desmond Castle 264
Doe Castle 383–4
Donegal Castle 397, 594 Dublin Castle 58–9
Dunamore Castle 207
Dunboy Castle 214
Dundrum Castle 513
Dungarvan Castle 163
Dunluce Castle 551
Dunseverick Castle 551
Enniscorthy Castle 151
Enniskillen Castle 561
Glenarm Castle 553
Glenveagh Castle 377–8
Grace O'Malley's Castle 353
Granuaile's Castle 346
Hillsborough Castle 516
Huntington Castle & Gardens 170
Johnstown Castle 148–9
Kearney's Castle 267
Kilkenny Castle 172
Kinbane Castle 551
King John's Castle 262
Leap Castle 408
Malahide Castle 112
Mullin's Castle 178
Oranmore Castle 315
Roscommon castle 422
Roslee Castle 363
Slane Castle 444
Trim Castle 450–51
Tullynally Castle 429
Castletownbere 214
Cathedral Quatter (Belfast) 474–80, **475**
  accommodation 473
  drinking 479, 480
  entertainment 480
  food 478–479
  shopping 480
Cavan 431–59, 454–5, **432–3, 454**
  beyond County Cavan 456–9
  food 455
  itineraries 434
caves
  Aillwee Cave 283
  Arigna Mining Experience 421–2
  Crag Cave 255
  Doolin Cave 286
  Marble Arch Caves 568
  Mermaid's Cave 551

Mitchelstown Cave 271–2
Oweynagat Cave 419–20
caving 287
Céide Fields 364–5, 592
cemeteries
  Abbeystrewry Famine Cemetery 205
  Caldragh Cemetery 566
  Huguenot Cemetery 73
children, travel with
  activities 43, 487, 519, 578
churches & cathedrals
  Ardfert Cathedral 254
  Carlisle Memorial Methodist Church 497
  Carlow Cathedral 167
  Cathedral of St Mary (Scattery Island) 301
  Cathedral of the Most Holy Trinity 158
  Christ Church 78–79
  Christ Church Cathedral (Waterford) 158
  Church of St Peter & Paul 410
  Down Cathedral 517
  Gallarus Oratory 249
  Galway Cathedral 311
  Holy Trinity Church (Fethard) 272
  Kilmalkedar Church 249
  Layd Old Church 553
  Saul Church 517
  St Anne's Cathedral (Belfast) 476
  St Anne's Church 193
  St Audoen's Catholic Church 88
  St Audoen's Church of Ireland 87–8
  St Canice's Cathedral 174
  St Columb's Cathedral 534
  St Fechin's Church 428
  St Mary's Collegiate Church 199
  St Nicholas Church 311
  St Patrick's Cathedral 84–5
  St Patrick's Church of Ireland Cathedral 521–2
  St Patrick's Roman Catholic Cathedral 522
  St Peter's Protestant Church 446
  St Peter's Roman Catholic Church 446
  St Stephen's Church 72
  St Audoen's Catholic Church 88
cinemas
  Irish Film Institute 79
  Light House 96–7

Nerve Centre 534
Odyssey Complex 485
Strand, The 484
Claddagh rings 317
Clare 279–301, **280**
  itineraries 281
Clare Island 593–4 Clifden 329–31, **329**
  accommodation 330
  beyond Clifden 332–5
  drinking 330, 331
  food 330
  shopping 330
Cliffs of Moher 289–91, **289**
  accommodation 293
  beyond the Cliffs of Moher 292–4
  drinking 293–4
  food 293
climate 36–7
Clonakilty 201–3, **201**
  accommodation 202, 205
  beyond Clonakilty 204–8
  drinking 206–7
  food 203, 205–7
Clonmacnoise 404–6, 593, **404**
  beyond Clonmacnoise 407–14
  food 405
coasteering 548
Cobh 197
Collins, Michael 203
Connemara National Park 318–20, **318**
  accommodation 319
  beyond Connemara National Park 321–3
Cooley Peninsula 449
Copper Coast 162
Cork 183–217, **184–5**
  accommodation 195–6, 210, 213
  drinking 197–8, 213
  food 195, 197, 198, 210, 214
  itineraries 186–7, 199, 215, **199, 215**
  shopping 195
Cork City 188–93, **189**
  accommodation 190
  beyond Cork City 194–200
  drinking 193
  food 190–2, 200
courses
  cooking courses 163, 164, 198, 581
  trapeze 480
credit cards 576
culture 596–7
Curragh, the 135–6
currency 576
Cushendall 553

cycling 43, 64
　Ballyhoura Mountain Bike Trails 265
　Bushmills-Giant's Causeway trail 549
　Comber Greenway 487
　Connemara 333
　Connor Pass 249
　Gap of Dunloe 228-9
　Great Western Greenway 347-8
　Inishowen 100 386
　Kilbroney Park 515
　Kilkenny Cycling Tours 176
　Lagan Towpath 493-4
　Mourne Mountains 511
　Old Rail Trail Greenway 411
　Priest's Leap 211
　Rathlin Island 546-7
　Sheep's Head 215
　St Mullins 180
　Waterford Greenway 161
　Wild Atlantic Way 586

D

Dalkey 111
deer 379, 605-6
Derry 527-55, **528**
　accommodation 539-40
　drinking 541
　food 541, 542
　itineraries 530, 535
Derry City 532-7, **532**
　accommodation 534
　beyond Derry City 538-42
　drinking 534
　food 536
　shopping 537
Devenish Island 564-5
Dingle 242-4, **242**
　accommodation 243, 246
　beyond Dingle 245-9
　drinking 248
　food 243, 248
　itineraries 247
disabilities, travellers with 15, 18, 42, 585
distilleries 86
　Ballykeefe Distillery 179
　Blackwater Distillery 165
　Clare Island Whiskey 347
　Clonakilty Distillery 202
　Jameson Distillery (Dublin) 95
　Micil Distillery 314
　Old Bushmills Distillery 549
　Old Jameson Whiskey Distillery 196-7
　Pearse Lyons Distillery 86
　Roe & Co 87
　Slane Irish Whiskey Distillery 444
　Teeling Distillery 86
　Titanic Distillers 485
　Tullamore Dew 409
diving, see scuba diving & diving
Docklands (Dublin) 100-6, **101**
　accommodation 103
　drinking 106
　food 104-5
dolmens
　Brownshill Dolmen 170
　Haroldstown Dolmen 170
　Knockroe Dolmen 170
　Legananny Dolmen 514
　Poulnabrone Dolmen 288
dolphins 244, 290, 299, 301, 394, 547
Donegal 373-99, **374**
　accommodation 381-3, 389-90, 397
　drinking 384, 390, 399
　food 382, 391, 396-8
　itineraries 375
Donegal town 397
Doolin 284-6
Down 503-25, **504-5**
　accommodation 513, 515, 517-8
　drinking 515, 516
　food 514, 516-7
　itineraries 506, 511, **511**
Dowth 440
drinking 14, 40, 580-1, see also distilleries, individual locations
　Dublin Literary Pub Crawl 61-62
driving tours, see road trips
Drogheda 446
Drumcliff 370
Dublin 48-113, **50-51**
　see also individual neighbourhoods
　Docklands (Dublin) 100-6, **101**
　Grafton Street & Stephen's Green 54-65, **56-7**
　itineraries 52-53
　Kilmainham 81-9
　Liberties, the 81-9, **82**
　Merrion Square & Georgian Dublin 66-74, **67**
　North of the Liffey 90-9, **92-3**
　Temple Bar 75-80, **76**
Dun Briste 364
Dungarvan 163-4
Dunmore East 161-2
Dursey Island 214

E

electricity 587
Ennis 301
Enniscorthy 151
Enniscrone 358-9
　beyond Enniscrone 360-5
　food 359
Enniskillen 560-2, **560**
　accommodation 561
　beyond Enniskillen 563-71
　food 561
etiquette 38

F

family travel 43, 487, 517, 578, see also children, travel with
Fanore 284
Fermanagh 557-71, **558**
　accommodation 567-9
　drinking 569
　food 566, 569
　itineraries 562, 559, **562**
ferry 574
festivals & events 37
　Baltimore Seafood & Wooden Boat Festival 208
　Blackwater Valley Opera Festival 165
　Carlow Arts Festival 167
　Carlow Fringe Festival 167
　Cat Laughs Comedy Festival 174
　City of Derry Jazz 539
　Clarinbridge Oyster Festival 315
　Clonakilty International Guitar Festival 202
　Connemara Pony Show 331
　Cork Harbour Festival 192
　Cork Midsummer Festival 192
　Cork on a Fork 192
　Cork World Book Fest 192
　Culture Night 74
　Dingle Food Festival 244
　Doolin Folk Festival 285
　Dublin International Film Festival 62
　Dublin Pride 62
　Dunmore East Bluegrass Festival 161
　Dwyer Weekend 158
　Electric Picnic 414
　Fastnet Film Festival 213
　Fermanagh Classic Fishing Festival 567
　Fleadh Nua 301
　Forbidden Fruit 62
　Foyle Film Festival 539
　Harvest Blues Festival 458
　Harvest Festival 158
　Imagine Arts Festival 158
　Kilkenny Arts Festival 174
　Kilkenny Roots Festival 174
　Kilkenny Tradfest 174
　Lisdoonvarna Matchmaking Festival 284
　May The Fourth Be With You Festival 387
　Mayo Dark Sky Festival 355-6
　New Year's Festival Dublin 103
　North West 200 Motorcycle Race 539
　Ould Lammas Fair 544
　Rose of Tralee International Festival 251
　Samhain 419
　Savour Kilkenny 174
　Spraoi 158
　St Patrick's Festival 62
　Summer in the City 158
　Taste of Wicklow Food Festival 133
　Waterford Walls Street Art Festival 157
　West Waterford Festival of Food 164
　Wexford Festival Opera 149
　Wexford Fringe Festival 149
　Wexford Spiegeltent Festival 149
　Winterval 158
　Writers Week 255
　Yulefest 174
Fethard 272
Field, The 323
film & television 39, 239, 287, 316, 323, 352, 516, 554
fishing 43, 227, 299, 409, 421, 566

food 40-1, 580-1, *see also individual locations*
foraging 41, 133, 163, 240, 244, 514, 570, 581
Fore Valley 428-9
forests, *see* national parks & nature reserves *and* parks & gardens
forts
 Cahergal 238
 Charles Fort 196
 Dún Aonghasa 326
 Dún Chonchúir 328
 Dún Dúchathair 326
 Dun na Sead 208
 Dunbeg Fort 247
 Fort Dunree 391
 Grianán of Aileách 389
 Leacanabuaile 238
 Navan Fort 523, 593
 Rath of the Synods 453
 Spike Island 198
Foynes 265

G

GAA 598-600
 Croke Park Stadium 110
 Experience Gaelic Games 110-11
 GAA Museum 110
 Kilkenny Hurlers statue 176
 Kilkenny Way, The 175
 Lár na Páirce Museum 272
 Nowlan Park GAA Stadium 175
gaeltachts 163, 207, 241, 316-7, 384, 499, 589
gaols
 Armagh Gaol 522
 Cork City Gaol 190
 Crumlin Road Gaol 498
 Kilmainham Gaol 89
Galtees, the 274-7, **275**
Galway 303-35, **304-305**
 drinking 315, 316
 food 314-35, 322
 itineraries 306-7
 itineraries 327, 334-5

Galway city 308-12, **309**
 accommodation 310
 beyond Galway city 313-7
 drinking 310
 food 312
 itineraries 311
Game of Thrones 516, 554
Garnish Island 216
gay travellers 191, 479, 584
geneology 262
Giant's Causeway 548
Glen of Aherlow 274-7, **275**
Glendalough 120-3
Glenveagh National Park 376-9, **377**
 accommodation 378
 beyond Glenveagh National Park 380-4
 food 377
golf 42
 Adare Manor Golf Resort 264
 Ballybunion Golf Club 255
 Ballyliffin Golf Club 391
 Castlebar Golf Club 355
 Greencastle Golf Club 391
 Lahinch Golf Club 293-4
 Mount Juliet 179
 Mulranny 355
 Portstewart Golf Club 542
 Powerscourt Golf Club 126
 Rosslare Golf Club 152
 Royal County Down Golf Club 509
 Royal Portrush 542
 Westport Golf Club 355
Grace O'Malley 346, 353
Grafton Street & St Stephen's Green 54-65, **56-7**
 accommodation 60-61
 drinking 61-5
 food 58-9, 65
 shopping 61, 63
Graiguenamanagh 180
Grand Canal 423-4
Great Famine, the 102, 105, 154, 205, 345, 348, 416-17, 569-70
Guinness Storehouse 83

H

health 581
Heaney, Seamus 540-1
highlights 10-21
hiking 18-19, 42-3
Hill of Tara 453

history 592-5
 early Christian sites 10-11, 120-3, 236-7, 246, 249, 301, 331, 404-6, 564, 566
 Great Famine, the 102, 105, 154, 205, 345, 348, 416-7, 569-70
 Irish independence 89, 91, 129, 203, 498
 medieval history 172-5, 178, 268-9, 411, 564
 pirates 346
 prehistoric sites 170, 191, 208, 236-7, 283, 288, 327, 347, 363, 364, 371, 389-90, 412, 413, 419, 436-41, 445-6, 453, 455, 494, 514-5, 523, 525, 592-3
 revolutionary history 151, 167, 391, 410, 416, 443, 471
 Troubles, the 491, 499, 500, 536-7, 595
 vikings 157-8, 406, 564, 593
 WWI 391, 484
 WWII 391
HMS *Caroline* 484
Holywood 519
horse riding 43, 240-1, 515
horses 136, 272
hot-air balloons 451
Howth 111

I

Inishbiggle 356
Inishmaan 328
Inishmore 326
Inishtrahull Island 390
Inistioge 179
insurance 581
Irish coffee 265
islands
 Abbey Island 239
 Achill Island 349-54
 Aran Islands 324-8
 Arranmore Island 384
 Blasket Islands 246, 248
 Boa Island 566
 Cape Clear Island 207
 Castle Island 421
 Clare Island 346-7, 593-4
 Devenish Island 564-5
 Dursey Island 214
 Garinish Island 216
 Inisfallen Island 232
 Inishbiggle 356
 Inishmaan 328

 Inishmore 326
 Inishtrahull Island 390
 Maharees Islands 248
 Omey Island 333
 Oxford Island 525
 Saltee Islands 154
 Scattery Island 301
 Skellig Islands 236-7
 Tory Island 382-3
 Trinity Island 421
 Valentia Island 239-40
 White Island 565
itineraries 26-35, *see also individual locations*

J

Joyce, James 74, 97, 113, 311, 594-5

K

Kavanagh, Patrick 457-8
kayaking & canoeing 42, 105-6, 162, 165, 180, 191, 206, 244, 262, 275, 323, 384, 455, 518, 565, 569
Kelly, Luke 60, 457
Kenmare 234
Kennedy, John F 154
Kerry 219-255, **220-21**
 itineraries 222-3
Kildare 115-39, **116**
 itineraries 117
 Kildare & the Curragh 134-9, **134**
 beyond Kildare & the Curragh 137-9
 food 135
Kilkee 296-7
Kilkenny 141, 171-81, **142**
 accommodation 178-9
 food 180
 itineraries 144
Kilkenny City 171-6, **172**
 accommodation 173-4
 beyond Kilkenny City 177-81
 drinking 175
 food 173
 shopping 175
Killala 365
Killarney
 accommodation 226
 drinking 231
 food 227
Killarney National Park 224-32, **225**
 accommodation 238

beyond Killarney
  National Park 233-41
 food 239-40
 itineraries 228-9, 230,
  234-5, **229**, **230**, **235**
Killary Harbour 323
Kilmainham 81-9, **82**
 accommodation 84
 drinking 86-7, 89
 food 85, 88-9
 shopping 85
Kilmainham Gaol 89
Kilmore Quay 152, 154
Kilrush 301
Kinsale 195
Kinvara 315
kite surfing 112, 248, 352
Knowth 440
Kylemore Abbey 322-3

L

Lahinch 293-4
lakes
 Lake Muskry 275
 Lough Bray 124
 Lough Corrib 316
 Lough Derravaragh 429
 Lough Erne 564, 565
 Lough Eske 398
 Lough Hyne 206
 Lough Key 421
 Lough Leane 231-2
 Lough Lene 429
 Lough Neagh 525
 Lough Ree 410-12
 Lough Swilly 391
 Lough Tay 126
 Muckross Lake 230
 Strangford Lough 518
language 588-9
Lennon, John 351
lesbian travellers 191,
 479, 584
Lewis, CS 487
LGBTIQ+ travellers 191,
 479, 584
Liberties, the 81-9, **82**
 accommodation 84
 drinking 86-7, 89
 food 85, 88-9
 shopping 85
libraries
 Armagh Robinson Library
  521
 Linen Hall Library 470
 Marsh's Library 85
 National Library of
  Ireland 71-2
lighthouses
 accommodation 577
 Baily Lighthouse 111

Blackhead Lighthouse
 555
Dunmore East lighthouse
 161
East Lighthouse 547
Erris lighthouses 357
Inisheer Lighthouse 327
Loop Head Lighthouse
 297-8
Poolbeg Lighthouse 106
Rue Point Lighthouse 547
Sheep's Head lighthouse
 215
Valentia Island
 Lighthouse 240
Limerick 257-65, **258**
 accommodation 264
 itineraries 276-7
Limerick city 260-2, **260**
 beyond Limerick city
  263-265
 drinking 261
Liscannor 293
Lisdoonvarna 284
Loop Head Peninsula
 295-9, **295**
 accommodation 296-7,
  301
 beyond the Loop Head
  Peninsula 300-1
 drinking 297
Lough Corrib 316
Lough Hyne 206
Louth 431-59, **432-3**
 accommodation 440, 447
 drinking 439, 449
 food 439, 443-5, 448
 itineraries 434

M

Mahareees Islands 248
Malahide 112
Malin Head 385-7, **386**
 accommodation 386
 beyond Malin Head
  388-91
 drinking 387
 food 389
markets
 Buttermarket 562
 Cobh Farmers Market
  200
 Dungarvan Farmers
  Market 163-4
 English Market 190
 Howth Market 111
 Kinsale Farmers Market
  200
 Marina Market 190-1
 Merrion Square Food
  Market 71

Midleton Farmers Market
 200
Milk Market 261
Moore Street Mall 96
People's Park market 113
St George's Market 473
Sunday Art Market 71
Mayo 337-57, **338-9**
 accommodation 346, 355
 drinking 345
 food 347
 itineraries 340
McCourt, Frank 261, 262
Meath 431-59, **432-3**
 food 446
 itineraries 434
Merrion Square & Georgian
 Dublin 66-74, **67**
 accommodation 69-70
 drinking 69, 73-4
 food 71-2, 73
Michelin restaurants 73, 91
Midlands, the 401-29, **402**
 accommodation 408, 411,
  419, 421, 423, 428
 drinking 409-10, 413, 423
 food 410, 420, 422-3
 itineraries 403
Miltown Malbay 294
Mizen Head 213-4
mobile phones 587
Monaghan 431-59, **432-3**
 accommodation 457
 itineraries 434
Monaghan town 459
monastic sites
 Bective Abbey 451
 Black Abbey 174-5
 Clare Island Abbey 346
 Clonmacnoise 404-6
 Corcomroe Abbey 288
 Dominican priory 423
 Duiske Abbey 180
 Dunbrody Abbey 153
 Ennis Friary 301
 Fore Valley Benedictine
  priory 429
 Glendalough 120-23
 Inisfallen priory 231
 Jerpoint Abbey 178
 Kells Priory 178
 Kilmacduagh 315
 Kylemore Abbey 322-3
 Mellifont Abbey 446-7
 Monasterboice 447-9
 Moyne Abbey 364
 Mt Melleray Abbey 165
 Rock of Cashel 268-9
 Ross Errilly Friary 316
 Scattery Island 301
 Selskar Abbey 147
 Sligo Abbey 369
 St Declan's Monastery
  164-5

 St Mary's Abbey 565
 St Molaise's House 565
 Teampall Chaoimháin
  327
 Tintern Abbey 153
 Turlough Round Tower
  345
money 576
mountain biking 43, 112,
 265, 500, 515, 570, 571
mountain climbing
 Achill Island 352
 Brandon Hill 180
 Carrauntoohil 232
 Comeragh Mountains 165
 Croagh Patrick 348
 Galtees, the 274-7
 Galtymore 276-7
 Mt Brandon 249
 Mt Errigal 381-382
 Slemish Mountain 554
 Slieve Donard 510
 Sugarloaf Mountain 127
Mt Errigal 381-382
Mullaghmore 366-7, **367**
 accommodation 367
 beyond Mullaghmore
  368-71
museums & galleries
 14 Henrietta Street 91
 Battle of the Boyne
  site 443
 Birr Castle science centre
  408-9
 Bishop's Palace 158
 Blasket Centre 246
 Brú Ború Heritage Centre
  267
 Cape Clear Heritage
  Centre 207
 Carlow County Museum
  167
 Carrickmacross Lace
  Gallery 458
 Cashel Folk Village 267
 Centre for Contemporary
  Art 534
 Chester Beatty 55
 City Assembly House 64
 Cobh Heritage Centre 197
 Connemara Heritage &
  History Centre 331
 Copper Coast Geopark
  Visitor Centre 162
 Copper Mine Museum 216
 Cork Butter Museum 193
 Cork City Gaol 190
 County Carlow Military
  Museum 167
 Crumlin Road Gaol 498
 Custom House Visitor
  Centre 103
 Down County Museum
  517

museums & galleries continued
Dunbrody Famine Ship 154
Eileen Hickey Irish Republican History Museum 497
Enniskillen Castle Museums 561
EPIC The Irish Emigration Museum 104
Foynes Flying Boat Museum 265
Francis Bacon Studio 94
GAA Museum 110
Giant's Causeway Visitor Centre 548
Golden Thread Gallery 480
GOMA (Gallery of Modern Art) 157
Headhunters Barber Shop & Railway Museum 562
Hill of Tara visitor centre 453
Home Place 539
Horse Country Experience 272
House of Waterford Crystal 158-9
Hugh Lane Gallery 94-5
Hunt Museum 261
Icon Factory 80
Irish Agricultural Museum 149
Irish Horse Museum 136
Irish Jewish Museum 63-64
Irish Museum of Modern Art 85-86
Irish Museum of Time 158
Irish National Heritage Park 149
Irish Silver Museum 157
Irish Wake Museum 158
Irish Whiskey Museum 60-61
James Joyce Centre 97
Jerpoint Glass 179
Kennedy Homestead 154
Kerry County Museum 251
Kerry Writers Museum 255
Kilbaha Gallery 297
Killarney National Park visitor centre 231
King House Historic & Cultural Centr 420
Lavelle Art Gallery 330
Ledwidge Museum, the 444
Lewis Glucksman Gallery 191
Limerick City Gallery of Art 261
Lismore Heritage Centre 165
Little Museum of Dublin 55
Loughcrew Megalithic Centre 445-6
Luan Gallery 410
Medieval Mile Museum 173
Medieval Museum 157-8
Metropolitan Arts Centre 476
Michael Collins Centre 203
Michael Collins House 203
Millmount Museum & Tower 446
Monaghan County Museum 459
Músaem Chorca Dhuibhne 247
Museum of Free Derry 536
Museum of Literature Ireland 59
Museum of Natural History 69-70
Museum of Style Icons 136
Nano Nagle Place 192
National 1798 Rebellion Centre 151
National Design & Craft Gallery 175
National Famine Museum 416-7
National Gallery of Ireland 68
National Leprechaun Museum 98
National Museum of Ireland - Archaeology 70-71
National Museum of Ireland - Country Life 345
National Museum of Ireland - Decorative Arts & History 95-6
National Print Museum 106
North Down Museum 519
Old Barracks Heritage Centre 238
Old Library & Book of Kells 58
Patrick Kavanagh Centre 458
People's Gallery 536-7
Quiet Man Museum, The 316
Radio Museum 190
Reginald's Tower 157
RHA Gallery 74
RMS *Lusitania* Museum 196
Roscommon County Museum 422
Skibbereen Heritage Centre 205
St Patrick Centre 517
Titanic Belfast 483
Titanic Experience 197
Tower Museum 534
Ulster American Folk Park 569-70
Ulster Folk and Transport Museum 519
Ulster Museum 491
Valentia Island Heritage Centre 240
Visual Centre for Contemporary Art 167
Waterford County Museum 163
Waterford Gallery of Art 157
Whitehead railway museum 555
Whitethorn Gallery 330
music 39, 457, 477, 478
 live music 62-3, 68, 77, 343, 478, 479, 534
 traditional music 14, 79-80, 158, 202, 285, 294, 310, 312, 515, 544
mythology 363, 439, 444-5, 453, 523, 549

N

national parks & nature reserves 13-14
Ballyteige Burrow Nature Reserve 154
Bog of Allen Nature Centre 138
Burren National Park 286-7
Castle Espie Wetland Centre 518
Cavan Burren Park 455
Clara Bog Nature Reserve 409
Connemara National Park 318-20
Cuilcagh Lakelands Unesco Global Geopark 566
Cuilcagh Mountain Park 455
Dursey Island 214
Glenveagh National Park 376-9
Inishtrahull Island 390
Knockomagh Wood Nature Reserve 206
Lough Beg 539-40
Lough Boora Parklands 409
Lower Lough Erne Islands Reserve 568
Murlough National Nature Reserve 513
Raven Nature Reserve 151
Slieve Bloom Nature Reserve 414
Westlight Seabird Centre 546-7
Wexford Wildfowl Reserve 151
Wild Nephin National Park 355-9
nature 151, 287, 394, 493, 525, see also individual animals *and* national parks & nature reserves
Newcastle 508-11, **508**
 accommodation 509
 beyond Newcastle 512-9
 food 509, 510
 itineraries 511, **511**
New Ross 154
Newgrange 438-41
nightlife 580-1, see also individual locations
north of the Liffey 90-99, **92-3**
 accommodation 94-5
 drinking 95, 97
 food 91, 96-7, 99
 nightlife 98-9

O

observatories 522, see also star gazing
Offaly, see Midlands, the
Oranmore 315
Oscar Wilde House 70
Oughterard 316

P

paddleboarding 352
parks & gardens
  Altamont Gardens 169–70
  Avondale Forest Park 129–30
  Bangor Castle Walled Garden 519
  Bantry House 210
  Belfast Botanic Gardens 490
  Birr Castle 408
  Blarney Castle 200
  Brigit's Garden 582
  Cappoquin House & Gardens 165
  Castlewellan Forest Park 514–5
  Cave Hill Country Park 500
  Crawfordsburn Country Park 519
  Delta Sensory Gardens 169
  Derrynane House 239
  Dromana House & Gardens 165
  Garden of Remembrance 98
  Garnish Island 216
  Glenariff Forest Park 553
  Hardymount Gardens 169
  Hillsborough forest park 516
  Huntington Castle & Gardens 170
  Iveagh Gardens 60
  Japanese Gardens 136
  Jerpoint Park 178
  John F Kennedy Arboretum 154
  Johnstown Castle Gardens 149
  Kells Bay House & Gardens 241
  Kilbroney Park 515
  Kilfane Glen 179
  Killarney House 231
  Killiney Hill Park 111
  Killruddery House & Gardens 131
  Killykeen Forest Park 455
  Kilmacurragh Botanic Gardens 130–31
  Lismore Castle Gardens 165
  Lough Key Forest Park 421
  Mount Congreve House & Gardens 159
  Mount Usher Gardens 131
  Nano Nagle Place 192
  National Botanic Gardens 112–3
  Ormeau Park 494
  Phoenix Park 109
  Powerscourt Estate 125
  Rossmore Forest Park 459
  Rothe House & Garden 174
  Sir Thomas & Lady Dixon Park 494
  Slieve Gullion Forest Park 525
  Tollymore Forest Park 511, 514
  War Memorial Gardens 86
  Woodstock Gardens 179
podcasts 39
Portrush 541
preparation 38
public holidays 587
public transport 575, see also individual locations

Q

Queen's Quarter & South Belfast 488–94, **489**
  accommodation 492
  drinking 494
  food 492, 493, 493–4
  nightlife 494
Quiet Man, The 316

R

rafting 112
responsible travel 582–3
Ring of Kerry 234–5
Ring Peninsula 163
RMS *Lusitania* 196
road trips
  Antrim Glens 552–3, **553**
  Binevenagh Scenic Drive 540
  Connemara 323
  Connor Pass 249
  Doolough Valley 346
  Glen of Aherlow Drive 275
  Glengesh Pass 397
  Hook Peninsula 153
  Inishowen 100 386
  Loop Head Drive 297
  Priest's Leap 211
  Ring of Kerry 234–5
  Skellig Ring 241
  Sky Road Loop 334–5, **335**
  Slea Head Drive 247
rock climbing 42, 112, 284, 449, 548
Rock of Cashel 268–269
Rock of Dunamase 413
Roscommon town 422–3
Rosslare 152
rowing 244, 384, 421
Royal Canal 423–4
rugby 262
Russborough House 132

S

safety 579
sailing 262, 449
Saltee Islands 154
Salthill 314–5
Schull 213
scuba diving & diving 43, 248, 249, 328, 384, 542, 548
seals 151, 216, 244, 493, 582
seaweed baths 163, 296, 359, 544
sheepdogs 323, 371
Sheep's Head 215
SIM cards 574
skateboarding 480
Skellig Islands 236–7
Skellig Michael 236–7
Skibbereen 205
slang 39
Slemish Mountain 593
Slieve League Cliffs 392–4, **393**
  accommodation 393
  beyond the Slieve League Cliffs 395–9
Sligo 337–41, 358–71, **338–9**
  accommodation 361, 363
  drinking 365, 369
  food 361–2, 365, 369
  itineraries 340
Sligo town 369
smoking 587
Sneem 234–5
spas 284, 296, 509, 544
Spiddal 317
SS *Nomadic* 483
St Patrick 517, 551, 554
stadiums
  Semple Stadium 272
  Thomond Park 262
stand-up paddleboarding 162, 165, 180, 244, 262, 352, 431, 449, 540
star gazing 570
  Mayo Dark Sky Park 355
Star Wars 239, 387
stone circles
  Beaghmore 571
  Drombeg Stone Circle 208
Stormont 485, 597
Strandhill 363
street art 96, 157, 478–479, 562
Strokestown 415–7, **416**
  accommodation 417
  beyond Strokestown 418–24
  drinking 416
surfing 43, 162, 284, 291, 294, 346, 352, 384, 399, 540, 541, 548
swimming 113, 314, 352, 398
Synge, JM 328

T

tap water 587
taxes 576
Temple Bar 75–80, **76**
  accommodation 80
  drinking 78–9
  food 80
  shopping 78–9
theatres
  Booley Theatre 165
  Bord Gáis Energy Theatre 102
  George Bernard Shaw Theatre 167
  Grand Opera House 469
  National Opera House 149
  Project Arts Centre 77
Thomastown 178–9
Tipperary 257–60, 266–77, **258**
  drinking 272
  food 271
  itineraries 276–7, **277**
Titanic 483, 486
Titanic Quarter & East Belfast 481–7, **482**
  drinking 484
  entertainment 485
  food 487
  shopping 487
Tory Island 382–3
tours
  bus 438
  food 65, 133, 176, 192, 312
  ghost 176
  taxi 500

tours continued
walking 95, 148, 176, 195, 262, 499, *see also* walking & hiking
train travel 575
Tralee 250-2, **251**
 beyond Tralee 253-5
 drinking 252
 food 252, 254
Tramore 162
travelling around Ireland 575
travelling to Ireland 574
Trim Castle 450, **450**
 beyond Trim Castle 452-3
Trinity College Dublin 55
Tyrone 557-71, **558**
 accommodation 564
 food 565
 itineraries 559

U

universities
 Queen's University 490
 Trinity College Dublin 55
 University College Cork 191
urban culture 20-21

V

Valentia Island 239-40

W

walking & hiking 42, *see also* tours
Achill Island 352
Ardmore cliff walk 164
Arthur Guinness Heritage Trail 135
Aughris Head 364
Ballybunion Cliff Walk 255
Bangor Trail 357
Beara Way 214

Benbulben 370-371
Black Mountain 500
Blue Stack Way 398
Brandon Hill 180
Bray Head Cliff Walk 131-2
Burren National Park 286-7
Busmills-Giant's Causeway trail 549
Cape Clear 207
Carrauntoohil 232
Causeway Coast Way 550
Cavan Way 455
Claggan Mountain Coastal Trail 356
Cliffs of Kilkee 296-7
Cliffs of Moher 290-1
Comeragh Mountains 165
Connemara National Park 319-20
Copper Mine Trail 216
Croagh Patrick 348
Cuilcagh Boardwalk Trail 566-7
Davagh Forest 571
Derry's City Walls 535
Devil's Bit 272
Doolin Cliff Walk 285-6
Dunmore East Coastal Walk 162
Eamonn an Chnoic Loop 273
Enniscrone coast 359
Enniskillen 562
Erris Head Loop Walk 356
Galtees, the 274-7
Galtymore 276-7
Galway's landmarks 311
Geokaun 240
Glanaclohy Loop Walk 207
Glenveagh National Park 378-9
Gobbins, the 555
Helvick Head Walking Trail 163
Howth Cliff Path Walk 111
Inisheer 327
Kilbroney Park 515
Killaspugbrone Coastal Walk 364
Letterkeen Walking Loops 356-7
Loop Head Walk 298
Lúb Dún Chonchúr

Looped Walk 328
Malin Head Trail 386
Miners' Way 127
Miners Way and Historical Trail 422
Mt Errigal 381-382
Muckross Lake 230
Mullaghmore Head Loop 367
Newcastle coastal path 509-10
Nore Linear Park 176
Nore Valley Walk 179
Priest's Leap 211
Raghly Cliff Walk 364
Rathlin Island 546-7
Roguey Cliff Walk 399
Roonivoolin walking trail 547
Saints' Road 249
Scilly Walk 196
Serpent's Lair 326
Slemish Mountain 554
Slieve Bloom Mountains 414
Slieve Donard 510
Slieve Gullion Forest Park 525
Slieve League Cliffs 393-4
St Patrick's Way 517
Sugarloaf Mountain 127
Three Castle Head 213
Titanic Quarter 486
Tory Island Loop trail 383
Urris Hills 391
Victorian Belfast 472
Whitehead coastal walk 554-5
Wicklow Mountains 119, 124
Wild Alpaca Way 387
waterfalls
 Aasleagh Falls 323
 Assaranca Waterfall 396
 Glenmacnass Waterfall 126
 Mahon Falls 165
 Powerscourt Waterfal 126
Waterford 141, 155-165, **142**
 accommodation 161-3
 food 164
 itineraries 144
Waterford city 155-9, **156**
 accommodation 158

 beyond Waterford city 160-5
 drinking 159
 food 157
waterparks 411
weather 3-7
West & North Belfast 495-501, **496**
 drinking 500
Westport 342-3, **342**
 beyond Westport 344-8
 drinking 343
 food 343
Wexford 141, 146-54, **142**
 accommodation 151
 food 151-2
 itineraries 144, 153
Wexford town 146-9, **147**
 accommodation 148
 beyond Wexford town 150
 food 148
whale watching 206, 208
whiskey 60-61, *see also* distilleries
White Island 565
Wicklow 115-39, **116**
 itineraries 117
Wicklow Mountains 118-33, **119**
 accommodation 126, 129-30
 beyond the Wicklow Mountains 128-33
 drinking 124
 food 124, 131-2
 shopping 125
Wild Atlantic Way 586
Wilde, Oscar 70
wildlife 12-13
windsurfing 248, 352

Y

yachting 213, 390
Yeats, WB 72, 363, 370, 601-2
yoga 480
Youghal 199

Map Pages **000**

NOTES